Professional Criminals

The International Library of Criminology, Criminal Justice and Penology
Series Editors: Gerald Mars and David Nelken

Titles in the Series:

Professional Criminals

Edited by

Dick Hobbs
University of Durham

Dartmouth
Aldershot • Brookfield USA • Singapore • Sydney

Published by
Dartmouth Publishing Company Limited
Gower House
Croft Road
Aldershot
Hants GU11 3HR
England

Dartmouth Publishing Company
Old Post Road
Brookfield
Vermont 05036
USA

British Library Cataloguing in Publication Data
Professional Criminals. – (International
Library of Criminology, Criminal Justice
& Penology)
 I. Hobbs, Dick II. Series
 344.1053

Library of Congress Cataloging-in-Publication Data
Professional criminals / edited by Dick Hobbs.
          p. cm.— (International library of criminology, criminal
     justice & penology)
       Includes bibliographical references and index.
       ISBN 1–85521–414–8
       1. Recidivists. 2. Criminals. 3. Crime. I. Hobbs, Dick.
  II. Series.
  HV6049.P75 1995
  364—dc20   94–39202
                                                                  CIP

ISBN 1 85521 414 8

Printed in Great Britain at the University Press, Cambridge

Contents

Acknowledgements

The editors and publishers wish to thank the following for permission to use copyright material.

Blackwell Publishers for the essay: Neal Shover and David Honaker (1991), 'The Socially Bounded Decision Making of Persistent Property Offenders', *The Howard Journal*, **31**, pp. 276–93.

Elsevier Science Limited for the essay: Marilyn Walsh and Duncan Chappell (1974), 'Operational Parameters in the Stolen Property System', *Journal of Criminal Justice*, **2**, pp. 113–29. Reprinted by permission of Elsevier Science Limited, Oxford.

Guildford Publications Inc. for the essay: Erving Goffman (1952), 'On Cooling the Mark Out: Some Aspects of Adaptation to Failure', *Psychiatry*, **15**, pp. 451–63.

The International Journal of Drug Policy for the essay: Vincenzo Ruggiero (1993), 'Brixton, London: A Drug Culture without a Drug Economy?', *The International Journal of Drug Policy*, **4**, pp. 83–90.

New Statesman and Society for the essay: Laurie Taylor (1983), 'Ducking and Diving', *New Society*, **6**, pp. 13–15.

Oxford University Press for the essay: Nicholas Dorn and Nigel South (1990), 'Drug Markets and Law Enforcement', *British Journal of Criminology*, **30**, pp. 171–88.

Routledge for the essays: John Mack (1964), 'Full-time Miscreants, Delinquent Neighbourhoods and Criminal Networks', *British Journal of Sociology*, **15**, pp. 38–53. Ordinary of Newgates Account: Mary Young (1741), London: John Applebee. Reprinted in P. Rawlings (ed.) (1992), *Drunks, Whores and Idle Apprentices: Criminal Biographies of the Eighteenth Century*, London: Routledge, pp. 121–36.

Sage Publications Inc. for the essays: John J. Gibbs and Peggy L. Shelly (1982), 'Life in the Fast Lane: A Retrospective View by Commercial Thieves', *Journal of Research in Crime and Delinquency*, **19**, pp. 299–330. Copyright © 1982 by Sage Publications Inc. Ken Levi (1981), 'Becoming a Hit Man: Neutralization in a Very Deviant Career', *Urban Life*, **10**, pp. 47–63. Copyright © 1981 by Sage Publications Inc. David F. Luckenbill (1981), 'Generating Compliance: The Case of Robbery', *Urban Life*, **10**, pp. 25–46. Copyright © 1981 by Sage Publications Inc. Julian Roebuck and Ronald Johnson (1962), 'The Jack-of-All-Trades Offender', *Crime and Delinquency*, **8**, pp. 172–81. Copyright © 1962 by Sage Publications Inc.

Taylor & Francis Inc. for the essay: Eloise Dunlap, Bruce D. Johnson and Ali Manwar (1994), 'A Successful Female Crack Dealer: Case Study of a Deviant Career', *Deviant Behavior*, **15**, pp. 1–25. All rights reserved.

The University of California Press for the essays: Patricia A. Adler and Peter Adler (1983), 'Shifts and Oscillations in Deviant Careers: The Case of Upper-Level Drug Dealers and Smugglers', *Social Problems*, **31**, pp. 195–207; Werner J. Einstadter (1969), 'The Social Organization of Armed Robbery', *Social Problems*, **17**, pp. 64–83; John Irwin and Donald R. Cressey (1962), 'Thieves, Convicts and the Inmate Culture', *Social Problems*, **10**, pp. 142–55; John Langer (1977), 'Drug Entrepreneurs and Dealing Culture', *Social Problems*, **24**, pp. 377–86; Edwin M. Lemert (1958), 'The Behavior of the Systematic Check Forger', *Social Problems*, **6**, pp. 141–9; Ned Polsky (1964), 'The Hustler', *Social Problems*, **12**, pp. 3–15; Neal Shover (1973), 'The Social Organization of Burglary', *Social Problems*, **20**, pp. 499–514.

The University of Chicago Press for the essay: Howard S. Becker (1960), 'Notes on the Concept of Commitment', *American Journal of Sociology*, **LXVI**, pp. 32–40.

Paul Warshow, Executor, for the essay: Robert Warshow (1948), 'The Gangster as Tragic Hero', *The Partisan Review*, pp. 240–44. Copyright © (1948) by R. Warshow.

John Wiley & Sons Limited for the essay: Robert Logie, Richard Wright and Scott Decker (1992), 'Recognition Memory Performance and Residential Burglary', *Applied Cognitive Psychology*, **6**, pp. 109–23.

Series Preface

The International Library of Criminology, Criminal Justice and Penology, represents an important publishing initiative designed to bring together the most significant journal essays in contemporary criminology, criminal justice and penology. The series makes available to researchers, teachers and students an extensive range of essays which are indispensable for obtaining an overview of the latest theories and findings in this fast changing subject.

This series consists of volumes dealing with criminological schools and theories as well as with approaches to particular areas of crime, criminal justice and penology. Each volume is edited by a recognised authority who has selected twenty or so of the best journal articles in the field of their special competence and provided an informative introduction giving a summary of the field and the relevance of the articles chosen. The original pagination is retained for ease of reference.

The difficulties of keeping on top of the steadily growing literature in criminology are complicated by the many disciplines from which its theories and findings are drawn (sociology, law, sociology of law, psychology, psychiatry, philosophy and economics are the most obvious). The development of new specialisms with their own journals (policing, victimology, mediation) as well as the debates between rival schools of thought (feminist criminology, left realism, critical criminology, abolitionism etc.) make necessary overviews that offer syntheses of the state of the art. These problems are addressed by the INTERNATIONAL LIBRARY in making available for research and teaching the key essays from specialist journals.

GERALD MARS
Visiting Professor of Risk Management, Cranfield University

DAVID NELKEN
Visiting Professor of Law (Criminology), University College London

Introduction

The concept of 'professional crime' enjoys a certain ambiguity within academic as well as populist textual formats, often overlapping with studies of organized crime, white-collar crime and, more recently, related sub-disciplinary alcoves such as drugs and youth gangs. However, the definitional ambiguity inherent in the term professional crime should not detract from the centrality of the concept. Indeed it is its ambiguous, rather ironic, connotations – suggesting a life world parallel to and reflective of normative society – that introduce a frisson of recognition to forms of behaviour that are all too often hidden from scholarly gaze by the banal hypocrisy of legalistic definition and by ignorance masquerading as moral outrage.

However, it is crucial to acknowledge the very particular problems that are posed to researchers by professional criminality. Researching this subject is both practically and ethically difficult, as active professional criminals have little to gain from exposing their world to an academic gaze. Further, if researchers focus upon those criminals who are no longer active, there is a real danger that the study of the inmates of prisons may produce studies of prison inmates. As Solway and Waters have indicated in a discussion concerned with field work among heroin addicts,

> If addicts are studied in jail, the result is a study of prisoners. If the ethnographer's goal is to understand addiction, he must resolve himself to entering the natural habitat of the addict, the streets, the back alleys, the shooting galleries (1977, p. 163).

Therefore until professional criminals can be persuaded to report their activities on the relevant revenue or census forms, ethnography would seem to offer the most obvious empirical option. However, the difficulties of gaining access and then establishing relationships, while maintaining academic credibility, are extreme in an environment that thrives upon its ability to avoid exposure. Consequently, ethnographic studies of professional crime, like good studies emanating from prisons, are rare. This book will utilize a range of sources, including ethnography, life histories, oral histories, biographies, autobiographies and journalistic accounts. In addition, this Introduction will stress the need to provide a structural frame for the activities of professional criminals for, like all economic actors, they operate within a specific cultural milieu that is defined and framed by a coalition of historical precedents.

Urbanization and the subsequent re-definition of economic relations marks the first acknowledgement of the existence of individuals whose identities were inextricably linked to a commitment to extract profit from criminal activity that extended beyond subsistence (Roebuck and Windham 1983; Salgado 1977; Howson 1971). For example, as the urban marketplace created a demand for game that could not be met by legitimate means, competent poachers were able to commit themselves full time to market engagement, thus raising their status to that of professional (Munsche 1981; Hay 1975; Sharp 1984). By the 18th century, however, professional criminality had established itself as a predominantly urban phenomenon, locating where the marketplace was most affluent (Low 1982) and where regimentation of the emerging working class (from whom professional criminals were predominantly recruited) was at its most ineffective (Stedman-Jones 1971). The areas in which this deviance was concentrated became highly functional to the evolving city for, as Rock has noted, ' . . . possibilities of random and unintended confrontation with deviants are considerably reduced' (1973, p. 30).

The emergence of these 'alternative geographies' (Shields 1991) was crucial for the symbolic, yet enduring, location of social organizations that enabled negotiated and ad hoc engagements, with variations on normative forms of enterprise (Hobbs 1988). These 'manors' can then be conquered and defended. They can be launched into conflicts that will endure for generations; they can exploit the indigenous resources by making special claims upon the area's commercial, manufacturing and leisure base.

Urbanization also brought an increased tendency to document contemporaneous social forms, and it is to these accounts that we must turn for an understanding of early professional crime (Chesney 1968; Tobias 1979). Rawlings has skilfully reproduced the at times ambiguous flavour of contemporary accounts of professional criminality in the form of popular pamphlets. The brief biography of Mary Young (Chapter 17) gives a flavour of the background, skills and culture of committed 18th-century criminals, suggesting a level of organization structured around the specific requirements of their criminal trades.

The journalistic adventures of the 'shadow criminologists' (Downes and Rock 1982, p. 58) amongst London's emergent working class succeed in situating crime within a cultural framework that was in harmony with the dominant commercial ethic of the age (Mayhew 1950). In addition, these writers acknowledged the evolution of a social form that was an intrinsic part of contemporary city life, with elements of structure and organization and (most importantly) with a master template located, not in the 'underworld', but within the normative economic relations of the overworld.

However, specific and focused academic studies of professional criminality did not come into existence until the University of Chicago's Department of Sociology initiated a qualitative shift towards sociological studies of aspects of urban life that had previously been ignored (Downes and Rock 1982, ch. 3). Yet the theoretical output of the Chicago School was inclined towards a model that appears to be contradicted by the vast wealth of empirical material now available. Social disorganization was regarded by many writers of the Chicago School as the primary dynamic that promoted criminogenic environments; this was deemed to be caused by a lack of both formal and informal controls within a community (Thomas and Znaniecki 1927).

The publication in 1937 of Edwin Sutherland's *The Professional Thief* is a landmark in criminological research for a number of crucial reasons. In his case study of Chic Conwell, a professional thief, Sutherland introduces readers to a concept of criminality, not as an all-encompassing monolith defined and identified by legal criteria, but as a fragment of activity to be understood as a separate behaviour system (see Hollingshead 1939). By ignoring legal dictats and concentrating upon cultural disposition, Sutherland offers a direct challenge to the dominant Chicagoan explanation of crime as being the result of social disorganization (see also Landesco 1968). What Sutherland discovered was a behaviour system that defined professional thieving in terms of the following characteristics: technical skill, consensus via a shared ideology, differential association, status and organization.

While support for this overtly sociological model is to be found in subsequent empirical work (Maurer 1955), the volatile nature of the marketplace appears to structure a social milieu within which Sutherland's concept of professional crime is hotly contested. For example, Lemert (Chapter 12) presents the cheque forger as a loner with few skills, while the President's Commission (Chapter 19) stresses the importance of 'hustlers' who are adaptable, engaging in a wide range of criminal activity. By not exhibiting consensus with other hustlers, they call into question the notion of a cohesive behaviour system as suggested by Sutherland.

Indeed, it is the status of specialist and the subsequent sub-cultural formations of criminal specialisms that have provoked the bulk of criticism of Sutherland's work amongst empirical criminologists. A further example is provided by Letkemann (1973), who uses the term 'rounders' to describe the all-purpose adaptive criminal. Yet Letkemann also emphasized that an explicit commitment to criminal activity as a means of making a living provided the best criterion for differentiating between professional and non-professional offenders. Consequently, Sutherland's model is not entirely discounted for there is support for the notion of an occupational group defined by its level of commitment to illegal economic activities (Becker in Chapter 2). Indeed, the most useful and historically relevant segment of Sutherland's theory remains the notion of a full-time commitment to crime as a pragmatic starting point for the study of what Block has defined as the 'serious crime community' (Block 1991(a), pp. 1–26).

Einstadter (Chapter 5) continued to dissect Sutherland's theory by exploring the sub-cultural possibilities that can emerge when a group of specialists share this commitment. Despite discovering consistency of practice and a measure of ideological coherence, Einstadter found that armed robbers were not reliant upon a system of tutelage, nor did they maintain relationships with quasi-legitimate agents such as 'fences' in order to maintain one foot in the straight world.

For the bulk of professional thieves, a cipher into the legitimate world who has the ability to turn loot into 'drinking vouchers' (cash) is crucial. Consequently, it is important to broaden the scope of any professional crime network analysis to include what Mack and Kerner (1975) have called 'background operators'. The dealer in stolen goods is pivotal to the competent and efficient functioning of any thief with a claim upon the status of professional. The work of Walsh (1977), Walsh and Chappell (Chapter 27), Steffensmeier (1986), Klockars (1974), Maguire and Bennett (1982, ch. 4) and Wright and Decker (1994, ch. 6) serve to place the trade in stolen goods within a milieu that is dominated by the mores of mainstream economic activity, thus shifting our attention away from an underworld and highlighting the everyday ambiguities of the overworld.

The work of Shover (Chapter 23) establishes that the social organization of burglary is closer to Sutherland's classic analysis than is suggested by the worlds of the cheque forger and the armed robber (as implied by Lemert and Einstadter). Shover proposes that it is the exigencies of burglary that necessitate the creation of networks of dependency, rather than non-instrumental cultural bonding based upon common occupational status. Further, although Shover acknowledges that these networks will continue to evolve due to changes in policing, security and technology, it is apparent that burglary as an occupation could never virtually disappear, as safe-blowing has for example (Chambliss 1972; Letkemann 1973; Hobbs 1995), or alter so radically as cheque forgery.

Wright and Decker (1994) locate their ground-breaking study of burglary neither within an amorphous marketplace nor within the structured social relations of a sub-culture. Instead, their emphasis is on the *generating milieu* of chaotic and tentative 'street life'. Few of their sample actually identified themselves as burglars, yet a significant number possessed a range of

> . . . specialised cognitive abilities related to burglary, commonly referred to as expertise. . . . Most had a consistent, workable scheme for assessing risk and reward schemes emited by potential targets . . . knew numerous ways to gain illicit entry to dwellings . . . had a general plan for searching targets quickly and efficiently . . . and understood how to convert the goods they stole into cash (p. 204).

Wright and Decker point out that this specialized knowledge, although also possessed by hustlers, rounders and other non-specialists, remains exclusive and is not retained by either non-criminals, specialist police personnel or convicted non-property offenders (Logie, Wright and Decker in Chapter 14).

The central theme of the all-purpose non-specialist criminal, the rounder or hustler (Holzman, Chapter 8; Polsky, Chapter 18; Roebuck and Johnson, Chapter 20) is likely to gain in analytic credibility as the concept of the market grows in importance within both criminal and non-criminal spheres; also as the labour force is fragmented into flexible coalitions of similarly economically-disposed individuals. For those engaged in criminal occupations, the temporary nature of these coalitions is ensured by the unpredictability of market forces and by the advantages to be gained from an ever-changing workplace and modus operandi.

This mobility and flexibility of professional criminal personnel and group activity have been attended by a perceived decline in the ethical base upon which it is claimed that the identity and solidarity of professional criminals are constituted (see, for instance, Maurer 1955). As in the straight world, there is a constant harking back to a golden age of predictability, stoicism, honour and reliability (Shover, Chapter 23, p. 346). Professional criminals are therefore as prone to bouts of nostalgia as any other individual, yearning for stability and a mythical age when justice, albeit rough, provided an ideological structure for their villainy that is in stark contrast to the amorphous nature of contemporary crime (see Kray 1991; Lambrianou 1992, Campbell 1991, ch. 6; Fraser 1994). In both fictional and empirical accounts, the depiction of an unwritten code or set of ethics providing a framework for a sharply delineated association of professional criminals is a powerful and pervasive concept that succeeds in drawing parallels with conventional professional communities. It thus draws on Sutherland's original template of a coherent group with 'a complex of abilities and skills, just as do physicians, lawyers or bricklayers' (1937, p. 197).

The most powerful claims for a self-contained code of ethics linked to professional criminals are to be found in studies of prison sub-cultures. Both Irwin (1970) and Irwin and Cressey (Chapter 10) stress that the most crucial aspect in determining an inmate's adaptation to prison is the culture that he brings with him. Further, the culture of the professional criminal is most easily adapted to prison regimes, for a criminal identity is one that carries currency both inside and outside the context of institutional confinement. In particular, currency is afforded to qualities of 'rightness' and 'solidness' and to attributes of 'honesty', 'responsibility' and 'loyalty'. It is vital for the criminal to,

... meet his obligations, pay his debts, keep his appointments, and most importantly never divulge information to anyone which may lead to the arrest of another person. His character, his 'rightness', is one of the most important dimensions of his life (Irwin 1970, p. 8).

Former identities are enhanced rather than erased. The professional's commitment to a criminal identity constitutes an important component in his adaptation to prison, confirming that prison is a constituent element of the broader criminal culture (Irwin and Cressey, Chapter 10. See also Cohen and Taylor 1972, ch. 7; McVicar 1982; Fraser 1994; Mason 1994).

However, for those writers with a penchant for 'free world' research, the code of professional criminal ethics appears to be little more than a rhetorical device that functions in the face of a constantly-changing working environment and ever-fluctuating personnel in order to maintain some sense of exclusive elite status (Taylor 1984, p. 76). As a report from the mid-1960s states: 'The shifting, transitory pattern of most professional criminals' working relationships was found to be accompanied by the absence of any strong ethical codes' (President's Commission, Chapter 19, p. 301).

A professional code of ethics may have been a feasible concept when the relevant organizations and technologies of professional crime required an ethical base as an instrumental foundation for competent practice. However, as can be observed from an analysis of armed robbery in Britain in the 1970s, when informants, security measures and police tactics combined to render these practices redundant, the criminal code was judiciously ousted by a rhetoric somewhat less than 'righteous', yet easily recognized by those more accustomed to the self-justifications of legitimate economic activity (Ball et al. 1978).

The most instructive concepts in terms of their potential for drawing a direct analogy with the legitimate economic order relate to notions of skill (Inciardi, Chapter 9), craft (McIntosh 1971) and competence (Shover, Chapter 23) – the everyday methodologies inherent in the committal of crime as work (Letkemann 1973). The question of what constitutes a competent performance is central to Luckenbill's 1981 study of armed robbery (Chapter 15). In this study the reader is introduced to the central problem for the robber: 'how do I gain and maintain compliance from my victims?' Luckenbill depicts robbery as a set of transactions managed by the robber, involving both himself and his victim in the accomplishment of four interrelated tasks. Once the robber has established his presence with the victim, the interaction must be transformed into 'the robbery frame'; the goods are handed over to the robber and, finally, the robber leaves the scene. The enabling device for the successful completion of these four stages in coercion based on physical force.

For an in-depth exploration of the maintenance of compliance we must look to Goffman (Chapter 7). Here, the victim's acceptance of failure is treated as crucial for the successful completion of a crime. In this particular case, Goffman concentrates upon the relationship between the confidence trickster and his victim or 'mark'. The skilful manipulation of the victim by the con-man and the role played by the mark, are presented here as central to the stage management of the ongoing felonious drama. However, unlike Luckenbill's study of the most confrontational of crimes, Goffman presents the con-game as an allegorical comment upon normative everyday interactions: the mark has an investment in the game that involves potential gain rather than the categorical deficit experienced by a victim in the course of a 'normal' robbery. The management of failure is therefore a more crucial aspect of this interaction than in the previous case. Further, the subsequent rationalizations of the victim serve to bring this particular aspect of professional crime closer to that found in non-criminal projects – for profit and loss, both actual and rhetorical, characterize all fraud and fraud-related interactions (Schur, Chapter 22).

In the same volume of *Urban Life* as Luckenbill's paper and constituting a canny piece of journal editing, Levi (Chapter 13) introduces the world of the professional killer. Utilizing frame analysis, his study is about the personal management of deviance and the neutralization, via 'reframing', of a criminal activity that is unlikely to find its professional status contested. By virtue of the exclusivity of their specialism, professional murderers, unlike professional thieves, are able to establish a rarefied niche within the labour market. Further, via reframing the victim as a target and receiving payment for his services, the professional murderer not only avoids self-stigmatization, but also enhances the status of murderer to that of a supremely rational market operative. The hit man commercializes a rarefied impersonal level of violence. He is the ultimate professional, a commodifier of death.

While there has been some debate concerning the existence or otherwise of a distinctive sub-culture of professional criminality that finds its mirror image in normative legitimate social settings, the emphasis on non-specialization (mentioned above in the work of the President's Commission, Letkemann, Holzman and Polsky) suggests that an exploration of the broader social maelstrom, of which professional criminals are but a segment, could be a profitable exercise. The adoption of entrepreneurship as a central ideological prop of contemporary society, has meant a merging of legitimate and illegitimate interests around a central theme of wealth accumulation (cf. Burrows 1991; Heelas and Morris 1992). Consequently the term professional criminal now carries with it an ambiguity that is entirely appropriate in a post-traditional order that shuns preconceived class-based notions of structural and ideological constraint. In turn, these notions are inextricably linked to social forms that were the direct product of a division of labour which, in late 20th century capitalism, shows every sign of obsolescence.

As Bauman has indicated, 'Cultural authorities turn themselves into market forces, become commodities, compete with other commodities, legitimize their value through the selling capacity they attain' (1992, p. 52). Accordingly, the shift by professional criminals towards entrepreneurial activities is indicative of the reproduction of post-traditional economic relations within the inscrutable parameters of illegal markets. The transformative capacities of the cultural and economic power that constitute professional criminality are ideally suited to the kinds of perpetual re-negotiations that regulate relations between both individuals and groups (Giddens 1979, pp. 65–6). They reproduce themselves in the form of constantly mutating social systems of culturally indeterminable origins and multifarious economic destinations.

In one of the few British studies that seeks to locate the enabling culture that nurtures professional criminality, Mack (Chapter 16) adopts a conventional class-orientated sub-cultural stance to this issue, concentrating upon the role of the traditional base from which most 'full-time miscreants' are culled. He also indicates the crucial role of competence in maintaining the networks that lend structure to serious criminal activity. However, our definitions of what constitutes criminal competence need to be as flexible as the marketplace itself if we are to advance our understanding of committed criminality. In an excellent and far-reaching analysis of the field, Mack and Kerner (1975) point out that our understanding of professional crime tends to be dominated by a continuing focus upon,

> The front line operators . . . the house breakers or the van or bank robbers, or the hijackers or fraudsters As a consequence, two vital categories are ignored, the 'service providers' and, most importantly, the 'background organisers (1975, p. 178).

Mack and Kerner continue by claiming that the high status of the front-line operator is somewhat illusory, and that it is the organization behind the front liners that warrants the focus of our attention. This is because professional criminal networks, like other systems of organized capitalism, are increasingly typified by profound and complex structures. These structures will be marked by local, regional, national and international characteristics, and may manifest themselves at street level as marginal and essentially disorganized. Yet, as with legitimate commerce and industry, it is the 'magic of the market' (Reuter 1984) rather than legal edicts or the myths promulgated by popular culture (cf. Warshow, Chapter 28; Hebdige 1974, p. 10; Hebdige 1977, pp. 56–8) that defines competent practice and expert status.

This ambiguity between criminal and legal commercial activity is best expressed by those writers concerned with the drugs trade (Langer, Chapter 11; Dorn and South, Chapter 3; Williams 1989). The scope and variety offered by drug dealing to those seeking to explore criminal entrepreneurial possibilities are considerable, the similarities between drug dealing and legitimate business highlighting yet again the problematics of utilizing the term professional crime in relation to an exclusive cultural and occupational space.

The problems inherent in attempting to develop criminal typifications within a marketplace that, despite being dominated by a single commodity, is as fragmented by class, race and gender as any legitimate economic sphere, can be examined by looking at the work of Ruggiero (Chapter 21) and Adler and Adler (Chapter 1). Drug economies will vary, and success or failure will inevitably be relative concepts for operatives engaging with markets which differ greatly in terms of refinement and intensity. Professional dealers who are able to sustain successful businesses will seek to invest in legal enterprises. On the other hand, the lack of opportunities for such investment within ghetto cultures (Ruggiero) compared to those of elite markets (Adler and Adler) is likely to curtail the prospect of longevity, thereby reducing the chances of skill, consensus, shared ideology and – most crucially – organization being allowed to develop.

It would appear, therefore, that what has traditionally been defined as professional crime has now ruptured into two distinctive forms of criminality. On the one hand we have the decline of key criminal activities that were previously central to the concept of professional crime (such as armed robbery) into haphazard, essentially amateur, excursions (Walsh 1986, ch. 3). These excursions are carried out with minimal planning, a low level of competence and, most importantly, no commitment to specialized criminality. For instance, only 11 per cent of Walsh's sample of robbers provided a self-description of thief or robber (1986, p. 57).

Concomitantly, there has emerged a highly flexible professional with the abilities and resources to engage in a myriad of entrepreneurial activities. These individuals do display a commitment, not to a sub-culture or occupational group, but to the prime motivational ethos of 'economic man' (Tobias 1968) – financial gain. Their practice is marked by competence in engaging and manipulating markets, with an emphasis placed upon those aspects of criminality that are amenable to organization with a view to maximizing profits. The division of labour within professional criminality assures that members of this latter group, via their control of relevant markets, are able to establish elements of continuity and stability that in every sense can be described as 'organized' (see Abadinsky 1991, ch. 1 for a concise discussion of the problems of defining organized crime).

The life world of the former 'disorganized' group stresses the ambiguity of motive that is to be found amongst professional criminals. This life world is stubbornly resistant to 'sub-systems of purposive, rational action' (Habermas 1984) and is exemplified by the narcissistic drive that is implicit in a 'life lived without a safety net' (Pileggi 1987, p. 39). Numerous first-hand accounts of 'life as party' (Shover and Honaker, Chapter 24) confirm the centrality of 'earning and burning money' (Katz 1988, p. 215) as a way of authenticating the professional criminal's commitment to a sub-cultural identity defined by conspicuous consumption and funded by crime (Hohimer 1981, p. 19; Wideman 1985, p. 131). The professional criminal cited by Taylor in Chapter 26 sums it up as follows:

> Well I'm a natural. I mean, I am a natural. I love it, I love the high life . . . I love the . . . going out to wine and dine, the fucking champagne and the birds, and living it up, and first class on the airplanes. Champagne fucking Charlie. You know. Ducking and diving; and, you know, wining and dining (p. 372).

Straddling both the economic and hedonistic strands of contemporary serious criminality are those emergent practitioners for whom market viability and hedonistic and/or addictive consumption merge seamlessly. The drugs trade does not constitute a homogenous economic activity; indeed, from the unlikely ranks of user-dealers can emerge some of the more committed, skilled and organized practitioners. As Dunlap et al. vividly and persuasively argue in Chapter 4, for user-dealers, consistency and longevity within the marketplace proffer more than economic viability. The fragmented nature of trading environments and their consequent cultures and the lack of enabling 'underworlds' has spawned criminal forms that are characterized more explicitly by the tribulations inherent in any small business than by the semi-mythical contingencies of traditional professional crime. Yet the criminal status of these non-traditional practitioners cannot be dismissed, for their lack of affiliation to traditional networks creates cognitive problems that must be resolved, along with the everyday accounting conundrums created by corner-shop economics:

> In the world of illegal drug sales, the opposition of government and the absence of formal training mean that individuals must discover by themselves how to deal with the complex contingencies involved in selling drugs. . . . They must learn how to obtain supplies of high quality drugs to sell; create retail sales units; recruit buyers; avoid arrest, incarceration, and violence from competitors or customers; and handle and account for large amounts of cash, while evading both formal and informal sanctions . . . Perhaps their most difficult challenge however is to limit their own drug consumption so that they sell to 're-up' or purchase more wholesale units of drugs (Chapter 4, pp. 46–7).

From this analysis of the contemporary drug trade, we can also observe the involvement of non-traditional operatives in criminal networks of various shape and intensity. In a move that finds parallels in the legitimate economy where labour (like the mode of production within which it is framed) has become fragmented and old forms of production have become redundant (Lash and Urry 1987; Piore and Sabel 1984), women are more likely to become involved in serious criminality (Taylor 1993; Hobbs 1995). Fagen (1994) has identified female involvement in the cocaine economy as indicative of crucial alterations to the social controls that previously prevailed in poor urban neighbourhoods, of changes to the structural circumstances of women living in these neighbourhoods and, most importantly, of a decline in the social status of young men: 'The declining status of young men may have diminished their "gatekeeper" and mediating roles in both conventional and street networks in poor neighborhoods' (Fagen 1994, p. 186). The very specific contingencies of cocaine markets were seen as relatively open to women able to achieve a measure of status that has traditionally been denied to them within street networks. Taken together, the contributions of Dunlap et al. and Fagen do suggest that the heavily gendered worlds of professional criminals may be showing signs of change in accord with the socioeconomic environments that host them.

Criminals enjoying their work and working to enjoy their leisure are not insignificant issues if we are to understand the cultures that nurture and sculpt professional crime. An understanding of the relationship between the two makes it possible to suggest that there is not some vast gulf between instrumental and non-instrumental crime, for the marketplace can, certainly in the case of drugs, create an environment that will enable both entrepreneurial and hedonistic engagement.

The enacted environments of professional criminality are therefore not homogenous spheres of activity. They will vary greatly, but in many crucial ways are largely indistinguishable from the entrepreneurial arenas for legitimate enterprise. These arenas are supportive of networks that function as enabling environments for a plethora of profit-making activities, some of which will be either partly or wholly criminal. It is worth stressing that the 'underworld', like other imaginary realms, is a convenient ideal location for fantasy; in the case of professional and organized crime, we are inclined to lurch mindlessly through the looking glass rather than stand back and consider the reflection.

The exclusivity of the professional criminals' milieu has been breached by the savagery of democratic enterprise culture; as a consequence, it is to mainstream commercial practice that we must turn for our understanding of 'full time miscreants' (Mack, Chapter 16). The cultural origins of those engaging in serious and committed criminality are no longer exclusively proletarian. Nevertheless, traditional analyses such as Mack's retain considerable relevance due to their capacity to define one aspect of both professional crime and entrepreneurial working-class culture.

However, such analyses need to be supplemented by studies that indicate the instrumental ambiguity of contemporary criminal enterprise (Block 1991(b)) and by others concerned with its relationship to the ideological frameworks and control strategies that sustain it (Hobbs 1988; Jennings et al. 1991). Further, the cultures that nurture professional crime now feature variations mirroring the range of activities that constitute the expert exploration of markets that have emerged comparatively recently (Dorn et al. 1992, pp. 31–62). While some of these settings reflect many of its practitioners' traditional schooling in rough places (Wideman 1985; Gibbs and Shelly, Chapter 6; Pruis and Irini 1980), the work of Block (1991(a), 1991(b)) and of Levi (1987) suggest that, as Chambliss has indicated, we can no longer distinguish crime from normal business. 'Much crime does not fit into a separate category. It is primarily a business activity' (Chambliss 1978, p. 53).

Both fraud and the drug trade represent generic criminal engagements with the marketplace that clearly indicate the merging of 'upper and underworld' (Levi 1987, p. 194). Specific structural changes to the marketplace, such as the deregulation of the London Stock Exchange in 1986, and key technological innovations particularly in the field of communications (Levi 1987, p. 3) have enabled professional criminals to attack information and/or money when and where it is most vulnerable in a similar way that the cosh, motor car, shotgun and thermic lance had enhanced the practice of previous generations of thieves (Hobbs 1995).

There is now a certain ambiguity regarding the cultural origins of professional criminals, social class proving an unreliable indicator of serious, committed contemporary criminality (Levi 1991, p. xix). Overlaps with other criminological categories are unavoidable, and the insularity of such idiosyncratic domains as white collar, professional, corporate or organized may in the future prove to be unhelpful to those seeking to understand phenomena that are difficult to define due to their illusive nature and covert operational formations. However, far from being redundant (Cressey 1972, p. 45), the term professional crime merely requires retuning to accord both with changing opportunity structures and with the consequent ideological shifts that mark the states of flux which are prime characteristics of modern societies. Once this retuning has been carried out, we will be able to focus upon professionals 'as fluid sets of mobile marauders in the urban landscape alert to institutional weakness in both legitimate and illegitimate spheres' (Block 1985, p. 245).

References

Abadinsky, H. (1991), *Organised Crime*, 3rd ed., Chicago: Nelson Hall.

Bauman, Z. (1992), *Intimations of Modernity*, London: Routledge.

Ball, J. et al. (1978), *Cops and Robbers*, London: Andre Deutsch.

Block, A. (1985), *East Side – West Side: Organising Crime in New York 1930–1950*, 2nd ed., New Brunswick: Transaction.

Block, A. (1991a), *Masters of Paradise*, New Brunswick: Transaction.

Block, A. (1991b), *The Business of Crime*, Colorado: Westview Press.

Burrows, R. (ed.) (1991), *Deciphering the Enterprise Culture*, London: Routledge.

Campbell, D. (1991), *That was Business, This is Personal*, London: Mandarin.

Chambliss, W.J. (1972), *Box Man*, New York: Harper & Row.

Chambliss, W.J. (1978), *On the Take*, Bloomington: Indiana University Press.

Chesney, K. (1968), *The Victorian Underworld*, Harmondsworth: Penguin.

Cohen, S. and Taylor, L. (1972), *Psychological Survival*, Harmondsworth: Penguin.

Cressey, D. (1972), *Criminal Organisation*, London: Heinemann.

Dorn, N. et al. (1992), *Traffickers*, London: Routledge.

Downes, D. and Rock, P. (1982), *Understanding Deviance*, Oxford: Clarendon Press.

Fagen, J. (1994), 'Women and Drugs Revisited: Female Participation in the Cocaine Economy', *The Journal of Drug Issues*, **24** (2), pp. 179–225.

Fraser, F. (1994), *Mad Frank*, London: Little Brown.

Giddens, A. (1979), *Central Problems in Social Theory*, London: Macmillan.

Habermas, J. (1984), *The Theory of Communicative Action*, Vol. 1, London: Heinemann.

Hay, D. (1975), 'Property, Authority and the Criminal Law' in D. Hay et al. (eds), *Albion's Fatal Tree*, London: Allan Lane.

Hebdige, D. (1974), 'The Kray Twins, A System of Closure', Occasional Paper 21, Centre for Contemporary Cultural Studies, Birmingham University.

Hebdige, D. (1977), 'Sub-Cultural Conflict and Criminal Performance in Fulham', Occasional Paper 25, Centre for Contemporary Cultural Studies, Birmingham University.

Heelas, P. and Morris, P. (eds) (1992), *The Values of the Enterprise Culture*, London: Routledge.

Hobbs, D. (1988), *Doing the Business: Entrepreneurship, Detectives and the Working Class in the East End of London*, Oxford: Clarendon Press.

Hobbs, D. (1994), 'Professional and Organised Crime' in M. Maguire, M. Morgan and R. Reiner (eds), *The Oxford Handbook of Criminology*, Oxford: Oxford University Press.

Hobbs, D. (1995), *Bad Business: The Culture and Practice of Contemporary Professional Criminals*, Oxford: Oxford University Press.

Hohimer, F. (1981), *Violent Streets*, London: Star.

Hollingshead, A.B.N. (1939), 'Behaviour Systems as a Field for Research', *American Journal of Sociology*, **4**, pp. 816–22.

Howson, G. (1971), *Thief Taker General*, New York: St Martins Press.

Irwin, J. (1970), *The Felon*, Englewood Cliffs, N.J.: Prentice-Hall.

Jennings, A. et al. (1991), *Scotland Yard's Cocaine Connection*, London: Arrow.

Katz, J. (1988), *Seductions of Crime*, New York: Basic Books.

Klockars, C. (1974), *The Professional Fence*, London: Tavistock.

Kray, R. (1991), *Born Fighter*, London: Arrow.

Lambrianou, T. (1992), *Inside the Firm*, London: Pan.

Landesco, J. (1968), *Organised Crime in Chicago*, 2nd ed., Chicago: University of Chicago Press.

Lash, S. and Urry, J. (1987), *The End of Organised Capitalism*, Cambridge: Polity Press.

Letkemann, P. (1973), *Crime as Work*, Englewood Cliffs: Prentice Hall.

Levi, M. (1987), *Regulating Fraud*, London: Tavistock.

Levi, M. (1991), 'Developments in Business Crime Control in Europe' in F. Heidensohn and M. Farrell (eds), *Crime in Europe*, London: Routledge.

Low, D.A. (1982), *Thieves' Kitchen: The Regency Underworld*, London: Dent.

Mack, J.A. and Kerner, H.J. (1975), *The Crime Industry*, Lexington: Saxon House, Lexington Books.

Maguire, M. and Bennett, T. (1982), *Burglary in a Dwelling*, London: Heinemann.

Mason, E. (1994), *Inside Story*, London: Pan.

Maurer, D.W. (1955), *The Whizz Mob*, New Haven: College and University Press.

Mayhew, H. (1950), *London's Underworld*, edited by P. Quennell, London: Spring Books.

McIntosh, M. (1971), 'Changes in the Organisation of Thieving' in S. Cohen (ed.), *Images of Deviance*, Harmondsworth: Penguin.

McVicar, J. (1982), 'Violence in Prisons' in P. Marsh and A. Campbell (eds), *Aggression and Violence*, Oxford: Blackwell.

Munsche, P.B. (1981), *Gentlemen and Poachers*, Cambridge: Cambridge University Press.

Pileggi, N. (1987), *Wise Guy*, London: Corgi.

Piore, M. and Sabel, C. (1984), *The Second Industrial Divide*, New York: Basic Books.

Pruis, R. and Irini, S. (1980), *Hookers, Rounders and Desk Clerks: The Social Organisation of a Hotel Community*, Toronto: Gage.

Reuter, P. (1984), *Disorganised Crime*, Cambridge Mass.: MIT Press.

Rock (1973), *Deviant Behaviour*, London: Hutchinson.

Roebuck, J. and Windham, G. (1983), 'Professional Theft' in G. Waldo (ed.), *Criminal Careers*, Beverly Hills: Sage.

Salgado, G. (1977), *The Elizabethan Underworld*, London: Dent.

Sharp, J.A. (1984), *Crime in Early Modern England, 1550–1750*, London: Longman.

Shields, R. (1991), *Places on the Margin: Alternative Geographies of Modernity*, London: Routledge.

Solway, I. and Waters, J. (1977), 'Working the Corner: The Ethics and Legality of Ethnographic Fieldwork Among Active Heroin Addicts' in R.S. Weppner (ed.), *Street Ethnography*, Beverly Hills: Sage.

Stedman-Jones, G. (1971), *Outcast London*, London: Oxford University Press.

Steffensmeier, D.J. (1986), *The Fence: In the Shadow of Two Worlds*, Totowa, N.J.: Rowman & Littlefield.

Sutherland, E. (1937), *The Professional Thief*, Chicago: University of Chicago Press.

Taylor, A. (1993), *Women Drug Users: An Ethnography of a Female Injecting Community*, Oxford: Clarendon Press.

Taylor, L. (1984), *In the Underworld*, Oxford: Blackwell.

Thomas, W.I. and Znaniecki, F. (1927), *The Polish Peasant in Europe and America*, 2nd ed., 2 Vols, New York: Knopf.

Tobias, J.J. (1968), 'The Crime Industry', *The British Journal of Criminology*, **II**, pp. 247–58.

Tobias, J.J. (1979), *Crime and Police in England, 1700–1900*, London: Gill and Macmillan.

Walsh, D. (1986), *Heavy Business*, London: Routledge & Kegan Paul.

Walsh, M.E. (1977), *The Fence*, Westport Conn.: Greenwood Press.

Wideman, J.E. (1985), *Brothers and Keepers*, New York: Penguin.

Williams, T. (1989), *The Cocaine Kids*, Reading, Mass.: Addison-Wesley.

Wright, R. and Decker, S. (1994), *Burglars on the Job, Street Life and Residential Break-Ins*, Boston: North Eastern University Press.

[1]

SOCIAL PROBLEMS, Vol. 31, No. 2, December 1983

SHIFTS AND OSCILLATIONS IN DEVIANT CAREERS:
THE CASE OF UPPER-LEVEL DRUG DEALERS AND SMUGGLERS*

PATRICIA A. ADLER
PETER ADLER
University of Tulsa

This is the first study of drug trafficking in the United States to penetrate the upper eschelons of the marijuana and cocaine business—the smugglers and their primary dealers. We spent six years observing and interviewing these traffickers and their associates in southwestern California and examining their typical career paths. We show how drug traffickers enter the business and rise to the top, how they become disenchanted due to the rising social and legal costs of upper-level drug trafficking, how and why they either voluntarily or involuntarily leave the business, and why so many end up returning to their deviant careers, or to other careers within the drug world.

The upper eschelons of the marijuana and cocaine trade constitute a world which has never before been researched and analyzed by sociologists. Importing and distributing tons of marijuana and kilos of cocaine at a time, successful operators can earn upwards of a half million dollars per year. Their traffic in these so-called "soft"[1] drugs constitutes a potentially lucrative occupation, yet few participants manage to accumulate any substantial sums of money, and most people envision their involvement in drug trafficking as only temporary. In this study we focus on the career paths followed by members of one upper-level drug dealing and smuggling community. We discuss the various modes of entry into trafficking at these upper levels, contrasting these with entry into middle- and low-level trafficking. We then describe the pattern of shifts and oscillations these dealers and smugglers experience. Once they reach the top rungs of their occupation, they begin periodically quitting and re-entering the field, often changing their degree and type of involvement upon their return. Their careers, therefore, offer insights into the problems involved in leaving deviance.

Previous research on soft drug trafficking has only addressed the low and middle levels of this occupation, portraying people who purchase no more than 100 kilos of marijuana or single ounces of cocaine at a time (Anonymous, 1969; Atkyns and Hanneman, 1974; Blum et al., 1972; Carey, 1968; Goode, 1970; Langer, 1977; Lieb and Olson, 1976; Mouledoux, 1972; Waldorf et al., 1977). Of these, only Lieb and Olson (1976) have examined dealing and/or smuggling as an occupation, investigating participants' career developments. But their work, like several of the others, focuses on a population of student dealers who may have been too young to strive for and attain the upper levels of drug trafficking. Our study fills this gap at the top by describing and analyzing an elite community of upper-level dealers and smugglers and their careers.

We begin by describing where our research took place, the people and activities we studied, and the methods we used. Second, we outline the process of becoming a drug trafficker, from initial recruitment through learning the trade. Third, we look at the different types of upward mobility displayed by dealers and smugglers. Fourth, we examine the career shifts and oscillations which veteran dealers and smugglers display, outlining the multiple, conflicting forces which lure them both into and out of drug trafficking. We conclude by suggesting a variety of paths which dealers

* An earlier version of this paper was presented at the annual meetings of the American Society of Criminology, Denver, Colorado, November, 1983. Correspondence to: Department of Sociology, University of Tulsa, Tulsa, Oklahoma 74104.
1. The term "soft" drugs generally refers to marijuana, cocaine and such psychedelics as LSD and mescaline (Carey, 1968). In this paper we do not address trafficking in psychedelics because, since they are manufactured in the United States, they are neither imported nor distributed by the group we studied.

and smugglers pursue out of drug trafficking and discuss the problems inherent in leaving this deviant world.

SETTING AND METHOD

We based our study in "Southwest County," one section of a large metropolitan area in southwestern California near the Mexican border. Southwest County consisted of a handful of beach towns dotting the Pacific Ocean, a location offering a strategic advantage for wholesale drug trafficking.

Southwest County smugglers obtained their marijuana in Mexico by the ton and their cocaine in Colombia, Bolivia, and Peru, purchasing between 10 and 40 kilos at a time. These drugs were imported into the United States along a variety of land, sea, and air routes by organized smuggling crews. Southwest County dealers then purchased these products and either "middled" them directly to another buyer for a small but immediate profit of approximately $2 to $5 per kilo of marijuana and $5,000 per kilo of cocaine, or engaged in "straight dealing." As opposed to middling, straight dealing usually entailed adulterating the cocaine with such "cuts" as manitol, procaine, or inositol, and then dividing the marijuana and cocaine into smaller quantities to sell them to the next-lower level of dealers. Although dealers frequently varied the amounts they bought and sold, a hierarchy of transacting levels could be roughly discerned. "Wholesale" marijuana dealers bought directly from the smugglers, purchasing anywhere from 300 to 1,000 "bricks" (averaging a kilo in weight) at a time and selling in lots of 100 to 300 bricks. "Multi-kilo" dealers, while not the smugglers' first connections, also engaged in upper-level trafficking, buying between 100 to 300 bricks and selling them in 25 to 100 brick quantities. These were then purchased by middle-level dealers who filtered the marijuana through low-level and "ounce" dealers before it reached the ultimate consumer. Each time the marijuana changed hands its price increase was dependent on a number of factors: purchase cost; the distance it was transported (including such transportation costs as packaging, transportation equipment, and payments to employees); the amount of risk assumed; the quality of the marijuana; and the prevailing prices in each local drug market. Prices in the cocaine trade were much more predictable. After purchasing kilos of cocaine in South America for $10,000 each, smugglers sold them to Southwest County "pound" dealers in quantities of one to 10 kilos for $60,000 per kilo. These pound dealers usually cut the cocaine and sold pounds ($30,000) and half-pounds ($15,000) to "ounce" dealers, who in turn cut it again and sold ounces for $2,000 each to middle-level cocaine dealers known as "cut-ounce" dealers. In this fashion the drug was middled, dealt, divided and cut—sometimes as many as five or six times—until it was finally purchased by consumers as grams or half-grams.

Unlike low-level operators, the upper-level dealers and smugglers we studied pursued drug trafficking as a full-time occupation. If they were involved in other businesses, these were usually maintained to provide them with a legitimate front for security purposes. The profits to be made at the upper levels depended on an individual's style of operation, reliability, security, and the amount of product he or she consumed. About half of the 65 smugglers and dealers we observed were successful, some earning up to three-quarters of a million dollars per year.[2] The other half continually struggled in the business, either breaking even or losing money.

Although dealers' and smugglers' business activities varied, they clustered together for business and social relations, forming a moderately well-integrated community whose members pursued a "fast" lifestyle, which emphasized intensive partying, casual sex, extensive travel, abundant drug

---

2. This is an idealized figure representing the profit a dealer or smuggler could potentially earn and does not include deductions for such miscellaneous and hard-to-calculate costs as: time or money spent in arranging deals (some of which never materialize); lost, stolen, or unrepaid money or drugs; and the personal drug consumption of a drug trafficker and his or her entourage. Of these, the single largest expense is the last one, accounting for the bulk of most Southwest County dealers' and smugglers' earnings.

consumption, and lavish spending on consumer goods. The exact size of Southwest County's upper-level dealing and smuggling community was impossible to estimate due to the secrecy of its members. At these levels, the drug world was quite homogeneous. Participants were predominantly white, came from middle-class backgrounds, and had little previous criminal involvement. While the dealers' and smugglers' social world contained both men and women, most of the serious business was conducted by the men, ranging in age from 25 to 40 years old.

We gained entry to Southwest County's upper-level drug community largely by accident. We had become friendly with a group of our neighbors who turned out to be heavily involved in smuggling marijuana. Opportunistically (Riemer, 1977), we seized the chance to gather data on this unexplored activity. Using key informants who helped us gain the trust of other members of the community, we drew upon snowball sampling techniques (Biernacki and Waldorf, 1981) and a combination of overt and covert roles to widen our network of contacts. We supplemented intensive participant-observation, between 1974 and 1980,[3] with unstructured, taped interviews. Throughout, we employed extensive measures to cross-check the reliability of our data, whenever possible (Douglas, 1976). In all, we were able to closely observe 65 dealers and smugglers as well as numerous other drug world members, including dealers' "old ladies" (girlfriends or wives), friends, and family members.

BECOMING A DRUG TRAFFICKER

There are three routes into the upper levels of drug dealing and smuggling. First, some drug users become low-level dealers, gradually working their way up to middle-level dealing. It is rare, however, for upper-level dealers to have such meager origins. Second, there are people who enter directly into drug dealing at the middle level, usually from another occupation. Many of these do extremely well right away. Third, a number of individuals are invited into smuggling because of a special skill or character, sometimes from middle-level drug trafficking careers and other times from outside the drug world entirely. We discuss each of these in turn.

Low-Level Entry

People who began dealing at the bottom followed the classic path into dealing portrayed in the literature (Anonymous, 1969; Blum *et al.*, 1972; Carey, 1968; Goode, 1970; Johnson, 1973). They came from among the ranks of regular drug users, since, in practice, using drugs heavily and dealing for "stash" (one's personal supply) are nearly inseparable. Out of this multitude of low-level dealers, however, most abandoned the practice after they encountered their first legal or financial bust, lasting in the business for only a fairly short period (Anonymous, 1969; Carey, 1968; Lieb and Olson, 1976; Mandel, 1967). Those who sought bigger profits gradually drifted into a full-time career in drug trafficking, usually between the ages of 15 and 22. Because of this early recruitment into dealing as an occupation, low-level entrants generally developed few, if any, occupational skills other than dealing. One dealer described his early phase of involvement:

> I had dealt a limited amount of lids [ounces of marijuana] and psychedelics in my early college days without hardly taking it seriously. But after awhile something changed in me and I decided to try to work myself up. I probably was a classic case—started out buying a kilo for $150 and selling pounds for $100 each. I did that twice, then I took the money and bought two bricks, then three, then five, then seven.

This type of gradual rise through the ranks was characteristic of low-level dealers; however, few reached the upper levels of dealing from these humble beginnings. Only 20 percent of the dealers we observed in Southwest County got their start in this fashion. Two factors combined to make it less likely for low-level entrants to rise to the top. The first was psychological. People who

---

3. We continued to conduct follow-up interviews with key informants through 1983.

started small, thought small; most had neither the motivation nor vision to move large quantities of drugs. The second, and more critical factor, was social. People who started at the bottom and tried to work their way up the ladder often had a hard time finding connections at the upper levels.[4] Dealers were suspicious of new customers, preferring, for security reasons, to deal with established outlets or trusted friends. The few people who did rise through the ranks generally began dealing in another part of the country, moving to Southwest County only after they had progressed to the middle levels. These people were lured to southwestern California by its reputation within drug circles as an importation and wholesale dealing market.

Middle-Level Entry

About 75 percent of the smugglers and dealers in Southwest County entered at the middle level. Future big dealers usually jumped into transacting in substantial quantities from the outset, buying 50 kilos of "commercial" (low-grade) marijuana or one to two ounces of cocaine. One dealer explained this phenomenon:

> Someone who thinks of himself as an executive or an entrepreneur is not going to get into the dope business on a small level. The average executive just jumps right into the middle. Or else he's not going to jump.

This was the route taken by Southwest County residents with little or no previous involvement in drug trafficking. For them, entry into dealing followed the establishment of social relationships with local dealers and smugglers. (Naturally, this implies a self-selecting sample of outsiders who become accepted and trusted by these upper-level traffickers, based on their mutual interests, orientation, and values.) Through their friendships with dealers, these individuals were introduced to other members of the dealing scene and to their "fast" lifestyle. Individuals who found this lifestyle attractive became increasingly drawn to the subculture, building networks of social associations within it. Eventually, some of these people decided to participate more actively. This step was usually motivated both by money and lifestyle. One dealer recounted how he fell in with the drug world set:

> I used to be into real estate making good money. I was the only person at my firm renting to longhairs and dealing with their money. I slowly started getting friendly with them, although I didn't realize how heavy they were. I knew ways of buying real estate and putting it under fictitious names, laundering money so that it went in as hot cash and came out as spendable income. I slowly got more and more involved with this one guy until I was neglecting my real estate business and just partying with him all the time. My spending went up but my income went down, and suddenly I had to look around for another way to make money fast. I took the money I was laundering for him, bought some bricks from another dealer friend of his, and sold them out of state before I gave him back the cash. Within six months I was turning [selling] 100 bricks at a time.

People who entered drug dealing at these middle levels were usually between the ages of 25 and 35 and had been engaged in some other occupation prior to dealing seriously. They came from a wide range of occupational backgrounds. Many drifted into the lifestyle from jobs already concentrated in the night hours, such as bartender, waiter, and nightclub bouncer. Still others came from fields where the working hours were irregular and adaptable to their special schedules, such as acting, real estate, inventing, graduate school, construction, and creative "entrepreneurship" (more aptly called hand-to-mouth survival, for many). The smallest group was tempted into the drug world from structured occupations and the professions.

Middle-level entrants had to learn the trade of drug trafficking. They received "on-the-job training" (Miller and Ritzer, 1977:89) in such skills as how to establish business connections, organize profitable transactions, avoid arrest, transport illegal goods, and coordinate participants

---

4. The exception to this was where low-level dealers rose on the "coattails" of their suppliers: as one dealer increased the volume of his or her purchases or sales, some of his or her customers followed suit.

and equipment. Dealers trained on-the-job refined their knowledge and skills by learning from their mistakes. One dealer recalled how he got "burned" with inferior quality marijuana on his first major "cop" [purchase] because of his inexperience:

> I had borrowed around $7,000 from this friend to do a dope deal. I had never bought in that kind of quantity before but I knew three or four guys who I got it from. I was nervous so I got really stoned before I shopped around and I ended up being hardly able to tell about the quality. Turned out you just couldn't get high off the stuff. I ended up having to sell it below cost.

Once they had gotten in and taught themselves the trade, most middle-level entrants strove for upward mobility. About 80 percent of these Southwest County dealers jumped to the upper levels of trafficking. One dealer described her mode of escalation:

> When I started to deal I was mostly looking for a quick buck here or there, something to pay some pressing bill. I was middling 50 or 100 bricks at a time. But then I was introduced to a guy who said he would front me half a pound of coke, and if I turned it fast I could have more, and on a regular basis. Pretty soon I was turning six, seven, eight, nine, 10 pounds a week — they were passing through real fast. I was clearing at least 10 grand a month. It was too much money too fast. I didn't know what to do with it. It got ridiculous, I wasn't relating to anyone anymore, I was never home, always gone. . . . The biggest ego trip for me came when all of a sudden I turned around and was selling to the people I had been buying from. I skipped their level of doing business entirely and stage-jumped right past them.

Southwest County's social milieu, with its concentration of upper-level dealers and smugglers, thus facilitated forming connections and doing business at the upper levels of the drug world.

Smuggling

Only 10 percent of Southwest County drug smugglers were formerly upper-level dealers who made the leap to smuggling on their own; the rest were invited to become smugglers by established operators. About half of those recruited came directly from the drug world's social scene, with no prior involvement in drug dealing. This implies, like middle-level entry into dealing, both an attraction to the drug crowd and its lifestyle, and prior acquaintance with dealers and smugglers. The other half of the recruits were solicited from among the ranks of middle-level Southwest County dealers.

The complex task of importing illegal drugs required more knowledge, experience, equipment, and connections than most non-smugglers possessed. Recruits had some skill or asset which the experienced smuggler needed to put his operation together. This included piloting or navigating ability, equipment, money, or the willingness to handle drugs while they were being transported. One smuggler described some of the criteria he used to screen potential recruits for suitability as employees in smuggling crews:

> Pilots are really at a premium. They burn out so fast that I have to replace them every six months to a year. But I'm also looking for people who are cool: people who will carry out their jobs according to the plan, who won't panic if the load arrives late or something goes wrong, 'cause this happens a lot. . . .And I try not to get people who've been to prison before, because they'll be more likely to take foolish risks, the kind that I don't want to have to.

Most novice smugglers were recruited and trained by a sponsor with whom they forged an apprentice-mentor relationship. Those who had been dealers previously knew the rudiments of drug trafficking. What they learned from the smuggler was how to fill a particular role in his or her highly specialized operation.

One smuggler we interviewed had a slightly larger than average crew. Ben's commercial marijuana smuggling organization was composed of seven members, not including himself. Two were drivers who transported the marijuana from the landing strip to its point of destination. One was a pilot. The dual roles of driver and co-pilot were filled by a fourth man. Another pilot, who operated both as a smuggler with his own makeshift crew and as a wholesale marijuana dealer who was supplied by Ben, flew runs for Ben when he wasn't otherwise occupied. The sixth member was Ben's enforcer and "stash house" man; he lived in the place where the marijuana was stored, distributed it to customers, and forcibly extracted payments when Ben deemed it necessary. The seventh member handled the financial and legal aspects of the business. He arranged for lawyers and bail bondsmen when needed, laundered Ben's money, and provided him with a legitimate-looking business front. Most of these family members also dealt drugs on the side, having the choice of taking their payment in cash ($10,000 for pilots; $4,000 for drivers) or in kind. Ben arranged the buying and selling connections, financed the operation, provided the heavy equipment (planes, vans, radios) and recruited, supervised, and replaced his crew.

Relationships between smugglers and their recruits were generally characterized by a benign paternalism, leading apprentices to form an enduring loyalty to their sponsor. Once established in a smuggling crew, recruits gained familiarity with the many other roles, the scope of the whole operation, and began to meet suppliers and customers. Eventually they branched out on their own. To do so, employees of a smuggling crew had to develop the expertise and connections necessary to begin running their own operations. Several things were required to make this move. Acquiring the technical knowledge of equipment, air routes, stopovers, and how to coordinate personnel was relatively easy; this could be picked up after working in a smuggling crew for six months to a year. Putting together one's own crew was more difficult because skilled employees, especially pilots, were hard to find. Most new smugglers borrowed people from other crews until they became sufficiently established to recruit and train their own personnel. Finally, connections to buy from and sell to were needed. Buyers were plentiful, but securing a foreign supplier required special breaks or networks.

Another way for employees to become heads of their own smuggling operations was to take over when their boss retired. This had the advantage of keeping the crew and style of operation intact. Various financial arrangements could be worked out for such a transfer of authority, from straight cash purchases to deals involving residual payments. One marijuana smuggler described how he acquired his operation:

> I had been Jake's main pilot for a year and, after him, I knew the most about his operation. We were really tight, and he had taken me all up and down the coast with him, meeting his connections. Naturally I knew the Mexican end of the operation and his supplier since I used to make the runs, flying down the money and picking up the dope. So when he told me he wanted to get out of the business, we made a deal. I took over the set-up and gave him a residual for every run I made. I kept all the drivers, all the connections— everything the guy had—but I found myself a new pilot.

In sum, most dealers and smugglers reached the upper levels not so much as a result of their individual entrepreneurial initiative, but through the social networks they formed in the drug subculture. Their ability to remain in these strata was largely tied to the way they treated these drug world relationships.[5]

SHIFTS AND OSCILLATIONS

We have discussed dealers and smugglers separately up to this point because they display distinct career patterns. But once individuals entered the drug trafficking field and rose to its upper levels, they became part of a social world, the Southwest County drug scene, and faced common problems and experiences. Therefore, we discuss them together from here on.

Despite the gratifications which dealers and smugglers originally derived from the easy money, material comfort, freedom, prestige, and power associated with their careers, 90 percent of those we observed decided, at some point, to quit the business. This stemmed, in part, from their initial

---

5. For a more thorough discussion of the social networks and relationships in Southwest County's drug world see Adler and Adler (1983).

perceptions of the career as temporary ("Hell, nobody wants to be a drug dealer all their life"). Adding to these early intentions was a process of rapid aging in the career: dealers and smugglers became increasingly aware of the restrictions and sacrifices their occupations required and tired of living the fugitive life. They thought about, talked about, and in many cases took steps toward getting out of the drug business. But as with entering, disengaging from drug trafficking was rarely an abrupt act (Lieb and Olson, 1976:364). Instead, it more often resembled a series of transitions, or oscillations,[6] out of and back into the business. For once out of the drug world, dealers and smugglers were rarely successful in making it in the legitimate world because they failed to cut down on their extravagant lifestyle and drug consumption. Many abandoned their efforts to reform and returned to deviance, sometimes picking up where they left off and other times shifting to a new mode of operating. For example, some shifted from dealing cocaine to dealing marijuana, some dropped to a lower level of dealing, and others shifted their role within the same group of traffickers. This series of phase-outs and re-entries, combined with career shifts, endured for years, dominating the pattern of their remaining involvement with the business. But it also represented the method by which many eventually broke away from drug trafficking, for each phase-out had the potential to be an individual's final departure.

Aging in the Career

Once recruited and established in the drug world, dealers and smugglers entered into a middle phase of aging in the career. This phase was characterized by a progressive loss of enchantment with their occupation. While novice dealers and smugglers found that participation in the drug world brought them thrills and status, the novelty gradually faded. Initial feelings of exhilaration and awe began to dull as individuals became increasingly jaded. This was the result of both an extended exposure to the mundane, everyday business aspects of drug trafficking and to an exorbitant consumption of drugs (especially cocaine). One smuggler described how he eventually came to feel:

> It was fun, those three or four years. I never worried about money or anything. But after awhile it got real boring. There was no feeling or emotion or anything about it. I wasn't even hardly relating to my old lady anymore. Everything was just one big rush.

This frenzy of overstimulation and resulting exhaustion hastened the process of "burnout" which nearly all individuals experienced. As dealers and smugglers aged in the career they became more sensitized to the extreme risks they faced. Cases of friends and associates who were arrested, imprisoned, or killed began to mount. Many individuals became convinced that continued drug trafficking would inevitably lead to arrest ("It's only a matter of time before you get caught"). While dealers and smugglers generally repressed their awareness of danger, treating it as a taken-for-granted part of their daily existence, periodic crises shattered their casual attitudes, evoking strong feelings of fear. They temporarily intensified security precautions and retreated into near-isolation until they felt the "heat" was off.

As a result of these accumulating "scares," dealers and smugglers increasingly integrated feelings of "paranoia"[7] into their everyday lives. One dealer talked about his feelings of paranoia:

---

6. While other studies of drug dealing have also noted that participants did not maintain an uninterrupted stream of career involvement (Blum *et al.*, 1972; Carey, 1968; Lieb and Olson, 1976; Waldorf *et al.*, 1977), none have isolated or described the oscillating nature of this pattern.

7. In the dealers' vernacular, this term is not used in the clinical sense of an individual psychopathology rooted in early childhood traumas. Instead, it resembles Lemert's (1962) more sociological definition which focuses on such behavioral dynamics as suspicion, hostility, aggressiveness, and even delusion. Not only Lemert, but also Waldorf *et al.* (1977) and Wedow (1979) assert that feelings of paranoia can have a sound basis in reality, and are therefore readily comprehended and even empathized with others.

You're always on the line. You don't lead a normal life. You're always looking over your shoulder, wondering who's at the door, having to hide everything. You learn to look behind you so well you could probably bend over and look up your ass. That's paraonia. It's a really scary, hard feeling. That's what makes you get out.

Drug world members also grew progressively weary of their exclusion from the legitimate world and the deceptions they had to manage to sustain that separation. Initially, this separation was surrounded by an alluring mystique. But as they aged in the career, this mystique became replaced by the reality of everyday boundary maintenance and the feeling of being an "expatriated citizen within one's own country." One smuggler who was contemplating quitting described the effects of this separation:

I'm so sick of looking over my shoulder, having to sit in my house and worry about one of my non-drug world friends stopping in when I'm doing business. Do you know how awful that is? It's like leading a double life. It's ridiculous. That's what makes it not worth it. It'll be a lot less money [to quit], but a lot less pressure.

Thus, while the drug world was somewhat restricted, it was not an encapsulated community, and dealers' and smugglers' continuous involvement with the straight world made the temptation to adhere to normative standards and "go straight" omnipresent. With the occupation's novelty worn off and the "fast life" taken-for-granted, most dealers and smugglers felt that the occupation no longer resembled their early impressions of it. Once they reached the upper levels of the occupation, their experience began to change. Eventually, the rewards of trafficking no longer seemed to justify the strain and risk involved. It was at this point that the straight world's formerly dull ambiance became transformed (at least in theory) into a potential haven.

Phasing-Out

Three factors inhibited dealers and smugglers from leaving the drug world. Primary among these factors were the hedonistic and materialistic satisfactions the drug world provided. Once accustomed to earning vast quantities of money quickly and easily, individuals found it exceedingly difficult to return to the income scale of the straight world. They also were reluctant to abandon the pleasures of the "fast life" and its accompanying drugs, casual sex, and power. Second, dealers and smugglers identified with, and developed a commitment to, the occupation of drug trafficking (Adler and Adler, 1982). Their self-images were tied to that role and could not be easily disengaged. The years invested in their careers (learning the trade, forming connections, building reputations) strengthened their involvement with both the occupation and the drug community. And since their relationships were social as well as business, friendship ties bound individuals to dealing. As one dealer in the midst of struggling to phase-out explained:

The biggest threat to me is to get caught up sitting around the house with friends that are into dealing. I'm trying to stay away from them, change my habits.

Third, dealers and smugglers hesitated to voluntarily quit the field because of the difficulty involved in finding another way to earn a living. Their years spent in illicit activity made it unlikely for any legitimate organizations to hire them. This narrowed their occupational choices considerably, leaving self-employment as one of the few remaining avenues open.

Dealers and smugglers who tried to leave the drug world generally fell into one of four patterns.[8] The first and most frequent pattern was to postpone quitting until after they could

---

8. At this point, a limitation to our data must be noted. Many of the dealers and smugglers we observed simply "disappeared" from the scene and were never heard from again. We therefore have no way of knowing if they phased-out (voluntarily or involuntarily), shifted to another scene, or were killed in some remote place. We cannot, therefore, estimate the numbers of people who left the Southwest County drug scene via each of the routes discussed here.

execute one last "big deal." While the intention was sincere, individuals who chose this route rarely succeeded; the "big deal" too often remained elusive. One marijuana smuggler offered a variation of this theme:

> My plan is to make a quarter of a million dollars in four months during the prime smuggling season and get the hell out of the business.

A second pattern we observed was individuals who planned to change immediately, but never did. They announced they were quitting, yet their outward actions never varied. One dealer described his involvement with this syndrome:

> When I wake up I'll say, "Hey, I'm going to quit this cycle and just run my other business." But when you're dealing you constantly have people dropping by ounces and asking, "Can you move this?" What's your first response? Always, "Sure, for a toot."

In the third pattern of phasing-out, individuals actually suspended their dealing and smuggling activities, but did not replace them with an alternative source of income. Such withdrawals were usually spontaneous and prompted by exhaustion, the influence of a person from outside the drug world, or problems with the police or other associates. These kinds of phase-outs usually lasted only until the individual's money ran out, as one dealer explained:

> I got into legal trouble with the FBI a while back and I was forced to quit dealing. Everybody just cut me off completely, and I saw the danger in continuing, myself. But my high-class tastes never dwindled. Before I knew it I was in hock over $30,000. Even though I was hot, I was forced to get back into dealing to relieve some of my debts.

In the fourth pattern of phasing-out, dealers and smugglers tried to move into another line of work. Alternative occupations included: (1) those they had previously pursued; (2) front businesses maintained on the side while dealing or smuggling; and (3) new occupations altogether. While some people accomplished this transition successfully, there were problems inherent in all three alternatives.

(1) Most people who tried resuming their former occupations found that these had changed too much while they were away. In addition, they themselves had changed: they enjoyed the self-directed freedom and spontaneity associated with dealing and smuggling, and were unwilling to relinquish it.

(2) Those who turned to their legitimate front business often found that these businesses were unable to support them. Designed to launder rather than earn money, most of these ventures were retail outlets with a heavy cash flow (restaurants, movie theaters, automobile dealerships, small stores) that had become accustomed to operating under a continuous subsidy from illegal funds. Once their drug funding was cut off they could not survive for long.

(3) Many dealers and smugglers utilized the skills and connections they had developed in the drug business to create a new occupation. They exchanged their illegal commodity for a legal one and went into import/export, manufacturing, wholesaling, or retailing other merchandise. For some, the decision to prepare a legitimate career for their future retirement from the drug world followed an unsuccessful attempt to phase-out into a "front" business. One husband-and-wife dealing team explained how these legitimate side businesses differed from front businesses:

> We always had a little legitimate "scam" [scheme] going, like mail-order shirts, wallets, jewelry, and the kids were always involved in that. We made a little bit of money on them. Their main purpose was for a cover. But [this business] was different; right from the start this was going to be a legal thing to push us out of the drug business.

About 10 percent of the dealers and smugglers we observed began tapering off their drug world involvement gradually, transferring their time and money into a selected legitimate endeavor. They did not try to quit drug trafficking altogether until they felt confident that their legitimate business could support them. Like spontaneous phase-outs, many of these planned withdrawals into legitimate endeavors failed to generate enough money to keep individuals from being lured into the drug world.

In addition to voluntary phase-outs caused by burnout, about 40 percent of the Southwest County dealers and smugglers we observed experienced a "bustout" at some point in their careers.[9] Forced withdrawals from dealing or smuggling were usually sudden and motivated by external factors, either financial, legal, or reputational. Financial bustouts generally occurred when dealers or smugglers were either "burned" or "ripped-off" by others, leaving them in too much debt to rebuild their base of operation. Legal bustouts followed arrest and possibly incarceration: arrested individuals were so "hot" that few of their former associates would deal with them. Reputational bustouts occurred when individuals "burned" or "ripped-off" others (regardless of whether they intended to do so) and were banned from business by their former circle of associates. One smuggler gave his opinion on the pervasive nature of forced phase-outs:

> Some people are smart enough to get out of it because they realize, physically, they have to. Others realize, monetarily, that they want to get out of this world before this world gets them. Those are the lucky ones. Then there are the ones who have to get out because they're hot or someone else close to them is so hot that they'd better get out. But in the end when you get out of it, nobody gets out of it out of free choice; you do it because you have to.

Death, of course, was the ultimate bustout. Some pilots met this fate because of the dangerous routes they navigated (hugging mountains, treetops, other aircrafts) and the sometimes ill-maintained and overloaded planes they flew. However, despite much talk of violence, few Southwest County drug traffickers died at the hands of fellow dealers.

Re-Entry

Phasing-out of the drug world was more often than not temporary. For many dealers and smugglers, it represented but another stage of their drug careers (although this may not have been their original intention), to be followed by a period of reinvolvement. Depending on the individual's perspective, re-entry into the drug world could be viewed as either a comeback (from a forced withdrawal) or a relapse (from a voluntary withdrawal).

Most people forced out of drug trafficking were anxious to return. The decision to phase-out was never theirs, and the desire to get back into dealing or smuggling was based on many of the same reasons which drew them into the field originally. Coming back from financial, legal, and reputational bustouts was possible but difficult and was not always successfully accomplished. They had to re-establish contacts, rebuild their organization and fronting arrangements, and raise the operating capital to resume dealing. More difficult was the problem of overcoming the circumstances surrounding their departure. Once smugglers and dealers resumed operating, they often found their former colleagues suspicious of them. One frustrated dealer described the effects of his prison experience:

> When I first got out of the joint [jail], none of my old friends would have anything to do with me. Finally, one guy who had been my partner told me it was because everyone was suspicious of my getting out early and thought I made a deal [with police to inform on his colleagues].

Dealers and smugglers who returned from bustouts were thus informally subjected to a trial period in which they had to re-establish their trustworthiness and reliability before they could once again move in the drug world with ease.

Re-entry from voluntary withdrawal involved a more difficult decision-making process, but was

---

9. It is impossible to determine the exact percentage of people falling into the different phase-out categories: due to oscillation, people could experience several types and thus appear in multiple categories.

easier to implement. The factors enticing individuals to re-enter the drug world were not the same as those which motivated their original entry. As we noted above, experienced dealers and smugglers often privately weighed their reasons for wanting to quit and wanting to stay in. Once they left, their images of and hopes for the straight world failed to materialize. They could not make the shift to the norms, values, and lifestyle of the straight society and could not earn a living within it. Thus, dealers and smugglers decided to re-enter the drug business for basic reasons: the material perquisites, the hedonistic gratifications, the social ties, and the fact that they had nowhere else to go.

Once this decision was made, the actual process of re-entry was relatively easy. One dealer described how the door back into dealing remained open for those who left voluntarily:

> I still see my dealer friends, I can still buy grams from them when I want to. It's the respect they have for me because I stepped out of it without being busted or burning someone. I'm coming out with a good reputation, and even though the scene is a whirlwind — people moving up, moving down, in, out — if I didn't see anybody for a year I could call them up and get right back in that day.

People who relapsed thus had little problem obtaining fronts, re-establishing their reputations, or readjusting to the scene.

Career Shifts

Dealers and smugglers who re-entered the drug world, whether from a voluntary or forced phase-out, did not always return to the same level of transacting or commodity which characterized their previous style of operation. Many individuals underwent a "career shift" (Luckenbill and Best, 1981) and became involved in some new segment of the drug world. These shifts were sometimes lateral, as when a member of a smuggling crew took on a new specialization, switching from piloting to operating a stash house, for example. One dealer described how he utilized friendship networks upon his re-entry to shift from cocaine to marijuana trafficking:

> Before, when I was dealing cocaine, I was too caught up in using the drug and people around me were starting to go under from getting into "base" [another form of cocaine]. That's why I got out. But now I think I've got myself together and even though I'm dealing again I'm staying away from coke. I've switched over to dealing grass. It's a whole different circle of people. I got into it through a close friend I used to know before, but I never did business with him because he did grass and I did coke.

Vertical shifts moved operators to different levels. For example, one former smuggler returned and began dealing; another top-level marijuana dealer came back to find that the smugglers he knew had disappeared and he was forced to buy in smaller quantities from other dealers.

Another type of shift relocated drug traffickers in different styles of operation. One dealer described how, after being arrested, he tightened his security measures:

> I just had to cut back after I went through those changes. Hell, I'm not getting any younger and the idea of going to prison bothers me a lot more than it did 10 years ago. The risks are no longer worth it when I can have a comfortable income with less risk. So I only sell to four people now. I don't care if they buy a pound or a gram.

A former smuggler who sold his operation and lost all his money during phase-out returned as a consultant to the industry, selling his expertise to those with new money and fresh manpower:

> What I've been doing lately is setting up deals for people. I've got foolproof plans for smuggling cocaine up here from Colombia; I tell them how to modify their airplanes to add on extra fuel tanks and to fit in more weed, coke, or whatever they bring up. Then I set them up with refueling points all up and down Central America, tell them how to bring it up here, what points to come in at, and what kind of receiving unit to use. Then they do it all and I get 10 percent of what they make.

Re-entry did not always involve a shift to a new niche, however. Some dealers and smugglers returned to the same circle of associates, trafficking activity, and commodity they worked with prior to their departure. Thus, drug dealers' careers often peaked early and then displayed a variety of shifts, from lateral mobility, to decline, to holding fairly steady.

A final alternative involved neither completely leaving nor remaining within the deviant world. Many individuals straddled the deviant and respectable worlds forever by continuing to dabble in drug trafficking. As a result of their experiences in the drug world they developed a deviant self-identity and a deviant *modus operandi*. They might not have wanted to bear the social and legal burden of full-time deviant work but neither were they willing to assume the perceived confines and limitations of the straight world. They therefore moved into the entrepreneurial realm, where their daily activities involved some kind of hustling or "wheeling and dealing" in an assortment of legitimate, quasi-legitimate, and deviant ventures, and where they could be their own boss. This enabled them to retain certain elements of the deviant lifestyle, and to socialize on the fringes of the drug community. For these individuals, drug dealing shifted from a primary occupation to a sideline, though they never abandoned it altogether.

LEAVING DRUG TRAFFICKING

This career pattern of oscillation into and out of active drug trafficking makes it difficult to speak of leaving drug trafficking in the sense of a final retirement. Clearly, some people succeeded in voluntarily retiring. Of these, a few managed to prepare a post-deviant career for themselves by transferring their drug money into a legitimate enterprise. A larger group was forced out of dealing and either didn't or couldn't return; their bustouts were sufficiently damaging that they never attempted re-entry, or they abandoned efforts after a series of unsuccessful attempts. But there was no way of structurally determining in advance whether an exit from the business would be temporary or permanent. The vacillations in dealers' intentions were compounded by the complexity of operating successfully in the drug world. For many, then, no phase-out could ever be definitely assessed as permanent. As long as individuals had the skills, knowledge, and connections to deal they retained the potential to re-enter the occupation at any time. Leaving drug trafficking may thus be a relative phenomenon, characterized by a trailing-off process where spurts of involvement appear with decreasing frequency and intensity.

SUMMARY

Drug dealing and smuggling careers are temporary and fraught with multiple attempts at retirement. Veteran drug traffickers quit their occupation because of the ambivalent feelings they develop toward their deviant life. As they age in the career their experience changes, shifting from a work life that is exhilarating and free to one that becomes increasingly dangerous and confining. But just as their deviant careers are temporary, so too are their retirements. Potential recruits are lured into the drug business by materialism, hedonism, glamor, and excitement. Established dealers are lured away from the deviant life and back into the mainstream by the attractions of security and social ease. Retired dealers and smugglers are lured back in by their expertise, and by their ability to make money quickly and easily. People who have been exposed to the upper levels of drug trafficking therefore find it extremely difficult to quit their deviant occupation permanently. This stems, in part, from their difficulty in moving from the illegitimate to the legitimate business sector. Even more significant is the affinity they form for their deviant values and lifestyle. Thus few, if any, of our subjects were successful in leaving deviance entirely. What dealers and smugglers intend, at the time, to be a permanent withdrawal from drug trafficking can be seen in retrospect as a pervasive occupational pattern of mid-career shifts and oscillations. More research is needed into the complex process of how people get out of deviance and enter the world of legitimate work.

REFERENCES

Adler, Patricia A., and Peter Adler
    1982 "Criminal commitment among drug dealers." Deviant Behavior 3:117–135.
    1983 "Relations between dealers: The social organization of illicit drug transactions." Sociology and Social Research 67(3):260–278.
Anonymous
    1969 "On selling marijuana." Pp. 92–102 in Erich Goode (ed.), Marijuana. New York: Atherton.
Atkyns, Robert L., and Gerhard J. Hanneman
    1974 "Illicit drug distribution and dealer communication behavior." Journal of Health and Social Behavior 15(March):36–43.
Biernacki, Patrick, and Dan Waldorf
    1981 "Snowball sampling." Sociological Methods and Research 10(2):141–163.
Blum, Richard H., and Associates
    1972 The Dream Sellers. San Francisco: Jossey-Bass.
Carey, James T.
    1968 The College Drug Scene. Englewood Cliffs, NJ: Prentice-Hall.
Douglas, Jack D.
    1976 Investigative Social Research. Beverly Hills, CA: Sage.
Goode, Erich
    1970 The Marijuana Smokers. New York: Basic.
Johnson, Bruce D.
    1973 Marijuana Users and Drug Subcultures. New York: Wiley.
Langer, John
    1977 "Drug entrepreneurs and dealing culture." Social Problems 24(3):377–385.
Lemert, Edwin
    1962 "Paranoia and the dynamics of exclusion." Sociometry 25(March):2–20.
Lieb, John, and Sheldon Olson
    1976 "Prestige, paranoia, and profit: On becoming a dealer of illicit drugs in a university community." Journal of Drug Issues 6(Fall):356–369.
Luckenbill, David F., and Joel Best
    1981 "Careers in deviance and respectability: The analogy's limitations." Social Problems 29(2):197–206.
Mandel, Jerry
    1967 "Myths and realities of marijuana pushing." Pp. 58–110 in Jerry L. Simmons (ed.), Marijuana: Myths and Realities. North Hollywood, CA: Brandon.
Miller, Gale, and George Ritzer
    1977 "Informal socialization: Deviant occupations." Pp. 83–94 in George Ritzer, Working: Conflict and Change. 2nd edition. Englewood Cliffs, NJ: Prentice-Hall.
Mouledoux, James
    1972 "Ideological aspects of drug dealership." Pp. 110–122 in Ken Westhues (ed.), Society's Shadow: Studies in the Sociology of Countercultures. Toronto: McGraw-Hill, Ryerson.
Redlinger, Lawrence J.
    1975 "Marketing and distributing heroin." Journal of Psychedelic Drugs 7(4):331–353.
Riemer, Jeffrey W.
    1977 "Varieties of opportunistic research." Urban Life 5(4):467–477.
Waldorf, Dan, Sheigla Murphy, Craig Reinarman, and Bridget Joyce
    1977 Doing Coke: An Ethnography of Cocaine Users and Sellers. Washington, DC: Drug Abuse Council.
Wedow, Suzanne
    1979 "Feeling paranoid: The organization of an ideology." Urban Life 8(1):72–93.

[2]

NOTES ON THE CONCEPT OF COMMITMENT[1]

HOWARD S. BECKER

ABSTRACT

The concept of commitment is widely used but has received little formal analysis. It contains an implicit explanation of one mechanism producing consistent human behavior. Commitments come into being when a person, by making a side bet, links extraneous interests with a consistent line of activity. Side bets are often a consequence of the person's participation in social organizations. To understand commitments fully, an analysis of the system of value within which side bets are made is necessary.

The term "commitment" enjoys an increasing vogue in sociological discussion. Sociologists use it in analyses of both individual and organizational behavior. They use it as a descriptive concept to mark out forms of action characteristic of particular kinds of people or groups. They use it as an independent variable to account for certain kinds of behavior of individuals and groups. They use it in analyses of a wide variety of phenomena: power, religion, occupational recruitment, bureaucratic behavior, political behavior, and so on.[2]

In spite of its widespread use, the appearance of the concept of commitment in sociological literature has a curious feature the reader with an eye for trivia will have noticed. In articles studded with citations to previous literature on such familiar concepts as power or social class, commitment emerges unscathed by so much as a single reference. This suggests what is in fact the case: there has been little formal analysis of the concept of commitment and little attempt to integrate it explicitly with current sociological theory. Instead, it has been treated as a primitive concept, introduced where the need is felt without explanation or examination of its character or credentials. As is often the case with unanalyzed concepts used in an *ad hoc* fashion, the term has been made to cover a wide range of common-sense meanings, with predictable ambiguities.

In what follows, I consider the uses to which the concept of commitment has been put and the possible reasons for its increasing popularity, indicate the nature of one of the social mechanisms to which the term implicitly refers, and develop a rudimentary theory of the social processes and conditions involved in the operation of this mechanism. Because the term has been used to express a varied assortment of ideas, it is fruitless to speculate on its "real" meaning. I have instead chosen one of the several images evoked by "commitment" and tried to make its meaning clearer. In doing so, I will unavoidably short-change those for whom the term evokes other of the associated images more strongly. The ultimate remedy for this injustice will be a classification and clarification of the whole family of images involved in the idea of commitment."[3]

[1] An earlier version of this paper was presented at the meetings of the Midwest Sociological Society, April, 1959. I wish to thank Eliot Freidson, Blanche Geer, Sheldon Messinger, and the *Journal*'s anonymous editorial consultants for their helpful comments.

[2] See the following examples: E. Abramson *et al.*, "Social Power and Commitment: A Theoretical Statement," *American Sociological Review*, XXIII (February, 1958), 15–22; Howard S. Becker and James Carper, "The Elements of Identification with an Occupation," *American Sociological Review*, XXI (June, 1956), 341–48; Bryan R. Wilson, "An Analysis of Sect Development," *American Sociological Review*, XXIV (January, 1959), 3–15; Philip Selznick, *TVA and the Grass Roots* (Berkeley: University of California Press, 1953); and Irving Howe and Lewis Coser, *The American Communist Party: A Critical History, 1919–57* (Boston: Beacon Press, 1957).

[3] Such a classification and clarification are not attempted here. For a pioneer effort see Gregory P. Stone, "Clothing and Social Relations: A Study of Appearance in the Context of Community Life" (unpublished Ph.D. dissertation, Department of Sociology, University of Chicago, 1959). I have also confined myself to consideration of the concept as it applies to individual behavior, though it often appears in analyses of the behavior of organizations.

I

Sociologists typically make use of the concept of commitment when they are trying to account for the fact that people engage in *consistent lines of activity*.[4] Howe and Coser, for instance, seek to explain the behavior of the follower of the Communist party line in this fashion: "The Stalinist did not commit himself to the use of Marxism; he committed himself to the claims of the Party that it 'possessed' Marxism."[5] By this they mean that the Stalinist did not undertake always to use Marxist styles of thought but that he did undertake always to honor the party's claim that it knew what the Marxist truth was. In short, they explain a man's persistent support of the shifting party line by referring to a commitment on his part to the belief that the party represented the source of correct Marxist knowledge.

The concept of commitment enjoys use in studies of occupational careers. We can explain the fact that men ordinarily settle down to a career in a limited field, and do not change jobs and careers with the alacrity of the proverbial economic man under changing market conditions, by referring to a process whereby they become committed to a particular occupation. James Carper and I found that graduate students in physiology originally wanted to become physicians but eventually developed commitments to the field of physiology such that they were no longer interested in the medical degree they had earlier desired so much.[6]

In these examples, and others that might be cited, commitment is used to explain what I have already called "consistent behavior." What are the characteristics of this kind of behavior, for which commitment seems so useful an explanatory variable?

To begin with, it persists over some period of time. The person continues to follow the party line; he remains in the same occupation. But the notion of a consistent line of activity implies more than this, for we often think of complexes of quite diverse kinds of activities as consistent. In fact, the examples just cited conceal a great diversity of activity. The Stalinist may engage in diametrically opposed lines of activity as the party line shifts. A person remaining in the same occupation may engage in many kinds of activity in the course of his career. The diverse activities have in common the fact that they are seen by the actor as activities which, whatever their external diversity, serve him in pursuit of the same goal. Finally, the notion of consistent lines of activity seems to imply a rejection by the actor of feasible alternatives. He sees several alternative courses open to him, each having something to commend it, but chooses one which best serves his purposes.

It is one of the central problems of social science, of course, to account for consistency, so defined, in human behavior. Many explanations have been forthcoming, but none has remained unscarred by critical attack. The volume of criticism suggests that sociologists are still looking for an unexceptionable explanation of consistent behavior. At the risk of doing violence, by reason of brevity, to some complex arguments, let me summarize these explanations and the criticisms that have been made of them.

Some of the most clearly sociological explanations (in the sense of being based most firmly in the process of social interaction) have been theories built around the related concepts of social sanction and social control. These theories propose that people act consistently because activity of some particular kind is regarded as right and proper in their society or social group and because deviations from this standard are punished. People act consistently, therefore, because it is morally wrong, practically inexpedient, or both, to do otherwise.

[4] Cf. Nelson N. Foote, "Concept and Method in the Study of Human Development," in *Emerging Problems in Social Psychology*, ed. Muzafer Sherif and M. O. Wilson (Norman, Okla.: Institute of Group Relations, 1957), pp. 29–53.

[5] *Op. cit.*, p. 521.

[6] Howard S. Becker and James Carper, "The Development of Identification with an Occupation," *American Journal of Sociology*, LXI (January, 1956), 289–98.

Such a theory, however, has still to explain consistently deviant behavior. Deviance is often explained by a circular process: a person who initially commits a minor infraction is increasingly alienated from normal society, therefore commits increasingly serious infractions, and so on.[7] Alternatively, it is explained as the result of a process of differential association:[8] the deviant has associated more with people who think his deviant act is proper than he has with those of the majority which thinks it is wrong. Again, deviance is explained by reference to a conflict between cultural goals which all members of the society value and a sharp restriction of institutionally legitimate means for achieving them;[9] this explanation, though, accounts only for the genesis of deviance and deals with the question of consistency only by assuming continuous presentation to the individual of the conflict. Serious objections have been raised as to the validity or area of applicability of all these theories; none constitutes a complete explanation of consistently deviant behavior.[10]

The second problem associated with theories based on the concept of social control, the fact that people obey social rules even when no sanctions would follow an infraction, has been dealt with by positing the internalization of a generalized other which constitutes the hidden audience that en-

[7] Talcott Parsons, *The Social System* (Glencoe, Ill.: Free Press, 1951), pp. 249–325.

[8] Albert K. Cohen, Alfred R. Lindesmith, and Karl F. Schuessler (eds.), *The Sutherland Papers* (Bloomington: Indiana University Press, 1956), pp. 7–29.

[9] Robert K. Merton, *Social Theory and Social Structure* (Glencoe, Ill.: Free Press, 1957), pp. 131–60.

[10] For some questions about the Parsons and Merton approaches see Albert K. Cohen, "The Study of Social Disorganiaztion and Deviant Behavior," in *Sociology Today: Problems and Prospects*, ed. Robert K. Merton, Leonard Broom, and Leonard S. Cottrell, Jr. (New York: Basic Books, 1959), pp. 461–74. For Sutherland's own critique of the theory of differential association see Cohen, Lindesmith, and Schuessler (eds.), *op. cit.*, pp. 30–41. See also Foote, *op. cit.*, p. 35.

forces the rules. This theory is quite generally accepted by sociologists but is just as generally criticized because it offers no reasonable explanation of how people choose one from among the many audiences they can mentally summon to observe any given act.

Other efforts to explain consistent lines of activity also meet criticism. Such activity is sometimes explained by the presumed existence of universally accepted cultural values which inform and constrain behavior. Thus a society is characterized by, let us say, a stress on the value of affective neutrality or the value of achievement; therefore, it is argued, people will consistently choose in any situation that alternative which allows expression of this value. Put another way, individuals will choose alternatives which are consistent with and logically deducible from such a basic value position. Such a theory has difficulty, first of all, in specifying what the basic values of a society are; those theorists who hold that modern society is characteristically ridden with value conflicts might claim such difficulty will be chronic. Second, such a theory does not explain the process by which values, so conceived, affect behavior. It is not likely, for instance, that people make logical deductions from value premises and act on them.

Explanations of consistent behavior are sometimes imported from psychology or psychoanalysis. They refer consistency of behavior to a stable structure of personal needs. They predicate that individuals have stable needs and consistently act so as to maximize the possibility of satisfying them. This kind of scheme is widely used in sociology, either alone or in eclectic combination. But the explanation of behavior by reference to needs not directly observable and, indeed, often inferred from the presence of the behavior they are supposed to explain often causes sociologists to feel queasy about employing it.

In short, many sociologists are dissatisfied with current explanations of consistent human behavior. In my view, use of the concept of commitment in current sociology constitutes an attempt to solve the problem of explaining consistent human behavior in a sociological way without the flaws often attributed to the theories just reviewed. The concept hints at a theory which would do this, but it only hints; it does not deliver the theory full blown. Such a theory would contain a definition of the nature of acts or states of commitment. It would specify the conditions under which commitments come into being. It would indicate the consequences for behavior of acts or states of commitment. In the remainder of this paper I consider some of these points, not attempting to construct such a theory entire, but giving a first approximation of answers to these questions.

In writing of these questions, I have deliberately narrowed the referent of "commitment" to one specific social-psychological mechanism, one of the mechanisms hinted at in the term. It should be clear that this mechanism is not offered as the only possible explanation of consistent human behavior. The present analysis simply undertakes to clarify the nature of one of a family of related mechanisms operating to produce this result.

II

What kind of explanation of consistent human behavior lies implicit in the concept of commitment? Clearly, the person is envisioned as having acted in such a way ("made a commitment") or being in such a state ("being committed") that he will now follow a consistent course. But, as the term is ordinarily used, the nature of this act or state of commitment is not specified; it appears to be regarded as either self-explanatory or intuitively understandable. If we use the concept in this way, the proposition that commitment produces consistent lines of activity is tautological, for commitment, whatever our intuitions about its independent existence, is in fact synonymous with the committed behavior it is supposed to explain. It is a hypothesized event or condition whose occurrence is inferred from the fact

that people act as though they were committed. Used in this way, the concept has the same flaws as those psychological theories which explain behavior by referring to some unobserved state of the actor's psyche, this state deduced from the occurrence of the event it is supposed to explain.

To avoid this tautological sin, we must specify the characteristics of "being committed" independent of the behavior commitment will serve to explain. Schelling, in his analysis of the process of bargaining,[11] furnishes a hypothetical example whose analysis may help us arrive at a characterization of the elements of one of the mechanisms that might be called "commitment." Suppose that you are bargaining to buy a house; you offer sixteen thousand dollars, but the seller insists on twenty thousand. Now suppose that you offer your antagonist in the bargaining certified proof that you have bet a third party five thousand dollars that you will not pay more than sixteen thousand dollars for the house. Your opponent must admit defeat because you would lose money by raising your bid; you have committed yourself to pay no more than you originally offered.

This commitment has been achieved by making a *side bet*. The committed person has acted in such a way as to involve other interests of his, originally extraneous to the action he is engaged in, directly in that action. By his own actions prior to the final bargaining session he has staked something of value to him, something originally unrelated to his present line of action, on being consistent in his present behavior. The consequences of inconsistency will be so expensive that inconsistency in his bargaining stance is no longer a feasible alternative.

The major elements of commitment present themselves in this example. First, the individual is in a position in which his decision with regard to some particular line of action has consequences for other interests

[11] Thomas C. Schelling, "An Essay on Bargaining," *American Economic Review*, XLVI (June, 1956), 281–306.

and activities not necessarily related to it.[12] Second, he has placed himself in that position by his own prior actions. A third element is present, though so obvious as not to be apparent: the committed person must be aware that he has made the side bet and must recognize that his decision in this case will have ramifications beyond it. The element of recognition of the interest created by one's prior action is a necessary component of commitment because, even though one has such an interest, he will not act to implement it (will not act so as to win his side bet) unless he realizes it is necessary.

Note that in this example commitment can be specified independent of the consistent activity which is its consequence. The side bet not to pay more and the additional interest this creates in sticking to the original offered price occur independent of the fact of refusing to pay more. Were we to interview this clever bargainer before the final bargaining session, he presumably would tell us that he understood his interests could now be served only by paying no more.

Thus, whenever we propose commitment as an explanation of consistency in behavior, we must have independent observations of the major components in such a proposition: (1) prior actions of the person staking some originally extraneous interest on his following a consistent line of activity; (2) a recognition by him of the involvement of this originally extraneous interest in his present activity; and (3) the resulting consistent line of activity.

We cannot, of course, often expect social life to be of the classic simplicity of this economic example. Rather, interests, side bets and acts of commitment, and consequent behavior will seem confounded and irremediably mixed, and it will require considerable ingenuity to devise appropriate

indexes with which to sort them out. But the economic example shows us the skeleton we can look for beneath the flesh of more complicated social processes.

III

If we confined our use of commitment to those cases where individuals have deliberately made side bets, we would seldom bring it into our analyses of social phenomena. What interests us is the possibility of using it to explain situations where a person finds that his involvement in social organization has, in effect, made side bets for him and thus constrained his future activity. This occurs in several ways.

A person sometimes finds that he has made side bets constraining his present activity because the existence of *generalized cultural expectations* provides penalties for those who violate them. One such expectation operates in the area of work. People feel that a man ought not to change his job too often and that one who does is erratic and untrustworthy. Two months after taking a job a man is offered a job he regards as much superior but finds that he has, on the side, bet his reputation for trustworthiness on not moving again for a period of a year and regretfully turns the job down. His decision about the new job is constrained by his having moved two months prior and his knowledge that, however attractive the new job, the penalty in the form of a reputation for being erratic and unstable will be severe if he takes it. The existence of generalized cultural expectations about the behavior of responsible adult males has combined with his recent move to stake his personal reputation, nominally extraneous to the decision about the new job, on that decision.

A person often finds that side bets have been made for him by the operation of *impersonal bureaucratic arrangements*. To take a simple instance, a man who wishes to leave his current job may find that, because of the rules governing the firm's pension fund, he is unable to leave without losing a considerable sum of money he has in that fund. Any decision about the new job in-

---

[12] So far, the definition of commitment proposed here parallels that of Abramson *et al.* (*op. cit.*, p. 16): "*Committed* lines are those lines of action the actor feels obligated to pursue by force of penalty .... Committed lines ... are sequences of action with penalties and costs so arranged as to guaran- their selection."

volves a financial side bet the pension fund has placed for him by its rules.

The situation of the Chicago schoolteacher presents a somewhat more complicated system of side bets made by the operation of bureaucratic arrangements. Teachers prefer to teach middle-class children. To do so, they must be assigned to a school containing such children. Teachers can request assignment to as many as ten different schools; assignments are made, as openings occur, to the teacher whose request for a given school is of longest standing. New teachers are assigned to schools for which there are no requests, the lower-class schools teachers like least. The desirable schools have the longest list of requests outstanding, while less desirable schools have correspondingly shorter lists. The teacher in the lower-class school who desires to transfer must, in picking out the ten schools she will request, take into account the side bets the operation of the bureaucratic transfer system has made for her. The most important such bet has to do with time. If she selects one of the most desirable schools, she finds that she has lost a bet about the time it will take her to get out of her present position, for it takes a long time to reach the top of the list for one of these schools. She can instead choose a less desirable school (but better than her present situation) into which she can move more quickly, thus winning the side bet on time. This system of bets constraining her transfer requests has been made in advance by the bureaucratic rules governing requests for transfer.[13]

One might ask in what sense the person's prior actions have made a side bet in these two instances. How has he, by his own act, placed himself in a position where his decision on a new job or request for transfer involves these other considerations? Is it not rather the case that he has had no part in it, being constrained by forces entirely outside himself? We can without sophistry, I think, locate the crucial action which has created the commitment in the person's acquiescence to the system, in his agreeing to work under the bureaucratic rules in force. By doing this, he has placed all the bets which are given in the structure of that system, even though he does not become aware of it until faced with an important decision.

Side bets constraining behavior also come into existence through the process of *individual adjustment to social positions*. A person may so alter his patterns of activity in the process of conforming to the requirements for one social position that he unfits himself for other positions he might have access to. In so doing, he has staked the ease of performance in the position on remaining where he is. To return to our earlier example, some Chicago schoolteachers chose to remain in a lower-class school for the lengthy period necessary to reach the top of the list for a very desirable middle-class school. When the opportunity to make the move came, they found that they no longer desired to move because they had so adjusted their style of teaching to the problems of dealing with lower-class children that they could not contemplate the radical changes necessary to teach middle-class children. They had, for instance, learned to discipline children in ways objectionable to middle-class parents and become accustomed to teaching standards too low for a middle-class school.[14] They had, in short, bet the ease of performance of their job on remaining where they were and in this sense were committed to stay.

Goffman's analysis of *face-to-face interaction*[15] suggests another way side bets are made through the operation of social processes. He notes that persons present to their fellows in any sequence of interaction an image of themselves they may or may not be able to live up to. Having once claimed to be a certain kind of person, they find it necessary to act, so far as possible, in an

---

[13] For a fuller account of the operation of this system see Howard S. Becker, "The Career of the Chicago Public Schoolteacher," *American Journal of Sociology*, LVII (March, 1952), 470–77.

[14] *Ibid.*, pp. 473–75.

[15] Erving Goffman, "On Face-Work," *Psychiatry*, XVIII (August. 1955), 213–31.

appropriate way. If one claims implicitly, in presenting himself to others, to be truthful, he cannot allow himself to be caught in a lie and is in this way committed to truthtelling. Goffman points out that the rules governing face-to-face interaction are such that others will ordinarily help one preserve the front he has put forward ("save face"). Nevertheless, a person will often find his activity constrained by the kind of front he has earlier presented in interaction; he finds he has bet his appearance as a responsible participant in interaction on continuing a line of activity congruent with that front.

This review of the social mechanisms through which persons make side bets extraneous to a particular line of activity that nevertheless later constrain that activity is not exhaustive. It serves only to point the direction for empirical study of side-bet mechanisms, in the course of which a more definitive classification might be made.

IV

As some of our examples indicate, commitments are not necessarily made conciously and deliberately. Some commitments do result from conscious decisions, but others arise crescively; the person becomes aware that he is committed only at some point of change and seems to have made the commitment without realizing it. By examining cases of both kinds, we may get some hints toward a theory of the genesis of commitments.

Such a theory might start with the observation that the commitment made without realization that it is being made—what might be termed the "commitment by default"—arises through a series of acts no one of which is crucial but which, taken together, constitute for the actor a series of side bets of such magnitude that he finds himself unwilling to lose them. Each of the trivial acts in such a series is, so to speak, a small brick in a wall which eventually grows to such a height the person can no longer climb it. The ordinary routines of living—the daily recurring events of every-

day life—stake increasingly more valuable things on continuing a consistent line of behavior, although the person hardly realizes this is happening. It is only when some event changes the situation so as to endanger those side bets that the person understands what he will lose if he changes his line of activity. The person who contributes a small amount of each paycheck to a nontransferable pension fund which eventually becomes sizable provides an apposite illustration of this process; he might willingly lose any single contribution but not the total accumulated over a period of years.

If this is the case with commitment by default, we might conjecture that it is also true of commitments resulting from conscious decisions. Decisions do not of themselves result in consistent lines of action, for they are frequently changed. But some decisions do produce consistent behavior. We can perhaps account for this variety of outcomes of decisions by the proposition that only those decisions bolstered by the making of sizable side bets will produce consistent behavior. Decisions not supported by such side bets will lack staying power, crumpling in the face of opposition or fading away to be replaced by other essentially meaningless decisions until a commitment based on side bets stabilizes behavior.[16]

We might also note that a consistent line of activity will often be based on more than one kind of side bet; several kinds of things valuable to the person may be staked on a particular line of activity. For instance, the man who hesitates to take a new job may be deterred by a complex of side bets: the financial loss connected with a pension fund he would lose if he moved; the loss of seniority and "connections" in his present firm which promise quick advance if he stays; the loss of ease in doing his work because of his success in adjusting to the

[16] The preceding paragraphs are adapted from Howard S. Becker, "The Implications of Research on Occupational Careers for a Model of Household Decision Making," in *Consumer Behavior*, Vol. IV: *Models of Household Decision Making*, ed. Nelson Foote (forthcoming).

particular conditions of his present job; the loss of ease in domestic living consequent on having to move his household; and so on.

V

For a complete understanding of a person's commitments we need one more element: an analysis of the system of values or, perhaps better, valuables with which bets can be made in the world he lives in. What kinds of things are conventionally wanted, what losses feared? What are the good things of life whose continued enjoyment can be staked on continuing to follow a consistent line of action?

Some systems of value permeate an entire society. To recur to Schelling's example of the canny house-buyer, economic commitments are possible only within the confines of a system of property, money, and exchange. A side bet of five thousand dollars has meaning only where money is conventionally valued.

However, it is important to recognize that many sets of valuable things have value only within subcultural groups in a society and that many side bets producing commitment are made within systems of value of limited provenience. Regional, ethnic, and social class subcultures all provide raw material for side bets peculiar to those sharing in the culture, as do the variants of these related to differing age and sex statuses. A middle-class girl can find herself committed to a consistently chaste line of behavior by the sizable side bet of her reputation that middle-class culture attaches to virginity for females. A girl who is a member of a social class where virginity is less valued could not be committed in this way; and, except for a few puritanical enclaves in our society, boys cannot acquire commitments of this kind at all, for male virginity has little value, and no side bet of any magnitude could be made with it.[17]

More limited subcultures, such as those

associated with occupational groups or political parties, also provide sets of valuables with which side bets can be made. These esoteric systems of value must be discovered if the commitments of group members are to be understood. For instance, the professional dance musician achieves job security by becoming known as a dependable man to a large group of employing bandleaders and to an even larger group of musicians who are not leaders but will recommend him for jobs they hear about. The dependable man is, among other things, a man who will take any job offered him unless he is already engaged; by doing this, he shows that he will not let a leader who needs a vital man down. His reputation for not letting leaders down has economic value to him, for leaders who believe in that reputation will keep him working. When he is offered a job that he does not, for whatever reason, want, he finds himself committed to taking it anyway; by failing to do so, he would lose the reputation for dependability and the consequent steady supply of jobs the value system of the music business has bet for him on his consistency in always taking whatever job is offered.[18]

In short, to understand commitments fully, we must discover the systems of value within which the mechanisms and processes described earlier operate. By so doing, we understand not only how side bets are made but the kind of counters with which they can be made; in fact, it is likely that we cannot fully penetrate the former without understanding the latter.

VI

The conception of commitment I have been proposing has certain disadvantages for empirical and theoretical work. In the first place, many of the difficulties faced in using other theories remain unresolved. People often have conflicting commitments,

---

[17] I hasten to say that this illustration is hypothetical; I do not know the facts of the differential distribution of evaluations of chastity.

[18] An earlier and somewhat different account of dance musicians' job security can be found in Howard S. Becker, "Some Contingencies of the Professional Dance Musician's Career," *Human Organization*, XII (Spring, 1953), 22–26.

and the theory proposed here offers no answer to the question of how people choose between the commitments they have acquired when such conflicts are activated. Problems like this do not magically disappear on the introduction of a new concept.

Furthermore, the limited conception of commitment I have suggested covers a limited area. Many kinds of consistent behavior will probably prove unexplainable in its terms. This is as it should be, for analytic precision comes through the breaking-down of global categories into more limited and homogenous classificatory types. However, the concept of commitment has been made to cover such a wide range of phenomena in ordinary discourse that confusion may arise from trying to limit its use. This difficulty should be met by clarifying analytically the several mechanisms that have been subsumed under commitment, the conditions under which they operate, and the ways they may be distinguished from one another.[19] It seems convenient to retain "commitment" to refer to the specific mechanism of constraint of behavior through previously placed side bets and use such terms as "involvement," "attachment," "vocation," "obligation," and so on, to refer to related but distinguishable phenomena. Un-

fortunately, we cannot make our concepts precise and at the same time keep the full range of evocative meaning they have acquired in ordinary discourse.

These disadvantages, serious as they are, must be weighed against the advantages that use of the concept confers. First, the idea of the side bet allows us to specify the elements of commitment independently of the consistent line of behavior they are used to account for and thus avoid tautology. Though it may not always be easy to find empirical indicators of the side bets constraining people's activity, side bets and consistent activity are in principle distinguishable, and we are thus able to avoid a common difficulty in the use of the concepts.

Beyond this, the conception of commitment I have sketched gives us the theoretical tools for assimilating the common-sense notion that people often follow lines of activity for reasons quite extraneous to the activity itself. While we are all aware of this fact, we have no conceptual language which allows us to put this insight to work in our research and theory. The concept of commitment furnishes the requisite terms. In addition, it outlines the mechanisms by which past actions link extraneous interests to a line of activity.

[19] See Stone, *op. cit.*, and Erving Goffman, "Role Distance" (unpublished paper).

COMMUNITY STUDIES, INC.
KANSAS CITY, MISSOURI

[3]

BRIT. J. CRIMINOL. VOL. 30 No. 2 SPRING 1990

DRUG MARKETS AND LAW ENFORCEMENT

NICHOLAS DORN and NIGEL SOUTH*

This paper examines the market in illegal drugs, law enforcement counter-measures, and their interaction in Britain. Doubt is cast on the conventional view that the drug market is monopolistic, dominated by a few big suppliers. A diverse set of enterprises, best distinguished by their qualitative features rather than their size, is described. These enterprises are faced by law enforcement agencies that have at their disposal formidable legislation which provides for life imprisonment and confiscation of assets of drug distributors. The British post-war history of legislation against distributors has been one of increasingly punitive measures, and although there is no evidence that this has restricted the distribution networks, it may have contributed to the increasing professionalization of the trade. The authors conclude that drug control policies would be more effective if less enthusiasm were expended in raising levels of penalties and more attention paid to the ways in which an irrepressible market may be shaped in more or less harmful forms by legislation and policing strategies.

Introduction

Debates within the drug policy field have for many years been dominated by a concern with individual users—epidemiology, treatment, education, and so on.[1] These are important perspectives. Over the last decade, however, things have changed somewhat: the drug question has been at least partly redefined as a question of crime control. We do not think that this is altogether a bad thing. There is, though, a need to take the crime control question more seriously. Fortunately, there is a body of work in the social sciences—economics, particularly the theory of the firm (economic enterprise), and criminology—that can be brought together to build a better understanding of drug distribution than that currently provided in the mass media and underpinning public debate.

Markets may be structured in a variety of ways. For example, there may be a monopoly, or near-monopoly, in which one or two enterprises or agencies provide the bulk of services; this can lead to a stable and often bureaucratized structure in which people occupy routine roles as functionaries. An oligopoly may exist, in which three or four enterprises constitute a cartel dominating the market. At the other extreme, there may be very active competition between a large number of enterprises which vary in

* Institute for the Study of Drug Dependence, 1 Hatton Place, London EC1N 8ND.

This is a revised version of a paper first presented at a workshop on the 'Side-effects of Drug Control Policy', Commission of the European Communities, Luxemburg, Oct. 1987. We should like to thank Gerald Mars, Peter Schioler, John Grieve, Geoff Pearson, Karin Murji, Alan Wright, Alan Waymont, Andrew Fraser, Jasper Woodcock, and several anonymous sources on both sides of the legal fence for comments on the ideas expressed in the paper. We also thank reviewers for the *British Journal of Criminology*.

[1] As reflected, for example, in the otherwise very useful and comprehensive collection edited by MacGregor (1989). The collection includes articles on drug users and the prison system (Tippell 1989) and on delinquent youth culture and drug use (O'Bryan 1989), but the areas of law enforcement and legislation receive scant attention.

NICHOLAS DORN AND NIGEL SOUTH

size, organizational structure, and market strategy; this leads to a fluid and unpredictable situation. It is conventional for economists, drug researchers, and the media to describe drug markets in terms of monopolies and cartels (organized crime, the Mafia, etc.).[2] This assumption may perhaps be reasonable in relation to some drug markets, for example those to be found in Italy in the 1970s. But in Britain today, we shall suggest, there is a competitive drug market, the structure of which is complex and in flux.[3]

In policing drug markets, law enforcement tends to take on some of the attributes of their opponents, the drug distribution enterprises. The prime movers on each side are entrepreneurs (Manning 1980; Auld, Dorn, and South 1986; Grieve 1987; Hobbs 1988). In the drug market, entrepreneurs sense new opportunities and organize their services accordingly. In modern law enforcement agencies, certain individuals who have innovative flair play a difficult and risky role of introducing new ideas and strategies (new ideas for covert operations, new legislation, etc.). There is a sense in which drug market entrepreneurs have an easier time than law enforcement entrepreneurs: the more creative the drug dealers, the more they will be able to keep ahead of their direct competitors and of the police. Law enforcement agents, working within a more established and bureaucratized organization, will face a variety of formal and informal sanctions if they are too unorthodox.

How, then, do drug enterprises and law enforcement agencies interact together, and what are the options for economic and social policy in this area? To answer this question fully requires empirical study of drug markets, of law enforcement agencies, and of the interactions of enterprises and law enforcement within the context of the economic, political, and cultural conditions within which they operate. Some of this work has been carried out by others, but it is incomplete and generally out of date, and much analytical and empirical work remains to be done. The remainder of this paper looks at specific aspects of the interface between drug markets and law enforcement, although for detailed case-study analysis of operational interactions the reader is referred to forthcoming work (Dorn and South 1991). For our present purposes we start from the law enforcement side of this interface.

[2] The most popular image of the drug distributor in Britain is that of the Mafia. In Italy, this term means something specific: a well-established economic community, based in such primarily licit businesses as construction, supported by extensive corruption of the political structure and of trade unions, and with a high degree of control over illegal business, including drug distribution. The term has entered the vocabulary and popular culture of many countries, and is still the subject of many newspaper reports. In Britain, however, the involvement of Italian *mafia* or *camorra* (Lewis 1989) has been minimal. A rare example of alleged Mafia involvement in the British drug market is the 1985 Di Carlo case (*Guardian*, 19 Aug. 1987). Di Carlo was a Mafia-connected businessman owning a variety of companies, including a decorating firm, a hotel, a wine bar, and a travel agency and exchange bureau, and used these businesses as fronts for importing drugs (*The Times*, 19 Aug. 1987; and personal communication, HM Customs and Excise source, 11 Aug. 1989).

[3] These conditions are not unique to drug markets in the developed world. In the context of another culture and economy, Jamaica, Headley (1989) describes the 'formation of a distinct urban lumpenproletariat of youthful males for whom street crime and involvement in a subterranean, informal economy have become normal, functional enterprises' (ibid. 70-1). The growth of the international drug trade in the 1970s and 1980s provided significant channels for the expansion of these enterprises. Headley documents a competitive and often violent drug market. Among the participants are groups similar to those we describe (below) as Opportunistic Irregulars. Headley notes that 'frequently, irregular income is also gained from illegalities such as burglary, stick-ups, prostitution, gun-running, ganja-trafficking, and becoming "top-ranking" enforcers for unscrupulous, corrupt politicians' (ibid. 73).

DRUG MARKETS AND LAW ENFORCEMENT

Law-making and Law Enforcement against Drug Distribution

The *content* of drug legislation in Britain has been influenced by earlier US legislation providing for life sentences, anti-laundering measures, and forfeiture[4] and confiscation[5] of assets. Similarly, the *organization and strategies* of law enforcement agencies in Britain have developed in broadly comparable ways to US enforcement agencies in relation to multiple jurisdiction, use of informants, and covert operations.

The relevant American legislation includes RICO (the Racketeer Influenced and Corrupt Organizations statute, 18 USC 1961–965); the CCE (Continuing Criminal Enterprise) legislation, which is part of the Comprehensive Drug Abuse, Prevention and Control Act, 1970; the Bank Secrecy Act implemented in 1970; the controlled Substances Act as amended in 1978; the Comprehensive Crime Control Act of 1984; and the Money Laundering Control Act of 1986. Each of these is concerned with the suppression of the forms of financial and other managerial activities that sustain criminal enterprises (Blau *et al.* 1983).

The US legislation is extensive and complex, and we can draw out only some key points here. RICO's concept of a racketeering 'enterprise', to which heavy penalties are attached, begins to address the central problem of organized crime—that an 'enterprise' gives the continuity needed to conduct and maintain the activities on which organized crime depends (Dombrink and Měeker 1986: 718). RICO is concerned with preventing illicit enterprises from interacting with licit enterprises. Any two proven interactions are regarded as constituting a pattern. CCE aims to suppress an enterprise which is shown to consist of an organizer and five or more other persons who commit drug offences. Both Acts provide for long prison sentences and forfeiture of the assets of those found guilty.

Under the Controlled Substances Act and the Comprehensive Crime Control Act, forfeiture of assets can occur even in the absence of a conviction. Whereas a conviction would require evidence of guilt 'beyond reasonable doubt', these Acts prescribe forfeiture *on the balance of evidence*. That is to say, the weight of evidence may be insufficient to merit conviction, but may be sufficient to allow the court to conclude that the individuals *probably* committed offences. In this case, the forfeiture extends to all property that was held at the time of the first probable offence. This is designed to prevent individuals and organizations transferring the proceeds of crime to friends, family, or other holding agents.

---

[4] The term 'forfeiture' has different meanings in Britain and the United States. In the British context it refers to the seizure of the material tools of crime (e.g. a crowbar, a car), seizure of money actually used in the carrying out of a crime, or of money that is shown to be the proceeds of crime where such money can be shown to directly relate to the offence before the court. Provision for such forfeiture is made under s.27 of the Misuse of Drugs Act 1971. Courts have also had recourse to forfeiture measures under the Powers of the Criminal Courts Act 1973, s.43, which makes provision for forfeiture of money or other property intended to facilitate the commission of *future* offences (see the Commentary on *R.* v. *Simms, Criminal Law Review*, Mar. 1988: 186–7). However, in the North American context, the term 'forfeiture' has roughly the same legal meaning as has confiscation in Britain (see n. 5), i.e. the seizure of all assets of a person convicted of drug supply unless the person can show that all or some part of his or her assets were not acquired from previous involvement in drugs supply, and quite regardless of whether those assets might be derived from any particular drugs offence or be likely to be used to finance future offences.

[5] As applied in the UK Drug Trafficking Offences Act, 1986, the term 'confiscation' means the seizure of all realizable assets of a person convicted of any 'drug trafficking offence', where such offences include the production, importation, supply, or possession with intent to supply drugs controlled under the Misuse of Drugs Act 1971 (see Drug Trafficking Offences Act 1986, s.38; and Nicol 1988), and where the defendant cannot show that these assets have been derived from sources other than trafficking. From October 1988, when the Criminal Justice Act 1988, Commencement No. 2 Order was made, trafficking offences are included in s.27 (1) of the Misuse of Drugs Act, so property of traffickers is now subject both to forfeiture (as tools of crime) and confiscation (proceeds of crime).

NICHOLAS DORN AND NIGEL SOUTH

Another relevant piece of US legislation is the Bank Secrecy Act. This requires banks to report any currency transaction exceeding $10,000 in value, or any transaction that is part of other transactions involving more than $100,000 per year. While there has been resistance from the banks, and problems in collating the mass of data being reported to the US Treasury, banking sector compliance has increased (Dombrink and Meeker 1986: 729–30). One response by illegal organizations is 'smurfing', which is the use of many small (and therefore unreported) transactions through a variety of different accounts (ibid. 731).

There is a long history of action by the US Internal Revenue Service. When the IRS observes a citizen living above the level of his or her declared income, it may impose a very high assessment of income and demand the corresponding tax. Unable to produce accounts that give a different picture, the person has to pay the tax or face forfeiture of property.

Each of these control tactics has been adopted by Britain in some form. The Drug Trafficking Offences Act of 1986 brought into force an obligation on the Crown Court to 'embark upon an enquiry to recover, under a Confiscation Order, the proceeds of drug trafficking . . . [T]he DTOA aims to confiscate the proceeds of drug trafficking and not merely the profits made by the offender' (Fortson 1988: 195). The breadth of the legislation aims to catch within it all proceeds of drug crime, considerably broadening the powers of financial investigation and penalty available to the courts well beyond those previously available under the Misuse of Drugs Act.[6] British legislation also allows the courts to impose a Restraint Order, 'freezing' all assets of suspected drug dealers before the police take action and hence preventing transfer of property. However, although asset confiscation in Britain is mandatory for convicted 'major' traffickers and suppliers, it cannot be imposed unless the person has been convicted (unlike the United States). The British banks are co-operating by giving hitherto confidential customer information to the authorities.

The impact of these new financial policing measures on the structure and organization of the drug market in Britain is now beginning to be assessed, but preliminary indications from senior police sources indicate that some distribution organizations are responding by keeping the financial side of their work at arm's length from the physical handling of the drug merchandise. This makes it difficult for enforcement agencies to build a case that will stand up in court. But this is just one of several aspects of enforcement that tends to keep the organization of the trade diffuse, rather than encouraging monopolistic structures.

Multiple Jurisdiction, Informants, Covert Operations, and the Shaping of the Market

In both the United States and Britain, there has been a movement away from sole jurisdiction (one agency) in law enforcement towards *multiple jurisdiction*, which means that several different agencies share responsibility for policing of any given geographical area (Punch 1985). This trend is partly a response to the problem of corruption: if there is just one police agency to 'buy off', then corruption is relatively easy—as illustrated by

---

[6] For a discussion of the development of the Drug Trafficking Offences Act in response to the perceived deficiencies of the Misuse of Drugs Act in the wake of the Operation Julie case (*R. v. Cuthbertson and others*, 1980. 2 *All England Law Reports*, 401) see Dorn and South 1989.

DRUG MARKETS AND LAW ENFORCEMENT

the wave of scandals in the New York Police Department leading to the Knapp Commission (1972) and by (relatively minor) scandals in the Metropolitan Police Drug Squad in London in the 1970s. The movement to multiple or overlapping jurisdiction can lead to problems of co-ordination (General Accounting Office 1983), but the fact that there are several agencies each engaged in surveillance of the same field does cut down the possibilities for major corruption since 'no single agency or agent can issue a license for an illegal operator' (Reuter 1983: 125). Today in Britain, for example, medium-scale drug dealing may attract a local drug squad, an area drug squad, a regional squad, a liaison officer from the National Drugs Intelligence Unit, and possibly Customs and Excise. In such conditions, with several agencies 'fishing in the same information pool', any one agency that is corrupted into protecting a drug distribution enterprise will sooner or later quite likely have such corruption discovered by one of the other agencies. The result is that *major* corruption of the kind needed to protect a large or monopolistic enterprise cannot easily be carried out. Hence monopolistic enterprises cannot easily emerge (in contrast with the situations when only one law enforcement agency has jurisdiction). Large enterprises may be able to operate successfully for a short while, but only small or medium enterprises can stay active in the longer term.

The use of informants is a key aspect of anti-drug policing. It involves relatively low-level members of drug distribution enterprises being offered the possibility of a reduction in sentence (or dropping of police action) in return for information about colleagues, managers, and principals (Shawcross and Young 1987). An informant recruited in the first instance through threats and plea-bargaining may subsequently go on the police 'payroll'. Other informants may initially be motivated by competitive considerations in relation to other enterprises, or a wish to square a grudge, or even simply by a wish to help the police or to curtail drug dealing in their community.

Because of legislative, media, public, and police interest in the 'big dealers', the informant system is handled in ways that focus upon getting information about operatives higher in the distribution system. Police try to move *up* — from users to minor employees of drug enterprises, from them to managers, and so on. In practice there are difficulties with this since principals (the more important figures in the business) will be better protected by cut-outs. At the same time, informants under pressure will tend to exaggerate the role of those whom they name. One possible counter-measure adopted by some drug distributors is to avoid operating continually in the same market in the same manner. Another counter-measure is to try to avoid detection by staying relatively small (although this has the disadvantage that it reduces the number of cut-outs between the principal and the police). Hence the informant system—a mainstay of policing in Britain—tends to break the market down into smaller and flexible enterprises and acts to discourage lasting monopoly structures.

The increasing use by police of *covert operations* has a broadly similar effect on the structure of the market. The term 'covert operations' covers a range of more active police operations, going beyond information-gathering to include provocative actions such as offering to trade with or otherwise assist drug enterprises in order to trap them on ground chosen by law enforcement agencies. By their nature, covert operations are demanding, risky, time-consuming, and absorb considerable levels of police resources. One of the primary difficulties for a unit involved in a covert operation is how to prevent the operation being unwittingly exposed by another law enforcement agency: liaison between agencies can reduce the risk of such accidents, but at the possible cost of

NICHOLAS DORN AND NIGEL SOUTH

'leakage' of information about the operation (Hurd 1989). Because these operations are so demanding, they are worth mounting only against substantial enterprises. It follows that the expansion of these techniques of law enforcement, which is happening in Britain and other European countries today (following the lead of the American Drugs Enforcement Administration and German agencies), tends to push against the larger drug enterprises harder than against smaller ones.

New emphases in law enforcement, such as covert operations and surveillance of cashflow, tend to structure the market into a series of smaller and flexible (e.g. multi-commodity) enterprises. Modern law enforcement may, in combination with the mass media, promulgate the myth of the monopolistic drug distribution enterprise, but it actually discourages such a market structure. Smaller is safer as far as drug distribution enterprises are concerned. Within this general tendency, there is considerable variation in organization of drug distribution enterprises, reflecting their diverse origins and local or regional circumstances.

Researching Drug Dealing

The following preliminary results have been derived using qualitative methods of investigation deployed within a framework developed out of reading of the international literature on criminal organizations, irregular economies, and law enforcement (e.g. Reuter 1983; Dorn and South 1987*b*; Grieve 1987).

We decided early in the research to adopt a Weberian methodological technique, that of the *ideal type* (Gerth and Mills 1970: 59). The reason for doing this was that different observers seemed to be giving us very different accounts of the structure of drug markets, their relations with other markets (whether legal or illegal), and the forms of drug distribution enterprises. For some observers, for example, drug markets are closely intertwined with other criminal activities such as robbery, fraud, terrorism, or street crime; for others, drug markets are entirely separate from other criminal markets, and indeed markets in different drugs (cannabis, heroin, etc.) are distinct from each other. We believed that one reason for this could be the different forms of evidence that tended to come the way of different observers. For example, cocaine and crack markets in parts of New York, as evidenced by Johnson *et al.* (1985, 1987) and our own New York fieldwork interviews in June 1989 seem rather different from West Coast marijuana markets; indeed, one would expect different settings to generate different drug distribution networks. Within Britain, HM Customs and Excise may most often come across specialist 'project teams' set up for the specific purpose of importing drugs, while a local police Drugs Squad may be better placed to observe the connections between long-established criminal families who have recently added drug distribution to a broader repertoire of illegal activities. Drug Wings in regional crime squads tend to come across both these types, among others, and so the view from their vantage point is relatively complex. From late 1989 onwards, independent quantitative data will become available (Wright and Waymont 1990) to enable elaboration of this point.[7]

[7] Alan Wright and Alan Waymont are carrying out a study based in the Department of Politics, Southampton University, and funded by the Police Foundation on behalf of ACPO and the National Drugs Intelligence Co-ordinator, entitled 'Drug Enforcement Strategies and Intelligence Needs'. Their questionnaire for interviewing Drug Squad officers includes a question based on our typology, and they have kindly offered to make data relating to this question available to us. It may be possible to run cross-tabulations to show how drug distributors are perceived differently according to whether officers are working in a local, regional, or national squad. We hope to report on this in 1990 or 1991.

DRUG MARKETS AND LAW ENFORCEMENT

Between April 1988 and early 1989 we carried out forty extended, semi-structured in-depth interviews with a variety of respondents on both sides of the legal fence, and ten background briefings with senior people in the criminal justice system. Our respondents have included:

- Senior Drug Squad officers, senior Customs and Excise officers, and NDIU (National Drugs Intelligence Unit) staff
- People and organizations concerned with bank disclosures and asset confiscation, including police 'Drug Profits Confiscation' specialists, and senior staff in a clearing bank
- Probation officers and other professionals concerned with convicted drug users/dealers
- Persons who have information about their own or others' involvement in drug distribution

We were fortunate in also gaining some limited degree of access to police files on particular cases and in being able to interview officers about these cases, asking them how drug dealers, money launderers, and their associates organize their businesses. None of the current cases are directly referred to here for two reasons: some cases are at the time of writing still being brought to trial or are *sub judice* and, additionally, we have given assurances that detailed 'insider' information given to us in confidence in this manner will be reported on by us no earlier than 1991, in order to protect current operational methods. Several of our respondents commented adversely on the BBC documentary *The Duty Men,* believing it to have exposed the current operational methods of HM Customs and Excise to a criminal underworld only too eager to learn. It is, however, significant that the Drug Squad officers who facilitated our research believe that their own investigative methods, and the defences put up by distributors, will have changed so much within two years that there will then be no harm in publicly airing what are today's operational secrets. This underscores a general point about the structures and organization of drug markets in Britain: they are in a state of flux.

Working through these steps, on the basis of the literature and empirical evidence, we postulate the existence of seven types of drug distributor in Britain today. The first three types are multi-commodity enterprises; that is to say, they deal with a variety of commodities, of which drugs are just some:

1. *Business Sideliners*: the licit business enterprise that begins to trade in drugs as a 'sideline'
2. *Criminal Diversifiers*: the existing criminal enterprise that diversifies its operations to include drugs
3. *Opportunistic Irregulars*: individuals or small groups who get involved in a variety of activities in the irregular economy, including drugs.

The next three types of enterprise are specialist drug distributors:

4. *Retail Specialists*: enterprises with a manager employing people in a variety of specialist roles to distribute drugs to users
5. *Mutual Societies*: friendship networks of user–dealers who support each other and sell or exchange drugs amongst themselves in a reciprocal fashion
6. *Trading Charities*: enterprises involved in the drug business because of ideological commitments to drugs (e.g. cannabis) as well as the profit motive.

177

NICHOLAS DORN AND NIGEL SOUTH

Finally, there is a seventh category:

7. *State-sponsored Traders*: enterprises that result from collaboration between control agents and others (for example, collaboration between police undercover agents and their informants who may be allowed to continue to trade; or covert 'buy–bust' operations, where police pose as buyers in order to entrap drug dealers and bust their operations).

We are not at this stage making any assumptions about the extent to which each type can be found throughout the country, but simply saying that there is some evidence for each type. Let us now look at each type of enterprise in rather more detail and present some of the evidence for each.

Discussion of the Seven Types of Drug Distribution Enterprises

1. *Business Sideliners* are licit economic units which get involved in drug distribution on the side. Examples include doctors who combine generous prescribing with collection of a fee for services; import–export agencies which provide a cover for shipment of drugs; and businesses with social and economic ties to areas of illicit drug production. As can be seen from this description, Sideliners can operate near the upper reaches of the distribution system, and/or in the middle: their common feature is their basis in a licit business enterprise. This has advantages in terms of the managers' experience of entrepreneurial activity, access to capital, ability to funnel cash through otherwise legitimate channels, public respectability, lack of police record, etc.

Historically, in Britain and elsewhere, it was doctors and pharmacists who were the source of pharmaceutical drugs such as morphine and heroin to people who use them for pleasure. The so-called British system, whereby responsible prescribing by doctors was intended to maintain those with a habit who could not be weaned off addictive drugs, was seen to be undermined from the early 1960s onwards by increased use of opiate-type (and other) drugs by 'new', young and working-class users. This was one of the considerations that prompted the British authorities to place restrictions on doctors and to license specific doctors, mostly psychiatrists in newly set up Drug Dependency Units ('the clinics'), to prescribe opiates for the treatment of dependency. The hope was that this more carefully regulated system of supply would be attractive enough to entice heroin users and hence displace the 'grey' market, and controlled enough to prevent further expansion of drug use. During the 1970s this system came under increasing strain, partly due to the clinics' increasing tendency to shift patients from heroin to substitutes such as methadone and from long-term prescriptions for injectable methadone to short-term prescriptions for oral forms of the drug, to patients' dissatisfaction. A small number of private British doctors responded to drug addicts' pleas by making available supplies of opiate-type drugs, in the face of mounting hostility from the psychiatrists running the Drug Dependency Units. In 1986, Ann Dally, a doctor in private practice and leader of an Association of Independent Doctors in Addiction, was admonished by the General Medical Council of the British Medical Association, after a sharp struggle within the profession, for doing just that (Ashton 1986). This was no doubt important symbolically to all those concerned, but by that time the market in imported heroin had grown so much as to considerably reduce its impact upon the broader drug market in Britain.

During the 1970s, supply of heroin from the Third World increased, the *coup de grace*

DRUG MARKETS AND LAW ENFORCEMENT

for Britain being the revolution in Iran and the conflict in Afghanistan from 1979 onwards. These events provoked an outpouring of heroin—first from Iran, as sections of the business community and intelligentsia emigrated to Britain, bringing their capital in whatever forms they could, and then from Pakistan as Afghan and Pakistani heroin that had previously been exported through Iran was rerouted southward, thorough Lahore and Karachi. For the first half of the 1980s at least, heroin from Pakistan and its environs dominated the British market.[8] Family links between British citizens of Pakistani descent and business interests in Pakistan provided opportunities for heroin importation as a sideline to other transactions, and the *hawallah* system of honouring verbal agreements and providing payment in a variety of ways over a period of time virtually eliminated the need to make immediate cash payments or to use conventional banking channels. As staff members of the National Drugs Intelligence Unit explained to us, such arrangements are relatively immune to the asset-tracing investigative methods favoured by enforcement agencies. If apprehended by enforcement agencies following the physical trail of the drugs from the producer country into Britain, the Sideliners may often present themselves as ordinary businessmen only peripherally or occasionally involved in trafficking—which, of course, they are:

Piecing together the information we have from varied sources, it would seem that much of the heroin in this country comes from Pakistan and is brought over by 'ordinary' English and Asian businessmen who, because they do not have a means for distributing the drug, sell it to local established 'underworld' figures. These, in turn, seem to be shifting their illegal activities from thieving to 'safer' drug dealing, although not exclusively, as we understand that local suppliers are accepting as payment for the heroin, stolen goods rather than money. (Griffiths and Barker 1984: 19)

This takes us on to our second category of drug distributor, the criminal who diversifies from 'traditional' crime to drugs. It also illustrates how, within the framework of the irregular economy there is a meshing between legal and illegal business practices, with exchanges of goods between the primarily licit businessman and the thief displacing exchanges of cash (Ferman and Ferman 1973; Auld, Dorn, and South 1986; Parker, Blakx, and Newcombe 1988: 105–8).

2. *Criminal Diversifiers.* During the late 1970s in Britain, it appears that increasing numbers of criminal enterprises already involved in criminal activities such as robbery, fraud, racketeering, and loan-sharking saw opportunities in drug distribution. It may have been that the increasingly heavy legal penalties legislated from the 1960s onwards and increasing pressure from police and HM Customs and Excise tended to discourage 'amateur' distributors and to leave the way open for more involvement of the security-conscious criminal enterprise. Such criminal 'firms' may have a continuing existence or, particularly in the case of major crime, may be temporary, bringing together a team of 'specialists' for a 'project' over a period of a few months or years, then perhaps dissolving before re-forming in a slightly different form in order to carry out another drug-related

---

[8] See O'Neil, Baker, and Gough 1984. Note, however, that although Pakistan was for the first half of the 1980s an important source of heroin for Britain, a considerable proportion of the opium from which the heroin was made was cultivated in Afghanistan, converted into heroin fairly close to the sites of cultivation, and then smuggled out through Pakistan (particularly through Karachi and Lahore). Some of it was diverted into Pakistan's own internal market, with the result that by the mid-1980s that country had a serious heroin problem. Pakistan is therefore not just a heroin producer country but a transit route and a consumer country as well.

NICHOLAS DORN AND NIGEL SOUTH

or non-drug project. Profits may be invested in a licit business (and, if this begins to trade in drugs, then it becomes more like type 1 above). Years of close engagement with middle-level police personnel mean that these Criminal Diversifier enterprises are most likely to provoke police corruption; a series of such scandals erupted during the 1970s (Cox, Shirley, and Short 1977).

The distinction between this type of enterprise and the Sideliners (described above) is that while the Sideliners are initially legitimate, the criminal firm began as an organization dedicated to unlawful gain. At the upper reaches of the distribution network, the organized criminal 'firm' is now a force to be reckoned with. As observed by Hartnoll and his colleagues: 'The illicit market has become more organized and has attracted the attention of criminal groups who, a few years ago, would not have been willing to become involved in drugs. This is particularly true of cannabis and in the past two years, of heroin' (Hartnoll, Lewis, and Bryer 1984: 22 4).

By the early 1980s it had become apparent to British police officers that a number of criminal gangs previously engaged in crimes other than drug distribution had begun to take considerable interest in this area. The profits from short-term involvement in drug distribution could be used to finance the longer term 'ordinary' criminal operations such as bank break-ins and wage snatches. It seems that the criminal entry into drug distribution was precipitated by the expansion of the drug market caused by the involvements of the other 'types': at a certain stage, probably at the end of the 1970s and beginning of the 1980s, a number of criminal gangs known to the police saw the opportunities in drug distribution and diversified into activity in this sector. Angela Burr has described this movement in Southwark in south London. Although her description may be somewhat romantic in comparison with weightier accounts (e.g. Hobbs 1988), it captures something of community attitudes:

The local 'mafiosi' style criminal subculture focuses around mob families (Taylor 1984). The notorious Richardson gang, for example, was a well known Bermondsey family. Nowadays, families from other ethnic groups, such as Turkish Cypriots, have also become big time criminals (villains). The latter are highly respected locally and looked upon as 'Robin Hood' types. 'They don't touch us, they only take from the rich' was a frequent comment, as was: 'If they find out someone's been mugging old ladies they do them over'. 'The Richardsons and Krays always used to give the old people a party at Christmas', they say appreciatively ... Although heroin trafficking and dealing has always been anathema to traditional criminals, by the end of the 1970s organised crime in Britain, realising the profits to be made from it, had begun to move into large-scale heroin trafficking, a trend reflected in North Southwark. (Burr 1987: 342)

Such diversification of 'traditional' British criminality is not confined to this area of London, as recent press reports and personal contacts with police and drug workers in East London testify (Rose 1989; Grieve, personal communication; Newham Drugs Advice Agency Staff, personal communication). However, for every successful Criminal Diversifier there are several less successful who hang around the fringes, trying to play the part and to pick up any tit-bits that may be available (see Hobbs 1988). This broader group of hangers-on merges into the next category to be described, the Opportunistic Irregulars.

3. *Opportunistic Irregulars* are large or small groups who respond to short-term market opportunities as these arise; they do not plan long-term operations. Their members are

DRUG MARKETS AND LAW ENFORCEMENT

highly 'streetwise', but generally lack the resources possessed by the Sideliners or Diversifiers. Irregulars have no legitimate business front and no capital to speak of; they may even be long-term unemployed. They generally have little experience of working in professional criminal enterprises, and indeed will usually be regarded as unreliable by those enterprises.

Some irregulars, particularly the younger and least experienced ones, will plan and execute a series of short-term exercises over a few minutes, hours, or days: stealing a wallet that is lying on the shop counter; ripping off a box of video recorders being delivered to a shop and selling them; buying or stealing drugs and re-selling them. They may or may not consume drugs, but in any case drug consumption will not be their primary motive; money and excitement are their main interests, and they will deal in whatever commodities and situations provide these. In parts of Britain they are called 'breadheads' (money-minded), in order to distinguish them from 'smackheads' (heroin-minded) (Parker, Blakx, and Newcombe 1988: 107–8; Pearson 1987: 127).

Other irregulars—for example, older people and petty criminal families— are still opportunistic in their approach but may plan some of their activities over a slightly longer time period. For example, from our fieldwork in a working-class housing estate in 'Seadown', a south-coast English town, we can point to the existence of localized networks of trading in a wide variety of goods that are evidently stolen or at least about which 'no questions are asked'. Drugs, including heroin, become merely one commodity among many in this kind of network:

> The 'Godmother' (as she is called on the estate) is known to be involved in money lending and receiving and dealing in stolen goods as well as heroin and other drugs . . . [These activities were] reflected in the underlife of a notorious local pub (since closed down and re-furbished) which, by the accounts of the local community police officer, local probation service and several tenant's representatives, had been literally a market place in a variety of illegal goods, drugs among them. (Fieldwork note, 1986)[9]

These styles of involvement in drug distribution are aspects of the 'irregular' parts of the broader informal economies. Irregular economies are irregular in the moral-legal sense (they are broadly illegal or on the borderline of legality), and also in the temporal sense. Activity in these settings

> takes the form of a bunching together of intensive periods of work (buying, selling, contacting, getting money together, etc.). In between these intensive bursts of activity the business of survival requires one to be always searching for further opportunities, and to be on the look-out for potential dangers. (Auld, Dorn, and South 1986: 172)

We turn now to three types of enterprise that tend to specialize in drugs rather than a range of commodities.

4. *Retail Specialists* are fairly stable, hierarchical organizations in which a 'manager' (or 'crew boss', in some of the North American literature) employs young adults to perform several specialized roles—protecting the drugs, fetching small deals for customers, collecting payment, keeping lookout, preparing diversions for police, discouraging rip-offs, etc. (see Preble and Casey 1969; Johnson *et al.* 1985). The work is broken down into

---

[9] From records of fieldwork from exploratory research carried out in April 1986, other aspects of which are reported in Dorn, James, and South 1987.

NICHOLAS DORN AND NIGEL SOUTH

a series of small job-roles, allowing easy hire and fire, high through-put, and easy control. Organizational size is variable: from one boss with about five employees, to a manager with several lieutenants and scores of workers. Employees of these enterprises may or may not be drug users themselves; the important organizational consideration is that they are not 'stoned' while working (being stoned would impair efficiency). The enterprise may work out of a fixed location (a house, a bar, or a pub) to which customers come; may work a certain limited area of public space; may move between a number of such sites; and/or may call at users' homes or other individual meeting places. This type of enterprise has been more commonly reported in the North American urban context (Johnson *et al.* 1985) than in Britain. However, Pearson's research in the north of England does suggest the emergence of simplified forms of such enterprises in Liverpool and Manchester (Pearson 1987: 127–8).

5. *Mutual Society.*   A Mutual Society, a term drawn from American usage, is an organization set up in order to provide mutual aid, insurance against sickness, etc. In the present context we are using the term to describe friendship networks of user-dealers. The term 'a cluster of user-dealers' has been coined by a senior Drug Squad officer to describe this relationship. Their primary interest is in drug *use*, but they frequently exchange, trade, and sell drugs when they have more than sufficient for their immediate needs, wish to repay a debt or to respond to a request, or wish to obtain cash in order to purchase a different drug or some other commodity. Members may support each other in a variety of ways, including co-operating to ensure the supply of drugs and to keep out unwelcome outsiders. The enterprise bears some resemblance to a co-operative.

One of the consequences of the drug scene becoming more commercialized and 'heavy' is that this type of distribution system is under greater pressure than it was some years ago. Here is a member of a Mutual Society describing these developments:

I mean at one time if you didn't have money one day you could go to a friend and say, well, lend me a quarter [of a gram] and I'll pay you back tomorrow. But now you can't do that sort of thing because people are very money-orientated, there's always a risk because there are so many people using it who, you know, you are worried that if you lay out on [give drugs to] one person then it is setting a precedent, even though you may have known them for eight or ten years. Maybe someone else in the room has heard you and they will say, 'You laid some on Dave yesterday, can you do the same for me?' And it escalates the situation . . . (Fieldwork note, 1986)

Another user recalls the 'good old days' when

it was more sociable. I mean to say, people used to give drugs to each other more or less to make their own time enjoyable . . . It was very much a social scene and people would use certain pubs and there was no real money involved. I mean to say, whatever money was involved was peanuts, was really just to cover your own costs of whatever prescription charge, or for your evening's drinking. Or if you didn't have the money and you weren't feeling too well, someone would always see you alright. (Fieldwork note, 1986)

Other researchers confirm these trends. Fraser and George (1988) write that 'using Dorn and South's (1987*a*) classification of drug enterprises, Seadown's heroin supply network can be described as maturing through a mutual society into a retail specialist'. They explain that when Seadown's relatively easy heroin supply became more erratic in the early 1980s, the shortages provoked

DRUG MARKETS AND LAW ENFORCEMENT

cooperative or entrepreneurial efforts to obtain illicit heroin, either from London, or by importing it directly through Seadown expatriates residing in Holland ... It was during this period that the drug using community developed its strong social links and ethos. [But] by the mid-1980s the increased commercialisation of the illicit non-pharmaceutical heroin distribution networks reached Seadown with three independent, but occasionally cooperating large heroin wholesalers quickly and firmly establishing a monopoly for local supply. None of the members of the three wholesaler groups were Seadown born. (Fraser and George 1988: 657)

One conclusion would seem to be that as soon as external factors—such as disruption to supply routes, or carefully targeted policing—begin to intrude, then the reciprocal relations of the Mutual Society begin to break down. Fraser and George describe the impact of more vigorous policing in the mid-1980s as 'dismantling the drug network's social centre as well as its distribution chain' (1988: 661), with the result that the network's members have generally shifted to heavy and rather demoralized consumption of alcohol (ibid. 658). Here we see the police completing the demolition job that began with the commercialization of a local distribution system previously based on mutuality.

6. *Trading Charities* result from a mixture of ideological commitments and commercial considerations. Some Trading Charities arose from the 'altruistic' motives of hippy-type individuals to provide drugs as a 'service to the community'; some from Rastafarian beliefs about the sacred nature of *ganja* (cannabis). For some groups and individuals these altruistic motives have become rather awkwardly joined up with an attitude which permits the accumulation of profit. But it is quite commonly the case that this type of enterprise 'does not yield much profit [because] entrepreneurial practices related to marketing behaviour have not been entirely coordinated or systemised. Although dealers are well-versed in the complex techniques needed to operate a successful dealership, they are not rigorous in the execution of these skills' (Langer 1977: 384).

Although individuals in Trading Charities will generally 'practice what they preach' and consume the drugs in which they trade, they differ from the user-dealers in Mutual Societies in so far as they do not expect customers to take turns in supplying them: the trading relationship is one-way, not reciprocal. Some individuals may, in the changed conditions of the 1980s, be ambivalent about their role:

John, a cannabis dealer, reports that he doesn't want any more customers and that he's thinking of stopping dealing altogether. He's only ever dealt in cannabis and has had most of his customers for several years. He started in the 1960s under the influence of 'alternative' ideas, and has just kept on since then, but he's not sure why he's doing it any more—maybe there was a point to it before, but he doesn't feel that there is now. However, he does make a bit of money out of it and quite likes the 'social round' associated with being a small 'friendly' dealer. Also he wants a supply for himself and it's easy enough to deal enough money to pay for this. (Fieldwork note, 1987)

Such modest aspirations may result in lesser rewards than would a greater involvement, but they also involve keeping a relatively low profile and hence greatly reduce the risk of apprehension.

7. *State-sponsored Enterprise.* The scale of State-sponsored Enterprises ranges from the globally significant (e.g. the CIA-supported heroin trade in the Far Eastern 'Golden Triangle' during the US presence in Vietnam, and more recently the Contra private

armies allegedly supported by Colonel Oliver North and his compatriots, and the activities of President Noriega of Panama, installed with the assistance of the United States); through the medium-level area police squad, whose members engage in covert 'buy–bust' operations; to local police drug squads turning a blind eye to small dealers in return for information from them about other drug enterprises. State-sponsored enterprises may be single-commodity organizations, but more often drugs will form part of a portfolio operation including arms sales, political intimidation, or prostitution services. Of necessity, such organizations will adopt a cover or front, varying with the environment, to present to others in the drug market. The motivations of the managers of these organizations may vary, and indeed many will oscillate over time between thinking of themselves as government agents and thinking of themselves as independent entrepreneurs. Their common (shared) features are links with state agencies, some degree of immunity from prosecution, and potential as focuses of corruption and scandal.

In Britain it is the Metropolitan Police, especially its Criminal Investigation Department, that has featured as the focus of drug-related corruption. Between 1968 and 1971, Detective Chief Inspector Kelaher became 'the most important police drugs man in the country' (Cox, Shirley, and Short 1977: 89). Under his leadership the Metropolitan Drug Squad made a number of mistakes, such as getting involved in drug deals, giving false evidence, recycling drugs back on to the market, and allowing some drug distributors to continue in business in return for information about others (ibid. 129–30). Only the persistence of HM Customs and Excise investigators and *Sunday Times* journalists eventually forced Scotland Yard to take remedial action. By 1989, however, the Metropolitan Police were again in trouble, with Detective Chief Inspector Tony Lundy allegedly having a corrupt relationship with an informant, Roy Garner, the latter being accused of trafficking in cocaine. Part of the case was heard *in camera* at the insistence of the defence (*Observer* 26th Feb. 1989: 3). The prime mover in bringing the case was again HM Customs and Excise, reinforcing our earlier point that there are limits to corruption when there is more than one enforcement agency working in the same area.

In outlining these varied forms which the drug distribution enterprise may take, we must of course acknowledge that the picture is blurred around the edges, and that organizational change may occur. At any given time, an enterprise may be staying the same, quantitatively and qualitatively; or changing size whilst retaining the same basic organizational structure and mode of operation; or changing into another form of organization, or a hybrid type. Such changes may be triggered by a variety of circumstances: the entry into or exit from the market of major criminal organizations; changes in practices of banks and other financial institutions; the expansion or contraction of alternative profitable means of investment; changes in the labour market; changes in enforcement strategies (as perceived by managers of drug distribution enterprises), etc. The next and penultimate section of this paper focuses upon aspects of the enforcement–market interaction.

Discussion: Small Is Not Always Beautiful

Drug markets and enforcement counter-measures are of interest not only in and of themselves but also because drugs enforcement is at the forefront of the more general

DRUG MARKETS AND LAW ENFORCEMENT

development of policing and penalties. The principles of asset investigations and of asset penalties have now been copied from the 1986 Drug Trafficking Offences Act to the 1988 Criminal Justice Act, and these new methods are applicable to any major crime netting over £10,000 gain for the criminal. The National Drugs Intelligence Unit, which currently has an information-sharing role but no operational or co-ordinating authority, could form the basis for a national drugs enforcement agency networking with European and other agencies and having more power to actually direct drugs operations within Britain (Hurd 1989). This development is seen by many senior police and customs officers as part of the broader development of a national police force, crowning a reorganized structure with up to ten regional forces dealing with serious crime while residual lower-level policing continues to be directed from the local level (Hirst 1989). Whether such reorganization actually occurs, and the linked question of whether assets seized from criminals will be used to make the national and/or regional organizations partly or wholly self-funding, remains to be seen. But the broader point, that drugs enforcement has been a harbinger of developments in broader areas of policing, is indisputable. So any observations that can be derived from a study of drugs enforcement may be of wider relevance.

The common thread running through this paper has been the suggestion that drug distribution enterprises and law enforcement agencies can be understood as organizations in interaction with each other. Drug distribution organizations provide a range of targets for law enforcement agencies; the latter develop an arsenal of strategies, which in turn provoke changes by the distributors. Certain developments on the enforcement side, in particular multiple jurisdiction, covert operations, and surveillance of cash-flow, press hardest against those distributors with larger and relatively static organizations, resulting in a market inhabited by a range of small, loose, and flexible organizations. Other developments, in particular the long-term cultivation of informants and a repeated escalation of penalties, have pushed the trade in the direction of becoming more security conscious, more prepared to use violence to deter informants and enforcement agents, and generally more brutal: the trading environment has been shaped in ways that attract high risk-takers. Taking these developments together, British drug markets are being shaped in the image of North American ones — fragmented, volatile, and increasingly violent. This has little to do with crack (which is simply the latest in a long line of 'horror drugs'), and more to do with trends in law enforcement. Continuing references to crack are an apologia for the disturbing consequences of politically popular policies. The increasing brutality thus encouraged can all too easily legitimize heavier law enforcement, and so the spiral of violence goes on. It seems easier for the legal apparatuses to reshape patterns of crime, including drug markets, than to prevent them.

Conclusion

We are now able to make some analytic distinctions that may be useful in broadening the debate. These are:

1. The general distinction between an analysis of the consequences of particular patterns of policing, sentencing and legislation, and a rejection of legal control of any kind.

185

NICHOLAS DORN AND NIGEL SOUTH

2. The distinction between financial enquiries as a technique of investigation and asset confiscations as a penalty on top of life imprisonment.
3. The distinction between the quantities of dangerous drugs provided by a market, and other dangers and forms of harm provided by that market.

On the first point, we note the tendency of some writers to slide from the proposition that particular drug control policies are worthy of close and critical analysis to the proposition that controlled drugs should be legalized (e.g. Wisotsky 1986). We think that proposals for a full-blown 'market solution' are not thought through, politically naive, and (worst of all) a waste of an opportunity to intervene positively in public policy-making.

Secondly, we feel a need to avoid getting into a for-or-against position in relation to the financial provisions of the Drug Trafficking Offences Act and the Criminal Justice Act. There is a very clear distinction between financial enquiries as a form of investigation (bank disclosures, Drug Profits Confiscation Teams, following the money trail), and asset confiscation as a form of penalty for all those convicted. There is a strand of opinion within the police that doubts the cost-effectiveness of going for asset confiscation in the case of everyone convicted of a trafficking offence; it simply takes a lot of time to investigate the finances of every small-time dealer convicted (Boothroyd 1989). Civil libertarians add that since the arrangements of small dealers (e.g. user-dealers, mutual societies) are more likely to be relatively unsophisticated, asset confiscation bears down more heavily upon them than upon the bigger and often more sophisticated distributors at whom the legislation was primarily aimed. We can follow both of these arguments. However, we do not necessarily follow the implication that asset confiscation should be focused upon the bigger villains. We have to ask whether the threat of confiscation of *all* one's assets on top of the threat of life sentences (which may easily in practice exceed ten years) pushes the market in the direction of greater or lesser sinfulness. We think that there are enough greedy and unpleasant people about who are prepared to respond by taking whatever measures are in their eyes likely to reduce the chances of being caught to the point where they can be discounted. The question therefore needs to be posed, does the structure of penalties, the 'tariff', require reassessment?

The final distinction is more general. Given that crimes such as drug distribution may be occasioned in ways which are more or less socially harmful (e.g with or without shootings), it follows that the policy of *harm minimization* can be invoked (ACMD 1984). This concept is now widely accepted as an aim in relation to drug consumers: minimizing the social, legal, and medical harms that may be associated with drug consumption, as well as trying to reduce drug consumption itself, are now accepted as the twin goals of prevention. It may now be time to discuss harm minimization in relation to drug distribution. The question is, given that we cannot totally prevent illegal drug markets (and there is reasonable consensus on that proposition—see e.g. Wagstaff and Maynard 1988), what sort of markets do we least dislike, and how can we adjust the control mix so as to push markets in the least *un*desired direction?

To pose this question is to reposition debates on drug markets within a social and ethical perspective that is currently notable by its absence. The thought crosses the mind, however, that the decriminalizers and the hard hats have already carved up the debate between them; the former having lost, the latter may now press their advantage

186

DRUG MARKETS AND LAW ENFORCEMENT

to the point of using the drugs-and-crime issue to justify re-introduction of the death penalty. It would not be the first time that drug control has been at the forefront of the evolution of law (Sheerer 1987).

REFERENCES

ACMD [ADVISORY COUNCIL ON THE MISUSE OF DRUGS] (1984), *Prevention*. London: HMSO.
ASHTON, M. (1986), 'Doctors at War', *Druglink*, 1/2: 14–16.
AULD, J., DORN, N., and SOUTH, N. (1986), 'Irregular Work, Irregular Pleasures: Heroin in the 1980s', in R. Matthews and J. Young, eds., *Confronting Crime*, 166–87, London: Sage.
BLAU, C., *et al.* (1983), *Investigation and Prosecution of Illegal Money Laundering: A Guide to the Bank Secrecy Act*. Washington, DC: Department of the Treasury, Internal Revenue Service.
BOOTHROYD, J. (1989), 'Drugs Act Forces Change of Tactics', *Police Review*, 17 February: 334–5.
BURR, A. (1987), 'Chasing the Dragon', *British Journal of Criminology*, 27/4: 333–57.
COX, B., SHIRLEY, J., and SHORT, M. (1977), *The Fall of Scotland Yard*. Harmondsworth: Penguin.
DOMBRINK, J., and MEEKER, J. (1986), 'Beyond "Buy and Bust": Nontraditional Sanctions in Federal Drug Law Enforcement', *Contemporary Drug Problems*, 13/4: 711–40.
DORN, N., JAMES, C., and SOUTH, N. (1987), *The Limits of Informal Surveillance: Four Case Studies in Identifying Neighbourhood Heroin Problems*. London: ISDD.
DORN, N., and SOUTH, N. (1987a), 'Some Issues in the Development of Drug Markets and Law Enforcement', paper to workshop on 'Drugs: Side Effects of Control Policies', Commission of the European Communities, Luxemburg, 22–23 Oct.
—— (1987b), 'Reconciling Policy and Practice', in Dorn and South (1987c).
——, eds. (1987c), *A Land Fit for Heroin? Drug Policies, Prevention and Practice*. London: Macmillan.
—— (1989), 'Profits and Penalties: New Trends in Legislation and Law Enforcement concerning Illegal Drugs'. Paper to British Sociological Association Annual Conference, Plymouth Polytechnic, March; forthcoming in D. Whynes and P. Bean, eds., *Policing and Prescribing: The British System of Drug Control*. London: Macmillan.
—— (1991), *Policing the Drugs Distribution Business*. London: Routledge.
FERMAN, L., and FERMAN, P. (1973), 'The Structural Underpinnings of the Irregular Economy', *Poverty and Human Resources Abstracts*, 8: 3–17.
FORTSON, R. (1988), *The Law on the Misuse of Drugs*. London: Sweet and Maxwell.
FRASER, A., and GEORGE, M. (1988), 'Changing Trends in Drug Use: An Initial Follow-up of a Local Heroin-using Community', *British Journal of Addiction*, 83: 655–63.
GENERAL ACCOUNTING OFFICE (1983), *Federal Drug Interdiction Efforts Need Strong Central Oversight*. Washington, DC: General Accounting Office.
GERTH, H., and MILLS, C. W. (1970), *From Max Weber: Essays in Sociology*. London: Routledge and Kegan Paul.
GRIEVE, J. (1987), 'Comparative Police Strategies: Drug-related Crime'. M.Phil thesis, Cranfield Institute of Technology.
GRIFFITHS, R., and BARKER, J. (1984), 'An Assessment of Drug Problems and Needs in Bermondsey and Rotherhithe and Recommendations for a Response: Report of a Local Working Party'. Feb. Mimeo.
HARTNOLL, R., LEWIS, R., and BRYER, S. (1984), 'Recent Trends in Drug Use in Britain', *Druglink*, 19: 22–4.

NICHOLAS DORN AND NIGEL SOUTH

HEADLEY, B. (1989), "'War Ina' Babylon": Dynamics of the Jamaican Informal Drug Economy', *Social Justice*, 15/3–4: 61–86.

HIRST, M. (1989), '1989; Year of the Super Forces?' *Police Review*, 28 Apr., pp. 857–9.

HOBBS, D. (1988), *Doing the Business: Entrepreneurship, the Working Class and Detectives in the East End of London*. Oxford: Clarendon Press.

HURD, D. (1989), Address to ACPO National Drug Conference, Preston, Lancs.

JOHNSON, B., GOLDSTEIN, P., PREBLE, A., SCHNEIDLER, J., LIPTON, D., SPUNT, B., and MILLER, T. (1985), *Taking Care of Business: The Economics of Crime by Heroin Abusers*. Lexington: Lexington Books.

JOHNSON, B., HAMID, A., MORALES, E., and SANABRIA, H. (1987), 'Critical Dimensions of Crack Distribution'. Paper presented to the American Society of Criminology, Montreal, 12 Nov.

KNAPP COMMISSION, THE (1972), *The Knapp Report on Police Corruption*. New York: George Braziller.

LANGER, J. (1977), 'Drug Entrepreneurs and Dealing Culture', *Social Problems*, 24/3: 377–86.

LEWIS, R. (1989), 'European Markets in Cocaine', *Contemporary Crises*, 13: 35–52.

MACGREGOR, S., ed. (1989), *Drugs and British Society*. London: Routledge.

MANNING, P. (1980), *The Narc's Game*. Cambridge, Mass.: MIT Press.

NICOL, A. (1988), 'Confiscation of the Profits of Crime' *Journal of Criminal Law*, 52: 75–83.

O'BRYAN, L. (1989), 'Young People and Drugs', in MacGregor (1989).

O'NEIL, P., BAKER, P., and GOUGH, T. (1984), 'Illicitly Imported Heroin Products: Some Physical and Chemical Features Indicative of their Origin', *Journal of Forensic Sciences*, 29/3: 889–902.

PARKER, H., BAKX, K., and NEWCOMBE, R. (1988), *Living with Heroin*. Milton Keynes: Open University Press.

PEARSON, G. (1987), *The New Heroin Users*. Oxford: Blackwell.

PREBLE, E., and CASEY, J. (1969), 'Taking Care of Business: The Heroin User's Life on the Street', *International Journal of the Addictions*, 4/1: 1–24.

PUNCH, M. (1985), *Conduct Unbecoming: The Social Construction of Police Deviance*. London: Tavistock.

REUTER, R. (1983), *Disorganised Crime: Illegal Markets and the Mafia*. Boston, Mass.: MIT Press.

ROSE, D. (1989), 'Great Train Robbers Dealt Cocaine', *Guardian*, 27 July, p. 8.

SHAWCROSS, T., and YOUNG, M. (1987), *Mafia Wars: The Confessions of Tommaso Buscetta*. London: Fontana.

SHEERER, S. (1987), 'Opiates and the Legal System in Europe since the Single Convention'. Paper to workshop on 'Drugs: Side Effects of Control Policy', Commission of the European Communities, Luxemburg, 22–23 Oct.

TAYLOR, L. (1984), *In the Underworld*. Oxford: Blackwell.

TIPPELL, S. (1989), 'Drug Users and the Prison System', in MacGregor (1989).

WAGSTAFF, A., and MAYNARD, A. (1988), *Economic Aspects of the Illicit Drug Market and Drug Enforcement Policies in the United Kingdom*. Home Office Research Study No. 95. London: HMSO.

WISOTSKY, S. (1986), *Breaking the Impasse in the War on Drugs*. New York: Greenwood Press.

WRIGHT, A., and WAYMONT, A. (1990), *Police Drug Enforcement Strategies and Intelligence Needs in England and Wales*. London: Police Foundation.

[4]

a successful female crack dealer: case study of a deviant career

Eloise Dunlap, Bruce D. Johnson, and Ali Manwar
National Development and Research Institute, Inc., New York

This paper traces the career of a successful female crack dealer in Harlem. "Rachel" is a deviant among deviants: a female in a male-dominated profession who caters to the "hidden" crack user rather than the stereotypical addict, uses techniques common among middle-class dealers rather than those more typical of her inner-city location, and is herself a crack addict who manages to avoid both arrest and dereliction. The paper describes how Rachel's career evolved around shifts in the drug market, from marijuana to cocaine to crack; illuminates an unknown side of the drug economy—the world of the older, better educated, middle class drug user; reveals how gender affects drug distribution in a profession dominated by males; and examines how those involved in deviant careers cope with social opprobrium and attempt to justify their activities. Rachel's relative success in her profession is attributed to a unique combination of historical contingencies, personal qualities, and career choices.

Selling drugs has been defined as a major social problem (Inciardi 1986; Bourgois and Dunlap 1993; Inciardi et al. 1993). Most of the

Received 15 January 1993; accepted 14 June 1993.

This paper was prepared under a project entitled "The Natural History of Crack Distribution" (1 R01 DA05126-04), supported by the National Institute on Drug Abuse (NIDA), and also under other projects funded by NIDA (1 R01 DA01926-07, 5 T32 DA07233-08, 1 R01 DA06615-02) and the National Institute of Justice (80-IJ-CX-0049S2, 87-IJ-CX-0064, 91-IJ-CX-D014). Narcotic and Drug Research, Inc. also provided support. The opinions expressed in this paper do not necessarily represent the official positions of either the U.S. Government or National Development and Research Institutes, Inc. The authors thank Ansley Hamid of John Jay College of Criminal Justice for his contributions to the research on which the paper is based.

Address correspondence to Eloise Dunlap, National Development and Research Institute, Inc., 11 Beach Street, New York, NY 10013

Deviant Behavior: An Interdisciplinary Journal, 15:1–25, 1994
Copyright © 1994 Taylor & Francis
0163-9625/94 $10.00 + .00

1

half million prison slots created since 1980 are occupied by persons imprisoned for drug sales, drug possession, or crimes committed to obtain drugs. Among illegal drugs, crack cocaine is recognized as presenting particularly severe social problems, and criminal penalties for crack sales, more severe than those for selling other drugs, are similar to penalties for burglary and robbery (Belenko et al. 1991).

Several studies have documented the role of females in criminal activity in general and in illegal drug use and sales in particular (Chambers et al. 1981; Inciardi 1986; Inciardi and Pottieger 1986; Sanchez and Johnson 1987; Dunlap and Johnson 1992a, 1992b; Bourgois and Dunlap 1993). The female prison population has doubled since 1980, with drug sales among the most common reasons for arrest (Sanchez and Johnson 1987; Bourgois and Dunlap 1993). Of all drug arrests of females, only arrests for the sale of heroin, cocaine, or crack are likely to result in imprisonment, but convictions since 1985 for such sales—especially for crack sales—account for much of the increase in the number of women in prison (Division of Criminal Justice Services 1988; Bureau of Justice Statistics 1992). Nevertheless, very little is known about females' participation in illegal drug sales, and virtually nothing is known about female crack dealers.

This paper presents a case study of Rachel (a pseudonym), a petite, attractive, outgoing African-American woman with a moderate Afro and fashionable appearance who looks much younger than her 40 years. A successful Harlem crack dealer, Rachel is a deviant among deviants, for several reasons. First, she is female in a traditionally male occupation. Second, her educational level, middle-class background, and professionalism are atypical of drug dealers. Third, her drug-related activities are distinctly different from those of both male crack dealers and other female dealers studied (cf. Dunlap and Johnson 1992a, 1992b; Maher and Curtis 1992): her thriving business serves not the stereotypical young, male addict but the older, employed, "hidden" user; and even though her activities occur in the depths of the inner city, she conducts her business according to practices common among middle-class dealers. Finally, Rachel is herself an addict who uses sizable amounts of crack several times a day, yet she has avoided both arrest and the usual consequences of personal crack use. Neatly balancing the various roles and competing social expectations placed on her, she stands at the intersection of the straight and drug subcultures, between middle-class and inner-city drug dealers, between drug abusers and more casual users.

Careful analysis of deviant cases often provides important insights, both theoretical and practical, about little understood phenomena (Becker 1963). Particularly helpful are informants who, like Rachel, are articulate enough to discuss their deviant behavior and explain the pressures and rewards that mold it. Rachel's case illustrates how the market for illegal drugs has shifted in the United States from marijuana to cocaine to crack; how drugs permeate inner-city communities, reaching older, better educated, middle-class professional people as well as the young, the uneducated, and the poor; how women fit into a sphere of activity heavily dominated by men; and how drug dealers justify their illegal activities and cope with moral opprobrium.

METHODS

Rachel's story is drawn from an ongoing, large-scale ethnographic research project, the "Natural History of Crack Distribution," designed to develop a systematic understanding of careers in drug (especially crack) sales. Under this project, information was collected on the structure, functioning, and economic aspects of cocaine and crack distribution in New York City, primarily in inner-city minority communities where selling crack has become a major career for many (Dunlap and Johnson 1992b). More than 300 crack dealers were observed and their activities noted in field records. More than 160 (approximately 130 males and 40 females) were interviewed and their responses recorded in field notes and on tape. Other papers provide details of the qualitative and quantitative methods used in the project, including respondent recruitment and interviewing procedures (Dunlap et al. 1990; Lewis et al. 1992), the transcription/retrieval of ethnographic texts for analysis by theme (Manwar et al. 1993), and techniques for assuring personal safety (Williams et al. 1992).

During ethnographic field work between 1989 and 1992, the senior author (Dunlap) developed close relationships with many crack dealers and their families. Her introduction to Rachel, whose cooperation was to prove crucial to the research, was arranged by a dealer for whom several others worked. With a college degree in psychology, Rachel quickly grasped the intent of the study and the importance of the issues to be examined. She was outgoing and friendly, and mutual rapport and trust soon emerged. As well as securing the ethnographer's personal safety (Williams et al. 1992), she also assured fellow dealers of the legitimacy of the research, which encouraged them to participate fully. Her story, elicited over a one-year period in ethnographic interviews and direct observations at her apartment (also her place of business), generated more than 700 pages of transcripts from tapes and field notes. The quoted material below is drawn from these transcripts.

Rachel speaks in a nonstandard English vernacular that combines the syntax used in the South (where she spent her childhood) with New York street talk, and incorporates what linguists call "code shifting" between standard English and African-American speech patterns (cf. Painter 1979). The quoted material below preserves her words, syntax, and speech rhythms, since "language symbolizes as well as expresses the distinctiveness of our personal identity and our most important group memberships and identifications: family, ethnicity, class, peer group, and lifestyle enclave" (Blauner 1989, p. 328; see also Blauner 1987).

BACKGROUND

Deviance Versus Legitimacy

Deviant careers are fundamentally different from legal ones. Government helps individuals to gain the resources and skills necessary to become legally employed, produce legal goods and services, and pay taxes, routinely providing legal-regulatory structures and financial support for the agencies (schools, families, employers, etc.) that supervise, educate, train, test, and reward these individuals. No such support is available to those in deviant careers, who "drift" into activities for which no formal training is available, learning "on the job" and receiving informal mentoring from other deviants (Matza 1964). In addition, the state and its social control agents (police, judges, treatment officials, etc.) protect persons pursuing legal careers, but those pursuing careers defined as illegal or immoral must consistently avoid the efforts of both social control agents and ordinary citizens to halt their activities.

In the world of illegal drug sales, the opposition of government and the absence of formal training means that individuals must discover by themselves how to deal with the complex contingencies involved in selling drugs (Faupel 1981; Waldorf et al. 1991). They must learn how to obtain supplies of high quality drugs to sell; create retail sales units; recruit buyers; avoid arrest, incarceration, and violence from competitors or customers; and handle and account for large amounts of cash, while evading both formal and informal sanctions. Individual dealers must develop informal rules or norms of conduct by which to conduct business (Zinberg 1984), determining what kinds of suppliers and customers to seek out; where and when to conduct sales; how to avoid the police and competitors; how to moderate personal crack use; how to spend cash income; and how to obtain shelter, food, and clothing. Perhaps their most difficult challenge, however, is to limit their own drug consumption so that they sell enough to "re-up," or purchase more wholesale units of drugs (Hamid 1992; Johnson et al. 1992).

Inner-City Versus Middle-Class Drug Careers

The limited literature on illicit drug sales suggests that there are two relatively distinct types of drug-selling careers, which for convenience may be labeled the "inner-city" and "middle-class" career types (Faupel 1981; Adler 1985; Johnson et al. 1985; Carpenter et al. 1988; Johnson et al. 1990; Waldorf et al. 1991; Reuter et al. 1990). Drug dealers representing the two types exhibit both similarities and differences.

In both types of drug-selling careers, dealers are primarily youths and young adults. Dealers themselves are typically among the heaviest users of the drugs they sell (and sometimes other drugs as well), although self-consumption is a rapid route to destitution (Reuter et al. 1990). Sales usually take place on an intermittent basis. Across several years, most dealers report cycles of "success" (characterized by many sales, high income, high levels of personal drug use, and high status in drug-consuming circles) and "failure" (characterized by low or no drug sale income, inability to obtain supplies of drugs, arrest, violence, and economic deprivation). Males dominate the upper level drug-dealing roles (e.g., importer, wholesale dealer, supplier); females typically act as freelancers or work with or for others, usually males (Johnson et al. 1992).

For present purposes, the differences between the two career types are more important than the similarities. Middle-class dealers almost always sell directly to steady customers in private settings—homes, cars, offices—rather than to buyers they do not know personally or who have not been recommended by their steady customers (Adler 1985; Waldorf et al. 1991). They generally get their supplies of drugs from a small number of "connections" and usually sell in relatively large quantities, measuring cocaine by the gram and marijuana by the ounce. Their retail sales average $50 or more. Violence is relatively uncommon, since middle-class dealers tend to avoid threatening situations. Most manage to avoid arrest because their activity is private, and they are rarely incarcerated since they have greater resources for legal defense. Inner-city dealers, in contrast, often lack access to private settings for sales and typically sell in public locations to buyers they do not know. While they may have some steady customers, high customer turnover is common (Johnson et al. 1985, 1990). They typically have numerous suppliers and usually sell smaller retail units at lower prices: $10 to $25 bags of cocaine or heroin, $3 to $20 vials of crack. Violence and the threat of violence, arrest, and incarceration are common among inner city drug dealers (Goldstein 1985).

The most important difference between the two kinds of dealers is probably the disparity in their resources and life skills. As children and young adults, most middle-class dealers had the advantages of realtively stable homes, stronger kinship and friendship networks, and more formal education. As adults, they have access to resources such as permanent housing, telephones, and cars, and to life skills such as literacy, some accounting expertise, and effective interpersonal relationships. Thanks to these resources and skills, middle-class dealers frequently either have legal incomes or access to them. The early family and educational backgrounds of inner-city drug dealers, in contrast, are often found to have been grossly deficient (Dunlap and Johnson 1992c; Bourgois and Dunlap 1993; Ratner 1993). Lacking resources and life skills, they are effectively excluded from legal employment in their late teens and early 20s. Most have left school, are homeless (unless they live with family or friends), and have no legal jobs or sources of income. Effectively, their only economic options are nondrug criminality (robbery, burglary, theft, prostitution) or drug sales, with crack sales, being the most profitable (Johnson et al. 1993).

Women as Crack Cocaine Users and Dealers

Today, women constitute a third to a half of all users of illegal drugs in the United States, with cocaine second only to marijuana as their drug of choice (Greenleaf 1989). However, the proportion of women involved in crack dealing—mostly at the lower levels of drug sales—is much smaller (Maher and Curtis 1992; Dunlap and Johnson

1992b; Inciardi et al. 1993). Selling is a career that carries harsh social penalties. In general, female dealers are viewed as having somehow overstepped their feminine bounds. They are stigmatized because, as society's "gatekeepers," they are viewed as being more responsible than males for upholding traditional values. Men often brand crack-using/selling women as "whores," a label resulting from the fact that some women engage in sex for crack or prostitute themselves to earn money for crack (Bourgois and Dunlap 1993; Ratner 1993; Inciardi et al. 1993).

The severe deprivation experienced by the typical female crack abuser and dealer in childhood, adolescence, and young adulthood has been documented elsewhere (Dunlap and Johnson 1992a, 1992b; Bourgois and Dunlap 1993), as have details of the typical careers of inner city female crack dealers (Dunlap 1992; Dunlap and Johnson 1992a, 1992b). Rachel's childhood and adolescence are described in a companion paper (Dunlap et al. 1993) in which her family life is shown to be more characteristic of middle-class than inner-city dealers.

Generally, female dealers try to avoid violence and are therefore more apt than males to cooperate with competitors instead of confronting them (Dunlap and Johnson 1992b). This tendency makes dealing relatively safer for females than for males. Some report that, faced with choice of dealing crack or prostituting themselves, they prefer the former because drug dealing gives them more control over what takes place, even though the amount of money they make is smaller (Dunlap and Johnson 1992b; Maher and Curtis 1992).

DEVELOPMENT OF A DRUG-DEALING CAREER

Rachel's Early Involvement with Drugs

As a child, Rachel moved from Mississippi to Harlem, where at 15 she met her future husband, a heroin and marijuana dealer with several uncles in the illegal drug business. She became pregnant at 16, gave birth to a daughter, and married the baby's father a year later. As a teenage mother, Rachel remained uninvolved in drug use or sales, yet through her husband's activities she was introduced to drug dealing and a network of users and dealers. Her husband also provided a model of behaviors that contributed to his success in drug dealing: legitimate employment in addition to illegal activities;

separation of drug involvement and family life; and expenditure of extra time and money on family rather than on street life.

After her daughter's birth, Rachel enrolled in an educational program targeting the poor, holding a program-related job as she worked toward her high school diploma. By 20 she had earned a high school equivalency degree. Then, when she was 21 and had been happily married for 5 years, her husband died suddenly of a kidney infection, leaving her to care alone for her 5-year-old daughter as well as her alcoholic mother. Rachel had negotiated adolescence without using drugs, had completed high school, held a legitimate job, lived in a household that was affluent by Harlem standards, and had well-developed household management and child-rearing skills. In short, by 21 she had acquired resources (housing and household furnishings, limited savings, close relationships with her husband's relatives) and skills (household maintenance, budgeting and accounting, child care, interpersonal negotiation) that would be valuable in her future career.

As a single black parent and informal custodian of an alcoholic mother, Rachel's new position placed conflicting demands upon her. In her bereavement, she began going to parties and smoking marijuana.

> With the marijuana, you know, it . . . started out as a social situation, you know . . . I would say that for myself, I was probably a late person, in trying any of . . . any of these drugs at all. You could go to a party, you know, when you smoking marijuana, everybody smoking it, you know, its, really—uh—nothing that you want to get over, you don't have worry about going into a special room or anything like that, you know. A lot of clubs and places, you know, and—um— a lot of people who you knew at the time, any people, say people . . . with money or—you know—like movers and shakers . . . it was all right, it was acceptable, you know?

Rachel's earnings at her poverty program job were insufficient for the lifestyle she wanted for herself and her family. Since she was already familiar with the drug business, she began selling marijuana, obtained from her husband's family.

> And then really, it's like—it's a good—you get a little chunk of money. A little boost in your checking account, and as you boost your checking account one time and you know you not planning to do it no more, then something will come up and maybe you want something, you know. . . . You don't be planning to do it, like be out

there, you know. . . . I made good money, okay. . . . I'm always working, so I always had a good job, okay. Let's say I figure it like this. I predict what I needed, and if I needed $1,000 then that's what I was gonna get. If I needed $500 then that's what I was gonna get. See, I'd make whatever I needed, you know. . . .

Rachel's success with her marijuana customers, most of whom were co-workers or other working-class drug users, increased her economic reliance on drug profits. At the same time, however, she was establishing herself as the provider for her family, a role that increased her commitment to conventional norms.

You see, it (drug dealing) was about different things then, you know. 'Cause I wanted to travel, and then—you know—the kid, and we gave her everything . . . and then [I] gotta look out for my mother and stuff, so it was about—it was all about business then, you know . . . I wanna give her [daughter] everything in the world. When she's into college, no struggling, no sleeping in no dorm with two and three people. You get your own room, your own telephone, your own refrigerator, your own everything, you know.

From Marijuana to Cocaine

Thus far, Rachel had used and sold only marijuana, avoiding heroin. However, the drug scene—customers, dealing activities, patterns and places of consumption—was changing. By the mid-1970s, cocaine use had begin to increase among nonheroin drug users in New York (Johnson et al. 1985; 1990). Rachel, still in her 20s, began snorting cocaine at social gatherings, although marijuana remained her dominant drug of consumption.

I was still working and stuff, you know, and I was still out there doing my thing (selling marijuana), and I used to deal with—you know— a lot of people of different ethnic origins, okay, and I can remember— I used to go camping a lot. And we take the van, you know, go upstate, and hustle on back down here to Manhattan, to the Bronx, get a load of herb, you know, take it up to the camp, you know . . . and then I noticed, I think it was probably like . . . one of the last times I went camping . . . we came down in the van and we had $200 and we (spent it) for cocaine! Instead of, you know, herb . . . Well, um . . . I started—all right, I started snorting cocaine, okay? But I didn't stop using marijuana on account of that, you know. Uh, I used marijuana and cocaine, sniffing cocaine, okay? Uh, a lot together, you know, and still basically under the same social situations. I . . . had a close friend that I worked with, and he got into the habit, like, um, bringing it to the job, okay? And you know, we started sniffing a little bit. But, um . . . I would still primarily (snort cocaine) in a social situation, you know.

By the early 1980s, Rachel, like many other inner-city marijuana users, had begun to consume cocaine more regularly. She continued to sell and use marijuana, although good quality marijuana was becoming hard to find.

The marijuana . . . it just got to a point where it was hard to get. I mean, it's not hard to get marijuana, herb is—you know—you can still get herb anywhere, but it's just not the same quality, you know. And if you been smoking herb a long time . . . it's nothing compared to what herb used to be. . . . The more cocaine started being utilized in the form of crack, the less good herb seem to be available, okay . . . when I was getting it, you know, for, um, other reasons, other than personal use, you know, there's people that I would get it from, you know . . . (and) the quality just started (going down). 'Til you . . . just start gradually moving away from it, you know . . .

While she used cocaine in the same social situations as she had smoked marijuana, the setting for cocaine use was slightly different.

Um, with cocaine, okay, you still . . . supposedly with "in" people, but you know—you kinda—it started moving to the back room a little bit, so naturally you can't—because a lot of places you couldn't go in the place, smoke coke openly, you know, but you could go the ladies room, and you know, all the ladies—quote ladies—was in there doing it, you know. Or if you went to a party at somebody's house, you know, there was always that special place where you could do . . . a line, you know, snorting a line of cocaine, or you could spoon, you know . . . years ago people used to wear those spoons around their neck, you know, little gold chain thing . . . you would announce it, you know, in a way . . . it was fashionable!

At 24, Rachel enrolled in college, again under a social welfare program, and eventually earned a bachelor's degree in psychology. She was accepted into and began a graudate program, but dropped out to work as a rehabilitation psychotherapist.

Career and Drug Use Changes

Rachel continued to supplement her legal income with marijuana dealing, always keeping her drug-related activities separate from her family life. Prior to 1985, she had been motivated primarily by the desire to provide her mother and daughter with a comfortable lifestyle, and her personal drug consumption was limited by her commitment to them. But after her daughter married and moved away and her mother died, her involvement with drugs began to change; she sold drugs more and more to support her own habit. Eventually she left her legal job, although she retained the appearance and attitude of a legitimate professional woman.

> See, I'm, not . . . not so much into it the way I was before, when all I thought about was the dollar. I just feel like being comfortable, you know—um—support my own particular habit, you know, keep myself cared for. There was a time when it was a lot different, it was just all about the dollar bill, you know . . . when my daughter was going to college I was dealing, you know, because I needed, I wanted the money, okay? That was my primary thing. After my mother died and . . . my daughter went away to college . . . it was easier to get high and stuff.

As supplies of good quality marijuana became increasingly difficult to acquire, Rachel drifted into crack selling. The switch was accomplished through the same male co-worker who had previously provided her with cocaine.

> This particular friend . . . was also, as it turned out, when I first started dealing with crack and then started, you know, again with the selling a little bit, with the same person, you know, we just escalated (from) one thing to the other. . . .

Selling crack as she had marijuana, in an open, convivial, "tea-pad" atmosphere, attracted attention, and Rachel soon recognized that even though she was making "crazy money" she would have to change her style of doing business. News of her high-quality crack traveled so fast that overnight she had lines of people seeking to buy it. Not only did such obvious drug dealing put her in jeopardy from her nondrug-using neighbors, whose friendship she valued, and from the authorities, it also made her more prone to robbery by crack users and other dealers.

> I mean it was like lines of niggers, you know what I'm saying. Oh, God. I remember one time . . . I had the line up from the door. It was like, oh, God, I can't do this . . . I mean, it was like, it was really ugly in the beginning, you know. . . . Money was so fast, people so crazy, it was ugly.

Rachel quickly ended such sales, although occasionally she is still pressured into dealing with strangers who have heard of the quality of her crack.

> . . . you know, I'm the type of person, I'm friendly with people, you know, so some time it be like, "yo, I heard . . ."—especially when . . . I got that good quality from Long Island, then it be—it's like a nickel, you know, see for $5, somebody gonna go, child—I got this bad [i.e., good] stuff . . . I sell it to them. But that—that's not really what I . . . [have for] my clientele per se.

Since the advent of crack, Rachel's neighborhood has become permeated with crack users and dealers, even though most residents are still working people with families. Shootings, robberies, assaults, and rape have become commonplace. Indeed, rape is so common that most of its victims no longer consider it a reportable crime.

> It's a lot more violence associated with this drug. With cocaine in general, okay. But with crack in particular, you know. I never knew anybody on this—on this block that got killed for cocaine, but I've known, in the last year, three people getting killed for this crack business. They'll pull a gun up to you in a minute. In a minute. The young guys . . . I'm talking about organized drug dealers, okay, the young ones that are really into it and working for real big movers and shakers in the drug business, okay. They have no respect for no one, male or female, okay? And they as soon whip it out on you as anything . . . seem like the taking of a life is not . . . important . . .

Relationships among crack users are different from marijuana users' social interactions, and Rachel had to readjust her selling strategy to accommodate the particular effects of crack on users. Whereas marijuana consumers enjoy a sociable environment with wine, music, and conversation, many of Rachel's crack customers wanted to be left alone, requiring only a safe, quiet place where they could consume their drug discreetly.

> . . . particularly for older customers, they don't like that feeling of being—you know—like moles under the ground or something . . . if you ever been in a (crack house), it's a awful, awful sight, you know what I'm saying.

Recognizing a need among middle class crack users for a safe haven, Rachel reorganized her business, developing techniques similar to those of the middle class/professional users and dealers studied by Waldorf et al. (1991) in the San Francisco Bay area. Some of her customers were former marijuana users who, like herself, had grown older and disliked the street crack users who were everywhere evident in the neighborhood.

With the demise of her obligations to her daughter, her mother, and her legal job, Rachel became more involved in drug consumption. In addition, the stress of dealing crack, combined with its easy availability and pleasurable high, encouraged her increased consumption.

> You see, I'm not the gun-toting mama type, you know what I'm saying. So . . . when it was like that, when it was like heavy at that time, it was like—I don't know, I would start to smoking too much my own damn self and then it was just—you know—when it's free . . .

Rachel in the Ethnographic Present

Four years after entering the crack market, Rachel is one of very few successful female crack dealers in the inner city. A freelancer, she operates as a "house connection"—a dealer who conducts drug sales from her apartment (Johnson, Dunlap, Manwar, and Hamid 1992). Most other freelancers are involved in networks of dealers who help one another to avoid robbery, competition, and arrest (Johnson, Dunlap, and Hamid 1992), but Rachel is not a part of any network. Nor does she fit comfortably into the established hierarchy of drug dealers, since she is neither a street dealer or lower level distributor like most other female crack dealers (Johnson, Hamid, and Sanabria 1991; Maher and Curtis 1992; Dunlap et al. 1992b) nor an upper level distributor.

Rachel's apartment, one of the few places where buyers can both buy and consume crack, is a sixth floor walk-up with bars on the windows and several locks on the door. Unlike the typical crack house, it is immaculate, much like the Harlem home of a typical lower middle-class nondrug user. The living room contains a worn but clean sofa, a coffee table, two end tables, a bookcase full of old books, a portable black and white TV, an ineffective table fan, and an old-fashioned entertainment set (a radio/record player/tape deck combination with a space for albums). A record player, long broken, and a stack of old albums provide evidence of Rachel's former marijuana-dealing days. Pictures of her mother, daughter, grandchildren, and son-in-law decorate the room, and she is eager to show visitors her family photo albums. The bedroom contains a single bed, a wardrobe, and a dresser with a mirror. The kitchen is furnished with an old table and chairs, refrigerator, stove, and a large barrel in one corner.

Rachel had more household possessions and more money when she was selling marijuana to supplement her income. During the early stages of her crack career, she lost possessions such as tape decks and color TVs by admitting "certain types" of customers into her apartment. Now, with her daughter educated and married and her mother deceased, she lives modestly, maintaining her business primarily to pay her rent and bills and to get high.

> So right now it ain't really all about (money) . . . it's like keeping a steady pace, keeping myself on a steady flow and just basically having what I want, you know, like that. And it works out better, and it's a lot easier 'cause it's a lot less headache. . . .

Despite her satisfaction with her current lifestyle, Rachel has occasional feelings of remorse about being "a bad person," a judgment she believes her customers reflect.

> No matter who's buying it, it's like they always wanna look at the person that's selling it . . . therefore that makes me—you know—the dealer is the bad guy . . . I mean . . . it's the fact that you're doing something shady and you're doing something wrong, you know. Especially, like I said, the way most of the time I dealt with it, it was a lot of professional people, people that I worked with and stuff like that. So it's like I'm the shady character, you know—'cause I'm the dealer. So somehow or another, that makes me the shady character.

To counter this view, Rachel and her suppliers, whom she chooses according to the same criteria of adherence to conventional norms as she does her customers, attempt to bolster one another's self-images as respectable professionals.

> They (suppliers) are also human beings who wanna be looked at in another light . . . They wanna be looked at respectable and decent, you know. So you go out to dinner with me, I'm also going with you. I'm making you look good, you make me, and we all pretending that we normal people out here just like everybody else, hob-knobbing downtown and where ever you wanna go, you know. So you feed into each other's egos, because you don't really want to look at yourself as a bad person.

Her relationships with her (male) dealing associates take two different forms. Some treat her as a businessperson, according her the same respect they would give any business owner. But others treat her like a street dealer, making her vulnerable to the violence ordinarily found in drug dealing. Over the years she has developed

the expertise required to offset the potential for violence with the
ability to handle difficult situations, managing to tread a thin line
between being a friendly, accommodating businesswoman and at-
tracting unwanted sexual attention.

> What I dislike . . . men get the wrong idea about you, you know.
> Even when you straight up . . . they always gotta look at you some-
> where lesser than what they are. If they being a businessman, why
> can't I be being a businessperson too? . . . They always feel like
> somehow or another—you know—there's supposed to be that little
> extra fringe benefit in there, you know . . . and especially if you try
> to treat 'em like a human being, you know, with respect. Oh, then—
> you know—you think—they start playing on you then, you know.
> Because if you try, then they wanna, "oh, would you like to go out
> to dinner." Then the next thing is, "cause you bought me a meal, I'm
> supposed to go to bed with you." And then that makes you a black
> bitch and all that kind of stuff . . . and stuck up, you know. Okay,
> I'm friendly, I'm a damn friendly personality, okay, and I like every-
> body, but then—you know—they read it all out of proportion . . .

STRATEGIES FOR A SUCCESSFUL DRUG-DEALING CAREER

In conducting her successful drug business, Rachel deviates considerably from the practices of most other drug dealers.

Catering to Working/Middle Class Users

Rachel's clients represent a hidden element in the world of illegal
drugs about whom little is known (cf. Hamid 1992). Many have
spouses and children who are unaware of their crack use. Their
average age is 30, although many are older, with adult children.
Some are newly middle class, the first in their families to have
college degrees or to own businesses. Despite their secure, long-
time positions, comfortable housing, and material wealth, however,
they find themselves in empty households and holding unfulfilling
jobs.

> I must say, of the people I know like myself . . . they older people, I
> have to say that, yeah. They're all older people . . . some of 'em got
> families and things like that, you know . . . everybody, everybody
> works. . . . I know some, to be frank, I know some doctors, you
> know. Two doctors, yeah, and, um, a couple of social workers, you
> know . . . They got a sense of black identity about them also, okay?
> And they do believe in something of a higher being, you know. I

mean, they know about faith and stuff like that . . . And they get high differently, you know, than the younger crowd . . . they don't get as paranoid, you know. And they don't want to talk about negative things . . . We be getting high but we be keeping talk about religion. What's happening to the black people in general, including ourselves. We can talk about these things, okay. . . .

Avoiding the Street Market

A key element in Rachel's success is her avoidance of both customers and dealers involved in the street crack market. Normally she declines to sell crack to street users or to anyone who threatens her or others. While she knows street dealers, she stays out of their territory and does not compete for their customers. In this way she avoids violence and maintains the safe, comfortable environment her customers prefer.

> Well, (I) try not to . . . get into no antagonistic situations, you know . . . You try to give a little respect to the neighbors around you, you know, so that they don't get too mad . . . they will tolerate you, you know. You try not to . . . go direct into no one's turf, and stuff like that. In other words, you have to maintain a low profile, you know. That's the main thing . . . And then . . . you know, like—I don't hit nobody, I don't rob nobody, I don't deliberately mess with people's heads, and I expect the same with them, okay . . . I think it's all in the way you treat people . . .

Maintaining Good Relations with Neighbors

Most crack users eventually lose their apartments (Dunlap 1992), but Rachel has lived in the same building for some 20 years and has established herself as a good neighbor to other long-time tenants, most of whom are not involved with drugs. Her neighborliness is motivated both by genuine affection for her neighbors and by an awareness that they could destroy her business. She retains their friendship (and avoids detection by the police) by restricting her business to a limited number of quiet, middle class customers.

> This is a quiet building and stuff like that. . . . I got neighbors that I've known, like, a long, long time, and (if I attracted the wrong clientele) I'd be outta here quick fast. 'Cause they got a law now, they kick you out . . . when you selling and they know.

Providing a Setting Appropriate to Clients' Needs

Aware of her customers' desire for a quiet, discreet atmosphere in which they can smoke crack without having to deal with the dangers of street life, Rachel strives to create a climate of tranquility in her apartment. She also makes much of the fact that she will not sell anything she would not smoke herself, which assures her customers that her crack is of high quality.

> I have it set up in a sense that now it's nice, easy, a social kind of situation. Person comes . . . they bring a certain amount of money, it's payday, you know, and . . . most of the time, they don't want to go out no more. They don't want to be seen, there's a lot of professional people, and they want to feel safe, you know. [I] sell it right to them, point blank period dot, and then smoke it with 'em too. You know what I'm saying? . . . And it's easy, it's subtle, it's quiet. Ain't a whole lot of noise, a whole lot of traffic . . . my main focus is to keep 'em comfortable.

Managing the Effects of Crack on Customers

Familiar with the negative physical and psychological reactions that crack consumption can cause, Rachel works hard to keep her customers from suffering "tension" (also a street name for crack). Her dimly lit bedroom provides those who prefer not to interact with others a place to be alone and those who are paranoid a place to feel safe.

> You don't know how this shit hits some people . . . If you could see some of the people that I have to tolerate, people come here because they know I have patience to deal with them, with the looking under the bed, and looking in the closet. They feel safe here . . .

Managing Customers' Finances

Many of Rachel's customers need help managing their drug habits. She knows when they get their paychecks, and also that if they arrive at her apartment with a full paycheck they may not have paid their bills or set anything aside for necessities. If she is aware that a customer needs money, she may cash his paycheck but then purchase a money order for him to take home.

> Whatever they come with, 9 times outta 10, sometime what I do is I'll take some off the top and—you know—'what did you say you needed?' . . . And I will go to the store and get it, get 'em whatever it is they needed . . . or even give 'em a money order or something. Especially the people that's living with families.

Controlling Unruly Customers

Rachel is quite capable of holding her own when customers attempt to "try her out" by violating her house rules. Prior to one interview, the ethnographer found Rachel scrubbing blood off the floor of the hall in front of her apartment. She reported that a customer had become violent—an unusual occurrence—and she had settled the matter. Since this was the second time this customer had acted this way, she barred him from returning. She keeps knives in her apartment for emergencies but no longer owns a gun, having devised other ways to discourage rowdy or threatening customers.

> Well, yeah, I got stuff like (knives), you know. I got quite a few of them . . . I just don't have weapons, I don't have a gun anymore, okay, 'cause it's hard for me to keep from not shooting somebody if I really did want to . . . and uh, I just went through last year a thing that—and it's like . . . I tried to kill that man. You don't come here and then bogart me around the house [i.e., act in a rough or bossy manner], okay, you can't do that, you know.

Choosing Suppliers Carefully

Rachel chooses stable suppliers who, like herself and her customers, lead superficially "normal" lives and have self-images of attachment to conventional norms and behaviors.

> . . . my best person, supplier, is a family man, you know, they have a home, everything. You know, nice people . . . Drive a nice car, nice kids, nice wife, the whole bit. That's the best kind of people to deal with, because they can't go but so far. You know, raunchy people, man, they'll be ready to take you off, you know, and then you gotta come out a whole 'nother bag, you know. Which I can do that too, but you see, why set yourself up for that?

Avoiding Unwanted Sexual Attention

Rachel knows that both clients and suppliers are drawn to her as an attractive woman, and she exploits this for business purposes. At the same time, she is aware that no special consideration is given female drug dealers and that the consequences of failing to anticipate and defuse potentially dangerous situations may be sexual harassment or physical harm.

> Being a female—you know, its good . . . 'cause they always think they gonna get something out the deal other than business, you know. I dress good, look good, you know. . . . (I) let them think whatever

they wanna think, you know. It ain't about stringing them on, because . . . when push come to shove, you know what talk more than anything else is the money. . . . Most of the time—you know—you just, you gotta handle it. You either gotta do one of two things . . . 9 times out of 10, you know, you can kinda talk your way out of it . . . use that reverse psychology in Psychology 101 on 'em . . . (But) sometime there are—you know—you just have to get downright, like, you just gotta act like a bitch. I mean you gotta get downright nasty, you know. See—but that's always a problem in that, you know—because then you don't want nobody coming back on you, you know. But . . . it depends on the kind of person you are, you know. Because it's like I don't sell my body.

Avoiding Arrest

By dealing discreetly, catering to a middle-class clientele, and being a responsible neighbor and tenant, Rachel has successfully avoided the police and has no arrest record. The threat of arrest is

> . . . important enough to me to do it (deal) the way I do it, you know. In other words, I'm not looking for the big profits no more, okay . . . it's very, very, very essential that I do not go to jail!

Another of her tactics for avoiding the police is to dress like a working woman when buying cocaine. On one occasion, when she encountered police who had staked out her supplier's apartment, her appearance plus some creative lies helped her to evade arrest.

> It's in the wintertime, right? Put my boots on, had nice leather boots, long coat, you should have seen me . . . I put my makeup on and stuff, like I'm going to work, okay? Earrings and everything, okay? So I get to where I got to go, right. . . . Soon as I went in there [i.e., into the area in which weight cocaine is sold], I felt it. I said, it's too quiet around here, and I turned around to make my move and come on out and they [undercover police] stopped me. Five of em, okay? But I was looking the part, so they say, "Where you going?" I said, "I'm getting ready to go to work. I heard my girlfriend, she gets in a lot of trouble on the job, and I ain't know whether she had got fired and I came to see about her." . . . He said, "You know about this place," and I said "I've heard terrible, terrible things about this place here, but I was so worried about my girlfriend that I had to take a chance and come anyway." So they said "Well, where?" I say "Apartment one, right over there" . . . They said, "Get the hell outta here."

Controlling Personal Consumption

For the most part, Rachel has avoided the pitfalls of excessive crack use. She manages to eat properly by requiring her customers to bring food, which she then cooks, serves, and shares with them, and she is careful to set aside money to pay the rent. She also avoids consuming too much of her own supply of crack. Unlike the average consumer, she does not "go on missions"—nonstop 3- to 5-day crack smoking binges without food or sleep. When one of her customers goes on a mission, consuming a substantial part of her supply of crack, she re-ups with money from her next well-heeled customer. She considers herself an intelligent crack user.

> You know, that's all a part of using your head. When you take care of your body, okay, and you put some knowledge up here in your head, if you are doing these things, it's because you want to survive after you do it. . . . See, a lot of people . . . just want to get high, and don't care nothing else other than that. Getting high, okay . . . for me [is] like some people want to take a martini after work, okay? Then you work and you do what you have to do. For me it's delayed gratification, is what I call it, okay?

LESSONS FROM A SUCCESSFUL DRUG-DEALING CAREER

Rachel is in many ways unique, a product of her singular personality, life history, and experiences, yet her very uniqueness sheds light on a number of aspects of illegal drug sales and use in the United States.

First, Rachel's career illuminates trends in the history of illegal drug use in New York and the United States. The shifts in her involvement, from one drug to another, were engendered not so much by her personal decisions as by macrolevel social and logistical forces (Johnson and Manwar 1991; Dunlap and Johnson 1992a, 1992b). Her introduction to cocaine in the mid-1970s, for example, was typical of many inner-city drug users of that era, who frequented "after-hours clubs" to snort cocaine when they could afford it (Williams 1978). More broadly, Rachel's business illustrates general shifts in the drug market in New York, from marijuana to cocaine to crack, showing how supply, demand, and consumption feed into one another. Her customers' drug choices and consumption patterns and her marketing practices reflect the availability of certain drugs. Availability in turn influences demand, which drives the market.

Second, Rachel's business illuminates an unknown side of the drug economy: the world of the older, better educated, employed, middle-class, violence-averse drug user (Hamid 1992; Waldorf et al.

1991). In the United States, the stereotypical crack user is young, violence-prone, poorly educated, and unemployed. In addition, entertainers and sports figures are widely viewed as being involved with drugs; actor Richard Pryor provides an example. But Mayor Marion Barry's arrest for crack use came as a surprise to many because his position as mayor of Washington, D.C. was inconsistent with such stereotypes. Middle-class drug users may consume drugs discreetly to protect their jobs and reputations, but they are no less a part of the illegal drug industry.

Third, Rachel illustrates the effects of being female in a profession dominated by males, a subject about which little is known despite recent increases in convictions of female drug offenders. Females are often stigmatized in the world of illegal drugs, but Rachel has managed to turn being female into an asset by cultivating a friendly, accommodating, caring, noncompetitive image. She exploits the fact that males find her attractive, but is able to defuse unwanted sexual attention with professionalism.

Finally, Rachel's attempts to be "normal" suggest the tension inherent in moving between the legitimate world and the world of illegal drugs. Her feelings of remorse, reflected in her need to see herself as other than "a bad person," are assuaged by her ability to justify her actions. She prides herself on providing high quality crack for her customers and a safe, congenial place to smoke it, and on her ability to avoid the police. But most important, she sees herself as a legitimate businessperson with a commitment to conventional norms and chooses associates—suppliers, other dealers, and customers—who share this self-image.

CONCLUSION

Rachel's success in her profession can be attributed to a unique combination of historical contingencies, personal qualities, and career choices. On the one hand, she is a product of a particular background and of the macrolevel social forces existing in a particular temporal and geographical context. Yet within this context, her unique personal characteristics—her intelligence, sense of professionalism, commitment to conventional values, skill as a businessperson, and self-discipline—have contributed to her position as a deviant among deviants, as have her surprising personal choices. Formerly a conventional black mother and nondrug user, she became involved with drugs relatively late, after her husband died.

She completed high school and college and was clearly capable of graduate work, yet abandoned the promise of a legitimate career for marijuana sales. And not until she was in her mid-30s did she shift from marijuana to crack. Together, these factors have contributed to the ingenious ways in which Rachel controls her environment, to the specific strategies she employs, and, ultimately, to her career success.

REFERENCES

Adler, Patricia A. 1985. *Wheeling and Dealing: An Ethnography of an Upper Level Drug Dealing and Smuggling Community.* New York: Columbia University Press.

Becker, Howard S. 1963. *Outsiders: Studies in the Sociology of Deviance.* Glencoe, IL: Free Press.

Belenko, Steven, Jeffrey Fagan, and Kolin Chin. 1991. "Criminal Justice Responses to Crack." *Journal of Research in Crime and Delinquency* 28:55–74.

Blauner, Robert. 1987. "Problems of Editing 'First-Person' Sociology." *Qualitative Sociology* 10:46–64.

Blauner, Robert. 1989. *Black Lives, White Lives: Three Decades of Race Relations in America.* Berkeley, CA: University of California Press.

Bourgois, Philippe, and Eloise Dunlap. 1993. "Exorcising Sex-for-Crack: An Ethnographic Perspective from Harlem" Pp. 97–132 in *Crack as Pimp: An Ethnographic Investigation of Sex-for-Crack Exchanges,* edited by Mitchell S. Ratner. New York: Lexington Books.

Bureau of Justice Statistics. 1992. Drugs and the Justice System. Rockville, MD: Center Clearinghouse. Dec. NCJ-133652.

Carpenter, Cheryl, Barry Glassner, Bruce D. Johnson, and Julia Loughlin. 1988. *Kids, Drugs, Alcohol, and Crime.* Lexington, MA: Lexington Books.

Chambers, Carl D., S. W. Dean, and M. Fletcher. 1981. "Criminal Involvement of Minority Group Addicts. Pp. 125–154 in *The Drugs-Crime Connection,* edited by James A. Inciardi. Beverly Hills, CA: Sage.

Division of Criminal Justice Services. 1988. *New York State Trends in Felony Drug Offense Processing 1983–1987.* Albany: DCJS

Dunlap, Eloise. 1992. "The Impact of Drugs on Family Life and Kin Networks in the Inner-city African American Single Parent Household." Pp. 181–207 in *Drugs, Crime and Social Isolation,* edited by Adele Harrell and George Peterson. Washington, DC: Urban Institute Press.

Dunlap, Eloise and Bruce D. Johnson. 1992a. "Structural and Economic Changes: An Examination of Female Crack Dealers in New York City and Their Family Life." Paper presented at the annual meeting of the American Society of Criminology, November, 1992. New Orleans, LA.

Dunlap, Eloise and Bruce Johnson. 1992b. "Who They are and What They Do: Female Dealers in New York City." Paper presented at the annual meeting of the American Society of Criminology, November, 1992. New Orleans, LA.

Dunlap, Eloise and Bruce D. Johnson. 1992c. "The Setting for the Crack Era: Macro Forces, Micro Consequences (1960–1992)." *Journal of Psychoactive Drugs* 24:307–321.

Dunlap, Eloise, Bruce D. Johnson, and Ali Manwar. 1993. "Rachel's Place: A Case Study of the Impact of Resources on Crack Use and Sales." Paper prepared for Urban Institute, Washington, D.C.

Dunlap, Eloise, Bruce D. Johnson, Harry Sanabria, Elbert Holliday, Vicki Lipsey, Maurice Barnett, William Hopkins, Ira Sobel, Doris Randolph, and Ko-Lin Chin. 1990, Spring. "Studying Crack Users and Their Criminal Careers: The Scientific and Artistic Aspects of Locating Hard-to-Reach Subjects and Interviewing Them About Sensitive Topics." *Contemporary Drug Problems* pp. 121–144.

Faupel, Charles E. 1981. "Drug Treatment and Criminality: Methodological and Theoretical Considerations." Pp. 183–206 in *The Drugs-Crime Connection*, edited by James A. Inciardi. Beverly Hills, CA: Sage.

Goldstein, Paul. 1985. "The Drug/Violence Nexus." *Journal of Drug Issues* 15:493–506.

Greenleaf, Vicki D. 1989. *Women and Cocaine: Personal Stories of Addiction and Recovery.* Los Angeles: RGA.

Hamid, Ansley. 1992. "Drugs and patterns of opportunity in the inner city." Pp. 209–239 in *Drugs, Crime and Social Isolation*, edited by Adele Harrell and George Peterson. Washington, DC: Urban Institute Press.

Inciardi, James A. 1986. *The War on Drugs: Heroin, Cocaine, Crime and Public Policy.* Palo Alto, CA: Mayfield.

Inciardi, James A., Dorothy Lockwood, and Anne E. Pottieger. 1993. *Women and Crack-Cocaine.* New York: MacMillan.

Inciardi, James A. and Anne E. Pottieger. 1986. "Drug Use and Crime among Two Cohorts of Women Narcotics Users: An Empirical Assessment." *Journal of Drug Issues* 16:91–106.

Jessor, Richard, John E. Donovan, and Francis M. Costa. 1991. *Beyond Adolescence: Problem Behavior and Young Adult Development.* New York: Cambridge University Press.

Johnson, Bruce. 1991. "Crack in New York City." *Addiction and Recovery* XX:24–27.

Johnson, Bruce D., Eloise Dunlap, Ali Manwar, and Ansely Hamid. 1992. "Varieties of Freelance Crack Selling." Paper presented at the annual meeting of the American Society of Criminology, November. New Orleans, LA.

Johnson, Bruce D., Eloise Dunlap, Ansley Hamid. 1992. "Changes in New York's Crack Distribution Scene." Pp. 360–364 in *Drugs and Society to the Year 2000*, edited by Peter Vamos and Paul Corriveau. Montreal: Portage Program for Drug Dependencies.

Johnson, Bruce D. , Paul J. Goldstein, Edward Preble, James Schmeidler, Douglas S. Lipton, Barry Spunt, and Thomas Miller. 1985. *Taking Care of Business: The Economics of Crime by Heroin Abusers.* Lexington, MA: Lexington Books.

Johnson, Bruce, Ansley Hamid, and Harry Sanabria. 1991. "Emerging Models of Crack Distribution." Pp. 56–78 in *Drugs and Crime: A Reader,* edited by Tom Mieczkowski. Boston: Allyn-Bacon.

Johnson, Bruce and Ali Manwar. 1991. "Towards a Paradigm of Drug Eras: Previous Drug Eras Help to Model the Crack Epidemic in New York City During the 1990s." Presentation at the American Society of Criminology, November, 1991. San Francisco, CA.

Johnson, Bruce E., Mangai Natarajan, Eloise Dunlap, Elsayed Elmoghazy. Forthcoming. "Crack Abusers and Noncrack Abusers: Profiles of Drug Use, Drug Sales, and Nondrug Criminality." *Journal of Drug Issues.*

Johnson, Bruce, Terry Williams, Kojo Dei, and Harry Sanabria. 1990. "Drug Abuse in the Inner City: Impact on Hard-Drug Users and the Community." Pp. 9–66 in *Drugs and Crime,* edited by Michael Tonry and James Wilson. Chicago: University of Chicago Press.

Lewis, Carla, Bruce D. Johnson, Andrew Golub, and Eloise Dunlap. 1992. "Studying Crack Abusers: Strategies for Recruiting the Right Tail of an Ill-Defined Population." *Journal of Psychoactive Drugs* 24:323–336.

Maher, L. and R. Curtis. 1992. "Women on the Edge of Crime: Crack Cocaine and the Changing Contexts of Street-Level Sex Work in New York City." *Crime, Law and Social Change* 18:221–258.

Manwar, Ali, Bruce D. Johnson, and Eloise Dunlap. 1993. "Qualitative Data Analysis with Hypertext: A Case of New York City Crack Dealers." Paper presented at the annual meeting of the American Sociological Association. August, 1993. Miami Beach, FL.

Matza, David. 1964. *Delinquency and Drift.* New York: Wiley.

Painter, Neil, Irvin. 1979. *The Narrative of Hosea Hudson.* Cambridge: Harvard University Press.

Ratner, Mitchell S. (ed). 1993. *Crack Pipe as Pimp: An Ethnographic Investigation of Sex-for-Crack Exchanges.* New York: Lexington Books.

Reuter, Peter, Robert MacCoun, and Patrick Murphy. 1990. *Money from Crime: A Study of the Economics of Drug Dealing in Washington, D.C.* Santa Monica, CA: Rand.

Sanchez, Jose E. and Bruce D. Johnson. 1987. "Women and the Drugs-Crime Connection: Crime Rates Among Drug Abusing Women at Rikers Island." *Journal of Psychoactive Drugs* 19:205–215.

Waldorf, Dan, Craig Reinarman, and Shegila Murphy. 1991. *Cocaine Changes: The Experience of Using and Quitting.* Delphia, PA: Temple University Press.

Williams, Terry. 1978. "The Cocaine Culture in After Hours Clubs." PhD dissertation. New York: Sociology Department, City University of New York.

Williams, Terry, Eloise Dunlap, Bruce D. Johnson, and Ansley Hamid. 1992. "Personal Safety in Dangerous Places." *Journal of Contemporary Ethnography* 21:343–347.
Zinberg, Norman E. 1984. *Drug Set and Setting: The Basis for Controlled Intoxicant Use.* New Haven, CT: Yale University Press.

[5]

THE SOCIAL ORGANIZATION OF ARMED ROBBERY*

WERNER J. EINSTADTER
Eastern Michigan University

Career robbery is examined with reference to Sutherland's previously postulated model of systematic or professional criminal collectivities; little resemblance is found. The social organization of career robbery is described as representing a distinct criminal group form, the content and characteristics of which reflect the unique stance of robbery as a form of criminal behavior.

In most criminological studies, when the group life of adult professional criminals is discussed a single theoretical model is employed. It is usually assumed that the adult professional criminal operates within the structural context of the *mob*. The model of the mob has been variously described in the literature but was most clearly formulated by Sutherland.[1]

A body of literature on professional crime has centered largely on an extension or modification of Sutherland's conception of the essential social characteristics of professional theft and his unifying theoretical statement of differential association.[2] As Clinard and Quinney have pointed out, however, empirical research concerning various types of professional crime has been sparse; this is especially true with regard to the social organization of various professional criminal groups.[3] No

* Adapted from sections of W. J. Einstadter, *Armed Robbery—A Career Study in Perspective*, unpublished doctoral dissertation, University of California, Berkeley, 1966. The study was supported in part by a grant from the National Institute of Mental Health #1-F3-MH-28, 204-01 (BEH)

[1] Edwin H. Sutherland, *The Professional Thief* (Chicago: University of Chicago Press, 1937), pp. 27-42.

[2] Edwin H. Sutherland and Donald R. Cressey, *Principles of Criminology* (7th ed., Philadelphia: J. B. Lippincott Co., 1966).

[3] Marshall B. Clinard and Richard Quinney, *Criminal Behavior Systems—A Typology* (New York: Holt, Rinehart and

studies appear to have been concerned specifically with a reexamination of Sutherland's conception of the social organization of the professional criminal.

The concept of the mob implies that professional criminal collectivities operate according to a number of common understandings, rules of conduct, or working relationships which are considered binding on all its members. These modes of conduct found among groups of professional thieves are presumed to have universal applicability to all professional criminal groups.

The purpose of this paper is twofold; first, it is an attempt to relate Sutherland's conception of the mob to professional robbery and to reassess its utility and relevance as a generic explanatory model; secondly, it is an effort to describe a specific type of criminal behavior system.

Methodology

Twenty-five convicted robbers on parole in California were studied. In addition to interview material, data gathered over several years from an equal number of convicted robbers who were confined were used. Official records were employed as supplementary material, to check the official criminal record, prior committments, and offense statements.

The respondents selected represent robbers who were considered to be professional or career robbers in that they all met the following criteria:

a) Each subject in company with others committed more than a single robbery prior to detection. Each subject either committed a series of robberies or several series of robberies separated by prison

Winston, Inc., 1967), p. 429. See their listing of the few representative studies in this area.

terms. In a number of instances there were robberies unknown to officials.

b) All were armed robbers. All employed weapons that were operative. None simulated weapons. Each instance of robbery was calculated and the subject fully intended to carry the act to its completion.

c) Each subject considered himself a robber and for various periods had spent considerable portion of his time in the engagement of robbery.

d) In all instances the subject's sole stated interest was robbery. In no case was the robbery incidental to some other form of crime, (e.g., rape, drug addiction).

The subjects, therefore, may be considered as representing more than just casual robbers, but individuals who engaged in this form of criminal conduct on a purposive, rational and sustained basis over various periods of time.

Findings

Sutherland describes a number of significant features that emerge in the group life of professional thieves which he considers the binding rules of the mob. As such, these rules develop into a formal code of ethics subscribed to by the professional thief much like other codes of conduct among legitimate professional groups.[4]

A comparison of the type of organization that develops among professional robbers with the type of organization that develops among professional thieves reveals little similarity as the following discussion will make clear. Whereas the professional thief finds his organizational counterpart in the legitimate professions, the professional or career robber may be compared more accurately with the legitimate businessman in the organizational form of the partnership.

Sutherland's thief is quite explicit

[4] Sutherland, *The Professional Thief*, pp. 35-42; 215ff.

in his description of the norms that develop in the mob. A review of the rules of the mob should prove revealing in highlighting the differences between the type of structure that is characteristic of groups of professional thieves and that of groups of armed robbers:

1. Gains are equally shared. A percentage is given to outsiders who assist the mob.

In general, robbers share equally with their associates whatever is taken. However, there is no sharing with outsiders as they do not exist for the robber. If someone has helpful knowledge about sites to rob or assist in some way in the robbery even if only tangentially, from the robber's point of view, he is not an outsider, but a member of the group and receives his share of the gain. Once robbery is discussed by a group with any amount of seriousness all become full partners and all consider themselves equally involved and have a stake in the success of the planned enterprise. Planning need not be extensive in order for this involvment to occur; there merely needs to be some discussion of robbery amongst a group that intends to carry it to completion.[5] Hence no one is ever considered an outsider to the group after preliminary discussions have taken place. The statement of one robber is illustrative:

(If) you compare notes with somebody, you are going to join them. In other words, my crime partner and I were talking to you and another fellow, and we were comparing notes, eventually the four of us are going to do something together, whether it be tonight, tomorrow night or the next night, regardless. By openly ad-

mitting to one another our situation, I think we find a binding point, where we, you say, I know a spot over there, let's go get it. And you say let's go get it, why, the four of you go instead of one or two.

2. Expenses of the mob come off the top.

The robber's expenses are minimal and are usually paid out of pocket by the individual concerned. Such outlays are in the nature of small business expenses and are managed quite informally from one robbery to the next. One respondent stated it simply:

I paid the gas and oil on the first job, the second time around somebody else got it. Usually it was just a couple of bucks and nobody expected anything back . . . .

Large expenses, such as the purchase of an automobile or the purchase of weapons are usually paid on a share-and-share-alike basis. Each contributes his amount to the total. In some instances, expenses are taken off the top, but this is not by any means a regular procedure. There is nothing formal about any of these arrangements, rather like any other informal group undertaking where there are expenses, there is a tacit agreement that each member contributes his share.

3. All loans are repaid out of the first sum of stolen money.

A number of robbers who were asked about this provision seemed perplexed and had no knowledge regarding this type of arrangement. These loans refer to an organized mob that needs capital to carry out its illegal enterprises. This rarely occurs in the sense that there are financial backers for the robber. When large sums of monetary outlays are necessary that can not readily be managed by the group, other methods than seeking a backer are employed. A group that generally commits the more sophisticated variety

[5] For a fuller discussion of the process of commitment involved in becoming a professional robber see Einstadter, *op. cit.*, pp. 31-66.

of robbery—(e.g., banks, large grocery chains)—where such outlays sometimes become necessary, may commit a number of small preliminary minor robberies before venturing to tackle a more formidable victim. Often such a group may rob a few smaller establishments to fund a contemplated large robbery which may require some additional equipment. Frequently such items are stolen directly.

4. A fourth rule described by Sutherland is concerned with a number of general understandings about the mob's action when a member is arrested. Basically, the understanding is that the mob helps the apprehended member by sharing the expenses of court costs if he is arrested "on business." Furthermore, a share of the *take* is saved for him and money is regularly set aside for bail to be used by any member.

The reply of one informant when queried about this procedure is graphically illustrative and provides a good summary:

> Hell, no, the guy went into this with his eyes wide open, oh, sure, we'd feel sorry for the guy, but, hell, he'd be on his own. If he were arrested we'd split to save our own necks. He'd be expected to keep his mouth shut, but that can only last for a little while. Whatever dough there was would be split amongst the guys out; if we get caught we'd come to an understanding later, but if he ratted he'd have nothing coming.

Robbers give little thought to being arrested while actively engaging in robbery. That such occurrence is an eventuality is recognized, but is given little weight. Should an arrest be made, the arrestee expects no assistance from his partners. Conversely, the group expects the member arrested to remain silent but is realistic enough to realize that this cannot be a permanent situation; nevertheless, it may apply sanctions if the arrested member gives information too readily.[6] In view of the seriousness of the offense, robbers are rarely released on bail once arrested. When bail is set, it is usually a high amount which the arrested member has difficulty in obtaining. Were a fund established by a robbery group to meet this need it would have to be a considerable sum, something prohibitive for most groups of robbers. Both the nature of the robbery venture and the type of group that emerges precludes this kind of foresight.

Hence there is little evidence in the social organization of robbers of group cohesion during periods of stress in the manner described by Sutherland. The robber's organization is a more fluid arrangement taking into account existing conditions; it is not conceived by those involved as a permanent group but more or less a loose confederation of individuals joined together for a specific purpose on a short-term basis. Among certain types of robbers specific role relationships do develop; however, these always are assumed to be temporary by the rob-

---

[6] An interesting parallel is found in military life. During war time, a soldier is expected to give only his name, rank, and serial number if captured. It is recognized that he might "break" due to "brainwashing" and torture but he is still considered a traitor by his side if he does and is sanctioned accordingly. As one informer put it, "He should do his own time and number." Sanctions may be applied in prison to the informing robber in the form of ostracism or violence. But often a curious reversal of intentions occurs. Since prison authorities usually are aware of the informing robber's "enemies," those who intend harm are placed in the ironic position of having to protect the informer since they would receive the blame in case any injury befalls him.

bery participants even though the association is of some duration. When this type of social organization exists no provision need be made for incapacitated members; each member considers himself on his own.

5. Members of the mob are to deal honestly with each other.

This rule generally applies to armed robber groups. As was pointed out under rule one, participants are expected to make even division of the stolen money, and are required to deal honestly in matters of robbery. But this expectation applies only to matters of the immediate present; hence robbers are not expected, for example, to reveal all their background or even be completely honest when they do. Most robbers anticipate that their partners will exaggerate about their past exploits as robbers, other criminal activities, prison experiences, dealings with women, etc., and openly tolerate a certain amount of these exaggerations when such information is supplied. Furthermore, robbers, as a rule, do not reveal too much about themselves to each other with the exception of current pressing problems, the stated reasons, which bring them into robbery. This lack of candor is respected. But there are "understandings" and cues which reveal much to the robber about his associates.

> . . . And, well, I don't know it's just kind of a thing, you meet some guy and you say, I like him, and he likes you, and so you start horsing around, well, you don't know each other, really, you don't know anything about each other, but eventually, it comes out, you know. You let it slip you ask him about something,—how do you like what you're doing,—and he says,—it's whole lot better than doing time. Then I knew, and I told him yeah, and you finally out on your backgrounds. So, we got to talking and talking about an easier way to make money . . . He

says 'I know a couple of guys, and we all got guns, and we can go out and hit a few places now, and then. If we don't hit it heavy, we won't get caught.' So, we started doing this stuff.
. . . .
. . . You are not exactly hanging around in a place for a long period of time, which we were. We were there, oh hell, six out of the seven nights a week. And, quite naturally, you learn to know somebody by their conversation, at least outwardly, you know them. And eventually, the money is going to drain out then a suggestion is going to come up, provided you feel that the person you are talking to is of your same caliber, and evidently when I met him at this particular time I felt that I could trust him, and I think there was, at my suggestion, if I remember correctly, that he come in with me. And between the two of us, why, we did a series of robberies.

Unless the robbers are acquaintances of long standing or are related and aware of each other's backgrounds, these understandings play a significant part in the trust relationship that becomes established.

6. Members voluntarily leaving the mob may ask to be taken back in, but it would not be proper for the leader of the mob to request they return.

This is another rule which is not applicable to armed robbers, indeed, there is serious question as to leadership in the first place. Any member is privileged to leave the group any time. He may also "sit one out" if he feels a particular robbery will be too dangerous for him, although this is not a frequent practice. Leaving robbery voluntarily is a rare occurrence; when it does occur it is temporary and returning presents no problems. There are no particular rules of etiquette that govern robbery group conduct as the group is not a tightly knit organization with fixed personnel and standards of behavior. The needs of the moment dictate the method of operation; there are few subtleties or niceties among robbers and in this respect also, a group of robbers bears little resemblance to the mob described by Sutherland's thief.[7]

7. Members of the mob are not held responsible for events which they cannot control.

This is the only rule that seems relevant; robbers as well as thieves do not appreciably blame each other too severely for certain blunders that are made.

> . . . We planned to get around $30,000 to $40,000 or $80,000 out of this bank; as it turned out, this one who was spending the money, he's quite a nervous fellow, anyhow, he went into the vault, had the assistant manager go into the vault, and there was a big sack. It must have been as big as a mail sack, and he picked it up and said, "What's in this?" It was locked, and the guy said it was non-negotiable securities, so the kid let it down. Turned out it was $40,000 . . . Anyhow he went out and cleaned out two or three of the cages and he got $10,000 out of that but . . . he thought he had more . . . we found out we had missed $40,000 so we were kinda grumbling at him for overlooking it but we figured he didn't have any experience and he wouldn't know how much paper would weigh anyhow . . .

Here a loss of $40,000 was rationalized away as insufficient experience. At a later time this same individual again made a costly error and again he was excused:

> So that time we got $16,500 and $17,000 . . . . again we passed up $80,000, I think it was, I forget the reason why they missed it. But again it was the same guy who goofed it up . . .

The fates enter heavily into robbers' lives in general, and this is merely an instance of the common tendency among robbers to use "fate" as a rationale of life. It's the "breaks" that count; you either have them or not. Fate is deemed to control the robber's destiny;[8] when the cards are right, when the dice are right, when the *setup* is perfect, nothing can go wrong but if luck is against you, "you haven't got a chance." It, therefore, becomes easy to excuse what would under ordinary circumstances be considered an unforgivable error. Also with this rationale the occasional violence that occurs may be explained away as an accidental twist of fate. The fate motif is probably more responsible for the group attitude of not holding members responsible for uncontrollable events than any other aspect in the robber's group life. This seeming reversion to magic on the part of the robber is difficult to explain. One would expect a lessening of this motif as the robber becomes more proficient, i.e., as he has learned to reduce the hazards and is more in control of the situation; however, such is not the case.[9] The fate motif is discernible in all levels of robbers' groups. It may be that robbery, no matter how well

---

[7] This has been recognized for criminal relationships in general. ". . . The social relationships of criminals are quite tenuous and much more likely to take the form of transient combination . . ." See Edwin M. Lemert, *Social Pathology* (New York: McGraw-Hill, 1951), p. 48.

[8] See Walter B. Miller, "Lower Class Culture as a Generating Milieu of Gang Delinquency," *J. of Social Issues*, XIV (1958), 5-19. Fate discussed as one of the focal concerns of the lower class.

[9] Primitive practices at least follow this pattern. Malinowski has noted in his study of Trobrianders that when they fished using the reliable method of poisoning and a rich catch was a certainty, magic was not practiced. On the other hand, when they fished in the open sea with its dangers, magical rituals were abundantly employed. See Robert K. Merton, *Social Theory and Social Structure* (2d ed. rev., New York: Free Press of Glencoe, 1957), p. 108.

planned, in view of its direct personal interaction, always presents the possibility of uncontrollable hazards and hence uncertainty.

8. No member of a mob should cut in on another member. This is another etiquette rule which forbids any mob member from "cramping the style" of another. The exception being an emergency or an inexperienced member who has only been given a minor role to perform.

Robbers, when necessary, help each other out in the performance of a robbery in the event of an "emergency." The rule appears to refer to mobs of pickpockets or shoplifters, and only in a very general way would be applicable to a group of robbers.[10]

9. The last mob maxim refers to the mob member's responsibility to do everything possible to fix a case for any other member of the mob who may have been arrested as a result of mob activities.

This raises the entire question regarding the practice of "fixing" cases, bribes, etc., as it exists today and would go beyond the confines of this paper. It is quite clear that the *fix* as described by Sutherland with reference to thieves is not practiced by contemporary armed robbers.

ARREST STRATEGY

If arrested, the strategy is to obtain the best "deal" with the prosecutor on the basis of the amount of information and evidence known to him. The "fixer" as described in the *Professional Thief* is unknown to the informants.

---

10 A recent study of department store shoplifting would indicate that this form of theft is no longer primarily a group phenomenon. See Mary Owen Cameron, *The Booster and the Snitch* (New York: Free Press of Glencoe, 1964), p. 58.

Members of robber troupes also express no feelings of obligation to help out a member arrested; the main concern is with maintaining their own individual anonymity.

The practice of obtaining the best "bargain" possible often requires the revelation of the crime partners' identities in exchange for a more favorable disposition; knowledge of the possibility of this occurrence creates considerable anxiety on the part of a group when one of its members is arrested. The result, therefore, is for all members to "split" and attempt to "ride it out" if possible, but it is a well known fact among robbers that the arrest of one usually spells the end for all. Hence, under present circumstances, the last thing a robber would think about is to attempt a "fix" even were it possible, for not only would he reveal his identity and suffer the likelihood of arrest, but he would also defeat a possible bargaining position of his associates.

Discussion

From the foregoing comparison it becomes obvious that the group of careerist robbers seems to bear only slight resemblance to the mob that Sutherland describes. How can one account for this difference? One obvious answer is simply that times have changed and so has the complexity of relationships in society. What was possible during the first quarter or more of this century is no longer feasible under present circumstances. The entire scope and function of law enforcement has changed, making certain criminal styles obsolete. One need only mention the revolutionary developments in systems of identification of criminals, modern communication, transportation methods, and methods of scientific investigation to stress the point.

The mob as an organized form of criminal activity must be related to a particular point in historical experience, a point where it served a purpose —a point where it was functional. During the first few decades of this century the "mob style" was particularly adapted to the social conditions of the day; the "fix" was possible because personal relationships were simpler and more direct.[11] Criminals, as well as others, knew each other personally with the resultant development of congeniality and rules of behavorial etiquette which guided the criminal mob both in its relationship among its own members and with outsiders. With the increasing complexity of society, these relationships were no longer possible and the mob was due to change. To paraphrase Bell, as the style of society changed, so did, in lagging fashion, its style of crime.[12]

There is, however, another reason why the robber's group differs from the mob. The mob, in general, referred to the organization of professional theft, which Sutherland distinguishes from robbery on the basis of style. Whereas the thief relies chiefly on wits, front, and talking ability, Sutherland declares, ". . . robbers, kidnappers and others who engage in the 'heavy rackets' are generally not regarded as professional thieves for they depend primarily on *manual dexterity*

or *force*."[13] However, there are those robbers who "use their wits, 'front,' and talking ability, and these are regarded by the professional thieves as belonging to the profession."[14] The robber's group also reflects the peculiar style of the robber; the elements of robbery require a different type of organization in order for the crime to be carried to completion. Furthermore, the robber's group reflects the life style of persons not concerned with the etiquette of relationships, nor the reciprocals inherent in group life, but chiefly concerned with accomplishing a specific goal—the rapid accumulation of money.

The armed robber's entire engagement in robbery differs from the professional thief's engagement in theft, even when the former possesses "wit, front, and talking ability." Both the quality and the nature of the commitment itself differ, with the robber being more compelled in his action in the sense of feeling restricted as to the alternative courses of action open to him.[15] He is in a "get-rich-quick enterprise" and as such needs to move quickly and strike swiftly when the opportunity presents itself. In his scheme of action, he simply does not have time for the amenities of the professional thief, nor can he appreciate the latter's moderate approach to profit.[16] The formal relationships of

---

[11] The fix still seems to be pervasive and widespread but in subtler form in relationship to organized crime. See Report by the President's Commission on Law Enforcement and Administration of Justice. *The Challenge of Crime in a Free Society 1967*, Chapter 7 passim.

[12] Daniel Bell, "Crime as an American Way of Life," *Antioch Review*, XIII (Summer 1953), 131-157.

[13] Sutherland, *Professional Thief*, p. 198 (emphasis supplied).

[14] *Ibid.*

[15] Einstadter, *op. cit.*, Chapter 12 passim.

[16] It is perhaps also imprecise to refer to the robber who engages in robbery on a persistent basis as professional in the sense that Sutherland refers to a thief as professional. More descriptive are the terms *career robber* or *careerist*. Others have found difficulty in applying Sutherland's professional criteria to criminal groups other than thieves. cf. Edwin M. Lemert "The Behav-

the mob are not functional for his needs; more adaptable to the style necessary for the accomplishment of his goal is the social organization represented by the partnership,[17] Much as the professional thief resembled other professionals, the careerist robber resembles the businessman who conducts his business through the tutelage of a partnership. The robber similarly works through a group of partners with whom he shares equally in what risks there are and invests his services to the total enterprise. As a partner he shares in the profits and losses of the operation. The partnership also provides opportunity for differentiation of various tasks necessary to carry out a robbery and to plan its strategy. Career robbery is conducted in and through partnerships; the lone systematic robber is rare.[18]

---

ior of the Systematic Check Forger" *The Other Side,* ed. Howard S. Becker (New York: Free Press of Glencoe, 1964), pp. 211-224.

[17] Webster defines partnership as "a relationship . . . involving close cooperation between parties having specified and joint rights and responsibilities (as in a common enterprise)." Robbers tend to refer to their associates as *crime partners.*

[18] Although robberies may be performed by a single person, careerists feel that a profitable robbery is rarely completed successfully alone. Groups have also been found to have greater probability of accuracy in solving problems, since groups of individuals have greater resources for ideas and capacity for dealing with error—hence the possibility for the robber to better plan his crimes. See generally D. C. Barnlund, "A Comparative Study of Individual, Majority and Group Judgment," *Journal of Abnormal and Social Psychology,* LVIII (January, 1959), 55-60; J. F. Dashiell, "Experimental Studies of the Influence of Social Situations on the Behavior of Individual Human Adults," *A Handbook of Social Psychology,* ed. C. Murchinson (Worcester: Clark University Press, 1935), pp. 1097-1158; H. V. Perlmutter and Ger-

Armed career robbers then develop a form of social organization that is essentially dissimilar to the model originally proposed by Sutherland for professional thieves, which by extension has been applied to all professional criminal activities. A closer examination of career armed robbery will serve to further distinguish this form of deviant action from other criminal behavior systems.

Functional Differentiation and Group Structure in Career Robbery

From the beginning the strategy or engineering of a *job* is a group product and must be viewed in an interaction context. An individual may present a solid robbery plan to his associates which is eventually acted upon, however, there is always deliberation by the group. Thus, partnership consensus must be reached prior to the commission of any act of robbery.

Although there is little discernible evidence of distinctive leadership roles, previous experiences of members are given due recognition. Where leaders are recognizable, they become most apparent in adroit partnerships, in the less definitive form of what might more appropriately be titled *planning consultants.* The role behavior is one of guiding rather than directing and in this sense fully meets the role expectations of the members of the partnership. Some members may become more persuasive than others, but dicta from partners are frowned upon and

---

maine de Montmollin, "Group Learning of Nonsense Syllables," *Journal of Abnormal and Social Psychology,* XLVII (October, 1952), 762-769; R. C. Ziller, "Group Size: A Determinant of the Quality and Stability of Group Decisions," *Sociometry,* XX (June, 1957), 165-173.

do not constitute the the basis of action. When there is divergence of opinion, there is majority rule of sorts, but as has been implied, there is no enforcement of majority rule on dissident members, rather the partners make accommodations.

It may be argued that in terms of the explicit goals of the partnership these types of arrangements are functional since to force an unwilling or dissident member to join in a robbery would only endanger the whole group. The success of the partnership depends on cooperative effort. The group then is a partnership of equals, each with a voice; what leadership arises comes out of mutual recognition of the expertise of an individual member which serve the group's goals.

These deliberations are informally structured, vary in duration of time, and are likely to occur anywhere the potential participants happen to be congregated—an automobile, a bar, a motel room—throughout, it is a rational and deliberative, albeit at times haphazard process of decision making. Once the decision is reached that a particular robbery or series of robberies is to be performed, there does not appear to exist a specific pattern of planning the robbery encounter. The planning of a robbery may vary from a simple drive around a neighborhod to "case a joint" to a series of complex maneuvers; the strategy employed depends on the type of robbery and the sophistication of those involved.

Prior to any robbery, however, no matter what the level of potential complexity, assignments are made as to the role each partner is to play in the encounter. In this effort the strengths and weaknesses of various members may be assessed and conclu-

sions reached as to the roles best fitted to each participant.[19] Again this decision is reached through group interaction; no single individual gives orders or assigns positions without group and individual consensus.

The account of one respondent who preferred not to participate directly in holdups but was a competent driver describes the process of how one such decision was reached.

> For one reason, I wasn't going in, that was the first reason. I told them that, but they wanted me to go in. Then they got talking about that he (another partner) was going to drive the car because one of them couldn't see good, and the second one, he's so damn nervous he'd probably take the key out and put it in his pocket and then couldn't find the key. We didn't think he would keep his head cool enough to stay in the car listening to the radio calls come in, especially if one came in that said there was a robbery in progress. Then we didn't know how to trust the fourth guy that just came in; we didn't know whether he might run off and leave all of us, if all three of us went in. He probably wasn't going to do it, but they were considering it. Well, anyway, it all boiled down to that I should be driving the car because I don't get excited and I drive well.

At other times a more flexible arrangement is used with assignments shifting from robbery to robbery. The

---

19 Robber partnerships confirm previous findings about group structure. Thus, for example, the fact that individuals vary in the ability to assume a given role has been shown by T. R. Sarbin and D. S. Jones, "An Experimental Analysis of Role Behavior," *Journal of Abnormal and Social Psychology*, LI (September, 1955), 236-241, and that particular traits are needed to meet certain role expectations as shown by, E. F. Borgatta, "Role-Playing Specification, Personality, and Performance, *Sociometry*, XXIV (September, 1961), 218-233; R. Rapoport and I. Rosow, "An Approach to Family Relationships and Role Performance," *Human Relations*, X (September, 1957), 209-221.

functional differentiation depends chiefly on what talents are available; however, the temperament of individual partners also may enter as a determinant.

> We switched around one time I went in with—at other times—went in. We sorta decided on the spur of the moment. All of us were pretty good, so it didn't matter. It sorta depended on how we felt at the time, you know, the mood we were in so we usually sorta decided beforehand; we agreed on who would go in . . .

A loose type of specialization results which is flexible and adaptable according to circumstances. In this way partnerships conform to fluctuations of member's moods and the possible eccentricities of various individuals. Individuality is never completely relinquished by the careerist. He cooperates but he is never subjugated. He fits himself into the allocated roles of the partnership to accomplish certain purposes but tries whenever possible to carry them out on his own terms. In so doing, he attempts to use the partnership as a vehicle to reach his goal—nothing more.

The Minimum Essentials—The Actor's Role

The successful completion of a robbery depends mainly on the coordination of various tasks that must be completed. Through coordination and specialization of roles of participants in the robbery, the robbery group not only assures more protection to itself but adds a measure of efficiency and shock in quickly overtaking the victim by a show of disciplined force. A well operating partnership need only have three men and successfully carry out profitable robberies. Sometimes the same results may be obtained by a dyad, but generally a group of three

men appears to be the most tactically effective unit.[20]

The typical career robbery triad consists of two men who enter the establishment armed; the third remains outside in the vicinity in an automobile, is usually armed but need not be.[21] Of the two men who perform the actual robbery, one is considered the "back-up." It is his function to watch any customers in the establishment, prevent any from leaving, and "cover" those that might enter while his partner gathers the cash. At times he assists also in gathering the *take* if there are no customers or other conditions that need his attention. The "wheel" or "wheelman" in addition to driving the get-away-car also acts as lookout or "pointman," and at times is given added responsibilities of a variety of sorts.

An example of a wheelman's role in a series of bank robberies is informative both of his role obligation and the rather sophisticated planning that may take place in some partnerships. Not all robberies committed by the careerist robber are this well planned and executed, but the interview excerpt describes the extent to which the systematic robber may go to assure his goal:

---

[20] Hare has pointed out that "in general, when the size of the group decreases, the strength of the affectional ties between members increases, with the dyad allowing the possibilities for the greatest degree of intimacy," A. Paul Hare, "Interpersonal Relations in the Small Group," *Handbook of Modern Sociology*, ed. Robert E. L. Faris (Chicago: Rand McNally, 1964), p. 252. When a dyad exists the partners as a rule are either close friends or are related.

[21] It has also been shown that where there is a need for fine coordination there is a tendency to restrict the size of the group. *Ibid.*, p. 253.

I. So then you had the place cased and then did you commit the robbery?

S. No. We decided against it for some reason. I think we might have kept refining our plans as we went along and what we had done was decided, well we found that there were a number of characteristics the bank had to have before it was acceptable into our situation; one, it had to have a nice getaway, so we could abandon one car if a police car or some citizen chased us; we didn't want to shoot anyone, you know, or shoot at them or be shot at, so we could leave this car and either jump over a fence or go through a culvert or through a walkway so no car could follow us and report it. Then we could go over and pick up another car and then take off. So not all banks would fit into this sort of category . . . Anyhow, my job was to go up the telephone pole and cut the telephone wires so they couldn't call the cops. And then as soon as I cut the wires then these two walk in the bank and then I would go down the pole and get in the car. We had a police radio so we could tell if the cops got a signal, I could drive up to the bank and honk; otherwise I could get into the car and give them one minute exactly to go clean out the bank.

I. How did you decide on the one minute?

S. Well, we figured how long it would take, if everyone cooperated, and we decided that one minute would probably be safe. So anyway they went in. They had the stocking caps up under these men's hats, snap brim hats, and then they had masks that dropped down, I think one of them had a stocking cap that pulled over and the other one had a mask that just dropped down. So as soon as they walked in the door they just dropped it; customers walked in and noticed it; they just walked out; they didn't believe there was a bank robbery going on. So I sat there and watched all of that. I was just sitting there listening to the radio and watching my watch. So anyhow, as soon as one minute was up, I left the parking place, looking carefully to see that there were no cops, and I drove up to the bank and just as I did, the guy inside, one was holding at bay and the other was getting the money, he got nervous or something. Anyway, he gathered up all he could and ran out the door just at the very minute I got to the door, just as we had rehearsed it, and I had the doors open for him. They jumped in the car and off we went. And all the customers and people out on the sidewalk just going like this and I don't think anybody chased us, although later we heard somebody did. It was some three blocks back. So we got about $10,000 out of that. We pulled the car up near a school and went down a little ravine and jumped into another car, drove it to one of the fellow's house and drove it right into his garage, pulled the garage door down, went out the back door and went into his cottage and got in there and stayed in there listening to the police radio . . . .

Additional men may be added depending on the size of the robbery and its felt complexity; however, these men perform no different roles from the basic triad. They assist those engaged in the holdup, that is, they become extra personnel.

The "wheelman" does not have assistants but often has additional responsibilities such as planning the escape route, obtaining the get-away car, arranging lodging, and acting as lookout. There is general agreement among career robbers that the "wheel" has the greatest responsibility at the critical period of escape; as such, he is required to be the most "mature" of the group.

No matter how many robbers participate in a robbery and no matter how functionally differentiated the partnership might be, the element of surprise and momentary domination of the scene must be maximized if the robbery is to be successfully completed.

Robberies are foiled if either a) the victim is not surprised, b) the coordination of the partnership is poor, c) the robbers do not completely dominate the scene. Violence is also likely to occur if any one or combinations of these conditions exist. The aim, therefore, is to so structure the situation that the victim is rendered helpless to resist and "cooperates" toward the successful completion of the crime. In the words of one robber, "It has to be a smooth operation or else someone is likely to get hurt." To accomplish this goal, robbers employ a number of tactics or styles with varying degrees of "smoothness" which reveal different levels of planning and proficiency depending in part on the type of partnership and in part on the situation.

Styles of Career Robbery

These robbery tactics may for purposes of discussion be divided into three categories and labeled according to style of approach.

1. *The Ambush*—This type of robbery is the least planned of all and depends almost entirely on the element of surprise. All participants literally attack an establishment guerrilla fashion and attempt to obtain whatever might be found in cash or other items of value. There is no sophistication in this style of robbery and it is considered the *lowest* form of robbery from the viewpoint of the careerist. There is almost randomness in the selection of the victim, with no thought as to what conditions might be present in the situation that may affect the outcome of the robbery. It is also the type of robbery where the chances of violence are high. As a rule it is a style employed by less systematic robbers.

2. *The Selective Raid*—In this form

there is a minimum of planning. Sites are tentatively selected and *cased* even though very briefly. Site conditions are analyzed to some degree before the robbery is attempted. There is a tentative plan of approach; however, the planning may be accomplished very casually and several robberies may be committed in rapid succession.

3. *The Planned Operation*—Robberies that fall into this category are well planned and well structured crimes where all aspects are carefully delineated in the group and each partner knows his part well. At times there may be rehearsals or "dry runs" so that all possible conditions are taken into account. Risks are held at a minimum.

It would be ideal, for purposes of analysis, if partnerships practiced one style during the life of the group. Such, however, is not the case. Each individual partnership practices different styles of robbery during its existence. Thus, for example, one partnership that is in the planning stages of a *planned operation* may commit a few *selective raids* to finance what is thought to be a more lucrative robbery. On the other hand, certain groups may practice only one style and become quite proficient in it. Generally, however, the *ambush* is a desperation measure for careerists and is resorted to only when an emergency occurs such as the threatened capture of the group where money for flight must be raised quickly.

Robbery Skills

This raises the issue of skills required to engage in robbery. Obviously the three robbery styles require different levels of planning ability and creative potential. A *planned operation* may be a highly sophisticated crime requiring unique creative capacities, whereas an *ambush* can be attempted by anyone. A number of skills, therefore, are necessary to plan the more resourceful types of robberies that are committed by the careerist. In order to engage in robberies other than the ambush, the robber must have a sense of organization, timing, ability to take into account unforeseen events, etc. But these are skills or capacities of planning which bring structure to the robbery; the robbery itself requires little skill or ability. The synthesizing of robbery requires talent; its commission does not. This is not the case with certain other professional crimes, the variety of which Sutherland speaks. Compare the pickpocket, who must learn intricate sets of muscular movements, learn to perfect the art of misdirection in order to become successful in his endeavor, or the booster who must learn techniques of concealment and misdirection to avoid detection as a shoplifter. The confidence man has to develop a high degree of front, wit, and talking ability, before he can carry out his swindle. All the robber needs, in the final analysis, is a revolver. This one attribute can make him the master of the situation. The skill involved in robbery pertains to the style employed and to the amount of planning of which the individual partnership is capable. These skills may be brought to robbery and need not necessarily be learned exclusively through interaction with other robbers.[22] They may, how-

ever, be modified and shaped to meet the conditions of the robbery situation. Noncriminal learning structures may provide the necessary qualifications which may easily be converted to robbery.

Military experience of a certain variety, for example, lends itself readily to robbery:

> . . . And I thought, well, with four of us—I can start running out squad training techniques—another of those I learned in the military and that possibly we could start . . . doing some fairly large things —One thing I had sort of in mind—I thought of taking . . . the golf prizes from the . . . Lodge which usually involves a couple hundred thousand dollars —and—doing it around the point by water—and we had actually run an intelligence project on this . . . My partner had made it a point to become acquainted with and questioned fairly thoroughly, if indirectly, a fellow that worked in the office there—the assistant to the accountant—and so we actually knew much of the scheduling around the handling of this money and the operation of the Lodge and we were going to make our approach by water—and with four of us operating as a commando unit, it would have gone quite smoothly. I approached the thing as I would approach a military problem. I ran general intelligence rather than just the sort of thing that usually in the criminal profession is called 'casing.' I had hoped to train my men to the —— disguise that didn't bear the earmarks of camouflage—whistles and so forth.

---

22 These findings are at variance with the "differential association tradition" which purports that criminal techniques are learned in association with other criminals. See Edwin H. Sutherland and Donald R. Cressey, *Principles of Criminology* (5th edition rev.; New York: Lippincott, 1955), pp. 74-81. What is being maintained here is that the planning skills required in robbery

are generic skills which are adaptable from a variety of noncriminal experiences and need not necessarily be learned *only* in association with other robbers. These capacities may be brought into the partnership from the outside. They may, however, be modified to meet specific requirements of robbery. See also Cressey's critique in Donald R. Cressey, *Other People's Money* (New York: The Free Press of Glencoe, 1953), and his review of the theory and criticism of literature in Donald R. Cressey, "Epidemiology and Individual Conduct: A Case from Criminology," *The Pacific Sociological Review* (Fall 1960), III, 47-54.

Business acumen may also be turned to robbery:

> I planned it just like I've seen businesses operate and what I did in my own 'front' business. We checked out details just like anybody running a firm. I didn't want anybody getting hurt or getting too excited, so I checked to see whether anybody had heart trouble in the bank through channels I knew about, that are open to employers . . .

These planning capacities may, of course, come from previous criminal experiences or indeed through association with robbers, but need not be limited to these sources.

The skills of robbery, therefore, center mainly around planning ability. The greater the organization aptitudes of the members of the partnership, the greater the number of *planned operations* in the career of the partnership. The greater the number of *planned operations*, the more successful the partnership becomes, the more likely the pattern will continue.

It is as a consequence of planning ability being brought to robbery that relatively newly formed partnerships may adopt more sophisticated styles from the beginning and are thus able to prolong their careers because of their expertise. Furthermore during the initial period they may be unknown robbers, a characteristic which tends to lessen the probability of detection.[23] Thus one bank robber states:

> It was really a well planned job and we knew exactly what to do. It was perfect . . . Now I'm known. I've been mugged and printed. I wouldn't think of trying anything. Hell, every time some-

---

23 This is also contrary to the professional thief whose professionalism depended on being accepted, tutored and recognized by other thieves. To the careerist robber, planning ability combined with anonymity are important factors in a successful career. See Sutherland, *Professional Thief*, p. 207.

body pulls something around here and even faintly resembles me, I better have a good alibi.

Patterns of Activity

Related to the particular styles of the robber partnership is the choice of victim. Although among careerists there is a definite victim preference, there is much divergence among partnerships as to the type of victim preferred; hence, few generalizations can be made; nevertheless, careerists would consider banks, loan companies, supermarkets, drug stores, bars, liquor stores, gas stations, corner groceries, a fair ranking of victims in descending order of profit but not necessarily in terms of preference. Intervening variables, i.e., the conditions sought or avoided in the robbery setting, are the important determinants in the selection of robbery victims. The victim is always viewed as part of a larger configuration; his profit-potential is never the sole consideration for the armed robber. These variables, however, become different objects of concern depending on the partnership. Identical sets of conditions may be perceived in completely opposite terms by different groups of armed robbers, and distinctive, nevertheless contradictory, rationales concerning these differential perceptions develop.

Thus, for example, contrast the different victim perception of supermarkets and the antithetical rationales concerning the optimum time that robberies should be perpetrated:

> There's usually quite a bit of money and there is usually quite a bit of disorganized activity. There is very little danger of being shot in the store. Many stores will have a look-out arrangement and an armed person at the look-out arrangement from say a walled mezzanine or something. A robber is very apt to be shot from concealment. There are enough

people moving about in a supermarket that this is not very apt to happen. Your safest bet is probably a supermarket . . . .

Yes, we preferred to take an action either when there were other people in the store, which would be during operating hours, or before they would have occasion to expect anyone to be able to enter and set up a defense . . . .

We didn't ever develop any real pattern relative to that (best time of day). We took one early in the morning when they were unloading supply trucks in the back—shortly after the time that we felt the safe would be open on its time lock. We've taken others in the late evening. Really there was—so far as we determined by operating it—no reason for taking it at one time of the day rather than at another . . . .

. . . the biggest factor was—was the place crowded? And we never did anything in the day time. So the biggest factor was how many people would be in—that was how many people would be in that place about the time we wanted to walk in. And this is why we cruised the streets. We may just stop at a place and walk right in and rob it, because there was no one in there . . . .

Say an average of three or four people in there, which is detrimental, you can't watch all of them at the same time. Banks, well, that's like a race track. You've always got people. So, in my thinking the less people the better. And even the supermarket there is always too many people in there, until absolute closing time, let them lock me in, and then I knew just where the two people were . . . .

As a consequence of these differing patterns of social perception of optimum robbery conditions and diverse interpretations as to the impact of these conditions, no unitary model of what robbers consider the ideal robbery setting is possible. Individual armed robbers all have varying opinions and rationales to such degree that the "perfect set-up" may be spoken about, but there is little commonality in its

explication among robbery partnerships.

The potential *take* thus never is the single criterion of victim choice, but the contingencies, as interpreted by each partnership, enter as important variables of victim selection. For this reason few careerists become bank robbers, although the lure of the vast sums to be had and the excitement involved are attractive. Generally, banks present a multiplicity of conditions to take into account; as a result they are considered only by the more accomplished partnerships as potential victims. Contrary to some accounts, banks fall prey more often to the amateur than the committed robber. Indeed those careerists who do specialize in bank robberies, tend to fear the amateur bank robber as a potential source of difficulty.

> The guy who sticks up a bank who doesn't know what he is doing makes it tough all around. He's never in control and somebody is liable to take advantage —some hero—then there is violence. This makes it hard for when some dude comes in who really means business they think he's just another amateur and things get out of control and somebody is liable to get hurt ——

Quantitatively, careerists tend to prefer what might be termed victims of the middle range: liquor stores, drug stores, and supermarkets.

Retail liquor establishments play a peculiar role as careerists' victims; they are popular yet not necessarily preferred. Their very prevalence in urban communities and ready availability most hours of the day and night, however, make them easy if not choice victims, lending themselves readily to serial robbery. A series of liquor store holdups can yield a handsome sum, even though the single store may only give small reward:

We hit nothing but liquor stores, sometimes two or three a night. We'd make 20, 50, 100 bucks a store—that's at the most 300 split three ways—you'd have to hustle to make it . . . .

Although it is difficult to point to any single victim preference, among armed robbers there are a number of themes of victim choice on which there is some unanimity.

Rationales, Myths and Values

Perhaps it is imprecise to speak of a victim from the point of view of the robber, for to him a victim in the usual sense of the term is rarely present in the crime situation.[24] Careerist partnerships make conscious efforts to choose as sites for robberies locales that are either parts of corporations or large organizations. The employee with whom the robbery encounter is made is considered to have nothing at stake since there is no personal loss for him, at most he is conceived of as an agent-victim. It is quite clear in the career robber's rationale that for an employee to worry about a sum of money that does not belong to him in the first place is foolish. He views the actual robbery encounter as an impersonal matter for in so doing he is not robbing a person but some amorphous mass—a bank, a supermarket, a loan company. In the actual robbery confrontation he may be dealing with a role incumbent but the role is only in the vaguest sense representative of the impersonal company which is the object of his attack. Hence it is inconceivable to the career robber that an

24 Cf. with Sykes' and Matza's discussion of the denial of the victim by delinquents. Gresham M. Sykes and David Matza, "Techniques of Neutralization: A Theory of Delinquency," *American Sociological Review*, Vol. XXII (December, 1957), 664-670.

agent-victim should resist, since there is no cause for resistance; no one loses personally. Careerists rarely rob the patrons who happen to be in an establishment at the time of the robbery, precisely because the encounter is deemed too personal.

The careerist robber frowns on other robbers who rob individuals, considers them amateur "hot heads" and "bums who make it hot for everybody." Small neighborhood grocery stores and gas stations are the domain not of the careerist but of the latter type of robber:

No, we'd only hit big markets. They're insured anyway. Nobody is out of pocket . . . Why should some small clerk put up a fuss? It isn't his money. They're not hurting . . .

The careerists' ambivalence about robbing liquor stores becomes clearer when one realizes that often these businesses are owner-operated. Under such circumstances it is difficult to avoid a person who may have "something at stake," but even in these circumstances there is always the insurance rationale.

I try to make sure the owner isn't around by knocking the place over late at night, figuring he'll have somebody working for him then who wouldn't care.
I. And if the owner is around?
S. The insurance would cover him anyway, but it's riskier. The employee doesn't care; the owner does, and he might be concerned . . .

Whenever possible, the careerist robber attempts to avoid the "human" in the situation; where it is unavoidable, he overcomes it by the rationale of recovery. Not unlike the soldier who makes a different object out of a human being by calling him the "enemy," the robber makes redefinitions in the very process of becoming a careerist. His victims are already de-personalized objects to him; robbing an impersonal business or company only makes it simpler, and as we shall see subsequently, more acceptable.

Next to the denial of the victims, the conception of honesty has an important place in the robber's rationale system. Sweeping aside the inherent paradox, the career robber views his form of acquisition as a not-too-dishonest enterprise. This appears at first glance as a peculiar stance, but becomes more intelligible when the behavioral elements that make up the robbery situation are examined. Robbery is an open, direct, face-to-face encounter coupled with a non-disguised coercive demand; there is no stealth or furtiveness as with a thief but a confrontation of unabashed power. It is this quality of candor that the robber equates with honesty, an apologia which in his own self-reflexive action makes the robbery career an object of worth, if not noble.

> No, I never thought of committing other kinds of crime. It just never occurred to me. I never thought about writing checks or stealing, somehow, I don't know—this will sound funny, but it just never seemed honest. It's funny. I can't really explain it . . .
>
> I. What do you mean, it wasn't *honest*?
> S. Well I just—I couldn't steal anything. You know—behind someone's back. When I took something I'd make no bones about it. I didn't hide or make out phony papers. I don't know, I guess it's just sorta being yourself—you just take it in front of the guy; you don't pussyfoot it around and do a lot of pretending . . .
>
> And something else—it's a lot cleaner. You feel better about it. You're a pretty big man standing there with your gun. Makes you feel oh—kinda important—big, somebody people don't mess with . . .

To the robber then the career gives

importance and is a noncontrived means of gaining a goal from a "faceless" victim in a situation in which, if all "play their cards right," no one suffers.

A considerable attraction of robbery is its challenge and its call to action—qualities which are savored by the careerist and discussed in the partnership. The review and *post-mortem* of each robbery adds further excitement and stimulation to the career. With each completed robbery a victory is achieved. In the *post-mortem* interaction each success binds the partnership further and provides the motive for continued involvement. In this fashion, each robbery serves to stimulate the next where there is always the chance of richer rewards. Thus the career continues, and with continued success there is the ever-present proof that "nothing can go wrong." A myth of invincibility gradually develops and takes shape, and often is the precursor to the dissolution of the partnership through capture.

As already pointed out, careerists do not think in terms of capture; although they are aware of the possibility, it is always a remote awareness. As the career unfolds for the individual robber confidence grows that no one can break his pattern—as long as he is careful. Continued interaction with his crime partners serves to reify the myth.

> Yeah, we thought we'd go on indefinitely, and not get caught. I think this is everybody's feeling—that they'll never get caught. I think everything that somebody does, that they are conscious of, they think they have this feeling that they'll never get caught. I heard it time after time. 'Shit, I had such a thing going for me that I thought I'd never get caught.' I really don't think that the consequences are really thought about at all.

Akin to the invincibility myth is the

myth of the *utopian heist*. This refers to what most careerists call the "big job," the most lucrative robbery. It is to be the final event which leads to retirement—the robbery that promises to end robbery. It is the ever-alluring pot of gold at the end of the rainbow —the solution to all the careerist's ills. In this connection, one must remember that the careerist's commitment to robbery is viewed by him as a temporary affair. To him robbery is a career escalator to more conventional endeavors.[25] He hopes to return triumphantly where he has previously failed. The "pot of gold" could lead him there quickly. Partnerships discuss the "big job," sometimes with fervor, as a realistic possibility. In the loosely knit group of the partnership the *utopian-heist* has a coalescing function. Moreover, it serves to focus the robbers' attention toward continued involvement.

When the rare "big job" is accomplished, events do not change for the rewards are dissipated only to start the cycle anew.

> . . . he and I took off and got us a couple of girls, and we went down to Mexico. Well, we had a heck of a time getting across the border, because we had to go cash it all into small bills. Part of it we left buried up around our homes. And we stayed down there about a week horsing around. Came back and decided we didn't want to go back to work, because it was too easy. And we started getting a little bit too rambunctious and almost every night we'd look for a place to rob. We weren't satisfied with what we had. Good clothes, the leisurely hours and the girls you could spend a lot of money on, and check into the biggest hotels, the nicest motels, all of this stuff

---

25 Howard S. Becker and Anselm C. Strauss, "Careers, Personality, and Adult Socialization," *American Journal Sociology*, LXII (November, 1956), pp. 253-263.

kinda went to make us go out every night for some more.

The Career Armed Robber as a Type

Viewed as a type, the individual careerist assumes the posture of a man whose round of life never quite seems to meet the standards of middle-class convention. He need not have a delinquent background nor have committed serious crimes prior to his career, but the rhythm of his existence has never been in tune with the conventional.

Typically, the careerist represents one who lives on the fringes, more a "night" dweller than a "day" dweller. In his circle of intimate acquaintances are the hustler, the bookie, the gambler, and the pimp; the bartender, the taxidriver, and the bellhop. Involvement in robbery does not remove him from this life arena but locks him more securely in it. The career, however, promises upward social mobility; thus the robbery ostensibly to finance a legitimate business, to open a motel, to enable a trip to start anew, but the style of life does not permit it. As the careerist reveals, he "blows it" and thus remains true to the "easy come, easy go" style of his social surroundings. Whereas the racketeer or organized criminal may achieve respectability for himself and his family, the career robber never tranlsates his economic gain into objects of legitimate social worth or more conventional style of life. Hence, the career does not change the existing life style; rather, it is an extreme expression of it and functions for the careerist as a transitory, if illusive, transcendent experience.

On those infrequent occasions when the careerist terminates the career on his own volition, the previous life cycle is usually resumed with reasonably appropriate accommodations as to costs and risks. The involuntary termination of the career, however, often leads to even further estrangement, for as Lemert has suggested, ". . . (when) the exconvict advances economically to the point where better positions become open to him, he may be rejected because of inability to obtain a bond or because his past criminal record comes to light. If the man's aspirational roles are low, he may adjust successfully as, say, a laborer or casual worker; otherwise, he nearly always shows the marks of his difficult struggle."[26]

The careerist thus eventually returns to his former milieu after the career is ended, whether he leaves it voluntarily or is forced to relinquish it by

---

[26] Lemert, *Social Pathology*, p. 331.

being caught and confined. In the latter instance, however, the stigmatic burden of the identified criminal makes it extremely difficult for him ever to lift himself above his circle:

> I did a lot of time for a few robberies. I'm not complaining, I shoulda known better . . . when you come out you're right back where you started only worse, nobody knows you and times have changed. So you knuckle under—you can make it—but you sure have to change your way of thinking. You can't be afraid of carrying a lunch bucket—if you don't you're sunk or you go back to capering and the same old shit starts over again.

The brief triumph leads to defeat or accommodation that must ultimately involve a reorganization of the self toward acceptance of a modified role as an actor on the social stage.

[6]

NCCD RESEARCH REVIEW

LIFE IN THE FAST LANE: A RETROSPECTIVE VIEW BY COMMERCIAL THIEVES

JOHN J. GIBBS
PEGGY L. SHELLY

[*In this issue of the* Journal, *the NCCD Research Centers are deferring their usual opportunity to present a report on their own work in order to share, with the* Journal's *readers, some interim findings from an important research effort that is still in progress. Through the strong collaborative links that exist between NCCD and the Graduate School of Criminal Justice at Rutgers University, we have been following with interest the research being conducted in the School's Center for the Study of Crime for Gain, a project funded by the National Institute of Justice and directed by Professor Richard Sparks. Ceding the "NCCD Research Review" space to a report solicited from our colleagues at Rutgers represents a small contribution on our part toward alleviating a chronic problem faced by researchers: the seemingly interminable lag time between the initiation of a research project and the public availability of the project's findings.*]

This article contains an analysis of interviews with commercial thieves. Both the interviews and analysis of them were shaped by the perspective that certain kinds of crime are like certain kinds of work. The article describes a variety of methods for illegally acquiring and distributing commercial goods, paths of entry into the business of commercial theft, and the relation between the work of the thief and his life style.

In October 1980, the National Institute of Justice awarded a research grant to the School of Criminal Justice at Rutgers University to establish the Center for the Study of the Causes of Crime for Gain. During the first eighteen months of funding the Center proposed to explain theoretically and examine empirically serious property crime, or

JOHN J. GIBBS: Assistant Professor, School of Criminal Justice, Rutgers University, Newark, New Jersey; Principal Investigator, Commercial Theft Project, Center for the Study of the Causes of Crime for Gain, Rutgers University. **PEGGY L. SHELLY:** Research Associate, Commercial Theft Project, Rutgers University.

The research on which this article is based was conducted as part of the Commercial Theft Studies Project of the Center for the Study of the Causes of Crime for Gain. The Center was established at Rutgers University under Grant Number 80-IJ-CX-0060 from the National Institute of Justice, United States Department of Justice. Points of view or opinions stated in this article are those of the authors and do not necessarily represent the official position or policies of the Department of Justice.

those crimes committed for pecuniary gain. In this article, we are concerned primarily with truck hijacking and commercial burglary. This article contains a description of the information that we gathered from thieves on how people go about planning and carrying out acts of theft.

The perspective that has shaped our research is that "crime for gain,"[1] of which property theft is a species, is much like legitimate work and that many of the factors that place constraints on or allow for the success of legitimate work operate as well in work of an illegitimate nature. We are interested here in examining opportunities for illegitimate work, the technology and skills associated with the work tasks, and the social controls that inhibit or induce involvement in illegitimate work.

As part of the Center's initial empirical work, it was agreed that a study of commercial burglary, including the theft of goods in transit, would be conducted. There were two major reasons for choosing large-scale commercial theft as the subject of the Center's first empirical investigation. First, we felt it likely a priori that large-scale thefts from factories, warehouses, retail stores, banks, port areas, airports, and the like were most likely to exemplify the major characteristics of "crime as work." We wanted to explore the issues of technology and of environmental constraint, of recruitment, of group organization, and of relations with other behavioral systems and offender groups (e.g., receivers of stolen property)—or all those things about crime that resemble legitimate work. All of these factors are more likely to be found when the target is a factory or container truck, and the property stolen is a large or expensive quantity of merchandise, than when the target is a residence and the property stolen is a small amount of cash. Second, the crime of commercial burglary is undoubtedly serious, in financial terms. In addition to the property lost through such thefts, protection against them entails large expenditures (ultimately passed on to consumers) for insurance, private and public police, and other security measures.

This article explores two kinds of "crime for gain," commercial burglary and truck hijacking, from the perspective of those who consider them their work. Our major purpose is to portray the world of the commercial thief, to face the problems he faces, to learn to do what he does, to see what he sees.

1. Sparks (1982:2) describes the meaning of "crime for gain" as follows: "The expression crime for gain is not now a recognized term of art in criminology.... We have so far used it, in our research, to refer in a general way to crimes which involve the misappropriation (through stealth, fraud, or threat) of money or other property—that is, to kinds of illegal acts done, in a plain sense, for material gain rather than (say) for their symbolic or expressive value. Paradigm cases of what we call 'crime for gain' would include such things as burglary, larceny, robbery, extortion, and fraud. There is an abundance of empirical evidence that most of those who commit crimes of this kind are (or at least appear to be) psychologically normal; and clearly the motivation behind their crimes is (by definition) not mysterious."

The basic methodological and analytical assumption underlying this article is that we can only understand a particular kind of crime by examining what the criminal is confronted with, the problems he must solve and the steps he must take to solve them (Levi, 1981:5). Our view is that exploring assumptive worlds of those involved in the behaviors we wish to subject to scientific scrunity is not just a useful heuristic technique; it is necessary for the development of explanatory constructs which make actions intelligible. The subjective experience of the thief, the meaning of events to him, is the context in which his actions can be understood (see Ryan, 1973:6–8).

STALKING THE COMMERCIAL THIEF

Our first step in obtaining the information we needed to describe the world of the commercial thief was defining and finding the kind of person we wanted to interview. After reviewing descriptions of professional thieves, full-time miscreants, good burglars, successful criminals, and big-time operators which collectively featured such inclusion criteria as planning, a code of conduct, a certain modus operandi, and stylish dress,[2] we decided to include in our sample individuals who had been involved in any large-scale commercial burglary, larceny, or robbery (excluding banks) that resulted or had the potential to result in a substantial financial gain.

Our plan was to interview a large number of commercial offenders and to use interview content in conjunction with data collected from agency files to classify them according to criteria contained in others' and our own definitions. We predicted that the use of complex criteria for sample selection would result in a restricted sample with limited variation in some factors of interest, and the application of the criteria would be difficult at best because much of the required information would not exist in institutional files or other sources of information that could be used to develop a sampling frame. We concluded that a very broad definition, which would yield a large pool of interview candidates, had many theoretical and operational advantages over a more precise definition.

Our initial experience in selecting a sample from institutional files

---

2. Sutherland (1937), Shover (1973), and Letkemann (1973) have all used definitions of professional thieves that incorporate some of these elements. Shover, for example, defined his "good thieves" as those who "... (1) [are] technically competent, (2) have a reputation for personal integrity, (3) tend to specialize in burglary, and (4) have been at least relatively successful at crime" (1973:501). Shover's operational definition of the good burglar is as follows: "[The] respondent must have (1) received $4000 or more on his largest score, and either (2) opened a safe at some time by drilling or burning, or (3) entered a place at some time by cutting a hole in the roof or wall" (1971:502). This definition is obviously too restrictive to be of much use to us.

convinced us that a broad definition was not merely desirable but also necessary if we wished to find anyone to interview. We began our search for interview candidates in the prisons of the state of New York. We were provided with a computer-generated list of the names of property offenders who were housed in selected institutions as of June 6, 1981. We restricted our attention to inmates who had entered the system since 1978 because the blotters containing offense description information for these inmates were much more accessible than those of prisoners who had become charges of the New York State correctional facilities before 1978. In order to obtain the best possible match with data on incidents of cargo theft and commercial burglary that we collected from the specialized detective squad of the City of New York Police Department, the Port Authority of New York/New Jersey, and the police department of a small metropolitan community, we further restricted the sampling frame by selecting only cases adjudicated in county courts located in the New York metropolitan area. We also limited our selection to the closest maximum and medium security institutions.

We reviewed the offense descriptions appearing on the blotters of 578 prisoners who (1) were convicted of a property offense by a county court located in the metropolitan area, (2) entered a state of New York institution on or after January 1, 1978, and (3) were housed in either of two institutions close to the metropolitan area. Our examination of the documents resulted in the discovery of 81 incident descriptions in which a commercial establishment was identified as the victim. Seven of those incidents met our criteria for inclusion in the sample—these were a theft from a commercial enterprise that resulted in a loss of $10,000 or more, a theft of goods in transit or storage from a nonretail commercial establishment that involved a substantial loss in quantity or dollars (e.g., several boxes of designer jeans from an air terminal storage area), or an attempted theft that would have resulted in a substantial loss if the offender had been successful (e.g., entering a fur storage area illegally with intent to steal).

There are several obvious flaws in the procedure we used for identifying interview candidates in the New York prison system. Our decision to review a person's blotter was based exclusively on whether he was presently sentenced for a property conviction. It is possible that there were men who had been convicted of property offenses in the past which would have met the criteria for inclusion in our interview sample who were not selected because they were confined at the time of sampling for something other than a property crime. It is possible also that those convicted of a property offense for which the blotter description did not meet our inclusion criteria could have an offense history that, if known, would make them prime candidates for interview.

The description of the conviction offense appearing on the inmate blotter was either extracted or derived from police reports or the presentence investigations usually prepared by probation officers. The considerable variation in the style and content of the blotter descriptions, which may reflect variation in the style and content of their sources, may have introduced considerable unreliability into our sampling scheme. For example, some descriptions of burglaries would contain only the address of the structure burglarized, with no indication as to whether the victim was a commercial establishment or a household. We know of no method within our time and budget limitations that could be used to estimate the number of cases that were classified as noncommercial because of lack of specificity in the blotter description of the offense.

Our rather disappointing experience in finding potential interviewees in New York State institutions led us to investigate other sources of interview candidates. We hypothesized that one reason for the small relative frequency of inmates in New York institutions whose records contained evidence of involvement in a large-scale commercial theft was that many criminal events of this kind involve interstate shipments and therefore can be processed as federal cases. We requested and were granted permission to conduct research in Otisville, the closest federal correctional institution.

The institutional records maintained at FCI Otisville contain (1) a presentence investigation which usually includes a complete description of the commitment offense, (2) a summary of the inmate's offense history which sometimes includes assessments by law enforcement authorities and others of the nature and extent of the prisoner's criminality, and (3) a copy of the offender's criminal record. A review of the records of the 265 prisoners housed in Otisville yielded a sample of 8 men who were serving a sentence for an offense that met our inclusion criteria or who had an arrest history for such an offense within the last decade.

We interviewed eleven of the fifteen men in our sampling frame. Although our goal was a sample of about fifty interviewees, we were not too discouraged by our sample size of eleven because (1) it allowed us to spend a great deal of time, from two to eight hours, with individual subjects, and (2) compared with others who have interviewed those who make their living by large-scale theft, our sample is not that small. For example, Levi, who studied the problem of long-firm fraud with an interview sample the same size as ours, states,

> My hope is that I have illuminated at least part of the setting within which fraud takes place, on the basis of a sample much larger than most studies of professional crime in England or America (1981:10).[3]

3. For a review of the sample size and techniques of selection used in other studies, see Gibbs and Shelly (1982: ch. 2).

METHOD OF INQUIRY

Before we went to prisons to interview thieves, we developed a series of questions to ask them. The questions reflect our theoretical perspective, and they are grouped into six general areas of inquiry: (1) extent of involvement in crime for gain; (2) social and cultural experience; (3) employment history and occupational choice; (4) descriptions of incidents of crime for gain; (5) identity and self-image; and (6) tricks of the trade. The last refers to probes designed to elicit descriptions of techniques of crime.

We called our questions an interview guide, rather than the more traditional term *interview schedule,* to emphasize our flexibility in approaching individual subjects and the exploratory nature of our inquiry. We did not expect to follow rigidly the sequence and syntax of the questions as they appear in the guide. We expected that questions would be reformulated and new areas for questioning would emerge as our interviews progressed. We intended to use the information furnished by one respondent to formulate questions that would be asked of subsequent respondents.[4]

Our strategy of inquiry does not yield a set of questions that meets conventional standards of reliability for research instruments. Indeed, reliability in this sense was not given high priority. Our primary goal was to elicit from each respondent a full description of how he went about his legitimate and illegitimate work. Accomplishing this goal required that we vary our approach from subject to subject. The relevance of questions varies among subjects and so too does the style of questioning. An approach that draws rich descriptions from one subject can yield a very disappointing response when used with another.

Some will view our variation in approach as contributing to error variance, and thereby diminishing reliability. Our position is that the modifications increase reliability by making the questions relevant and understandable to individual subjects.

Those who read our interview transcripts will see that the approach we used with some subjects, or, more accurately, the tack some respondents took, resulted in much irrelevant information. In these interviews, some respondents seemed almost to be testing to see whether the interviewer was really interested in them as individuals, and not just exploiting them for information, by talking about matters that were not connected with the interviewer's expressed interests and observing the interviewer's response. Other subjects may have thought that the interviewer was genuinely interested in the most trivial aspects of their lives. In both cases, it was incumbent upon the interviewer to listen attentively and respond with appropriate questions.

---

4. The progressive increase in the length of our interviews from first to last is a consequence of our approach.

Sometimes these situations evolved into implied contracts between the interviewer and interviewee that allowed the interviewer to ask questions in a more direct manner than would have been prudent to do otherwise. The bargain struck was if the interviewer would listen to and discuss certain matters of particular importance to the subject, the subject owed the interviewer honest answers about other matters.

THE SAMPLE AND SETTING AS THREATS TO VALIDITY

One often hears that studies of confined criminals result in misrepresentative descriptions of the world of crime because only the inept are caught. The position is by now so well entrenched in the minds of criminologists that it is almost an involuntary response to the stimulus "data were gathered from a sample of prisoners with an extensive history of..." Other criticisms of the use of prison populations are (1) incarceration is considered a personal failure that can distort one's view of the past, and (2) crime, like other behaviors, should be studied in the context in which it occurs (see Shover, 1971:31–35).

These criticisms have merit. We strongly support the idea of studying crime in natural settings. Beyond the practical limits to this approach, however, it is not well suited to examining developmental aspects. There may well be differences between those who are caught in any one time period and those who are not. Until a study comparing the groups is conducted, however, we will not know the extent of these differences or how they affect descriptions and explanations of criminal behavior. We also think it is likely that today's prison cell colors one's memory of the streets of yesterday. This is a specific instance of the more general observation that one's present circumstances affect what one remembers. Again, assessing the precise effects of circumstantial influences on memory warrants scientific scrutiny.

In the absence of such comparative information, we can only speculate about the likely effects. We think it is very likely that our sample of commercial thieves is representative of more than the bungling habitual failure area of the distribution of commercial thieves, the schlemiel tail. There is evidence that suggests that most thieves do time. Gould et al. (1966) interviewed fifty criminals who had been involved in crimes "... committed for personal economic gain by individuals whose major source of income is from criminal pursuits and who spend a majority of their working time in illegal enterprises..." (1966:10). Every member of the interview sample, which consisted of thirty-one incarcerated subjects and nineteen subjects who were at liberty (1966:17), had served a prison sentence (1966:45). More recently, most of our interviewees reported that they considered prison a cost of doing business, they expected to get caught eventually, and they did not know many people who were persistently involved in theft who had not served time.

It could be argued, of course, that our unrepresentative sample is likely to furnish a biased estimate of the proportion of thieves who get caught. Gould et al. also note the possibility of bias when they point out in a footnote that "it should be noted that we may not have found any professional criminal who had never been in jail or prison simply because such criminals would not be known to the police who were our major source of contact with criminals" (1966:45).

There are a number of reasons why we would expect a substantial proportion of commercial thieves, even the best, to have spent some time in prison. Even the most competent criminal may be apprehended when he is caught unaware of improvements in police or social control techniques, organization, or personnel (see Levi, 1981:10). And, once caught, even the biggest of big-time operators cannot "fix" all of the cases all of the time. Shover notes that the ability of criminals to fix cases has been overstated in the literature; ironically, ". . . Sutherland's professional thief, who was probably largely responsible for creating the image of the virtual infallibility of the 'fix,' had himself served at least five different terms in confinement" (1971:32). Gould et al. found that criminal-official dealings revolved around trading information to reduce penalties, not the use of financial or political influence to avoid prosecution (1966:46–47). Criminals with the right connections may not serve as much time as their less well-connected counterparts, but there is a good chance that their names will appear on prison rosters at some time.

Another reason we suspect that most people who have been involved in the business of commercial theft have served time is, in some circles, doing time is considered a prerequisite for becoming a thief. A prison record is evidence that a man has paid his dues as a thief. It establishes his reputation as a man who can be trusted, a man who can take the heat, a man who is willing to take a risk. A record is a calling card. If people know a man has done time, they are more likely to approach him with an offer.

We would also expect commercial thieves to have confinement histories because prisons, jails, and reformatories are where men learn skills and make contacts. They provide the isolation from conventional influences and the concentration of criminal influences that shape futures in the crime business. Letkemann makes the following observation about ". . . those who consider it [crime] as their work" (1973:1):

> None of my respondents suggested any degree of specialization before their first prison sentence—it was during prison that the illegitimate career took form and structure. Prison helps the criminal realize that the haphazard and impulsive character of delinquency can no longer be afforded (p. 129).

Even if we could guarantee that a representative sample of the population of commercial thieves can be found in prison, we still would not be out of the methodological woods. A man's perspective on the past can be altered by his incarceration. Interviews conducted with criminals while they are still on the streets actively involved in their work could produce more accurate results. There would be less chance of memory decay, and the man on the street should be able to describe current life on the streets more realistically than his confined counterpart.

The "street" as an interview setting, however, has some disadvantages when compared with prison. Life on the streets has been described by some thieves as a fast-paced cycle of obtaining money and spending it. It is a hectic and exciting life style that does not promote reflection and rumination. The penitentiary, on the other hand, spawns self-inventory. In prison cells, men take stock of their lives, and review their pasts, sometimes in great detail. Although prison inventory taking may be skewed toward negative assessments, it stimulates the mind to search for descriptions of past events. The thief in prison probably has a more appropriate mind set for a retrospective interview than does the thief on the streets (see Levi, 1981:329).

Other reasons why interviewing in prison may be preferable to the streets are (1) thieves in prison generally have more time available to talk; in the streets the interviewer has to compete for time with many other activities and interests; (2) thieves in prison have less reason to be secretive about their activities[5]; and (3) the places available for interviews on the streets (e.g., bars) may promote social discourse but impede validity.

STRATEGY OF ANALYSIS

The observations presented in this article are the result of a thematic analysis of interview content. Our examination of the interviews was guided by our theoretical perspective and the observations of others who have explored the world of the thief. Our method of analysis was to attempt to verify themes and explanations that emerged from one interview in all others. This required reformulation and refinement of observations until descriptions of themes that reliably spelled out the perspectives of our subjects were developed.

5. Some of the men we interviewed had been testified against by former associates. This made them more willing to describe very detailed accounts of the incidents because they were not too concerned about implicating others.

Another factor that promotes openness in prison is that concerns that were potent on the streets may be pale by comparison when a man is confined. Information on techniques and other subjects appears less deserving of concealment when a man is serving time.

Most of the remainder of this article is devoted to our observations about those involved in crime for gain. A great deal of excerpted material is included, not only to bring the content categories to life with the words of those who have had experience in the world of theft but also to provide the reader with examples of the kinds of interview content from which we drew our conclusions.

THE WORK OF THIEVES

Work structures our lives. It influences when we eat and sleep, who our friends are, and how often we see them. Our theoretical framework, and the perspective of most of the men we interviewed, is that crime is a kind of work. The remainder of this article will be devoted to describing how commercial thieves go about their work and how it affects other aspects of their lives.

The work of the thief requires that he complete one and sometimes two tasks without getting caught by the police. He must obtain property, and if it is other than money, he must sell the property. In this section, we will describe the methods our men used to procure goods and the channels they used for distribution. We will illustrate the close connection between the kind and amount of property appropriated and the method of distribution. Our interest is in charting the ways in which substantial amounts of property of many different kinds are illegally acquired and sold.

ON THE JOB WITH THE BURGLAR

The men in our sample can be classified, roughly, into two categories. The men in the first category, burglars, shared one defining characteristic: The primary target of their thefts was cash. The first form of commercial burglary we will describe is one of the simplest illegal acquisition-distribution systems. It requires the most technical sophistication of all the systems (see also Letkemann on this point, 1973:51), and as much acquisition planning as other methods, but only rarely does it require a distribution system. Cash, the most liquid of all assets, requires resale only in the unusual case where it must be laundered.

The most sophisticated and specialized of the three men we interviewed who were primarily involved in burglary was a member of a crew concentrating on theft from supermarkets. The number of men needed on any one job varied between two and six, and members of the crew possessed skills in opening safes with tools, torches, and explosives, and bypassing alarm systems by using simple electronic devices, a voltage meter, batteries, wire, alligator clips, wire snips, and a battery-operated soldering iron. Additional tools of their trade included a police scanner radio and walkie-talkie radios for communication within the crew.

Supermarkets are prime targets for those interested in stealing cash because supermarkets, along with some bars and restaurants, are among the kinds of businesses that have been least affected by the credit revolution. They still deal in large amounts of cash, and they will probably continue to do so for some time.

In selecting a particular supermarket as a target, the thief tries to maximize payoff and minimize risk. He looks for markets with a substantial amount of cash on the premises that are located in relatively isolated areas which feature escape options. The thief watches the market for a few days to estimate sales and cash on hand by noting the manager's deposit pattern at the local bank, which is usually located in the same shopping center. He also surveys the area to plan escape routes.

Supermarkets located in shopping centers surrounded by a wooded area on three sides and adjacent to a major highway are considered ideal targets. They are so vulnerable that one man refers to them as gift scores:

> *#11:* . . . if you've got houses in the back, you know, you've got to say, "Well Jesus there's a risk that someone can see me climbing up on the roof," you know. So naturally, I look for shopping centers that are built on the edge of town, preferably close to a highway. . . . You pull off the exit, there's the shopping center, usually it's set back from the road, there's woods all around it, a motel down the street, a coffee shop that's open all night, so you've got all kinds of places where you can park your car, right, you can get dropped off with your tools, one guy can go down and park the car at the motel, walk around the back of the building, scoot into the bushes, come down and be a watch already. . . .

A supermarket in a shopping center is also an attractive target because the buildings are connected, a feature that is seen as enhancing the chances of escape:

> *#11:* . . . it's a lot more difficult for them to surround a shopping center than it would be to surround one single building. . . . I just go out the back. There's no way he can get around that building fast enough. If the car pulls in around the back, I go out the front. You know, so the chances are good that I'll get away, especially with the doors locked. They're not positive that somebody's in there yet because they haven't seen anybody, you know, so usually they'll check the doors and call the manager, and they wait until the manager comes, and then they go inside the building. By that time, I'm long gone.

Once the target is selected, the place has been "cased," the crew goes into action:

> *#11:* Well, two guys would usually go in, right, you'd go up on the roof, two guys chop a hole. . . . So you have two guys inside that move the safe, do the actual work. So now you've gotta have a guy outside. You've gotta have a watch, you know, a guy out there with a walkie-talkie and a police scanner and he's watching for you, telling you when you can make noise and when you can't, when the cop's checking and when he isn't. You know, and so on. And then, a lot of places you'll find that you can't park the car close by, it's dangerous to park a car close by . . . so you have a driver who drops everybody off with the tools. . . . Maybe he can park in an area toward town where he can be like a first watch. . . . So it's a nice system, sometimes we even used two watches, one down the road, one up the road.

Not all the jobs attempted by this crew were as well planned or as well staffed as what has been described. As we will see later in this article, this crew made some spectacular errors in planning and operation, and under certain conditions (e.g., financial difficulties) they would attempt some high-risk thefts called kamikazi scores.

A second of our subjects worked as a commercial burglar, and used techniques and methods of target selection that were somewhat similar to those we have just described; for example, he expressed the principles of maximizing payoff in target selection:

> *#10:* That's just the way it was. We'd just watch and see. Studied a joint for days. If we had to, weeks. If it seemed easy enough that we could make a score out of it, we'd take it down. If it didn't, if the money went to the bank every night, we wouldn't touch it, wouldn't touch it. What's the use of going in, making a hit, if you've got something to lose?

This thief also prefers retail stores with a large volume of cash sales as targets, and he actually enters stores to see what kind of safe is used and to estimate the potential payoff:

> *#10:* Well, you just watch, that's all. . . . They open the registers when you're walking by, and you see how much. The lady comes by or the guy comes around and they take so much out of each register and he leaves them so much. They'll take all the 20's, 50's, and 100's. . . . You figure if he grabs underneath and pulls out a chunk like this here, you know he's got over $5,000, you know, easy. . . . I could estimate what they had, maybe $30,000 during the night. . . .

This thief differed from the other commercial burglar we have described in several ways: (1) He reported that he usually worked with only one partner; (2) his target selection was broader in kind; (3) he used less sophisticated tools; (4) he didn't know how to open certain kinds of safes (e.g., "cannon balls"); and (5) he would steal merchandise in addition to cash. These differences are obviously connected. If he was less sophisticated and skilled than our other man, and his work crew was smaller, we would expect him to have more difficulty getting at the well-protected liquid asset, cash. If he could not get at the cash after he entered a commercial establishment, we would expect him to appropriate the next most liquid asset, consumer goods of general market appeal, to make the risk worthwhile. This is precisely what he reported he did:

> *#10:* If we couldn't take the safe, we'd take the merchandise. Like anything that was expensive, rings, radios, anything you could steal that could get a good quantity out of. Small stuff. One day we stole tapes. Stole over 10,000 tapes. . . . Tapes, you know, with music on them and stuff. . . . We had stacks and stacks, real stacks of tapes.

Once the thief acquires goods, he must convert them into cash. He needs a distribution channel through which he can market his goods. The most direct and most profitable channels for the thief are sales to the consumer and to retail outlets. These are the channels our man used to market his tapes. Below, he tells us that not only did he function as a retailer and wholesaler for his own stolen property but he also provided these services for others.

> *#10:* We stole like over 10,000 of them, and then we sold them for a buck a piece.
> *Interviewer:* Who did you sell them to?
> *#10:* We sold them to anybody that bought them. Anybody that wanted them we sold them to. Stores, they'd buy them for a buck a piece, I think they had a $3.00 tag on them.
> *Interviewer:* Would you go around to stores and say, "I got a deal on these tapes, do you want to buy some?"
> *#10:* All the guys I used to deal with, just the guys I used to deal with, like certain guys.
> *Interviewer:* So you had like customers?
> *#10:* Yeah.
> *Interviewer:* How did you meet these people?
> *#10:* I met a lot in the rubbish business, a lot on the street. You know, "hey, I'm lookin' for TV sets," or "I'm lookin' for that." So I'd say, "if I can get anything I'll let you know."
> *Interviewer:* Does the word just sort of come out on the street? When people are looking for something, they know you're in that business?
> *#10:* I wasn't really in a business. It was something where if I needed money, I did it. Like TV sets like for $25 or $30. I used to buy a lot of stolen stuff. I used to resell, that's all. A lot of stuff I used to rob, a lot of stuff I used to buy.

The third man we interviewed whose major activity was burglary was primarily involved in thefts from residences. However, he did commit some commercial burglaries, and he is currently serving a sentence for the robbery of $50,000 worth of gold and diamonds from a retail jewelry store. We will concentrate on his household burglaries to illustrate how differences in choice of target, household or commercial establishment, can affect other aspects of crime.

Unlike commercial establishments, especially retail stores like supermarkets, households do not operate in the public domain. This limits the amount of information that can be obtained about them. It is especially difficult to estimate the amount of cash or other easily convertible assets that are contained in a residence. In comparison with the commercial burglar, the residential burglar is at a disadvantage because the data necessary to maximize payoff are not as available. The household burglar does have some information related to concentration of assets that can be used for target selection. He knows that certain neighborhoods are inhabited by wealthy people; and people who live in Tudor houses are more likely to have jewels than people who live in Quonset huts.

The problems of entry also differ for the household and the commercial burglar. There is an association between protective devices and concentration of assets, and, as would be expected, entering a home does not require as much skill and muscle or tool power as does entering a commercial building. Nevertheless, there are risks involved in residential burglary, and our man's major concern on the job was ease of entry and risk of confrontation with a member of the household:

> *#4:* Yeah, when you case out an apartment building usually you have to go into the apartment, and you go up on the roof. Usually, there's an emergency door that's open all the time. First, you go up on the roof, you look down and check out the fire escapes 'cause they lead to the windows. You go back down, you start ringing bells to see if anybody's home. If no one's home, you go back up on the fire escape, open the window and go into the apartment. . . . Now private houses were easier. You know, just open a window and you go in. Or you break down the door and go in, whatever. . . . A house, usually we go about 2 o'clock. . . . If you see mail in the mailbox at 2 o'clock in the afternoon you know no one's home or they're very late sleepers, so we ring the bell and check it.

Our residential burglar and his partner seldom had a particular dwelling in mind when they went to work. They usually cruised in their car looking for an appropriate target. After entering a dwelling, they searched bedrooms for cash and jewels. However, they were prepared to appropriate a variety of property to make the risk of entry worthwhile.

A variety of property, especially a small number of unrelated items like a camera, a stamp collection, and a piece of luggage, is not the kind of product package that you take to a major criminal fence to sell, even if you happen to know one. Small quantities of these kinds of goods are usually sold directly to the consumer by the thief, or they require the services of the small, primarily legitimate, retailer. Finding a retail distributor for small high-value goods is easy:

> *Interviewer:* How do you know who buys stuff, do you just hear the word?

#4: You meet them. . . . I just meet them, I just meet people. Here for instance, I know certain people, they go to certain places, they tell you where you go to sell something. So I go there and I'm selling something, like I ask them, "Can I talk in front of this guy?" "Yea, yea," they say. "I got this and this," I say. I used to pull out a little statue, diamonds, and lay them on the table, and the other guy would see this and he'll give me his card. He'll catch me outside as I'm getting into my car. He'll come running out and say, "Look, I'll give you a better price."

The last man we interviewed whom we classify primarily as a burglar began as an employee thief, stealing, he says, "things off the job, saws, copper, tools, tires, you name it, I'll steal it. . . . You know anything I know I could sell." The reason for his crime at work was to support a drug habit (heroin and cocaine), and, as his habit increased, he found that he had to branch out into crime as work to meet expenses.

His form of crime as work did not differ in many ways from his crime at work. He concentrated on construction sites as targets, and stole tools, equipment, and materials. Although he stole from what we would technically classify as a commercial establishment, his approach was very similar to that of our household burglar. He went out cruising in his car looking for scores:

#2: . . . you just go cruising around, things pop up. Believe me, they pop up. Right in front of you. Right in front of your eyes. . . . Alright, true story. I was driving by a construction site and there was a welding machine, brand new, chained to the building. I checked the job out. The guard was there. Now I know this guy has gotta eat lunch. I know this guy has gotta do something. So I wait. Two hours. He leaked. I go on the job, cut the chain, and now I've gotta put it in the trunk of my car. I can't lift it by myself. There's this fork lift. What do I do for a living? I run a machine. I start the machine up. . . . This is what I do for a living, alright. Start the machine up, pick it up, throw it in the trunk of my car, and goodbye $275. . . .

The kind of property this man usually stole limited his distribution options. Most of his thefts did not involve goods that had mass market appeal, and he didn't steal quantities large enough to interest a big-league fence. Anyhow, he preferred the most direct distribution channel, from producer, the thief, to the consumer, a buyer who purchases the materials or equipment for his own use:

#2: I didn't like doing business with fences because if the thing was worth like $200, they'd wanna give you $100 so they could make $100. . . . I'd go to. . . say you need that tape recorder, I'm coming right to you 'cause I know you need that tape recorder and you're willing to pay. If it's worth $200, you'll be willing to pay tops. The least I'll sell it to you for is $150.

HIJACKING AND GRAND LARCENY FROM TRUCKS

A second broad occupational classification of the men we interviewed is the theft of goods in transit from trucks. Trucks are attractive targets because (1) they contain large quantities of goods; (2) the goods are ready for transport; and (3) goods are less protected in the truck than they are in a producer's or wholesaler's warehouse or in storage in a retail store.[6]

Our interviewees described a number of acquisition-distribution systems for property taken from trucks. The most elementary is to drive away in the truck when the driver goes in a building to make a delivery. In the interview excerpt below one of our men describes this basic acquisition pattern:

> *#5:* There were certain areas, right, certain days of the week, you know, certain areas that would get deliveries, we'd go in that area, we'd walk up and down the street and we'd spot a truck, mostly we'd spot a truck as it pulls up; like standing on the corner or sitting on the stoop and watch them take off what they're going to deliver and watch them go into the building or apartment.... By the time they go in the building I usually jump in the truck. It don't take more than 3 or 4 seconds, more like 10 seconds.... You use what you call a pulley, some people call it a slap hammer, it's a rod about so long, you got a screw at the end, and you got like a weight in the middle that you slide up and down, slide it up and down the bar, screw that into the ignition and you just hit it and it comes up and you can stick anything in there and it starts.

This thief preferred to steal delivery trucks transporting household appliances. He read the paper to see which department stores were having sales, waited two or three weeks for the delivery wave resulting from the sale to begin, and then went to the areas where he knew from experience these stores delivered on certain days. A second method of target selection involved making deals with people in his neighborhood. Some neighbors called him to tell him when they were having goods, usually furniture, delivered to their homes. When the delivery man went in to verify the order with the customer, our man made off with the truck, and the customer received a substantial discount for his trouble.

This man was by no means exclusively a furniture and appliance thief. He would steal and sell anything. He boasted of successfully marketing truckloads of rags, watermelons, and sparkling water. These particular loads were the result of cruising for a score. When riding around in a car searching for a load to take, the major concern is minimizing risk. The strike must be quick and clean. This limits the time available to case the target. When the opportunity to take the truck arose, our

---

6. Our analysis of the method of entry into warehouses leads us to question how well protected goods are in warehouses (see Gibbs and Shelly, 1982: ch. 4).

man sprang into action. Sometimes he did not know what the truck was carrying.

This man not only stole a variety of goods but he also used a variety of distribution channels. He sold to fences but more often he sold directly to the consumer, his neighbors. He is the only thief we talked with who had grass-roots community involvement as a component of his acquisition-distribution system:

> *#5:* . . . half the time I'd just pull up in the street and sell it. . . . If you're in a certain neighborhood where people know you, it would be safe. Never go to a strange neighborhood.
>
> *Interviewer:* So you'd stay within neighborhoods? The cops wouldn't bother you or anything?
>
> *#5:* Well, you'd have somebody watching the corner, you know. Like sometimes I'd go out by myself and do this and I've placed people, you know, stand on both corners and I'd place people to help me unload the stuff. I'd put it in the backyard and throw some paper stuff over it and I'd take it and leave the truck. You know, not leave it but move the truck and come back.

Four of the men we interviewed were involved primarily in illegally appropriating entire trailer loads of goods. There was, however, considerable variation in the method of acquisition. Two of the subjects reported that their thefts usually involved collusion with employees of the trucking company or the truck depot. The other two claimed that this kind of cooperation was rare.

Both of the men whose method usually required duplicity on the part of the victim organization's employees started stealing trailers by simply driving a tractor into a depot, coupling it with the trailer, and driving away. In the interview excerpt appearing below one of our men reminisces:

> *#7:* We were out there every night, we really thought this was a job, "It ain't stealing, it's a job." In them years, it was easy. I'm talking about the 1960's the last time I did something like that and went to jail for it, you could go anywhere in the metropolitan area and go into any trucking yard and walk around. It was like shopping. Just walk around until you see something that you want. We had trailers; we had tractors. We had our own tractors which were stolen they weren't really ours but we put a claimer on them. They were ours, put in our own yard. Big yard and garages. Go take a tractor, go in, driver would hook up to it, and just go out. We would take it, and unload, and dump the empty somewhere. Let's say dump it in New York or Staten Island. Y'know away from where you got the stuff.
>
> *Interviewer:* No one would ever question you when you were pulling out with the stuff?
>
> *#7:* No, nobody is there. No not during them years.

As this method of theft became more popular in the mid-1960s, it

became necessary to pay terminal employees for the privilege of stealing, and many truck drivers took advantage of the opportunity to make
some extra money by selling their loads and reporting them stolen:

> *#7:* Alot of times when you are looking for stuff it comes to you. Guys
> come. They say look I have a trailer load of this; they give it up. They give
> it up and turn themselves in and say they got robbed.
> *Interviewer:* How often does that happen?
> *#7:* It happens alot. Alot of them are give-ups. Or you have the guards at
> the big railway yards, the big piggyback yards, they got the guards at the
> gate they let you get out.
> *Interviewer:* So you pay them a certain amount?
> *#7:* Yeah, they get paid, yeah everybody's out to get a buck. Everybody's
> out to make money. Everybody's got a little bit of greed. Y'know a guy
> making $10,000 a year, the guy is busting his ass. He wants to buy a
> house. Somehow you make contact. You make contacts because he's
> working there, he's working with guys you know. Most guys in that busi-
> ness, the trucking business, truck drivers, they're all thieves. They won't
> get a gun and shoot nobody. But take a case of this or a case of that. But
> then it comes to a point where they want a whole trailer. You get friendly
> with the guards, learn their likes and dislikes. Pretty soon you know
> them.

The thief who steals the contents of tractor trailers without the
explicit cooperation of the driver must accomplish a number of tasks
that differ from those of the man who is in collusion with the driver. The
two essential tasks are to stop the truck and to manage the
driver/victim properly. Below one of our hijackers describes the accomplishment of these tasks as simple matters:

> *Interviewer:* How do you stop a truck?
> *#8:* It stops at a light.
> *Interviewer:* And you just go up and say move over Jack?
> *#8:* That's right.
> *Interviewer:* And then what do you do with the driver?
> *#8:* You put him in the car, you drive around for maybe two, three hours
> and you let him off. Make sure he's got money in his pockets so he can get
> where he's got to go. . . . I mean usually the guy's alright. What are you
> gonna leave him handcuffed to a pole in Jersey, out in the wilderness? I
> mean the guy's got to have money in his pocket, if he ain't got money in
> his pocket, he ain't going nowhere. He'll be out there for years, you know.
> I'm not looking to hurt a guy. You just say, "Listen, stay here for 20
> minutes and then leave. Nobody's gonna hurt you."

Once the driver is kidnapped, the stolen truck is taken to a prearranged spot where the goods are transferred to a second truck in which
they will be taken to the buyer. The stolen truck is driven some distance
from the switch area and abandoned.

The acquisition component of the acquisition-distribution system for stealing tractor trailers does not require a great deal of technical sophistication. As is the case with the mechanics of taking the truck, selecting the target is a simple matter. The thief tries to steal truck loads of high-value, low-volume consumer goods; for example, our two hijackers told us independently that a load of razor blades would be an ideal score. Sometimes, hijackers receive information about possible scores from tipsters; they, in turn, receive 10 percent of the value of the score to the hijacker if their information is accurate and useful. Other times, the thief judges the content by the container. He knows that certain companies carry certain kinds of loads and he bases his target decision on this knowledge.

The key to success in the business of theft of entire trailer loads of goods is distribution. People in the acquisition end of the business prefer to have a buyer for the load before they steal it. The buyer is usually a big-league fence who distributes the goods to legitimate distributors.

There is some variation in how these criminal middlemen conduct business. Some operate as factors. They promise the thief one-third of the wholesale value of the goods or some percentage of the sale price and sell the goods to a legitimate wholesaler or retailer for two-thirds of the wholesale value or more. They do not take possession of the goods. They arrange to have the thief deliver to the buyer, or to have the buyer pick up the load from the thief. Other criminal middlemen function as wholesalers. They buy stolen merchandise by the trailer load and store it until they find a suitable buyer. They keep their inventory in rented garages or yards.

The experiences of our subjects indicate that it is not unusual for the motivated and enterprising thief to advance from acquisition to distribution. Three of our four men who were in the business of appropriating trailer loads of goods eventually operated as major-league fences. The remaining thief sold stolen property in less-than-trailer-load lots in addition to hijacking.

Our fences informed us that the most important aspect of distribution is, as might be expected, whom you know. They told us that, over the years (each of these men was at least thirty-five), they met the thieves, truckers, and legitimate businessmen who comprised their distribution networks. The network, which includes those involved in both crime at work and crime as work, is not something that emerges full blown when one decides to become a fence. As in most other businesses, the network develops in a snowball fashion:

> #7: Y'know being around that type of environment you learn people who buy that type of thing. You get to know people who handle those things, who make the buy. There is always a guy who could handle something. People who own big shopping centers maybe would buy.

Interviewer: Where did you get to know these people, how did you get to know them?

#7: I don't know, it's a strange thing. When a guy is a thief all his life he always gets to meet these people. You know, you get to meet them. You would know this guy, he being a thief and you being a thief, and he knows somebody else. Everybody has a little larceny in them. Most people have it. Even legitimate businessmen. Men in big shopping centers. We have taken loads of stuff to big shopping centers. One time we got a load of copper, went to a big wire company that made copper quarter-inch wire. When we loaded it off the truck, they were putting it in the machine, and it was coming out in the other side of the machine thick as your hair. He was paying above the going price just to get it. Legitimate businessmen. He needed the copper for orders. It was during the shortage. Here's a guy who took a shot with a multi-million dollar business.

Interviewer: You heard about him from somebody else?

#7: Well, yes I met him through somebody else. The guy I went through was one of the bigger thieves.

A NOTE ON SPECIALIZATION

The way we have been portraying our subjects so far may give the impression that they specialized in one criminal activity; this impression is contrary to the observations of Gould et al. (1966), Letkemann (1973), and Shover (1971). Our findings do not dispute those of these researchers, however. Indeed, they support them. The previous section describes the primary activities of our men or their major criminal enterprise. Most of these men had been involved in a variety of criminal activities. For example, one of the more criminally diversified subjects admitted involvement in burglary (commercial and household), robbery (commercial and personal), assault (with and without a weapon), larceny, sale of dangerous drugs, and collecting for a loan shark. In addition, he had been convicted of arson and corrupting the morals of a minor, but he denied involvement in the former and guilt in the latter. This man's legitimate employment record showed corresponding variability: construction worker, amusement-variety store operator, rubbish collector, car carrier driver, foundry worker, and agent for go-go dancers.

The variety of criminal work performed by the men in our sample over their lives is probably not much different from the variety of legitimate work performed by most men over their lives. Many men experiment with jobs or simply flounder in the job market, or perhaps in life in general, in their formative years. As they grow older, they usually recognize the need to forge some preference-skill-opportunity convergence, and they settle into a line of work (see Sparks, Greer, and Manning, 1982: ch. 5).

Most of the men we interviewed reported what Letkemann calls "having a line" and describes as ". . . a generalized work preference and a related repertoire of skills, which can be adapted to various related crimes should reasons of practicality, economics, and unique opportunities so dictate" (1973:35).

Some of our subjects felt that the broader the definition of one's line, within the limits of good taste and property crime, of course, the better off one is. In this respect, it is like level of measurement: You can always go down the scale but you cannot go up it. Some of our interviewees observed that the man who specializes reduces opportunities and increases risk:

> *#6:* I wouldn't hijack all the time because it's no good. So you do a little swag, you know. Somebody's got something they want to sell, they want to sell this thing. Alright, I'll give you a good price and I'll sell that. There's all other ways to make money.

DEVELOPING A LINE

Developing a crime line is not a linear process, and there are a number of different paths of entry into the business. Some of our men were proponents of the "born under a bad sign" explanation. These men saw themselves as almost predestined to a life of crime—one which they began shortly after birth:

> *#10:* . . . I was only 5, 5½ years old. . . . I ended up being friends with this kid. And then we started stealing. Small things, you know, we'd see fifty cents, we went and robbed it, that's right. I'd do it like a damn fool and he'd do the same thing and robbing other places here and there. . . . Like the penny arcade, like candy and stuff, you know, stealing candy for our friends.

A variation on this explanation is exposure to a disorganized environment (see Shover, 1971:66). Some men considered their early crimes the result of economic deprivation and restricted opportunity, while others attributed them to internalization of neighborhood values.

Other men, who committed their first offenses much later in life, at twenty-seven, for example, blamed economic desperation and a sudden opportunity to make big money. For these men, the devil usually came in the shape of a long-lost friend:

> *#11:* Someone tooted the horn at me so I looked and it was an old friend of mine that I hadn't seen for about 10 years, and he's driving a brand new car, big Pontiac Grand Prix, waves me into the car, so I jump into the car, and I said, "Jesus, how you doing? How you been?" "Good, how you doing," you know. We went to have coffee and renew old relationships, and I said, "Jesus, you look like you're doing really good, you've got a

320   J. J. GIBBS, P. L. SHELLY

brand new car," you know. He was dressed nice, and I said, "How are you doing it?" He takes out his wallet, and he couldn't fold it, you know, it wouldn't fold shut, that's how much money he had—50's, 100's—this is back in the 60's and he's got all this money. So he says, "You still working at the jewelry store." I says, "Yes, I am." He says, "Well, if you ever decide to get out of there let me know," you know. And after I quit the job I called him, you know. It was a few days later, probably after a week or so went by I realized well, "Gee, things don't look too good." I got in touch with him, and I said, "Well I quit my job and I'm broke." And at that time I separated from my wife. I was staying with my mother, I went back and stayed with my mother. So he says, "Well, I have a market that I'm going to do and you can come along with me on that," and all of a sudden I was hoping he'd say well maybe in a couple of months.

Shover notes (1971:66–68) that service in the armed forces can predispose some men to a criminal life style. Three of the interviewees saw some connection between their service experiences and their involvement in crime for gain:

> *#6:* I ran a messhall for the officers mess, I ran the officer's club, I really enjoyed it, and then that's when I started drinking. . . . I had a good time with booze, yeah, I think, well you know, what do they say, you know, "When you're in the army you drink, all soldiers drink," and I drank too, you know, you drink a beer, you start with a beer and then you go up to bigger things.
> *Interviewer:* But in the army you picked up some skills. Managerial skills?
>
> *#6:* Yes, cooking, I picked up a few skills . . . more or less. But I also did a little conniving when I was in the army too. Nothing big but, you know enough to make a living. . . . Black market, you know, black market stuff, that's all.

No matter what is seen as the reason for the original descent or ascent into crime, our subjects invariably considered the jail as a place where the crime line takes shape. Shover notes that for many of the burglars he interviewed confinement resulted in

> . . . a more complete embracement of a deviant identity. This is because, as Irwin (1970) has suggested, the prison experience produces considerable polarization among inmates. Those who identify with the more sophisticated deviants frequently spend a great deal of time fantasizing about—and in some cases actually planning—future *scores* (Irwin, 1970). This process commonly serves as the mechanism for the creation and/or reinforcement of personal commitments to crime and criminal others. As a result one may become obligated to continue stealing after release (1971:84).

We know it is trite to write this in 1982—it might be trite even if it were 1892—but jails and prisons are schools for crime. For our men, the jail provided the environment in which technical skills were introduced and acquisition and distribution networks developed. It was a place in which one became seasoned and acquired veteran status. It was a marketplace for ideas.

> *#11:* ... And we did meet some burglars there [in county jail] that were pretty good burglars. We had opened a round door by then, and they had never opened one, and so we had a lot in common. And we used to get together, you know, shoot the breeze, talk about different scores, different mistakes, you know, things that each other had ran into, or things they picked up, you know, swapping information, ideas.... And we used to talk about alarm systems and this and that, ideas we got from people in jail, what they were gonna do, and we'd talk about when we got out, "We'll try something like that."

> *#10:* Well, you might say, everything I've learned, I've learned in jail. That's where it comes from really. I didn't learn it on the street. Most of my thing was when I was in county jail, I think on my first bit, let me see, I went to the county jail when I was 16. In jail, in the county jail a lot of guys meet there and you have bull sessions and they explain how to do it, "This is how you rob a safe, how you do this," and you go by things that they told you. And you did it yourself, tried it out, and it worked. You know what to look for, how to break an alarm system, how to wire, everything, and people would explain, this is right down the line, everything would be explained.

Doing time is to the thief as combat is to the soldier or going ten rounds is to the boxer. It is a confirmation of veteran status, a sign that the man has faced the harshest reality of the occupation and survived. It is an indication that he is a stand-up, knock-around, sure-enough guy who can be trusted:

> *#6:* Most of the guys that I know, we've all been back and forth to jail so we know we can trust 'em.

> *#10:* Well, you know who's been in jail, and who hasn't been in jail around the neighborhood, who you can depend on, who you can't depend on.

HIGH ROLLING IN THE FAST LANE

Life in the fast lane is a luxury and necessity, pleasure and business, for the thief. In this section, we will describe the relation between the work of the thief and his life style. We will explore the links between his demonstrative spending, business promotion, fatalism, and need for excitement.

No matter what the perceived motivation or intention for beginning a life in crime, most of the thieves we interviewed agreed that one reason for remaining a thief is the attraction of life in the fast lane. The hedonistic abandon indulged in by some thieves after a score—the free spending on wine, women, clothes, and cars—has value in its own right as excitement. It is also important as an expression of autonomy and status. Some of the descriptions furnished by our subjects are like caricatures of Miller's lower class focal concern—excitement (Miller, 1958). Men spend thousands of dollars reveling with friends and acquaintances. Below two of our subjects recount the benefits of their prestigious occupation, at times with almost giddy self-consciousness:

> *#6:* ... You're thinking of making money and popularity, "Here comes such and such," a guy you know he's with such and such or he's associated with these people. There's a lot of prestige in it because they think you're a gangster, you're a wise guy, whatever terminology you want to use, you know, you're a knock-around guy. Always dresses nice, always looks good. You walk in a bar, you'll find a line of drinks, already. As soon as you walk in, "Here comes so and so, you know," and there's a lot of prestige. ... Girls at the time, they get a kick out of going out with a guy that they know is a knock-around guy or stand-up guy. And they think right away, "He's this guy or that," you know, but they says, you know, "there's an aroma around you, about you". ... I walked in. Here's so and so, "Give him a drink as soon as he walks in." Naturally years ago you could never buy anybody a drink but now you can walk in and buy the whole bar a drink, so it will cost you $500, what difference does it make? You have it in your pocket. Alright so maybe you only clear $5,000 or $6,000 a piece. So now next week or so what's $6,000, according to the way you live. That's no money at all. So maybe you'll hijack another truck in two weeks. And you do it until you get to where you want. ... I never put my money that I made in business. I used to party a lot. Now my partying, don't mix me with anybody else, I don't smoke dope or I don't take any dope, my parties is to be around people, I love to be around my friends, and you know, you own the bar, or you own the nightclub you're in, and you can go for $2,000 a week with no problem. 'Cause you're out every night.

> *#11:* I went to this movie once. ... There was safe-crackers in it and it showed them bypassing an alarm system. And I felt, "Gee look at that, that's exciting." It's gotta be exciting or else they wouldn't of made a film out of it. So, I was actually living that life. It was exciting in a way, in the beginning it was exciting. You know driving down the road, I got a hundred in my pocket. I got nice clothes, I'm living good. Another thing about that is in the beginning they didn't know. I spent money. People knew I had money, but they didn't know where I got it. Word got around. I was seen with different small time people. You're seen with different people like this guy, word gets around. Word gets around quick. Word of mouth is the best advertising. Before you know it, I was affiliated with gangsters. "He hangs around gangsters. That's where he gets his money." It sorta gives you status. Women like that. For some reason that type of excitement draws women. I don't know why. I notice that. I always had some broad come up to me and say, "You're a crook, aren't you?" It was exciting for them to be around gangsters. Somebody that they thought lived

dangerously. . . . Well, like I said you know money generates power. Do you know what I mean? If you got money you can do anything you want. . . . You don't have any responsibilities. Do anything you want. You don't have to go to work. You can go to the park, go party tonight, go up to Cape Cod. It's nice, the only ones who can do that are the ones with money. They can afford it.[7]

Living life in the fast lane requires a tremendous amount of money. From conversations with our subject about expenditures, we estimated that some spent over $50,000 a year on entertainment alone. Most of the men we interviewed could not pay for a fraction of these expenses with the money made on any legitimate job they held; only four of them were legitimately employed at the time of their arrest. Their expensive habits were supported almost exclusively through the proceeds of criminal enterprise.

Most thieves do not go out on scores every day. The most common pattern described was one or a series of jobs followed by a period of leisure and job searching. During this period of relative inactivity, thieves sometimes borrow from their neighborhood bankers, shylocks, to maintain the life style to which they have become accustomed:

> #6: . . . let's use hijacking, you're not supposed to do one every week because the odds are too much against you, alright. But what happens in the meantime is that you're spending whatever you made the last time. So the idea is to try to cover yourself all the time. Like I never invested my money. You always owed shylocks money, or you owed somebody money because you're partying, you have to pay your house bills, your bills go on. So the next score comes, you're bailing yourself out. . . . But you're never supposed to do a score when you're desperate, when you're broke. Because you're vulnerable to make mistakes. You have pressure on you, you've gotta do it, you've gotta do it, and that's when you get caught.

One would think that if a thief were having a difficult time meeting expenses, he would cut back as the rest of us do in such circumstances. Is the thief so hedonistic that he can't reduce his consumption? Is his self-esteem so attached to ostentatious spending that a public display of austerity is out of the question? Perhaps. However, as the thief sees it, image maintenance has more than psychological benefits; it is good business. "You have to have money to make money. . . . look prosperous to get prosperous. . . . look like you're working to get a job. . . . and so on. . . ."

Unless a thief is strictly a lone operator who steals only cash, he needs at least a rudimentary distribution system to do business. Since the thief cannot advertise in the usual places people selling services and products do, he typically must establish a network of personal contacts

7. There is also a drug addict's version of the thieves' life style. It includes the purchase and consumption of huge quantities of drugs with friends and crime partners.

to conduct business. He keeps abreast of developments by making the rounds or the circuit. The thief advertises that he is active in the trade by circulating, dropping in the taverns, restaurants, and clubs that are frequented (and sometimes staffed and owned) by core members of the local acquisition-distribution network.

The traditions and conventions associated with making the rounds can be expensive. The thief may be expected to buy a costly round of drinks or pick up a dinner tab or two. To display less than the utmost generosity can mean that the thief lost his heart or balls, his willingness to take a risk; therefore he is being careful with his money. For the fence, it may mean he doesn't have enough money to cover a score if one comes his way. Such interpretations of one's actions can put one out of business. Nobody likes to deal with a loser:

> *#7:* Especially if people think you're earning money, if they think you've got money, they're gonna come to you more, it's a fucking game really, if you've got a good front, if you're always dressed, if you've always got money in your pocket, if you know how to carry yourself, they look at your car, look at what this guy's earning, they ain't worrying about getting paid now, see, so they're gonna come to you because they think you've got money.

Theoretically, support for life in the fast lane could come from money from scores that has been invested. One of the guiding principles of the thief is to invest part of the score. The other is never go out on a score when you need money. While all our subjects accepted the validity of these cardinal rules, they all violated them at some time or other:

> *#6:* I don't like to live on anybody else's, I like to live on my own. But see, then you're getting in something so involved, you've gotta do it anyway. Like I said, if you're younger, if you want to do everything like partying, back and forth to Vegas all the time, you gamble a little bit, you know, and you spend it as fast as you can make it. In other words, I didn't invest it in anything else to keep me going so I wouldn't have to take a truck or I wouldn't have to go rob this store or rob this factory or whatever it is that comes up. You let yourself get desperate, you should never do that.

The failure of these men to plan financially, even in the short run, can be explained, in part, by their fatalistic posture. These men assumed, realistically, that getting caught was inevitable:

> *#7:* Yeah, you're crazy, 'cause you know you're going to be caught. There's no way you would not get caught. . . . You take a long shot, you make a big score, and retire. You're not doing that. . . . This is a never-ending thing—you're in Connecticut, you're in Pennsylvania, you're in New York, you're all over the joint. I mean, you're bound to meet agents, undercover, or you're bound to meet rats, that will set you up, turn you in. Which I got set up in, once.

#8: Percentage wise you've gotta get caught. . . . you've gotta get caught, your luck can run thin. You're gonna get caught for something, even if it's not for the hijacking or the possession of stolen property, you must get caught for something. Because now, today, they made it a profitable business to tell on people. And even if the person didn't do it.

The uncertainty that the thief lives with is not whether he will be caught; the question is when. A restricted future time perspective and a hedonistic life style are compatible with such fatalistic assumptions. We would expect the thief to live fast and live well for today.

The benefits of life in the fast lane are a sufficient condition for some men to continue stealing. Others, however, continue to steal because they find the action exciting. There is a thrill associated with theft and wheeling and dealing in hot property:

#2: Sometimes I got off, you know. I got over like a fat rat, you know. It was exciting. . . .
Interviewer: What's it like when you're cruising and you see something, what kind of feelings do you have?
#2: Well, what I'm trying to say, if a girl was walking down the street with no clothes on, "WOW, look at this, you know, WOW, beautiful broad walking down the street with no clothes on," visualize that and that's how I feel. . . . You know she's yours. Like that, like that, it was exciting. It really was. Then it was exciting, now I get the chills when I think about it. . . .

#8: I don't know why I chose this life. I like the excitement, I like the, I just like the excitement, I like when the adrenalin starts pumping for some reason when I'm out there. I can work on this thing and this and this and this. I can have seven, eight different things going on at one time. It's not boring. It's not an everyday routine.

#11: I was hooked after that, that was it, it was almost like heroin I think, you know. I had shot the vein and that was it. I was ready to go, and it scared the hell out of me. And I'll tell you, I'll be honest with you, I think that thrill has a lot to do with it. People climb mountains and get scared, people jump out of airplanes and get scared, they do all kinds of crazy things that they're risking their life at, just for, I think, it's that thrill, that thrill of excitement, you know, excitement. People watch TV and watch things like this on TV and get excited, you know. They go to the movies to see that stuff. Here I am; wound up doing it, but the end result is the money, the profit, I got $2,000. . . . That was a lot of money, you know, hard cold cash, you know. I could get up on the floor and start dancing about it, you know.

The frenetic and variable pace of the life of the thief precludes full-time legitimate employment in most cases. The few who did have legitimate occupations were in businesses that were closely associated with illegal acquisition-distribution networks, for example, taverns, restaurants, scrap, and salvage.

The thief requires flexibility in his home and work life. When the opportunity for the score is there, he must be prepared to respond. Some of our subjects described it as being on call twenty-four hours a day:

> *Interviewer:* Sounds like it's 24 hours a day. Do you have a regular schedule where you go to bed at 11 and get up at 7 and to go to work at . . .
> *#6:* No, any hour, get called any hour. Or you have to meet a guy—maybe a guy's working nights himself—"Meet me at 2 in the morning at a diner and I'll have something for you" or "meet me in New York." Maybe he was going out on a date, after that took a ride, and "then meet me in the Bronx or in Brooklyn." Back alleys. Before a flight. . . .
> *#7:* But this business is a 24-hour-a-day business because you're not settling at just one. It's 24 hours a day. I got called one time at 1 o'clock in the morning, "come on let's go," I didn't even know what he had. But I came, he had a whole load of something, he's gotta get rid of it. Alright, it's constant, it's 24 hours, it's a business.

Although being on call all day every day certainly indicates some consistency, as we pointed out previously, these men do not engage in criminal activity on a regular basis. Some men report that they go out on scores only when they need money or when they are invited to go out on a good score. Others provide descriptions of criminal activities that are like those of the junkie's run or drunkard's binge. In the excerpt appearing below, one of subjects describes the pattern of his colleague:

> *#11:* I thought I was hooked. This guy went crazy, he went and bought tools, he went up and down the commercial boulevards every night, you know, one step ahead of the cops, because they're looking for it, they'd cruise up the street with their lights out trying to catch this guy. He just went crazy, he couldn't steal enough.

CONCLUSION

In this article, we have described some aspects of the work and life style of men who are by self-definition thieves. We have painted our portrait in broad strokes, and thereby lost some of the interesting variation among thieves. This was necessary to avoid writing a number of short biographies on individual thieves. Our job was to describe what was common among thieves, not to bring attention to the unique.

The patterns we have presented describe some of our subjects all of the time, and all of our subjects some of the time. In the future, we hope to collect information on a greater number and wider variety of thieves to see whether our patterns hold.

Our objective was to describe the work of thieves, and to explore the interaction between crime at work and life style. There remains plenty of rich content in our interviews to be explored and described: How much do thieves make? How do they divide up the proceeds of the score? How many people work together? How do they get caught? We can provide short answers to some of these questions in this article. A more detailed description will be provided in the future.

Thieves make and spend what the average citizen would consider enormous amounts of money. When asked to estimate their income for the year before their incarceration (and in smaller time units), most of the subjects could not provide us with an answer. Thieves think in terms of scores, and they informed us there is a great deal of variation in score payoff; so much variation that they could not compute an average that would describe their income accurately.

We made some computations based on information they furnished on entertainment expenses, average score, and frequency of theft. If the information our subjects provided us with is accurate, most of them made in excess of $75,000. Some made considerably more.

Most of the commercial burglars we interviewed worked with one partner. In most cases, they were more than business associates; they were best friends who worked and played together. Partners always divided the score money right down the middle.

The hijackers and the first commercial burglar we described worked in crews. The specific members of the work crew could change from job to job, but members were selected from a small group of people. There was usually a core member or members who would organize, plan, and go out on every score. Most crews divided the proceeds of the score equally among members. However, there were some reports of scores for which participants received various percentages of the score for their work and risk taking.

Most thieves get caught, they say, because other thieves get caught. The men we interviewed put to rest forever the notion of honor among thieves. Thieves also get caught because they make mistakes. We will end this article with a description of the most spectacular error told to us.

> *#11:* I've had alot of things happen to me on burglaries and the first time we ever used the explosives. Sam[8] came out of prison. While he was in Attica he met a guy from Canada who was a burglar, full-time burglar and the guy used nitroglycerin and he showed Sam how to make it. So he made up a batch, this guy, you know, pour this acid, pour this acid and you pour this stuff and you stir it up, and there you go, you've got nitroglycerin, pure nitroglycerin. So Fred and I went down to a market to try this stuff out; a couple of mobbed up guys were with us on this burglary and they thought we were nuts, you know. I was scared of the stuff, you know. He's got this bottle full of nitroglycerin, I really don't know any-

8. Names have been changed to protect the preposterous.

thing about it, maybe the guy made a mistake, maybe if you yell too loud it will go off, you know, so we went inside this supermarket. I really didn't like this store because it was a free-standing building, it was all by itself, you know, they could surround it. So we chopped a hole in the roof, went inside the building, moved the safe out of the office into a back room. It wasn't really a back room, they had a storage room, but it was on the side of the building rather than in back of the building. We moved the safe in there and flipped it up on its back and we put a bolt in the door, by that time we had an iron called a burning bar. We made a miniature burning bar, we had the little mini-cage, little bolts. It was just enough to put a hole in a safe. So we take the safe to the back door, put it on its back, put a hole through the door, and fill it up with water, fill it right up with water, and when it goes off, naturally, the water doesn't move, the water's already pressed so it blows the door off, it blows the sides off, you know, just blows the safe up. So Fred had about 6 ounces of this stuff, and the guy says 2 is plenty, 2 ounces is more than enough. And he had a hose, like the older kind, a clear carburetor hose, you can see the gas line through it, and he used this hose to pour the nitro in. Had a cork in the top with a plastic cap down through the center of the core, ok, the wires coming out to a real wire, it was like an extension that we could run 200 feet away, and plug into an outlet. Naturally, the dc current would set the cap off and set the explosives off. Well when he filled the hose up, you know, the thing was full, of course the hole in it was small, but he used all of it, he used the whole 6 ounces. I said, "Jesus I think you're using a little too much, what do you think." He says, "Nah, I want to make sure it's opened, I don't want to look bad in front of these guys, in case we don't get the money." So you can imagine what happened. We went to the end of the store room, he was gonna plug in and I says, "Wait, look, I'm gonna go on the other side of the room," to the back door where we usually go in and out of, you know. Completely from here to here I went, and he stayed down on the end. So he plugged it in and I heard boom, boom, loud thing, you know, it was a loud noise. I ran outside and one of the guys says, like he thought it was all planned or what have you, "Are the lights supposed to go out outside?" All the spotlights exploded. So I said, "I don't know, let me go see," so I run back inside and here's Fred coming, staggering from the back room in a daze, he's like feeling his body to see if he had any arms or legs, I says "are you ok," "I gotta get out of here," and he takes off out the door, you know. I go outside and he's just wandering through the woods, he's in shock. So I thought, "Well hell, I might as well see what happened," you know, so I run across the back of the store and I threw these swinging doors open and I hear, shhhhhh . . . macaroni, spaghetti, beans, corn, the place looked like, oh it was a mess, it was everywhere, I forgot what they call that dish, but I mean it was just all over the walls, spaghetti was hanging from the ceiling, that Chef-Boy-R-Dee macaroni, oh it was a mess and I'm sliding in the syrup stuff that was on the floor and I go into the storeroom and the door to the cooler was inside the cooler, they blew it right inside the door, I swear, and there was egg yolk running, you know, there must have been 40 dozen eggs, they broke and they were all over the floor, water, all the pipes were gone, water just spraying, it was raining, it was just like it was raining in there. What had happened was, we had definitely used too much nitroglycerin, the side of the safe came off, and when it came off it was just like a cannonball, it went through every one of those canned goods. It left a hole, a trail right through all those stacks and rows of cases of goods, right, destroyed them, just ripped right through the cans and cases and everything. The roof of the round door, I mean this was a big door, the door was like this, weighs 350 pounds, I look up and there's a hole in the roof, a great big hole. I think the safe door is still in orbit, I swear 'cause it was gone. I asked the guy on rounds outside, "Did you hear anything come down, loud noise out there?" "No, I didn't hear nothing." I'm scared to death, maybe the thing went over the other side of town and came down on somebody's car or in some guy's bedroom. Oh my God, you know. It really scared me. Fred, you know, he was standing inside the cases and the thing went shoooooo, you know, it was a mess. He had this gook all over him, you know. And the drawers, the bottom of the safe was still there, that was the only thing left was the bottom of the safe and it was embedded in the floor, it was like tile, embedded. The trays were completely flat, all those plastic trays, and the coins were mangled, dimes embedded in the quarters, and the bags were still there so I picked up the bags, what I could find, you know, it was really a mess, I left and went home. But that was our first experience with nitroglycerin.

Interviewer: I'm surprised you used it again, after that.

#11: We used less.

REFERENCES

GIBBS, J. J., and P. L. SHELLY
  1982 *Commercial Theft Studies Project Final Report.* Newark, N.J.: Center for the Study of the Causes of Crime for Gain, School of Criminal Justice, Rutgers University.

GOULD, L. C., et al.
  1966 "Crime as a Profession: A Report on Professional Criminals in Four American Cities." Final Report to the President's Commission on Law Enforcement and Administration of Justice.

LETKEMANN, P.
  1973 *Crime as Work.* Englewood Cliffs, N.J.: Prentice-Hall.

LEVI, M.
  1981 *The Phantom Capitalist.* London, England: Heinemann.

MILLER, W. B.
  1958 "Lower Class Culture as a Generating Milieu of Gang Delinquency." *Journal of Social Issues* 14: 5–19.

RYAN, A., ed.
  1973 "Introduction." *The Philosophy of Social Explanation.* London, England: Oxford University Press.

330   J. J. GIBBS, P. L. SHELLY

SHOVER, N. E.
  1971   "Burglary as an Occupation." Ph.D. diss.: University of Illinois at Urbana-Champaign.
  1973   "The Social Organization of Burglary." *Social Problems* 20 (4): 499–514.

SPARKS, R. F.
  1981   "Center for the Study of the Causes of Crime for Gain Annual Report 1980–1981." Newark, N.J.: School of Criminal Justice, Rutgers University.

SPARKS, R. F., A. GREER, and S. A. MANNING
  1982   "Theoretical Studies Project Final Report." Newark, N.J.: Center for the Study of the Causes of Crime for Gain, School of Criminal Justice, Rutgers University.

SUTHERLAND, E. H.
  1937   *The Professional Thief.* Chicago: University of Chicago Press.

[7]

On Cooling the Mark Out[†]

Some Aspects of Adaptation to Failure

Erving Goffman[*]

IN CASES OF CRIMINAL FRAUD, victims find they must suddenly adapt themselves to the loss of sources of security and status which they had taken for
granted. A consideration of this adaptation to loss can lead us to an understanding of
some relations in our society between involvements and the selves that are involved.

In the argot of the criminal world, the term "mark" refers to any individual who is a victim or prospective victim of certain forms of planned illegal exploitation. The mark is the sucker—the person who is taken in. An instance of the operation of any particular racket, taken through the full cycle of its steps or phases, is sometimes called a play. The persons who operate the racket and "take" the mark are occasionally called operators.

The confidence game—the con, as its practitioners call it—is a way of obtaining money under false pretenses by the exercise of fraud and deceit. The con differs from politer forms of financial deceit in important ways. The con is practiced on private persons by talented actors who methodically and regularly build up informal social relationships just for the purpose of abusing them; white-collar crime is practiced on organizations by persons who learn to abuse positions of trust which they once filled faithfully. The one exploits poise; the other, position. Further, a con man is someone who accepts a social role in the underworld community; he is part of a brotherhood whose members make no pretense to one another of being "legit." A white-collar criminal, on the other hand, has no colleagues, al-though he may have an associate with whom he plans his crime and a wife to whom he confesses it.

The con is said to be a good racket in the United States only because most Americans are willing, nay eager, to make easy money, and will engage in action that is less than legal in order to do so. The typical play has typical phases. The potential sucker is first spotted, and one member of the working team (called the outside man, steerer, or roper) arranges to make social contact with him. The confidence of the mark is won, and he is given an opportunity to invest his money in a gambling venture which he understands to have been fixed in his favor. The venture, of course, is fixed, but not in his favor. The mark is permitted to win some money and then persuaded to invest more. There is an "accident" or "mistake," and the mark loses his total investment. The operators then depart in a ceremony that is called the blowoff or sting. They leave the mark but take his money. The mark is expected to go on his way, a little wiser and a lot poorer.

Sometimes, however, a mark is not quite prepared to accept his loss as a gain in experience and to say and do nothing about his venture. He may feel moved to

* A.B. Univ. of Toronto 45; M.A., Sociology, Univ. of Chicago 49; Instr., Dept. of Social Anthropology, Univ. of Edinburgh, and field research in the Shetland Islands 49-51; admitted to candidacy for Ph.D. in Sociology, Univ. of Chicago; Rsc. Asst., Division of Social Sciences, Univ. of Chicago 52-. For bibliography, see Reference Lists section of this issue.

† Terminology regarding criminal activity is taken primarily from D. W. Maurer, *The Big Con* (New York, Bobbs-Merrill, 1940), and also from E. Sutherland, *The Professional Thief* (Chicago, Univ. of Chicago Press, 1937). The approach that this paper attempts to utilize is taken from Everett C. Hughes of the University of Chicago, who is not responsible for any misapplications of it which may occur here. The sociological problem of failure was first suggested to me by James Littlejohn of the University of Edinburgh. I am grateful to Professor E. A. Shils for criticism and to my wife, Angelica S. Goffman, for assistance.

complain to the police or to chase after the operators. In the terminology of the trade, the mark may squawk, beef, or come through. From the operators' point of view, this kind of behavior is bad for business. It gives the members of the mob a bad reputation with such police as have not yet been fixed and with marks who have not yet been taken. In order to avoid this adverse publicity, an additional phase is sometimes added at the end of the play. It is called cooling the mark out. After the blowoff has occurred, one of the operators stays with the mark and makes an effort to keep the anger of the mark within manageable and sensible proportions. The operator stays behind his team-mates in the capacity of what might be called a cooler and exercises upon the mark the art of consolation. An attempt is made to define the situation for the mark in a way that makes it easy for him to accept the inevitable and quietly go home. The mark is given instruction in the philosophy of taking a loss.

When we call to mind the image of a mark who has just been separated from his money, we sometimes attempt to account for the greatness of his anger by the greatness of his financial loss. This is a narrow view. In many cases, especially in America, the mark's image of himself is built up on the belief that he is a pretty shrewd person when it comes to making deals and that he is not the sort of person who is taken in by anything. The mark's readiness to participate in a sure thing is based on more than avarice; it is based on a feeling that he will now be able to prove to himself that he is the sort of person who can "turn a fast buck." For many, this capacity for high finance comes near to being a sign of masculinity and a test of fulfilling the male role.

It is well known that persons protect themselves with all kinds of rationalizations when they have a buried image of themselves which the facts of their status do not support. A person may tell himself many things: that he has not been given a fair chance; that he is not really interested in becoming something else; that

the time for showing his mettle has not yet come; that the usual means of realizing his desires are personally or morally distasteful, or require too much dull effort. By means of such defenses, a person saves himself from committing a cardinal social sin—the sin of defining oneself in terms of a status while lacking the qualifications which an incumbent of that status is supposed to possess.

A mark's participation in a play, and his investment in it, clearly commit him in his own eyes to the proposition that he is a smart man. The process by which he comes to believe that he cannot lose is also the process by which he drops the defenses and compensations that previously protected him from defeats. When the blowoff comes, the mark finds that he has no defense for not being a shrewd man. He has defined himself as a shrewd man and must face the fact that he is only another easy mark. He has defined himself as possessing a certain set of qualities and then proven to himself that he is miserably lacking in them. This is a process of self-destruction of the self. It is no wonder that the mark needs to be cooled out and that it is good business policy for one of the operators to stay with the mark in order to talk him into a point of view from which it is possible to accept a loss.

In essence, then, the cooler has the job of handling persons who have been caught out on a limb—persons whose expectations and self-conceptions have been built up and then shattered. The mark is a person who has compromised himself, in his own eyes if not in the eyes of others.

Although the term, mark, is commonly applied to a person who is given short-lived expectations by operators who have intentionally misrepresented the facts, a less restricted definition is desirable in analyzing the larger social scene. An expectation may finally prove false, even though it has been possible to sustain it for a long time and even though the operators acted in good faith. So, too, the disappointment of reasonable expectations, as well as misguided ones, creates a need for consolation. Persons who participate in what is recognized as a confidence game are found in only a few social settings, but persons who have to be cooled out are found in many. Cooling the mark out is one theme in a very basic social story.

For purposes of analysis, one may think of an individual in reference to the values or attributes of a socially recognized character which he possesses. Psychologists speak of a value as a personal involvement. Sociologists speak of a value as a status, role, or relationship. In either case, the character of the value that is possessed is taken in a certain way as the character of the person who possesses it. An alteration in the kinds of attributes possessed brings an alteration to the self-conception of the person who possesses them.

The process by which someone acquires a value is the process by which he surrenders the claim he had to what he was and commits himself to the conception of self which the new value requires or allows him to have. It is the process that persons who fall in love or take dope call getting hooked. After a person is hooked, he must go through another process by which his new involvement finds its proper place, in space and time, relative to the other calls, demands, and commitments that he has upon himself. At this point certain other persons suddenly begin to play an important part in the individual's story; they impinge upon him by virtue of the relationship they happen to have to the value in which he has become involved. This is not the place to consider the general kinds of impingement that are institutionalized in our society and the general social relationships that arise: the personal relationship, the professional relationship, and the business relationship. Here we are concerned only with the end of the story, the way in which a person becomes disengaged from one of his involvements.

In our society, the story of a person's involvement can end in one of three general ways. According to one type of ending, he may withdraw from one of his involvements or roles in order to acquire

a sequentially related one that is considered better. This is the case when a youth becomes a man, when a student becomes a practitioner, or when a man from the ranks is given a commission.

Of course, the person who must change his self at any one of these points of promotion may have profound misgivings. He may feel disloyal to the way of life that must be left behind and to the persons who do not leave it with him. His new role may require action that seems insincere, dishonest, or unfriendly. This he may experience as a loss in moral cleanliness. His new role may require him to forgo the kinds of risk-taking and exertion that he previously enjoyed, and yet his new role may not provide the kind of heroic and exalted action that he expected to find in it.[1] This he may experience as a loss in moral strength.

There is no doubt that certain kinds of role success require certain kinds of moral failure. It may therefore be necessary, in a sense, to cool the dubious neophyte in rather than out. He may have to be convinced that his doubts are a matter of sentimentality. The adult social view will be impressed upon him. He will be required to understand that a promotional change in status is voluntary desirable, and natural, and that loss of one's role in these circumstances is the ultimate test of having fulfilled it properly.

It has been suggested that a person may leave a role under circumstances that reflect favorably upon the way in which he performed it. In theory, at least, a related possibility must be considered. A person may leave a role and at the same time leave behind him the standards by which such roles are judged. The new thing that he becomes may be so different from the thing he was that criteria such as success or failure cannot be easily applied to the change which has occurred. He becomes lost to others that he may

---

[1] Mr. Hughes has lectured on this kind of disappointment, and one of his students has undertaken a special study of it. See Miriam Wagenschein, "'Reality Shock': A Study of Beginning School Teachers," M.A. thesis, Dept. of Sociology, Univ. of Chicago, 1950.

find himself; he is of the twice-born. In our society, perhaps the most obvious example of this kind of termination occurs when a woman voluntarily gives up a prestigeful profession in order to become a wife and a mother. It is to be noted that this illustrates an institutionalized movement; those who make it do not make news. In America most other examples of this kind of termination are more a matter of talk than of occurrence. For example, one of the culture heroes of our dinner-table mythology is the man who walks out on an established calling in order to write or paint or live in the country. In other societies, the kind of abdication being considered here seems to have played a more important role. In medieval China, for instance, anchoretic withdrawal apparently gave to persons of quite different station a way of retreating from the occupational struggle while managing the retreat in an orderly, face-saving fashion.[2]

Two basic ways in which a person can lose a role have been considered; he can be promoted out of it or abdicate from it. There is, of course, a third basic ending to the status story. A person may be involuntarily deprived of his position or involvement and made in return something that is considered a lesser thing to be. It is mainly in this third ending to a person's role that occasions arise for cooling him out. It is here that one deals in the full sense with the problem of persons' losing their roles.

Involuntary loss seems itself to be of two kinds. First, a person may lose a status in such a way that the loss is not taken as a reflection upon the loser. The loss of a loved one, either because of an accident that could not have been prevented or because of a disease that could not have been halted, is a case in point. Occupational retirement because of old age is another. Of course, the loss will inevitably alter the conception the loser has of himself and the conception others have of him, but the alteration itself will

------

[2] See, for example, Max Weber, *The Religion of China* (H. H. Gerth, tr.); Glencoe, Ill., Free Press, 1951; p. 178.

not be treated as a symbol of the fate he deserves to receive. No insult is added to injury. It may be necessary, none the less, to pacify the loser and resign him to his loss. The loser who is not held responsible for his loss may even find himself taking the mystical view that all involvements are part of a wider con game, for the more one takes pleasure in a particular role the more one must suffer when it is time to leave it. He may find little comfort in the fact that the play has provided him with an illusion that has lasted a lifetime. He may find little comfort in the fact that the operators had not meant to deceive him.

Secondly, a person may be involuntarily deprived of a role under circumstances which reflect unfavorably on his capacity for it. The lost role may be one that he had already acquired or one that he had openly committed himself to preparing for. In either case the loss is more than a matter of ceasing to act in a given capacity; it is ultimate proof of an incapacity. And in many cases it is even more than this. The moment of failure often catches a person acting as one who feels that he is an appropriate sort of person for the role in question. Assumption becomes presumption, and failure becomes fraud. To loss of substance is thereby added loss of face. Of the many themes that can occur in the natural history of an involvement, this seems to be the most melancholy. Here it will be quite essential and quite difficult to cool the mark out. I shall be particularly concerned with this second kind of loss—the kind that involves humiliation.

It should be noted, parenthetically, that one circle of persons may define a particular loss as the kind that casts no reflection on the loser, and that a different circle of persons may treat the same loss as a symbol of what the loser deserves. One must also note that there is a tendency today to shift certain losses of status from the category of those that reflect upon the loser to the category of those that do not. When persons lose their jobs, their courage, or their minds, we tend more and more to take a clinical or naturalistic view of the loss and a nonmoral view of their failure. We want to define a person as something that is not destroyed by the destruction of one of his selves. This benevolent attitude is in line with the effort today to publicize the view that occupational retirement is not the end of all active capacities but the beginning of new and different ones.

A consideration of consolation as a social process leads to four general problems having to do with the self in society. First, where in modern life does one find persons conducting themselves as though they were entitled to the rights of a particular status and then having to face up to the fact that they do not possess the qualification for the status? In other words, at what points in the structures of our social life are persons likely to compromise themselves or find themselves compromised? When is it likely that a person will have to disengage himself or become disengaged from one of his involvements? Secondly, what are the typical ways in which persons who find themselves in this difficult position can be cooled out; how can they be made to accept the great injury that has been done to their image of themselves, regroup their defenses, and carry on without raising a squawk? Thirdly, what, in general, can happen when a person refuses to be cooled out, that is, when he refuses to be pacified by the cooler? Fourthly, what arrangements are made by operators and marks to avoid entirely the process of consolation?

In all personal-service organizations customers or clients sometimes make complaints. A customer may feel that he has been given service in a way that is unacceptable to him—a way that he interprets as an offense to the conception he has of who and what he is. The management therefore has the problem of cooling the mark out. Frequently this function is allotted to specialists within the organization. In restaurants of some size, for example, one of the crucial functions of the hostess is to pacify customers whose self-conceptions have been injured by wait-

resses or by the food. In large stores the complaint department and the floorwalker perform a similar function.

One may note that a service organization does not operate in an anonymous world, as does a con mob, and is therefore strongly obliged to make some effort to cool the mark out. An institution, after all, cannot take it on the lam; it must pacify its marks.

One may also note that coolers in service organizations tend to view their own activity in a light that softens the harsher details of the situation. The cooler protects himself from feelings of guilt by arguing that the customer is not really in need of the service he expected to receive, that bad service is not really deprivational, and that beefs and complaints are a sign of bile, not a sign of injury. In a similar way, the con man protects himself from remorseful images of bankrupt marks by arguing that the mark is a fool and not a full-fledged person, possessing an inclination towards illegal gain but not the decency to admit it or the capacity to succeed at it.

In organizations patterned after a bureaucratic model, it is customary for personnel to expect rewards of a specified kind upon fulfilling requirements of a specified nature. Personnel come to define their career line in terms of a sequence of legitimate expectations and to base their self-conceptions on the assumption that in due course they will be what the institution allows persons to become. Sometimes, however, a member of an organization may fulfill some of the requirements for a particular status, especially the requirements concerning technical proficiency and seniority, but not other requirements, especially the less codified ones having to do with the proper handling of social relationships at work. It must fall to someone to break the bad news to the victim; someone must tell him that he has been fired, or that he has failed his examinations, or that he has been by-passed in promotion. And after the blowoff, someone has to cool the mark out. The necessity of disappointing the expectations that a person has taken for granted may be infrequent in some organizations, but in others, such as training institutions, it occurs all the time. The process of personnel selection requires that many trainees be called but that few be chosen.

When one turns from places of work to other scenes in our social life, one finds that each has its own occasions for cooling the mark out. During informal social intercourse it is well understood that an effort on the part of one person (ego) to decrease his social distance from another person (alter) must be graciously accepted by alter or, if rejected, rejected tactfully so that the initiator of the move can save his social face. This rule is codified in books on etiquette and is followed in actual behavior. A friendly movement in the direction of alter is a movement outward on a limb; ego communicates his belief that he has defined himself as worthy of alter's society, while at the same time he places alter in the strategic position of being able to discredit this conception.

The problem of cooling persons out in informal social intercourse is seen most clearly, perhaps, in courting situations and in what might be called de-courting situations. A proposal of marriage in our society tends to be a way in which a man sums up his social attributes and suggests to a woman that hers are not so much better as to preclude a merger or partnership in these matters. Refusal on the part of the woman, or refusal on the part of the man to propose when he is clearly in a position to do so, is a serious reflection on the rejected suitor. Courtship is a way not only of presenting oneself to alter for approval but also of saying that the opinion of alter in this matter is the opinion one is most concerned with. Refusing a proposal, or refusing to propose, is therefore a difficult operation. The mark must be carefully cooled out. The act of breaking a date or of refusing one, and the task of discouraging a "steady" can also be seen in this light, although in these cases great delicacy and tact may not be required, since the mark may not be deeply involved or openly committed.

Just as it is harder to refuse a proposal than to refuse a date, so it is more difficult to reject a spouse than to reject a suitor. The process of de-courting by which one person in a marriage maneuvers the other into accepting a divorce without fuss or undue rancor requires extreme finesse in the art of cooling the mark out.

In all of these cases where a person constructs a conception of himself which cannot be sustained, there is a possibility that he has not invested that which is most important to him in the soon-to-be-denied status. In the current idiom, there is a possibility that when he is hit, he will not be hit where he really lives. There is a set of cases, however, where the blowoff cannot help but strike a vital spot; these cases arise, of course, when a person must be dissuaded from life itself. The man with a fatal sickness or fatal injury, the criminal with a death sentence, the soldier with a hopeless objective—these persons must be persuaded to accept quietly the loss of life itself, the loss of all one's earthly involvements. Here, certainly, it will be difficult to cool the mark out. It is a reflection on the conceptions men have —as cooler and mark—that it is possible to do so.

I have mentioned a few of the areas of social life where it becomes necessary, upon occasion, to cool a mark out. Attention may now be directed to some of the common ways in which individuals are cooled out in all of these areas of life.

For the mark, cooling represents a process of adjustment to an impossible situation—a situation arising from having defined himself in a way which the social facts come to contradict. The mark must therefore be supplied with a new set of apologies for himself, a new framework in which to see himself and judge himself. A process of redefining the self along defensible lines must be instigated and carried along; since the mark himself is frequently in too weakened a condition to do this, the cooler must initially do it for him.

One general way of handling the problem of cooling the mark out is to give the task to someone whose status relative to the mark will serve to ease the situation in some way. In formal organizations, frequently, someone who is two or three levels above the mark in line of command will do the hatchet work, on the assumption that words of consolation and redirection will have a greater power to convince if they come from high places. There also seems to be a feeling that persons of high status are better able to withstand the moral danger of having hate directed at them. Incidentally, persons protected by high office do not like to face this issue, and frequently attempt to define themselves as merely the agents of the deed and not the source of it. In some cases, on the other hand, the task of cooling the mark out is given to a friend and peer of the mark, on the assumption that such a person will know best how to hit upon a suitable rationalization for the mark and will know best how to control the mark should the need for this arise. In some cases, as in those pertaining to death, the role of cooler is given to doctors or priests. Doctors must frequently help a family, and the member who is leaving it, to manage the leave-taking with tact and a minimum of emotional fuss.[3] A priest must not so much save a soul as create one that is consistent with what is about to become of it.

A second general solution to the problem of cooling the mark out consists of offering him a status which differs from the one he has lost or failed to gain but which provides at least a something or a somebody for him to become. Usually the alternative presented to the mark is a compromise of some kind, providing him with some of the trappings of his lost status as well as with some of its spirit. A lover may be asked to become a friend; a student of medicine may be asked to switch to the study of dentistry;[4] a boxer may become a trainer; a dying person

may be asked to broaden and empty his worldly loves so as to embrace the All-Father that is about to receive him. Sometimes the mark is allowed to retain his status but is required to fulfill it in a different environment: the honest policeman is transferred to a lonely beat; the too zealous priest is encouraged to enter a monastery; an unsatisfactory plant manager is shipped off to another branch. Sometimes the mark is "kicked upstairs" and given a courtesy status such as "Vice President." In the game for social roles, transfer up, down, or away may all be consolation prizes.

A related way of handling the mark is to offer him another chance to qualify for the role at which he has failed. After his fall from grace, he is allowed to retrace his steps and try again. Officer selection programs in the army, for example, often provide for possibilities of this kind. In general, it seems that third and fourth chances are seldom given to marks, and that second chances, while often given, are seldom taken. Failure at a role removes a person from the company of those who have succeeded, but it does not bring him back—in spirit, anyway—to the society of those who have not tried or are in the process of trying. The person who has failed in a role is a constant source of embarrassment, for none of the standard patterns of treatment is quite applicable to him. Instead of taking a second chance, he usually goes away to another place where his past does not bring confusion to his present.

Another standard method of cooling the mark out—one which is frequently employed in conjunction with other methods—is to allow the mark to explode, to break down, to cause a scene, to give full vent to his reactions and feelings, to "blow his top." If this release of emotions does not find a target, then it at least serves a cathartic function. If it does find a target, as in "telling off the boss," it gives the mark a last-minute chance to re-erect his defenses and prove to himself and others that he had not really cared about the status all along. When a blow-up of this kind occurs, friends of the

---

[3] This role of the doctor has been stressed by W. L. Warner in his lectures at the University of Chicago on symbolic roles in "Yankee City."

[4] In his seminars, Mr. Hughes has used the term "second-choice" professions to refer to cases of this kind.

mark or psychotherapists are frequently brought in. Friends are willing to take responsibility for the mark because their relationship to him is not limited to the role he has failed in. This, incidentally, provides one of the less obvious reasons why the cooler in a con mob must cultivate the friendship of the mark; friendship provides the cooler with an acceptable reason for staying around while the mark is cooled out. Psychotherapists, on the other hand, are willing to take responsibility for the mark because it is their business to offer a relationship to those who have failed in a relationship to others.

It has been suggested that a mark may be cooled out by allowing him, under suitable guidance, to give full vent to his initial shock. Thus the manager of a commercial organization may listen with patience and understanding to the complaints of a customer, knowing that the full expression of a complaint is likely to weaken it. This possibility lies behind the role of a whole series of buffers in our society—janitors, restaurant hostesses, grievance committees, floorwalkers, and so on—who listen in silence, with apparent sympathy, until the mark has simmered down. Similarly, in the case of criminal trials, the defending lawyer may find it profitable to allow the public to simmer down before he brings his client to court.

A related procedure for cooling the mark out is found in what is called stalling. The feelings of the mark are not brought to a head because he is given no target at which to direct them. The operator may manage to avoid the presence of the mark or may convince the mark that there is still a slight chance that the loss has not really occurred. When the mark is stalled, he is given a chance to become familiar with the new conception of self he will have to accept before he is absolutely sure that he will have to accept it.

As another cooling procedure, there is the possibility that the operator and the mark may enter into a tacit understanding according to which the mark agrees to act as if he were leaving of his own accord, and the operator agrees to preserve the illusion that this was the case. It is a form of bribery. In this way the mark may fail in his own eyes but prevent others from discovering the failure. The mark gives up his role but saves his face. This, after all, is one of the reasons why persons who are fleeced by con men are often willing to remain silent about their adventure. The same strategy is at work in the romantic custom of allowing a guilty officer to take his own life in a private way before it is taken from him publicly, and in the less romantic custom of allowing a person to resign for delicate reasons instead of firing him for indelicate ones.

Bribery is, of course, a form of exchange. In this case, the mark guarantees to leave quickly and quietly, and in exchange is allowed to leave under a cloud of his own choosing. A more important variation on the same theme is found in the practice of financial compensation. A man can say to himself and others that he is happy to retire from his job and say this with more conviction if he is able to point to a comfortable pension. In this sense, pensions are automatic devices for providing consolation. So, too, a person who has been injured because of another's criminal or marital neglect can compensate for the loss by means of a court settlement.

I have suggested some general ways in which the mark is cooled out. The question now arises: what happens if the mark refuses to be cooled out? What are the possible lines of action he can take if he refuses to be cooled? Attempts to answer these questions will show more clearly why, in general, the operator is so anxious to pacify the mark.

It has been suggested that a mark may be cooled by allowing him to blow his top. If the blow-up is too drastic or prolonged, however, difficulties may arise. We say that the mark becomes "disturbed mentally" or "personally disorganized." Instead of merely telling his boss off, the mark may go so far as to commit criminal violence against him. Instead of merely blaming himself for failure, the mark may inflict great punishment upon himself by attempting suicide, or by acting so as to make it necessary for him to be cooled out in other areas of his social life.

Sustained personal disorganization is one way in which a mark can refuse to cool out. Another standard way is for the individual to raise a squawk, that is, to make a formal complaint to higher authorities obliged to take notice of such matters. The con mob worries lest the mark appeal to the police. The plant manager must make sure that the disgruntled department head does not carry a formal complaint to the general manager or, worse still, to the Board of Directors. The teacher worries lest the child's parent complain to the principal. Similarly, a woman who communicates her evaluation of self by accepting a proposal of marriage can sometimes protect her exposed position—should the necessity of doing so arise—by threatening her disaffected fiancé with a breach-of-promise suit. So, also, a woman who is de-courting her husband must fear lest he contest the divorce or sue her lover for alienation of affection. In much the same way, a customer who is angered by a salesperson can refuse to be mollified by the floorwalker and demand to see the manager. It is interesting to note that associations dedicated to the rights and the honor of minority groups may sometimes encourage a mark to register a formal squawk; politically it may be more advantageous to provide a test case than to allow the mark to be cooled out.

Another line of action which a mark who refuses to be cooled can pursue is that of turning "sour." The term derives from the argot of industry but the behavior it refers to occurs everywhere. The mark outwardly accepts his loss but withdraws all enthusiasm, good will, and vitality from whatever role he is allowed to maintain. He complies with the formal requirements of the role that is left him, but he withdraws his spirit and identification from it. When an employee turns sour, the interests of the organization suf-

fer; every executive, therefore, has the problem of "sweetening" his workers. They must not come to feel that they are slowly being cooled out. This is one of the functions of granting periodic advancements in salary and status, of schemes such as profit-sharing, or of giving the "employee" at home an anniversary present. A similar view can be taken of the problem that a government faces in times of crisis when it must maintain the enthusiastic support of the nation's disadvantaged minorities, for whole groupings of the population can feel they are being cooled out and react by turning sour.

Finally, there is the possibility that the mark may, in a manner of speaking, go into business for himself. He can try to gather about him the persons and facilities required to establish a status similar to the one he has lost, albeit in relation to a different set of persons. This way of refusing to be cooled is often rehearsed in phantasies of the "I'll show them" kind, but sometimes it is actually realized in practice. The rejected marriage partner may make a better remarriage. A social stratum that has lost its status may decide to create its own social system. A leader who fails in a political party may establish his own splinter group.

All these ways in which a mark can refuse to be cooled out have consequences for other persons. There is, of course, a kind of refusal that has little consequence for others. Marks of all kinds may develop explanations and excuses to account in a creditable way for their loss. It is, perhaps, in this region of phantasy that the defeated self makes its last stand.

The process of cooling is a difficult one, both for the operator who cools the mark out and for the person who receives this treatment. Safeguards and strategies are therefore employed to ensure that the process itself need not and does not occur. One deals here with strategies of prevention, not strategies of cure.

From the point of view of the operator, there are two chief ways of avoiding the difficulties of cooling the mark out. First, devices are commonly employed to weed out those applicants for a role, office, or relationship who might later prove to be unsuitable and require removal. The applicant is not given a change to invest his self unwisely. A variation of this technique, that provides, in a way, a built-in mechanism for cooling the mark out, is found in the institution of probationary period and "temporary" staff. These definitions of the situation make it clear to the person that he must maintain his ego in readiness for the loss of his job, or, better still, that he ought not to think of himself as really having the job. If these safety measures fail, however, a second strategy is often employed. Operators of all kinds seem to be ready, to a surprising degree, to put up with or "carry" persons who have failed but who have not yet been treated as failures. This is especially true where the involvement of the mark is deep and where his conception of self had been publicly committed. Business offices, government agencies, spouses, and other kinds of operators are often careful to make a place for the mark, so that dissolution of the bond will not be necessary. Here, perhaps, is the most important source of private charity in our society.

A consideration of these preventive strategies brings to attention an interesting functional relationship among age-grading, recruitment, and the structure of the self. In our society, as in most others, the young in years are defined as not-yet-persons. To a certain degree, they are not subject to success and failure. A child can throw himself completely into a task, and fail at it, and by and large he will not be destroyed by his failure; it is only necessary to play at cooling him out. An adolescent can be bitterly disappointed in love, and yet he will not thereby become, at least for others, a broken person. A youth can spend a certain amount of time shopping around for a congenial job or a congenial training course, because he is still thought to be able to change his mind without changing his self. And, should he fail at something to which he has tried to commit

himself, no permanent damage may be done to his self. If many are to be called and few chosen, then it is more convenient for everyone concerned to call individuals who are not fully persons and cannot be destroyed by failing to be chosen. As the individual grows older, he becomes defined as someone who must not be engaged in a role for which he is unsuited. He becomes defined as something that must not fail, while at the same time arrangements are made to decrease the chances of his failing. Of course, when the mark reaches old age, he must remove himself or be removed from each of his roles, one by one, and participate in the problem of later maturity.

The strategies that are employed by operators to avoid the necessity of cooling the mark out have a counterpart in the strategies that are employed by the mark himself for the same purpose.

There is the strategy of hedging, by which a person makes sure that he is not completely committed. There is the strategy of secrecy, by which a person conceals from others and even from himself the facts of his commitment; there is also the practice of keeping two irons in the fire and the more delicate practice of maintaining a joking or unserious relationship to one's involvement. All of these strategies give the mark an out; in case of failure he can act as if the self that has failed is not one that is important to him. Here we must also consider the function of being quick to take offense and of taking hints quickly, for in these ways the mark can actively cooperate in the task of saving his face. There is also the strategy of playing it safe, as in cases where a calling is chosen because tenure is assured in it, or where a plain woman is married for much the same reason.

It has been suggested that preventive strategies are employed by operator and mark in order to reduce the chance of failing or to minimize the consequences of failure. The less importance one finds it necessary to give to the problem of cooling, the more importance one may have given to the application of preventive strategies.

I have considered some of the situations in our society in which the necessity for cooling the mark out is likely to arise. I have also considered the standard ways in which a mark can be cooled out, the lines of action he can pursue if he refuses to be cooled, and the ways in which the whole problem can be avoided. Attention can now be turned to some very general questions concerning the self in society.

First, an attempt must be made to draw together what has been implied about the structure of persons. From the point of view of this paper, a person is an individual who becomes involved in a value of some kind—a role, a status, a relationship, an ideology—and then makes a public claim that he is to be defined and treated as someone who possesses the value or property in question. The limits to his claims, and hence the limits to his self, are primarily determined by the objective facts of his social life and secondarily determined by the degree to which a sympathetic interpretation of these facts can bend them in his favor. Any event which demonstrates that someone has made a false claim, defining himself as something which he is not, tends to destroy him. If others realize that the person's conception of self has been contradicted and discredited, then the person tends to be destroyed in the eyes of others. If the person can keep the contradiction a secret, he may succeed in keeping everyone but himself from treating him as a failure.

Secondly, one must take note of what is implied by the fact that it is possible for a person to be cooled out. Difficult as this may be, persons regularly define themselves in terms of a set of attributes and then have to accept the fact that they do not possess them—and do this about-face with relatively little fuss or trouble for the operators. This implies that there is a norm in our society persuading persons to keep their chins up and make the best of it—a sort of social sanitation enjoining

torn and tattered persons to keep themselves packaged up. More important still, the capacity of a person to sustain these profound embarrassments implies a certain looseness and lack of interpenetration in the organization of his several life-activities. A man may fail in his job, yet go on succeeding with his wife. His wife may ask him for a divorce, or refuse to grant him one, and yet he may push his way onto the same streetcar at the usual time on the way to the same job. He may know that he is shortly going to have to leave the status of the living, but still march with the other prisoners, or eat breakfast with his family at their usual time and from behind his usual paper. He may be conned of his life's savings on an eastbound train but return to his home town and succeed in acting as if nothing of interest had happened.

Lack of rigid integration of a person's social roles allows for compensation; he can seek comfort in one role for injuries incurred in others. There are always cases, of course, in which the mark cannot sustain the injury to his ego and cannot act like a "good scout." On these occasions the shattering experience in one area of social life may spread out to all the sectors of his activity. He may define away the barriers between his several social roles and become a source of difficulty in all of them. In such cases the play is the mark's entire social life, and the operators, really, are the society. In an increasing number of these cases, the mark is given psychological guidance by professionals of some kind. The psychotherapist is, in this sense, the society's cooler. His job is to pacify and reorient the disorganized person; his job is to send the patient back to an old world or a new one, and to send him back in a condition in which he can no longer cause trouble to others or can no longer make a fuss. In short, if one takes the society, and not the person as the unit, the psychotherapist has the basic task of cooling the mark out.

A third point of interest arises if one views all of social life from the perspective of this paper. It has been argued that a person must not openly or even privately commit himself to a conception of himself which the flow of events is likely to discredit. He must not put himself in a position of having to be cooled out. Conversely, however, he must make sure that none of the persons with whom he has dealings are of the sort who may prove unsuitable and need to be cooled out. He must make doubly sure that should it become necessary to cool his associates out, they will be the sort who allow themselves to be gotten rid of. The con man who wants the mark to go home quietly and absorb a loss, the restaurant hostess who wants a customer to eat quietly and go away without causing trouble, and, if this is not possible, quietly to take his patronage elsewhere—these are the persons and these are the relationships which set the tone of some of our social life. Underlying this tone there is the assumption that persons are institutionally related to each other in such a way that if a mark allows himself to be cooled out, then the cooler need have no further concern with him; but if the mark refuses to be cooled out, he can put institutional machinery into action against the cooler. Underlying this tone there is also the assumption that persons are sentimentally related to each other in such a way that if a person allows himself to be cooled out, however great the loss he has sustained, then the cooler withdraws all emotional identification from him; but if the mark cannot absorb the injury to his self and if he becomes personally disorganized in some way, then the cooler cannot help but feel guilt and concern over the predicament. It is this feeling of guilt—this small measure of involvement in the feelings of others—which helps to make the job of cooling the mark out distasteful, whereever it appears. It is this incapacity to be insensitive to the suffering of another person when he brings his suffering right to your door which tends to make the job of cooling a species of dirty work.

One must not, of course, make too much of the margin of sympathy connecting operator and mark. For one thing, the operator may rid himself of the mark by application or threat of pure force or open insult.[5] In Chicago in the 1920's small businessmen who suffered a loss in profits and in independence because of the "protection" services that racketeers gave to them were cooled out in this way. No doubt it is frivolous to suggest that Freud's notion of castration threat has something to do with the efforts of fathers to cool their sons out of oedipal involvements. Furthermore, there are many occasions when operators of different kinds must act as middlemen, with two marks on their hands; the calculated use of one mark as a sacrifice or fall guy may be the only way of cooling the other mark out. Finally, there are barbarous ceremonies in our society, such as criminal trials and the drumming-out ritual employed in court-martial procedures, that are expressly designed to prevent the mark from saving his face. And even in those cases where the cooler makes an effort to make things easier for the person he is getting rid of, we often find that there are bystanders who have no such scruples.[6] Onlookers who are close enough to observe the blowoff but who are not obliged to assist in the dirty work often enjoy the scene, taking pleasure in the discomfiture of the cooler and in the destruction of the mark. What is trouble for some is Schadenfreude for others.

This paper has dealt chiefly with adaptations to loss; with defenses, strategies, consolations, mitigations, compensations, and the like. The kinds of sugar-coating have been examined, and not the pill. I would like to close this paper by referring briefly to the sort of thing that would be studied if one were interested in loss as such, and not in adaptations to it.

A mark who requires cooling out is a person who can no longer sustain one of his social roles and is about to be removed from it; he is a person who is losing one of his social lives and is about to die one of the deaths that are possible for him. This leads one to consider the ways in which we can go or be sent to our death in each of our social capacities, the ways, in other words, of handling the passage from the role that we had to a state of

---

[5] Suggested by Saul Mendlovitz in conversation.
[6] Suggested by Howard S. Becker in conversation.

having it no longer. One might consider the social processes of firing and laying-off; of resigning and being asked to resign; of farewell and departure; of deportation, excommunication, and going to jail; of defeat at games, contests, and wars; of being dropped from a circle of friends or an intimate social relationship; of corporate dissolution; of retirement in old age; and, lastly, of the deaths that heirs are interested in.

And, finally, attention must be directed to the things we become after we have died in one of the many social senses and capacities in which death can come to us. As one might expect, a process of sifting and sorting occurs by which the socially dead come to be effectively hidden from us. This movement of ex-persons throughout the social structure proceeds in more than one direction.

There is, first of all, the dramatic process by which persons who have died in important ways come gradually to be brought together into a common graveyard that is separated ecologically from the living community.[7] For the dead, this is at once a punishment and a defense. Jails and mental institutions are, perhaps, the most familiar examples, but other important ones exist. In America today, there is the interesting tendency to set aside certain regions and towns in California as asylums for those who have died in their capacity as workers and as parents but who are still alive financially.[8] For the old in America who have also died financially, there are old-folks homes and rooming-house areas. And, of course, large cities have their Skid Rows which are, as Park put it, ". . . . full of junk, much of it human, i.e., men and women who, for some reason or other, have fallen out of line in the march of industrial progress and have been scrapped by the indus-

trial organization of which they were once a part."[9] Hobo jungles, located near freight yards on the outskirts of towns, provide another case in point.

Just as a residential area may become a graveyard, so also certain institutions and occupational roles may take on a similar function. The ministry in Britain, for example, has sometimes served as a limbo for the occupational stillborn of better families, as have British universities. Mayhew, writing of London in the mid-nineteenth-century, provides another example: artisans of different kinds, who had failed to maintain a position in the practice of their trade, could be found working as dustmen.[10] In the United States, the jobs of waitress, cab driver, and night watchman, and the profession of prostitution, tend to be ending places where persons of certain kinds, starting from different places, can come to rest.

But perhaps the most important movement of those who fail is one we never see. Where roles are ranked and somewhat related, persons who have been rejected from the one above may be difficult to distinguish from persons who have risen from the one below. For example, in America, upper-class women who fail to make a marriage in their own circle may follow the recognized route of marrying an upper-middle class professional. Successful lower-middle class women may arrive at the same station in life, coming from the other direction. Similarly, among those who mingle with one another as colleagues in the profession of dentistry, it is possible to find some who have failed to become physicians and others who have succeeded at not becoming pharmacists or optometrists. No doubt there are few positions in life that do not throw together some persons who are there by virtue of failure and other persons who are there by virtue of success. In this sense, the dead are sorted but not segregated, and continue to walk among the living.

THE UNIVERSITY OF CHICAGO

---

[7] Suggested by lectures of and a personal conversation with Mr. Hughes.

[8] Some early writers on caste report a like situation in India at the turn of the nineteenth century. Hindus who were taken to the Ganges to die, and who then recovered, were apparently denied all legal rights and all social relations with the living. Apparently these excluded persons found it necessary to congregate in a few villages of their own. In California, of course, settlements of the old have a voluntary character, and members maintain ceremonial contact with younger kin by the exchange of periodic visits and letters.

[9] R. E. Park, *Human Communities;* Glencoe, Ill.; Free Press, 1952; p. 60.

[10] Henry Mayhew, *London Labour and the London Poor;* London, Griffin, Bohn, 1861; Vol. II, pp. 177-178.

[8]

0091-4169/82/7304-1774
THE JOURNAL OF CRIMINAL LAW & CRIMINOLOGY
Copyright © 1983 by Northwestern University School of Law

Vol. 73, No. 4
Printed in U.S.A.

CRIMINOLOGY

THE SERIOUS HABITUAL PROPERTY OFFENDER AS "MOONLIGHTER": AN EMPIRICAL STUDY OF LABOR FORCE PARTICIPATION AMONG ROBBERS AND BURGLARS*

Harold R. Holzman**

I. INTRODUCTION

It is generally believed that there exists a sizable number of persistent property offenders who earn their livelihood through criminal activity. Such persons are usually termed "professional" or "career" criminals. The traditional perspective, represented by Sutherland,[1] views the "professional criminal" as a highly skilled specialist. A newer perspective has emerged, however, which views "career" criminals as opportunistic generalists who spend most of their time searching ("hustling") for chances to commit property-related offenses.[2] While there may be some debate about the degree of specialization present among such criminals, there seems little controversy with respect to the notion that serious habitual property offenders are seldom members of the conventional labor force.

---

* The paper was derived from the author's doctoral dissertation: "The Persistent Property Offender and the Concept of Professional Criminality: The Case of Robbery and Burglary." University of Maryland, 1979.

** Research Consultant, Columbia, Maryland. Ph.D., University of Maryland 1979; M.A., University of Maryland, 1968; B.A., State University of New York, 1966.

[1] E. SUTHERLAND, THE PROFESSIONAL THIEF 3, 197-98 (1937).

[2] *See generally* L. GOULD, E. BITTNER, S. MESSINGER, K. KOVAK, F. POWLEDGE & S. CHANELES, CRIME AS A PROFESSION 25 (1966); R. WINSLOW, SOCIETY IN TRANSITION 133-35 (1970); Inciardi, *Vocational Crime* in HANDBOOK OF CRIMINOLOGY 299 (D. Glaser ed. 1974); Staats, *Changing Conceptualizations of Professional Criminals: Implications for Criminology Theory*, 15 CRIMINOLOGY 49, 57 (1977); Walker, *Sociology and Professional Crime* in CURRENT PERSPECTIVES ON CRIMINAL BEHAVIOR 87 (A. Blumberg ed. 1974).

The traditional perspective represented by Sutherland,[3] suggests that the basis for this assumed non-participation in the conventional labor force lies in the offender's value system. The offender is thought to view conventional jobs as demeaning and unproductive. In contrast, proponents of the emerging generalist perspective believe that persistent property offenders simply do not have the time for legitimate employment since they are constantly searching for opportunities to commit property crimes. Winslow characterized the assumptions of the traditional perspective in respect to labor force participation as stemming from a "normative compliance model" while the generalist perspective position emanated from a "utilitarian compliance model."[4] Regardless of the basis of their positions, however, both perspectives portrayed the "professional" as obtaining his livelihood from crime.

The labor force participation of persistent property offenders has never been a very controversial issue and has seldom been the focus of empirical research. This article presents data, however, which suggest that labor force participation in specified populations of known recidivists is much more extensive than had been previously thought. Over three out of four of the recidivist robbers and burglars whose careers were examined were found to have been employed at the time of their arrest for their latest offense.

II. THE TARGET POPULATION

The target population studied here was drawn from the 1974 *Survey of Inmates of State Correctional Facilities*. This survey was conducted in January, 1974 by the United States Census Bureau under the sponsorship and general direction of the Law Enforcement Assistance Administration, United States Department of Justice.[5] Most of the data used for the present study have not been previously analyzed.

The target population comprised 29,474 men who had at least two convictions resulting in incarceration for robbery, burglary, or a combination of the two. The average number of adult incarcerations for the

---

[3] *See generally* E. SUTHERLAND, *supra* note 1.

[4] *See* R. WINSLOW, *supra* note 2, at 224-34.

[5] JUST. DEP'T, SURVEY OF INMATES OF STATE CORRECTIONAL FACILITIES 1974, Advance Report [hereinafter cited as 1974 SURVEY]. The survey involved the drawing of a stratified random sample of 10,359 inmates, based on size of institution. Approximately one out of 18 of the some 191,400 inmates incarcerated in state correctional facilities at the time of data collection were selected for a personal interview of about 20 minutes duration, touching upon their social, economic and official criminal histories. Of the 10,359 selected, 8,869 inmates were interviewed directly. Using the total enumeration of prisoners as determined by the January 31, 1974 Census of State Correctional Facilities, United States Census Bureau personnel performed a series of weighting procedures on the interview sample, which, in effect, generated survey findings for the entire population of 191,400 inmates.

population averaged slightly over three. When juvenile incarcerations were included, each offender had done "hard time" an average of four times. Thus, the target population was composed of persons committed to persistent involvement in property crime.

The present offense of all members of the target population was robbery, burglary, or some other property offense. Since the objective of the 1974 survey was to examine the careers of recidivistic robbers and burglars whose criminal behavior could be reasonably assumed to be rational economic activity akin to conventional income-producing pursuits, individuals with known histories of heroin addiction and sex offenses were excluded from the target population. Similarly, individuals serving time for expressive acts alone, e.g., assault, were excluded from the target population since a person with a history of robbery or burglary could possibly "reform" but, due to factors unrelated to economic objectives, find himself in prison years after his last property crime.[6] Given the selection criteria used, it can reasonably be assumed that the members of the target population were actively pursuing careers in

---

6 These criteria were used in defining the target population:

(1) *Inmates*: Only individuals who were serving sentences were included in the target population. Individuals who were being held pending trial or sentencing were not included in the target population since data on their present offense was incomplete.

(2) *Males*: Most studies of predatory property offenders involve males. This is traditionally a predominantly masculine area of endeavor—witness the fact that 97% of the inmates of state correctional facilities are men. 1974 SURVEY, *supra* note 5, at 24. Therefore, the present research has been designed to deal only with males.

(3) *N + 1 Incarcerations*: The present research deals with persistent offenders. In this research, a persistent offender has been defined as an individual who, in spite of an initial incarceration, has chosen to continue his criminal behavior. Incarceration is a serious career contingency and represents, in effect, a test of one's commitment to a crime as a vocation.

(4) *Drug Usage*: The survey obtained information about the use of narcotics among respondents. *Id.* at 27. Among other questions was one about "daily or almost daily" use of heroin and methadone. *Id.* at 7. The use of heroin may well have significant effects on an individual's lifestyle, altering his alternatives for income-producing activities and thus putting him quite apart from other workers in both legitimate and illegitimate occupations. Hence, individuals who were heroin users or were recovering from heroin addiction at the time of their present offense were excluded from the target population.

(5) *Sex Offenders*: As with heroin addiction, involvement in sex offenses was seen as possibly representing motivation toward criminality unlikely to be related to economic considerations—considerations which are central to both traditional and the newer generalist concept of professional criminality.

(6) *Latest Incarceration for an Expressive Act*: The last refinement of the population involved selecting out individuals whose latest incarceration involved (a) homicide, (b) assault, (c) minor drug offenses, e.g., possession, not including offenses involving sale, (d) arson, (e) weapons offenses, or (f) drugged or drunken driving and did not include a concomitant conviction for robbery or burglary. The rationale for this procedure was that these offenses alone can be seen as involving expressive rather than instrumental acts. A person with a history of robbery or burglary could possibly "reform" but, due to factors unrelated to economic objectives that might have played a role in his earlier criminal career, could find himself in prison years after his last burglary or robbery. Simply because an individual may renounce crime as an occupation does not mean that he can escape what Wolfgang and Ferracuti called the "subculture of violence." M. WOLFGANG & F. FERRACUTI, THE SUBCULTURE OF VIOLENCE (1966).

property crime for essentially rational economic motives, i.e., crime as work.[7]

Table 1 shows the target population by type of offender and race. A "robber" was defined as an individual with at least two incarcerations for robbery and none for burglary. "Burglars" had at least two incarcerations for burglary and none for robbery. "Generalists" had at least one incarceration for each.

TABLE 1

TYPE OF OFFENDER BY RACE FOR THE TARGET POPULATION

Race of Offender	Type of Offender			
	Total	Burglars	Robbers	Generalists
White	15,601 (100%)	10,081 (65%)	2,100 (13%)	3,420 (22%)
Black	13,873 (100%)	5,862 (42%)	3,302 (24%)	4,709 (34%)
Total	29,474 (100%)	15,943 (55%)	5,402 (18%)	8,129 (27%)

Property offenses other than robbery and burglary were not uncommon in the criminal history of the target population. Approximately three out of every five of the white offenders and two out of five of the black offenders had been convicted at least once of a property crime other than robbery or burglary. White burglars were most likely to have been convicted of some other property offense, with sixty-five percent having such a conviction. Overall, the criminal histories of the target population were dominated by property crimes (including robbery and burglary) with over four out of five reporting property offenses as their only source of conviction. Along with the population average of four incarcerations, these data further suggest that those in the target population were persistently involved in serious property crimes and therefore clearly "career criminals."

III. THE FINDINGS

Given the widespread notion that serious habitual property offenders tend not to be active in the legitimate world of work, one would expect that the labor force participation for persistent property offenders

---

[7] In cases of persons who reported that their present incarceration followed a parole violation, survey respondents were asked if their return to prison was caused by a conviction for a new offense. If so, this new offense became a present offense and was used in determining his eligibility for inclusion in the present study's target population.

would be less than fifty percent.[8] The data indicate, however, that some seventy-eight percent of target population was, in fact, employed at the time of arrest for their present offense, with approximately ninety-five out of one hundred of those employed having full-time jobs.[9] Not only were nearly eighty percent of the target population employed, but the members of this group also held their last full-time job, for over one year on the average.

The extent of labor force participation (L.F.P.) by the target population is comparable to the participation of the general population.[10] The L.F.P. of white offenders is 76%, nearly matching the 79.6% for the general population (see Table 2). Blacks in the target population had a higher rate of labor force participation (81.6%) than did non-whites in the United States population (74.9%).[11] The analysis of the L.F.P. of the target population which follows suggests that habitual property offenders may be very much a part of the conventional world of work.

---

[8] Labor force participation rates rather than unemployment rates were used in the analysis. The definitions of unemployment and labor force participation used in the data analysis were derived from the BUREAU OF LABOR STATISTICS, U.S. DEP'T OF LABOR, HANDBOOK OF LABOR STATISTICS 1973 (1974)—the same source from which definitions for the data collection instrument were drawn. Unemployed persons were defined as "all persons who did not work during the survey week, who made specific efforts to find a job within the past four weeks and who were available during the survey week except for temporary illness." *Id.* at 2. Labor force participants included "(1) full-time workers, (2) persons involuntarily working part-time and (3) unemployed persons seeking full-time jobs." *Id.* at 3.

Virtually none (less than .5%) of the offenders who were without a job at the time of their arrest for present offense were seeking work. Therefore, non-workers could not technically be called unemployed—rather they were non-participants in the labor force. Hence, labor participation rates were used.

[9] Persons involuntarily working part-time are classed as labor force participants. Since it could not be determined if a respondent was working part-time involuntarily when arrested, it was assumed that such was the case and he was accorded the status of a labor force participant. Part-time employment among white offenders was slightly less than four percent. The rate for blacks was nearly eight percent.

[10] The median year of incarceration for the target population was 1971. This year was chosen as the reference year for comparison between the target population and the general population.

[11] Labor force participation and occupational data concerning blacks in the United States for 1971 is consistently presented under the heading of "black and other" and "Negro and other races." Data on the racial composition of the United States in 1970 indicate that some 90% of all non-whites in the population were black. U.S. BUREAU OF THE CENSUS, STATISTICAL ABSTRACT OF THE UNITED STATES: 1971. Therefore, the general population data used in comparisons with black offenders in the target population can be assumed to give a reasonably accurate picture of where the offenders stood in relation to blacks as a group in American society.

Furthermore, given the well-documented employment discrimination that blacks face in the United States, inclusion of data from the L.F.P. of other racial minorities, e.g., Chinese or Japanese, with that of blacks might serve to slightly inflate the L.F.P. figure for the aggregate of "non-white" above that which exists for blacks alone. Hence the L.F.P. comparisons presented, if they err at all, do so in a conservative direction—pushing the L.F.P. of the general black population up toward that of black offenders.

A.   LABOR FORCE PARTICIPATION: WHITE PERSISTENT OFFENDERS

Table 2 presents labor force participation rates for white males.[12] Significantly, the labor force participation rates for the age groups shown, although less than those of the general population, are well over fifty percent. Labor force participation rates include persons actually working and those seeking employment. Men in the target population between the ages of sixteen and seventeen and between eighteen and nineteen display a higher labor participation rate than individuals in the general population of comparable age.[13] Given the generally recognized association between persistent involvement in "street crime" and lack of interest in formal education, it might be expected that younger members of the target population would tend not to be enrolled in high school or college and thus be free to participate in the labor market. The data indicate that young offenders were more active in the labor market than their conventional peers. Thus, many young offenders were free to work and in fact chose to do so.

---

[12] Mean age was 28.8 years for whites. *See supra* note 10 for reference year for comparison.

[13] The comparisons presented in Tables 2 through 4 were tested for statistical significance. The N's in these comparisons were so large as to assure statistical significance for even the most trivial differences, e.g., 81.5% versus 82.0%. Hence, although virtually all of the comparisons (except those where the percents were actually equal) were significant at the .01 level, these tests are not indicated in the tables themselves.

TABLE 2

COMPARISON OF LABOR FORCE PARTICIPATION (L.F.P.) FOR
OFFENDER POPULATION AND MALES IN THE UNITED STATES
POPULATION BY AGE AND RACE (1971)

Age	White		Non-White[a]	
	L.F.P. Rate U.S. Males[14]	L.F.P. Rate Offenders	L.F.P. Rate U.S. Males	L.F.P. Rate Offenders
	1971			
16-17	49.2%	75.5%	32.4%	73.3%
18-19	67.8%	75.6%	58.9%	75.4%
20-24	83.2%	79.4%	81.5%	82.0%
25-34	96.3%	74.3%	92.9%	84.6%
35-44	97.0%	77.6%	92.0%	91.2%
45-54	94.7%	80.9%	86.9%	85.5%
55-64	82.6%	b	77.8%	b
65 and over	25.6%	b	24.5%	b
Total Population	79.6%	76.0%	74.9%	81.6%

a. All non-white offenders studied were black. United States data for 1971 for blacks are
consistently presented under the heading of "black and other" or "Negro and other
races."

b. Population estimates are so low as to be of questionable reliability.

The occupations of the whites in the target population are shown in
Table 3. White persistent offenders are much more active in all varieties
of manual labor[15] than white men in the general population. Conversely, white offenders are under-represented in white collar jobs. Participation in relatively unskilled service occupations by members of the
two populations is the same. Of interest, however, is the fact that white
offenders are clearly over-represented in skilled (craft) and semi-skilled
occupations; some three out of every five offenders were so employed
prior to incarceration.

---

[14] GOV'T PRINTING OFFICE, EMPLOYMENT AND TRAINING REPORT OF THE PRESIDENT
232 (1976).

[15] Manual labor in Table 3 is comprised of the occupations "craft and kindred," "operatives" and "unskilled labor (non-farm)."

TABLE 3

COMPARISON OF OCCUPATIONAL DATA FOR OFFENDER POPULATION
AND MALES IN THE UNITED STATES POPULATION BY RACE (1971)[16]

Type of Occupation	White		Non-White[a]	
	Percent of U.S. Males	Percent of Offenders	Percent of U.S. Males	Percent of Offenders
Professional, tech., administrative and managerial	29.9%	10.1%	13.2%	5.7%
Sales and clerical	12.9%	4.5%	9.3%	5.7%
Craft and kindred	20.6%	34.6%	13.2%	20.2%
Operatives	17.4%	25.2%	26.5%	28.8%
Unskilled labor (non-farm)	6.6%	15.0%	17.5%	22.8%
Service (except private hh)	7.4%	7.4%	15.2%	15.5%
Other	5.2%	2.8%	4.1%	1.3%
Total	100%	100%	100%	100%

a. All non-white offenders studied were black. United States data for 1971 for blacks are consistently presented under the heading of "black and other" and "Negro and Other."

Table 4 compares income levels in the target population with those in the general population. The average income of the white offender is well below that of conventional white workers. However, as the table shows, income levels for offenders age sixteen to nineteen and twenty to twenty-four exceed those of comparable conventional groups by a sizable margin. This may be explained by the fact that young persistent offenders are less likely to be in low paying activities such as military service or work/study lifestyles as would their conventional peers. Like the labor participation rates, these data indicate that young persistent offenders are participants in the conventional work force.

---

[16] BUREAU OF LABOR STATISTICS, U.S. DEP'T OF LABOR, HANDBOOK OF LABOR STATISTICS (1977).

TABLE 4

COMPARISON OF ANNUAL INCOME FOR MALES IN UNITED STATES
POPULATION WITH OFFENDER POPULATION BY AGE
AND RACE (1971)[17]

Age	White		Black	
	U.S. Males	Offenders	U.S. Males	Offenders[a]
14-15	$377	b	$430	b
16-19	$1,403	$4,080	$1,159	$2,867
20-24	$4,614	$5,887	$3,613	$3,968
25-34	$9,271	$7,006	$6,192	$4,875
35-44	$11,488	$7,090	$6,465	$5,650
45-54	$11,503	$7,335	$6,525	$4,480
55-64	$9,755	b	$5,329	b
65 and over	$5,221	b	$2,937	b
Total Population	$8,203	$6,117	$4,888	$4,240

a. Income for offenders was calculated as the average income for the twelve months prior to incarceration.
b. Population estimates are so low as to be of questionable reliability.

B. LABOR FORCE PARTICIPATION: BLACK PERSISTENT OFFENDERS

In examining labor participation data for black persistent offenders[18] in Table 2, one is struck by the fact that the labor force participation of black offenders more closely resembles that of the general non-white population than the participation of white offenders resembles that of whites in conventional society. The differences in labor force participation rates are of a lesser magnitude with some younger age groups displaying more activity in the labor market than conventional peers. The labor force participation rate for black offenders sixteen and over appears greater than that for the general black population (81.6% versus 74.9%). While this no doubt is, in part, due to the very much higher rate of participation in the target population's sixteen to seventeen age group and also the higher rate for the eighteen and nineteen age group, which together constitute almost half of black offenders, it is evidence of the similar position of black offenders and non-offenders in the labor market. This impression of similarity is reinforced when average income by age is considered.[19]

Furthermore, a comparison of occupational involvement[20] indicates yet another area of similarity between black offenders and the general non-white population. In four out of seven occupational categories

---

[17] U.S. BUREAU OF THE CENSUS, CURRENT POPULATION REPORTS, SERIES P-60, NO. 85, CONSUMER INCOME (1972).
[18] Mean age of black persistent offenders was 25.9 years.
[19] *See supra* Table 4, at 1782.
[20] *See supra* Table 3, at 1781.

there is less than a five percent difference between offenders and conventional citizens. A very slight difference was found between the two populations in the area of service jobs. Black offenders do lag considerably behind the general non-white population in "white collar" jobs. The black offenders are somewhat more active than the general non-white population in "blue collar" occupations, showing greater participation at all skill levels. The two groups seem, in general, to resemble one another occupationally. Occupational data, then, appear to support previously discussed indicators of black offenders' involvement in the labor market, creating the impression that the position of the persistent black offender as a worker is not radically different from his non-offender counterpart.

IV. DISCUSSION OF FINDINGS

A. "MOONLIGHTING" IN CRIME

This study's findings fail to support the prevailing view that professional criminals are not active participants in the legitimate world of work. The persistent property offenders under study here may be characterized as "moonlighters" in crime.

While the sociological school of criminology has always maintained that crime and criminals are in general "normal," it has not yet come to hold the view that legitimate workers may also be predatory criminals such as robbers and burglars. For either practical or ideological reasons, e.g., the respective positions of the traditional and generalist perspectives on the issue,[21] the two roles seem to be viewed as somewhat antithetical. When crime is associated with workers in conventional occupations, it is almost always white collar crime, e.g., fraud, occupational crime, or larceny by workers against their employer or fellow employees. In the following excerpt from an article entitled "Avocational Crime," Gilbert Geis notes the failure of criminologists to deal objectively with moonlighting in crime, but he also conveys an unwillingness to accept predatory crime as moonlighting:

> The matter does not concern only the proportional amount of time devoted to law-abiding and criminal activity, however, but also involves those aspects of a person's being and behavior which come to define all of him. A man who commits armed robbery offenses, and who also spends much of his time as a factory worker, sandpapering furniture, will be defined most fundamentally as an "armed robber." A streetwalking prostitute who devotes most of her nonworking hours to seeing to it that her children are well raised will be called a "whore," not a "mother." Conversely, a man who violates tie-in agreement laws or who carries on outlawed insider transactions will be defined as a "businessman" or as a "stockbroker," and a woman from Oak Park with four children who steals regularly at Marshall Field's will be identified as a "suburban housewife."

---

[21] *See supra* notes 1-4 and accompanying text.

The anomalous and seemingly discordant nature of the legal and illegal
activities may be regarded in part as the reason for the varied identifications. Suburban housewives who shoplift (and are caught at it) are relatively rare. But this hardly stands up logically; furniture sandpaperers
who are armed robbers are not very common either.[22]

Several authors, however, have recognized the fact that moonlighting in crime might be fairly common. In the field of sociology, Ned
Polsky[23] was among the first to discuss such activity. He briefly men-
tions this phenomenon in his occupational study of pool hustlers. Polsky
argues that there should be more research on patterns of criminal activity, suggesting that crime is ideal for moonlighting because it requires
little time, is highly profitable, and has flexible working hours.[24] Similarly, Bluestone[25] suggests in his analysis of the participation of poor
people in urban labor markets that economists have tended to overlook
widespread but unconventional means by which persons in the lower
socio-economic strata of society supplement their legitimate income,
e.g., by various forms of criminal activity. Like Polsky,[26] he emphasizes
the positive features of moonlighting: (1) higher wages than conventional jobs; (2) better working conditions; and (3) a sense of independence.[27] Levitan[28] saw criminal activity by the urban poor as a means
of acquiring the much needed income that their conventional jobs in
semi/unskilled occupations could not provide. Clearly, these researchers
are suggesting that multiple jobholding routinely reaches beyond the
boundaries of the conventional world of work into the realm of predatory criminal activity.

B.   MULTIPLE JOBHOLDING IN THE CONVENTIONAL LABOR MARKET

Understanding patterns of multiple jobholding that occur within
the conventional labor market may help one better understand the phenomenon of crime as a second job. Multiple jobholding or secondary
employment (moonlighting) has been defined as (1) having jobs as a
wage or salary worker with two employers or more; (2) being self-employed and also holding a wage or salary job; or (3) working as an un-
paid family worker but also having a secondary wage or salary job. The
primary job is that job at which one works the greatest number of

---

[22] Geis, *Avocational Crime* in HANDBOOK OF CRIMINOLOGY 275-76 (D. Glaser ed. 1974).

[23] N. POLSKY, HUSTLERS, BEATS AND OTHERS 91-92, 101-03 (1967).

[24] *Id.*

[25] Bluestone, *The Tripartite Economy: Urban Labor Markets and the Working Poor*, 5 POVERTY
AND HUMAN RESOURCES 15, 26 (1970).

[26] *See supra* text accompanying note 23.

[27] *See supra* note 25.

[28] *See generally* S. LEVITAN, G. MANGUM & R. MARSHALL, HUMAN RESOURCES AND LA-
BOR MARKETS 133-34 (1976).

hours.[29]

Moonlighting is common among both white and blue collar workers; the principal objective in secondary employment being the acquisition of additional income.[30] Multiple jobholding is especially critical for unskilled workers and some segments of the semi-skilled labor force who do not earn enough from their primary job to provide subsistence for themselves and their families.[31] These persons are commonly referred to as the "working poor."[32] Furthermore, many blue collar workers have been viewed as being caught in an "economic squeeze" in which, although earning an income which provides well for their basic needs, they cannot afford the "middle class" style of life which they very much desire.[33] The jobs of these semi-skilled workers do not provide fast promotions and in some cases fail to provide any promotion opportunities at all; hence, if one is without overtime work, savings, and/or a working spouse, moonlighting is the only means of acquiring desired material goods.[34]

In mid-1971,[35] a United States Labor Department survey revealed that four million people, or 5.1% of all employed workers, were multiple jobholders.[36] Almost eight out of ten multiple jobholders were male. Secondary employment was highest among teachers and protective service workers (e.g., policemen and firemen); eighteen and sixteen percent, respectively.[37] In general, workers in jobs with flexible hours were found to be more apt to have second jobs.[38] Secondary jobs tended not to be in the same major occupational group as primary jobs.[39]

Patterns of moonlighting differed for non-whites and whites. Nearly half again as many whites as non-whites were multiple jobholders (5.3% versus 3.8%).[40] While one of every three whites was self-employed in his or her second job, only a quarter of blacks moonlighted in their own businesses.[41] The racial differences among multiple jobhold-

---

[29] Hayghe & Michelotti, *Multiple Jobholding in 1970 and 1971*, 94 MONTHLY LAB. REV. 38 (1971).

[30] S. WOLFBEIN, EMPLOYMENT AND UNEMPLOYMENT IN THE UNITED STATES 264-67 (1964).

[31] S. LEVITAN AND R. TAGGART III, EMPLOYMENT AND EARNINGS INADEQUACY (1974).

[32] *See* S. LEVITAN, G. MANGUM & R. MARSHALL, *supra* note 28, at 340.

[33] Rosow, *The Problem of the Blue-Collar Worker*, in AN ANTHOLOGY OF LABOR ECONOMICS: READINGS AND COMMENTARY 941, 942-45 (R. Marshall & R. Perlman ed. 1972).

[34] *See generally* B. MABRY, ECONOMICS OF MANPOWER AND THE LABOR MARKET 217 (1973).

[35] *See supra* note 10.

[36] *See* Hayghe & Michelotti, *supra* note 29, at 40.

[37] *Id.* at 40.

[38] *Id.*

[39] *Id.* at 41.

[40] *Id.* at 40.

[41] *Id.* at 41.

ers are perhaps reflective of general racial differences in labor force participation. It has been noted that professional and skilled workers find it easier to moonlight because their specialized experience and training are more valuable to prospective employers.[42] Since minorities tend to be underrepresented in these groups, they may be at a disadvantage in finding second jobs. The nature of the secondary employment market may be structured so as to minimize the participation of lower income individuals who may need this source of additional income the most.

There is some evidence to suggest that skilled workers who are unable to obtain secondary employment as wage workers may attempt to earn additional money by starting their own businesses. In 1971, blue collar workers were two and one half times as likely to operate farms (a form of self-employment) than other occupational groups.[43] Nearly a quarter of all blue collar moonlighting involved agricultural entrepreneurial activity. In attempting to explain the dramatic rise from 166,000 to 728,000 between May, 1970 and May, 1971 in the number of self-employed persons in non-agricultural industries with little concomitant rise in the total number of moonlighters, Michelotti and Hayghe[44] state "it may be that some persons who wanted but could not find a wage or salary job turned to self-employment in order to earn additional income."[45]

C. ROBBERS AND BURGLARS AS SELF-EMPLOYED MOONLIGHTERS

The rates of labor force participation by members of this study's target population were so high as to indicate that conventional jobholding was much more the rule than the exception among these persistent property offenders.[46] Given the relatively brief time periods in which both robberies and burglaries can be committed, as opposed to the roughly forty hour weekly schedule that characterizes most conventional work, it is reasonable to view such criminal activity by an employed person as a secondary rather than a primary job. In the context of multiple jobholding, robbers and burglars can be looked upon as *self-employed* since their activities are usually not conducted on a salary or wage basis but rather involve a profit and loss structure akin to conventional entrepreneurial endeavors. In essence, then, the target population was moonlighting as self-employed businessmen and their business was crime.

The decision of members of the target population to seek secondary

---

[42] *See* S. WOLFBEIN, *supra* note 30, at 267.
[43] *See* Hayghe & Michelotti, *supra* note 29, at 41-42.
[44] *Id.*
[45] *Id.*
[46] *See supra* Table 2, at 1780.

employment as entrepreneurs rather than salary or wage earners may be partly a function of their position in the conventional labor market. Table 5 shows the occupational status scores for the members of the target population in comparison to the mean scores by occupational grouping for the male population of the United States. Based on data gathered in the 1970 decennial census, Nam, LaRocque, Powers and Holmberg[47]

TABLE 5

OCCUPATIONAL STATUS SCORES FOR UNITED STATES MALES (1970)
WITH AVERAGE OCCUPATIONAL SCORES OF TARGET POPULATION BY
RACE AND OFFENSE

Occupational Status Scores for Males in U.S. by Job Category[48]		Average Occupational Status Scores for Whites in Target Population		Average Occupational Status Scores for Blacks in Target Population	
Professional and technical	84				
Managers, officials, and proprietors (except farm)	75				
Sales and clerical	53				
Craftsmen	49				
		Robbers	44.5		
		Generalists	42.9		
		Burglars	41.1		
				Robbers	37.4
				Generalists	37.2
				Burglars	35.1
Operatives	35				
Service (except private hh)	32				
Laborers (except farm)	15				

derived these scores using average levels of education and income for incumbents of 589 occupations. Hence, these scores allow one to compare the socioeconomic position of the target population with that of other men in the conventional world of work. On the basis of their oc-

---

[47] C. Nam, J. LaRocque, M. Powers & G. Holmberg, Occupational Status Scores: Stability and Change, Proceedings of the Social Statistics Section, American Statistical Association 570-75 (1975).

[48] *Id.*

1788   *HAROLD R. HOLZMAN*   [Vol. 73

cupational status scores, the members of the target population can best
be characterized as semi-skilled workers. Since semi-skilled workers tend
to (1) have fewer marketable skills than other better trained and better
educated occupational groups and (2) have less flexible working hours
than some other occupational groups, they are at a disadvantage in obtaining secondary employment as wage earners. Hence, entrepreneurial
activity might have been the only secondary employment available to
the semi-skilled workers of the target population.

D.   MOONLIGHTING AND CRIMINAL CAREERS IN ROBBERY
     AND BURGLARY

In light of the income level and occupational status of the target
population, i.e., as semi-skilled workers, one could reasonably assume
that a substantial proportion of these individuals could be classified as
either the "working poor" or victims of the "economic squeeze"; the latter condition seen as being endemic among blue collar workers.[49] Obtaining secondary employment in wage jobs is relatively difficult for
such persons. Moonlighting in entrepreneurial activity then may not
only be desirable—it may be necessary.

While perhaps not possessed of conventionally marketable skills,
the target population was not without other personal resources. To varying degrees, they possessed experience and perhaps skill as burglars
and/or robbers. As Polsky[50] and Bluestone[51] note, participation in
criminal activity as secondary employment is of such character as to
quickly provide one with income without interfering with one's conventional occupational responsibilities. Since these men are already convicted felons, they are not likely to be dissuaded from criminal activity
by fear that apprehension and conviction will damage their prospects
for legitimate employment; the damage is already done. More importantly perhaps, these men have already made a considerable investment
in their criminal careers. It would seem that when they are in need of
economic assistance, they draw upon this investment, i.e., they continue
to pursue a criminal career.

E.   A NOTE ON THOSE NOT IN THE LABOR FORCE

Virtually all (99.5%) of those offenders without a job indicated that
they were not seeking employment.[52] This finding is itself of some sig-

---

[49] *See generally* Rosow, *supra* note 33, at 942-45; Wool, *What's Wrong with Work in America?—
A Review Essay*, 96 MONTHLY LAB. REV. 38, 39 (1973).

[50] *See* N. POLSKY, *supra* note 23.

[51] *See* Bluestone, *supra* note 25.

[52] H. Holzman, The Persistent Property Offender and the Concept of Professional Criminality: The Case of Robbery and Burglary 137-39 (1979) (dissertation).

nificance to the study since it suggests that some twenty-two percent of the target population may have had no interest in legitimate employment. This would indicate that some persistent offenders, although a minority, may conform to the existing conceptions of the "professional criminal." Two out of three of those not in the labor force reported that they *did not want to work*.[53] Furthermore, only about one in twenty of those who did not want a job reported that their age or participation in school and/or training influenced their decision not to seek work.

The finding that a sizable minority of the target population did not have nor want a job at the time of their arrest for present offense is not unexpected. Both the generalist and specialist conceptions of the professional criminal are based on empirical research, although this research has used rather small samples that were not as rigorously defined as the target population in the present study. It is interesting to note, however, that Petersilia, Greenwood and Lavin,[54] who studied a sample of forty-nine incarcerated armed robbers with at least one prior prison term, found employment rates roughly comparable to those presented here. Furthermore, some of the individuals studied by Petersilia and her associates may have been similar to this study's generalists, since over one out of every three[55] stated that they were burglars who had switched to robbery.[56] It thus appears that as one better defines the population of "career" criminals under study, previously unnoticed behavior patterns emerge.

V. MOONLIGHTER OR CRIMINAL?—IMPLICATIONS FOR CRIMINOLOGICAL THEORY

The findings of this study pose a question quite germane to criminological theory: are persistent robbers and burglars to be viewed as criminals who also have conventional jobs or as semi-skilled workers who moonlight as criminals? Since most criminological theories focus upon an attempt to explain deviance rather than conformity, the prevalence of conventional work force participation among "hard core" criminals is theoretically intriguing.

Among the major schools of contemporary criminological thought,

---

[53] *Id.*

[54] J. PETERSILIA, P. GREENWOOD & M. LAVIN, CRIMINAL CAREERS OF HABITUAL FELONS (1977).

[55] *Id.* at 23.

[56] The examination of the criminal histories of the generalists in the target population indicated that the last incarceration for over four out of five of these men was for robbery. This would suggest that these men were first active in burglary and then switched to robbery. This supposition is supported by the findings of a recent study by Peterson, entitled "Doing Crime: A Survey of California Prison Inmates," in which it was found that recidivists do tend to be apprehended for those offenses in which they are most active.

only control theory takes the position that conformity, not deviance, must·be explained.[57] Control theorists believe that crime, delinquency and other forms of deviance are not caused by forces which motivate people to transgress norms but rather are simply not prevented by internal and external controls.[58] Reckless sees criminal behavior as the product of a series of struggles between countervailing forces involving what he calls inner containment and outer containment of deviance. The individual is pushed toward deviance by internal drives and impulses (e.g., discontent), and also pressured or pulled toward deviance by environmental factors, (e.g., delinquent peers or poverty). Conversely, inner controls (e.g., good self concept, ego, or strength), work to minimize deviance as do outer controls (e.g., parents or official agents of social control). Matza[59] sees juveniles as "drifting" in and out of delinquency due to situational factors, e.g., peer pressure, which join to push the youngster into deviance in a specific instance.

Advocates of control theory stress the situational nature of the personal decision to commit crime and suggest that commission of a proscribed act may indeed seem appropriate to an indiviual at "time A" and inappropriate at "time B." It is this flexibility that was characterized by Matza as "drift" in his discussion of the etiology of juvenile delinquency. Hence, the control perspective views the offender as a subjective human being who occasionally indulges in brief episodes of criminality rather than viewing him as simply an object to be feared, rehabilitated, or punished. Control theorists would therefore not be surprised that the persistent burglar spends his days as a factory worker.

The earlier discussion regarding multiple jobholding, the nature of blue collar secondary employment, and the conventional and criminal economic activities of the target population are consistent with control theory. Semi-skilled workers with prior criminal histories are subjected to economic pressures. Having already "served time," they do not fear the stigma of criminalization. Their experience in successfully committing property crime suggests that an individual can indulge in many lucrative but illegal episodes before being caught, i.e., the risk of apprehension is low. They possess skills which they believe will enhance the possibility of profit while reducing the risk of being caught. The forces of inner containment are temporarily suppressed. A semi-skilled worker thus comes to moonlight in crime. The worker's position in the marketplace, his entire repertoire of skills, his financial situation and his fund of

---

57 T. HIRSCHI, CAUSES OF DELINQUENCY (1969).

58 *See generally* F. NYE, FAMILY RELATIONSHIPS AND DELINQUENT BEHAVIOR 3-4 (1958); Reckless, *A New Theory of Delinquency and Crime* 25 FED. PROBATION 42 (1961).

59 D. MATZA, DELINQUENCY AND DRIFT 42-46 (1964).

personal experiences conjoin not only to make him a multiple jobholder but a recidivistic property offender as well.

VI.   CONCLUSION

Twentieth century criminologists have tended to make much of the relationship between crime and unemployment. Even with the renewed popularity of deterrence and incapacitation justifications for long term incarceration, rehabilitation still has very wide currency in the United States. Traditionally, rehabilitation depends heavily on occupational training and job placement. The results of the present study suggest that known recidivists in robbery and/or burglary are very likely to be legitimately employed while continuing to pursue their criminal careers. Furthermore, when one examines the occupational status of these recidivists in light of the literature on moonlighting, it seems reasonable to view their continued involvement in property crime as secondary employment of an entrepreneurial genre.

In respect to their political implications, the findings of this study might be interpreted in several very different ways. The opponents of rehabilitation might suggest that this study represents further evidence of the ineffectiveness of traditional correctional treatment. Expensive vocational education programs in prison could be depicted as merely sharpening the skills of would-be careerists in burglary. Why not simply opt for more use of lengthy incapacitation with the hope that it would chasten the offender while it protected society?

The interpretation of radical criminologists might be quite different. They might suggest that the underclasses of a capitalist society are forced to participate in "underground" economies, stealing, or purchasing the fruits of crime simply to survive. These criminologists might declare that the rising unemployment among America's middle class will finally teach liberals and conservatives alike what the term "working poor" really means. The critical criminologist might see moonlighting in crime by habitual offenders as perhaps foreshadowing more part-time criminal activity by the so-called law-abiding majority of workers as the general economic situation worsens.

This study's findings can also be interpreted as providing evidence that the central focus of the criminal justice system's rehabilitative efforts needs to be changed. Although the average age of the offender in the target population was only twenty-seven, the average number of incarcerations—not convictions—was four. Taken with the evidence of moonlighting, these data suggest that the solution to career criminality might rest with a program of correctional intervention before that criminal career is well established. In essence, perhaps it is time to take another serious look at "childsaving."

This study's results also have important implications for the study of criminal careers of persistent property offenders. The finding of an unexpectedly high rate of labor force participation in the target population suggests that both traditional and newer conceptions of the professional criminal need to be reexamined with regard to their perspective on the position of the serious habitual property offender in the world of work. Any new theoretical hypotheses concerning "crime as work" must account for conventional labor force participation among serious habitual property offenders.

[9]

VICTIMOLOGY: An International Journal
Volume I, Number 3, Fall 1976, pp. 446–461
© Copyright 1976 Visage Press, Inc. *Printed in U.S.A.*

The Pickpocket and His Victim

The pickpocket has been widely discussed in both history and literature. While first romanticized in the *Satyricon* of Petronius, the earliest
vivid descriptions of the pickpocket and his tactile arts appeared in a
collection of Tudor and early Stuart tracts, pamphlets, and ballads which
detailed the life and times of the rogues and vagabonds of Elizabethan
England.[1] Mayhew's (1862) *London Labour and London Poor*, provided a
description of the pickpocket to a more recent popular audience, and
Charles Dickens' discussion of *Fagin's* school for pickpockets in *Oliver
Twist* has had an impact on both nineteenth and twentieth century imagi-
nations.

Yet an overview of the history of crime suggests that while the stealth
and cleverness of the pickpocket has been widely known, he has been the
subject of only minimal analytical study during recent times. Furthermore, our current knowledge of pickpocket activities has generally been
drawn from less than a dozen studies and commentaries generated during
the last one hundred years. In 1868, for example, Edward Winslow Martin's *Secrets of the Great City* offered a descriptive portrait of New York
pickpockets, indicating who they were, where they operated, and how they
were integrated as a group. Edward Crapsey's (1872) *The Nether Side of
New York* provided statistical data on the number of pickpockets who
worked the southern end of Manhattan Island, combined with their arrest

---

[1] The majority of these rogue pamphlets and ballads were first published during the
sixteenth century, and have been reprinted in Viles and Furnivall (1880), Wheatley and
Cunningham (1891), Chandler (1907), and Judges (1930). Their historical reliability has
been examined by Aydelotte (1913: 76–78, 114–139).

and conviction rates. Thomas Brynes' *Professional Criminals of America*, first published in 1886 and updated in 1895, described the criminal behavior system of the pickpocket with a discussion of the career histories of seventy-one professional pickpockets who were operating in New York during the latter part of the nineteenth century. More recently, Edwin Sutherland's (1937) *The Professional Thief* examined the structure of the pickpocket mob as it was related to the wider professional underworld. And finally, David W. Maurer's (1964) *Whiz Mob* viewed the behavior patterns of pickpockets as reflected by their technical argot.[2]

Not unlike studies of other criminal behavior systems, the efforts of Maurer, Sutherland, and their predecessors focused only minimally on the victim of the pickpocket. The literature, for example, can tell us little as to how the pickpocket locates and selects his victim, what victim losses amount to, what a pickpocket's attitudes towards the victim are, or how a pickpocket typically deals with a victim who detects the act of theft while it is in progress. Within this context, the following discussion reviews the nature and structure of pickpocket operations, and attempts to provide data and insight into pickpocket/victim interaction based on extensive field research with twenty professional pickpockets during 1976 in Dade County (Miami), Florida.

The Professional Pickpocket

Although the literature has referenced various types of pickpockets, ranging from the rank amateur to the seasoned expert, traditional conceptions have designated the pickpocket as a *professional thief* (Sutherland, 1937; Maurer, 1964; Inciardi, 1975). Along with a delimited group of sneak thieves, safe and house burglars, forgers and counterfeiters, shoplifters, and confidence men, the seasoned pickpocket is conceived of as a highly specialized, non-violent criminal who makes a regular business of stealing. He devotes his entire working time and energy to larceny, operating with proficiency and possessing an extensive body of skills and knowledge that is utilized in the planning and execution of his work. He is a graduate of a developmental process that includes the acquisition of specialized experience and attitudes. He makes crime his way of life, identifying himself with an underworld that extends friendship, understanding, sympathy, congeniality, security, recognition, and respect. And finally, he is able to steal for long periods of time without extended terms of incarceration as a result of his abilities to deal with his victims and the various elements of social control.

---

[2] While much of our data on pickpockets have been drawn from these studies and commentaries, other descriptive information can be found in Mayhew (1862), Farley (1876), Pinkerton (1886), Buel (1891), Willard (1900), Hapgood (1903), Felstead (1923), Dearden (1925), O'Connor (1928), Ingram (1930), Dressler (1951), Campion (1957), and Varna (1957).

The pickpocket, reflecting this notion of professionalism, is known in the underworld as a _class cannon:_

> . . . class cannon means experience, skill, connections and a sense for knowing when to steal and when not to steal . . . it means that the _cannon_ (picking pockets) is part of your life . . . it means that you're not one of those amateurs who spend their time _grinding up nickels and dimes_ (inept stealing for low stakes).[3]

The seasoned professional pickpocket, or _class cannon_, most often works in a _mob_ of two, three, or four members, each playing a specific role in the total operation.[4] This operation typically includes the selection of the _mark_ (victim), the locating of the money or valuables on his person, maneuvering him into position, the act of theft, and the passing of the stolen property. Pickpockets work in crowded areas—amusement centers, public gambling attractions, transportation depots—those which draw victims with money in their possession and where a pickpocket can operate unnoticed.

The Pickpocket and His Victim

The pickpockets interviewed for this study were all drawn from the Miami, Florida area, and were contacted during the period January–April 1976. A total of twenty were interviewed extensively, and the author's entree' into this criminal fraternity occurred during prior research with the professional underworld, and is described in Inciardi (1975, 1977).

The Miami area was especially suited for a study of this type because for some fifty years, it has been considered by the underworld as a pickpocket mecca. Numerous pickpockets, both professional and amateur, travel to Miami from the northeastern and midwestern cities to victimize the northern winter tourists. The area offers a large congested population of _marks_, most of whom are carrying substantial amounts of money in a carefree and relaxed attitude. One _class cannon_ from New York City indicated:

> The city is full of suckers just waiting to be hit. They come down here with plenty of money and they're not thinking about trouble . . . they're not thinking about being hit, just about having a good time and what they can brag about to their friends back home.

Also:

> It's like New York at Christmas time . . . everybody rushing here, there, trying to do things. Their pockets are full and their heads empty . . . you can pull down their drawers and they might not notice.

---

[3] This quotation was drawn from Inciardi (1977), who provides a more complete description of the _class cannon_.

[4] Most mobs only have three members, while a few pickpockets work alone.

Or similarly:

> It's easy to catch them off guard . . . all they're thinking about is where to spend
> their money next. Also, down here they don't have friends who are cops or lawyers
> or judges who can put on extra pressure.

Although most of the Miami area is generally congested during the
winter season, there are a variety of locations which have excessive
numbers of potential *marks* – the race tracks, fair grounds, the Jai Alai
fronton, the Miami Beach Convention Hall and Dinner Key Auditorium,
the Miami Seaquarium, the airport, and the crowded streets of downtown
Miami and Miami Beach. While most pickpockets work all of these areas,
some have preferences which reflect a recurrent pattern. For example:

> The killer whale at the Seaquarium is my best confederate (partner). When the
> show is over and everyone starts pushing their way out of the area on to the next
> attraction, this dumb fish takes a practice jump that catches everybody. When they
> look up, I *go down* (steal a wallet).

> . . . Jai Alai is a good spot. There's plenty of people, plenty of action, and plenty of
> money. When a player scores a point and everyone yells and jumps, that's the time
> for a hit.

And at the race tracks:

> . . . down around the middle of the race you look around to see who's win-
> ning . . . he's usually going crazy – yelling and cheering and all that. When his
> horse crosses the line he's thinkin' only about that horse, and that's when I *beat*
> (steal from) him.[5]

While the Miami cannons indicate favorite locations, most have few
preferences in terms of specific victims. Maurer (1964:103–107) has suggested that some pickpockets will prefer elderly men (*paps*) since their
reaction time is slow, or middle age men (*bates*) because they carry more
money than others. Such preferences generally fade in the vacation area
setting. The primary factor to the Miami *cannon* is whether his potential
mark is a tourist. He looks at a person's attitude, dress, and behavior, and
combines this information with his occupational intuition about whether
his victim has money.

By contrast, however, *all* of the pickpockets interviewed do not look
upon women as potential victims. In fact, the pickpocket who steals from
women (a *moll buzzer* or *hanger binger*) has always been considered as low

---

[5] By contrast, however, this pickpocket also commented that theft is difficult after a
winner has collected his earnings:
   . . . but once he comes from the windows with his hard won cash, forget about him.
He gets suspicious, thinking that everyone around him is a thief or a mugger.

class in the underworld fraternity. Maurer (1964: 103-105) offers several explanations for this phenomenon. First, there is the Freudian notion that the pickpocket is a latent homosexual, that the act of theft is symbolic of the sex act and hence, the choice of a male victim is an unconscious and symbolic expression of homosexual urges. An alternative suggestion is that males have been the traditional carriers of money, thus excluding women as potential victims. Finally, within the underworld, those who have also preyed on women have generally victimized cripples, drunks, or the retarded, and are considered as acting without skill or courage.

The pickpockets contacted in Miami verbalized an alternative set of reasons for stealing from only male victims, essentially in terms of the relative ecology of risk. For example:

> Women carry all kinds of things these days, even money, but the ones from the cities worry about the (purse) snatchers, so they keep their bags closed or under the arm. This makes things difficult or damn near impossible. Also, even if they're just carrying it by the strap, first, you have to open it, then you have to find the wallet. All of this can be too obvious.

Also:

> . . . then you have the ones who shove a roll of bills down between their tits (bosom) — usually vacationers — or they pin a little purse to the bra. Now I like tits, but I don't want anyone screamin' that I grabbed them in a public place.

Finally:

> Let's face it. The girls can be good *marks* . . . well, let's say possible *marks* . . . they carry more. But if they see you you've got trouble. They scream, attract attention and make a hell of a ruckus.

In addition to the selection of locations for picking pockets and the choice of potential *marks,* the professional *cannon* adjusts his activity and manner to that of his victims. He tries to remain inconspicuous and mesh with his environment, avoiding everything that will draw attention to him. He refrains from the use of his technical argot in public places. And he will dress accordingly. At the race tracks he will appear as a northern tourist — bermuda shorts, flowered shirt, and white shoes. On the Miami Beach streets, some will look like a pensioner — tired, slow-moving, perhaps a bit disheveled.

Once the act of theft takes place, the cannon will *pass* (hand over) the *loot* (wallet, money, or other valuables) to a mob member, and leave the immediate area.[6] Pickpockets claim that their interaction with the victim

---

[6] The dynamics of picking pockets and passing of the stolen goods are described at length by Maurer (1964).

is minimal. While they may *track a mark* (observe or follow a victim) for some time, the act of theft takes place in less than a second. This is done quietly and without *bumping,* jostling, or disturbing the victim in any way. On this latter period, *class cannons* suggest that bumping into a victim and stealing from him while he is off balance is just not done by professionals:

> . . . jostling the *mark* is for the amateurs, T.V. writers, and dreamers. Don't wake up the mark is what we always think. If you do, he sees your face, he thinks, he remembers.

When a *cannon* is caught by his *mark,* which is claimed to occur only one in a hundred times, the thief can generally talk his victim out of pressing charges:

> Problems come only when he makes a big stink and someone calls a cop. But that's not too often. Just give 'em his money back and then some . . . tell him he's gonna have to go to court, give up the *loot* to the police as evidence . . . tell 'em it will spoil his vacation . . . he'll just take his money and let you split.

Victim losses in Miami are relatively extensive. Among the twenty pickpockets interviewed, their average annual income was estimated at $23,000, with $9,200 reported as the seasonal income while in Miami. This would suggest that these twenty thieves alone would be responsible for some $184,000 in cash thefts. Yet, while this sum may seem extensive, losses to the individual victim are generally small by comparison. The *cannons* studied here reported that they *track* no more than ten to fifteen victims each day, while *making a score* (finding money in excess of $5) on half that number. As such, while some *scores* may, although rarely, be in the hundreds of dollars, the average is $10 to $25. Finally, the pickpocket looks upon his *mark* simply as fair game. His stealing is detached and impersonal, and he has no hatred or contempt for the victim. On the other hand, however, they rationalize their behavior by defining their actions as parallel to the dishonest practices of businessmen or law enforcement officials; or they devalue their victims by suggesting that the latter could easily absorb their losses:

> What's 50 bucks to a guy like that . . . he'll blow ten times that at the track tomorrow.
> They don't even feel it . . . if they can afford to stay on the *beach* (Miami Beach) they can afford to throw a few hundred my way.
> They've no gripe. They're ripped off every day by the storekeepers, waiters, hotels . . . What I get is nothin' compared to what those legal types do.

Conclusion

During the course of this research, several pickpockets clearly indicated how to avoid becoming a *mark:*

Anybody carrying lots of money is asking for trouble . . . some people use their wallets as a portable safety deposit box . . . you can't be *beat* (robbed) if you don't have much.

Some guys carry their money in their shoe or their wallet in their boot . . . you can't steal from them . . . others have it in a money belt. It's the guys that put a wallet in the pants or coat that are easy.

The sign that says 'Beware of Pickpockets' is our best friend. People see the sign, feel their wallets, just telling us where it is.

My advice is to wear tight trousers . . . it's hard to pull a wallet from there.

Watch out for the *double bump* . . . That's when a *cannon* jostles you — a fake jostle sort of, just to watch you feel for your *poke*. Then he moves in — if you get bumped, watch out.

REFERENCES

Aydelotte, Frank.
    1913   Elizabethan Rogues and Vagabonds. Oxford: Clarendon.
Buel, J. W.
    1891   Sunlight and Shadow of America's Great Cities. Philadelphia: West Philadelphia Publishing Co.
Byrnes, Thomas.
    1886   Professional Criminals of America. New York: G. W. Dillingham.
    1895   Professional Criminals of America. New York: G. W. Dillingham.
Campion, Daniel.
    1957   Crooks Are Human Too. Englewood Cliffs, N.J.: Prentice-Hall.
Chandler, Frank Wadleigh.
    1907   The Literature of Roguery. Boston: Houghton Mifflin.
Crapsey, Edward.
    1872   The Nether Side of New York. New York: Sheldon.
Dearden, R. L.
    1925   The Autobiography of a Crook. New York: Dial Press.
Dressler, David.
    1951   Parole Chief. New York: Viking Press.
Farley, Phil.
    1976   Criminals of America. New York: Author's Edition.
Felstead, Sidney T.
    1923   The Underworld of London. New York: Dutton.
Hapgood, Hutchins.
    1903   The Autobiography of a Thief. New York: Fox, Duffield.
Inciardi, James A.
    1975   Career in Crime. Chicago: Rand McNally.
    1977   "In Search of the Class Cannon: A Field Study of Professional Pickpockets," in Robert S. Weppner (ed.), The Street Ethnography of Crime and Drugs. Beverly Hills: Sage.
Ingram, George.
    1930   Hell's Kitchen. London: Herbert Jenkins.
Judges, Arthur V. (ed.).
    1930   The Elizabethan Underworld. London: Routledge.
Martin, Edward Winslow.
    1868   Secrets of The Great City. Philadelphia: National.
Maurer, David W.
    1964   Whiz Mob: A Correlation of The Technical Argot of Pickpockets with their Behavior Pattern. New Haven: College and University Press.

Mayhew, Henry.
    1862   London Labour and The London Poor. Vol. IV, Those That Will Not Work,
                comprising Prostitutes, Thieves, Swindlers and Beggars, by several contribu-
                tors. New York: Dover Publications (1968 edition).
O'Connor, John.
    1928   Broadway Racketeers. New York: Horace Liveright.
Pinkerton, Allan.
    1886   Thirty Years a Detective. New York: G. W. Dillingham.
Sutherland, Edwin H.
    1937   The Professional Thief. Chicago: University of Chicago Press.
Varna, Andrew.
    1957   World Underworld. London: Museum Press.
Viles, Edward, and F. J. Furnivall (eds.).
    1880   The Rogues and Vagabonds of Shakespeare's Youth. London: N. Truber.
Wheatley, Henry B., and Peter Cunningham.
    1891   London Life, Past and Present, vol. 3. London: John Murray.
Willard, Josiah Flynt (pseud. Josiah Flynt).
    1900   Notes of An Itinerant Policeman. Boston: L. C. Page.

                                            James A. Inciardi
                                            Department of Sociology
                                            University of Delaware
                                            Newark, DE 19711

[10]

THIEVES, CONVICTS AND THE INMATE CULTURE

JOHN IRWIN and DONALD R. CRESSEY
Departments of Anthropology and Sociology
University of California, Los Angeles and Santa Barbara

In the rapidly-growing literature on the social organization of correctional institutions, it has become common to discuss "prison culture" and "inmate culture" in terms suggesting that the behavior systems of various types of inmates stem from the conditions of imprisonment themselves. Use of a form of structural-functional analysis in research and observation of institutions has led to emphasis of the notion that internal conditions stimulate inmate behavior of various kinds, and there has been a glossing over of the older notion that inmates may bring a culture with them into the prison. Our aim is to suggest that much of the inmate behavior classified as part of the prison culture is not peculiar to the prison at all. On the contrary, it is the fine distinction between "prison culture" and "criminal subculture" which seems to make understandable the fine distinction between behavior patterns of various categories of inmates.

A number of recent publications have defended the notion that behavior patterns among inmates develop with

* We are indebted to the following persons for suggested modifications of the original draft: Donald L. Garrity, Daniel Glaser, Erving Goffman, and Stanton Wheeler.

a minimum of influence from the outside world. For example, in his general discussion of total institutions, Goffman acknowledges that inmates bring a culture with them to the institution, but he argues that upon entrance to the institution they are stripped of this support by processes of mortification and dispossession aimed at managing the daily activities of a large number of persons in a small space with a small expenditure of resources.[1] Similarly, Sykes and Messinger note that a central value system seems to pervade prison populations, and they maintain that "conformity to, or deviation from, the inmate code is the major basis for classifying and describing the social relations of prisoners."[2] The emphasis in this code is on directives such as "don't interfere with inmate interests," "don't lose your head," "don't exploit inmates," "don't weaken," and "don't be a sucker." The authors' argument, like the argument in other of Sykes' publications is that the origin of these values is situational; the value system arises out of the conditions of imprisonment.[3] Cloward stresses both the acute sense of status degradation which prisoners experience and the resulting patterns of prison life, which he calls "structural

accommodation."[4] Like others, he makes the important point that the principal types of inmates—especially the "politicians" and the "shots"—help the officials by exerting controls over the general prison body in return for special privileges. Similarly, he recognizes the "right guy" role as one built around the value system described by Sykes and Messinger, and points out that it is tolerated by prison officials because it helps maintain the status quo. Cloward hints at the existence in prison of a *criminal* subculture when he says that "the upper echelons of the inmate world come to be occupied by those whose past behavior best symbolizes that which society rejects and who have most fully repudiated institutional norms." Nevertheless, his principal point is that this superior status, like other patterns of behavior among inmates, arises from the *internal* character of the prison situation. McCleery also stresses the unitary character of the culture of prisoners, and he identifies the internal source of this culture in statements such as: "The denial of validity to outside contacts protected the inmate culture from criticism and assured the stability of the social system," "A man's status in the inmate community depended on his role there and his conformity to its norms," "Inmate culture stressed the goals of adjustment within the walls and the rejection of outside contacts," and "Status has been geared to adjustment in the prison."[5]

The idea that the prison produces its own varieties of behavior represents a break with the more traditional notion that men bring patterns of behavior with them when they enter prison, and use them in prison. Despite their emphasis on "prisonization" of newcomers, even Clemmer and Riemer noted that degree of conformity to prison expectations depends in part

---

[1] Erving Goffman, "On the Characteristics of Total Institutions," Chapters 1 and 2 in Donald R. Cressey, Editor, *The Prison: Studies in Institutional Organization and Change*, New York: Holt, Rinehart and Winston, 1961, pp. 22-47.

[2] Richard A. Cloward, Donald R. Cressey, George H. Grosser, Richard McCleery, Lloyd E. Ohlin, and Gresham M. Sykes and Sheldon L. Messinger, *Theoretical Studies in Social Organization of the Prison*, New York: Social Science Research Council, 1960, p. 9.

[3] *Ibid.*, pp. 15, 19. See also Gresham M. Sykes, "Men, Merchants, and Toughs: A Study of Reactions to Imprisonment," *Social Problems*, 4 (October, 1957), pp. 130-138; and Gresham M. Sykes, *The Society of Captives*, Princeton: Princeton University Press, 1958, pp. 79-82.

[4] Cloward, *et al., op. cit.*, pp. 21, 35-41.
[5] *Ibid.*, pp. 58, 60, 73.

on prior, outside conditions.[6] Schrag has for some years been studying the social backgrounds and careers of various types of inmates.[7] Unlike any of the authors cited above, he has collected data on both the pre-prison experiences and the prison experiences of prisoners. He relates the actions of inmates to the broader community as well as to the forces that are more indigenous to prisons themselves.[8] Of most relevance here is his finding that anti-social inmates ("right guys") "are reared in an environment consistently oriented toward illegitimate social norms,"[9] and frequently earn a living via contacts with organized crime but do not often rise to positions of power in the field. In contrast, asocial inmates ("outlaws") are frequently reared in institutions: "The careers of asocial offenders are marked by high egocentrism and inability to profit from past mistakes or to plan for the future."[10]

However, despite these research findings, even Schrag has commented as follows: "Juxtaposed with the official organization of the prison is an unofficial social system originating within the institution and regulating inmate conduct with respect to focal issues, such as length of sentence, relations among prisoners, contacts with staff members and other civilians, food, sex, and health, among others."[11] Garrity interprets Schrag's theory in the following terms, which seem to ignore the findings on the pre-prison careers of the various inmate types:

> Schrag has further suggested that all inmates face a number of common problems of adjustment, as a consequence of imprisonment and that social organization develops as a consequence. When two or more persons perceive that they share a common motivation or problem of action, a basis for meaningful interaction has been established, and from this interaction can emerge the social positions, roles, and norms which comprise social organization. Schrag suggests that the common problems of adjustment which become the principal axes of prison life are related to time, food, sex, leisure, and health.[12]

Garrity himself uses the "indigenous origin" notion when he says that "the axial values regarding shared problems or deprivations provide the basis for articulation of the broad normative system or 'prison code' which defines positions and roles in a general way but allows enough latitude so that positions and roles take on the character of social worlds themselves."[13] However, he also points out that some prisoners' reference groups are outside the prison, and he characterizes the "right guy" as an "anti-social offender, stable, and oriented to crime, criminals, and inmates."[14] "The 'right guy' is the dominant figure in the prison, and his reference groups are elite prisoners, sophisticated, career-type criminals, and other 'right guys.'"[15] Cressey and Krassowski, similarly, seem confused about any distinction between a criminal subculture and a prison subculture. They mention that many inmates of Soviet labor camps "know prisons and maintain criminalistic values," and that the inmates are bound together by a "crim-

[6] Donald Clemmer, *The Prison Community*, Re-issued Edition, New York: Rinehart, 1958, pp. 229-302; Hans Riemer, "Socialization in the Prison Community," *Proceedings of the American Prison Association*, 1937, pp. 151-155.
[7] See Clarence Schrag, *Social Types in a Prison Community*, Unpublished M.S. Thesis, University of Washington, 1944.
[8] Clarence Schrag, "Some Foundations for a Theory of Correction," Chapter 8 in Cressey, *op. cit.*, p. 329.
[9] *Ibid.*, p. 350.
[10] *Ibid.*, p. 349.
[11] *Ibid.*, p. 342.

[12] Donald R. Garrity, "The Prison as a Rehabilitation Agency," Chapter 9 in Cressey, *op. cit.*, pp. 372-373.
[13] *Ibid.*, p. 373.
[14] *Ibid.*, p. 376.
[15] *Ibid.*, p. 377.

inalistic ideology,"[16] but they fail to deal theoretically with the contradiction between these statements and their observation that the inmate leaders in the labor camps are "toughs" or "gorillas" rather than "right guys" or "politicians." Conceivably, leadership is vested in "toughs" to a greater extent than is the case in American prisons because the orientation is more that of a *prison* subculture than of a criminal subculture in which men are bound together with a "criminalistic ideology."

It is our contention that the "functional" or "indigenous origin" notion has been overemphasized and that observers have overlooked the dramatic effect that external behavior patterns have on the conduct of inmates in any given prison. Moreover, the contradictory statements made in this connection by some authors, including Cressey,[17] seem to stem from acknowledging but then ignoring the deviant subcultures which exist outside any given prison and outside prisons generally. More specifically, it seems rather obvious that the "prison code"—don't inform on or exploit another inmate, don't lose your head, be weak, or be a sucker, etc.—is also part of a *criminal* code, existing outside prisons. Further, many inmates come to any given prison with a record of many terms in correctional institutions. These men, some of whom have institutional records dating back to early childhood, bring with them a ready-made set of patterns which they apply to the new situation, just as is the case with participants in the criminal subculture. In view of these variations, a clear understanding of inmate conduct cannot be obtained simply by viewing "prison culture" or "inmate culture" as an isolated system springing solely from the conditions of imprisonment. Becker and Geer have made our point in more general terms: "The members of a group may derive their understandings from cultures other than that of the group they are at the moment participating in. To the degree that group participants share latent social identities (related to their membership in the same 'outside' social groups) they will share these understandings, so that there will be a culture which can be called *latent*, i.e., the culture has its origin and social support in a group other than the one in which the members are now participating."[18]

We have no doubt that the total set of relationships called "inmate society" is a response to problems of imprisonment. What we question is the emphasis given to the notion that solutions to these problems are found within the prison, and the lack of emphasis on "latent culture"—on external experiences as determinants of the solutions. We have found it both necessary and helpful to divide inmates into three rough categories: those oriented to a criminal subculture, those oriented to a prison subculture, and those oriented to "conventional" or "legitimate" subcultures.

THE TWO DEVIANT SUBCULTURES

When we speak of a criminal subculture we do not mean to imply that there is some national or international organization with its own judges, enforcement agencies, etc. Neither do we

---

[16] Donald R. Cressey and Witold Krassowski, "Inmate Organization and Anomie in American Prisons and Soviet Labor Camps," *Social Problems*, 5 (Winter, 1957-58), pp. 217-230.

[17] Edwin H. Sutherland and Donald R. Cressey, *Principles of Criminology*, Sixth Edition, New York: Lippincott, 1960, pp. 504-505.

[18] Howard S. Becker and Blanche Geer, "Latent Culture: A Note on the Theory of Latent Social Roles," *Administrative Science Quarterly*, 5 (September, 1960), pp. 305-306. See also Alvin W. Gouldner, "Cosmopolitans and Locals: Toward an Analysis of Latent Social Roles," *Administrative Science Quarterly*, 2 (1957), pp. 281-306 and 2 (1958), pp. 444-480.

imply that every person convicted of a crime is a member of the subculture. Nevertheless, descriptions of the values of professional thieves, "career criminals," "sophisticated criminals," and other good crooks indicate that there is a set of values which extends to criminals across the nation with a good deal of consistency.[19] To avoid possible confusion arising from the fact that not all criminals share these values, we have arbitrarily named the system a "thief" subculture. The core values of this subculture correspond closely to the values which prison observers have ascribed to the "right guy" role. These include the important notion that criminals should not betray each other to the police, should be reliable, wily but trustworthy, cool headed, etc. High status in this subculture is awarded to men who appear to follow these prescriptions without variance. In the thief subculture a man who is known as "right" or "solid" is one who can be trusted and relied upon. High status is also awarded to those who possess skill as thieves, but to be just a successful thief is not enough; there must be solidness as well. A solid guy is respected even if he is unskilled, and no matter how skilled in crime a stool pigeon may be, his status is low.

Despite the fact that adherence to the norms of the thief subculture is an ideal, and the fact that the behavior of the great majority of men arrested or convicted varies sharply from any "criminal code" which migh be identified, a proportion of the persons arrested for "real crime" such as burglary, robbery, and larceny have been in close contact with the values of the subculture. Many criminals, while not following the precepts of the subcul-

ture religiously, give lip service to its values and evaluate their own behavior and the behavior of their associates in terms relating to adherence to "rightness" and being "solid." It is probable, further, that use of this kind of values is not even peculiarly "criminal," for policemen, prison guards, college professors, students, and almost any other category of persons evaluate behavior in terms of in-group loyalties. Whyte noted the mutual obligations binding corner boys together and concluded that status depends upon the extent to which a boy lives up to his obligations, a form of "solidness."[20] More recently, Miller identified "toughness," "smartness," and "autonomy" among the "focal concerns" of lower class adolescent delinquent boys; these also characterize prisoners who are oriented to the thief subculture.[21] Wheeler found that half of the custody staff and sixty per cent of the treatment staff in one prison approved the conduct of a hypothetical inmate who refused to name an inmate with whom he had been engaged in a knife fight.[22] A recent book has given the name "moral courage" to the behavior of persons who, like thieves, have shown extreme loyalty to their in-groups in the face of real or threatened adversity, including imprisonment.[23]

Imprisonment is one of the recurring problems with which thieves must cope. It is almost certain that a thief will be arrested from time to time, and the subculture provides members with patterns to be used in

[19] Walter C. Reckless, *The Crime Problem*, Second Edition, New York: Appleton-Century-Crofts, 1945, pp. 144-145; 148-150; Edwin H. Sutherland, *The Profesisonal Thief*, Chicago: University of Chicago Press, 1937.

[20] William Foote Whyte, "Corner Boys: A Study of Clique Behavior," *American Journal of Sociology*, 46 (March, 1941), pp. 647-663.
[21] Walter B. Miller, "Lower Class Culture as a Generating Milieu of Gang Delinquency," *Journal of Social Issues*, 14 (1958), pp. 5-19.
[22] Stanton Wheeler, "Role Conflict in Correctional Communities," Chapter 6 in Cressey, *op. cit.*, p. 235.
[23] Compton Mackenzie, *Moral Courage*, London: Collins, 1962.

order to help solve this problem. Norms which apply to the prison situation, and information on how to undergo the prison experience—how to do time "standing on your head"—with the least suffering and in a minimum amount of time are provided. Of course, the subculture itself is both nurtured and diffused in the different jails and prisons of the country.

There also exists in prisons a subculture which is by definition a set of patterns that flourishes in the environment of incarceration. It can be found wherever men are confined, whether it be in city jails, state and federal prisons, army stockades, prisoner of war camps, concentration camps, or even mental hospitals. Such organizations are characterized by deprivations and limitations on freedom, and in them available wealth must be competed for by men supposedly on an equal footing. It is in connection with the *maintenance* (but not necessarily with the *origin*) of this subculture that it is appropriate to stress the notion that a minimum of outside status criteria are carried into the situation. Ideally, all status is to be achieved by the means made available in the prison, through the displayed ability to manipulate the environment, win special privileges in a certain manner, and assert influence over others. To avoid confusion with writings on "prison culture" and "inmate culture," we have arbitrarily named this system of values and behavior patterns a "convict subculture." The central value of the subculture is utilitarianism, and the most manipulative and most utilitarian individuals win the available wealth and such positions of influence as might exist.

It is not correct to conclude, however, that even these behavior patterns are a consequence of the environment of any particular prison. In the first place, such utilitarian and manipulative behavior probably is characteristic of

the "hard core" lower class in the United States, and most prisoners come from this class. After discussing the importance of toughness, smartness, excitement and fate in this group, Miller makes the following significant observation:

> In lower class culture a close conceptual connection is made between "authority" and "nurturance." To be restrictively or firmly controlled is to be cared for. Thus the overtly negative evaluation of superordinate authority frequently extends as well to nurturance, care, or protection. The desire for personal independence is often expressed in terms such as "I don't need *nobody* to take care of me. I can take care of myself!" Actual patterns of behavior, however, reveal a marked discrepancy between expressed sentiments and what is covertly valued. Many lower class people appear to seek out highly restrictive social environments wherein stringent external controls are maintained over their behavior. Such institutions as the armed forces, the mental hospital, the disciplinary school, the prison or correctional institution, provide environments which incorporate a strict and detailed set of rules defining and limiting behavior, and enforced by an authority system which controls and applies coercive sanctions for deviance from these rules. While under the jurisdiction of such systems, the lower class person generally expresses to his peers continual resentment of the coercive, unjust, and arbitrary exercise of authority. Having been released, or having escaped from these milieux, however, he will often act in such a way as to insure recommitment, or choose recommitment voluntarily after a temporary period of "freedom."[24]

In the second place, the "hard core" members of this subculture as it exists in American prisons for adults are likely to be inmates who have a long record of confinement in institutions for juveniles. McCleery observed that, in a period of transition, reform-school graduates all but took over inmate society in one prison. These boys called themselves a "syndicate" and engaged in a concentrated campaign of argu-

---

[24] *Op. cit.,* pp. 12-13.

ment and intimidation directed toward capturing the inmate council and the inmate craft shop which had been placed under council management. "The move of the syndicate to take over the craft shop involved elements of simple exploitation, the grasp for a status symbol, and an aspect of economic reform."[25] Persons with long histories of institutionalization, it is important to note, might have had little contact with the thief subculture. The thief subculture does not flourish in institutions for juveniles, and graduates of such institutions have not necessarily had extensive criminal experience on the outside. However, some form of the convict subculture *does* exist in institutions for juveniles, though not to the extent characterizing prisons for felons. Some of the newcomers to a prison for adults are, in short, persons who have been oriented to the convict subculture, who have found the utilitarian nature of this subculture acceptable, and who have had little contact with the thief subculture. This makes a difference in their behavior.

The category of inmates we have characterized as oriented to "legitimate" subcultures includes men who are not members of the thief subculture upon entering prison and who reject both the thief subculture and the convict subculture while in prison. These men present few problems to prison administrators. They make up a large percentage of the population of any prison, but they isolate themselves —or are isolated—from the thief and convict subcultures. Clemmer found that forty per cent of a sample of the men in his prison did not consider themselves a part of any group, and another forty per cent could be considered a member of a "semi-primary group" only.[26] He referred to these

men as "ungrouped," and his statistics have often been interpreted as meaning that the prison contains many men not oriented to "inmate culture" or "prison culture"—in our terms, not oriented to either the thief subculture or the convict subculture. This is not necessarily the case. There may be sociometric isolates among the thief-oriented prisoners, the convict-oriented prisoners, and the legitimately oriented prisoners. Consequently, we have used the "legitimate subcultures" terminology rather than Clemmer's term "ungrouped." Whether or not men in this category participate in cliques, athletic teams, or religious study and hobby groups, they are oriented to the problem of achieving goals through means which are legitimate outside prisons.

BEHAVIOR PATTERNS IN PRISON

On an ideal-type level, there are great differences in the prison behavior of men oriented to one or the other of the three types of subculture. The hard core member of the convict subculture finds his reference groups inside the institutions and, as indicated, he seeks status through means available in the prison environment. But it is important for the understanding of inmate conduct to note that the hard core member of the thief subculture seeks status in the broader criminal world of which prison is only a part. His reference groups include people both inside and outside prison, but he is committed to criminal life, not prison life. From his point of view, it is adherence to a widespread criminal code that wins him high status, not adherence to a narrower convict code. Convicts might assign him high status because they admire him as a thief, or because a good thief makes a good convict, but the thief does not play the convicts' game. Similarly, a man oriented to a legitimate subculture is by definition committed to the values

---

[25] Richard H. McCleery, "The Governmental Process and Informal Social Control," Chapter 4 in Cressey, *op. cit.*, p. 179.
[26] *Op. cit.*, pp. 116-133.

of neither thieves nor convicts.

On the other hand, within any given prison, the men oriented to the convict subculture are the inmates that seek positions of power, influence, and sources of information, whether these men are called "shots," "politicians," "merchants," "hoods," "toughs," "gorillas," or something else. A job as secretary to the Captain or Warden, for example, gives an aspiring prisoner information and consequent power, and enables him to influence the assignment or regulation of other inmates. In the same way, a job which allows the incumbent to participate in a racket, such as clerk in the kitchen storeroom where he can steal and sell food, is highly desirable to a man oriented to the convict subculture. With a steady income of cigarettes, ordinarily the prisoners' medium of exchange, he may assert a great deal of influence and purchase those things which are symbols of status among persons oriented to the convict subculture. Even if there is no well-developed medium of exchange, he can barter goods acquired in his position for equally-desirable goods possessed by other convicts. These include information and such things as specially-starched, pressed, and tailored prison clothing, fancy belts, belt buckles or billfolds, special shoes, or any other type of dress which will set him apart and will indicate that he has both the influence to get the goods and the influence necessary to keeping and displaying them despite prison rules which outlaw doing so. In California, special items of clothing, and clothing that is neatly laundered, are called "bonaroos" (a corruption of *bonnet rouge,* by means of which French prison trusties were once distinguished from the common run of prisoners), and to a lesser degree even the persons who wear such clothing are called "bonaroos."

Two inmates we observed in one prison are somewhat representative of high status members of the convict subculture. One was the prison's top gambler, who bet the fights, baseball games, football games, ran pools, etc. His cell was always full of cigarettes, although he did not smoke. He had a job in the cell block taking care of the laundry room, and this job gave him time to conduct his gambling activities. It also allowed him to get commissions for handling the clothing of inmates who paid to have them "bonarooed," or who had friends in the laundry who did this for them free of charge, in return for some service. The "commissions" the inmate received for doing this service were not always direct; the "favors" he did gave him influence with many of the inmates in key jobs, and he reputedly could easily arrange cell changes and job changes. Shortly after he was paroled he was arrested and returned to prison for robbing a liquor store. The other inmate was the prison's most notorious "fag" or "queen." He was feminine in appearance and gestures, and wax had been injected under the skin on his chest to give the appearance of breasts. At first he was kept in a cell block isolated from the rest of the prisoners, but later he was released out into the main population. He soon went to work in a captain's office, and became a key figure in the convict subculture. He was considered a stool pigeon by the thieves, but he held high status among participants in the convict subculture. In the first place, he was the most desired fag in the prison. In the second place, he was presumed to have considerable influence with the officers who frequented the captain's office. He "married" another prisoner, who also was oriented to the convict subculture.

Since prisoners oriented either to a legitimate subculture or to a thief subculture are not seeking high status within any given prison, they do not look for the kinds of positions considered so desirable by the members of the convict subculture. Those oriented to legitimate subcultures take prison as it comes and seek status through channels provided for that purpose by prison administrators—running for election to the inmate council, to the editorship of the institutional newspaper, etc.—and by, generally, conforming to what they think administrators expect of "good prisoners." Long before the thief has come to prison, his subculture has defined proper prison conduct as behavior rationally calculated to "do time" in the easiest possible way. This means that he wants a prison life containing the best possible combination of a maximum amount of leisure time and a maximum number of privileges. Accordingly, the privileges sought by the thief are different from the privileges sought by the man oriented to prison itself. The thief wants things that will make prison life a little easier—extra food, a maximum amount of recreation time, a good radio, a little peace. One thief serving his third sentence for armed robbery was a dish washer in the officers' dining room. He liked the eating privileges, but he never sold food. Despite his "low status" job, he was highly respected by other thieves, who described him as "right," and "solid." Members of the convict subculture, like the thieves, seek privileges. There is a difference, however, for the convict seeks privileges which he believes will enhance his position in the inmate hierarchy. He also wants to do easy time but, as compared with the thief, desirable privileges are more likely to involve freedom to amplify one's store, such as stealing rights in the kitchen, and freedom of movement around the prison. Obtaining an easy job is managed because it is easy and therefore desirable, but it also is managed for the purpose of displaying the fact that it can be obtained.

In one prison, a man serving his second sentence for selling narcotics (he was not an addict) worked in the bakery during the entire term of his sentence. To him, a thief, this was a "good job," for the hours were short and the bakers ate very well. There were some rackets conducted from the bakery, such as selling cocoa, but the man never participated in these activities. He was concerned a little with learning a trade, but not very seriously. Most of all, he wanted the eating privileges which the bakery offered. A great deal of his time was spent reading psychology, philosophy, and mysticism. Before his arrest he had been a reader of tea leaves and he now was working up some plans for an illegal business involving mysticism. Other than this, his main activity was sitting with other inmates and debating.

Just as both thieves and convicts seek privileges, both seek the many kinds of contraband in a prison. But again the things the thief seeks are those than contribute to an easier life, such as mechanical gadgets for heating water for coffee and cocoa, phonographs and radios if they are contraband or not, contraband books, food, writing materials, socks, etc. He may "score" for food occasionally (unplanned theft in which advantage is taken of a momentary opportunity), but he does not have a "route" (highly organized theft of food). One who "scores" for food eats it, shares it with his friends, sometimes in return for a past or expected favors, but he does not sell it. One who has a "route" is in the illicit food selling business.[27] The inmate oriented to the convict subculture, with its emphasis on displaying ability to manipulate the environment, rather than on pleasure, is the inmate with the "route." The difference is observable in the case of an inmate assigned to the job of clerk

[27] See Schrag, "Some Foundations for a Theory of Correction," *op. cit.*, p. 343.

in the dental office of one prison. This man was known to both inmates and staff long before he arrived at the institution, for his crime and arrest were highly publicized in the newspapers. It also became known that he had done time in another penitentiary for "real crime," and that his criminal exploits had frequently taken him from one side of the United States to the other. His assignment to the dental office occurred soon after he entered the prison, and some of the inmates believed that such a highly-desirable job could not be achieved without "influence" and "rep." It was an ideal spot for conducting a profitable business, and a profitable business was in fact being conducted there. In order to get on the list to see the dentist, an inmate had to pay a price in cigarettes to two members of the convict subculture who were running the dental office. This practice soon changed, at least in reference to inmates who could show some contact with our man's criminal friends, in or out of prison. If a friend vouched for a man by saying he was "right" or "solid" the man would be sitting in the dental chair the next day, free of charge.

Generally speaking, an inmate oriented to the thief subculture simply is not interested in gaining high status in the prison. He wants to get out. Moreover, he is likely to be quietly amused by the concern some prisoners have for symbols of status, but he publicly exhibits neither disdain nor enthusiasm for this concern. One exception to this occurred in an institution where a thief had become a fairly close friend of an inmate oriented to the prison. One day the latter showed up in a fresh set of bonaroos, and he made some remark that called attention to them. The thief looked at him, laughed, and said, "For Christ's sake, Bill, they're *Levi's* (standard prison blue denims) and they are always going to be Levi's." The thief may be

accorded high status in the prison, because "rightness" is revered there as well as on the outside, but to him this is incidental to his being a "man," not to his being a prisoner.

Members of both subcultures are conservative—they want to maintain the status quo. Motivation is quite different, however. The man oriented to the convict subculture is conservative because he has great stock in the existing order of things, while the man who is thief oriented leans toward conservatism because he knows how to do time and likes things to run along smoothly with a minimum of friction. It is because of this conservatism that so many inmates are directly or indirectly in accommodation with prison officials who, generally speaking, also wish to maintain the status quo. A half dozen prison observers have recently pointed out that some prison leaders—those oriented to what we call the convict subculture—assist the officials by applying pressures that keep other inmates from causing trouble, while other prison leaders—those oriented to what we call the thief subculture—indirectly keep order by propagating the *criminal* code, including admonitions to "do your own time," "don't interfere with others' activities," "don't 'rank' another criminal." The issue is not whether the thief subculture and convict subculture are useful to, and used by, administrators; it is whether the observed behavior patterns originate in prison as a response to official administrative practices.

There are other similarities, noted by many observers of "prison culture" or "inmate culture." In the appropriate circumstances, members of both subcultures will participate in fomenting and carrying out riots. The man oriented to the convict subculture does this when a change has closed some of the paths for achieving positions of influence, but the thief does it when privileges of the kind that make life easier are taken away from him. Thus, when a "prison reform" group takes over an institution, it may inadvertently make changes which lead to alliances between the members of two subcultures who ordinarily are quite indifferent to each other. In more routine circumstances, the thief adheres to a tight system of mutual aid for other thieves—persons who are "right" and "solid"—a direct application in prison of the norms which ask that a thief prove himself reliable and trustworthy to other thieves. If a man is "right," then even if he is a stranger one must help him if there is no risk to himself. If he is a friend, then one must, in addition, be willing to take *some* risk in order to help him. But in the convict subculture, "help" has a price; one helps in order to gain, whether the gain be "pay" in the form of cigarettes, or a guarantee of a return favor which will enlarge one's area of power.

RELATIONSHIPS BETWEEN THE TWO SUBCULTURES

In the routine prison setting, the two deviant subcultures exist in a balanced relationship. It is this total setting which has been observed as "inmate culture." There is some conflict because of the great disparity in some of the values of thieves and convicts, but the two subcultures share other values. The thief is committed to keeping his hands off other people's activities, and the convict, being utilitarian, is likely to know that it is better in the long run to avoid conflict with thieves and confine one's exploitations to the "do rights" and to the members of his own subculture. Of course, the thief must deal with the convict from time to time, and when he does so he adjusts to the reality of the fact that he is imprisoned. Choosing to follow prison definitions usually means paying for some service in cigarettes or in a returned service; this is the cost of doing easy time. Some thieves adapt in a more general way to the ways of convicts and assimilate the prisonized person's concern for making out in the institution. On an ideal-type level, however, thieves do not sanction exploitation of other inmates, and they simply ignore the "do rights," who are oriented to legitimate subcultures. Nevertheless, their subculture as it operates in prison has exploitative effects.[28]

Numerous persons have documented the fact that "right guys," many of whom can be identified as leaders of the thieves, not of the convicts, exercise the greatest influence over the total prison population. The influence is the long run kind stemming from the ability to influence notions of what is right and proper, what McCleery calls the formulation and communication of definitions.[29] The thief, after all, has the respect of many inmates who are not themselves thieves. The right guy carries a set of attitudes, values and norms that have a great deal of consistency and clarity. He acts, forms opinions, and evaluates events in the prison according to them, and over a long period of time he in this way determines basic behavior patterns in the institution. In what the thief thinks of as "small matters," however—getting job transfers, enforcing payment of gambling debts, making cell assignments—members of the convict subculture run things.

It is difficult to assess the direct lines of influence the two deviant subcultures have over those inmates who are not members of either subculture when they enter a prison. It is true that if a new inmate does not have definitions to apply to the new prison situation, one or the other of the deviant subcultures is likely to supply them. On

---

[28] See Donald R. Cressey, "Foreword," to Clemmer, *op. cit.*, pp. vii-x.
[29] "The Governmental Process and Informal Social Control," *op. cit.*, p. 154.

the one hand, the convict subculture is much more apparent than the thief subculture; its roles are readily visible to any new arrival, and its definitions are readily available to one who wants to "get along" and "make it" in a prison. Moreover, the inmate leaders oriented to the convict subculture are anxious to get new followers who will recognize the existing status hierarchy in the prison. Thieves, on the other hand, tend to be snobs. Their status in prison is determined in part by outside criteria, as well as by prison conduct, and it is therefore difficult for a prisoner, acting as a prisoner, to achieve these criteria. At a minimum, the newcomer can fall under the influence of the thief subculture only if he has intimate association over a period of time with some of its members who are able and willing to impart some of its subtle behavior patterns to him.

Our classification of some inmates as oriented to legitimate subcultures implies that many inmates entering a prison do not find either set of definitions acceptable to them. Like thieves, these men are not necessarily "stripped" of outside statuses, and they do not play the prison game. They bring a set of values with them when they come to prison, and they do not leave these values at the gate. They are people such as a man who, on a drunken Saturday night, ran over a pedestrian and was sent to the prison for manslaughter, a middle class clerk who was caught embezzling his firm's money, and a young soldier who stole a car in order to get back from a leave. Unlike thieves, these inmates bring to the prison both anti-criminal and anti-prisoner attitudes. Although it is known that most of them participate at a minimum in primary group relations with either thieves or convicts, their relationships with each other have not been studied. Further, criminologists have ignored the possible effects the "do rights" have on the

total system of "inmate culture." It seems a worthy hypothesis that thieves, convicts and do rights all bring certain values and behavior patterns to prison with them, and that total "inmate culture" represents an adjustment or accommodation of these three systems within the official administrative system of deprivation and control.[30] It is significant in this connection that Wheeler has not found in Norwegian prisons the normative order and cohesive bonds among inmates that characterize many American prisons. He observes that his data suggest "that the current functional interpretations of the inmate system in American institutions are not adequate," and that "general features of Norwegian society are imported into the prison and operate largely to offset any tendencies toward the formation of a solidary inmate group. . . ."[31]

BEHAVIOR AFTER RELEASE

If our crude typology is valid, it should be of some use for predicting the behavior of prisoners when they are released. However, it is important to note that in any given prison the two deviant subcultures are not necessarily as sharply separated as our previous discussion has implied. Most inmates are under the influence of *both* subcultures. Without realizing it, inmates who have served long prison

---

[30] "But if latent culture can restrict the possibilities for the proliferation of the manifest culture, the opposite is also true. Manifest culture can restrict the operation of latent culture. The problems facing group members may be so pressing that, given the social context in which the group operates, the range of solutions that will be effective may be so limited as not to allow for influence of variations resulting from cultures associated with other identities." Becker and Geer, *op. cit.*, pp. 308-309.

[31] Stanton Wheeler, "Inmate Culture in Prisons," Mimeographed report of the Laboratory of Social Relations, Harvard University, 1962, pp. 18, 20, 21.

terms are likely to move toward the middle, toward a compromise or balance between the directives coming from the two sources. A member of the convict subculture may come to see that thieves are the real men with the prestige; a member of the thief subculture or even a do right may lose his ability to sustain his status needs by outside criteria. Criminologists seem to have had difficulty in keeping the two kinds of influence separate, and we cannot expect all inmates to be more astute than the criminologists. The fact that time has a blending effect on the participants in the two deviant subcultures suggests that the subcultures themselves tend to blend together in some prisons. We have already noted that the thief subculture scarcely exists in some institutions for juveniles. It is probable also that in army stockades and in concentration camps this subculture is almost nonexistent. In places of short-term confinement, such as city and county jails, the convict subculture is dominant, for the thief subculture involves status distinctions that are not readily observable in a short period of confinement. At the other extreme, in prisons where only prisoners with long sentences are confined, the distinctions between the two subcultures are likely to be blurred. Probably the two subcultures exist in their purest forms in institutions holding inmates in their twenties, with varying sentences for a variety of criminal offenses. Such institutions, of course, are the "typical" prisons of the United States.

Despite these differences, in any prison the men oriented to legitimate subcultures should have a low recidivism rate, while the highest recidivism rate should be found among participants in the convict subculture. The hard core members of this subculture are being trained in manipulation, duplicity and exploitation, they are not sure they can make it on the out-

side, and even when they are on the outside they continue to use convicts as a reference group. This sometimes means that there will be a wild spree of crime and dissipation which takes the members of the convict subculture directly back to the prison. Members of the thief subculture, to whom prison life represented a pitfall in outside life, also should have a high recidivism rate. However, the thief sometimes "reforms" and tries to succeed in some life within the law. Such behavior, contrary to popular notions, is quite acceptable to other members of the thief subculture, so long as the new job and position are not "anti-criminal" and do not involve regular, routine, "slave labor." Suckers work, but a man who, like a thief, "skims it off the top" is not a sucker. At any rate, the fact that convicts, to a greater extent than thieves, tend to evaluate things from the perspective of the prison and to look upon discharge as a short vacation from prison life suggests that their recidivism rate should be higher than that of thieves.

Although the data collected by Garrity provide only a crude test of these predictions, they do support them. Garrity determined the recidivism rates and the tendencies for these rates to increase or decrease with increasing length of prison terms, for each of Schrag's inmate types. Unfortunately, this typology does not clearly make the distinction between the two subcultures, probably because of the blending process noted above. Schrag's "right guys" or "antisocial offenders," thus, might include both men who perceive role requirements in terms of the norms of the convict subculture, and men who perceive those requirements in terms of the norms of the thief subculture. Similarly, neither his "con politician" ("pseudosocial offender") nor his "outlaw" ("asocial offender") seem to be what we would characterize as the ideal-type member of the convict subculture. For example, it is said that relatively few of the former have juvenile records, that onset of criminality often occurs after a position of respectability has already been attained in the civilian community, and that educational and occupational records are far superior to those of "right guys." Further, outlaws are characterized as men who have been frequently reared in institutions or shifted around in foster homes; but they also are characterized as "undisciplined troublemakes," and this does not seem to characterize the men who seek high status in prisons by rather peaceful means of manipulation and exploitation. In short, our ideal-type "thief" appears to include only some of Schrag's "right guys"; the ideal-type "convict" seems to include some of his "right guys," some of his "con politicians," and all of his "outlaws." Schrag's "square Johns" correspond to our "legitimate subcultures" category.

Garrity found that a group of "square Johns" had a low parole violation rate and that this rate remained low no matter how much time was served. The "right guys" had a high violation rate that decreased markedly as time in prison increased. In Garrity's words, this was because "continued incarceration [served] to sever his connections with the criminal subculture and thus to increase the probability of successful parole."[32] The rates for the "outlaw" were very high and remained high as time in prison increased. Only the rates of the "con politician" did not meet our expectations—the rates were low if the sentences were rather short but increased

___
[32] *Op. cit.*, p. 377.

systematically with time served.

Noting that the origins of the thief subculture and the convict subculture are both external to a prison should change our expectations regarding the possible reformative effect of that prison. The recidivism rates of neither thieves, convicts, nor do rights are likely to be significantly affected by incarceration in any traditional prison. This is not to say that the program of a prison with a "therapeutic milieu" like the one the Wisconsin State Reformatory is seeking, or of a prison like some of those in California, in which group counseling is being used in an attempt to change organizational structure, will not eventually affect the recidivism rates of the members of one or another, or all three, of the categories. However, in reference to the ordinary custodially-oriented prison the thief says he can do his time "standing on his head," and it appears that he *is* able to do the time "standing on his head"—except for long-termers, imprisonment has little effect on the thief one way or the other. Similarly, the routine of any particular custodial prison is not likely to have significant reformative effects on members of the convict subculture—they will return to prison because, in effect, they have found a home there. And the men oriented to legitimate subcultures will maintain low recidivism rates even if they never experience imprisonment. Garrity has shown that it is not correct to conclude, as reformers have so often done, that prisons are the breeding ground of crime. It probably is not true either that any particular prison is the breeding ground of an inmate culture that significantly increases recidivism rates.

[11]

DRUG ENTREPRENEURS AND DEALING CULTURE

JOHN LANGER
Monash University

Using the concept of a dealing culture, this paper describes the skills and ideology of middle-level marijuana and hashish dealers in Melbourne, Australia. This analysis, together with a summary of early research on the marketing of psychedelics refutes the "pusher" stereotype of the drug dealer.

The illegal distribution and marketing of psychedelic drugs have been the subject of several studies over the last decade (Carey, 1968; Goode, 1970; Mouledoux, 1972; Atkyns and Hanneman, 1974). The individual who engages in this activity on a regular basis is usually described by his customers as a "dealer." It is the purpose of this paper to offer a summary of the findings on drug "dealing" and to present an account of some of the properties of a "dealing culture."

Early studies report that the popular imagery used to describe the seller of narcotics had been readily transferred to the seller of psychedelics (Carey, 1968: 30-1). Anyone who sold drugs of any kind was defined as a "dope pusher": a strange looking man, employed by a complex criminal apparatus, who seduced innocent youngsters into a life of dissipation by giving away drugs under false pretences. His victims would unwittingly "get hooked" and have to pay vast sums to support their uncontrollable habit. Rejecting this portrayal of drug distribution, sociologists examined the marketing of psychedelics from the perspective of those involved. Research based on this "relativist position" (Young, 1971) revealed a substantial discrepancy between the official interpretation of non-narcotic drug entrepreneurship and the empirical reality of the drug scene. Goode (1970: 251-57), for example, showed that marijuana was not sold by a small number of highly organized criminals, but rather, it was distributed for cash and often without payment among friends—unsystematically and in varying quantities. He reports that forty-four per cent of his respondents claimed to have sold marijuana at least once. Commenting on these findings in relation to the pusher stereotype, he states that:

> It is not simply that the user must purchase his drug supply from the sellers to consume the drug, but the user and seller are largely indistinguishable; there is no clear-cut boundary between them. Selling and using involve parallel activities and association. The seller and the user inhabit the same social universe (1970: 254-5).

When the value orientations of individuals using and selling psychedelics were examined, the official characterization of the dope pusher was again challenged. The use of non-narcotic drugs functioned as both a symbolic representation of, and an agent for, a set of values subsequently designated as the counterculture, the alternative culture, the new bohemia or hippiedom (Davis, 1967; Roszak, 1968; Yablonsky, 1968; Westhues, 1972; Cavan, 1972). Goode (1970: 4) pointed out that the immense increase in non-narcotic drug use in the past decade was an organic outgrowth of a newly evolving way of life. Young (1971: 124-162) suggested that, unlike the vast majority of drug-using subcultures, there were "pronounced ideological overtones associated with marijuana use." He elaborated this observation by describing a "fit" between "bohemian subterranean values"—hedonism, spontaneity, expressivity, anti-materialism, consciousness expansion—and the pharmacological properties of marijuana and LSD. Reich (1970: 208-81) along similar if somewhat rhapsodic lines, stated that psychedelic drugs were makers of revolution, repelling false consciousness and breaking through the closed system of indoctrination and domination. Roszak (1968) noted that if the counterculture was seen as an "exploration of the politics of consciousness", the psychedelic experience was a method of that exploration.

The use of psychedelics being intricately linked to the countercultural ideology, prompted sociologists to take a similiar view of the marketing of these drugs. Mouledoux (1972: 119) reported that "the dealership" was not simply a business organization but contained commitments "to lure men away from the contemporary world." Dealers often defined themselves as instrumental in promoting social and personal change, by creating new modes of perception through the dispensation of psychedelics. Carey (1968: 92) found that the pusher myth presented by the authorities and other experts contradicted the world of drug dealing. Dealers, he observed, were "in it for a little money and lots of pleasure." The economic ethos of the dealing scene is its formative years was traditional (Weber, 1930: 58-67). It did not rest on rationally and systematically seeking profit but had such secondary qualities as personal, customer-seller contact, moderate earnings and good relations among competitors.

Dealers were found to be convivial, easy-going, sloppy and free-wheeling, with time to spend being friendly (Carey, 1968: 72-3). The exchange of "dope" for money carried with it a series of elaborate rituals and dialogues emphasizing the collective values and sentiments of all drug users and blurring status lines between customer and purchaser (Goode, 1970: 254-5). The desire to obtain profit was played down and those dealers suspected of being interested in drugs for monetary reasons were subject to severe sanctions and ostracized by customers (Mouledoux, 1972: 117). Generally, the "value" of drugs was as much a social concern as an economic one. This group of businessmen represented a "kind of island of tribalism within a sea of commercial ethic" (Goode, 1970: 250).

Clearly, the dealer committed to the values of the counterculture and its "hand-loose ethic" (Suchman, 1968) could not also be devoted to ruthless profit-seeking. The counter-culture morality of antimaterialism, hedonism and self-expression opposed a desire for profit. Thus, by locating drug distribution within the context of the countercultural value system, sociologists were able further to discredit the pusher stereotype. To think of the drug dealer as preying on a hapless victim and profiting from the consequent misery was a ludicrously incorrect view of the state of affairs (Goode, 1970: 255).

Since the completion of these studies there has been little follow-up research in the social world of marketing psychedelic drugs.[1] Based on a particular network of "middle-range" dealers in Melbourne Australia, this paper reports apparent changes in the dealing scene. Primarily, it will discuss some of the properties and the maintenance of what might be called a "dealing culture"—a shared set of understandings and codes of behaviour which provide dealers with the basis for evaluating the relevance of their activities, establishing their practical affairs as entrepreneurs and locating their identity in the drug scene (Becker, 1967; Cavan, 1972).

METHODOLOGICAL CONSIDERATIONS

The distribution of psychedelic drugs proceeds through the workings of an elaborate social and economic hierarchy with many internal differences and distinctions (see Carey, 1968; Mouledoux, 1972; Goode, 1970). Drugs flow downward from a few "top dealers," producers or importers to middle level dealers and then to street sellers with corresponding

---

[1] One recent study has attempted to look at drug distribution in terms of an innovation–diffusion paradigm (Atkyns and Hanneman, 1967). However, the definition of a drug dealer - anyone who currently or formerly sold in any quantity any psychedelic substance appears too sweeping for understanding the social world of dealers themselves.

increases in price. (Because of the climate in Australia, marijuana can be grown readily and then distributed at any level in the hierarchy.)

This study concentrates on one section of the distribution hierarchy—that loosely comprised by dealers generally known as middle men or as in the "middle level" or the "middle range." These dealers make bulk purchases from "outlets" or "contacts" above and sell to clients in large quantities, who in turn sell to others at street level.

Middle level dealers constitute a more stable section of the distribution hierarchy than those on lower levels. A career in "street dealing" is often short-lived, lasting from a few months to a few days (Carey, 1968: 68-93). This fluid state of affairs makes it difficult to establish parameters of significant categories based on the actor's definitions of the situation. At the middle level, however, the career of the dealer lasts longer. It takes more time to develop the reliable contacts and customers necessary for middle-range marketing. In the process, the dealer's work becomes more routine than at the lower levels.

Middle-level dealers also have more complete knowledge of the dynamics of marketing psychedelics illegally. To arrive at the middle level, a dealer's career passes through a series of distinct stages—from initial stages of drug experimentation to the decision to sell drugs on a regular basis. At each stage knowledge is acquired about the processes which constitute the role of "dope dealer." Hence, if relative position in the distribution hierarchy is used as an index for knowledge about the dealing scene, it could be argued that middle level dealers would have a more comprehensive understanding about marketing drugs than lower level dealers.

Beginning with certain key respondents—dealers known personally to the researcher—an informal system of referrals developed. One dealer would inform a colleague about the research, encourage his co-operation, and finally set a place and time for meeting. This procedure was repeated until nine case-studies were developed, over a period of eight months in 1973 and 1974. These were based on a number of lengthy, unstructured interviews as well as several weeks observation of the day-to-day affairs of dealers. All the dealers can be described as middle-level entrepreneurs purchasing from contacts higher up and servicing a number of lower level dealers. All had been dealing between two and five years.

DEALING TECHNIQUES

Fundamental to the dealing culture is a "complex of techniques" (Sutherland, 1937: 197-200) which the dealer must have to work as an underground entrepreneur. Dealing techniques rest on three separate but not necessarily exclusive categories of knowledge and skill—entrepreneurial, interactional and pharmacological.

Entrepreneurial knowledge pertains to skills required to operate a dealership by means of the purchase and distribution of drugs. The dealer as a purchaser and retailer must be aware of a series of distinct courses of action and codified tasks which make up the practical affairs of his market behavior. To the extent that dealers "take the initiative and in the pursuit of profit in some discernible form, manipulate other persons and resources, they are acting as entrepreneurs" (Barth, 1964: 6). At the most basic level a middle-range dealer must have a series of entrepreneurial implements and strategies to carry out his work. House (1974: 115) provides a number of useful concepts for understanding the dealer's entrepreneurial knowledge.

(1) Initial resources the dealer must have in order to perform his work. The most important resource is a series of regular business contacts where a dealer can "score dope in bulk" when he wants it and at the price that he wants to pay, as well as a regular clientele of lower level dealers to whom he can sell his goods. He must also have time to spend in the mechanics

of dealing—sampling possible purchases, transporting and storing stock safely, weighing and dividing the product into saleable quantities, visiting contacts, entertaining clients, talking to colleagues about business arrangements, and just getting stoned.

(2) Profits, an ultimate resource, one of the final goals of business. The main profit for dealers is cash income from sales after covering for overhead—living expenses, transportation costs, waste through personal use of the product. Important secondary rewards also emerge as the dealers become established—prestige, power and positive self-image. One of the recurrent themes in terms of potential monetary gain is the ever present quest for the "good deal." This quest involves obtaining a large quantity of very potent marijuana or hashish at what would be seen as a fair price. The "good deal" is the best way a dealer can ensure profits as well as satisfied, steady customers. Recognizing a good deal presupposes a comprehensive knowledge of the current market value of drugs which fluctuate on a daily basis. Once the arrival of a "shipment" is made public by a contact, the dealer may have to go into direct competition with his colleagues to obtain it—risking more money in the hope of greater return for his initial investment.

(3) Conversions whereby one kind of resource is used to produce another resource or profit. This process becomes most apparent when dealers discuss their net assets in terms of the potential purchases of certain quantities of drugs.

> You start off with a certain amount of money, say 300 dollars. With that you can afford a pound of grass. So you buy a pound and sell it for 35 dollars an ounce and make 200 dollars. You've got 500 dollars. Take out a certain amount for living expenses, buy another pound of grass and maybe a bit of hash or acid until you work up enough money for 2 pounds and the price goes down. The more money you've got, the more you can spend, the cheaper you can get the dope. There's no point in putting your money in the bank, you are just cutting out your profits.

(4) Dealers' plans for selling. These strategies provide an essential framework for the interactional skills and knowledge with which dealers manage their practical affairs. Drug entrepreneurship is an interpersonal process requiring extended periods of time in face-to-face situations with business associates. On one hand, this interaction takes the form of congregating regularly with one's peers—other middle range dealers—over matters of mutual business concern. One respondent described the situation:

> You don't associate with people who just smoke; you associate with people who deal. You relate to people who are at the same stage as you in the dope thing because it is much easier and you can talk about the scene and deals coming up.

Interaction with business colleagues is one of the most important activities in conducting entrepreneurial affairs. The ability to participate actively in these discussions is part of the technical knowledge one must have to be considered a genuine middle-level dealer. On the other hand, interactional skills are directed specifically towards one's customers. Dealers are aware of the "sociogenic" (Goode, 1970: 21) nature of psychedelic use and conduct their business accordingly. As one dealer reported

> No matter what happens in terms of money and amounts of dope bought, the dealer settles the deal on a social level.

The ability to be congenial with customers is seen as important to maintain a successful entrepreneurship. This interaction usually takes the form of smoking with customers, discussing possible future deals, or dispensing largesse to prospective clients.

Dealers, however, interpret these aspects of socializing with customers in very business-like terms. One dealer observed that:

> You need a bit of salesmanship; you have to create an air of confidence so that people buying are at ease and will come back. If you are dealing, people expect you to roll strong joints or lay dope on them, and you do that—that's salesmanship.

Interaction with customers is based on dealers' understanding of buyers' suppositions about the social nature of drug use. Rather than being naive participants in the sociability which accompanies drug use, dealers incorporate it into their sales technique. Face-to-face contact with customers is a matter of practical sales strategy and meaningful interaction is reserved for gatherings with one's dealer colleagues.

Practicing one's interactional skills includes methods by which dealers manage their "front stage" performance while making purchases or selling to customers. The sum total of these methods might be described as a dealing "style"—a series of behavioral and linguistic conventions which are used in interpersonal business situations and shared in common by middle-level dealers. These conventions include specified verbal exchanges, complex forms of etiquette, personal poise and confidence. A whole series of discreet cues, stances and gestures go to make up this dealing style. One dealer, recalling a meeting with a major outlet stated

> You need an air of coolness. You don't walk in like a fool. You need to impress them with good deals that have come off for you and good deals that you know are going to happen. It's the little things that makes you cool.

In this context "being cool" is used as an index for evaluating dealing style. It is a measure of professional conduct and those who are perceived to be most cool accrue most status rewards.

A final cluster of dealing skills focusses on the knowledge that dealers acquire about the pharmacological properties of marketable drugs. Despite the fact that their "specialization" was marijuana and hashish, dealers felt obliged to obtain first-hand experience and information about a wide range of drugs.

> If I couldn't talk about drugs and the things that I was selling, I wouldn't be accepted as a dealer. A dealer is the person who is knowledgeable about drugs, who's experienced, who has tried most of the stuff around.

The respondents had tried almost all the drugs marketed illegally as well as others sold over the counter or on prescription. The role of dealer in the drug scene required an expertise which would be readily available upon request.

"GETTING BUSTED"

No matter how skillfully dealers use their technical knowledge in business or how cool their operation is, one of the common contingencies of their entrepreneurial affairs is "getting busted." Getting busted occurs when dealers are confronted by representatives of law enforcement agencies—the drug squad, customs agents or other governmental services in connection with distributing illicit drugs. The "bust" often takes the form of raid on a dealer's residence to locate and confiscate the "stash" and arrest those selling the drugs. Although this is a common format, busts can take place almost anywhere and at any time. Dealers report being stopped in cars and while walking along the street. Even if the police find no incriminating evidence, the dealer is "clean" and no arrest ensues, the visit is still categorized as a bust. If drugs are found in any quantity, a set of procedures follows which include a trip to police headquarters for questioning, signing statements, and getting bail. What actually happens to a dealer when he is busted, the basic legal mechanics of a bust, vis à vis the authorities, seems less important for this discussion than the way this experience is interpreted in the dealing culture.

Middle-level dealers are aware of the risks involved in distributing large quantities of illegal drugs and know the rate of arrest in high. Every dealer interviewed knew at least two or more of his colleagues who had been busted. When a colleague is arrested the usual, general explanation is in terms of the dealer's "uncoolness." Being uncool involves failure to follow basic dealing procedures, and inadequate use of available technical knowledge. The authorities are rarely credited with skill, initiative, or finesse in the performance of their duty. For dealers the bust is always seen in terms of their own negligence.

> A dealer is someone who follows the rules. If he does this he doesn't get busted. Cops are stupid anyway.

Paradoxically, getting busted also functions in the dealing culture as a positive social episode, and individuals who have been arrested, charged, and taken to court are viewed by their peers as having encountered first-hand all that can be experienced as a professional dealer. After a bust, the dealer is granted full dealing identity—he has come through the final rite of passage into true "dealerhood." Interaction with the police through a bust allows information to filter back into the dealing scene. For example, dealers who are arrested and charged for their business activities are usually set free on bail. They return to their colleagues to describe the bust, police tactics, and general legal procedures. Over a number of months or years a pool of information about law enforcement institutions collects within the dealing culture to be passed on to each successive generation of dealers. This information becomes part of the stock of technical knowledge of drug entrepreneurship.

DEALING IDEOLOGY

According to Lofland (1969: 197-99) the ideology of any group performs at least two functions. It defines events and provides a range of strategies for coping with occurrences. Ideologies function to protect adherents from stasis and situations whose meaning is unclear. It is thus that the dealing culture provides a code by which drug entrepreneurs use a range of strategies in order to anticipate and structure events in their practical affairs. Ideologies also function to lend moral validity to behavior. Groups whose behavior is stigmatized will construct attitudes and moralities which repudiate conventional rules and institutions and minimize the moral nature of their transgressions (Becker, 1963: 38-9; Skyes and Matza, 1957).

A major element in the ideological structure of dealing culture, described by all respondents, is the belief that dealers serve an important social function by providing certain scarce goods and services for a distinctly formulated community need. Dealers describe the drug scene as flourishing and wide-spread across the general population. They see themselves as a group which has a legitimate claim to exist, given the community desire for illegal psychedelics. One dealer stated that:

> Virtually, the person who gets out of the common herd of smokers and bothers to hassle up some dope is doing those people (the customers) a favour. This is the way the whole relationship (between dealer and client) is looked at.

In similar terms:

> Most dealers come in contact with an extremely wide circle of people that the ordinary person wouldn't and you get the opportunity to meet the people who are interested in deals.

Dealers justify their activities further in terms of their accumulated pharmacological expertise, used when advising customers about purchases.

> By virtue of the fact that I am a dealer I can try all grades and types of dope and have
> knowledge about lots of drugs.

Another dealer explained:

> People ask you about a particular type of drug, a particular type of grass or hash and
> you can talk about it right off, give some advice.

Emphasis is placed on the fact that drugs are not "pushed" according to popular imagery—
they are sold or "dealt" in relation to customer demand. Dealers intepret their entrepreneurial
role as a genuine response to an articulate and well-formed need among certain groups.

Noticeably absent from dealers descriptions of their social function is the claim that they
are engaged in "turning people on" in order to facilitate the incidence of consciousness
expansion and personal growth. One respondent explained

> I'd like to think that my role was making people more aware through dope, but it's not.

The belief that the use of psychedelics creates individual and societal changes through
changed states of consciousness appears to have faded into the background and become an
historical referent within present day dealing culture. Dealers describe these ideals and
beliefs of the counterculture as unrealistic, unfounded and misleading. The dealer who
endorses these values is condemned as naive and untutored in the ways of drugs and drug
entrepreneurship. One dealer noted that:

> The counterculture mystique about dope is from a lack of knowledge or experience—it's
> for the 'hippies' . . . . You can't mix dealing and the counterculture.

Another respondent stated:

> You don't treat drugs as a mystical thing because (they) are business.

In general, dealers at this level are cynical and even disdainful of belief in the potential value
of psychedelics.

This cynicism may be related to a development in the ways contempory business ethics
and social action intermingle. Reflecting on their entrepreneurial activities, dealers have
constructed a basic socio-economic account, primitive though it may be, which presents
the capitalist economy as an "unalterable order of things" forcing individuals involved in a
system of market relationships to conform to capitalist rules of action (Weber, 1930: 64). In
dealers, own terms: "All of society is based on a capitalist rip-off, and that's just the way
things go." Hence, the profit which dealers actively seek as part of a system of market
relationships is seen merely as an extension of "the way things are in the world."

A similar pattern emerges when dealers discuss their sense of exploitation. What they see
as the basic structure of a capitalist economy—that is, the exploitation of one's fellows for
the sake of gaining advantage, either economically or socially is also seen as basic to the
distribution and marketing of psychedelic drugs. Dealers see themselves pushed and pulled
in a chain of exploitation down through the distribution hierarchy. They are exploited by
their customers as well as "the people above." They believe that they take all the major
risks and are constantly in legal or financial danger, while contacts above make vast fortunes

and customers "score dope" easily without hassle. Profits are rare. But if profits are made, they are considered deserved and justifiable.[2]

Dealers confirm the validity of their practical affairs by building into their ideology "evidential sensitivity to the immorality of normals" (Lofland, 1969: 199). They are quick to point out the hypocrisy displayed by the "straight" world in its attitudes and unfounded suppositions about certain drugs and in its own drug taking behavior.

> Everyone in society takes drugs, at all levels. Straight people are into drugs as much as anyone else—different kinds of drugs, like alcohol.

The belief is held by most dealers that "smoking dope," even in large quantities over time, is less harmful than the use of many of the licit drugs taken by the majority of the population. Dealers view drug taking as a general and wide-spread societal phenomenon; they sense that the legal differentiation of psychoactive substances is a set of arbitrary divisions which may have political, economic or even religious motives.

The moral hypocrisy attributed to convential society crystallizes further when dealers evaluate certain institutions concerned with illegal drug use. The assertion most often voiced was that the agencies of social control were corrupt and secretly engaged in criminal activities of various kinds, including the victimization of dealers. Numerous instances were reported describing how police agents would "perform a bust, confiscate drugs and money, pocket the money and then resell the drugs."[3] Other pejorative views of the medical profession and other social welfare agencies concerned their uninformed and brutal handling of people on "bad trips." Also, mass media, especially the press, were seen to present a distorted, naive and sensational portrayal of the drug scene and the role of the dealer in order to sell papers. By interpreting the social actions of individuals and institutions in straight society as morally hypocritical, dealers are able to justify their own illegal behavior.

SUMMARY

This paper has suggested that dealing psychedelics has moved from a hang-loose ethic linked with the values of the counterculture to a specific attitude which sanctions the accumulation of profit for services rendered. It must be noted however that, although dealers have an expressed desire to make profit from their entrepreneurial activities, they rarely do so. Respondents report that their earnings from dealing could only support them part of the time. In most cases they had to seek out menial jobs to meet their expenses. Some, in fact, accepted full time employment for several months, leaving their dealerships aside until they had accumulated capital and market conditions were right for investment. However, no matter what other work was pursued their pivotal status and self-identification remained that of the dealer.

The reason dealing does not yield much profit may be partly explained by the fact that entrepreneurial practices related to marketing behavior have not been entirely co-ordinated or systematized. Although dealers are well-versed in the complex of techniques needed to operate a successful dealership, they are not rigorous in the execution of these skills. For example, there is much waste of their product through constant personal use, gift-giving or entertaining. This pattern has been documented by Carey (1968) in his earlier study and seems to persist. Another factor may be that dealers do not keep written accounts of their sales and stock turn-overs since records of this kind provide incriminating evidence in

---

[2] These comments appear to represent the plaintive cry of the "middle-man" in all walks of economic life.

[3] It is claimed that the police understate the amount of the drug seized during a bust. They then take the discrepant amount and resell it to special contacts who place it back on the market.

case of arrest. However, without the use of rational book-keeping, systematic accumulation of profits is difficult (Weber: 1947, 164-6). The frequency of "rip-offs" for drugs or money is high. These incidents are usually perpetrated by other dealers above or below the middle level and sometimes by one's peers. Obviously the dealer's own criminal activity leaves no recourse for legal action. Thus investments are regularly lost and capital accumulation must start again.

A further explanation for the unprofitability of dealing might be offered in terms of dealers' ambivalence about their own entrepreneurial activities. By making large profits from marketing drugs, dealers come much closer to the societal stereotype of the dope pusher,— and this is a self-image they emphatically reject. By remaining relatively unrewarded in monetary terms, dealers hold an image of themselves and their activities which does not fit this stereotype.

Dealers state they are profit oriented, yet make little money. This leads the researcher into a methodological dilemma concerning the truth of respondents reports about their social behavior and their actual behavior and its consequences. This dilemma may indicate some sort of general limitation inherent in the approach used in this study. Whatever the outcome of this methodological question, the discrepancy between dealers professed profit motives for dealing and the lack of pecuniary results from their business transactions casts further doubt on the accuracy of the dope pusher stereotype. Dealers may state that they are "in it for the money," but the results of their entrepreneurial ventures in monetary terms do little to substantiate this claim.

In concluding we should consider the social policy implications of the unprofitability of dealing. If dealers at the middle-level of the distribution hierarchy make little profit, the recent legal trends to reduce penalties for private possession and use of psychedelics such as marijuana and hashish and the simultaneous move to increase punishment for the drug distributor must be re-examined. The claim that punishment of dealers is necessary because they profit from unsuspecting victims is belied by the evidence submitted in this paper.

REFERENCES

Atkyns, R.L. and G.J. Hanneman
  1974 "Illicit drug distribution and dealer communication behavior." Journal of Health and Social Behavior 15 (March): 36-43.
Barth, F.
  1964 The Role of the Entrepreneur in Social Change in Northern Norway. Oslo: University of Oslo Press.
Becker, H.
  1963 Outsiders: Studies in the Sociology of Deviance. New York: The Free Press.
  1967 "History, culture and subjective experience: an exploration of the social bases of drug induced experiences." Journal of Health and Social Behavior 8 (June): 163-76.
Carey, J.T.
  1968 The College Drug Scene. Englewood Cliffs, New York: Prentice-Hall.
Cavan, S.
  1972 The Hippies of the Haight. St. Louis: New Critics Press.
Davis, F.
  1967 "Why all of us may be hippies someday." Transaction 5 (December): 10-18.
Goode, E.
  1970 The Marijuana Smokers. New York: Basic Books.
House, J.D.
  1974 "Entrepreneurial career patterns of residential real estate agents in Montreal." Canadian Review of Sociology and Anthropology 11 (2): 110-124.
Lofland, J.
  1969 Deviance and Identity. Englewood Cliffs, New Jersey: Prentice-Hall.
Mouledoux, J.
  1972 "Ideological aspects of drug dealership." pp. 110-122 in K. Westhues (ed.) Society's Shadow: Studies in the Sociology of Countercultures. Toronto: McGraw-Hill, Ryerson.

Reich, C.A.
    1970 The Greening of America, New York: Random.
Roszak, T.
    1969 The Making of a Counterculture: Reflections on Technological Society and Its Youthful
          Opposition. New York: Doubleday.
Suchman, E. A.
    1968 "The 'hang loose' ethic and the spirit of drug use." Journal of Health and Social Behavior 9
          (June): 146-55.
Sutherland, E.H.
    1937 The Professional Thief. Chicago: University of Chicago Press.
Sykes, G.M. and D. Matza
    1957 "Techniques of neutralization: a theory of delinquency." American Sociological Review 22,
          (December): 667-670.
Weber, M.
    1965 The Protestant Ethic and the Spirit of Capitalism. Translated by Talcott Parsons, London,
          Unwin.
    1947 The Theory of Social and Economic Organization. New York: Free Press.
Westhues, K.
    1972 Society's Shadow: Studies in the Sociology of Countercultures. Toronto: McGraw-Hill Ryerson.
Yablonsky, L.
    1968 The Hippie Trip, New York: Pegasus.
Young, J.
    1971 The Drugtakers. London: Paladin.

[12]

THE BEHAVIOR OF THE SYSTEMATIC CHECK FORGER

EDWIN M. LEMERT
University of California

The concept of behavior systems in crime was first approximated in this country in Hall's analysis of several types of larceny in terms of their historical, legal, and social contexts. (15) Later the concept was made explicit and formulated into a typology by Sutherland and by Sutherland and Cressy. (32, 34, 21, 26, 14, 4, pp. 579-589) Although this has hitherto inspired only a few monographic studies, there seems to be a growing consensus that focusing attention on specific orders of crime or making behavior systems the unit of study holds considerable promise for criminological research. (27, p. 134)

Because this paper proposes to assess the usefulness of Sutherland's formulation of the behavior system in analyzing or understanding the behavior of the systematic check forger, the typology outlined in his study of the professional thief will be employed. The five elements of the behavior system of the thief are as follows: (1) stealing is made a regular business; (2) every act is carefully planned, including the use of the "fix"; (3) technical skills are used, chiefly those of manipulating people; this differentiates the thief from other professional criminals; (4) the thief is migratory but uses a specific city as a headquarters; (5) the thief has criminal associations involving acquaintances, congeniality, sympathy, understandings, rules, codes of behavior, and a special language. (31, 32, 6, pp. 256-262, 27, 5, Ch. V, 10, Ch. IV, 23, 37)

Altogether seventy-two persons currently serving sentences for check forgery and writing checks with insufficient funds were studied. Three additional check offenders were contacted and interviewed outside of prison. The sample included eight women and sixty-seven men, all of whom served time in California correctional institutions.

Thirty of the seventy-five check criminals could be classified as systematic in the sense that they (1) thought of themselves as check men; (2) had worked out or regularly employed a special technique of passing checks; (3) had more or less organized their lives around the exigencies or imperatives of living by means of fraudulent checks. The remaining forty-five cases represented a wide variety of contexts in which bogus check passing was interspersed with periods of stable employment and family life, or was simply an aspect of alcoholism, gambling, or one of a series of criminal offenses having little or no consistency.

FINDINGS

Projected against the typology of professional theft, the behavior of the persons falling into the systematic check forgery category qualified only in a very general way as professional crime. In other words, although it is possible to describe these forgeries as *systematic*, it is questionable whether more than a small portion of them can be subsumed as *professional* under the more general classification of professional theft. A point-by-point comparison will serve to bring out the numerous significant differences between systematic forgery and professional theft.

1. *Forgery as a "regular business."* It is questionable whether check men look upon their crimes as a "regular business" in the same way as do members of "other occupational groups" who "wish to make money in safety."

(34, p. 240) In virtually all cases the motivation proved to be exceedingly complex. This fact was self-consciously recognized and expressed in different ways but all informants revealed an essential perplexity or conflict about their criminal behavior. The following statement may be taken as illustrative:

> Nine out of ten check men are lone wolves. Those men who work in gangs are not real check men. They do it for money; we do it for something else. It gives us something we need. Maybe we're crazy. . . .

The conflicts expressed involved not merely the rightness or wrongness of behavior; they also disclosed a confusion and uncertainty as to the possibility of living successfully or safely by issuing false checks. All of the cases, even the few who had a history of professional thieving, admitted that arrest and imprisonment are inevitable. None knew of exceptions to this, although one case speculated that "It might be done by an otherwise respected business man who made one big spread and then quit and retired."

The case records of the systematic check forgers gave clear testimony of this. Generally they had but short-lived periods of freedom, ranging from a few months to a year or two at the most, followed by imprisonment. Many of the cases since beginning their forgery careers had spent less total time outside prisons than within, a fact corroborated by the various law-enforcement officers queried on the point.

Many of the check men depicted their periods of check writing as continuous sprees during which they lived "fast" and luxuriously. Many spoke of experiencing considerable tension during these periods, and two cases developed stomach ulcers which caused them to "lay off at resorts." A number gambled and drank heavily, as-

sertedly to escape their internal stress and sense of inevitable arrest. A number spoke of gradual build-up of strain and a critical point just before their arrest at which they became demoralized and after which they "just didn't care any more" or "got tired of running." The arrests of several men having a very long experience with checks resulted from blunders in technique of which they were aware at the time they made them. Some of the men gave themselves up to detectives or F. B. I. agents at this point.

In general the picture of the cool, calculating professional with prosaic, matter-of-fact attitudes towards his crimes as a trade or occupation supported by rationalizations of a subculture was not valid for the cases in question.

2. *Planning as an aspect of forgery.* In regard to the second element of professional theft—planning—the behavior of check forgers is again divergent. Actually the present techniques of check passing either preclude precise planning or make it unnecessary. Although systematic check passers undeniably pay careful attention to such things as banking hours, the places at which checks are presented, and the kinds of "fronts" they employ, these considerations serve only as generalized guides for their crimes. Most informants held that situations have to be *exploited as they arise,* with variation and flexibility being the key to success. What stands out in the behavior of systematic check forgers is the rapid tempo — almost impulsiveness — with which they work.

The cases seemed to agree that check forgers seldom attempt to use the "fix" in order to escape the consequences of their crimes. The reason for this is that although one or a small number of checks might be made good, the systematic forger has too many bad checks outstanding and too many victims to mollify by offering restitution. Although the forger may be prosecuted on the basis of only one or two checks, ordinarily the prosecuting attorney will have a choice of a large number of complaints upon which to act. About the best the check forger can hope for through fixing activities is a short sentence or a sentence to jail rather than to prison.

3. *Technical skills.* Although the systematic check man relies upon technical skills — those of manipulating others — these are usually not of a high order, nor do they require a long learning period to master. From the standpoint of the appearance of the check or the behavior involved at the time of its passing, there need, of course, be no great difference between passing a bad check and passing a good check. This is particularly true of personal checks, which are at least as favored as payroll checks by check men.

When check men impersonate others or when they assume fictitious roles, acting ability is required. To the extent that elaborate impersonations are relied upon by the forger, his check passing takes on qualities of a confidence game. Most of the check men showed strong preference, however, for simple, fast-moving techniques. A number expressed definite dislike for staged arrangements, such as that of the "out of town real estate buyer" or for setting up a fictitious business in a community, then waiting several weeks or a month before making a "spread" of checks. As they put it, they "dislike the slow build-up involved."

4. *Mobility.* Like the thief, the systematic forger is migratory. Only one check man interviewed spoke of identifying himself with one community, and even he was reluctant to

call it a headquarters. Generally check men are migratory within regions.

5. *Associations.* The sharpest and most categorical difference between professional theft and systematic forgery lies in the realm of associations. In contrast to pickpockets, shoplifters, and con men, whose criminal techniques are implicitly cooperative, most check men with highly developed systems work alone, carefully avoiding contacts and interaction with other criminals. Moreover, their preference for solitude and their secretiveness gives every appearance of a highly generalized reaction; they avoid not only cooperative crime but also any other kinds of association with criminals. They are equally selective and cautious in their contacts and associations with the noncriminal population, preferring not to become involved in any enduring personal relationships.

A descriptive breakdown of the thirty check forgers classified as systematic bears out this point. Only four of the thirty had worked in check passing gangs. Two of these had acted as "fences" who organized the operations. Both were close to seventy years old and had long prison records, one having been a receiver of stolen property, the other having worked as a forger. Both had turned to using gangs of passers because they were too well known to detectives either to pass checks themselves or to permit their handwriting to appear on the checks. The other two forgers who had worked in gangs were female drug addicts who had teamed up with other female addicts.*

---

*One may question whether they were systematic check forgers in a true sense; other informants state that "such people are not real check men; they are just supporting a habit." Their self-definitions and the organization of their lives centers around drug addiction rather than forgery.

Three other systematic check forgers did not work directly with other criminals but had criminal associations of a *contractual* nature. One old-time forger familiar with the now little-used methods for forging signatures and raising checks usually sold checks to passers but never had uttered (passed) any of his own forgeries. Two men were passers who purchased either payroll checks from a "hot printer" or stolen checks from burglars. Apart from the minimal contacts necessary to sell or obtain a supply of checks, all three men were lone operators and very seclusive in their behavior.

Six of the thirty systematic forgers worked exclusively with one other person, usually a girl or "broad."* The check men seemed to agree that working with a girl was equivalent to working alone. These pairs ordinarily consisted of the check man and some girl not ordinarily of criminal background with whom he had struck up a living arrangement and for whom he felt genuine affection. The girl was used either to make out the checks or to pass them. In some cases she was simply used as a front to distract attention. Some men picked up girls in bars or hotels and employed them as fronts without their knowledge.

The remaining seventeen of the thirty systematic check forgers operated on a solitary basis. The majority of these argued that contact with others is unnecessary to obtain and pass a supply of checks. Most of them uttered personal checks. However, even where they made use of payroll

---

*One of the "pair" workers consisted of two homosexual females. The other non-man-woman pair was made up of two brothers, both of whom had substantial prison records. They worked up and down the West Coast, alternating in making out checks and playing the part of passer.

or corporation checks they contrived to manufacture or obtain them without resorting to interaction with criminal associates or intermediaries. For example, one Nisei check man arranged with a printer to make up checks for a fraternal organization of which he represented himself as secretary-treasurer. Another man frequented business offices at noon time, and when the clerk left the office, helped himself to a supply of company checks, in one instance stealing a check writing machine for his purposes.

It was difficult to find evidence of anything more than rudimentary congeniality, sympathy, understandings, and shared rules of behavior among the check forgers, including those who had worked in gangs. Rather the opposite seemed true, suspicion and distrust marking their relationships with one another. One organizer of a gang, for example, kept careful account of all the checks he issued to his passers and made them return torn off corners of checks in case they were in danger of arrest and had to get rid of them. Only two of the thirty forgers indicated that they had at times engaged in recreational activities with other criminals. Both of these men were lone wolves in their work. One other lone wolf stated that he had on occasion had dinner with another check man he happened to know well and that he had once or twice entered into a rivalry with him to see who could pass a check in the most difficult place.

The two men who had organized gangs of check passers worked with a set of rules, but they were largely improvised and laid down by the fence rather than voluntarily recognized and obeyed by the passers. The other check men with varying degrees of explicitness recognized rules for passing checks — rules learned almost entirely on an individual trial-and-error basis. The informants insisted that "you learn as you go" and that one of the rules was "never use another man's stunt."

Such special morality as was recognized proved to be largely functional in derivation. Thus attitudes toward drinking and toward picking up women for sexual purposes were pretty much the result of individual perceptions of what was likely to facilitate or hamper the passing of checks or lead to arrest. Many of the men stated that since they were dealing primarily with business, professional, and clerical persons, their appearance and behavior had to be acceptable to these people. "Middle class" is probably the best term to describe their morality in most areas.

Careful inquiries were made to discover the extent to which the check men were familiar with and spoke an argot. Findings proved meager. Many of the men had a superficial acquaintance with general prison slang, but only four men could measurably identify and reproduce the argot of check forgery or that of thieves. Three more could be presumed to have some familiarity with it. Only one of these spoke the argot in the prison setting. Another said that he never used the argot either in prison or on the outside, except years previously when once in a great while he had "let down at a thieves' party." There were only two men who spoke of themselves as being "on the scratch."*

---

*The attitude of the lone wolf check man toward the argot is illustrated by the following quotation:

It's just the older men in here [San Quentin] who use argot, or some of the young guys who think they are tough. I know the argot but when I hear it I tell them to talk English. Most people on the outside know it anyway. Why call a gun a heater? What is gained by it. . . ?

INTERPRETATION

How can these findings be reconciled with the specific statement of Sutherland's informant (31, p. 77)** that "laying paper" is a form of professional theft most often worked in mobs? The answer to this apparent contradiction requires that a distinction be made between forgery of *the nineteenth and early twentieth centuries and that of the present day.* In the past forgery was a much more complex procedure in which a variety of false instruments such as bank notes, drafts, bills of exchange, letters of credit, registered bonds, and post office money orders as well as checks were manufactured or altered and foisted off. A knowledge of chemicals, papers, inks, engraving, etching, lithography, and penmanship as well as detailed knowledge of bank operations were prime requisites for success. The amounts of money sought were comparatively large, and often they had to be obtained through complex monetary transactions. (7) The technological characteristics of this kind of forgery made planning, timing, specialization, differentiation of roles, morale, and organization imperative. Capital was necessary for living expenses during the period when preparations for the forgeries were being made. (24, 25, pp. 338-441, 7) Intermediates between the skilled forger and the passers were necessary so that the latter could swear that the handwriting on the false negotiable instruments was not theirs and so that the forger him-

---

These findings coincide with Maurer's. (22) He states that the argot of check forgery is relatively unspecialized and that forgers seldom have an opportunity to use it.

**Maurer refers to check forgery as a branch of the "grift," and also speaks of professional forgers without, however, defining the term. Yet he recognizes that check forgers are usually lone wolves. (22)

self was not exposed to arrest. A "shadow" was often used for protection against the passer's temptation to abscond with the money and in order to alert the others of trouble at the bank.* "Fall" money was accumulated and supplied to assist the passer when arrested. Inasmuch as forgery gangs worked together for a considerable length of time, understandings, congeniality, and rules of behavior, especially with regard to the division of money, could and did develop. In short, professional forgery was based upon the technology of the period.

Although precise dating is difficult, the heyday of professional forgery in this country probably began after the Civil War and lasted through the 1920's. (29) It seems to have corresponded with the early phases of industrialization and commercial development before business and law-enforcement agencies developed methods and organization for preventing forgery and apprehending the offenders. Gradually technological developments in inks, papers, protectographs, and check-writing machines made the forging of signatures and the manufacture of false negotiable instruments more difficult. According to one source, for example, raised drafts have been virtually nonexistent since 1905. (29) Similarly, at the present time raising of checks is quite rare. The establishment of a protective committee by the American Bankers Association in 1894, related merchants' protective agencies, and improvements in police methods have made the risks of organized pro-

*Pinkerton enumerates the following roles of the forgery gang: (1) backer, (2) forger, (3) middleman, (4) presenter, (5) shadow; Maurer (22) without specifying the historical period to which his description applies, distinguishes the following as check forger roles: (1) connection, (2) fence, (3) passer. (24)

fessional forgery exceedingly great. (24, 22)

Check gangs have always been vulnerable to arrest but this vulnerability has been multiplied many times by the large amounts of evidence left behind them in the form of countless payroll checks. Vulnerability is also heightened by the swiftness of communication today. If one person of a check-passing gang is arrested and identifies his associates, it becomes a relatively simple matter for police to secure their arrest. A sexually exploited and angered female companion may easily do the same to the check man. This goes far to explain the extreme seclusiveness of systematic check forgers and their almost abnormal fear of stool pigeons or of being "fingered." The type of persons who can be engaged as passers — unattached women, bar waitresses, drug addicts, alcoholics, petty thieves, and transient unemployed persons — also magnifies the probabilities that mistakes will be made and precludes the growth of a morale which might prevent informing to the police. These conditions also explain the fact that when the forger does work with someone it is likely to be one other person upon whom he feels he can rely with implicit confidence. Hence the man-woman teams in which the woman is in love with the man, or the case of the two homosexual girls, or of the two brothers mentioned previously.

Further evidence that organized forgery is a hazardous type of crime, difficult to professionalize under modern conditions, is indicated by the fact that the organizer or fence is apt to be an older criminal with a long record, whose handwriting methods are so well known that he has no choice other than to work through passers. Even then he does it with recognition that arrest is inevitable.

A factor of equal importance in

The Systematic Check Forger 147

explaining the decline of professional organized forgery has been the increasingly widespread use of business and payroll checks as well as personal checks. Whereas in the past the use of checks was confined to certain kinds of business transactions, mostly involving banks, today it is ubiquitous. Attitudes of business people and their clerical employees have undergone great change, and only the most perfunctory identification is necessary to cash many kinds of checks. Check men recognize this in frequent unsolicited comments that passing checks is "easy." Some argue that the form of the check is now relatively unimportant to passing it, that "you can pass a candy bar wrapper now days with the right front and story."* It is for this reason that the systematic check man does not have to resort to criminal associates or employ the more complex professional procedures used in decades past.

These facts may also account for the presence among lone-wolf check forgers of occasional persons with the identification, orientation, skills, codes, and argot of the thief. Case histories as well as the observations of informants show that older professional criminals in recent decades have turned to check passing because they face long sentences for additional crimes or sentencing under habitual criminal legislation. They regard checks as an "easy racket" because in many states conviction makes them subject to jail sentences rather than imprisonment. Check passing may be a last resort for the older criminal.

The presence of the occasional older professional thief in the ranks of

check forgers may actually token a general decline and slow disappearance of professional thieving. One professional thief turned check passer had this to say:

> I'm a thief — a burglar — but I turned to checks because it's getting too hard to operate. Police are a lot smarter now, and they have better methods. People are different nowadays too; they report things more. It's hard to trust anyone now. Once you could trust cab drivers; now you can't. We live in a different world today.**

THE CHECK FORGER AS AN ISOLATE

The preference of many systematic check forgers for solitary lives and their avoidance of primary-group associations among criminals may also be explicable in terms of their educational characteristics and class origins. The history of forgery reveals that in medieval times it was considered to be the special crime of the clerical class, as indeed it had to be inasmuch as the members of this class monopolized writing skills. (36, pp. 5-31) It also seems to be true from the later history of the crime that it has held a special attraction for more highly educated persons, for those of higher socioeconomic status and those of "refined" or artistic tastes.*** The basic method of organized forgery is stated to have been invented and perfected in England, not by criminals but by a practicing barrister of established reputation in 1840. (28, 8) An early gang of forgers organized by a practicing physician is also described by Felstead. (11) A number of studies directed to the differentiating characteristics of check criminals point to

---

*Detectives in Santa Monica, California showed the writer a collection of checks successfully passed with such signatures as: "I. M. A. Fool," "U. R. Stuck," and others not printable. For a discussion of the crudeness of bogus checks accepted by business people see. (30)

**There is evidence that there has been a sharp absolute decline in the number of pickpockets in recent years and that most of the so-called "class cannons" (highly skilled) operating now are fifty years of age or over. (23)

***See footnote page 148.

an "above average" intelligence and formal education. This refers to the general population as well as to the criminal populations with which they have been compared. (3, 12, 17, p. 87, 18, p. 40)

All of this is not to say that less-educated persons do not frequently pass bad checks but rather that the persons who persist in the behavior and develop behavior systems of forgery seem much more likely than other criminals to be drawn from a segment of the population distinguished by a higher socioeconomic status. Generally this was true of the systematic forgers in this study. Eight of the thirty had completed two or more years of college. Fourteen of the thirty had fathers who were or had been in the professions and business, including a juvenile court judge, a minister, a postmaster of a large city, and three very wealthy ranch owners. One woman came from a nationally famous family of farm implement man-

***This is the thesis of Rhodes (28); two of the four participants in the famous Bank of England forgery in 1873 were college educated, one being a Harvard graduate. See Dilnot (7); forgers coming from "good" families are described by Adam (1); fourteen of the nineteen persons tried for forgery at Newgate Prison in England during the later eighteenth and early nineteenth centuries were what can be termed "middle" and "upper" class, including three army or navy officers (one who commanded the royal yacht of Queen Caroline, consort of George IV), one banker, one physician Cambridge graduate, one prosecuting attorney, two engravers (one by appointment to George III), three "gentlemen" of good connections; and three bank clerks. Two of the three men who had "poor parents" had married women of "good means." Tegg (35) and Bonger (4, pp. 429, 430, 437) give data from France and Italy which support this idea. A number of writers have commented on the fact that forgery has been quite common among the educated classes of India, particularly the "wily Brahmins." (1, 9, pp. 3-6, 16)

ufacturers. Four others had siblings well established in business and the professions, one of whom was an attorney general in another state. Two of the men had been successful businessmen themselves before becoming check men.

The most important implication of these data is that systematic check forgers do not seem to have had criminal antecedents or early criminal associations. (19, 20) For this reason, as well as for technical reasons, they are not likely to seek out or to be comfortable in informal associations with other criminals who have been products of early and lengthy socialization and learning in a criminal subculture. It also follows that their morality and values remain essentially "middle" or "upper" class and that they seldom integrate these with the morality of the professional criminal. This is reflected in self-attitudes in which many refer to themselves as "black sheep" or as a kind of Dr. Jekyll-Mr. Hyde person. Further support for this interpretation comes from their status in prison where, according to observations of themselves and others, they are marginal so far as participation in the primary groups of the prison is concerned.

CONCLUSION

The cases and data presented suggest that present-day check forgery exists in systematic form but does not appear to be a professional behavior system acquired or maintained through associations with other criminals. The technical demands of contemporary check forgery preclude efficient operation on an organized, cooperative basis. In addition to these factors the class characteristics and backgrounds of systematic forgers incline them to avoid intimate association with other criminals.

REFERENCES

1. Adam, H. L., *Oriental Crime* (London: T. Werner Laurie, 1908).

2. ————, *The Story of Crime* (London: T. Werner Laurie, 1908).

3. Berg, I., "A Comparative Study of Forgery," *Journal of Applied Psychology*, 28 (June, 1944), 232-238.

4. Bonger, W. A., *Criminality and Economic Conditions* (Boston: Little, Brown, 1916).

5. Cavan, R. S., *Criminology* (New York: Crowell, 1948).

6. Clinard, M. B., *Sociology of Deviant Behavior* (New York: Rinehart, 1957).

7. Dilnot, G., *The Bank of England Forgery* (New York: Scribners, 1929).

8. ————, *The Trial of Jim the Penman* (London: Geoffrey Bles, 1930).

9. Edwards, S. M., *Crime in India* (London: Oxford University Press, 1924).

10. Elliott, M., *Crime in Modern Society* (New York: Harper and Bros., 1942).

11. Felstead, T. S., in *Famous Criminals and Their Trials* (New York: Doran, 1926).

12. Fox, V., "Intelligence, Race and Age as Selective Factors in Crime," *Journal of Criminal Law and Criminology*, 37 (July-August, 1946), 141-152.

13. Fregier, H. A., *Les Classes Dangereuses de la population dans les grandes villes* (Paris: Chex J. B. Balliére, 1840).

14. Gruhle, H. W. and L. Wetzel, Eds. "Verbrechentype" (cited in Bonger, W. A., *op. cit.*, p. 581).

15. Hall, Jerome, *Theft, Law and Society*, 2nd. Ed. (Indianapolis: Bobbs - Merril, 1952).

16. Hardless and Hardless, *Forgery in India* (Chunar: Sanctuary, 1920).

17. Hooton, E. A., *The American Criminal*, Vol. I (Cambridge: Harvard University, 1939).

18. Lawes, L., *Life and Death in Sing Sing* (New York: Sun Dial Press, 1938).

19. Lemert, E., "An Isolation and Closure Theory of Naive Check Forgery," *Journal of Criminal Law and Criminology*, 44 (September-October, 1953), 296-307.

20. ————, "Generality and Specificity in Criminal Behavior: Check Forgery Considered," paper read before American Sociological Society, September, 1956.

21. Lindesmith, A. R. and H. W. Dunham, "Some Principles of Criminal Typology," *Social Forces*, 19 (March, 1941), 307-314.

22. Maurer, D. W., "The Argot of Check Forgery," *American Speech*, 16 (December, 1941), 243-250.

23. Maurer, D. W., *Whiz Mob* (Gainesville, Florida: American Dialect Society, No. 24, 1955).

24. Pinkerton, W. A., "Forgery," paper read before Annual Convention of the International Association of Chiefs of Police, Washington D. C., 1905.

25. ————, *Thirty Years a Detective* (New York: G. W. Carleton, 1884).

26. Puibaraud, L., *Les Malfaiteurs de profession* (Paris: E. Flammarion, 1893).

27. Reckless, W. C., *The Crime Problem*, 2nd Ed. (New York: Appleton Century, 1955).

28. Rhodes, H. T. F., in *The Craft of Forgery* (London: J. Murray, 1934).

29. Speare, J. W., *Protecting the Nation's Money* (Rochester: Todd Protectograph Co., 1927).

30. Sternitsky, J. L., *Forgery and Fictitious Checks* (Springfield: Charles C. Thomas, 1955).

31. Sutherland, E. H., *The Professional Thief* (Chicago: University of Chicago, 1937).

32. ————, "The Professional Thief," *Journal of Criminal Law and Criminology*, 28 (July-August, 1937), 161-163.

33. ————, *Principles of Criminology*, Rev. (New York: Lippincott, 1947).

34. Sutherland, E. H. and D. Cressey, *Principles of Criminology*, 5th Ed. (New York: Lippincott, 1955).

35. Tegg, T., *The Chronicles of Crime*, Vols. I, II (London: Camden Pelham, 1841).

36. Tout, T. F., *Medieval Forgers and Forgeries*, Bulletin of the John Rylands Library, 5, 3, 4, 1919.

37. Von Hentig, H., "The Pickpocket: Psychology, Tactics and Technique," *Journal of Criminal Law and Criminology*, 34 (May-June, 1943), pp. 11-16.

[13]

BECOMING A HIT MAN
Neutralization in a Very Deviant Career

KEN LEVI

OUR KNOWLEDGE ABOUT DEVIANCE management is based primarily on behavior that is easily mitigated. The literature dwells on unwed fathers (Pfuhl, 1978), and childless mothers (Veevers, 1975), pilfering bread salesmen (Ditton, 1977), and conniving shoe salesmen (Friedman, 1974), bridge pros (Holtz, 1975), and poker pros (Hayano, 1977), marijuana smokers (Langer, 1976), massage parlor prostitutes (Verlarde, 1975), and other minor offenders (see, for example, Berk, 1977; Farrell and Nelson, 1976; Gross, 1977). There is a dearth of deviance management articles on serious offenders, and no scholarly articles at all about one of the (legally) most serious offenders of all, the professional murderer. Drift may be possible for the minor offender exploiting society's *ambivalence* toward his relatively unserious behavior (Sykes and Matza, 1957). However, excuses for the more inexcusable forms of deviant behavior are, by definition, less easily come by, and the very serious offender may enter his career with few of the usual defenses.

AUTHOR'S NOTE: I would like to thank Sharon Barnartt, Jack Douglas, Edgar Mills, Daniel Rigney, and two anonymous reviewers for their helpful criticisms and suggestions.

EDITOR'S NOTE: Drawing from frame analysis, Ken Levi examines how the stigma of being a "professional killer" is managed by a neutralization process of "reframing." Levi's contribution to our understanding of the social organization of profes-

URBAN LIFE, Vol. 10 No. 1, April 1981 47-63

48   URBAN LIFE   APRIL 1981

This article will focus on ways that one type of serious offender, the professional hit man, neutralizes stigma in the early stages of his career. As we shall see, the social organization of the "profession" provides "neutralizers" which distance its members from the shameful aspects of their careers. But for the novice, without professional insulation, the problem is more acute. With very little outside help, he must negate his feelings, neutralize them, and adopt a "framework" (Goffman, 1974) appropriate to his chosen career. This process, called "reframing," is the main focus of the present article. Cognitively, the novice must *reframe his experience* in order to enter his profession.

THE SOCIAL ORGANIZATION OF MURDER

Murder, the unlawful killing of a person, is considered a serious criminal offense in the United States, and it is punished by extreme penalties. In addition, most Americans do not feel that the penalties are extreme enough (Reid, 1976: 482). In overcoming the intense stigma associated with murder, the hit man lacks the supports available to more ordinary types of killers.

Some cultures allow special circumstances or sanction special organizations wherein people who kill are insulated from the taint of murder. Soldiers at war, or police in the line of duty, or citizens protecting their property operate under what are considered justifiable or excusable conditions. They receive so much informal support from the general public and from members of their own group that it may protect even a sadistic member from blame (Westley, 1966).

Subcultures (Wolfgang and Ferracuti, 1967), organizations (Maas, 1968), and gangs (Yablonsky, 1962) that unlawfully promote killing can at least provide their members with

sional murder provides insights into an area of deviance rarely addressed in social analysis, but its significance, as the author suggests, extends to other realms of social activity in which detachment is a requisite characteristic of managing the activity.

an "appeal to higher loyalties" (Sykes and Matza, 1957), if not a fully developed set of deviance justifying norms.

Individuals acting on their own, who kill in a spontaneous, "irrational" outburst of violence, can also mitigate the stigma of their behavior.

> I mean, people will go ape for a one minute and shoot, but there are very few people who are capable of thinking about, planning, and then doing it [Joey, 1974: 56].

Individuals who kill in a hot-blooded burst of passion can retrospectively draw comfort from the law which provides a lighter ban against killings performed without premeditation or malice or intent (Lester and Lester, 1975: 35). At one extreme, the spontaneous killing may seem the result of a mental disease (Lester and Lester, 1975: 39) or dissociative reaction (Tanay, 1972), and excused entirely as insanity.

But when an individual who generally shares society's ban against murder, is fully aware that his act of homicide is (1) unlawful, (2) self-serving, and (3) intentional, he does not have the usual defenses to fall back on. How does such an individual manage to *overcome his inhibitions* and *avoid serious damage to his self-image* (assuming that he does share society's ban)? This is the special dilemma of the professional hit man who hires himself out for murder.

RESEARCH METHODS

Information for this article comes primarily from a series of intensive interviews with one self-styled "hit man." The interviews were spread over seven, tape-recorded sessions during a four-month period. The respondent was one of fifty prison inmates randomly sampled from a population of people convicted of murder in Metropolitan Detroit. The respondent told about an "accidental" killing, involving a drunken bar patron who badgered the respondent and finally forced his hand by pulling a knife on him. In court he claimed self-defense, but the witnesses at the bar claimed

50   URBAN LIFE   APRIL 1981

otherwise, so they sent him to prison. During the first two interview sessions, the respondent acted progressively ashamed of this particular killing, not on moral grounds, but because of its "sloppiness" or "amateurishness." Finally, he indicated there was more he would like to say. So, I stopped the tape recorder. I asked him if he was a hit man. He said he was.

He had already been given certain guarantees, including no names in the interview, a private conference room, and a signed contract promising his anonymity. Now, as a further guarantee, we agreed to talk about him in the third person, as a fictitious character named "Pete," so that none of his statements would sound like a personal confession. With these assurances, future interviews were devoted to his career as a professional murderer, with particular emphasis on his entry into the career and his orientation toward his victims.

Was he reliable? Since we did not use names, I had no way of checking the veracity of the individual cases he reported. Nevertheless, I was able to compare his account of the hit man's career with information from other convicted murderers, with police experts, and with accounts from the available literature (Gage, 1972: Joey, 1974; Maas, 1968). Pete's information was generally supported by these other sources. As to his motive for submitting to the interview, it is hard to gauge. He apparently was ashamed of the one "accidental" killing that had landed him in prison, and he desired to set the record straight concerning what he deemed an illustrious career, now that he had arrived, as he said, at the end of it. Hit men pride themselves on not "falling" (going to jail) for murder, and Pete's incarceration hastened a decision to retire—that he had already been contemplating, anyway.

A question might arise about the ethics of researching self-confessed "hit men" and granting them anonymity. Legally, since Pete never mentioned specific names or specific dates or possible future crimes, there does not seem to be a problem. Morally, if confidentiality is a necessary condition to obtaining information about serious offenders, then we have to ask: Is it worth it? Pete insisted that he had retired from the profession. Therefore, there seems to be no "clear and imminent danger" that would justify the violation of confidentiality, in the terms set forth by the American Psychological Association (1978: 40). On the other hand, the *possibility* of danger does exist, and future researchers will have to exercise their judgment.

Finally, hit men are hard to come by. Unlike more lawful killers, such as judges or night watchmen, and unlike run-of-the-mill murderers, the hit man (usually) takes infinite care to conceal his identity. Therefore, while it is regrettable that this paper has only one case to report on, and while it would be ideal to perform a comparative analysis on a number of hit men, it would be very difficult to obtain such a sample. Instead, Pete's responses will be compared to similar accounts from the available literature. While such a method can never produce verified findings, it can point to suggestive hypotheses.

THE SOCIAL ORGANIZATION OF PROFESSIONAL MURDER

There are two types of professional murderers: the organized and the independent. The killer who belongs to an organized syndicate does not usually get paid on a contract basis, and performs his job out of loyalty and obedience to the organization (Maas, 1968: 81). The independent professional killer is a freelance agent who hires himself out for a fee (Pete). It is the career organization of the second type of killer that will be discussed.

The organized killer can mitigate his behavior through an "appeal to higher loyalties" (Sykes and Matza, 1957). He also can view his victim as an enemy of the group and then choose from a variety of techniques available for neutralizing an offense against an enemy (see, for example, Hirschi,

52   URBAN LIFE   APRIL 1981

1969; Rogers and Buffalo, 1974). But the independent professional murderer lacks most of these defenses. Nevertheless, built into his role are certain structural features that
help him avoid deviance ascription. These features include:

(1) *Contract.* A contract is an unwritten agreement to
provide a sum of money to a second party who agrees, in
return, to commit a designated murder (Joey, 1974: 9). It is
most often arranged over the phone, between people who
have never had personal contact. And the victim, or "hit," is
usually unknown to the killer (Gage, 1972: 57; Joey, 1974:
61-62). This arrangement is meant to protect both parties
from the law. But it also helps the killer "deny the victim"
(Sykes and Matza, 1957) by keeping him relatively anonymous.

In arranging the contract, the hired killer will try to find
out the difficulty of the hit and how much the customer
wants the killing done. According to Pete, these considerations determine his price. He does not ask about the motive
for the killing, treating it as none of his concern. Not knowing the motive may hamper the killer from morally justifying
his behavior, but it also enables him to further deny the
victim by maintaining his distance and reserve. Finally, the
contract is backed up by a further understanding.

> Like this guy who left here (prison) last summer; he was out
> two months before he got killed. Made a mistake some-
> where. The way I heard it, he didn't finish filling a contract
> [Pete].

If the killer fails to live up to his part of the bargain, the
penalties could be extreme (Gage, 1972: 53; Joey, 1974: 9).
This has the ironic effect that after the contract is arranged,
the killer can somewhat "deny responsibility" (Sykes and
Matza, 1957), by pleading self-defense.

(2) *Reputation and Money.* Reputation is especially important in an area where killers are unknown to their customers, and where the less written, the better (Joey, 1974:

58). Reputation, in turn, reflects how much money the hit man has commanded in the past.

> And that was the first time that I ever got 30 grand . . . it's based on his reputation. . . . Yeah, how good he really is. To be so-so, you get so-so money. If you're good, you get good money [Pete].

Pete, who could not recall the exact number of people he had killed, did, like other hit men, keep an accounting of his highest fees (Joey, 1974: 58, 62). To him big money meant not only a way to earn a living, but also a way to maintain his professional reputation.

People who accept low fees can also find work as hired killers. Heroin addicts are the usual example. But, as Pete says, they often receive a bullet for their pains. It is believed that people who would kill for so little would also require little persuasion to make them talk to the police (Joey, 1974: 63). This further reinforces the single-minded emphasis on making big money. As a result, killing is conceptualized as a "business" or as "just a job." Framing the hit in a normal businesslike context enables the hit man to deny wrongfulness, or "deny injury" (Sykes and Matza, 1957).

In addition to the economic motive, Pete, and hit men discussed by other authors, refer to excitement, fun, game-playing, power, and impressing women as incentives for murder (Joey, 1974: 81-82). However, none of these motives are mentioned by all sources. None are as necessary to the career as money. And, after a while, these other motives diminish and killing becomes only "just a job" (Joey, 1974: 20). The primacy of the economic motive has been aptly expressed in the case of another deviant profession.

> Women who enjoy sex with their customers do not make good prostitutes, according to those who are acquainted with this institution first hand. Instead of thinking about the most effective way of making money at the job, they would be doing things for their own pleasure and enjoyment [Goode, 1978: 342].

54   URBAN LIFE   APRIL 1981

(3) *Skill.* Most of the hit man's training focuses on acquiring skill in the use of weapons.

> Then, he met these two guys, these two white guys . . . them two, them two was the best. And but they stayed around over there and they got together, and Pete told [them] that he really wanted to be good. He said, if [I] got to do something, I want to be good at it. So, they got together, showed him, showed him *how to shoot.* . . . And gradually, he became good. . . . Like he told me, like when he shoots somebody, he always goes for the head; he said, that's about the best shot. I mean, if you want him dead then and there. . . . And these two guys showed him, and to him, I mean, hey, I mean, he don't believe nobody could really outshoot these two guys, you know what I mean. *They know everything you want to know about guns, knives, and stuff like that* [Pete].

The hit man's reputation, and the amount of money he makes depend on his skill, his effective ability to serve as a means to *someone else's ends.* The result is a focus on technique.

> Like in anything you do, when you do it, you want to do it just right. . . . On your target and you hit it, how you feel: I hit it! I hit it! [Pete].

This focus on technique, on means, helps the hit man to "deny responsibility" and intent (Sykes and Matza, 1957). In frame-analytic terms, the hit man separates his morally responsible, or "principal" self from the rest of himself, and performs the killing mainly as a "strategist" (Goffman, 1974: 523). In other words, he sees himself as a "hired gun." The saying, "If I didn't do it, they'd find someone else who would," reflects this narrowly technical orientation.

To sum up thus far, the contract, based as it is on the hit man's reputation for profit and skill, provides the hit man with opportunities for denying the victim, denying injury, and denying responsibility. But this is not enough. To point out the defenses of the professional hit man is one thing, but it is unlikely that the *novice* hit man would have a totally professional attitude so early in his career. The novice is at a point where he both lacks the conventional defense against the stigma of murder, *and* he has not yet fully acquired the exceptional defenses of the professional. How, then, does he cope?

THE FIRST TIME: NEGATIVE EXPERIENCE

Goffman defines "negative experience" as a feeling of disorientation.

> Expecting to take up a position in a well-framed realm, he finds that no particular frame is immediately applicable, or the frame that he thought was applicable no longer seems to be, or he cannot bind himself within the frame that does apparently apply. He loses command over the formulation of viable response. He flounders. Experience, the meld of what the current scene brings to him and what he brings to it— meant to settle into a form even while it is beginning, finds no form and is therefore no experience. Reality anomically flutters. He has a "negative experience"—negative in the sense that it takes its character from what it is not, and what it is not is an organized and organizationally affirmed response [1974: 387-379].

Negative experience can occur when a person finds himself lapsing into an old understanding of a situation, only to suddenly awaken to the fact that it no longer applies. In this regard, we should expect negative experience to be a special problem for the novice. For example, the first time he killed a man for money, Pete supposedly became violently ill:

> When he [Pete], you know, hit the guy, when he shot the guy, the guy said, 'You killed me' . . . something like that, cause he struck him all up here. And what he said, it was just, I mean, *the look right in the guy's eye,* you know. I mean he looked like: *why me?* Yeah? And he [Pete] couldn't shake that. Cause he remembered a time or two when he got cut, and all he wanted to do was get back and cut this guy that cut him. And this here. . . . No, he just could not shake it. And

56   URBAN LIFE   APRIL 1981

then he said that at night-time he'll start thinking about the
guy: like he shouldn't have looked at him like that. . . . I mean
actually [Pete] was sick. . . . He couldn't keep his food down, I
mean, or nothing like that. . . . [It lasted] I'd say about two
months. . . . Like he said that he had feelings . . . that he
never did kill nobody before [Pete].

Pete's account conforms to the definition of negative experience. He had never killed anyone for money before. It
started when a member of the Detroit drug world had spotted Pete in a knife fight outside an inner city bar, was apparently impressed with the young man's style, and offered
him fifty dollars to do a "job." Pete accepted. He wanted the
money. But when the first hit came about, Pete of course
knew that he was doing it for money, but yet his orientation
was: revenge. Thus, he stared his victim in the *face,* a characteristic gesture of people who kill enemies for revenge
(Levi, 1975: 190). Expecting to see defiance turn into a look
of defeat, they attempt to gain "face" at the loser's expense.

But when Pete stared his victim in the face, he saw not an
enemy, but an innocent man. He saw a look of: "Why me?"
And this *discordant* image is what remained in his mind
during the weeks and months to follow and made him sick.
As Pete says, "He shouldn't have looked at him like that."
The victim's look of innocence brought about what Goffman
(1974: 347) refers to as a "frame break:"

> Given that the frame applied to an activity is expected to
> enable us to come to terms with all events in that activity (in-
> forming and regulating many of them), it is understandable
> that the unmanageable might occur, an occurrence which
> cannot be effectively ignored and to which the frame cannot
> be applied, with resulting bewilderment and chagrin on the
> part of the participants. In brief, a break can occur in the ap-
> plicability of the frame, a break in its governance.

When such a frame break occurs, it produces negative
experience. Pete's extremely uncomfortable disorientation
may reflect the extreme dissonance between the revenge

frame, that he expected to apply, and the unexpected look of innocence that he encountered and continued to recall.

SUBSEQUENT TIME: REFRAMING THE HIT

According to Goffman (1974: 319), a structural feature in frames of experience is that they are divided into different "tracks" or types of information. These include, "a main track or story line and ancillary tracks of various kinds." The ancillary tracks are the directional track, the overlay track, the concealment track and the disattend tract. The disattend track contains the information that is perceived but supposed to be *ignored*. For example, the prostitute manages the distasteful necessity of having sex with "tricks' by remaining "absolutely . . . detached. Removed. Miles and miles away" (1978: 344). The existence of different tracks allows an individual to define and redefine his experience by the strategic placement of information.

Sometimes, the individual receives outside help. For example, when Milgram in 1963 placed a barrier between people, administering electric shocks, and the bogus "subjects" who were supposedly receiving the shocks, he made it easier for the shockers to "disattend" signs of human distress from their hapless victims. Surgeons provide another example. Having their patients completely covered, except for the part to be operated on helps them work in a more impersonal manner. In both examples, certain crucial information is stored away in the "concealment track" (Goffman, 1974: 218).

In other cases help can come from guides who direct the novice on what to experience and what to block out. Beginning marijuana smokers are cautioned to ignore feelings of nausea (Becker, 1953: 240). On the other hand, novice hit men like Pete are reluctant to share their "experience" with anyone else. It would be a sign of weakness.

In still other cases, however, it is possible that the subject can do the reframing *on his own*. And this is what appears to have happened to Pete.

> And when the second one [the second hit] came up, [Pete] was still thinking about the first one. . . . Yeah, when he got ready to go, he was thinking about it. *Something changed.* I don't know how to put it right. Up to the moment that he killed the second guy now, he waited, you know. Going through his mind was the first guy he killed. He still seeing him, still see the *expression on his face*. Soon, the second guy walked up; I mean, it was like just his mind just *blanked out* for a minute, everything just blanked out. . . . Next thing he know, he had killed the second guy. . . . *He knew what he was doing,* but what I mean, he just didn't have nothing on his mind. Everything was wiped out [Pete].

When the second victim approached, Pete says that he noticed the victim's approach, he was aware of the man's presence. But he noticed none of the victim's personal features. He did not see the victim's face or its expression. Thus, he did not see the very thing that gave him so much trouble the first time. It is as if Pete had *negatively conditioned* himself to avoid certain cues. Since he shot the victim in the head, it is probable that Pete saw him in one sense; this is not the same kind of experience as a "dissociative reaction," which has been likened to sleep-walking (Tanay, 1972). Pete says that, "he knew what he was doing." But he either did not pay attention to his victim's personal features at the time of the killing, or he blocked them out immediately afterward, so that now the only aspect of his victim he recalls is the victim's approach (if we are to believe him).

After that, Pete says that killing became *routine*. He learned to view his victims as "targets," rather than as people. Thus, he believes that the second experience is the crucial one, and that the disattendance of the victim's personal features made it so.

Support from other accounts of hit men is scant, due to a
lack of data. Furthermore, not everything in Pete's account
supports the "reframing" hypothesis. In talking about later
killings, it is clear that he not only attends to his victims'
personal features, on occasion, but he also derives a certain
grim pleasure in doing so.

> [the victim was] a nice looking woman. . . . She started weep-
> ing, and [she cried], 'I ain't did this, I ain't did that' . . . and
> [Pete] said that he shot her. Like it wasn't nothing . . . he
> didn't feel nothing. It was just money [Pete].

In a parallel story, Joey, the narrator of the *Killer,* also
observes his victim in personal terms.

> [The victim] began to beg. He even went so far as to tell us
> where had stashed his money. Finally, he realized there was
> absolutely nothing he could do. He sat there quietly. Then,
> he started crying. I didn't feel a thing for him [1974: 56].

It may be that this evidence contradicts what I have said
about reframing; but perhaps another interpretation is possible. Reframing may play a more crucial role in the original
redefinition of an experience than in the continued maintenance of that redefinition. Once Pete has accustomed himself to viewing his victims as merely targets, as "just
money," then it may be less threatening to look upon them
as persons, once again. Once the "main story line" has
been established, discordant information can be presented
in the "overlay track" (Goffman, 1974: 215), without doing
too much damage. Indeed, this seems to be *the point* that
both hit men are trying to make in the above exerpts.

THE HEART OF THE HIT MAN

For what I have been referring to as "disattendance" Pete
used the term "heart," which he defined as a "coldness."

When asked what he would look for in an aspiring hit man, Pete replied,

> See if he's got a whole lot of heart . . . you got to be cold . . . you got to build a coldness in yourself. It's not something that comes automatically. Cause, see, I don't care who he is, first, you've got feelings [Pete].

In contrast to this view, Joey (1974: 56) said,

> There are three things you need to kill a man: the gun, the bullets, and the balls. A lot of people will point a gun at you, but they haven't got the courage to pull the trigger. It's as simple as that.

It may be that some are born with "heart," while others acquire it in the way I have described.

However, the "made rather than born" thesis does explain one perplexing feature of hit men and other "evil" men whose banality has sometimes seemed discordant. In other aspects of their lives they all seem perfectly capable of feeling ordinary human emotions. Their inhumanity, their coldness, seems narrowly restricted to their jobs. Pete, for example, talked about his "love" for little children. Eddie "The Hawk" Ruppolo meekly allowed his mistress to openly insult him in a public bar (Gage, 1972). And Joey (1974: 55) has this to say about himself:

> Believe it or not, I'm a human being. I laugh at funny jokes, I love children around the house, and I can spend hours playing with my mutt.

All of these examples of human warmth indicate that the cold heart of the hit man may be less a characteristic of the killer's individual personality, than a feature of the professional framework of experience which the hit man has learned to adapt himself to, when he is on the job.

DISCUSSION

This article is meant as a contribution to the study of deviance neutralization. The freelance hit man is an example of an individual who, relatively alone, must deal with a profound and unambiguous stigma in order to enter his career. Both Pete and Joey emphasize "heart" as a determining factor in becoming a professional. And Pete's experience, after the first hit, further indicates that the inhibitions against murder-for-money are real.

In this article "heart"—or the ability to adapt to a rationalized framework for killing—has been portrayed as the outcome of an initial process of reframing, in addition to other neturalization techniques established during the further stages of professionalization. As several theorists (see, for example, Becker, 1953; Douglas, 1977; Matza, 1969) have noted, people often enter into deviant acts first, and then develop rationales for their behavior later on. This was also the case with Pete, who began his career by first, (1) "being willing" (Matza, 1969), (2) encountering a frame-break, (3) undergoing negative experience, (4) being willing to try again (also known as "getting back on the horse"), (5) reframing the experience, and (6) having future, routine experiences wherein his professionalization increasingly enabled him to "deny the victim," "deny injury," and "deny responsibility." Through the process of reframing, the experience of victim-as-target emerged as the "main story line," and the experience of victim-as-person was downgraded from the main track to the disattend track to the overlay track. Ironically, the intensity of the negative experience seemed to make the process all the more successful. Thus, it may be possible for a person with "ordinary human feelings" to both pass through the novice stage, and to continue "normal relations" thereafter. The reframing hypothesis

62   URBAN LIFE   APRIL 1981

has implications for other people who knowingly perform stigmatized behaviors. It may be particularly useful in explaining a personal conversion experience that occurs despite the relative absence of deviant peer groups, deviant norms, extenuating circumstances, and neutralization rationales.

REFERENCES

American Psychological Association (1978) Directory of the American Psychological Association, Washington, DC: Author.

BECKER, H. (1953) "Becoming a marijuana user." Amer. J. of Sociology 59: 235-243.

BERK, B. (1977) "Face-saving at the singles dance." Social Problems 24, 5: 530-544.

DITTON, J. (1977) "Alibis and aliases: some notes on motives of fiddling bread salesmen." Sociology 11, 2: 233-255.

DOUGLAS, J., P. RASMUSSEN, and C. FLANAGAN (1977) The Nude Beach. Beverly Hills: Sage.

FARRELL, R. and J. NELSON (1976) "A causal model of secondary deviance; the case of homosexuality." Soc. Q. 17: 109-120.

FRIEDMAN, N. L. (1974) "Cookies and contests: notes on ordinary occupational deviance and its neutralization." Soc. Symposium (Spring): 1-9.

GAGE, N. (1972) Mafia, U.S.A. New York: Dell.

GOFFMAN, E. (1974) Frame Analysis. Cambridge, MA: Harvard Univ. Press.

GOODE, E. (1978) Deviant Behavior: An Interactionist Approach. Englewood Cliffs, NJ: Prentice-Hall.

GROSS, H. (1977) "Micro and macro level implications for a sociology of virtue— case of draft protesters to Vietnam War." Soc. Q. 18, 3: 319-339.

HAYANO, D. (1977) "The professional poker player: career identification and the problem of respectability." Social Problems 24 (June): 556-564.

HIRSCHI, T. (1969) Causes of Delinquency. Berkeley: Univ. of California Press.

HOLTZ, J. (1975) "The professional duplicate bridge player: conflict management in a free, legal, quasi-deviant occupation." Urban Life 4, 2: 131-160.

JOEY (1974) Killer: Autobiography of a Mafia Hit Man. New York: Pocket Books.

LANGER, J. (1976) "Drug entrepreneurs and the dealing culture." Australian and New Zealand J. of Sociology 12, 2: 82-90.

LESTER, D. and G. LESTER (1975) Crime of Passion: Murder and the Murderer. Chicago: Nelson-Hall.

LEVI, K. (1975) Icemen. Ann Arbor, MI: University Microfilms.

MAAS, P. (1968) The Valachi Papers. New York: G. P. Putnam.

MATZA, D. (1969) Becoming Deviant. Englewood Cliffs, NJ: Prentice-Hall.

PFUHL, E. (1978) "The unwed father: a non-deviant rule breaker." Soc. Q. 19: 113-128.

REID, S. (1976) Crime and Criminology. Hinsdale, IL: Dryden Press.

ROGERS, J. and M. BUFFALO (1974) "Neutralization techniques: toward a simplified measurement scale." Pacific Soc. Rev. 17, 3: 313.

SYKES, G. and D. MATZA (1957) "Techniques of neutralization: a theory of delinquency." Amer. Soc. Rev. 22: 664-670.

TANAY, E. (1972) "Psychiatric aspects of homicide prevention." Amer. J. of Psychology 128: 814-817.

VEEVERS, J. (1975) "The moral careers of voluntarily childless wives: notes on the defense of a variant world view." Family Coordinator 24, 4: 473-487.

VERLARDE, A. (1975) "Becoming prostituted: the decline of the massage parlor profession and the masseuse." British J. of Criminology 15, 3: 251-263.

WESTLEY, W. (1966) "The escalation of violence through legitimation." Annals of the American Association of Political and Social Science 364 (March) 120-126.

WOLFGANG, M. and F. FERRACUTI (1967) The Subculture of Violence. London: Tavistock.

YABLONSKY, L. (1962) The Violent Gang. New York: Macmillan.

KEN LEVI is Assistant Professor of Sociology at the University of Texas at San Antonio. He has written papers on homicide, violence, and religious commitment.

[14]

APPLIED COGNITIVE PSYCHOLOGY, VOL. 6, 109–123 (1992)

Recognition Memory Performance and Residential Burglary*

ROBERT LOGIE†

Department of Psychology, University of Aberdeen, U.K.

RICHARD WRIGHT and SCOTT DECKER

Department of Administration of Justice, and Center for Metropolitan Studies, University of Missouri–St Louis, St Louis, U.S.A.

SUMMARY

This paper reports two studies of recognition memory performance in groups of juvenile residential burglars. Memory performance of the burglars was compared in Experiment 1 with police officers and a group of adult householders. In Experiment 2 a second group of juvenile burglars was compared with a group of juvenile offenders who had no experience of housebreaking. All groups were asked first to identify houses in photographs that would be attractive or otherwise to burglars. Subsequently, subjects were given a surprise recognition test where, in some photographs, physical features had been changed. Recognition memory for information about physical features of houses was significantly better for the burglary group than for the police officers, who in turn were better than members of the law-abiding public. In Experiment 2 the juvenile burglars' recognition memory performance was significantly better than the other offenders. These results are interpreted in terms of the burglary subjects possessing a level of expertise associated with their experience of offending. This is a finding with implications for criminology and for the application of cognitive psychology to crime prevention, an area of considerable practical importance.

INTRODUCTION

Much of the early literature on the role of expertise in memory performance concentrated on expert chess players (e.g. de Groot, 1965; Chase and Simon, 1973). More recently, Morris, Tweedy, and Gruneberg (1985) have studied memory for football scores among experts in football knowledge. A major conclusion from these studies is that memory performance in experts is only superior to novices when the material to be remembered is structured in a fashion that matches the knowledge structure of the individual. Thus chess masters can remember chess positions better than novices only if the positions are taken from an actual game. When chess pieces are placed

*Prepared, in part, under grant No. 89-IJ-CX-0046 from the National Institute of Justice, Office of Justice Programs, U.S. Department of Justice. Points of view or opinions expressed in this document are those of the authors and do not necessarily represent the official position or policies of the U.S. Department of Justice.

† Part of this work was carried out when Robert Logie was at the Medical Research Council Applied Psychology Unit, Cambridge, U.K.

0888–4080/92/020109–15$07.50

Received 2 May 1990
Revised 7 August 1990

randomly on the board, chess masters are no better than novice players. Likewise, individuals with extensive football knowledge can remember impressive numbers of scores only if the scores match existing knowledge in terms of league positions or recent form. Similar results have been reported in other domains of expertise, including reading electronic circuit diagrams (Egan and Schwartz, 1979), bridge playing (Charness, 1979), the game 'GO' (Reitman, 1976), computer programming (McKeithen, Reitman, Reuter, and Hirtle, 1981), and map-reading (Gilhooly, Wood, Kinnear, and Green, 1988).

Complementary to this continuing interest in the psychology literature, research in criminology is beginning to examine the role of expertise or specialized knowledge among offenders in relation to decision-making (e.g. about whether or not to commit an offence) and perception of the physical environment in which crimes are committed (Cornish and Clarke, 1986; Bennett and Wright, 1984). A recent study by Taylor and Nee (1988) has specifically suggested the role of prior learning in burglars' exploration of their environment. However, this approach is in its early stages and remains controversial. Furthermore, the work that has been done in this arena has concentrated almost exclusively on adult offenders, in spite of the fact that many house burglars are known to be youngsters (Home Office Statistics, 1987; Sessions, 1989).

An interesting question to ask is whether the findings from research on other forms of expertise might generalize to individuals with experience of residential burglary, a group that is rarely available for any kind of research. Also, it would be interesting to explore whether a 'cognitive' approach to the study of offenders is likely to be fruitful. If it proves to be so, it will serve to demonstrate the applicability of cognitive psychology to a topic of considerable public concern.

The study reported here addressed these issues by asking two basic questions. First, do residential burglars have a specialized knowledge or expertise? Second, if they do, is this expertise evident in memory performance with relevant material?

EXPERIMENT 1

Method

Subjects
Three groups of subjects were chosen for study, and these are described below.

Residential burglars. The 'burglar' group comprised ten male, juvenile offenders who had been convicted of one or more offences of residential burglary, and who were in a British juvenile remand centre at the time of the interview. Their ages ranged from 15 to 17 years, with a mean age of 16.1 years and a standard deviation of 10 months.

A remand centre, by its very nature, is a short-stay institution, but we were eager to select offenders who were still 'close to their crime' and who had not been in a longer-term facility. Data collection was a time-consuming and often frustrating process, and the ten interviews were conducted over a period of 7 months. However, this made it extremely unlikely that the offenders would have colluded in their responses.

Police officers. This group consisted of 14 male police officers from the Criminal Investigation Department of a medium-sized British city. Twelve of the officers held the rank of detective constable, and their ages ranged from 27 to 40, with a mean age of 31 years 3 months, and a standard deviation of 4 years. There was one detective sergeant, aged 34 and one detective inspector, aged 46. All of the interviews were conducted in 1 day, and each officer was requested to avoid giving details of the interview to his colleagues.

Householders. The third group comprised ten members of the general public who were householders. Their ages ranged from 21 to 60 years, with a mean age of 39 years and a standard deviation of 11 years.

They were chosen from a larger panel of volunteers who were members of the Medical Research Council Applied Psychology Unit, Cambridge, U.K. Members of this panel tend to have had at least 12 years of full-time education, and many have attended a college or university. These subjects were chosen because they have a vested interest in preventing burglary, and have been exposed to some crime prevention literature, but have no involvement in committing such offences.

Materials

Target photographs. Black-and-white photographs were taken of 20 houses. Six of the houses were detached, eight were semi-detached, and six were terraced. There were six photographs of a full front view of each house, and two close-up shots showing details of the front door. The photographs were arranged as follows:

1. A full view of the front of the house as it looked normally, with no additional features.
2. One close-up of the front door showing details of a latch-type lock.
3. A full view of the front of the house with a 'dead-bolt' or mortice lock fitted to the door.
4. A close-up of the front door showing the 'dead bolt' or mortice lock.
5. A full view of the front of the house with a 'beware of the dog' sign clearly visible.
6. A full view of the front of the house with a burglar alarm clearly visible.
7. A full view of the front of the house with a hedge or fence superimposed on the photograph.
8. A full view of the front of the house with a car parked in the driveway or in the road out front.

This allowed for a possible six sets of photographs, constructed such that each house was shown in each of six conditions across the sets. Within one set, however, a given house was shown in one condition only. For example, a particular house would be shown in set one as a straight house with no factors added, in set two with a burglar alarm, in set three with a 'beware of the dog' sign (but no burglar alarm) and so on for each factor. In contrast, another house might have a burglar alarm in set one, a mortice lock in set two and so on. Examples of some of the photographs are shown in Figure 1.

Within any one set, the five factors were represented three times; once each on

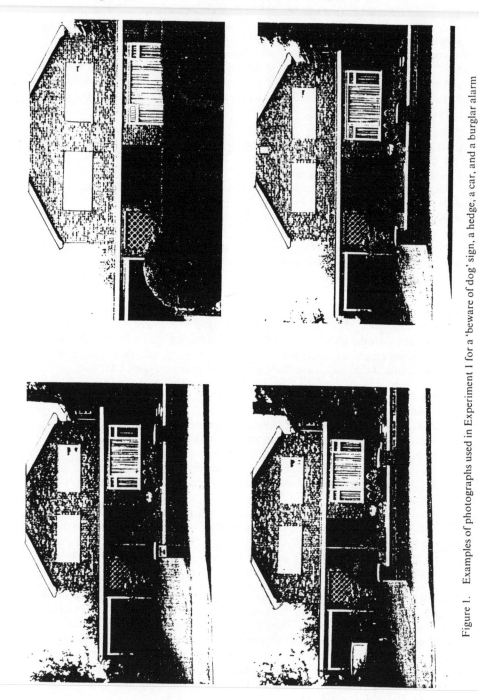

Figure 1.   Examples of photographs used in Experiment 1 for a 'beware of dog' sign, a hedge, a car, and a burglar alarm

a terraced, a semi-detached and a detached house. In addition, the 'straight' houses comprised one that was terraced, one that was detached, and three that were semi-detached.

In practice, for some of the photographs it was not possible realistically to superimpose a hedge, fence, or burglar alarm. These limitations resulted in the construction of two sets of target photographs for use in the experiment.

Recognition photographs. The sets of photographs for recognition were based on the target sets. Within each set, half of the photographs were identical copies of those in the corresponding target set. The remainder involved a change to the original photograph, comprising in some cases the addition of a factor to a house that was a 'straight' house in the target set. In other cases a factor was removed from the original. Within each set of photographs, and for each factor, one house had that factor removed for the recognition test, while a second house had it added.

Interpolated checklist. In order to ensure a reasonable retention interval between target presentation and the recognition test we administered a 'burglary checklist'. The checklist comprised a list of 30 physical features of houses that might affect the attractiveness of a house to a burglar, for example 'newspapers stuffed in the letter box', 'television on', 'double glazing', and so on. For the purposes of this study the checklist was regarded as interpolated material to fill the gap between target presentation and recognition test, and the data will not be reported here. All of the physical features manipulated in the target photographs also were included in the checklist. Further details about the checklists are given in Wright and Logie (1988).

Procedure

Subjects were first shown the photographs from one of the target sets, presented individually in a different random order for each subject. The subjects were required carefully to examine each photograph, and indicate whether the depicted house would be attractive or unattractive to a burglar. They were asked to make their decision on the basis of the information as it was presented in the photograph, without the possibility of returning at some later time to commit the offence. Half of the subjects were given the first set of photographs, with the remainder being shown the second set. This part of the procedure took about 10 minutes with 30 seconds presentation time for each photograph.

Subjects were then given items from the checklist. The experimenter read out each of the items in turn, and subjects were asked whether that particular feature would make a house more attractive, less attractive, or would make no difference to a burglar. The subjects were requested to consider these factors without reference to any particular house. This part of the procedure lasted about 5 minutes.

Subjects were then asked a number of questions. In the case of the burglars, these were questions about their age and number of previous convictions. The police were asked about their age, rank, and their experience in investigating residential burglary. The householders were questioned about their age, whether their house had ever been broken into, and about any measures they had taken to make their house less attractive to a burglar. All subjects were asked for their opinion regarding which features of a house make it most vulnerable or most secure with respect to burglary. This part of the procedure took around 5 minutes.

Finally, subjects were shown the set of photographs for recognition. The photographs were presented one at a time in a different random order for each subject. Subjects were asked to state whether the photograph was an identical copy of the one they had seen earlier, or whether there was a change. Subjects were allowed a maximum of 10 seconds for each photograph and were not pre-warned of this part of the procedure.

Results

There were no significant differences between the two photograph sets for any of the factors studied. Therefore results from both sets were combined for the main analyses.

Target selection
Target selection data are of interest for the present paper in so far as they highlight differences in the choices of the three groups of subjects studied. They are also of interest to the extent that they are likely to be 'noticed' by subjects in each group, thereby increasing the chances of good subsequent recognition memory performance on these items. Summary data are shown in Table 1 in terms of mean percentage of responses that were 'attractive' or 'unattractive'.

Table 1.   Percentage of 'attracted' responses to photographs of target houses, by factor studied and subject group in Experiment 1

Factor	Burglars	Police	Householders
Straight house	58	64	64
Mortice lock	60	52	53
Burglar alarm	23	17	20
Hedge or fence	83	83	60
'Beware of dog'	30	36	23
Car	3	12	50

The mean percentage data were analysed by means of a chi-square test to examine whether the groups differed in the attractiveness of particular factors. An analysis over all factors resulted in $\chi^2 = 66.3$, d.f. $= 10$, $p < .001$, indicating a large discrepancy between groups across factor types. An examination of Table 1 seems to suggest that this was due primarily to an aversion by the burglars and police to the presence of a car. The householders, on the other hand, were ambivalent about this factor. The other imbalance between the groups was that a hedge or fence was seen as very attractive by both the police and the burglars, but its importance was missed by the householders.

An alarm acted to make the house seem unattractive to all three groups, while the presence of a lock appeared to make very little difference. The suggestion that a dog was in the house was a less attractive proposition for all three groups. However, the householders felt that a dog would be rather more of a deterrent than did either of the other two groups.

Recognition data

We next studied the extent to which factors shown to be important in target selection affected recognition memory. These are the data of most interest for this paper, and they are shown in Table 2 in terms of percentage correct recognitions. Since this involved a two-choice recognition procedure, chance performance is 50 per cent. It is clear that the burglar group achieved the highest overall recognition score. An analysis of variance on the recognition scores indicated that the group means were significantly different from one another (F 1,31 = 5.2; $p < .01$). Individual comparisons between means indicated that the burglary group had higher scores than the police, although the effect was weak, $t(22) = 2.04$; $p = .054$. The burglars also had higher scores than the control subjects $t(18) = 3.272$, $p < .01$. However, the police did not have significantly higher scores than the control subjects, $t(22) = 1.53$; $p > .1$. Looking at individual factors shown in Table 2, the burglars showed better recognition performance than the other two groups on all of the factors. The police were better than the householders only for locks, 'beware of dog' signs, and cars.

Table 2. Percentage of correct recognitions for each factor and subject group in Experiment 1

Factor	Burglars	Police	Householders
Lock	75.0	69.6	50.0
Beware of dog	72.5	69.6	55.0
Hedge or fence	95.0	78.6	78.0
Alarm	77.5	71.4	73.0
Car	82.5	73.2	60.0
Mean recognition	80.5	72.5	63.2

It is possible that subjects had a response bias to answer 'same', since many of the changes were quite small. We therefore separated the data for those items where a change had occurred, to investigate whether the change had been noticed. These data are shown in Table 3. From the table it is clear that the burglars recognized changes in the photographs more readily than the other two groups. The mean scores were compared by means of *t*-tests. The burglars had significantly higher scores than the householders ($t = 5.17$; d.f. = 18; $p < .005$). The police also recognized changes more readily than did the householders ($t = 3.85$; d.f. = 22; $p < .005$). However, the comparison between the police and the burglar group failed to reach significance ($t = 1.63$; d.f. = 22).

Discussion

These data suggest that our 'burglar' group had slightly better recognition memory performance than did the police, and both these groups performed rather better than the householders.

The recognition test pragmatically was a test of incidental memory for features in the initial target set. However, the target selection data can be taken to indicate

116   *R. Logie* et al.

Table 3. Percentage of correct recognitions of change
for each factor and subject group in Experiment 1

Factor	Burglars	Police	Householders
Lock	80	64	38
Beware of dog	60	57	38
Hedge or fence	80	68	63
Alarm	80	79	38
Car	90	71	38
Mean recognition	78	68	47

the extent to which the three groups may initially have noticed the presence of a particular factor. The assumption was that factors which did not influence reported target attractiveness would have been processed less efficiently. In this respect an alarm, a hedge or fence, a 'beware of dog' sign, and a car in the driveway, all appeared to make houses less or more attractive for the burglars and the police, whereas the presence of a mortice lock made very little difference to target selection for these groups. In contrast, the householders' selections were influenced only by alarms and 'beware of dog' signs.

Comparing this pattern of findings with the recognition memory data, it appears that all of the factors were remembered well by the burglars, including the presence or absence of a lock. Previously they had indicated that the presence of a lock had little to do with their choice of house. To a lesser extent the same was true for the police group. Householders did not appear to remember the 'beware of dog' signs which they previously had considered in their target selections, although they did remember whether an alarm was present during the recognition test. In contrast, a hedge or fence was reasonably well remembered by this group, although it had not been considered important during target selection. What is remarkable about this last finding is that the householders and the police, on over 20 per cent of occasions, did not accurately remember whether or not a very large item such as a hedge had been present in the original photograph.

From these data it appears that the initial target selection was a reasonable predictor of recognition memory for the burglar and police groups, but was rather less good as a predictor for the householder group. This is consistent with the notion of some form of expertise in the burglar and police groups affecting their incidental recognition memory performance, with the burglar group showing evidence of a somewhat higher level of expertise than the police.

One possible objection to our findings concerns the choice of householders as a control group. Such a group does provide a useful baseline for comparison. As individuals concerned with preventing burglary, they would have some element of relevant 'expertise' derived from intuition and from crime prevention campaigns.

What are the possible objections to the use of members of the general public as control subjects? There are three possible differences with the burglary group that might present a problem; namely age, social class, and educational level. The argument about educational level is relatively straightforward. If we choose individuals who are of a higher educational level than our other two groups, the most reasonable prediction would be that their memory performance would be improved as a result of their education. Our choice of a control group with a higher educational level than the burglars is therefore conservative. One objection might be that educational level is not an adequate measure of general memory ability. However, educational level is an established measure of general ability in the absence of standardized test scores, and is widely used clinically as one indication of pre-morbid ability in studies of ageing or of brain damage (for a review see Crawford, 1989).

Although our burglars tend to come from the lower socioeconomic classes, this is also unlikely to be a confounding factor. There is no reason to expect that a low socioeconomic level will improve memory performance. If anything the evidence is to the contrary. For example, Richardson (1987) has shown that people from the lower socioeconomic classes typically do less well on standard tests of memory and are unable to take advantage of mnemonic techniques.

Finally, one prediction on the basis of age would be that, with greater experience of life, individuals tend to improve their memory ability. If this is the case, the householders (who were older) should be better than the burglars, and our choice of control group again is conservative. A second possibility is that memory performance decreases with age and this, rather than expertise, accounts for our findings. The majority of the evidence on the effects of age suggest that, all other things being equal, memory performance does not deteriorate appreciably within the age range of our sample (e.g. Rabbitt, 1988).

A further possible objection to Experiment 1 is that the factors manipulated were all related to burglary. This gives an indication as to which of these factors seem to be important for burglars and which do not. However, there is still a remote possibility that the burglar group happened to be generally more observant or 'streetwise' than our two comparison groups. This possibility is even more remote for the contrast with the police group, since they are given training in observation (but see Woodhead, Baddeley, and Simmonds, 1979). In Experiment 2 we included changes for the recognition test, involving factors which on the basis of previous research (e.g. Bennett and Wright, 1984) could be considered neutral with respect to burglary. In addition, in Experiment 2 we investigated the extent to which a burglary group differed from a control group consisting of youngsters who had been convicted of offences other than housebreaking (e.g. crimes of violence).

EXPERIMENT 2

Method

Subjects
The 29 subjects in this experiment were boys in a British, independent, residential and day school for children with special educational needs (formerly a 'List-D' school). This sample comprised roughly half of the total number of children in the school, the vast majority of whom were boys. There were no *a-priori* selection criteria, except that all of the subjects should be male. All of the boys in half of the classes in the school were asked by a member of staff if they wished to participate. All subjects were informed that participation was entirely voluntary and confidential, and that they were under no pressure to take part. None of the boys who were asked to participate refused to do so. All of the boys that we interviewed had been charged with one or more criminal offences ranging from making hoax telephone calls to attempted murder.

Subjects were divided into the following groups.

Burglar group
The burglar group comprised 19 boys, aged 14 years 3 months to 16 years 7 months, with a mean age of 15 years 2 months and a standard deviation of 7.9 months. All of these subjects had been involved in one or more housebreaking offences. Most subjects had committed other offences as well.

Control group
The control group consisted of 10 boys, aged 11 years to 16 years, with a mean age of 14 years, and a standard deviation of 17.8 months. The mean age of this group was not significantly different to that of the burglar group ($t = 1.67$; d.f. $= 27$). Allocation to the control group required that the youngster had not committed any housebreaking offences, but had committed other offences. They had been involved in, among other things, car theft, assault, vandalism, and truancy. We were confident that none had taken part in housebreaking.

Materials

The materials for target selection were the same as those used for Experiment 1, except that a third set of photographs was made up from the possible six sets. In each set there were photographs of two additional houses, with no specific factor included. Three complementary sets of photographs also were used for the recognition test. However, in each set there were two changes that were considered to be neutral with respect to burglary. These involved: (1) a change in angle of about 30 degrees from which the house was viewed in the photograph; (2) a photograph of the house from the same angle as for target selection, but taken from a few metres further away, thus including more of the front pavement, or more of the house itself. An example of a neutral change is shown in Figure 2.

The checklist included ten more items than that used for Experiment 1, and all of these additional items were considered neutral with respect to burglary. As in the earlier experiment, this was included as a filler task.

Procedure

The procedure was identical to that for Experiment 1, except that the expanded target set required 11 minutes to administer, while the checklist took approximately 7 minutes, and the recognition procedure required 11 minutes. The questionnaire for the burglar group was the same as for the offenders in Experiment 1. For the control subjects the questionnaire addressed the specific offences for which they had been charged. The questionnaires took approximately 5 minutes for both groups.

Results

Target selection
The mean percentage 'attractive' and 'unattractive' responses for target selection are shown in Table 4. These data were subjected to an overall chi-square analysis which revealed $\chi^2 = 9.4$, d.f. $= 5$, $.05 < p < .1$, suggesting that any differences between

Figure 2. Examples of photographs used in Experiment 2 for a 'neutral' change

the groups are not as dramatic as those shown in Experiment 1. However, each factor was investigated by means of Kolmogornov–Smirnov tests, which showed that the responses to alarms differed significantly between the groups ($p < .05$), and the attractiveness of the 'straight' houses was higher for the control group than it was for the burglars ($p < .001$).

Table 4.   Percentage of 'attracted' responses to photographs of target houses, by factor studied and subject group in Experiment 2

	Burglars	Controls
Straight houses	59	71
Lock	67	60
Alarm	23	40
Cover	68	59
Dog	32	48
Car	39	43

Recognition memory

The mean percentage recognition memory performance data are shown in Table 5 for the two groups. A t-test comparing the two groups revealed $t = 3.34$; d.f. $= 27$; $p < .005$. It is clear from Table 5 that subjects in the control group were performing at chance on the recognition test, while the burglar group were performing significantly above chance on this test. Also from Table 5, it appears that both groups of subjects were performing at about the same level on the neutral items.

Table 5.   Percentage of correct recognitions for each factor and subject group in Experiment 2

Factor	Burglars	Controls
Lock	45	38
Beware of dog	55	35
Hedge or fence	71	52
Alarm	64	49
Car	67	62
Neutral	61	60
Mean recognition	61	50

As before, we examined the recognition memory performance only for those photographs where a change was made. These data are shown in Table 6. The mean recognition scores for the two groups were compared with a t-test. This showed that the burglar group maintain their advantage ($t = 2.63$; d.f. $= 27$; $p < .01$) over the control group.

Correlations

Finally, we investigated the extent to which recognition memory performance correlated with individual subject variables. During the interview we obtained information about the age (years and months) of each subject, the number of burglaries in which

Recognition Memory Performance and Residential Burglary 121

Table 6. Percentage of correct recognitions of change for each factor and subject group in Experiment 2

Factor	Burglars	Controls
Lock	40	30
Beware of dog	53	30
Hedge or fence	71	45
Alarm	61	50
Car	64	64
Neutral	48	28
Mean recognition	56	41

they had been involved, and the total number of crimes in which they had been involved. Although there was no significant difference in age between the control and burglary subjects, we wished to investigate whether the recognition memory performance was related to experience with offending rather than age. Spearman rank correlation coefficients are shown in Table 7. From the table, it is clear that experience with offending, rather than a difference in age, accounts for the differences in recognition memory performance.

Table 7. Spearman rank correlation coefficients between age, number of burglaries, number of offences of all types, and recognition memory performance in Experiment 2

	Age	Burglaries	Offences
Recognition memory	.249	.541**	.416*
Age		.211	.076
Burglaries			.831**

$*p < .05$; $**p < .01$.

Discussion

As with Experiment 1, the group of burglars tested showed superior recognition memory performance relative to a group of controls. In this case the controls were matched on age and social class with the burglars. The memory advantage for the burglary group did not extend to factors that were neutral with respect to burglary. This supports the notion that the burglary group have a level of expertise that is reflected in recognition memory for information related to their offending.

The target selection and checklist data showed some small differences between the groups. As regards target selection, it appears that for the burglars a house with a hedge or fence was more attractive than a straight house, whereas for the controls the reverse was the case. The same was true, to a lesser extent, for locks, with subjects more or less agreeing on the remaining three factors.

It is interesting to compare the results of Experiment 2 with those of Experiment 1. A formal comparison is not appropriate because there were procedural differences between the experiments. However, the target selection responses for the burglar group in Experiment 2 (Table 4) are remarkably similar to those for the burglary group in Experiment 1 (Table 1). The attractiveness of a hedge or fence is diminished somewhat, as is the effect of a car being present, but even here the effects follow similar trends.

CONCLUSION

The results of two experiments have provided support for the hypothesis that juvenile offenders acquire a level of expertise that affects both their apparent willingness to select targets for burglary, and their ability to remember details related to that expertise.

That it may affect their willingness to select a particular property suggests that altering the physical environment may diminish the attractiveness of a property as a target for burglary, with implications for crime prevention. Thus on the basis of these data hedges and fences make houses rather more attractive to burglars, the type of lock makes little difference, and alarms and signs of occupancy make houses rather less likely as target choices. This pattern of results, including the rather counterintuitive result for locks, is in line with those reported for adult offenders (Bennett and Wright, 1984; Waller and Okihiro, 1978; Walsh, 1980).

The notion that there is a relationship between expertise and memory performance is by no means new. However, the finding that offenders have a level of expertise associated with their crime is important for criminology and psychology alike.

It is important for criminology in terms of its contribution to crime prevention and an understanding of the offender. For example, the extent to which criminal behaviour is rational is currently a topic of considerable debate among criminologists (e.g. Cornish and Clark, 1986). Carroll and Weaver (1986) note that while interview-based field studies of criminals have found strong evidence of technical and interpersonal skill and knowledge relevant to specific crime opportunities, laboratory research generally has uncovered little to suggest that offenders are highly rational in their approach to committing crimes. Our findings, derived in an essentially laboratory setting, support the view that at least the offence of burglary appears to involve the application of acquired expertise, which is consistent with a process of rational decision-making. Clearly, the burglary groups were attuned to factors that objectively are important in determining the potential risks involved in committing offences against various targets. Moreover, the fact that our research involved juvenile offenders, suggests that this expertise is acquired fairly early on in a burglar's career.

The finding is important for psychology because it demonstrates that conclusions drawn from studies of expertise in chess and of more conventional skills (see Ericsson, 1990 for a review) generalize to studies of a population that is rarely studied by cognitive psychologists. Further, seldom are the methods of experimental cognitive psychology applied to studies of offenders. In doing so, this study illustrates the potential applicability of cognitive psychology to the important activity of crime prevention.

REFERENCES

Bennett, T. and Wright, R. (1984). *Burglars on burglary*. Aldershot: Gower.
Carroll, J. and Weaver, F. (1986). Shoplifters' perceptions of crime opportunities: A process-

tracing study. In D. Cornish and R. Clarke (eds), *The reasoning criminal: rational choice perspectives on offending* (pp. 19–38). New York: Springer-Verlag.

Charness, N. (1979). Components of skills in bridge. *Canadian Journal of Psychology*, **33**, 1–16.

Chase, W. G. and Simon, H. A. (1973). The mind's eye in chess. In W. G. Chase (ed.), *Visual information processing*. (pp. 215–281). New York: Academic Press.

Cornish, D. and Clarke, R. V. G. (eds) (1986). *The reasoning criminal: rational choice perspectives on offending*. New York: Springer-Verlag.

Crawford, J. (1989). Estimation of premorbid intelligence: a review of recent developments. In J. R. Crawford and D. M. Parker (eds), *Developments in clinical and experimental neuropsychology* (pp. 55–74). New York: Plenum.

Egan, D. W. and Schwartz, B. J. (1979). Chunking in the recall of symbolic drawings. *Memory and Cognition*, **7**, 149–158.

Ericsson, K. A. (1990). Theoretical issues in the study of exceptional performance. In K. Gilhooly, M. Keane, R. Logie and G. Erdos (eds), *Lines of Thinking: reflections on the psychology of thought*, Vol. 2 (pp. 5–28). Chichester: Wiley.

Gilhooly, K. J., Wood, M., Kinnear, P. R. and Green, C. (1988). Skill in map reading and memory for maps. *Quarterly Journal of Experimental Psychology*, **40A**, 87–107.

de Groot, A. D. (1965). *Thought and choice in chess*. The Hague: Mouton.

Home Office (1987). *Criminal statistics: England and Wales 1986*. London: Her Majesty's Stationery Office.

Kinnear, P. and Wood, M. (1987). Memory for topographic contour maps. *British Journal of Psychology*, **78**, 395–402.

McKeithen, K. B., Reitman, J. S., Reuter, H. H. and Hirtle, S. C. (1981). Knowledge organisation and skill differences in computer programmers. *Cognitive Psychology*, **13**, 307–325.

Morris, P. E., Tweedy, M. and Gruneberg, M. M. (1985). Interest, knowledge and the memorization of soccer scores. *British Journal of Psychology*, **76**, 415–425.

Rabbitt, P. M. A. (1988). Social psychology, neurosciences and cognitive psychology need each other (and gerontology needs all three of them). *Psychologist*, **1**, 500–506.

Reitman, J. (1976). Skilled perception in GO: deducing memory structures from inter-response times. *Cognitive Psychology*, **8**, 336–356.

Richardson, J. T. E. (1987). Social class limitations on the efficacy of imagery mnemonic instructions. *British Journal of Psychology*, **78**, 65–77.

Sessions, W. (1989). *Crime in the United States—1988*. Washington, DC: U.S. Government Printing Office.

Taylor, M. and Nee, C. (1988). The role of cues in simulated residential burglary. *British Journal of Criminology*, **28**, 396–401.

Walleer, I. and Okihiro, N. (1978). *Burglary: the victim and the public*. Toronto: University of Toronto Press.

Walsh, D. (1980). *Break-ins: burglary from private houses*. London: Constable.

Woodhead, M. M., Baddeley, A. D. and Simmonds, D. C. V. (1979). On training people to recognize faces. *Ergonomics*, **22**, 333–343.

Wright, R. and Logie, R. H. (1988). How young house burglars choose targets. *Howard Journal of Criminal Justice*, **27**, 92–104.

[15]

GENERATING COMPLIANCE
The Case of Robbery

DAVID F. LUCKENBILL

ONE OF THE CENTRAL ideas in interactionist social psychology is that coorientation is vital for concerted action (Mead, 1934; Shibutani, 1961: 40-48; Scheff, 1967). When individuals are cooriented, they operate from a common definition of the situation, a common frame for interaction. When individuals operate from a common frame, they can coordinate their respective actions to form a joint act. While coorientation usually has been studied in situations of cooperation, it also must appear in situations of conflict, such as coercion (Simmel, 1950; 182-185; Schelling, 1963: 83).

Coercion requires two roles, a source and a target. In coercion, the source exacts compliance from the target, despite a conflict of interests, by means of actual or threatened punishment. A problem for social psychologists is to determine how the source manages to get the target, to adopt a particular coercive frame and act in a manner consistent with it (compare Horai and Tedeschi, 1969; Miller et al., 1969; Tedeschi et al., 1971; Tedeschi et al., 1973: 53-83). What must the source do to generate the

AUTHOR'S NOTE: I wish to thank John Baldwin, Donald R. Cressey, and Tamotsu Shibutani for their instructive comments on the larger work of which this article is a part. I also wish to thank Reynaldo Baca and Joel Best for their assistance.

EDITOR'S NOTE: David Luckenbill focuses on robbery performances as a resource for understanding the conditions under which compliance is generated in coercion

URBAN LIFE, Vol. 10 No. 1, April 1981 25-46
© 1981 Sage Publications, Inc.

26   URBAN LIFE   APRIL 1981

target's compliance? How must the source communicate the coercive frame, and how must the source manipulate punitive resources to exact compliance? Put differently, under what conditions will the target reject the proposed frame and comply with the source's demands? Conversely, under what conditions will the target reject the proposd frame and oppose the source? This paper seeks to determine the conditions under which the source generates the target's compliance in a particular type of interpersonal coercion.

Research on this problem had been limited to certain types of coercion. It has focused on situations where the source uses the deprivation of existing resources or expected gains as the means for exacting compliance. Research generally has ignored situations where the source employs noxious stimulation to generate compliance. This is especially true when noxious stimulation takes the form of physical force, the actual or threatened infliction of bodily pain (see Goode, 1972; Wrong, 1976: 183-195). This limitation probably stems from the fact that most research on coercion uses laboratory experimentation. To be sure, experimentation is a useful method, providing substantial control over causal and extraneous conditions (Scheff, 1967b). However, there are limits to the punitive resources which sources can use in laboratory experimentation. Researchers can provide subjects with resources for inflicting either severe yet imaginary punishment, e.g., depriving targets of a large amount of play money, or real yet mild, noncorporal punishment, e.g., depriving targets of relatively small earnings from task performances. For ethical reasons, researchers cannot provide subjects with resources for inflicting genuine, severe punishment, causing targets physical injury.

---

based on physical force. Luckenbill suggests that the coercive frame is a collective transaction consisting of four time-ordered stages, each of which involves an important task which offender and victim accomplish together. Drawing from the robbery data, Luckenbill offers several hypotheses regarding the conditions under which voluntary compliance is generated in coercion based on force.

This investigation tries to determine the conditions under which the source generates the target's compliance in coercion based on physical force. Given a lack of research addressing this problem, my task is to develop hypotheses from the comparative analysis of actual cases of coercion. Although several types of transactions could be used as the data base, robbery is used to study the generation of compliance in coercion.[1] After describing the stages of joint action in robbery, some hypotheses about coercion are developed.

METHODOLOGICAL STRATEGY

Robbery is a transaction in which an offender (operating as the source) unlawfully takes goods from the possession of a victim (operating as the target), against his/her will, by means of force.[2] Two principal types of robbery are distinguished in the criminal law: "Aggravated robbery" means that the offender employs a weapon, while "robbery" signifies that the offender is unarmed. In this study, robbery refers to both types.

The data were drawn from cases of robbery and attempted robbery over a one-year period in one Texas city. Sampling was of a multistage design. Between February 1976 and March 1977, 732 cases of robbery and attempted robbery were reported to the police. Cases occurring in alternate months of that period were selected for analysis. For these six months, a roster of 354 cases was constructed. Of these cases, 93 were then excluded; 54 cases because the police had determined that the event was not a robbery or attemptd robbery, and 39 cases because there was too little information on the event. The remaining 261 cases comprised the sample for investigation; 179 cases were successful robberies, and 82 cases were attempted robberies.

28   URBAN LIFE   APRIL 1981

To understand the dynamics of robbery these transactions were reconstructed. Two types of information were used to reconstruct cases. First, official documents, including police field reports, detective follow-up reports, victim and witness statements, and, when available, offender statements, provided information on the central participants, who said and did what to whom, the chronology of action, and the orientations of the victim, bystanders, and, when available, offender. In reconstructing the event, each individual document was scrutinized for information regarding its development. This information was used to prepare separate accounts of the transaction. When all of the documents for a case were exhausted, a summary account was constructed, using the individual accounts as primary resources.[3] Second, for some of the cases, the account was augmented with in-depth interviews with one or both opponents. Interviews with 35 victims regarding 39 cases and 16 incarcerated offenders regarding 38 cases were conducted. All of the offenders spoke at length about the cases in which they were apprehended and convicted, and five offenders also discussed 22 cases in which they were not apprehended.

DYNAMICS OF THE ROBBERY PERFORMANCE

Employing analytic induction, a sequential model of robbery was developed from a comparative analysis of the cases. In this model, the robbery transaction consists of four stages, each involving an important task which the offender and victim usually accomplish together. First, the offender establishes co-presence with the victim. Second, the offender and victim develop coorientation toward a common robbery frame. Third, one or both opponents transfer the material goods. Fourth, the offender leaves the setting. Accomplishing all four tasks constitutes robbery: the offender obtains goods from the victim without apprehension during the operation.

STAGE 1

After selecting a victim, the offender moves into co-presence with the victim.[4] Co-presence is established in a particular manner. The offender moves into striking range, into a position where he/she can attack, without arousing suspicion and provoking unmanageable opposition.

The offender employs one of two strategies to establish co-presence. In 91 cases (35%), the offender used speed and stealth to rush the unwitting victim. Here, the offender locates behind "lurk lines," points behind which the victim's senses cannot penetrate (Goffman, 1971: 293), and prepares for the strike. Then, without advance warning, the offender quickly moves into the victim's presence with punitive resources at the ready:

> *Case 403.* The offender walked to the side of the gas station and saw the attendant helping several customers. He walked back to the rear of the station to wait for the customers to leave. The customers left a few minutes later. The offender donned a ski mask, pulled a handgun from his pocket, and walked to the side office window. He peered inside and saw the attendant sitting behind the desk reading. The offender crept up to the office door and pointed his handgun at the attendant. In a harsh tone of voice, the offender announced, "This is a stick up, man. Give me the money."

Although alarmed, the victim is not given the opportunity to launch an effective defense.

In 170 cases (65%), the offender established co-presence by managing a normal appearance, attempting to behave as someone the victim would see as an ordinary, legitimate part of the setting (see Goffman, 1971: 238-333). In a grocery store, for instance, the offender enters under the guise of a customer intent on purchasing goods:

> *Case 113.* The offender entered the convenience store and moved to the cooler, getting a carton of milk. He then walked to the cashier's counter where the lone clerk was located

30   URBAN LIFE   APRIL 1981

and placed the carton on the counter. The clerk noted the price of the milk and began to ring up the sale. Before the clerk hit the last register key, the offender stuck his hand in his pocket and said, "I've got a gun. Give me all the money in the register." The clerk was startled by the demand.

Or on a street in the late evening, the offender stops a passerby, making a legitimate request for information.

Both strategies require the victim's unawareness of the offender's intention. For the offender to successfully rush the victim, the victim should not spot the offender's preparations or approach. Similarly, for the offender to successfully manage a normal appearance, the victim should be convinced that the offender is the kind of person he/she claims to be (see Goffman, 1971: 268-284). Generally, the victim is unaware of the offender's operation until co-presence is firmly established; the victim is oblivious to the offender until the rush is accomplished, or the offender's presentation of self is convincing. In 48 cases (18%), however, the offender alarmed the victim, and the victim responded by laying low, consulting the offender about the grounds for alarm, or opposing the offender by attacking or fleeing from the setting.

When the offender fails to establish co-presence without alarming the victim and provoking strong opposition, the robbery is jeopardized. In two cases (1%), the robbery broke down because the offender failed to establish co-presence before alarming the victim: The victim fled before the offender moved into striking range. In two other cases (1%), the robbery broke down even though the offender established co-presence: The victim outwardly expressed alarm and prepared to attack. Certainly, given a relatively weak victim, the offender will continue with the robbery. But a seemingly capable victim, ready to attack, can cause the offender to forfeit the venture:

Case 61. The victim, an off-duty but uniformed police officer who was working part-time for a local business, walked up

to the bank's night deposit drawer and dropped the deposit
bag inside. He then heard someone running toward him
from behind. He turned around and saw the hooded offender, wielding a tire iron, standing behind him. The victim,
fearing impending robbery, reared back to strike the offender. The offender appeared surprised to see this particular
person making the regular night deposit. The offender shouted,
"Oh shit," dropped his tire iron, and tried to run past the
victim. The victim managed to strike the offender with his
fist. But unhurt, the offender ran from the scene.

STAGE II

After establishing co-presence, a task accomplished in 257
cases, the offender and victim reorient their interaction,
transforming their encounter to a common robbery frame.
The robbery frame consists of two elements: (1) To avoid
death or injury, the victim should suppress opposition and
permit the offender to take his/her goods. (2) To obtain the
victim's goods, the offender should control the victim's
conduct by means of force and make or supervise the
transfer. When the opponents establish and act in terms of
a common robbery frame, robbery usually is consummated.

Two variants of the transformation process appeared in
the cases. In one variant, involving 80 cases (31%), the
offender cast the victim in an acquiescent role; the victim
was expected to not interfere while the offender took the
goods. In a second variant, involving 177 cases (69%), the
offender cast the victim in a participatory role; the victim
was expected to assist the offender in the transfer.

In either case, the transformation process involves a
succession of moves between the offender and victim. The
offender opens the process with a move designed to provide
the victim with the robbery frame. In 56 cases (22%), the
offender opened with incapacitating force—bodily pain which
debilitates or immobilizes the victim for a time. In the
remaining 201 cases (78%), the offender opened with a
command for compliance backed with a threat of punish-

ment. The offender's choice of opening depends on two conditions. First, in deciding between incapacitating force and a command backed by a threat of force, the offender considers the victim's likely response to a threat given the strength of the offender's punitive resources. When the offender has what he/she considers to be lethal resources,[5] such as a firearm or knife, he/she envisions that a command backed with a threat will intimidate the victim into immediate compliance:

> *Offender #2:* You know, if somebody came up to me and said, "Give me your money," and he had a gun or machete, I'd give him everything. I mean, it would scare the hell out of me. It would scare the hell out of anybody.

Believing the victim will comply if threatened with lethal resources, the offender opens with a command backed by a threat of force. In every case where the offender had a gun or knife, he/she opened with a command backed by a threat.

When the offender has what he/she considers to be nonlethal resources,[6] such as a club or bare hands, he/she envisions that a command backed by a threat will bring opposition, for nonlethal resources will not intimidate the victim into submission:

> *Offender #7:* In strongarms, you have to put him out of commission for a few minutes. When you haven't got a gun or knife, he won't do anything. He'll tell you to go to hell or turn on you. So all you can do is knock him out.

Believing the victim will oppose if threatened with nonlethal resources, the offender opens with incapacitating force. In 78% of the cases where the offender possessed a club or bare hands, he/she opened with incapacitating force.

A second condition is the victim's value to the transaction. The victim may be necessary, either to sustain the fiction before outsiders that the offender and victim are involved in a respectable activity, or because the victim has knowledge and skill needed for the robbery:

> *Offender #7:* (The victim is) really important. He knows how to open the safe and he can open the registers. It's funny. You got to have him, but you can't let him think you need him. . . . You want to make him think you'd just as soon kill him as anything else, you know, that you don't need him. But you really do. If he won't open the safe, you're dead. You might as well leave.

When the victim is considered unnecessary, the offender opens with incapacitating force or a command backed by a threat of force, depending on the strength of his/her punitive resources. When the victim is cast in an acquiescent role, there is a strong relationship between the mode of opening and the strength of the offender's resources: if the offender has lethal resources, he/she always opens with a command backed by a threat of force; if the offender has nonlethal resources, he/she almost always opens with incapacitating force. But when the victim is considered necessary, the offender always opens with a command backed by a threat of force, independent of the strength of his/her punitive resources. In cases where the victim is cast in a participatory role, there is no relationship between the mode of opening and the strength of the offender's resources.

Except for one case (1%) where the robbery broke down because the offender and victim did not share a common language, and 28 cases (11%) where the victim was felled, the opening move surprised the victim. The move violates the expected tenor of action which the victim normally experiences in the setting. Momentarily shocked and disoriented, the victim delays routine action in order to determine whether the move should be taken as a sign of a prank or exploitation. Thus, attention focuses on the tenability of the robbery frame (see LeJeune and Alex, 1973).

34   URBAN LIFE   APRIL 1981

In reassessing the situation, the victim may ask the offender if he/she is serious. The offender responds in ways which indicate that he/she is serious and the proposed frame should be adopted: the offender states that he/she is serious, repeats the command, or uses force. The victim also looks for cues in assessing the tenability of the proposed frame, such as the offender's appearance, armament, and comportment. When the offender appears cold and hardened or tense and nervous, when he/she is armed, or when he/she uses force or acts as though force is imminent, the victim suspends doubts and considers the proposed frame believable.

Accepting the robbery frame as tenable, the victim adjusts, either accepting or challenging the frame. In 151 cases (66% of the 228 remaining cases), the victim complied; in 77 cases (34%), the victim opposed. In 28 of the latter cases, the victim noncomplied, refusing to adopt the role in which he/she had been cast; in 49 cases, the victim resisted, trying to block or overcome the offender.

The manner in which the victim responds depends on two conditions. First, the victim considers the offender's capacity to inflict death or serious injury. The offender is considered capable when he/she appears to possess lethal resources and to be in a position to use them, and when the victim cannot mobilize resources for opposition. Second, the victim evaluates the offender's intent regarding the use of force—whether the offender intends to inflict punishment only for opposition or regardless of opposition. If the offender appears capable of inflicting severe punishment and the use of force seems contingent on opposition, the victim complies:

> *Victim #4:* I wasn't going to try anything because he had a pistol. When he's got a piece, you give him the money. That's all there is to it. If you try anything, he might shoot you.

When the offender appears incapable of inflicting serious injury, the victim resists:

> *Victim, Case 429:* He stuck his hand in his shirt and told me, "I'm sorry too but this is a holdup." I asked him, "Where's the gun?" I wasn't going to give him any money if he didn't have a gun. Sometimes robbers try to bluff you. They just say they have a gun, but they really don't. If he showed a gun, I would have given him the money. He never showed a gun, so I never gave him money.

And when the victim believes the offender intends to use force regardless of the victim's response, the victim also resists. However feasible its success may seem, resistance offers a chance for avoiding death or injury:

> *Case 401:* The offender pulled a hunting knife from his pocket, walked to the cashier's counter, and stated, "I want all your money." The clerk stood motionless behind the counter. The offender responded to such inaction by raising the knife over his head and shouting, "I'm going to kill you and take the money." Fearing impending death, the clerk grabbed the offender's arm and tried to take away the knife.

The victim's response provides the offender with feedback. When the victim complies, then he/she ratifies the robbery frame. But when the victim opposes or appears to oppose, the frame is in doubt.[7] The offender can respond to opposition in any of several ways: in 31 cases (36% of the 85 remaining cases), the offender issued a warning against further opposition; in 8 cases (9%), the offender coupled a command for compliance with prodding force—bodily pain short of debilitating or immobilizing the victim; in 20 cases (24%), the offender used incapacitating force; and in 26 cases (31%), the offender forfeited the robbery.

The way the victim opposes affects the offender's response. When the victim does not try to block or overcome the offender, then salvaging the robbery is the most feasible response, adopted in almost every case. But, when the victim resists and seems capable of overcoming the offender, then salvaging the robbery is not feasible; in half of these cases, the offender forfeited the robbery.

How the offender salvages the robbery depends on the same conditions involved in opening the transformation. When the offender has lethal resources, he/she will warn or prod the victim in order to demonstrate capacity and determination and thereby intimidate the victim:

> *Offender #7:* I wouldn't kill anybody. But sometimes I'd hit them. Like this one guy, you know, was stalling around, saying he didn't know the combination of the safe. So I just smacked him on the side of the head with the gun and said, "Open it." So he suddenly remembers the combination. I guess he figured I'd waste him if he kept stalling.

But when the offender has nonlethal resources, he/she will use additional force to exact compliance:

> *Offender #10:* So we hit him on the head, you know, to knock him out. . . . But I guess we didn't hit him hard enough because he started fighting back. He fought pretty good. I guess he thought he was fighting for his life. So we just hit him harder, you know, to take him out.

In addition, when the victim is considered unnecessary, the offender attempts to salvage the robbery by warning, prodding, or incapacitating the victim, depending solely on the strength of his/her resources. But when the victim is considered necessary, the offender tries to salvage the robbery by warning or prodding the victim, independent of the strength of his/her resources.

Except for 16 cases in which the victim eventually was felled, the offender's salvaging attempt usually provides the victim with information questioning the utility of the victim's preceding move. On the one hand, when the offender warns or prods the victim for intentional opposition, he/she typically brandishes a weapon, moves into striking range, informs the victim that only opposition will bring punishment, or takes charge of the victim's allies, thereby altering the conditions which the victim considers in organizing action. Such alterations bring a redefinition of the offender's capacity or intent and a shift from opposition to compliance:

Case 139: The offender stated, "You see this bag? Well pick it up and give me only the cash." The clerk stared at him. The offender said, "I have a gun. If you make a sound, I'll shoot you." The clerk did not see a gun and thought the offender was bluffing. She responded, "The cash register is locked and I don't know how to open it." The offender responded, "You know how to open it. I saw you open it." The clerk stood silent, thinking about what to do. The offender pulled out a pistol, pointed it at her and stated, "Stop fucking around or I'll shoot you." The clerk spotted the pistol and feared that the offender might kill her for further opposition. She opened the cash register and give him $280.

On the other hand, when the offender prods the victim for a move which the victim deems compliance but the offender considers noncompliance, the victim believes that the offender will use force indiscriminately, and shifts from compliance to resistance. In cases where the victim shifts to or maintains opposition, the offender eventually forfeits the robbery.

When the offender and victim orient themselves toward a common robbery frame, movement toward the transfer is facilitated. But when the victim is not oriented toward the frame, and the offender fails to promote its acceptance, movement toward the transfer breaks down. In 11 cases (4% of the 257 cases entering Stage II) where the victim refused to acquiesce, and in 33 cases (13%) where the victim refused to adopt the participatory role, the robbery collapsed:

Case 157: The two offenders walked up to the cashier's counter where the victim was standing. Offender #2 pulled out a small pistol, pointed it at the victim, and stated, "Hand over all the money." The victim looked at the gun and realized that the two men intended to rob her. Angered, the victim said sharply, "I'll give you nothing, you son-of-a-bitch." Before either offender could respond, the victim turned, rapped on the front window behind her, and caught the attention of two friends walking by. She yelled, "Get the police. I'm being robbed." One of the friends saw offender #2 holding a pistol on the victim. To scare the offenders, the friend rapped on the window, pointed to the parking lot, and shouted, "There's a police car over there." The offenders quickly ran out the front door.

STAGE III

After the offender and victim establish a common robbery frame, a task accomplished in 213 cases, one or both accomplish the transfer. This is a relatively simple task in which valued goods are excavated and transferred from the victim to the offender.

The transfer takes two forms. In 85 cases (40%), it seemed to follow a predetermined design; the offender wanted particular goods, leaving others untouched. For example, the victim is ordered to turn over the paper currency but not the coin change or merchandise. In 128 cases (60%), the transfer appeared to follow a search-and-seizure design; the offender took whatever valuables he/she discovered.

The role in which the victim is cast becomes important in this stage. In the 69 cases (32%) where the victim was cast in an acquiescent role, the offender used his/her knowledge and skill to make the transfer alone. But in the 144 cases (68%) where the victim was cast in a participatory role, the victim gave the goods to the offender. When the victim performs a participatory role, the offender supervises the transfer. In all cases, the offender surveyed the victim's operation, offering an implicit or explicit threat of punishment should the victim have failed to fulfill the role. In 112 cases (78% of the 144 cases), the offender also instructed the victim on how to make the transfer, e.g., to place the money in a paper bag. In 36 cases (25%), the offender attempted to certify that the victim delivered the full stock of requested goods, e.g., ordering the victim to open the second, unused cash register to see whether it has additional money.

Several obstructions can hinder the transfer and disrupt the robbery. First, the victim may not hold to the robbery frame. When the offender shifts attention from the victim to the transfer, he/she may move outside striking range or drop armed surveillance of the victim. Detecting an opening, the victim may launch an attack or attempt to flee. The offender may reinstitute the frame by moving back into striking range or warning the victim. But in 5 cases (2% of the 213 cases entering Stage III), the offender forfeited the robbery. Second, the entrance of outsiders can disrupt the robbery. When women or children (who may be defined as nonthreatening) enter the setting, the offender orders them to acquiesce and turns to the transfer. In 6 cases (3%), however, police officers or men entered the setting, and the offender fled. Third, the offender or victim may not have the knowledge and skill needed to make the transfer. When a victim who has been cast in a participatory role is unable to secure the goods, the offender usually adjusts the demand, requesting those goods which the victim can provide. But in 4 cases (2%), the offender simply forfeited the venture. When a victim has been cast in an acquiescent role and the offender lacks the knowledge and skill to secure the goods, the transfer falters. If the victim has been debilitated, the offender can recast the victim in a participatory role and enlist his/her aid. In 3 cases (1%), however, the victim's aid could not be enlisted, for he/she had been debilitated. Consequently, the transfer collapsed:

> *Case 443:* Hearing the buzzer signaling a customer's entrance, clerk #1 walked to the front of the store. He saw offender #1 standing behind the cashier's counter. Spotting

clerk #1, offender #1 moved toward him and, without saying a word, hit him on the head with a club. Clerk #1 fell to the floor unconscious. In the meanwhile, offender #2 moved to the back room. Spotting clerk #2 in the open rest room, offender #2 moved up behind him and struck him on the head with a club. Clerk #2 fell unconscious. The offenders then moved behind the cashier's counter and attempted to open the cash register. They were unsuccessful, even though they had depressed the main key six times (as shown by the register tape). The offenders left the store empty handed.

STAGE IV

Once the goods are transferred, a task accomplished in 195 cases, the offender leaves the setting. This involves one task, of course, but in most cases, two tasks are involved: the offender physically moves away from the victim; and the offender separates personal from situated identity, attempting to avoid identification by those who observed the event. Failure to leave the setting in either sense can lead to apprehension.

To facilitate leaving, the offender employs one or more of several strategies. He/she may adhere to a plan for expedient and stealthy departure. For instance, before entering the store, the offender parks the getaway car outside the victim's view; after the robbery the offender dashes from the store and runs for the car. By the time the victim gets outside and looks for the offender, the offender is gone. A second strategy is concealing personal identity from the victim. The offender may wear a mask or alter his/her physical appearance. One offender, for instance, would shield his brunette hair with a blond wig. A third strategy is containing the victim. In 170 cases (87%), the offender tried to hinder the victim's possible pursuit. In 94 of these cases, the offender verbally contained the victim, warning against attempts to follow, observe the getaway, or contact anyone before he/she could leave:

> *Case 414:* The offender announced, "Okay, I'm leaving. Don't try anything because my friend is outside and he will

blow your head off if you try anything." He cut the phone cord with a pocket knife. He then moved to the front door, looked back at the two clerks, and walked out. The clerks, fearing they may be killed if they attempted to pursue or observe the offender, held their positions behind the cashier's counter for several minutes. One of the clerks then went next door to phone the police.

In another 76 cases, the offender physically contained the victim. The offender bound the victim's hands and feet, placed the victim in a closet, or used force to preclude pursuit:

Case 400: The clerk bent down, grabbed the money, and handed it to the offender. The offender took the money and, as the clerk started to stand up, hit her on top of the head with the butt of the pistol. She fell to the floor, startled by the blow but not injured. As soon as he had hit the clerk, the offender turned and walked from the office and out the front door, some fifty feet away. The clerk laid on the floor for what seemed like hours, trembling and afraid to get up and summon aid.

When the offender fails to move away from the victim, apprehension is likely. In 3 cases (2% of the 195 cases entering Stage IV), the victim or a coalition convened by the victim pursued and corralled the offender for the police. When the offender fails to conceal his/her personal identity, apprehension is possible. In 13 cases (7%), the victim or opposing coalition pursued the offender and learned his/her personal identity; this information was given to the police, and the offender was subsequently captured.

DISCUSSION

Robbery transactions usually involve the joint contribution of the offender and victim in accomplishing four tasks. First, the offender establishes co-presence with the victim, moving into striking range without the victim's awareness or readiness to defend against robbery. Second, the offender and victim transform their encounter toward a common

42   URBAN LIFE   APRIL 1981

robbery frame. Third, one or both opponents transfer the victim's goods. Fourth, the offender leaves the setting. Achievement of all four tasks results in robbery, while failure to accomplish any one task may result in disintegration of the transaction.

Using data on robbery, particularly on the second and third stages of the transaction, several generalizations can be advanced regarding the conditions necessary for generating voluntary compliance in coercion based on force.[8] First, the generation of compliance requires effective communication between the source and target (see Schelling, 1963). In order to assess the source's intent and respond to that assessment, the target requires understandable information. The source must communicate coherently, completely, and in a common language. Communication failing in any of these respects brings discussion over the meaning of the source's action. When discussion fails, the transaction collapses:

> *Case 2:* The offender entered the bank and moved directly to the teller's cage occupied by teller #1. The offender, his hand in his pocket, gave teller #1 a note written in Spanish. Teller #1 took the note and examined it. She announced, "I can't read Spanish. What do you want?" The offender, apparently unable to speak English, started to tremble. He looked furtively about the setting, turned around, and walked out. Teller #1 took the note to teller #2. Teller #2, fluent in Spanish, stated that the note was an order to give the offender all of her money or she would be killed.

Second, compliance requires the target to define the particular coercive frame as tenable. On the one hand, this means the target must approach the situation with a cognitive perspective amenable to defining the source's action as an indication of coercion (see Emerson, 1970). On the other hand, this requires the source to manage an appearance consistent with the particular coercive frame. The target is likely to define the frame as tenable when the source appears serious. In robbery, the offender is considered serious when he/she appears cold and hardened or tense and nervous and manipulates punitive resources in a threatening manner. If the target does not interpret the source's action as an indication of impending coercion, then he/she will not orient self to act according to that frame:

> *Case 91:* Leaning against the counter, holding a pistol, and sporting a broad grin, the offender said casually, "Be cool. This is a robbery." Spotting the pistol yet noting the offender's wide smile, clerk #1 turned to clerk #2, who was stocking shelves, and announced, humorously, "Hey, we're being robbed." Clerk #2 laughed and then stated, "Is that right?" At this point, the offender raised his pistol and told clerk #1 in a loud, harsh, voice, "Look, goddamn it, this is a robbery. Put all the money in a bag or I'll blow your fucking head off." Both clerks realized the offender was serious.

Third, the generation of compliance requires the source to manipulate punitive resources in a way that demonstrates the capacity to punish yet a judiciousness in the administration of punishment. To be sure, the level of force used to exact compliance is shaped by two conditions. One is the strength of the source's punitive resource's: the greater the strength of the source's resources, the more likely the source will use limited force, such as a threat or prodding force; the lesser the strength of the source's resources, the more likely the source will use massive force, such as incapacitating force. The relation between resource strength and level of force used is constrained by a second contingency, the value of the target to the transaction: When the target is deemed necessary to the source's goal achievement, the source is confined to using limited force, independent of the strength of his/her resources; when the target is not considered necessary, the source will use limited or massive force, depending on the strength of his/her resources.

However, to generate compliance, the source must manipulate punitive resources in a way that imparts at least two kinds of information to the target. First, the source must convey to the target that he/she has the capacity to inflict

44   URBAN LIFE   APRIL 1981

threatened punishment, that he/she possesses superior resources and can convert them into punishment (see Singer, 1958; Tedeschi, 1970; Baldwin, 1971; Michener et al., 1973). Assuming the victim could not convene an opposing coalition, when the victim believed the offender possessed lethal resources and was positioned within striking range, he/she complied. However, when the victim believed the offender did not have lethal resources or was not in the position to use them, he/she resisted. Thus, compliance is facilitated when the source manages an appearance of superior strength and advantageous position. Second, the source must convey that punishment is contingent on opposition. This information is effectively transmitted by issuing a clear threat or warning that punishment will only follow opposition. When the offender issued a threat or warning, the victim believed that the offender intended to punish only opposition. Given this judgement, the victim either complied or opposed, depending on the capacity of the offender to inflict punishment. But when the offender verbally suggested an intent to injure the victim or used prodding force in response to a move which the victim considered compliance, the victim believed that the offender planned to inflict punishment independent of the victim's action. Given this judgement, the victim opposed; opposition offered a chance for avoiding harm. Thus, compliance is facilitated when the source makes it the most attractive and profitable line of action.

NOTES

1. Robbery, like some other forms of criminal violence, is illicit coercion, typically involving strangers. These features may restrict its usefulness in generalizing to other types of coercion based on physical force. In licit coercion, such as some instances of parental control of children, the source is confined to the use of limited force. To employ massive force is to render the transaction illicit. However, when the source plans to exploit the target illegally, massive force may be acceptable to the source. In coercion involving family and friends, the source may

be restricted to limited force, for massive force would jeopardize the intimacy of the relationship. But such a restriction may not be present in such transactions as police capture of felons, skyjacking, and robbery, for these usually involve strangers who do not wish to build an intimate relationship.

2. The roles of offender and victim can each be filled by one or more individuals.

3. Parties to the transaction sometimes gave differing accounts of the event. For the most part, these discrepencies centered on the specific dialogue. Accounts were consistent with respect to the basic development of the event.

4. Because robbery generally involves only the offender and victim, and is usually designed in this way, my focus is on their activities. The behavior of bystanders will be examined only in passing.

5. Firearms and knives may be considered as "lethal" resources, for, as the interviewed offenders claimed, the offender defines them, and thinks the victim also defines them, as deadly. (See Conklin 1972: 112-119.) In 21% of the cases, the victim did not see the firearm or knife, but was informed by the offender that he/she possessed such a weapon. In some cases, the offender concealed a genuine weapon so as not to alarm bystanders, but in other cases, the weapon may have been a fiction. Whether the weapon was real or not appears to matter little, for the offender operated in the same fashion: He/She sought to intimidate the victim by claiming that he/she had the capacity to inflict death or serious injury.

6. Clubs and bare hands may be considered as "nonlethal " resources, for, as the interviewed offender claimed, the offender defines them, and believes the victim defines them, as nondeadly. (see Conklin 1972: 112-119.)

7. In 8 cases where the victim intended to comply, the offender defined the victim's move as noncompliance. In these cases, the victim qualified a part of the robbery frame, explaining that while he/she would provide whatever was available, he/she could not satisfy all of the offender's demands because of obstacles beyond control.

8. These generalizations pertain to situations in which the target has the opportunity to consciously select a course of action; they ignore cases where the target is incapacitated.

REFERENCES

BALDWIN, D. (1971) "Thinking about threats," J. of Conflict Resolution 15: 71-78.
CONKLIN, J. (1972) Robbery and the Criminal Justice System. Philadelphia: J. B. Lippincott.
EMERSON, J. (1970) "Nothing unusual is happening," in T. Shibutani (ed.) Human Nature and Collective Behavior. New Brunswick: Transaction Books.
GOFFMAN, E. (1971) Relations in Public. New York: Harper & Row.
GOODE, W. (1972) "The place of force in human society," Amer. Soc. Rev. 37: 507-519.

46   URBAN LIFE   APRIL 1981

HORAI, J. and J. TEDESCHI (1969) "The effects of threat credibility and magnitude of punishment upon compliance," J. of Personality and Social Psychology 12: 164-169.

LeJEUNE, R. and N. ALEX (1973) "On being mugged: the event and its aftermath," Urban Life and Culture 2: 259-287.

MEAD, G. (1934) Pp. 42-51 in C. Morris (ed.) Mind, Self and Society, Chicago: Univ. of Chicago Press.

MICHENER, H., E. LAWLER, and S. BACHARACH (1973) "Perception of power in conflict situations," J. of Personality and Social Psychology 28: 155-162.

MILLER, N., D. BUTLER, and J. McMARTIN (1969) "The ineffectiveness of punishment power in group interaction," Sociometry 32: 24-42.

SCHEFF, T. (1967a) "Toward a sociological model of consensus," Amer. Soc. Rev. 32: 32-46.

―――― (1967b) "A theory of social coordination applicable to mixed-motive games," Sociometry 30: 215-234.

SCHELLING, T. (1963) The Strategy of Conflict. Cambridge, MA: Harvard Univ. Press.

SHIBUTANI, T. (1961) Society and Personality: An Interactionist Approach to Social Psychology. Englewood Cliffs, NJ: Prentice-Hall.

SIMMEL, G. (1950) The Sociology of Georg Simmel, K. Wolff (ed.) New York: Macmillan.

SINGER, J. (1958) "Threat-perception and the armament-tension dilemma," J. of Conflict Resolution 2: 90-105.

TEDESCHI, J. (1970) "Threats and promises," in P. Swingle (ed.) The Structure of Conflict. New York: Academic Press.

―――― B. SCHLENKER and T. BONOMA (1973) Conflict, Power and Games. Chicago: Ave.

TEDESCHI, J., T. BONOMA and R. BROWN (1971) "A paradigm for the study of coercive power," J. of Conflict Resolution 15: 197-224.

WRONG, D. (1976) Skeptical Sociology. New York: Columbia Univ. Press.

DAVID F. LUCKENBILL is Assistant Professor, Department of Criminal Justice and Sociology, University of Illinois, Chicago Circle. He is engaged in research on interpersonal coercion, deviance and social organization, and deviant careers.

[16]

FULL-TIME MISCREANTS, DELINQUENT NEIGHBOURHOODS AND CRIMINAL NETWORKS*

John Mack

THIS PAPER is an interim report on some work now being done on systems of criminal activity. The first part describes the criminal output—in terms of full-time practitioners—of an urban industrial territory. The second part describes a delinquent neighbourhood and sketches the wider criminal network which is today the more typical form of criminal sub-culture. The third part gives some interpretations of the data provided by these and other studies in the sociology of crime, and suggests some further lines of inquiry.

It should perhaps be emphasized that while the activities described here illustrate some of the basic and traditional sources of crime—professional criminals, organized criminals, and, in general, groups habituated to a criminal way of life—these activities provide no more than a fraction of the crimes which are made known to the police in the country as a whole, and which derive from a great variety of situations. The work described here is concerned with only a few of the many kinds of behaviour technically classified as criminal. This concentration on one thing at a time is a necessary condition of any inquiry which aims at the advancement of knowledge about criminals. The fact that many other types of crime and criminal are left unnoticed here does not imply that their existence is queried or denied.

I. FULL-TIME CRIMINALS

In Worktown, an urban territory of 100,000 population, there are twelve full-time criminals, of whom nine are full-time 'travelling' criminals: i.e. operating mainly outside their area of residence. The twelve have been thinned out from a longer list agreed by the police forces concerned. Eight of the twelve are heavy-weight or at least middle-weight operators; the remaining four are smaller fry. In the

* Part of this paper was read to the Scottish branch of the B.S.A., in February 1963. The fieldwork for the Full-time Criminal and Network studies is the responsibility of M. Ritchie. The studies were financially assisted by the Scottish Home and Health Department to whom grateful acknowledgment is hereby made.

38

FULL-TIME MISCREANTS

remainder of this section we shall confine ourselves in the main to the eight more formidable characters, six of whom are travelling criminals. It is a small group, but it constitutes the main contribution of the territory to the organized crime of the region and beyond.

The precise definition of 'full-time' criminal—a term we prefer to 'professional' criminal—is that although the people concerned have some nominal occupation which they practise more or less regularly, they are known to be engaged in or available for criminal activities at all times. Secondly, the main classes of crime in which they are engaged are crimes against property, or more generally, crimes of dishonesty. Some of them are also violent but the violence is marginal to their main activity. Thirdly, they have been engaged in continuous criminal activity for a considerable period to date. All of the twelve have so far had a criminal span, operating from this territory, of not less than seventeen years: i.e. the youngest is 34. Some younger men are still coming on but have not yet made the grade since they might conceivably give up.

The territory consists in the main of two towns; one large and one small. The bulk of the adult population are industrial workers or engaged in the usual services, transport and other, of an industrial area. All of the full-time criminals fall into the social-occupational classes of semi-skilled and unskilled workers.

The eight more formidable characters fall into two distinct groups:

The first four (whom we shall call AA, BB, CC, and DD) are psychologically unremarkable. They show no signs of emotional unbalance. They appear to be above average intelligence. Their childhood home backgrounds are either unknown—two come from Ireland—or fairly respectable. Two of the four have a slight juvenile record—one with two periods of probation, the other one absolute discharge. Two have regular work records. The other two live mainly on public funds as well as on undisclosed sources of income. All four have a fairly stable family life, two being regularly and two irregularly married. All have children living regularly under the same roof with them.

Details of the four are as follows:

AA (now 52) arrived here from Ireland at about age 30. He has had occasional jobs as motor driver but is now mostly on relief. The police find him a friendly character, easy to get on with. His professional specialism is that of key-making and duplicating, particularly safe keys. He moves about all the time and is known for his specialism throughout the region. He looks sleepy and stupid, but participates in remarkable feats of organization and planning on a small scale.

BB (now 42) arrived from Ireland when 19. He also is a motor driver to trade but is seldom in work. He is known to the police, who have a sneaking regard for him, as a friendly, sociable character with no violence in him. BB is an expert house-breaker, ranked high in ability

JOHN MACK

by the police; he has many associates and travels widely throughout the region.

CC (now 34). CC's life-style was transformed about age 24. Although he had one minor juvenile offence he came from a fairly respectable home. But he got into bad company in his late teens; and hung around street corners with criminals. Now he is always clean and tidy, a home-lover, non-drinker, non-smoker, devoted to his children, a fairly regular worker, keen on physical fitness and to all outward appearances a good citizen. On the darker side of his ordinary life he is said to be a money-lender at his work on a considerable scale.

Underneath his fair-seeming surface he is a persistent house-breaker and safe-blower, is seldom inactive, travels widely, and has a wide range of criminal associates, including one or two connections in England. Quiet, reserved and uncommunicative, he is regarded by the police with a certain grudging respect, as a quite rational and able criminal who may conceivably stop when he has acquired a respectable modicum of capital.

DD (now 37). There is no information about DD's early background. His present house is better than average; his children are well looked after. He is on the whole a steady worker but gambles a lot. Views on his temperament differ. Police in his own town find him cheerful and companionable, always smiling, salutes his police friends in the street. Police in the neighbouring town find him sullen and withdrawn. DD is an outstandingly able contriver and executant of burglaries big and small, based on complete information. He appears to be the ablest of these criminals. He may however be surpassed by CC who never gives anything away. The two are thought to work together from time to time.

The second group (WW, XX, YY and ZZ) are thought to be not too bright. Two of them are markedly unbalanced characters; a third has a record of violence, including assaults on the police. All four have poor work records. All four are regarded by the police as surly, unsociable, unpleasant characters. Three had poor home backgrounds as children. Three have juvenile records, one including a term in an Approved School, one (post-16) a Borstal sentence, and one both Approved School and Borstal.

Details of the four are as follows:

WW (now 38) has no juvenile record but had a bad childhood home background. A violent and uncontrolled character. An excessive drinker and persistent drunkard, goes wild when drunk and suffers from persecution feeling and terror of renewed imprisonment. Has been known to threaten to murder police for putting him in prison but this indicates his horror of imprisonment rather than his likely behaviour. No record of assaults on police.

40

FULL-TIME MISCREANTS

Poor work record; lives on public relief. Does not travel. Depredations all within area, mostly house-breakings.

XX (*now 36*). A lone wolf with magpie tendencies; mixes with no one; dour and unco-operative with the police. A non-stop house-breaker: seems unable to resist stealing anything on sight, including worthless articles which he hides on the hill-side. When XX is caught 'the police office looks like Woolworths'.

A difficult child; slept out; avoided school; mother alleged a fall as a small child resulting in a fractured skull.

Approved School at 12 for 10 thefts: released at $16\frac{1}{2}$ and committed 6 thefts in 2 months for which he was in quick succession admonished, fined, admonished, sent to Approved School, and returned to Approved School having absconded. Later was sent to Borstal.

No work record. Adult professional specialism is breaking into houses (in a vigilant area avoided by other criminals) when the owners are in residence but asleep. Main activity is local but has been convicted in London and elsewhere.

YY (*now 36*). Described by police as an evil and dangerous man—inclined to be violent—spat in general direction of police at last sentence. Has never been in regular employment. First came to the notice of the police at the age of 11 years and as a juvenile spent a period on probation and one in Approved School. Adult convictions consist mainly of theft by house-breakings with a sprinkling of assaults and breaches of the peace; his latest charge in 1960 involved the use of explosives; he has twice served terms of imprisonment in England (1 year and 3 years). Associate of ZZ.

ZZ (*now 35*) has the biggest public reputation. Taught safe-blowing when young in company with other young criminals including CC and DD, and in turn has passed on the teaching to others including WW. A persistent safe-blower on a large scale; undeterrable; 'no thrill like facing a safe at 2 a.m. and blowing it'. Slight juvenile record. 28 days Remand Home at 16. Immediately after sent to Borstal. Wide range of associates. Has been known through heartlessness or stupidity to require younger men to carry explosives at great personal risk to them. Seldom talks to the police. Active over a very wide area, including English Midlands.

The main difference between the two groups is shown in the table overleaf. While it is known that the first group are continuously active, they are seldom caught or charged and seldom sent to prison. The second group are likewise continuously active during all the free time they have but they are frequently caught and are seldom out of prison.

The question arises—how do we know that the first group *are* full-time criminals? (The available evidence is by definition not sufficient to convict them in a court of law.) The claim is supported (*a*) by the

JOHN MACK

Full-Time Miscreants—Time spent in prison

	Years at Risk (from age 17 years)	Years in Prison (or Borstal)
AA (52 years)	35	1¾
BB (42 years)	25	3⅝
CC (34 years)	17	3⅛
DD (38 years)	21	2¾
	98	11½

AA, BB, CC, DD: Proportion of adult years spent in prison, etc., 12%

WW (38 years)	21	11¼
XX (35 years)	18	16¾
YY (36 years)	19	7⅝
ZZ (34 years)	17	15
	75	50⅜

WW, XX, YY, ZZ: Proportion of adult years spent in prison, etc., 64%

Note (i): No allowance is made in this table for remission of sentence.
Note (ii): ZZ is at present serving a sentence of 7 years imprisonment imposed on him in June 1963; this is not included in the above table.

knowledge of various C.I.D. groups of a series of successful crimes by each; (*b*) by indications in their household spending of undisclosed sources of income; (*c*) by the discovery of one or the other in police road blocks and in other suspicious circumstances; and (*d*) by the disclosures of accomplices (after their capture) who tell all but whose evidence does not convict.

The next stage in the study of a group of criminals of this kind would be to trace the network of collaboration and information which links them together with each other and with lesser criminals in a social and economic system of communication and exchange, and which extends far beyond Worktown. There is *inter alia* a special link between Worktown and a town in the London area.

Methods of carrying out such a study are now under consideration. We go on meantime in this paper to discuss other examples of criminal inter-connections in other parts of the country, not necessarily connected with Worktown.

II. DELINQUENT AREAS AND CRIMINAL NETWORKS

Existing studies of criminal sub-cultures are concerned in the main with territorial clusters of criminal-producing households—criminal

FULL-TIME MISCREANTS

areas or neighbourhoods.[1] Since these areas are usually quite small, we prefer the terms 'neighbourhood' or 'precinct'. There were in the past many examples of criminal neighbourhoods. But territorial location is becoming less and less important in modern society. Just as the nation is no longer composed of small socially self-contained towns and villages, but of cities and regions in which neighbours are less important than colleagues, so also with crime. The majority of persistent criminals today live in a neutral neighbourhood, or keep on the move. A criminal community may be predominantly a network of communications over a wide region with some kind of foothold in various neighbourhoods but not tied to these neighbourhoods. The important thing is no longer a place but a system of social relationships and functions, including a status system. These systems carry on, with changes of tempo and vigour, with ups and downs, a criminal way of life, an adaptable tradition that moves with the times.

There are in fact no *criminal* areas left, i.e. areas in which known criminals are known to reside in sizeable groups. This would make it too easy for the police, who are now able to go anywhere, by day or night. But there are in every conurbation a number of *delinquent* neighbourhoods. These are so defined because they produce delinquents (i.e. young offenders) in exceptionally large numbers of whom a very large selection go on to crime (that is, graduate from juvenile to adult offending).[2] Delinquent neighbourhoods have therefore a strong connection with criminals, but most of these when grown up use the place only as an occasional port of call, a part of a wider network.

The distinguishing mark of these neighbourhoods is that their social tone is directed against the values and practices of the wider society. The people in them accept dishonesty and minor violence as a way of life. It is for most of them a passive acceptance. The majority of households avoid being convicted for criminal behaviour and the majority of these do so by not behaving criminally.

One such neighbourhood we have begun to study in some detail. Most of the work has still to be done. But some preliminary results are interesting. We began by making a crime map of an urban territory. 27 precincts, blocks of criss-crossing streets, stood out as having a high delinquent content. 19 were located in older housing districts: 8 in inter-war-built housing schemes: none in post-war housing schemes. These latter schemes had not had time to build up the concentrations already established in the older districts. The period covered is 1946–58. Of the three precincts with the highest crime rating one is in an old near-central district and the remaining two are in schemes built in the nineteen-thirties. The figures were respectively: 23, 36 and 45 first offenders per year per 1,000 households on an annual average over twelve years.[3] Since houses and households are much more tightly packed in the older area the actual density of offenders and of offending

43

JOHN MACK

households *per acre* is greater than in the inter-war-built schemes. But the latter have still a long life in front of them; the older areas are due for demolition and redevelopment.

The precinct with the highest crime-rate has been studied in more detail up to 1960. It consists of a pocket of 1,100 houses—mainly the product of slum clearance and 'rehousing' building policy. Measured for first *and subsequent* offenders, i.e. *all* persons against whom charges are proved, the sector has produced 110 offenders per thousand households, or 11 per 100 households, on an annual average for the 12 years 1948–60. The two highest density streets (536 houses in all) have 16 offenders per 100 houses per year. The highest density street (252 houses) produced 20 offenders per 100 houses per year.

How many of these households are actively criminal or delinquent at any one time? This has been calculated for the worst street, counting households producing *two or more offenders* over a period of ten years. The answer is 32 per cent. Another 7 per cent of households have a record of one offence only in the period. These are infectedly rather than actively criminal. In sum: three out of five households in the worst area in this region have no criminal record at all, and only one out of three is criminally active.

The most striking figure is that of those who graduate from delinquency to crime. Of the total of juvenile entrants into delinquency from the worst street in the 12 years 1946–58, viz. 135, no fewer than 39 or 29 per cent have become adult criminals. The national figure is probably well under 5 per cent. The degree of incorrigibility of the entry is shown by the Borstal figures. The two worst streets sent to Borstal a proportion of its young men at least ten times as high as the Scottish rate. The total was 27 in the period from the 532 houses. This is roughly 52 per 1,000 households which would if generalized for all Scotland give an annual Borstal entry of 5,000. The average annual entry into Borstal in 1958–60 was 400–500. Moreover this group shows an 80 per cent 'failure' compared with a general failure proportion of 50 per cent in the period (calculated over a period of 10 years after release).

Some sketches of life in this neighbourhood will illustrate its tone and atmosphere:

The Training of the Young

'Between the ages of 4 and 8 the main activity is to pick up the lumps of coal or other merchandise thrown on the sides of the track from the railway wagons by the older boys. The wee ones are hardly able to lift their feet over the wire, but they manage it. 8–12 they become very active: as Mr. M. observed, a 9-year-old could carry a hundredweight of coal on his back. 12 upwards the boys, young adults and adults are sometimes very agile. They wear a harness over their shoulders to keep

44

FULL-TIME MISCREANTS

their hands free. This is favoured particularly by the D——'s of 47 X Street. One 20+ very agile: was on a slowly moving truck when the police were closing in on him. He threw the bag full of coal on to the spikes of the railings about 7 ft away, jumped from the moving train on to the bag, then jumped down 12 ft and got away. Various devices were used to stop the trains some years ago. On several occasions the signals were interfered with. Drivers sometimes found sleepers across the rails; when they got out to remove the sleepers the coal-stealers swarmed on to the trucks. It was just like the Wild West. The coal-stealers threw the coal either in between the middle rails, or on the side next to X street. They then go and reclaim their own coal from where they have thrown it, having a strong sense of private property in what they steal.'

A Moral Improvement

'The Railway Police dogs had a considerable effect on the inhabitants of this area. Before the dogs came they used to steal whisky from the bonded store and sell it to the people in the nearby pub. The dogs made this much more difficult. The thieves were thrown back from the railway on to the street. After that the whisky was stolen from the pub, which was a slight moral improvement on the former situation. This pub has now been demolished.'

Rude Social Health

'The place gives an impression of rude social health. The young in particular have an active life with plenty of recreational activity and room to play in. One gets the impression of a thoroughly self-contained community going about its business with great vigour. As one observer remarked, it is just like a big tinker encampment. Although the excitement was quite marked when we were there, the whole place was very quiet.'

This impression of rude social health is perhaps mistaken. The factors* in the area report that they have requests for transfer from almost everyone in the scheme. Many of the tenants are untransferable, because of rent arrears among other things. But all seem to want, or go through the motions of signifying that they want, to get out.

A CRIMINAL NETWORK

The idea of a criminal network is useful in any attempt to understand organized crime over a fairly wide industrial region.

Such a network is probably a very loose affair with its various parts, usually dormant, coming into operation as circumstances determine. You can always (one is told) get a man to do a job, either because you know whom you want already, or because you can get someone to put

---

* Anglicé—housing managers or rent collectors.

JOHN MACK

you on to him. Prisons are important centres for the exchange of information of this kind, and for following what is going on in the outside world from a criminal point of view. Although the morning newspapers are not given out in one large prison until afternoon and then only to a few privileged prisoners or to untried prisoners, the speed of the prison grape-vine is such that an item appearing in the newspaper can go all round the prison before any single newspaper can have got into the hands of any prisoner. Moreover the active criminals in prison can interpret the news more accurately than can the ordinary reader. When they read of a safe-blowing or a bank robbery, they have a shrewd idea about the people involved. They will know who would do this kind of thing in this particular way and also which of them is already in prison or outside. Sometimes, even more strikingly, news is passed into a prison or Borstal before it can be printed: thus the writer was told of a slashing in a cinema in a neighbouring town, on the same evening as it happened, and twelve hours before the episode appeared in the newspaper, the informant being a Borstal resident.

Every prison officer or chaplain, every police detective or crime journalist, is aware of the existence of an intelligence system of this kind, supported by a persisting system of relationships, a common acceptance of a privately enforced code of conduct, and a generally recognized status system. But systematic evidence for its existence, of the kind demanded by sociologists, is uncommonly hard to get. The people who have the practical knowledge, on both sides, generally keep this knowledge to themselves. Valuable work has been done on prison social systems, in U.S.A. and to a lesser extent in this country, and this throws light incidentally on the wider criminal social system of which prisons are a part.[4] Apart from this the main work of delineating the criminal sub-culture, the system of organized criminal relationships which exists in any big industrial region, must so far begin with such information as emerges when the curtain is lifted by a spectacular High Court trial. Evidence of this kind is available for the industrial region centring on Clydeside. Three big trials took place in this region in the five years up to 1960: viz. the Paisley Road bank robbery in July 1955 —trial in January 1956; the Manuel murders 1956–58, trial in May 1958; and the Shettleston Road bank robbery in April 1959, followed by the capture of the chief miscreants in May 1959, the escape of Samuel McKay in July 1959, the trial in September 1959, the recapture of McKay in July 1960, and his trial in November 1960.

The most striking criminal episode in the period was that of the pursuit and capture of the murderer Manuel, as outlined in the court proceedings and in a narrative by the detective* who was principally

* Detective-Superintendent A. Brown, since deceased. The narrative is in the Scottish *Daily Express*, October 19-30, 1959. See also John Gray Wilson: *The Trial of Peter Manuel:* London, 1959.

FULL-TIME MISCREANTS

responsible for his conviction. This gives some grounds for holding that a network exists and throws some light in particular on the economic system, the status system and the value system, which are part of it.

The narrative is remarkable for the large number of well-known people (criminally speaking) who come into it.

The first name to come up is that of a notorious gang leader of the inter-war years. This man, as it turned out, had reformed since the war: his intervention in this case was intended to help in the tracing of the gun used in one of Manuel's murders. The next name to be connected with the case is that of Samuel McKay. This is of great interest, for McKay was the leading criminal figure in the region in the period up to 1960. A National Assistance form found under a vase in Manuel's sitting-room bore the name 'Mr. McKay', and the telephone number of the Gordon Club, a well-known gambling club with which Samuel McKay was associated. Manuel told some remarkable stories about this.

The background of one of the stories is that the people connected with the Gordon Club were determined to discourage the setting up of rival clubs. Criminal enterprises, like non-criminal, tend towards oligopoly. One rival was proposing to open a club in a building round the corner. The proprietor of the building received by post a bomb with the explosive left out. The message this conveyed was that next time the bomb would be live and would not come by post. This was no empty threat. About this time a bookmaker's office had been bombed on two occasions and was a few months later to be put out of action by fire. And this particular threat, the non-live bomb, was in fact traced back to the Gordon Club. EE, co-proprietor of the club with Samuel McKay, was charged, convicted and sent for nine months to prison for the crime of sending it. There is reason to believe that he was not actively concerned in sending the bomb, though he may have known of it. But he did not talk, and duly served his time.

Manuel's story, which comes into the extraordinary address to the jury made by himself as his own defending counsel, was that McKay took him to see EE who was in prison awaiting trial on the bomb charge. During this visit, Manuel alleged, he was asked to prevent the prospective victim of the bomb incident, the rival proprietor, from giving evidence against EE. 'That', said Manuel, 'was the business I had with McKay, he wanted me to wait until the night before the trial and get hold of this —— and give him a right doing so that he would land in hospital and wouldn't be able to go to the trial. . . .'

It is difficult to judge the accuracy of this story. It is probably nearer the truth than some other accounts offered by Manuel to explain why McKay and he came together at this time. But irrespective of the details of the story it does illustrate rather well the nature of the relationship between the two men. It throws some light for example on the criminal status-system. Note the implied high status of McKay. It is quite feasible

JOHN MACK

that he in his role of criminal tycoon should employ Manuel as a junior executive. Note secondly the implied low status of Manuel. This also is consistent with the other data we have. Manuel appears to have been a relatively unimportant figure before his trial. He was a man of the second rank, a strong-arm man and a relative outsider to the McKay circle. McKay admitted to knowing him for some years but only as a minor figure.

Further indications show how status (in the sense of high status) is acquired in this sub-culture. McKay appears to have achieved his position in three ways. First by money. Secondly by fear. He is thought to be a violent man in the sense that he threatens the use of violence to enforce his will on other criminals and even on non-criminals. (It should be noted that there is little record of personal violence on his part.) Thirdly by skill in outwitting the forces of law and order. McKay's most notable exploit, already noted, was to escape from prison and to remain 'on the run' for a year. This happened in 1959–60, in the last year of his active career to date, but it crowned a reputation already won for agility in avoiding capture.

The EE episode shows us something of the value-system accepted by criminals. EE was ready to serve the prison sentence imposed on him without complaining. Why? Not because of a feeling of loyalty to his colleagues—there is no loyalty between thieves as such—but because of a common repudiation of the police-enforced code of the wider society. These people have their own sanctions, and prefer to operate them in their own way. They may use betrayal to the police as an occasional method of enforcement but this is rare.

A further episode in the Manuel case illustrates several aspects of the network—its intelligence and economic system and the limited range of the group code. This is the surprising behaviour of FF. This episode first came into the light of day at the trial of Manuel in 1958 in the course of evidence concerning the murder of Mrs. Watt, her sister, and her daughter in September 1956. At the trial FF told how he had helped Manuel to procure the gun which killed these women. The business, which involved two other dealers, both with bad criminal records, was transacted in a series of meetings in Gallowgate public houses.

The surprising behaviour of FF consists in the fact that he had told this story a year earlier, and to the police at that. He had gone to Mr. Watt, husband and father of two of the murdered women, and had then been persuaded to confide in the police. It is on the face of it unusual that one criminal should inform against another on such a serious charge. All this was before Manuel had become notorious. Why should FF break the code? If there is a criminal network throughout the west of Scotland, and if Manuel was part of it, why should FF betray him? The answer appears to be that Manuel was not a member of the

48

FULL-TIME MISCREANTS

particular corner of the network to which FF belonged. He was an outsider. He didn't 'run with' the Gallowgate crowd. In his own area (he was known to the Lanarkshire police but *not* to the Glasgow police) he did belong. It is also possible that Manuel was distrusted as a deep or queer type. A fellow-prisoner in Peterhead Prison describes him as excessively self-centred and withdrawn. But the main suggestion one gets from all this is that the network, such as it is, is sustained by a common code of not talking to the police, which is strong in local groups or between habitual associates, but does not stretch to casual associates from a distance, and does not stand up well to a major exposure.

Similar considerations may explain the sentences in the Paisley Road bank robbery trial in 1956. Two English and three local men were tried. The Englishmen got eight years and six years respectively. One local minor figure got three years; the other two were discharged. Scottish criminal opinion probably approved the system of private information which may have resulted in these disposals.

We have space here for only a brief reference to the Shettleston Road bank robbery. This was a very well-planned crime but it led to the final capture and imprisonment of McKay and the collapse of the Gordon Club group. In this major engagement one imagines the police came out finally on top. This may not be a final verdict, since the greater part of the money stolen was not recovered. But it is probable that all of the stolen money was spent by McKay in his expensive year on the run. What is certain is that the network in the shape described here, with its apex in McKay, is now a matter of history. There are no well-known figures left. But it goes on in a more anonymous shape. For it has connections with the wider culture in its more dubious economic aspects.

One main connection is with the gambling world. The Gordon Club has been succeeded by a number of other gambling clubs some of which harbour criminals (according to a recent statement by the Chief Constable of Glasgow). On a lower level there are less conspicuous trades, notably that of scrap merchant. The nature of this business attracts criminals who wish to dispose of stolen goods. Some of these concerns are simply fronts for criminal activities: most have no criminal connections: a number in between have a criminal corner to their business. There are several well-known resetters of this kind. They oblige the police from time to time by turning someone in. This is usually a person from outside the district and who is inexperienced, a first offender who doesn't know the ropes. One low character, with no place of business, has a habit of informing on juveniles who refuse to take the very low prices he offers them for stolen goods. These might be regarded as society's devices for preventing first offenders and juvenile delinquents from becoming persistent criminals. It should be added that some resetters, probably most, will not touch youngsters.

JOHN MACK

III. SUMMARY AND INTERPRETATION

1. A number of organized crimes are planned and carried through by miscreants who spend most of their time in prison. These might be described as habitual or full-time prisoners.

2. A number of organized crimes, at least as numerous as those first referred to, are planned and carried through by miscreants who seldom go to prison. These might be described as habitual or full-time criminals.[5]

3. The habitual prisoners tend to exhibit the characteristics associated with psychological maladjustment or deviance.

4. The habitual criminals give the impression of psychological normality. Although their behaviour deviates sharply from the norms of the wider society, which favour law-abiding and property-and-person-respecting behaviour, the reasons for this deviance are not psycho-pathological: they refer to the *social* as distinct from the *personal* history of the criminals in question.

5. It is not possible to estimate the relative proportion of full-time prisoners and full-time criminals in the total of full-time miscreants. The Worktown study described in I above suggests that there are as many full-time criminals as there are full-time prisoners.

6. Most British criminological studies of individual miscreants have concentrated on full-time and habitual prisoners to the neglect of the possibly equally large group of full-time and habitual criminals. The preponderance of personal-pathological tendencies, mild and serious, in the group of full-time prisoners, has co-operated with the broadly psycho-pathological interest of many of the investigators to produce the impression that the 'real' criminal, the habitual and persistent offender, is in most cases a maladjusted individual, a miscreant whose deviant behaviour is to be explained in terms of his personal-clinical history.

7. The general trend of thought suggested by the present studies goes therefore to reinforce the current shift of emphasis in British criminological thought from a psycho-pathological to a sociological approach to the subject: i.e. from the study of crime as a symptom of personal maladjustment to the study of criminality as a normal aspect of the social structure.

8. The move from one emphasis to another is unlikely to be excessively enlightening in the long run. A repudiation of the entire psycho-pathological approach in the manner of Sutherland[6] is as silly in its own way as a repudiation of the Sutherland-sociological approach in the manner of Glueck.[7] It is desirable that the attempt be made to lay down rules for a fruitful co-operation between the two complementary approaches. One might regard the psychiatric approach, or more generally the clinical-psychological approach, as describing and explaining how certain individuals with certain propensities and suscepti-

FULL-TIME MISCREANTS

bilities, developed or acquired in ways which can now be delineated in specific detail, are propelled or inducted into a criminal way of life. Similarly the sociological approach might be regarded as having as its main concern the description and analysis of the criminal way of life which is already there to receive the pathologically propelled individuals.

9. These individuals are far from exhausting the range of types of criminal. In their case the two factors are needed to explain the criminal outcome—the pathological propellant on the one hand and the receiving apparatus of an already existing and ongoing system of criminal activity on the other. The propellant renders them crime-susceptible. The receptor takes up and actualizes their susceptibility.

10. There are other pathologically propelled criminals—violent criminals in the main—whose propellant is self-actualizing, whose form of criminal activity is instinctive not learned.[8] These need no sub-culture, and are indeed complete outsiders to any sub-culture. But even they—like Manuel—need the system of economic exchange and communications which the sub-culture sustains.

11. The studies reported above, together with similar studies else-where, enable us to sketch the main outlines of the *general* criminal system[9] of activity in societies such as ours. It appears that while most persistent criminals may carry out their specific criminal operations on their own, or in small groups unconnected with any wider group, they also share a network of relationships over a wide geographical area. They have a common code of conduct enforced by internal group sanctions. They have a rough-and-ready status system. They carry on a regular acquisitive activity which has its distinctive economic and technical aspects—indeed they operate in a manner not unlike that of a profession or trade, as for example doctors or dockers, in which the way of making a living is also a way of life. They recruit and train young people, and they also recruit adults who were not apprenticed to the trade in early life. They have a private communication network and a technical language and expertise of their own. They play as well as work together. They form, in short, a sub-culture, a criminal sub-culture.

12. The extreme or single-minded clinical approach to crime would interpret the criminal sub-culture as a coming together of already maladjusted individuals. Thus one theory of delinquent neighbourhoods holds that such neighbourhoods are simply reception areas for indivi-duals and households already predisposed to crime by pathological factors.[10] This theory has still to be tested in detail. At present one can say that it does not accord with ordinary observation. The delinquent neighbourhood described above has its quota of sick delinquents, people who are crime-prone by reason of some predisposing factor in their family or personal or obstetric history. But a bigger proportion of its actively delinquent members appear to become delinquent and

JOHN MACK

later criminal because they are only too well-adjusted to their local community.

13. The main contribution of sociology to the study of criminal sub-cultures is to suggest that these are shaped on the same model as the principal non-criminal sub-cultures. The general structure of any sub-culture, or of any lasting group, is best traced through its leadership pattern. The medical or legal professions, or the universities, are by and large sustained and adapted to change by their more able members. It is suggested that the general criminal sub-culture over any wide area of modern society is likewise maintained and developed by its more able members, those who have high status acquired through exceptional competence in criminal activity and in keeping out of the hands of the police. It is notable that the full-time *criminals* studied above, those who on the whole avoid capture, are to all appearance well-balanced individuals with little or no juvenile record and with none of the personal or family history of the maladjusted individual criminal. There is other evidence of this kind in the recent Cambridge study *Robbery in London*. 81 per cent of the perpetrators of the organized van robbery type of crime in 1957 got away.[11] The leaders at least of these criminal enterprises are probably as normal, psychologically speaking, as any random group of stock-brokers, quite as intelligent, and physically, perhaps more agile.

14. The general conclusion this work points to can now be summarily stated. It is that criminality is a normal aspect of the social structure, a permanent feature of any complex society, an ongoing social activity like the practice of medicine or police work or university teaching or stevedoring. It is sustained, like these other activities, by a sub-culture of people and groups most of whom are tolerably well-adjusted to their sub-culture and most of whose leaders are not only socially and personally competent but are also exceptionally able individuals. It is the latter, the successful criminals, who maintain and keep up to date the criminal system of activities. They thereby render it the more able to receive into its flinty bosom that less successful miscreant, the habitual prisoner, who is often of lower intelligence, who is very often propelled into crime by pathological drives, and who is by the nature of the case more continuously accessible to clinical observation than is his abler colleague.

15. One remaining and ever-recurring question remains to be considered. How do these so-called able and non-pathological criminals come to take up a criminal way of life? It is clear from all the existing evidence, which is derived mainly from the study of delinquent neighbourhoods, that even in a heavily delinquent and criminal-producing area only a minority of the young learners enter into the criminal sub-culture as life members. What is it that propels into crime those of them who are not crime-susceptible on pathological grounds but who

nevertheless become full-time criminals? It is almost invariably assumed in discussion of this point that the propellant or selective factor must be pathological, or at least derivable from some special developmental circumstances in the personal history or family group-environment of the person concerned. But this simply begs the question at issue. It is perfectly feasible to hold that the same process is at work in the production of normal criminals as operates in the manning of the ranks of sociologists, or policemen, or decision makers, or any other more respectable occupational group. It is simply that process of social selection which is to be found in all social systems and which in our particular social system works by a combination of chance, choice, and paternal cheque-book.

NOTES

[1] See for example *British Journal of Criminology*, vol. 3, editorial Note, p. 209 (1962). See also T. Morris: *The Criminal Area*, London, 1958, chs. I–VI, for an effective summary of work in this field.

[2] Robert E. Forman discusses in *Journal of Criminal Law, Criminology and Police Science*, vol. 54 (1963), pp. 317–21, the question of how delinquent an area must be to be labelled delinquent.

[3] These and similar figures given here are of course official figures and therefore exclude undetected offenders. R. E. Forman, op. cit., holds that although much delinquency goes unrecorded in these high-rate areas, the more serious and persistent delinquents do tend to receive official attention. 'This would imply that rate differences between ecological areas probably reflect real differences in behaviour' (p. 318).

[4] D. Clemmer, *The Prison Community*, New York, 1958; G. M. Sykes, *The Society of Captives*, Princeton, 1958; D. R. Cressey (ed.), *The Prison*, New York, 1961; Terence and Pauline Morris, *Pentonville*, London, 1963.

[5] Most studies of full-time miscreants fail to make this essential distinction between 'habitual criminal' and 'habitual prisoner'. A conspicuous exception is the recent study by D. J. West, *The Habitual Prisoner*, London, 1962.

[6] E. H. Sutherland and D. R. Cressey,

Principles of Criminology, fifth edition, New York, 1955, ch. 7.

[7] Sheldon Glueck, 'Theory and Fact in Criminology', in *British Journal of Delinquency*, vol. vii (1956), pp. 92–109.

[8] See Sheldon Glueck, op. cit., p. 94.

[9] By '*general* criminal system' is intended a contrast with the specialized sub-cultural studies now being pursued in U.S.A. Cf. Marshall Clinard in *British Journal of Criminology* vol. 3 (1962), p. 113—'Sociological research has shown the existence of pronounced differences in normative structures of sub-cultures involving persons of different age-groups, social classes, occupations, social, religious and ethnic groups, neighbourhoods and regions. In addition there are some even more limited sub-cultures such as those among teenage gangs, prostitutes, alcoholics, drug addicts, homosexuals, professional and organized criminals. Even institutions for the treatment of deviants, such as prisons, are actually sub-cultures with their own social systems.' See also Cloward, R. A., and Ohlin, L. E., *Delinquency and Opportunity*, Glencoe, Illinois, 1960.

[10] Cf. D. H. Stott, 'Spotting the Delinquency-Prone Child', *Howard Journal*, vol. 10 (1959), no. 2.

[11] F. H. McLintock and E. Gibson, *Robbery in London*, London, 1961, p. 127, table.

[17]

THE

ORDINARY *of* NEWGATE,

His ACCOUNT of the

Behaviour, Confession, and Dying Words,

OF THE

MALEFACTORS,

Who were Executed at TYBURN,

On WEDNESDAY the 18th of *March*, 1740.[1]

BEING THE

First EXECUTION in the MAYORALTY

OF THE

Rt. Hon. *HUMPHREY PARSONS*, Esq;

LONDON:

Printed and Sold by JOHN APPLEBEE, in *Bolt-Court*, near

the *Leg-Tavern, Fleet-street.* M,DCC,XL.

(Price SIX-PENCE.)

[Part I, p. 7]

Mary Young, alias *Jenny Diver*,[2] and *Elizabeth Davis*, alias *Catherine* the Wife of *Henry Huggins*, were indicted for assaulting *Judith Gardener* on the King's Highway, putting her in Fear, and taking from her 12s. in Money, the Money of the said *Judith*, in the Parish of St. *Mary Woolchurch*, *January* 17.

... *Mary Young*, alias *Jenny Diver*, about 36 Years of Age, born in *Ireland*, as I was informed, but she denied it, calling herself an *English* Woman, being unwilling to declare either her Country or Family, desiring to be excused in that Point. She had good Education at School, and was instructed in the Principles of Religion, and the Knowledge of other Things which was required, in order to fit her for doing Business. She lived with her Parents, and did not go to Service, but came up to *London*, where she soon became a good Proficient in the tricking Arts of the Town, as now she hath found to her sad Experience. A few Years ago she passed for a Wife to a Prisoner in *Newgate*, whom she daily attended, and supplied him with Victuals, and likewise gave Charity to the other Prisoners under Sentence, and to some on the Common Side. She was thought to be one of the most artfullest Pick-pockets in the World; she was a constant Street-walker, where she exercised her Skill. About 2 Years, or 2 Years and half, she was Transported, for picking the Pocket of a Gentlewoman in St. *Paul's Church Yard*, at the Feast of the Sons of the Clergy; for which Fact she was tried at the *Old Bailey*, and was ordered to be Transported; but she had not been gone long, before she and her supposed Spouse returned to *London*, where she has been a constant Practitioner ever since. She was then tried by another Name, it being usual for such Persons to change their Names upon every Occasion. On *Saturday* the 17th of *Jan* last, as she was walking along the Streets, between 6 and 7 at Night, she met with *Judith Gardener* by the Corner of the *Mansion-house*, a Man held up *Judith*'s Arm with such Force, that she was like to have lost the Use of it; *Mary* came up before the Woman, and put her Hand into her Pocket, *Judith* being frighted, cryed out she was robbed, and like to be murdered; upon this the Man run away, and a Scuffle ensuing, *Davis* taking the Man's Part, came in for her Share in the Fray, and was taken up and convicted for the same Robbery with *Mary Young*. The Man having made his Escape, *Young* and *Davis* were carried to *Devonshire Square*, and several other Places in the City, in order to carry them before a Justice, but not finding one in the Way, they came back to the *Old Bailey*, where the Court was sitting, they was brought before my Lord Mayor, who was pleased to commit them. It is observable of them, viz. *Mary Young* and *Elizabeth Davis*, that the Robbery was committed, and they sent to *Newgate* on *Saturday* the 17th of *Jan* and on *Monday* the 19th, a Bill of Indictment was found against them, and on *Tuesday* the 20th, they were tried, capitally convicted, and receiv'd Sentence of Death.[3] *Mary Young* behaved well while under Sentence, and was very devout to all outward Appearance, often crying at Prayers, and singing of Psalms. She declared that *Elizabeth Davis* had no Hand in the Robbery which she suffered for, and that she wou'd persuade the World (if possible) that she was not the Woman, that she was represented to be; but had always lived a sober Life,

ORDINARY OF NEWGATE'S *ACCOUNT*: MARY YOUNG

(if you believe her) but she could not deny the robbing of *Judith Gardener*, on the 17th of *Jan.* last, and that she was Transported by the Name of *Jane Web*, in *April* Sessions 1738.[4] She believed in Christ her only Saviour, repented of all her Sins, and was in Peace with all the World.

* * * * * * * *

[Part II, p. 5]
The following is a particular Account of the Transactions of the Life of Mary Young, *alias* Jenny Diver, *&c, &c, &c.*

AS I am in a few Days to suffer for what I most justly deserved, and am to give an Account to the righteous Judge of all Things for my past wicked Transactions, I thought it a Duty incumbent on men, as I could no other Way make Restitution, to publish an Account of my past mispent miserable Life; I know in doing this, I shall give much Offence to those Persons who have been Partners in my Crimes, and Partakers of ill got Goods; but let them consider 'ere 'tis too late, that the Course they are now pursuing, will one Day or other bring them into my sad State! I know if it was possible to speak with the Tongue of Men and Angels, without they beg of God, and have a sincere Desire to reform my unhappy Exit, as that of many Others before me, will be rather an Encouragement to pursue their wicked Practices, than work in them a Desire of reforming, as I must confess with all the Agonies of Horror, Remorse and anguish of Mind, it was formerly with me! But Oh! that they felt the Racks and Tortures I now do! how would they wish! what would they give! had they reformed by timely Advice. I do sincerely hope that my untimely Exit may be a Warning to all unhappy Persons, and that they would take Example by me, and shun the fatal Rock on which I split. I hope those I have any Ways offended or injured, will forgive my past Transactions, for which I am very sorry, and do heartily repent of; as the following Account contains a sincere and faithful Narrative of my Facts; and the various Methods taken in the Performance of 'em, I hope as I have made a true Discovery, that my Companions will forgive me for so doing; and I beg that God would grant them his Grace and enable them for the future to take to some honest, though ever so mean, an Employ. The Hopes of which has engag'd me to say thus much.

Mary Young, alias *Murphew*, alias *Webb*, alias *Jenny Diver*, (whose *true* Name was *Mary Young*) was so great a Proficient in her Art, that she got the Name amongst her Companions of *Jenny Diver*, alias *Diving Jenny* from her great Dexterity in picking Pockets; she followed this Profession between 14 and 15 Years; was born in the *North* of *Ireland*, but was entirely ignorant of her Family. When she was about 10 Years of Age,[5] she was put to School by an old Woman whom she used to call by the Name of *Nurse*, who bestowed some small Matter of Learning upon her, as Reading, Writing, and Plain-Work, which latter she was dextrous at, being reckon'd an extraordinary Workwoman with her Needle. When she was about 15 Years of Age, having an itching Desire to see *London*, and Quarrelling with the old Woman who kept her, she made Enquiry for any Vessel bound for

DRUNKS, WHORES AND IDLE APPRENTICES

England, and soon finding one for her Purpose, she made an Agreement with the Captain who was to sail in three Days: Now her next Scheme was, how to leave the old Woman, and to get her Cloaths handsomely away, and Money to bear her Expences in her Passage, and when she came to *England*, to live on, 'till she could get into some Business, for as yet, she had not imbib'd any Principle to wrong or defraud any body, as she herself confess'd.

There was a young Fellow who had paid his Addresses to her in the Quality of a Suitor, for the Space of a Month, now this Person being very sollicitous to persuade her to become his Wife, she told him there was but one Way to make them both happy, and that was to go to *England*, telling him the old Woman her Nurse, would never consent for her to marry him, and if he really loved her, as he pretended, he would soon comply with her Request; the young Fellow being overjoy'd at this Proposal, promised her he would, when she had so done, she told him how she had already made an Agreement with the Captain, who was to sail in about three days, and directed him where he lived, desiring him to get Things in Readiness by that Time, he promised her he would, and accordingly took his Leave; as soon as the appointed Time came, the Morning when they were to sail, the young Fellow who was a Servant to a Gentleman of Fortune, and being willing to bring his new Bride a handsome Sum to support Expences, robb'd his Master of upwards [p. 6] of 80*l.* and his Gold Watch; and both getting secretly Aboard, she for fear of her Nurse, and he for fear of being discovered, the Ship hoisted Sail, and arrived two Days after at the City of *Liverpoole*, in *Lancashire*. As soon as they came Ashore, *Jenny* being Sea-sick, her Spark proposed to stay two or three Days, in order to refresh themselves before they proceeded for *London*; so he, for fear of being known, got a Lodging at a private House in that City; now the Day being come in which they designed to depart, he pack'd up her Cloaths, and his own, and put them in the Hands of the Waggoner in order to be carried to *London*, proposing themselves to follow, and so walk easy Day's Journeys, till such Time they should get safe to Town. As soon as they had so done, they went to a publick House in order to get some Refreshment before they set out; and as soon as they came in, who should be there but a Person who was sent in Quest of him by his Master; the young Spark was extremely surprized, and would have retreated faster than he came in, but it was too late, for the Person seized him, and told him he was his Prisoner, and immediately upon this hurry'd him with a great Mob before the Mayor. As soon as they came there (*Jenny* following him at some Distance, for in the Hurry and Confusion no Body took Notice of her) she heard him confess the Robbery of his Master, but never mention'd one Syllable about her; now just before this Accident, he had given her 10 Guineas, in order to put in a little Purse which she had, the rest of the Money and the Watch being found on him, he was committed to Prison; as soon as *Jenny* heard this, she went aside to a Publick House and wrote him a Letter, expressing a great Concern for this Misfortune, and promised to return his Things that were pack'd up for *London*, and likewise the Money which she had of him when it was in her Power; so done, she made the best of her Way to Town, never as she confessed, being the least dismayed at this Accident.

ORDINARY OF NEWGATE'S *ACCOUNT*: MARY YOUNG

After the Hurry was a little over, she was as good as her Word; for as soon as she arriv'd at *London* she sent his Things, and some Time after that his Money. He was cast (which was after she had been in *London* some Time) for his Life, but was transported afterwards. As soon as she arrived at *London*, she got acquainted with one *A. M --- p*,[6] who was her Country-woman, who took a Lodging for her near *Long Acre*, where she proposed to take in Plain Work; but Business not coming in according to Expectation, *M --- y*[7] takes her aside one Day, and thus expostulates the Case with her, says she, *Jenny* Trading being dead, suppose we was to take a new Method of Life, which at present you are a Stranger to; but what I am acquainted with; *Jenny* being mighty desirous to know what it was, why reply'd the other, if you'll go along with me this Evening, you shall be instructed in this new Art; but I must first swear you to Secrecy, for Fear if you shou'd not like it, you should discover; upon which *Jenny* promised she would obey her Directions in all Particulars, and swearing Secrecy she was admitted into the Society that Evening, which consisted of four Persons, two Men and a Woman with herself; their Business that Evening was to go upon *Cheving the Froe*, (that is, *Cutting off Women's Pockets*;) in order to do this they attended the Theatres after the Play was over; she was appointed (as being a young Novice in the Art) to stand *Miss Slang all upon the Safe*, (that is, *to stand safe at a Distance as if not one of the Gang, in order to receive the Things stollen.*) They got that Night 2 Diamond Girdle Buckles, and a Gold Watch, which they fenced at a Lock for 70*l*. now *Jenny* had but 10*l*. for her Share, by Reason that she did the least Execution, and was in least Danger.

Jenny finding Money coming in pretty fast this Way, applied her Time very diligent in this new Study; and in order that she might be well vers'd in this new Employ, and learn the Cant Language, one of her Companions used to come every Day to instruct her in the Theory of her new Calling, as well as the practical Part; in order to which, she used to set aside two Hours every Day for this Purpose, and soon became a good Scholar, and well versed in the aforesaid Tongue; *Jenny*'s Master coming often to instruct his new Pupil, they contracted such a Respect for each other, that they agreed to live together.

By this Time *Jenny* was grown a compleat Artist, and got great Reputation amongst her Companions. One Day when they were all out together upon Business, at a noted Meeting-house in the *Old Jewry*, where abundance of People were crowding, in order to get in, *Jenny* being very genteely dressed, she observ'd a Gentleman who was a very *Rum Muns*, (that is, *a great Beau*) who had a very handsome *Glim Star*, (that is, *a Ring*) upon his *Feme*, (that is, *Hand*) which she longed to make, so giving the Hint to her Companions to *Bulk the Muns forward*, (that is, *Push*) they pushed him quite in; whereupon the Meeting being pretty full, as soon as he was in, *Jenny* held up her Hand to the young Spark, that he might help her forward, which he perceiving, very complaisantly gave her his Hand, in order to assist her, which she readily accepting of, she griped his Hand very fast, and while she had hold of his Hand, the People who were on the outside striving for Entrance, and *Jenny*'s Companions pushing forward, in the Scuffle she

DRUNKS, WHORES AND IDLE APPRENTICES

squeez'd his Hand so hard, that he was glad to get it away, and did not perceive her take off his Diamond Ring, which as soon as she had effected, she slip'd behind her Companions, saying at the same Time, it is in vain to get in, I'll come another Time, when there's less Crowd; her Companions convey'd her clean off, before the Gentleman had Time to miss his Ring, who called out to stop the Woman, but 'twas too late, for she had brush'd off with the Booty, this gain'd her great Applause amongst her Companions, who now appointed her an equal Share of every Thing they got.

The next Exploit that *Jenny* went on was, *Slanging the Gentry Mort rumly with a sham Kinchin*, that is, (*Cutting well the Women big with Child*) which was thus perform'd, *Jenny* had got 2 false Arms made, and Hands, by an ingenious Artist, and dressing herself very genteely, like a Citizen's Wife big with Child, with a Pillow artfully fixed under Coats for that Purpose, and her Arms fix'd on, she by the Contrivance of the Pillow hid her real ones under her Petticoat, and the artificial ones came across her Belly; dressed in this Condition, with one of the Gang in the Habit of a Footman, she takes a Chair and goes, (it being on a Sunday Evening) to the Meeting-house already mention'd; now it was so contriv'd by the rest of the Gang, that one should go before as a Scout, and bring Word to the supposed Footman in what Part of the Meeting set the *rummest Froes*; and likewise to *Saweer clearly*, (that is, *to keep a good look out*) that they should have *Vid Loges (repeating Watches)* by their Side, that *Jenny*'s Footman might place his Mistress accordingly. Now it was so ordered, that our big-belly'd Lady was plac'd in a Pew between 2 elderly Ladies who had both repeating Watches by their Side; she sat very quietly all the Time of the Service, but at the Conclusion of the last Prayer, the Audience being standing, she took both the Ladies Watches off, unperceiv'd by them, and *tip'd* 'em to one of her Companions, who was ready planted for the Purpose (and who went and tip'd them to *Slang upon the Safe*; and then went back to be ready for Business) Now the Congregation breaking up, every body was in a Hurry to get out, and the Gang surrounding the Ladies in order to make a greater Croud, and help *Jenny* off if she should be *smoak'd*.

The two Ladies had no sooner got out of the Pew to the Door, but they missed their Watches, and made a terrible Outcry, which alarmed that Part of the Audience, who enquiring what was the Matter, was answered that the Ladies had lost their Watches, and being asked again who took them, answered, nobody, without the D – – l and the big-belly'd Woman had, who was now got far enough off. Nay, says one of the Ladies, that's impossible, for she never moved her Hands from her Lap, all the Time of the Service. This Accident gathered a great Mob round the Ladies, some enquiring, others confounded at the Strangeness of the Robbery: In the mean while *Jenny* was slipp'd out to a House hard by, and had alter'd her Dress, and delivered herself of her great Belly, and returned with the utmost Precipitation to her Companions, in order to be assisting in the helping of with more Moveables, who was very busy with the rest of the Crowd, and while they were astonished at the Accident, they took Opportunity to make the Gentleman's *Loges* and *Tales*, (or Men's repeating Watches) and to *Chive* the *Froes* of their *Bungs*, (or cut off the Women's Pockets.)

126

ORDINARY OF NEWGATE'S *ACCOUNT*: MARY YOUNG

They were succesful that Day, for no sooner was they got to the *Biding* (or Place where they divide the Booty) but they examined the Contents of their Booties, which was three *Bungs*, with *Lowers* (Purses) in each *Lower* there were ten *Ridges* (or Guineas) and two *Vid Loges*. These, with the Money they had got, and 2 *Tales* (or Swords) amounted to 30 *Ridges* a Piece, after they had *fenced* the *Loges*, &c. which was all carried abroad, and disposed of by *R — — J — — n*,[8] since dead.

[p. 8]After this Robbery, the Gang consulted together, and thought it proper not to steer that Way for some Time, for Fear of being discover'd. *Jenny* got so great a Name by this last Affair, that they all swore to act for the future according to her Directions in every Thing, which she thanked them for, and then made the following Speech.

"It is now 2 Years since I entered into this honourable Society, and I think it is a Duty incumbent upon me to advise for our general Preservation, that the following Articles ought to be made for the Use of our Gang.

I. That no one else be admitted without the Consent of the whole Gang.

II. That no one presume to go upon any thing by him or herself upon Pain of being entirely turn'd off, and left to shift.

III. That if any new Member be propos'd by any of the Gang, that he or she shall be a Month upon Trial, and all that Time shall be instructed at convenient Seasons in the *Cant Tongue*, so that they may speak intelligibly to nobody but the Gang.

IV. That if any of the Gang should happen to be taken upon any one Action, that the rest shall stand by him, or her, and swear any thing in order to get such releas'd; and if convicted, a sufficient Allowance to be given him or her in Prison out of the Common Stock, that they may live in a Gentleman or Gentlewoman-like Manner. These Articles were agreed to and sign'd by 'em all".

Their next Adventure was in St. *James*'s-Park upon a fine Day, when abundance of People of Fashion were walking. In that Place, *Jenny* being well dressed, and her sham great Belly, with one of the Gang in the Habit of a Servant attending her, they took the Opportunity coming out at *Spring Garden* Gate, when a great Concourse of People were crouding, for the sham Lady to make a false Step and Stumble; presently abundance of good-natur'd Gentlemen and Ladies seeing a big-belly'd Woman ready to fall, was very busy striving who should first lend their Assistance, notwithstanding which, the Lady fairly contriv'd to fall down, and when they went to help her up, she made Signs, and gave 'em to understand that she had so hurt herself by the Fright, that she could not presently recover so as to be able to stand upon her Legs; by this Time more People came up to see what was the Matter, and she had so order'd it as to fall just in the Middle of the Passage; and while the Croud was gazing on, and commiserating the Case of the poor supposed distressed Lady, the rest of the Gang were very busy in speaking with their Pockets, Diamond Girdle Buckles, &c. They manag'd their Business so dextrously, that they got by this Adventure, two Diamond Girdle Buckles, a Gold Watch, a Gold Snuff Box and two Purses which contain'd upward of twenty Guineas; the next Day the Buckles, Watch, &c.

DRUNKS, WHORES AND IDLE APPRENTICES

were advertized, and a large Reward offer'd for them; which $M---y^9$ proposed to restore for the Reward, when *Jenny* started up and ask'd who would venture Home with them? I, says $M---y,^{10}$ would you? do you not consider the Consequence of returning them? why reply'd the other, there is no Questions to be ask'd, What then, replied *Jenny*, suppose there is not, apprehend you no farther Consequence than that; no, replied the other; why then resumed *Jenny*; my Reason is this; suppose you go Home with them and get the Reward offered; here lies the Case, the Parties injured, will, though they ask you no Question, take particular Notice of your Person, and some time or other when you are out upon Business, you may be *smoak'd*, and then perhaps all may be *blown*; so my Advice is, that whatever Things may be got, though we can *Fence* 'em but for two Thirds of the Value offer'd, yet it is much the safer Way, and less dangerous. This Reason the Gang applauded much, and presently consented to send them to their usual *Fence*, (who was one who used to trip over to *Holland* very often upon the Smuggling Business, and who gave most Money for Goods got in that Manner) and the Gang for the future very seldom made Restitution, but generally dealt with this *Fence*.

Some small Time after this last Adventure, 2 of the Gang fell Sick, and were rendered uncapable of turning out upon Business for some Time; now *Jenny* and her *Quondam Spouse* were obliged to turn out by themselves upon the *Slang mort Lay*, described in the following Adventures. *Jenny* being dressed as a big-belly'd Woman already mention'd, and her Spouse as a Footman in a Livery, used to take the Opportunity of the Master of the House's Absence in a genteel [p. 9] Street, when the Lady's pretended Footman knocking at the Door, ask'd if the Lady of the House was at Home, and being answer'd yes, used to say, my Lady here is taken ill and desires to speak with your Mistress; and so when she had introduc'd herself and Servant, they was not idle upon the Occasion, but generally made what they could that lay in the Way. One Day *Jenny* and her Servant being upon Business of this Nature in *Burr Street*, near *Wapping*, *Jenny*'s Servant knocked at the Door, and a Person coming and enquiring his Business, my Lady, says he there, pointing to *Jenny*, is a little out of Order, and being some Distance from Home, desires to speak with your Mistress; the Servant desired the Lady to Walk in, and said, she would fetch her Mistress presently, who was above Stairs.

So directly in goes *Jenny* grunting and groaning as if she was half dead. Down comes the Mistress, and sends the Maid in a hurry up Stairs for the Chamber-pot; while she went to fetch the Smelling Bottle. While they were gone, *Jenny* took the Opportunity of opening the Drawer, and taking out a fine dress'd suit, worth 60 Guineas, which she presently put in a Place made on purpose on the Inside of her large Hoop, and was got sitting in her Chair by the Time the Lady return'd in a very moving melancholy Posture, pretending to be almost dead. As soon as the Lady came, and her Servant with the Pot, the pretended Footman was ordered into the Kitchen, who had till then attended his Mistress; but out of Decency, was desired to walk down till his Mistress wanted him; while he was in the Kitchen, he took the Opportunity to convey half a dozen Silver Spoons, a Salt, and a

ORDINARY OF NEWGATE'S *ACCOUNT*: MARY YOUNG

Pepper-Box in his Pocket; and as the Lady and her Maid above Stairs were very busy in applying her Smelling-Bottle to Madam's Nose, she took the Opportunity to convey the Lady's Purse out of her Pocket, when she had so done, pretending to be a little Better, ask'd the Lady's Pardon for the extraordinary Trouble she had given her, and returning many Thanks for her great Care and Kindness, desired her Man might be call'd to get a Coach, which he did in a Trice, and order'd the Coachman to drive to Mr. – – – naming an eminent Merchant near *Tower Street*, at the same Time taking Leave of the Lady, and inviting her to the aforesaid Merchant's; but as soon as the Coachman had drove out of Sight, he was order'd to stop, and Madam *Jenny* pretending she could not ride easy in a Coach: Here *John*, says she, give the Coachman a Shilling, and let eim [him] go about his Business. As soon as this was done, *John* and his Mistress retreated another Way, and went clean off with the Booty; two or three Facts of this Nature put a Stop to their farther Proceedings, the Circumstances which attended the committing of, being put into the public Papers, so that they thought it safest to desist from any more Tricks of this Nature.

Some few Days after, *Jenny*'s Companion's recovering, they pursued their old Adventures with great Success; for in less than 3 Years they acquir'd above 300 Pounds a-piece, besides Expences by these illegal Practices.

About this Time the Gang agreed to go in the Country upon Business there; so they took a Progress down to *Bristol*, in the Time of the Fair, kept there in the Summer Season. Here they thought it necessary to admit a new Member, whom they found at that Place; who was esteemed a good Hand upon *The Twang Adam Cove*; that is (*could draw him in by a fine Tongue, or Way of talking those, whom they had a Design to impose upon*) him they admitted after reading the foremention'd Articles, and swearing him to Secrecy; here it was thought proper to metamorphose one of them into the Habit of a Servant in Livery. The 2 Women pass'd for Gentlewomen, Merchants Wives in *London*, and who had come down to see the Fair, and the 2 Men for Persons who came down as dealers, and in order that they might more safely accomplish their intended Designs, they lodg'd at separate Places, their Reason for so doing was, that if any of the Gang was detected, the others might appear for their Characters, as Acquaintance accidentally meeting there; they had their Lessons so perfect, that each knew one another's meaning almost by a Nod: One Day the whole Gang being in the Fair, they espy'd a West Country Clother, who had just received a Parcel of Money, to the amount of 100 Pounds, which he had given to a Servant, and order'd him to carry it to his Lodgings, and lock it up in his Bureau, and likewise gave him a Key, and bad him return in about an Hour to the Sign of the *Fountain*, a Tavern in the *High Street*. The Whole Gang upon this, follows the Fellow and jostles him in the Croud, but he was so careful of his Bag that they could not get it from him [p. 10] by this Means; so they were obliged to have recourse to the following Stratagem.

One of the Gang steps after him out of the Fair, and giving him a Tap of the Shoulder; Friend, says he, did not you part from your Master just now, and did not he order you to go Home with a Bag of Money. *Yea*, replied the Countryman, *and what then*? oh! says he, your Master has alter'd his

DRUNKS, WHORES AND IDLE APPRENTICES

Mind, and is upon the Point of Agreement for some Goods with my Mistress, and desires you will bring it, in order to pay for 'em, at the – – – naming a House where *Jenny* and the rest of the Gang were gone to. *Oh! moighte weell, moighte weell!* says the poor credulous Fellow. *I'se go wi you*; so Cheek by Jole they go along together.

In the mean Time, *I* – – –,[11] who was dressed as the supposed Lady's Servant, amused the Countryman with what a handsome rich Lady his Mistress was, and how gloriously he lived with her; and how free she always used him.

By this Time they drew towards the House where the rest of the Gang was waiting. When they came there, *Jenny*'s supposed Servant introduced the Countryman (who artfully as they pass'd along, got his Master's Name, unknown to the poor ignorant Fellow.) When they entered the Room, who is this honest Man says *Jenny*, Oh! Madam, it is Mr. *S* – – –'s Servant, come according to his Master's Orders. Oh! honest Friend says she, sit down, your Master is just gone a little Way, and will return presently, but you must stay till he comes back; *Yea, Yea, Madam*, says the Countryman, *I shall weat on your Lediship*. Come honest Friend says she, will you drink a Glass of Wine; *No Ise thank you Madam*. Come, Come, don't be bashful, you shall drink, so pouring out a Glass of Wine, he drank it off; come now you must drink another towards your Master's Health. *S'Bleed Madaum*, says the Countryman, *Ise drink that, thof 'twas a whole Mile to the Bottom*; so taking the Glass in his Hand, drank it off; now says *Jenny*, you must drink my Health, the Countryman with the two first Glasses being pretty much spiritted, chatter'd, *ads Waudds, Madam, that Ise do thof it was as deep as the Sea; an I codd* ---- and so off it goes; well done, honest Friend, says *Jenny*.

Now every Glass the poor Countryman drank, was mix'd with a certain Quantity of liquid Laudanum.

As soon as she had done this, Here *John*, says she, take this honest Fellow, and treat him handsomely till his Master comes, and then I'll send for him in again; so the poor Countryman making twenty aukward Scringes and Scrapes, goes out, and was convey'd to a more close Room convenient for the Purpose, along with his new Acquaintance.

When they had been there about half an Hour, and drank three or four Glasses of more Wine, the Countryman began to yawn, and in some small Time after, fell fast asleep. As soon as he perceived this, the Signal was given, and the Gang came in, and took the poor Fellows Bag of Money, paid the Reckoning, and ordered the Servant not to disturb the poor Man, who was weary, but let him have his Nap out. They went away, and going seperately to their Lodgings, they got their Things in Readiness, and then made the best of their Way for *London*, leaving the poor Country Fellow to curse his new Acquaintance.

They made so many Things at this Fair, that when they came to Town, and *Fenced* them, they shared Thirty Pounds a-piece, besides Expences.

By these Means, the Gang supported themselves in the most splendid Manner, sometimes living very profusely, like People of Quality; only they kept up what they term'd a common Stock, to support themselves in Case

ORDINARY OF NEWGATE'S *ACCOUNT*: MARY YOUNG

of any Disaster, which was thus raised. When any Booty was got and sold, a Tenth Part was put by, to relieve the Gang in Time of Need, and the remaining Part, was equally divided amongst them.[12]

The usual Places of *Jenny* and the Gang's Resort in *London*, when there was no extraordinary Crowd in other Places, was the *Change*, the *Bridge*,[13] &c. One Day being upon Business at the last mentioned Place about 5 o'Clock in the Evening, the Gang espy'd a Lady very well dressed, on Foot, walking over, and when she had got about half Way, a sudden Hurry of Carts and Coaches coming over at the same Instant, she stood up at the Door in order to avoid them. One of the Gang, being genteely dressed, steps up at the same Time, and says, *Have a Care, Madam*; and so standing before her, catches hold of both her Arms, that she should not be at Liberty to *Tout* the rest, and holds them up: In the mean Time [p. 10] *Jenny*, and the rest of the Gang, were very busy with her, and they was so dexterous, that before the Coaches got by, they made her Pocket, and walked off with it. As soon as the Hurry was over, the Lady dropp'd the supposed Gentleman a fine Curtsey, and humbly thank'd him for his great Care, and so took her Leave, little dreaming of her Loss; for they found in the Pocket upwards of 30 Guineas, a gold Snuff box worth 6 Guineas, and a Case of silver Instruments.

The next Day being upon Business, the Corner of *Change-Alley*, they got a Pocket-Book, in which was two hundred Pound Bank-Notes, which they sold to their old Friend *J – n*,[14] for 130*l*. ready Cash.

Jenny now took genteel Lodgings not far from *Covent Garden*; and living in a very gay Manner, kept a Servant to wait on her and her supposed Spouse. They lodged in this Place, that they might be the readier to attend the Theatre, and convey their Booties soonest off.

One Night when his Majesty was at the Play-House, the Gang dressed *Jenny* up very gay, like a Person of Quality, and going in a Chair with her Footman before her, she got a Place in the Middle of the front Boxes; but having no Opportunity to do any Thing while the Play was performing, she came out before the Entertainment was over, handed by a young Beau, whom she had pick'd up. She sounding him, found him a Country young Gentleman, lately come from *York*.

The Spark being very much enamour'd with his new Mistress, desired the Honour of conducting her Home to her Lodgings. Laird, Sir, says she, that's impossible, for I am married, and if I should let a strange Gentleman wait upon me Home, what do you think my Spouse would say? Then, Madam, quoth the Youngster, permit me the Pleasure of waiting on you to drink a Glass of Wine. Sir, says she, it is what I don't care to do, but added with a Sigh, if I thought you was a Man of Honour, I durst venture to drink a Glass of Wine, for sure there is no Harm in that, but I am told that there is so few Men of Honour, it is hard trusting. Madam, reply'd the enamoured Spark eagerly, I would sooner kill myself than hurt your Reputation. With this last Expression *Jenny* seemed to be overcome, and went with the Spark to the *Rose*, the Corner of the Theatre, and calling for a Room, he said a hundred fine Things to his new Acquaintance. After *Jenny* had drank a Glass, and sat a Quarter of an Hour, she seemed uneasy, and wanted to be

DRUNKS, WHORES AND IDLE APPRENTICES

gone; our Spark used many Intreaties for her Stay, but in vain, for she positively insisted upon going (for as yet she had not given the Gang necessary Directions upon this new Affair, so to be sure she could not stay) then the young Spark insisted upon going with her, but she begged he would not trouble himself, yet with much Intreaty on his Side, this last Request was, with some seeming Difficulty, granted.

Then he called the Drawer, and ordered a Hackney Coach to be got ready, and handed the Lady in with much Complisance. *Jenny* order'd the Coachman to drive slowly to her Lodgings, naming the Place where she lived, and as they were going Home, he pressed hard for the Pleasure of seeing her again. She told him, she expected her Husband would be out of Town in two or three Days, and in that Time he might call upon her. By this Time the Coach came to the Door, so *Jenny* requesting the Favour, that the Spark would sit still till she got out, and get himself out at some other Place for fear of her Husband, she would be glad to see him in two or three Days, and in that Time prepare for his Reception.

The young Gallant, so overjoy'd, took his Leave; so *Jenny* got out of the Coach, and going up Stairs, found the Gang come there before, for it seems the Signal was for her to stay till the Play was done, and she coming out before, they had missed her. As soon as she entered the Room they began to upbraid her, for being out of the Way, for it seems by wanting her they lost their Right Hand, for they made but one Gold Snuff-Box that Night; but she soon pacified them, by telling them her Adventure, and what she intended to do, the appointed Evening being come, in which *Jenny*'s Spark was to appear, he came dressed very gay with a gold Watch in his Pocket, a gold hilted Sword by his Side, a Diamond Ring upon his Finger, and a Gold headed Cane dangling in his Hand.

Jenny being ready to receive him, had dressed up two of the gang in rich Liveries, and *M – – –*[15] as her waiting Woman very gay, and the Lodgings being genteel, all Things seemed to look very grand.

[p. 12]The young Spark seeing this Grandeur, seemed quite amazed, and to be sure thought her some Person of Quality, as he afterwards privately told her; by and by up comes a Bottle of Wine, and some rich Sweetmeats, then the Footman was ordered to withdraw. Now Sir, says *Jenny*, you must think I have a great Respect for you, to be so free with you in this manner, I hope you are a Gentleman of more Honour than to tattle of a Lady's Favours. The young Gentleman reply'd, he would sooner cut his Tongue out; after some small Discourse, *Jenny* gave him to understand that she did not expect her Husband till very late that Evening, so the Spark begged hard, that during that Time she would make him happy in her Arms; in short, she so contriv'd Matters that she made him believe none of her Servants knew any Thing of the Affair of his Stay, except her faithful Chambermaid and Confident; so conducting him into her Bedchamber, the young Spark being eager to enjoy his Mistress, soon slipped off his Cloaths and got into Bed, she pulled hers off more slowly, pretending to be very bashful, upon which he jump'd out of Bed in order to assist her, as she was unbuckling her Shoes, she pretending to be modest, catched hold of his Hand, and seeming to admire his Ring, took it off his Finger and put it upon

ORDINARY OF NEWGATE'S *ACCOUNT*: MARY YOUNG

hers; as soon as she had got into Bed, the Signal was given from the supposed Maid, who knock'd at the Door, and told her that her Master was come Home: *Jenny* immediately jumped out of Bed, Lord! says she, what shall I do, I am inevitably ruin'd! Madam, says her Lover, what shall I do? Oh Sir! says she, I have hit it, get into Bed and cover yourself all over Head and Ears, and I'll take your Cloaths and hide 'em, least perchance he should take it into his Head to come into this Room, and in the mean Time I'll go and persuade him that I'm not well, and perhaps I can make him lie by himself to Night, which if I do than I can have the Pleasure of being with you this Evening.

The Spark immediately did as he was ordered, and *Jenny* slipp'd on her Night Gown, &c. and went out of the Room, and lock'd the Door after her, when she came into the Place where the rest of the Gang was, they held a Consultation; the result of which was, immediately to quit the Lodgings and leave poor *Pill Garlick*[16] in the Lurch, which was immediately put in Execution, and the poor unfortunate *Enamoretta* left locked up by himself, who no Doubt cursed his New Acquaintance, which for the future 'tis thought gave him a Caution how he enter'd into Intreagues of this Nature; they examined the Contents of this Booty, which amounted when the Moveables was *Fenced* to 250*l.* Now *Jenny* had the greatest Share of this Booty, because she did the most Execution; her Share coming to upwards of 50*l.*[17]

After this Robbery the Gang retired into the Country, where they carried on their Adventures very successfully for the Space of half a Year, when coming to Town they pursued their old Courses as Occasion offered.

She lay in *Newgate* almost 4 Months, and then was Transported; during the Time of her Confinement she turned *Fence*, and bought such Things as came in her Way, she having a quantity of Money by her, and knowing this Business could no ways affect her, she being Cast already; and when she went away she had as many Goods of one Sort or other, as would almost have loaded a Waggon. When she came on Board she was treated in a quite different Manner from the rest of the Transports, and was put ashore at the first Port they came to in *Virginia*. *Jenny* staid no longer there than to see the Country, for Business in her Way could not be transacted there; so after she had diverted herself as long as she thought proper, she agreed with a Gentleman for her Passage who was bound for *England*, who brought her over. When she came back, she did not chuse immediately to come to Town, but went and took a Progress round the Countries; and after she had sufficiently tired herself, and the Country People with her Exploits, she came to *London*, where she with some others used to resort about *London-Bridge*, the *Royal Exchange*, the Play-Houses, and St. *Paul's*.[18]

In *April* 1738, in the Mayorlty of Sir *John Barnard*, she was try'd by the Name of *Jane Web*, for picking the Pocket of Mrs. *Rowley*, who had been at St. *Paul's* to hear the Rehearsal; one Mr. *Addy* who detected her was offered 50*l.* not to appear against her on her Trial; but he like an honest Man refused it. At the very Time Mr. *Addy* seized her for picking the Pocket of Mrs. *Rowley*, she was going to pick the Pocket of Dr. *Best's* Lady. Another Person who appeared against her on her Trial, said he saw her pick

DRUNKS, WHORES AND IDLE APPRENTICES

20 Pockets that Day, and had known her to have been a Pickpocket these five Years; she was found guilty, and was ordered for Transportation, and accordingly was Transported, but returned again, [p. 13] and followed her old Practices, till she was detected for robbing Mrs. *Gardener* near the *Mansion-House*, on the 17th of *Jan.* last, for which Robbery she was capitally convicted, and suffered.

All the while she was under Sentence of Death, she never omitted coming the Chapel, behaving herself very devout, and seemingly very penitent for her past wicked Life. The Day before she died she sent for the Nurse that nursed her Child, (who lives in *Little-Britain*) which is about three Years of Age, and begged that she would now and then see it, and telling her the Child would be taken Care of; desiring her to give it good Advice, and instill good Notions into it, when she came capable to receive her Admonitions; which the Nurse faithfully promised to perform while she lived; on which *Jenny* reply'd, I don't doubt of your Love for my poor Child, and so God bless and protect you; Pray for my poor Soul while I am living, for I have greatly offended my good God.

The Morning she went to Execution she seem'd very composed; but when the Officer came to halter her in the *Press Yard*, she was very much shocked. She was conveyed to the Place of Execution in a Mourning Coach, attended by the Revd. Mr. *Broughton*,[19] who went and prayed to her in the Cart, after some Time allowed her for her Devotions, she went off the Stage, crying to God to have Mercy on her, Christ have Mercy on me, Lord receive my Spirit, Sweet Jesus receive my Spirit, &c. After she had hung the usual Time, she was cut down, and convey'd to *Pancrass*, in order to be interr'd in the Church-yard.

She confessed the Fact for which she died for.[20]

NOTES

1 The hanging took place in 1741.

2 The slang term 'diver' for a pickpocket predated Young by at least 150 years. 'Jenny Diver' was a part in John Gay's hugely popular play, *The Beggar's Opera* (1728). Young seems to have been the only person at that time to whom this name was applied; when, as Jane Webb, she was convicted for picking pockets in 1738, one newspaper referred to her as 'Jane Webb alias Jenny Diver': *London Daily Post, and General Advertiser*, 12 April 1738, 19 April 1738.

3 OBSP, 20 January 1741. According to another account Young and Davis both pleaded at the trial that they were pregnant ('pleaded their bellies'), which, if successful, would at least put the execution off and, in all probability, would lead to a reduction of the sentence to transportation. But the 'jury of matrons' – women impanelled to examine those who made such pleas – found them both 'Not Quick with Child', and they were condemned: *Daily Post*, 21 January 1741; *London Daily Post, and General Advertiser*, 21 January 1740–1. However, Elizabeth Davis, also known as 'Catherine the Wife of Henry Huggins', had her sentence reduced to transportation for seven years; she was transported to Virginia in January 1739: *London Evening Post*, 10–12 March 1741; P.W. Coldham, *The Complete Book of Emigrants in Bondage: 1614–1775*, Baltimore, 1988, p. 212; *Daily Gazetteer*, 21 January 1741.

ORDINARY OF NEWGATE'S *ACCOUNT*: MARY YOUNG

4 OBSP, 12–15 April 1738, trial of Jane Webb. The woman robbed was a Mrs Rowley. According to her, she was held by two men while Webb stole from her. Mr Astley, who appears to have been a law officer of some kind, said of Webb, 'I have known her for a Pick-pocket these 5 Years, and saw her pick 20 Pockets that Day. She is so well known, that I could have brought a Dozen People to have prov'd this'. Mr Addy, another prosecution witness, alleged that friends of Webb had tried to bribe him. Six people appeared for the defence to give evidence of Webb's good character: Mary Cherry, Ann Carter, Francis Fletcher, Mary Robes, John Taylor and Thomas Welch. One newspaper reported that after her arrest and as she was being taken to Newgate 'she attempted to stab the Person who apprehended her'. The same newspaper commented that 'This Webb is reckoned one of the Tip-top Hands at Picking of Pockets, and well known at Newgate by the Name of Mrs. *Murphy*; she belongs to a large Gang of Pickpockets that attend the Play-houses, &c. who declare if it costs *Two Hundred Pounds she shan't go abroad*': *London Daily Post, and General Advertiser*, 12 April 1738, 19 April 1738; *Weekly Miscellany*, 21 April 1738; *The Country Journal: or, the Craftsman*, 22 April 1738; Coldham, *The Complete Book of Emigrants*, p. 849. There is some confusion here over the person called Murphew or Murphy; Rev. Mr. Gordon, *The Life and Circumstantial Account of the Extraordinary and Surprising Exploits, Travels, Robberies and Escapes, of the famous Jenny Diver, The most noted Pickpocket of her Time, Who was executed for a Street robbery, on the 18th of March, 1740. With an Introduction Written by Herself. To which is added A Narrative of the chief Transactions of Harry Cook, And also the Gang to which he belonged. Written by the Rev. Mr. Gordon, Ordinary of Newgate*, London, n.d., has Ann Murphew, a common corruption of Murphy, as the person who introduced Young to crime, but according to newspapers (above) and the *Gentleman's Magazine*, March 1741, vol. ii, pp. 161–2, Young called herself Murphy. See also note 6 and *passim*.
5 That is, about 1714, assuming she died at the age of 36 years.
6 According to Gordon, *The Life and Circumstantial Account of . . . Jenny Diver*, p. 7, this is Ann Murphew. According to Coldham, *The Complete Book of Emigrants*, an Ann Murphy was sentenced to be transported in April 1746, although there is no record of her being sent abroad.
7 Gordon, *The Life and Circumstantial Account of . . . Jenny Diver*, p. 7, has 'Murphew'.
8 Roger Johnson: ibid., p. 10.
9 Murphew: ibid., p. 12.
10 Murphew: ibid., p. 12.
11 Johnson: ibid., p. 15.
12 Henry Fielding wrote, in 1751, of the existence of a similarly organized gang: H. Fielding, *An Enquiry into the Causes of the Late Increase of Robbers and Related Writings*, ed. M.R. Zirker, Oxford, 1988, p. 76.
13 London Bridge: Gordon, *The Life and Circumstantial Account of . . . Jenny Diver*, p. 17.
14 Johnson: ibid., p. 17.
15 Murphew: ibid., p. 19.
16 'Pill Garlick' was normally a term of sympathy applied to oneself, along the lines of 'poor me'; here it is used in the slightly less sympathetic way of 'poor fool'. It carries the implication of someone who has been left out, as here the 'Spark' is unaware what is going on.
17 '70*l*.': Gordon, *The Life and Circumstantial Account of . . . Jenny Diver*, p. 21.
18 The Gordon biography breaks here (at p. 21) and continues at p. 39: ibid.

DRUNKS, WHORES AND IDLE APPRENTICES

19 Thomas Broughton (1712–77), a methodist who became, in 1743, secretary of the Society for Promoting Christian Knowledge. He wrote *Serious Advice and Warning to Servants. More especially those of the Nobility and Gentry*, London, 1746 (6th edn, 1800) about Matthew Henderson, who was hanged for the murder of Lady Dalrymple.

20 Including Young, twenty people were ordered to be hanged on 18 March, which, even for those bloody times, was a large number. It was announced beforehand that foot and horse soldiers from General Wood's regiment would guard the procession from Newgate to Tyburn. Such precautions were not usual. There may have been a fear that Young's gang would rescue her (see *Gentleman's Magazine*, in this note), but there was also a rumour circulating about a week before that an armed attempt was to be made to rescue some Irish prisoners. This alleged plot was discovered by another condemned prisoner, Richard Quail, and, according to the Ordinary, both Young and Davis confirmed Quail's account. The truth of this story is left uncertain by the fact that Quail, who might have expected some sort of reward, was hanged along with the others: *Daily Post*, 12 March 1741, 14 March 1741, 16 March 1741, 19 March 1741; *London Daily Post, and General Advertiser*, 19 March 1740–1; *Daily Gazetteer*, 18 March 1741, 21 March 1741; *London Evening Post*, 12–14 March 1741; Ordinary of Newgate's *Account*, 18 March 1740–1, Part I, p. 17, Part II, p. 20.

Although the soldiers were almost certainly there to prevent a rescue, they may have had another, incidental function, to protect the prisoners, or some of them, from the crowd: the Ordinary, having described the escort of soldiers, continued: 'In this Manner were they convey'd through a vast Multitude of People to *Tyburn*, some of whom, notwithstanding the Guard of Soldiers, were very rude and noisy, hallooing, throwing Brickbats, Mud, &c. at the unhappy Prisoners, as they passed' (Ordinary of Newgate's *Account*, 18 March 1740–1, Part II, p. 17). However, such behaviour may have been directed, not at the prisoners, but at the soldiers, or at the other members of the crowd: B. Mandeville, *An Enquiry into the Causes of the Frequent Executions at Tyburn*, London, 1725. The *Gentleman's Magazine*, March 1741, vol. ii, pp. 161–2, reported the hanging day: '*Mary Young* went to *Tyburn* in a Mourning Coach, veil'd, and strongly guarded, there being a Design form'd to rescue her. . . . She appeared gaily dressed even to the last, yet deeply affected with her approaching Fate. Her Concern was so sensibly expressed, when she took Leave of her little Child, a few Days before her Execution, that (a weekly Writer says) it drew Tears into the Eyes of the Turnkey. *So far does Affliction with a genteel Behaviour and Dress move Compassion beyond what is shewn to the Generality of Objects seen there; at least it was another sort of Compassion. We are more nearly concerned for Persons under these terrible Circumstances when they are at last sensible of their Crimes and wish they had acted a more rational and honest Part. Whereas there is some Difficulty in pitying those abandoned Wretches, who do not pity themselves; tho' it might be juster to say, that we cannot sympathize with them – we must pity them.*

[18]

THE HUSTLER*

NED POLSKY
New York City

"Such and such a man spends all his life playing every day for a small stake. Give him every morning the money that he may gain during the day, on condition that he does not play—you will make him unhappy. It will perhaps be said that what he seeks is the amusement of play, not gain. Let him play then for nothing; he will lose interest and be wearied."—*Blaise Pascal*

"They talk about me not being on the legitimate. Why, lady, nobody's on the legit when it comes down to cases; you know that."—*Al Capone*[1]

The poolroom hustler makes his living, or tries to do so, by betting his opponents in various types of pool or billiard games; and as part of the playing and betting process he engages in various deceitful practices. The terms "hustler" for such a person and "hustling" for his occupation have been in poolroom argot for decades, antedating their application to prostitutes. Usually the hustler plays with his own money, but often he makes use of a "backer." In the latter event the standard arrangement is that the backer, in return for assuming all risk of loss, receives half of the hustler's winnings.

As a necessary and regular part of their work, hustlers break certain of America's generally agreed-upon moral rules, and because of this they are stigmatized by respectable outsiders. More knowledgeable outsiders see the hustler as one who violates an ethic of fair dealing, as a quasi-criminal who systematically "victimizes" people. Less knowledgeable outsiders (the large majority of outsiders) regard hustlers as persons who, whatever they may actually do, certainly do not hold down respectable jobs; therefore this group

also stigmatizes hustlers—"poolroom bums" is the classic phrase—and believes that society would be better off without the hustler. Hustling, to the degree that it is known to the larger society at all, is classed with that large group of social problems composed of morally deviant occupations.

However, in what follows I try to present hustlers and hustling on their own terms. Insofar as I treat of problems they are not the problems posed by the hustler but for him; not the difficulties he creates for others, but the difficulties that others create for him.

My approach is basically that of Everett Hughes to occupational sociology. In this paper I deal chiefly with questions about the work situation: How is the hustler's work structured? What skills are required of him? Whom does he interact with on the job? What does he want from them, and how does he try to get it? How do they make it easy or hard for him?

PREVIOUS RESEARCH

A bibliographic check reveals no decent research on poolroom hustling, sociological or otherwise. Apart from an occasional work of fiction in which hustling figures, there are merely a few impressionistic accounts in newspapers and popular magazines. With a couple of exceptions, each article is based on interviews with only one or two hustlers. No article analyzes hustling on any but the most superficial level, or even provides a well-rounded

* This the first third of a larger study, which will appear in complete form in Ned Polsky, *Hustlers, Beats, and Other Reflections on Our Time*, Chicago: Aldine Publishing Company, forthcoming. For criticism of an earlier draft I am indebted to Howard Becker and Erving Goffman.
[1] The Pascal quotation is from *Pensées*, V. Al Capone's remark is quoted in Paul Sann, *The Lawless Decade*, New York: Crown Publishers, 1957, p. 214.

4 SOCIAL PROBLEMS

description of hustling. The fullest survey of the subject not only omits much that is vital, but contains numerous errors of fact and of interpretation.[2]

The desirability of a study of hustling first struck me upon hearing comments of people who saw the movie *The Hustler* (1961, re-released spring 1964). Audience members who are not poolroom habitués regard the movie as an accurate portrait of the contemporary hustling "scene." Now, the movie does indeed truly depict some social characteristics of pool and billiard hustlers and some basic techniques of hustling. But it neglects others of crucial importance. Moreover, the movie scarcely begins to take proper account of the social structure within which hustling techniques are used and which radically affects their use. *The Hustler* is a reasonably good but highly selective index of the poolroom hustling scene as it existed not later than 30 years ago. And as a guide to today's hustling scene—the terms on which it presents itself and on which the audience takes it—the movie is quite misleading.

―――――――

[2] The compendium of misinformation and cockeyed interpretation is Jack Olsen's "The Pool Hustlers," *Sports Illustrated*, 14 (March 20, 1961), pp. 71-77. Jack Richardson's "The Noblest Hustlers," *Esquire*, IX (September, 1963), pp. 94, 96, 98, contains a few worthwhile observations; but it is sketchy, ill-balanced, and suffers from editorial garbling—all of which make it both confusing and misleading for the uninitiated. One article conveys quite well the lifestyle of a particular hustler: Dale Shaw, "Anatomy of a Pool Hustler," *Saga: The Magazine for Men*, 23 (November, 1961), pp. 52-55, 91-93. Useful historical data are in Edward John Vogeler's "The Passing of the Pool Shark," *American Mercury*, 48 (November, 1939), pp. 346-351. For hustling as viewed within the context of the history of pool in America, see Robert Coughlan's "Pool: Its Players and Its Sharks," *Life*, 31 (October 8, 1951), pp. 159 ff.; though Coughlan's account of the game's history contains errors and his specific consideration of hustling is brief (p. 166), the latter is accurate.

METHOD AND SAMPLE

My study of poolroom hustling extended over eight months. It proceeded by a combination of: (a) direct observation of hustlers as they hustled; (b) informal talks, sometimes hours long, with hustlers; (c) participant observation—as hustler's opponent, as hustler's backer, and as hustler. Since methods (b) and (c) drew heavily on my personal involvement with the poolroom world, indeed are inseparable from it, I summarize aspects of that involvement below.

Billiard playing is my chief recreation. I have frequented poolrooms for over 20 years, and at one poolroom game, three-cushion billiards, am considered a far better than average player. In recent years I have played an average of more than six hours per week in various New York poolrooms, and played as much in the poolrooms of Chicago for most of the eight years I lived there. In the course of traveling I have played occasionally in the major rooms of other cities, such as the poolrooms on Market Street in San Francisco, on West 25th Street in Cleveland, and the room on 4th and Main in Los Angeles.

My social background is different from that of the overwhelming majority of adult poolroom players. The latter are of lower-class origin. As with many American sports (e.g., baseball), pool and billiards are played by teenagers from all classes but only the players of lower-class background tend to continue far into adulthood. (And as far as poolroom games are concerned, even at the teenage level the lower class contributes a disproportionately large share of players.) But such differences—the fact that I went to college, do highbrow work, etc.—create no problems of acceptance. In most good-sized poolrooms the adult regulars usually include a few people like myself who are in the poolroom world but not of it. They are there because they like to play, and are readily accepted because they like to play.

The poolroom I play in most regularly is the principal "action room" in New York and probably in the country, the room in which heavy betting on games occurs most often; sometimes, particularly after 1:00 A.M., the hustlers in the room well outnumber the non-hustlers. Frequently I play hustlers for money (nearly always on a handicap basis) and occasionally I hustle some non-hustlers, undertaking the latter activity primarily to recoup losses on the former. I have been a backer for two hustlers.

I know six hustlers well and during the eight months of the study I talked or played with over 50 more. All are now usually based in New York, except for two in Chicago, two in Cleveland, one in Philadelphia, one itinerant hustler whose home base is Boston and another whose home base is in North Carolina. However, the hustlers based in New York are of diverse regional origins; almost a third grew up in other states and started their hustling careers in other states.

It is not possible to demonstrate the representativeness of this sample because the universe (all U.S. pool and billiard hustlers) is not known exactly. But the hustlers I asked about the number of real hustlers in America, i.e., the number of people whose exclusive or primary occupation is hustling, generally agree that today the number is quite small. In response to my queries about the total number of poolroom hustlers, one hustler said "thousands" and another said "there must be a thousand," but the next highest estimate was "maybe 400" and somewhat lesser estimates were made by 19 hustlers. Moreover, the three hustlers making the highest estimates have rarely been out of New York, whereas over half the others either come from other parts of the country or have made several road trips. It

seems safe to assume that the sample is at least representative of big-city hustlers. Also, it is highly probable that it includes the majority of part-time hustlers in New York, and certain that it includes a good majority of the full-time hustlers in New York.

POOLROOM BETTING: THE STRUCTURE OF "ACTION"

Hustling involves betting one's opponent, by definition. But the converse is not true. The majority of poolroom games on which opponents bet do not involve any element of hustling. In order to understand how hustling enters the picture, one must first establish a perspective that encompasses all betting on poolroom games, hustled or not.

In pool or billiard games, the betting relationship has three possible modes: (1) player bets against player; (2) player(s) against spectator(s); (3) spectator(s) against spectator(s). In most games only the first mode occurs, but combinations of the first and second are frequent, and slightly less so are combinations of the first and third. Combinations of all three are uncommon, but do occur when there is more "ready action" offered to the player(s) by the spectator(s) than the player(s) can, or wish(es) to, absorb. I have never seen the second mode occur alone, nor a combination of second and third. I have seen the third mode occur alone only twice—at professional tournaments. The betting relationship, then, involves the mode player-vs.-player, whatever additional modes there may be.

If two mediocre players are betting, say, upwards of $15 per game, and at another table two excellent players are playing for only a token amount, the first table will invariably draw many more people around it. The great majority of spectators, whether or not they bet much and whatever their own degree of playing skill, are attracted more by the size of the action than the quality of the performance. (A visiting Danish billiardist tells me this is not so in Europe, and also that betting on poolroom games is far less frequent than in America.)

There is an old American poolroom tradition that players should make some kind of bet with each other, if only a small one. This tradition remains strong in every public poolroom I know. (It is weak in the pool or billiard rooms of private men's clubs and YMCAs, weaker still in student unions, and virtually nonexistent in faculty clubs.) When one player says to another, "Let's just play sociable," as often as not he means that they should play for only a dollar or two, and at the very least means that they should play "for the time" (the loser paying the check). It is only some of the newer and least skilled players who refuse to bet at all (want to "split the time"), and nearly always they rapidly become socialized to the betting tradition by a carrot-and-stick process— the stick being that it is often hard to get a game otherwise, the carrot that better players are always willing to give poorer ones a handicap (a "spot"). Most of the regular players will not even play for the check only, but insist on a little money changing hands "just to make the game interesting." The player who claims that just playing the game is interesting enough in itself is regarded as something of a freak.

Although few serious bettors (hustlers excepted) care for big action, nearly all (including hustlers) want fast action. They may not want to bet much per game, but they want the cash to change hands fairly quickly. Consequently, in an action room the standard games are redesigned for this purpose. Some are simply shortened: players gambling at snooker will re-move all the red balls but one; or three-cushion billiard players will play games of 15, 20, or 25 points instead of the usual 30, 40, or 50. In straight pool (pocket billiards), where the standard game is 125 or 150 points, good players are usually reluctant to play a much shorter game because scoring is so easy—any good player can occasionally run more than 50 points—that shortening the game makes it too much a matter of chance. Therefore, in an action room one finds most of the pool players playing some variant of the game that requires high skill and minimizes luck, and that therefore can be short (take only 5 to 20 minutes per game). Today the chief of these variants are "nine ball" and "one pocket" (also called "pocket apiece").

Every poolroom has at least one "No Gambling" sign on display, but no poolroom enforces it. The sign is merely a formal gesture for the eyes of the law (and in some cities required by law). It is enforced only in that the proprietor sometimes may ask players to keep payoffs out of sight— not to toss the money on the table after the game—if the room is currently heaty, e.g., if an arrest has recently been made there. Police are never really concerned to stop the gambling on poolroom games, and everyone knows it. (But police sometimes check to see that the minimum age law is observed, so proprietors will often ask youths for identification.) Betting is so taken for granted that in most poolrooms the proprietor —the very man who displays a "No Gambling" sign over his desk—will on request hold the players' stake money.

However, in no poolroom does the house take a cut of the action; i.e., the proprietor gets no fee for permitting gambling or holding stake money, and wouldn't dream of asking for one. His payment from bettors is simply that they comprise most of his custom (in equipment rental).[8] And hustlers, as he and they well know, count in this regard far beyond their numbers, for they play much oftener and longer than other customers; indeed, they virtually live in the poolroom.

NON-HUSTLED POOLROOM GAMBLING

Hustling is *not* involved when the games played for money are any of the following:

(a) *Non-hustler vs. non-hustler.* A "sociable" game in which the bet is a token one. The only betting is player vs. player.

(b) *Non-hustler vs. non-hustler.* A game for significantly more than a token amount. The players play even-up if they are fairly equal. If they are aware of a significant difference in skill levels, the weaker player is given an appropriate handicap. Usually the betting is just between players; rarely, one or both players will bet spectators; spectators do not bet each other.

(c) *Hustler vs. non-hustler.* The players are aware of the difference in skills, and this is properly taken into account via an appropriate spot. Usually the betting is only player vs. player, though sometimes spectators bet players or each other. The hustler tries to avoid this type of game, and agrees to it only when he has nothing better to do.

(d) *Hustler vs. hustler.* Each player knows the other's mettle, if only by reputation ("Minnesota Fats" vs. "Fast Eddy" in *The Hustler,* for example). The hustler, contrary to the impression given by the movie, does *not* prefer this type of game (though he does prefer it to the foregoing type) and does *not* regard it as hustling. But he plays it often because he often can't get the kind of game he wants (a true "hustle") and this alternative does offer him excitement—not only the greatest challenge to his playing skill, but the most action. The average bet between two hustlers is much higher than in any other type of poolroom contest.[4] And the betting modes 2 and 3 (player vs. spectator, spectator vs. spectator) occur much more often.

Be that as it may, the hustler much prefers to hustle, which means to be in a game set up so as to be pretty much a sure thing for him, a game that "you're not allowed to lose" as the hustler puts it. In order to achieve this, to truly hustle, he engages in deception. The centrality of deception in pool or billiard hustling is perhaps best indicated by the fact that the poolroom hustlers' argot originated that widespread American slang dictum, "never give a sucker an even break."[5]

THE HUSTLER'S METHODS OF DECEPTION

The structure of a gambling game determines what methods of deception, if any, may be used in it. In many games (dice, cards, etc.) one can deceive one's opponent by various techniques of cheating. Pool and billiard games, though, are so structured

---

[8] The only non-bettor whose payment is somewhat related to the size of the action is the rack boy (if one is used), the person who racks up the balls for the players after each frame. The bigger the action, the larger the tip he can expect; and if one player comes out very much ahead he tips the rack boy lavishly. The rack boy's position is thus analogous to that of the golf caddie, except that a rack boy is used in only about half of hustler-vs.-hustler contests and in but a tiny fraction of other contests. Sometimes he is an employee (sweeper, etc.) of the poolroom, but more often is a spectator performing as rack boy on an *ad hoc* basis.

[4] When two high-betting hustlers agree to play each other there is often a real race among poorer spectators to offer rack-boy services because, as previously indicated, if one is engaged for such a session he can expect a good tip. I witnessed one six-hour session between hustlers in which the winning hustler came out $800 ahead and tipped the rack boy $50.

that this method is virtually impossible. (Once in a great while, against a particularly unalert opponent, one can surreptitiously add a point or two to one's score—but such opportunity is rare, usually involves risk of discovery that is judged to be too great, and seldom means the difference between winning and losing anyway; so no player counts on it.) One's every move and play is completely visible, easily watched by one's opponent and by spectators; nor is it possible to achieve anything via previous tampering with the equipment.

However, one structural feature of pool or billiards readily lends itself to deceit: on each shot, the difference between success and failure is a matter of a fraction of an inch. In pool or billiards it is peculiarly easy, even for the average player, to miss one's shot deliberately and still look good (unlike, say, nearly all card games, where if one does not play one's cards correctly this is soon apparent). On all shots except the very easiest ones, it is impossible to tell if a player is deliberately not trying his best.

The hustler exploits this fact, so as to deceive his opponent as to his (the hustler's) true level of skill (true "speed"). It is so easily exploited that, when playing good opponents, usually the better hustlers even disdain it, pocket nearly every shot they have (intentionally miss only some very difficult shots), and rely chiefly on related but subtler techniques of failure beyond the remotest suspicion of most players. For example, such a hustler may strike his cue ball hard and with too much spin ("english"), so that the spin is transferred to the object ball and the object ball goes into the pocket but jumps out again; or he may scratch (losing a point and his turn), either by "accidentally" caroming his cue ball into a pocket or by hitting his cue ball hard and with too much top-spin so that it jumps off the table; or, most commonly, he pockets his shot but, by striking his cue ball just a wee bit too hard or too softly or with too much spin, he leaves himself "safe" (ends up with his cue ball out of position, so that he hasn't another shot). In such wise the hustler feigns less competence than he has.

Hustling, then, involves not merely the ability to play well, but the use of a kind of "short con." Sometimes the hustler doesn't need to employ any con to get his opponent to the table, sometimes he does; but he always employs it in attempting to keep his opponent there.

The best hustler is not necessarily the best player among the hustlers. He has to be a very good player, true, but beyond a certain point his playing ability is not nearly so important as his skill at various kinds of conning. Also, he has to possess personality traits that make him "rocklike," able to exploit fully his various skills—playing, conning, other—in the face of assorted pressures and temptations not to exploit them fully.

The Hustler's Cardinal Rule

As the foregoing indicates, the hust-

---

[5] Its pool-hustler origin is noted by Vogeler (*op. cit.*, p. 347), a reliable observer. It is recorded in none of the slang sourcebooks (Mencken, Mathews, Berrey and Van den Bark, *et al.*) except Harold Wentworth and Stuart Berg Flexner's *Dictionary of American Slang* (New York: T. Y. Crowell, 1960), p. 527. Wentworth and Flexner do not attempt to account for the phrase's origin. They claim that it dates to *ca.* 1835, but this seems impossibly early. The only source they cite is its use as the title of a 1941 W. C. Fields movie. Actually, Fields used the phrase earlier in his *Poppy* (1936), where it is his exit line and the last line of the movie. Fields' partiality to the phrase is quite in keeping with Vogeler's account of its origin, as Fields spent much of his boyhood in his father's poolroom, was an excellent player, and built his funniest vaudeville act around his pool-playing skill (at the act's climax he sank 15 balls with one shot). Cf. Douglas Gilbert, *American Vaudeville* (New York: Whittlesey House, 1940), pp. 273-274.

ler's cardinal rule is: *don't show your real speed.* Of course, an exception is permitted if by some miracle the hustler finds himself hustled, finds himself in a game with someone he thought would be easy but who turns out to be tough. But this is not supposed to happen, and it rarely does. For one thing, hustlers generally know each other, or of each other, and their respective skill levels. Secondly, any type of pool or billiard game is overwhelmingly a game of skill rather than luck—even in the chanciest type of poolroom game the element of skill counts for much more than in any card game whatsoever—and this means it is possible to rate the skill levels of various players (to "handicap" them) along small gradations with a high degree of accuracy. For example, if one has seen the three-cushion billiard players X and Y play various people over a period of time, it is possible to arrive at the judgment "On a 30-point game, X is 2 or 3 points better than Y" and to be dead right about it in at least 8 out of 10 contests between them.

The corollaries of the hustler's chief rule are: (a) The hustler must restrain himself from making many of the extremely difficult shots. Such restraint is not easy, because the thrill of making a fancy shot that brings applause from the audience is hard to resist. But the hustler must resist, or else it would make less believable his misses on more ordinary shots. (b) He must play so that the games he wins are won by only a small margin. (c) He must let his opponent win an occasional game.

It may be thought that once a hustler has engaged an opponent, a bet has been agreed upon and the stake money put up, and the game has started, the hustler might safely let out all the stops. This would be terribly short-sighted.

In the first place, as noted earlier, the typical non-hustler bets only a small amount on the game. The hustler's only hope of making real money,

therefore, is to extend the first game into a series of games, entice his opponent into doubling up when he is behind, etc. If the hustler does this well, the opponent will hang on for a long time, may even come back after the first session to play him on another day, turn into a real "fish" (the poolroom term for an inferior opponent who doesn't catch on that he's outclassed, and keeps coming back for more). And when the opponent starts demanding a spot, as sooner or later he will, the hustler can offer him his (the hustler's) average winning margin, or even a little better, and still have a safe game.

Secondly, there are spectators to take into account. Some of them will bet the hustler if he offers the non-hustler a seemingly fair spot. More importantly, some of them are potential opponents. Nearly all poolroom spectators are also players (except for the inevitable contingent of poor and lonely old men, who use the poolroom as a poor man's club). The hustler doesn't want to look too good to spectators either.

He knows that as he beats various opponents his reputation will rise, and that increasingly he'll have to offer spots to people, but he wants to keep his reputation as low as possible as long as possible with as many people as possible. He also knows that he has to play superbly on occasion—that he will play fellow hustlers when there's no other action around, and that then he must show more skill—but he wants to keep these occasions few. (It helps considerably, by the way, that because hustler-vs.-hustler games occur when hustlers give up hope of finding other action, these games usually take place after midnight when there aren't so many non-hustler potential victims around to watch.)

The sooner everyone in the poolroom knows the hustler's true speed, the sooner he exhausts the real hustling possibilities among the room's regular players. Then, either he must move on to a room where he's less known or, if he stays in the room, has to take games he shouldn't take or else restrict his pickings to strangers who wander in.

JOB-RELATED SKILLS AND TRAITS

Although the hallmarks of the good hustler are playing skill and the temperamental ability to consistently look poorer than he is, there are other skills and traits that aid him in hustling. Some are related to deceiving his opponent, some not.

Chief of these is argumentative skill in arranging the terms of the match, the ability to "make a game." The prospective opponent, if he has seen the hustler play, may when approached claim that the hustler is too good for him, or ask for too high a spot, i.e., one that is fair or even better than that. The hustler, just like the salesman, is supposed to be familiar with standard objections and with ways of overcoming them.

Another side of the ability to make a game reveals itself when the prospective opponent simply can't be argued out of demanding a spot that is unfair to the hustler, or can be convinced to play only if the hustler offers such a spot. At that point the hustler should of course refuse to play. There is often a temptation to do otherwise, not only because the hustler is proud of his skill but because action is his lifeblood (which is why he plays other hustlers when he can't find a hustle), and there may be no other action around. He must resist the temptation. In the good hustler's view, no matter how badly you want action, it is better not to play at all than to play when you are disadvantaged; otherwise you are just hustling yourself. (But the hustler often will, albeit with the greatest reluctance, agree to give a fair spot if that's the only way he can get action.)

The hustler, when faced, as he very often is, with an opponent who knows him as such, of course finds that his ability to make a game assumes greater importance than his ability to feign lack of skill. In such situations, indeed, his game-making ability is just as important as his actual playing ability.

On the other hand, the hustler must have "heart" (courage). The *sine qua non* is that he is a good "money player," can play his best when heavy action is riding on the game (as many non-hustlers can't). Also, he is not supposed to let a bad break or distractions in the audience upset him. (He may pretend to get rattled on such occasions, but that's just part of his con.) Nor should the quality of his game deteriorate when, whether by miscalculation on his part or otherwise, he finds himself much further behind than he would like to be. Finally, if it is necessary to get action, he should not be afraid to tackle an opponent whom he knows to be just about as good as he is.

A trait often working for the hustler is stamina. As a result of thousands of hours of play, all the right muscles are toughened up. He is used to playing many hours at a time, certainly much more used to it than the non-hustler is. This is valuable because sometimes, if the hustler works it right, he can make his opponent forget about quitting for such a "silly" reason as being tired, can extend their session through the night and into the next day. In such sessions it is most often in the last couple of hours, when the betting per game is usually highest, that the hustler makes his biggest killing.

Additional short-con techniques are sometimes used. One hustler, for example, entices opponents by the ancient device of pretending to be sloppy-drunk. Other techniques show more imagination. For example, a hustler preparing for a road trip mentioned to me that before leaving town he was going to buy a soldier's uniform: "I walk into a strange room in uniform and I've got it made. Everybody likes to grab a soldier."

Finally, the hustler—the superior hustler at any rate—has enough flexibility and good sense to break the "rules" when the occasion demands it, will modify standard techniques when he encounters non-standard situations. An example: Once I entered a poolroom just as a hustler I know, X, was finishing a game with non-hustler Y. X beat Y soundly, by a higher margin than a hustler should beat anyone, and at that for only $3. Y went to the bathroom, whereupon I admonished X, "What's the matter with you? You know you're not allowed to win that big." X replied: "Yeah, sure, but you see that motherfucking S . . . over there? [nodding discreetly in the direction of one of the spectators]. Well, about an hour ago when I came in he and Y were talking, and when S . . . saw me he whispered something to Y. So I had a hunch he was giving him the wire [tipping him off] that I was pretty good. And then in his middle game it looked like Y was stalling a little [missing deliberately] to see what I would do, so then I was sure he got the wire on me. I had to beat him big so he'll think he knows my top speed. But naturally I didn't beat him as big as I *could* beat him. Now he'll come back cryin' for a spot and bigger action, and I'll nail him." And he did nail him.[6]

THE ART OF DUMPING

As we saw, the structure of a pool or billiard game makes it virtually im-

possible for the hustler to cheat his opponent. By "stalling" (deliberately missing some shots, leaving himself out of position, etc.) and by "lemoning" or "lemonading" an occasional game in the session (winning in a deliberately sloppy and seemingly lucky manner, or deliberately losing the game), the hustler keeps his opponent on the hook and entices him into heavier action, but such deception falls short of outright cheating. However, in examining betting we saw that there is considerable variation in the interpersonal superstructure of the game, i.e., that there are several possible types of betting relationships between and among players and spectators. One of these varieties does lead to outright cheating by the hustler—not cheating of his opponent, but cheating some spectators.

When two hustlers play each other, not only is the betting between players relatively heavy, but the betting of spectators against players is also, typically, at its height. Therefore, two hustlers sometimes will agree before their session that if, on any game, there is a good disparity between the amounts of action that each gets from spectators, the player with the most to gain from side bets with spectators will win the game and the players will later share the profits. The amount that spectators bet each other is of course irrelevant to such calculations; and in such circumstances the amount that the players bet each other automatically becomes a phony bet, strictly for deluding the spectators.

For example, one such game I know of went as follows: Hustler A played hustler B for $70. A's side bets with spectators totaled $100 and B's side bets with spectators totaled $380. Therefore A deliberately lost to B, paying him $70 and paying $100 to spectators, with B collecting $70 from A and $380 from spectators. Later, in private B gave A $310 (the $70 that A had "lost" to B, the $100 that A had paid to the audience, plus $140 or one-half

---

[6] This sort of situation is unusual. One part of the poolroom code, adhered to by virtually all regular players, holds that a player is supposed to watch out for himself in the matches he gets into, find out for himself whom he can and cannot beat. Ordinarily one does not warn a player about who is superior or who the hustlers are, unless one is a close friend of that player. (And even if one is a friend, the code demands that such warning be given only before any match is in prospect; that is, once a player has started to "make a game" with another, third parties are supposed to stay out.)

the overall amount won from the audience). Each player thus made $140 on the deal.

Sometimes the hustlers will set up the audience for such disparity in side betting, via previous games in the session. An example: Hustler X played hustler Y for $20 per game. By pre-arrangement, both players refused to make side bets with spectators on the first three games and player Y deliberately lost the first three games. At the end of the third game Y became enraged, claiming that bad breaks had beat him, that X was just lucky, etc.; he raised his bet with X to $50 and also offered to bet spectators. Naturally, he got lots of action from spectators —and just as naturally he won the fourth game.

More commonly, however, such setting up does not occur. Rather, the hustlers will agree before their session that they will play each other in earnest and the bets between them will be real, but that if there is a disparity in side betting with spectators on a given game and one player gives the other a prearranged signal (gives him "the office" as the hustler's argot has it), the player with the most side action will win.

In the hustler's argot, the above type of deliberate losing is called "dumping." It is always distinguished from "lemoning" (where deliberate losing is strictly a means of conning one's nonhustler opposing player). Though all hustlers use the verb "to dump" in referring to a game that the hustler deliberately loses for the purpose of cheating spectators, hustlers vary in the object they attach to the verb. Some hustlers would say that the hustler who lost "dumped the game," others that he "dumped to" his opponent, and others that he (or both players in collaboration) "dumped the bettors." Some hustlers on occasion prefer a nominal use: "the game was a dump."

Because dumping involves outright cheating and could lead to serious, indeed violent, reprisals if discovered, it is the aspect of hustling that hustlers are most evasive about. A profession not merely has "open secrets" which only novices and outsiders don't know about, but, as Erving Goffman noted, also has "strategic secrets" which professionals often talk about among themselves but try to keep from outsiders, and "dark secrets" which professionals not only try to keep from outsiders but seldom talk about even with each other. Dumping falls in the "dark secret" category. No hustler likes to own up to dumping, even in talk with other hustlers. One learns about dumping indirectly, via hustlers' comments on other hustlers, hardly ever via a hustler's direct admission that he has engaged in it. It is my impression that such reticence is always pragmatic rather than moral, i.e., that no hustler has strong compunctions about dumping and that every long-time hustler has dumped at least on occasion.

Although dumping is a possibility whenever two hustlers playing each other make unequal amounts of side bets with spectators,[7] it actually occurs in only a minority of such situations, perhaps a sixth of them. For dumping is risky even when it is not literally discovered, i.e., sometimes the spectators' suspicions are aroused even though nothing can be proven; and hustlers can't afford to have this happen often, because it would kill their chances of side betting.

In this regard there are two kinds of spectator-bettors that the hustler distinguishes and takes account of: First, there are the ignorant majority of spectators who don't know about dumping; the hustler doesn't want talk, much less actual knowledge, of dumping to reach their ears. Second—and equally important to the hustler because, though they are in the minority,

---

[7] Under certain special circumstances dumping can also occur when there are no bets with spectators or such bets are approximately equal on both sides. See below.

they bet more—there are some knowledgeable spectators (including other hustlers) who know about dumping but *also* know that it occurs in only a minority of hustler-vs.-hustler contests and therefore will often risk a bet. That is to say, just as some horse players assume that at certain tracks there probably will be one race per day that is fixed (one race "for the boys") and are willing to discount this because it's only one race out of eight or nine, similarly there are poolroom spectators who will bet on one hustler against another because they know that dumping occurs but seldom. (Among the knowledgeable spectators there are also, of course, some cautious types who refuse to make such bets because of a possible dump, even though they know the odds are against it.)

In sum, the fact that spectators will bet players in hustler-vs.-hustler games not only permits dumping but at the same time restrains the extent of it. Hustlers must severely limit their dumping, both to prevent it becoming known to the ignorant and, just as importantly, to prevent knowledgeable spectators from feeling that hustlers *generally* dump when they play each other. No hustler wants to get a reputation as a dumper; therefore he cautiously picks his spots. As a result, dumping provides only a small portion of his true hustling income, i.e., his "sure-thing" income. The great bulk of such income derives from his games with non-hustler opponents.

THE HUSTLER AND HIS BACKER

The hustler frequently uses a backer, who pays the losses if the hustler loses and receives 50% of any winnings. Contrary to the movie *The Hustler,* a backer hardly ever assumes any managerial function. All he does is put up the hustler's stake money in return for a half share in the profits.

Once in a very great while, a hustler will work out a standing agreement for backing, i.e., have someone agree to back him regularly. There is no time limit specified for such an arrangement; the deal lasts only as long as both parties consent to it.

But almost always—again contrary to the movie—the hustler has no standing agreement with a backer. Rather, he looks for backing on an *ad hoc* basis as the occasion for backing arises. The "occasion" is not that the hustler decides, in the abstract, to play on someone else's risk capital; it is a specific match with a particular opponent, whose handicap terms (if any) the hustler has already arranged or knows he can get. Indeed, even a top-notch hustler rarely can get backing without being able to tell the backer who the prospective opponent is and what the terms of the game are; the hustler has to convince the backer that the particular deal is a good one.

After tentatively arranging a game with his opponent, the hustler asks one of his acquaintances in the room to back him, and if he can't find backing in the room he phones a potential backer to hurry on down with some cash. Sometimes the hustler enters the poolroom with his backer in tow.

The backer specifies the maximum amount per game that he is willing to invest, but makes no guarantee about a total investment. That is, if the hustler starts to lose, the backer can pull out after any game. And if the hustler starts winning, he cannot then bet only his "own" money and dispense with the backer; the backer is in for 50% of the profit made on the entire session.

Under what conditions does the hustler seek a backer? The obvious answer is that when the hustler is broke or nearly broke (as he very often is), he looks for backing, and when he has his own money to invest he plays with that. This is indeed how the average hustler operates. The superior hustler, however, figures more angles than that. As one of the most intelligent hustlers explained to me: "If you've got lockup action [a game impossible to lose] and you're broke or maybe you need a bigger stake, you should first try like hell to *borrow* the dough. It's crazy to cut somebody in on action like that unless you have to. The other big thing—what some of these jerks don't understand—is that when you have a real tough game you should *always* look for a backer, even if you've got the dough. You should take out insurance."

The backer, then, should not assume he is being approached for backing because the hustler can raise stake money no other way (though this is usually the case), but has to consider the possibility that it's because the hustler has a very difficult game he wants to "insure."

Also, the backer must consider the possibility that he may be dumped by the hustler: If the hustler is playing a colleague, they may have agreed that one of them will win the good majority of games and that they will later split the profits. (When both hustlers making such an agreement are using backers, the decision as to which hustler will lose is more or less arbitrary. If one hustler is using a backer and the other is not, it is of course the former who agrees to lose.) Or, if the hustler is playing a non-hustler with whom no such collusion is possible, he may deliberately lose on the backer's money until the backer quits, and then, after the backer has left the room or on some other occasion, the hustler, playing with his own money, will slaughter the opponent he has set up on the backer's money.

All in all, it takes as much sophistication to be a good backer as to be a good hustler.

THE HUSTLER AS CON MAN

As several parts of this study illustrate in detail, hustling demands a continuous and complicated concern with how one is seen by others. Attention to this matter is an ineluctably pervasive requirement of the hustler's trade, and is beset with risks and contradictions. The hustler has not only the concerns that one ordinarily has about being esteemed for one's skills, but develops, in addition to and partly in conflict with such concerns, a complex set of special needs or desires about how others should evaluate him, reactions to their evaluations, and behaviors designed to manipulate such evaluating.

The hustler is a certain kind of con man. And conning, by definition, involves extraordinary manipulation of other people's impressions of reality and especially of one's self, creating "false impressions."[8] Now, if one compares the hustler with the more usual sorts of con men described by David Maurer in *The Big Con*, part of the hustler's specialness is seen to lie in this: the structural contexts within which he operates—the game, the setting of the game within the poolroom, the setting of the poolroom within the larger social structure—are not only more predetermined but more constraining. Structures do not "work for" the poolroom hustler to anywhere near the extent that they often do for other con men, and hence he must involve himself in more personal ways with active, continuous conning.

The point is not simply that the hustler can't find an ideal structural context, but that much less than the ordinary con man is he able to bend a structure toward the ideal or create one *ab ovo* (come up with an analogue

---

[8] Of course conning is only a matter of degree, in that all of us are concerned in many ways to manipulate others' impressions of us; and so one can, if one wishes, take the view that every man is at bottom a con man. This form of "disenchantment of the world" is central to Herman Melville's *The Confidence Man* (perhaps the bitterest novel in all of American literature) and to the sociological writings of Erving Goffman. Its principal corollary is the view expressed by hustlers, by professional criminals, and by Thorstein Veblen, that all businessmen are thieves.

of the con man's "store"). That is, the hustler is far less able to be a "producer" or "director" of ideal social "scenes." To a much greater degree he must work in poor settings, and to a correspondingly greater degree he must depend on being a continuously self-aware "actor."[9] (In this connection, note the ease with which many passages of this essay could be restated in dramaturgical or Goffmaniacal terms.)

The nature and degree of the hust-

ler's concern about the evaluation of him by another person varies, of course, with the specific kind of "other" that the person represents. For the hustler the three main types of significant others are: outsiders, intended or actual victims, and colleagues. As later parts of this study will illustrate, his shifting concerns about each group relate not only to particular work situations but to his general lifestyle and career line.[10]

---

[9] The kinds of structural problems faced today by the pool or billiard hustler are by no means all endemic. Some are the result of recent social change (see Polsky, *op. cit.*).

On the other hand, such change does not create structural problems for all types of hustling. Today the golf hustler, for example, finds that with precious little "acting" he can (a) get heavy action from non-hustlers, (b) lose the good majority of the 18 holes and still clean up, and at the same time (c) not be suspected as a

hustler. The structure of the game of golf itself, the peculiar structurally predetermined variations in the betting relationship as one makes the round of the course ("presses," etc.), and the present setting of the game within the larger society—all these combine to create a situation that is tailor-made for hustling. But that is another story.

[10] The latter two-thirds of this study deals mainly with hustlers' careers and the relation of hustling to larger social structures and social change.

[19]

Professional Crime

Professional Commission on Law Enforcement and Adminstration of Justice

Persons whose income is gained primarily from the full-time pursuit of criminal activity account for a large proportion of certain crimes, particularly major thefts, and theft-related offenses, committed in the United States. No data are available on exactly how many crimes are committed by professionals nor how many criminals fall into the professional category, but both figures are undoubtedly substantial. Fuller understanding of the nature of professional crime could be a first step toward developing new techniques and approaches for control and prevention of this form of criminality.

Existing information about professional crime is fragmentary, and much of it may be outdated. A primary source is Edwin H. Sutherland's classic description of theft as a way of life, "The Professional Thief", but that work, though helpful, was published in 1937 and describes the life of a thief in the period between 1905 and 1925. Other books published since have focused on particular types of criminal activity normally engaged in by professionals including confidence game operations, [1] pickpocketing,[2] professional robbery and burglary,[3] and receiving stolen goods.[4] These few studies provide the basic information on professional crime available in the literature. Although differences in emphasis and coverage exist among them, they present a reasonably coherent, though necessarily incomplete, description of certain types of professional criminal activity.

In order to supplement this material, the Commission sponsored a pilot field research study in four cities—Atlanta, Chicago, New York, and San Francisco—during the summer of 1966.[5] The study differed from previous research in that it used police and prosecutors as well as professional criminals as primary informants. Each consultant spent approximately half of his field time, or about 10 days, conferring with police and district attorneys on the problems of professional crime in their cities. In addition, some of the consultants observed the police in action and examined relevant materials in the files of special intelligence units. Law enforcement agents provided most of the leads to professional criminals.[6]

The consultants spent the balance of their time in the field (about 10 to 15 days each) locating and talking with professional criminals. The number of criminals interviewed varied from a low of eight in one city (Chicago) to 19 in another (San Francisco), with a total of 50 being interviewed. About two-thirds of the total number were in jail or prison at the time of their interviews. Although compared with prior studies the combined samples amounted to a relatively large number of informants, it is obvious that such a survey, conducted under such tight time limitations, could not result in a detailed comprehensive picture of professional crime in the United States. But the data collected are useful for obtaining some insights about professional criminals and the life they lead. Combined with relevant data from previous studies, they provide the basis for the material in this chapter.

For purposes of the Commission-sponsored study, professional crime was defined as: "Crime committed for personal economic gain by individuals whose major source of income is from criminal pursuits and who spend the majority of their working time in illegal enterprises."

Organized crime and white-collar crime were specifically excluded. And while the definition was comprehensive enough to cover a variety of crimes such as killing or strong-arming for hire, professional arson and even prostitution, the principal emphasis of the Commission's study, following the pattern of earlier studies, was on essentially predatory crimes where the victim does not consent and where the actors usually function not as employees but as entrepreneurs. This approach tends to focus on theft and theft-related offenses, including such crimes as receiving stolen goods, shoplifting, pickpocketing, auto theft, burglary, forgery, confidence games, and various kinds of fraud.

This definition differs from traditional definitions in that it does not include any requirement that professionals have specially developed skills or that they have any particularly close association with other professionals. In Sutherland's classic study, the professional thief was described as having "a complex of abilities and skills * * * developed * * * by education" which "can be secured only in association with professional thieves."[7] Obviously this difference in definition affected the characteristics found to be associated with professional criminals. Thus prior studies found that professional criminals were often highly specialized, and that they tended to be quite loyal to members of their professional groups. The Commission-sponsored study, on the other hand, found that professional criminals tended to be generalists, to operate in a variety of loose associations with other professionals, and to exhibit no particular loyalty to their fellows.

1 D.W. Maurer, "The Big Con" (N.Y.: Pocketbooks, Inc., 1949).
2 D.W. Maurer, "Whiz Mob" (New Haven: College and University Press, 1953).
3 J.B. Martin, "My Life in Crime" (N.Y.: Harper Brothers, 1952).
4 See J. Hall, "Theft, Law, and Society" (2d ed. Indianapolis: Bobbs-Merrill, 1952).
5 The Office of Law Enforcement Assistance, Justice Department, funded the project. Brandeis University administered the project grant. The project's coordinator was Prof. Leroy Gould at Yale University. Professor Gould was assisted by five field consultants, two advisors, and one research assistant.
6 Some of those contacted through the police referred the staff to other professional criminals.
7 E. H. Sutherland, "The Professional Thief," (Chicago: Uni. of Chicago Press, 1937), pp. 197-198.

There is no way of knowing whether these different findings reflect only the difference in definition, or whether they reflect in addition changes in the character of professional crime.

The purpose of this chapter is to summarize the concededly inadequate data regarding professional crime, contained in the available literature and in the report of the Commission's study, and to speculate about possible lines of fruitful inquiry. The chapter adopts the broad definition used by the Commission-sponsored study. The significance of professional criminals so defined lies in part simply in the amount of crime that they are apparently responsible for. It is obvious that any group which is engaged in criminal activity on a relatively full-time basis will be responsible for crime out of all proportion to its numbers. Moreover, unlike many occasional criminals, professionals typically make no significant contribution to society through legitimate activity. Their significance lies also in the fact that, compared to many of the criminal types dealt with in the Commission's report, professional criminals are a relatively rational and competent group of persons who are involved in crime because it is a profitable business. It would appear therefore, that the traditional sanctions of the criminal law could be highly effective in dealing with many types of professional crime. But if law enforcement efforts are to succeed, more must be known about who professional criminals are and how they operate.

THE EXTENT OF PROFESSIONAL CRIME

There are no accurate statistics on the amount of professional crime. Published studies contain only estimates of career earnings of individual professional criminals, illustrative "touches," estimated average weekly earnings of various types of professional mobs, and other data of this order.[8]

The lack of accurate data on professional crime is in part a reflection of the general absence of adequate statistics on crime, as discussed more fully in chapter 10. But there are particular difficulties in measuring professional crime. The professional and nonprofessional often engage in the same type of criminal activity. Even if crime reporting improves, it will still be difficult to distinguish the professional's work from that of the amateur. The task is complicated by the fact that the kinds of crimes committed by professionals change over a period of time.

Nevertheless, there is reason to believe that professional criminals are responsible for a large proportion of all property crimes committed and probably an even larger proportion of total property loss through such crimes. Available information indicates, for example, that there are a large number of professional criminals, all of whom, by definition, work at crime on a relatively full-time basis, and some of whom are reported to have very high incomes, sometimes exceeding $100,000. And it is apparent that thefts involving the loss of large amounts of valuable merchandise require the sorts of

contacts with fences and commercial establishments that professionals develop.

There is evidence that the more successful professionals tend to spend substantial portions of their working time in developing lucrative opportunities and planning their criminal activity. A week, month, or even longer period may be spent in preparing for a particularly promising venture. As a result, "scores" tend to be good and the risk of apprehension low. The run-of-the-mill professional criminal, on the other hand, finds it necessary to spend more time in actual stealing to meet expenses and maintain himself at a comfortable and free-spending standard of living. Members of rackets, such as picking pockets and other forms of low-paying larceny, spend virtually all of their time this way.

The Commission's study produced some vivid descriptions of the day-to-day life of the typical professional, the flavor of which is captured by the term "hustling."[9] For the small-time professional criminal, hustling means moving around the bars and being seen; it means asking "what's up." It means "connecting" in the morning with two others who have a burglary set up for the evening, calling a man you know to see if he wants to by 10 stolen alpaca sweaters at $5 each, and scouting the streets for an easy victim. It means being versatile: passing checks, rolling a drunk, driving for a stickup, boosting a car, burglarizing a store. It is a planless kind of existence, but with a purpose—to make as much money as can be made each day, no holds barred. While the more successful professional criminals hustle to some extent, they can afford to be much more purposeful and choosy in their criminal activities.

The Commission's study revealed that run-of-the-mill professionals regularly gather at certain bars and restaurants which in effect function as criminal job placement centers. These centers do for the professional criminal what want ads, employment offices, and businessmen's luncheons do for legitimate business. Through contact with other criminals, professionals learn of jobs to be pulled and of openings in groups planning to pull them. Contacts of this type also enable the professional to keep abreast of the latest techniques, and to gather information regarding criminal opportunities. These centers tend to attract the low-status professional criminal; apparently the successful practitioner in crime does not go to the employment office.

CHARACTERISTICS OF PROFESSIONAL CRIME

SKILLS

Sutherland drew a sharp distinction between the professional and the amateur thief based upon their relative skills. Under his classification, a person might steal as a full-time occupation, but he would not be a professional if he lacked the comprehensive complex of technical skills, personal contacts, and knowledge necessary in order to make a good living at crime in comparative safety. Sutherland's professional thief was contemptuous of the

---

8. For example, Martin's professional burglar estimated that he was in on $250,000 worth of thieving over a 4-year period. Martin, supra note 3, p. 139. This contrasts with the "scores" made by big con-men which during the 1920's were reported to run to $375,000. Maurer, "The Big Con," supra, note 1, pp.26-30.

At the other extreme, $15,000 is said to be a better than average income for a pickpocket, as of 1955. Maurer, p. 38.

9 This term was often encountered in Atlanta and San Francisco where it is most likely to be used to describe the activities of run-of-the-mill professionals, rather that the more successful ones.

98

amateur's crude techniques, low income, and inability to avoid arrest. He therefore avoided association with amateurs and excluded them from the complex of reciprocal expectations and services which characterized his own way of life. But even under this definition, the professional criminal's skills vary significantly in kind [10] and degree. The big-time jewel thief and the "ropers" and "insidemen" who contrive to extract thousands of dollars from wealthy victims in the big con game are at one end of the spectrum. At the other are petty thieves, short con operators, and pickpockets who, though technically competent, lack the techniques needed to make big scores consistently.

Clearly there is an even greater range in skills when all persons who work at crime on a relatively full-time basis are classified as professionals. Nevertheless even this group is, as a whole, a relatively competent one. Many of its members possess, in addition to particular skills, the ability to plan and carry out detailed operations, to manipulate people. to analyze problems and implement solutions. It is clear that professional crime represents the loss to society of the potential contributions of a capable group of people, as well as the channeling of their energies into destructive activities.

SPECIALIZATION

There is evidence that some individual professional criminals tend to specialize in a limited number of related rackets. Many exclude certain kinds of activities: thus some of the professional criminals who were interviewed in the course of the Commission's study said that they would not use violence. But in general the Commission's study indicated that professionals in the middle and lower status levels tend to be versatile. [11] Even the better professional criminal is not always free to follow his preferred line of work, since it may not be either profitable or safe at all times. Under these circumstances he may undertake activities at which he is not especially skilled.

GROUP ACTIVITY

Earlier studies described the relationship between professional criminals as relatively structured. Sutherland, in describing the professional thief of 40 years ago, and Maurer, in his treatment of professional confidence men and pickpockets, stressed the idea that professional criminals enjoy a sense of identity and solidarity and work within a set of well-defined norms and codes of loyalty, helpfulness, and honesty in dealing with one another.

The Commission-sponsored study, directed at a broader group of criminals, found that only the more successful members of this group could be so characterized. It found that the associations or gangs which run-of-the-mill professionals form to commit their crimes tend to be unstable, and that this instability results in part from the diversity of their activities. Different crimes require different kinds of personnel, amounts of financial backing, and types of fencing operations. Consequently, groupings and relations with loan sharks and fences may

change from operation to operation. Even the few relatively stable groups which the consultants heard about brought in other professional criminals for certain jobs, and some members of the group might hire out from time to time on other jobs.

The shifting, transitory pattern of most professional criminals' working relationships was found to be accompanied by the absence of any strong ethical codes. Few of the professional criminals interviewed, for example, seemed to feel bound by any "no ratting" rule. Typically they appeared to take it for granted that others would do whatever necessary to protect themselves—to avoid imprisonment or reduce a sentence—and that they, therefore, should do likewise. As one professional criminal commented: "The one who gets his story told first gets the lightest sentence." There was little resentment expressed about this. It was treated like the weather—a fact of life. Further, criminals expected to be cheated by their colleagues, or by most colleagues. Many of those interviewed reported having been cheated by fences and even by their partners in a particular venture. Victimization of one professional group by another is apparently also fairly common, limited only by fear of reprisal.

There were exceptions to this general pattern, however. Some professional criminals stated that they had worked with certain individuals whom they trusted completely. And relative stability was found among the really successful professional criminals in New York and Chicago. In Chicago, for example, there is a group of between 50 and 200 "heavy" professional thieves who concentrate on such criminal activities as burglary, robbery, and cartage theft. It is said that this group, or at least the core members of the group, are quite stable and quite highly organized, and apparently they exert a considerable amount of control over their own regular members, as well as over persons who work with them only on occasional jobs.

CHANGING CRIMINAL OPPORTUNITIES

As conditions in society change, certain criminal occupations become relatively unprofitable, and other opportunities develop. The nature of crime will tend to change accordingly. Criminal activity like legitimate business activity may respond to the market, to supply and demand curves, and to technological developments. Professional crime, guided by the profit motive, can be expected to be particularly responsive to such factors. One example is the reported decline in safecracking. This is apparently due in part to such factors as increased law enforcement surveillance and mobility, and improvements in the design of safes. Undoubtedly the fact that safes no longer play as important a role has also contributed to the decline—modern economic transactions involve the transfer of credits much more than the transfer of cash. Thus it may have become both more difficult and riskier to rob safes, and also less profitable. At the same time, more promising opportunities for crime have arisen. One of these is check-passing. The Commission's study

[10] A classification frequently encountered is the distinction between the "light" rackets in which stealing is accomplished by stealth or by manipulating the victim, and the "heavy" rackets in which force, or its threat, is used.

[11] A notable exception are pickpockets who are relatively unsuccessful members of the professional crime group, and yet are highly specialized.

learned that nearly every burglar nowadays is also in the check business. One professional burglar said that in one period of several weeks between burglaries he passed over $20,000 of stolen checks. A generation ago burglars did not even look for checks to steal.

A good illustration of the effect of the development of a new market is auto theft and crimes relating to the automobile, such as auto stripping and auto "boosting" (stealing goods from parked cars), activities which are reported to be thriving in the cities surveyed. The Commission's study found also that there has been a rapid rise in recent years in home improvement and related frauds, a rise which corresponds roughly to the increase in privately owned homes. Some law enforcement officials think that in many cities these frauds currently constitute the most profitable source of income for professional criminals.

Professional criminals are also reported to be turning from robbing banks, picking pockets, and operating confidence games to other opportunities, but documentation for such new trends is scanty.

Careful research into changes in the general patterns of crimes committed by professionals and the factors that caused such changes would provide us with more insight into the nature of professional criminality and might provide a basis for designing better methods of crime prevention and control. It might also make it possible to begin to anticipate and plan for such changes.

KEY ASPECTS OF PROFESSIONAL CRIME

The services of the fence and the loan shark appear to be essential to the operations of many professional criminals. Since a great many professionals may depend on a very few such figures, they may constitute a particularly vulnerable aspect of professional crime. The "fix" appears to be of similar importantce to the success of professional criminality.

THE FENCE

Nearly all professional theft is undertaken with the aim of selling the goods thereafter. Although the thief himself may retail his stolen merchandise,[12] he probably will prefer to sell to a fence. He thereby increases his safety by reducing the risk that he will be arrested with the goods in his possession, or that they will be stolen in turn from him. He also avoids the dangers associated with the disposal process itself. In addition, large quantities of goods which may be perishable or otherwise quickly lose their value, or for which there is a specialized demand, will require a division of labor and level of organization beyond the capacity of an individual thief operating as his own retailer. The professional thief thus needs a "middleman" in the same way and for some of the same reasons as the farmer, manufacturer, or other producer.

The types of thefts recorded by the Commission study staff in New York and Chicago suggest the presence of big-time fences who can handle large quantities of specialized goods. For example, in Chicago there recently occurred a cartage theft of $250,000 worth of merchandise and Green Stamps from a Sperry and Hutchinson warehouse and another cartage theft of copper metal valued at over $400,000. To dispose of such quantities of specialized goods requires connections with commercial firms. Most likely a highly accomplished fence served as a middleman between the thieves and the eventual buyers.[13]

As an illustration of the level of efficiency which may be attained by professionals working in cooperation with fences, the Commission's study learned from the New York City police that within the space of approximately 1 month following the recent increase in that city's cigarette sales tax, an entire system for distributing bootlegged cigarettes had been set up and was operating smoothly. The out-of-State suppliers, the truckers, and both the wholesale and retail distributors had been organized, and the system was operating on a scale capable of handling full truckloads of untaxed cigarettes shipped in from the South.

Some fences engage in fencing as a supplement to their legitimate businesses, often on a more or less regular basis. The consultants learned of clothing and appliance delaers who regularly serve as outlets for stolen goods. The major outlets for stolen jewels in one of the cities studied were reported to be legitimate jewelry merchants. Other fences deal primarily or wholly in stolen goods, and are therefore professional criminals themselves.

Some narcotics pushers act as fences, taking stolen goods instead of cash for narcotics. While dealing with addicts is generally regarded as more dangerous than dealing with nonaddicts, it is also more profitable. The addict in need of a "fix" does not bargain well.

Little research has been done on fencing,[14] despite its central role in professional crime. More information is needed about the nature of the market for illicit goods and the extent to which demand for various types of goods affects the incidence of theft. More should also be learned about the relationship of legitimate and illegitimate markets. Little is known about the pattern of distribution of stolen goods. When stolen automobiles are excluded, only a very small proportion of the total amount of goods stolen is returned to its owners. The redistribution of goods through theft and resale might constitute a significant subsidy to certain groups in our society; its curtailment might have significant side effects which should be explored. Finally, it would be desirable to have more information about the organization and operations of large-scale fencing operations, to aid in the development of better methods of law enforcement.

THE LOAN SHARK

The loan shark also performs a key function by providing professional criminals with capital and emergency funds. The literature of professional crime contains few references to loan shark activity. Both Sutherland and Maurer[15] describe a practice whereby mem-

12 Most professional shoplifters are thought to bypass fences and sell directly to the public. See Mary O. Cameron, "The Booster and the Snitch" (Glencoe, Ill.: The Free Press, 1964), p. 57. Martin's burglar had considerable experience retailing the goods he had stolen (supra, note 3).
13 See also John F. Lyons, "Lucrative Looting." Wall Street Journal, July 28, 1965, for an analysis of the role played by fences in the theft and distribution of large quantities of mercury and synthetic rubber.

14 Jerome Hall's report, supra note 4, is the only systematic study of fencing published. Sutherland, Maurer, and Martin, however, provide some additional descriptive and analytic material (supra, notes 7, 1, and 3).
15 Sutherland, supra note 7, pp. 31, 35-36, Ill; Maurer, "Whiz Mob," supra note 2, pp. 137-138.

100

bers of a professional criminal gang establish their own emergency fund. Each member of the gang contributes an equal share to the fund which he may receive back if he leaves the gang. If he is arrested while working with the gang, he has access to as much of the fund as he needs for a bail bond, legal fees, or related expenses. This sort of arrangement appears to be an extension of the natural interdependence of a closely knit group and tends to reinforce the solidarity of the group.

The loan shark functions quite differently. He may meet professional criminals' needs for cash in emergencies, but his activity often has secondary effects which tend to be detrimental to his clients.

Professional criminals may turn to the loan shark to finance crimes which require extra amounts of capital—to buy the tools, or whatever may be needed for the operation, or to bribe public officials. The professional criminal may be willing to pay usurious interest rates (sometimes reported to be as high as 100 percent per week for highly risky loans) if he expects his activities to be particularly lucrative. He may also need emergency financing when apprehended, to pay bail and legal costs. To repay the money borrowed plus interest upon his release, the criminal will often engage in further criminal activities, often more risky than those he ordinarily undertakes. If rearrested, he must post bond again and incur additional legal fees. This pattern may be repeated a number of times before he is finally brought to trial. The high interest charged by the loan shark may thus itself precipitate criminal activity.

The interaction between loan sharking and professional crime doubtless is far more complicated than was discovered during the course of the Commission's brief study. The study staff was told that some "legitimate" businessmen provide loans to criminals occasionally. And there was some evidence that professional criminals regard loan sharking as a relatively safe and profitable racket, and that those who make a big score or otherwise accumulate enough capital frequently set themselves up as loan sharks. But further study is needed on these as well as other facets of the relationshp between professional crime and the loan shark.

THE FIX

There is evidence that the professional criminal frequently bribes public officials to increase his security against law enforcement activity.[16] The fix may be applied in advance to forestall intervention by the police and thereby reduce a major occupational hazard of his profession. Or it may be used after the fact to alleviate the usual consequences of apprehension—to obtain reduced charges or a lighter sentence, or to arrange for preferential treatment. In some communities the professional must himself deal directly with the appropriate officials. In others there may be a local "fixer" who has connections with the party in power and who may be tied in with organized crime. Here the professional criminal need only deal with the fixer as a middleman.[17]

Maurer reports that in some cities there are several fixers, each handling the fix for a different type of a racket. Specialization attaches even in the world of bribery.

Attorneys, bondsmen, politicians, and other ostensibly legitimate persons may be fixers. A fixer may also be a fence, the insideman in a big con game, or a member of organized crime. Cash is the usual commodity used to purchase immunity, but sometimes a case may be fixed for credit or as a favor.

The extent of fixing today is difficult to document. The Commission's study, which did not focus on this aspect of professional crime, encountered little evidence of the sort of fixing described here. The fact that police, judges, and prosecutors probably are better paid and trained today may mean that individually they are less susceptible to bribery. The increased bureaucratization of police operations and personnel practices may also make policemen less subject to corruption from above. And the decline of the big city political machine may have contributed to a decline in organized fixing. On the other hand, professional criminals still operate with considerable success, and it seems likely that they need some protection to do so.

RELATIONS WITH ORGANIZED CRIME

Professional crime may or may not be carried on in structured groups. In some ways it can be loosely analogized to legitimate business activity. But its essence is not business; it is outright theft or theft-related conduct. Organized crime, on the other hand, tends to bear a closer resemblance to the operations of business. It involves thousands of criminals working in well-organized, highly structured operations engaged in activites involvng the supplying of illegal goods and services-such as gambling, narcotics, and prostitution-to cooperative customers; it often involved infiltration into legitimate businesses and labor unions.

Regrettably, little is known of the nature and extent of the relationship between professional and organized crime. This is hardly surprising given the limited facts known about either activity. But it is apparent that a variety of working arrangements exist between professional criminals and organized crime, which are of substantial significance for both categories of crime. There is some evidence, for example, that the fences and loan sharks with whom professional criminals deal are frequently part of the organized crime operation. And there is some indication that organized crime exerts significant power and control over professional crime. The Commission's study staff was informed, for example, that in Chicago the syndicate occasionally provides the services of an arbitrator to settle disputes among the members of a large theft gang. And the syndicate apparently hires professional criminals, on occasion, to do particular jobs such as homicide. But organized crime may also be victimized by professionals. Martin's professional criminal frequently hijacked syndicate trucks and distilleries.

---

16 See generally, Maurer, "The Big Con," supra, note 1, pp. 216-251; Sutherland, supra, note 7, pp. 118, 210-222.

17 Martin's professional burglar found that: "With the exception of shooting the Mayor or the President, there isn't anything he can't straighten out. For money, lots of money." Martin, supra, note 3, p. 247. However,

it is also reported that "right towns" in which complete immunity can be purchased are becoming increasingly scarce.

CONCLUSION

The professional criminal's energy and talents are devoted not merely to committing profitable crimes, but to avoiding the legal consequences of such activity. His methods range from simply taking full advantage of all rights accorded him by the system of criminal justice to actual corruption of the system. It is obvious that sophisticated methods of law enforcement are necessary to deal with the phenomenon of professional crime. A more sophisticated understanding of professional crime is a clear prerequisite.

Present knowledge about professional crime is clearly inadequate. The literature is limited in scope and may be outdated. The Commission's pilot study could obviously do little more than touch on issues deserving of further exploration. But even this brief study gave some indication of the potential that further research has for improved methods of law enforcement.

Some similarities, for example, have been noted between professional crime and ordinary business activity. Further study may lead to the application of the techniques of economic analysis, business, and marketing to the problem of diverting and channeling professional criminal activity. More information about the direction of future change in the types of crimes professionals tend to commit would help planners to build crime prevention components into new business devices and law enforcement agencies to allocate their resources more efficiently. Greater concentration on key figures such as the loan shark or fence may provide a greater return per law enforcement dollar and greatly inhibit professional criminal activity. Further research may produce sufficient information to justify allocation of a larger proportion of law enforcement resources to dealing with professional crime.

The development of more information about the skills and versatility of the professional criminal may also be of direct use to law enforcement and correctional agencies. Correctional programs might take more account of the competence exhibited by the typical professional—with the purpose of channeling his existing capabilities into legitimate fields. The apparent versatility exhibited by professional criminals suggests that the traditional organization of police agencies into specialized squads—such as robbery, burglary, auto theft, and bunco—requires reconsideration. It suggests also the need for a much greater degree of communication between law enforcement agents with information on professional criminals. Detectives tend to be too reluctant to share their information sources with other detectives, or to supply information to any centralized intelligence unit which may exist. Also the traditional complaint orientation of police departments is not appropriate for dealing with persons who are engaged continuously, rather than episodically, in criminal activities.

Chicago provides one exception to the traditional pattern of police organization in relation to the problem of professional crime. In 1963 the Chicago Police Department established an intellgence unit, locally referred to as the C.I.U., which has the responsibility for gathering, and disseminating to other detectives, information about persons in the Chicago area who are known to be, or are highly suspected of being, regularly engaged in big-time professional crime. The members of this unit concentrate not on crimes, but on criminals. When a crime is committed that appears likely to have been committed by someone on whom they have a file, the C.I.U. tries to link their suspects to the crime. There is a different intelligence unit assigned to organized crime.

Other cities should experiment with the development of a similar intelligence function. By developing and sharing knowledge about the operations of professional criminals among different jurisdictions, it is likely that far greater success can be achieved in controlling professional crime.

[20]

The Jack-of-All-Trades Offender
A Comparative Study*

JULIAN ROEBUCK

Assistant Professor, Department of Sociology and Anthropology, San Jose State College
Classification and Case Worker, Department of Corrections, Washington D. C., 1952-57;
Instructor, University of Maryland, 1949-51

B.A. (Social Science), 1941, Atlantic Christian College; M.A. (Sociology), 1944, Duke
University; Ph. D. (Sociology), 1957, University of Maryland

RONALD JOHNSON

Associate Professor, Department of Psychology, San Jose State College
Assistant Professor, San Jose State College, 1957-59; Instructor, University of Minnesota,
1956-57

B.A. (Psychology), 1949, University of Minesota; M.A. (Sociology), 1950, Denver
University; Ph. D. (Child Development), 1959, University of Minnesota

Seventy-one criminals with long arrest histories that revealed
no pattern or concentration on a specific variety of crime were
compared with the remainder of a total sample of 400 criminals,
nearly all of whom did show a pattern in their criminal activities.
The writers hypothesized that a comparison of the no-pattern
group with the remainder of the offenders would reveal differences that would show why these 71 criminals did not evince any
particular pattern. They also hypothesized that the no-pattern
group might consist of two subgroups—one bright and highly
mobile (in terms of shifts toward more "advanced" types of crime),
and a second so dull that more experienced criminals would
not accept them as apprentices. However, bright, mobile offenders were almost nonexistent in the no-pattern group, indicating
that criminal progression of adult criminals takes place within,
not between, specific types of crime. While intellectually dull,
the no-pattern group was no more so than the whole sample, so
that lack of intellectual ability does not seem to be the cause of
their lack of pattern. The introverted, "marginal" character of
their personal relations suggests that these offenders showed no
pattern because they did not have close enough contact with
other criminals to learn effective techniques. Because of their
naïveté in criminal operations and consequently their frequent
incarceration, they were shunned by other criminals. Thus, they
were further limited in their opportunities to learn a single,
"sophisticated" pattern of crime.

* This article continues a study of a sample
group of prisoners classified according to
criminal typologies, in support of the authors' theory that a typology based on specific
arrest patterns is a useful approach to the
study of crime. See Julian Roebuck and
Ronald Johnson, "The Negro Drinker and
Assaulter as a Criminal Type," Crime and
Delinquency, Jan., 1962, pp. 21-33.

THE quest for an all-inclusive theory by which criminal behavior can be predicted or explained has long intrigued laymen, literary men, lawyers, judges, penologists, and scholars in the physical and social sciences. Usually, the orientation of the searcher foretells the typology and makes for etiological approaches to crime and delinquency that are varied if not often contradictory, inconsistent, and inadequate.

Students of human behavior who have interested themselves in criminology have suggested a number of general theories for use in criminological research. These include differential association, culture conflict, and class conflict; ecological, psychodynamic, and constitutional theories; containment, *anomie,* and delinquent subculture. All of these theories have been repudiated by articulate critics, who have pointed to certain negative cases that cannot be explained by a particular theoretical frame of reference. . . . In any case . . . there has been a movement away from general theories to account for all criminal behavior, with a corresponding increase of interest in the development of separate theories as explanations of specific patterns of crime.[1]

Crime is relative in time and space; different geographical areas are represented by different kinds of crimes and by different kinds of criminals. For example, smuggling is prevalent in border regions as is the illegal manufacture of corn whiskey in Southern hill regions, while teen-age "jack rolling" is a city phenomenon. For this reason, researchers might accomplish more if they confined their quest to one particular group at a time and if they sought for criminal typologies which vary according to political jurisdiction, geographical area, and a specific prison population, instead of seeking for a universal criminal type.

With regard to research on prison populations, many sociologists have found that certain groups of prisoners have many personal and social characteristics in common. However, despite this finding, these researchers have persisted in a fruitless search for one general criminal and delinquent type instead of examining several specific types.[2] Some have compared samples of offenders with control groups of nonoffenders, but have failed to study the frequency with which certain personality characteristics occur in those offenders who have particular types of criminal patterns, such as robbery, housebreaking, intoxication, etc.[3] Other sociologists have classified offenders for purposes of analysis into general criminal categories—sex offenders, property offenders, or murderers. Further, their classifications have usually been based on one particular criminal charge which resulted in one particular arrest, conviction, or commitment.[4]

Typologically speaking, one swallow does not make a summer: one robbery does not necessarily indicate a robber. Behavioral sciences deal with behavior patterns, and we believe that if patterns exist, much information can be acquired by studying them. In our opinion, the following questions represent the crux of the typology problem: Are patterns present in offenders' criminal histories? Are cer-

---

[1] Roebuck and Johnson, *op. cit.,* p. 22.

[2] Ruth S. Cavan, *Criminology, 2nd ed.* (New York: Thomas Y. Crowell, 1955), pp. 32-67.

[3] Walter C. Reckless, *The Crime Problem, 2nd ed.* (New York: Appleton-Century-Crofts, 1955), p. 111.

[4] John Lewis Gillin, *The Wisconsin Prisoner: Studies in Criminogenesis* (Madison, Wisc.: University of Wisconsin Press), 1946.

174   JULIAN ROEBUCK AND RONALD JOHNSON

tain social and personal characteristics in these histories related in some way to their criminal patterns? Or to their *lack* of a criminal pattern?

We hypothesized that individual offenders could be classified according to criminal pattern categories based on past criminal records, and that, thus classified, they exhibit personal and social characteristics common to the category. This is not the same thing as saying, "Criminals in general have many personal and social characteristics in common," a statement all too frequently made. On the contrary, marked *differences* will be found between groups of offenders assigned to different criminal pattern categories.

Many offenders show a considerable amount of predictability in their behavior, concentrating on a single type of offense. Offenders within a single type (for example, armed robbers) resemble one another quite closely in the constellation of background factors which presumably disposed them toward crime. On the other hand, offenders of different types (for example, armed robbers versus assaulters) differ considerably from one another in the incidence of these background factors.[5] The tremendous variability in the backgrounds of criminals suggests that any

general theory of crime must fail at predicting certain forms of criminality and can be only moderately successful at predicting who will enter into other types of crime. For example, differential association, one of the major sociological-criminological theories, does not account for those whose crimes follow a pattern of drinking and assault although it seems to account relatively adequately for other types of crime, such as armed robbery.[6] The similarity in background among members of any one offender type suggests that separate theories of crime can—indeed, must—be constructed for differing criminal types.

Criminals often concentrate on one type of crime and, in fact, may specialize on a certain technique, or *modus operandi*, within this type. The technique may be significant in determining the direction of police investigation. In many instances, in fact, the police in large cities have combined or cross-filed their *modus operandi* files with their "rap sheets," in a rough attempt at classifying by criminal type those who have been arrested. Most large law-enforcement agencies have appropriately titled spaces on the reverse side of their fingerprint blanks for noting the specific techniques used in the commission of each specific crime.[7] Given a filling-station holdup by a lone-wolf bandit wearing a stocking over his face, the police investigator may well check his "m.o. file" and then begin to check up on the whereabouts of criminals who specialize in this form of activity.

[5] Julian Roebuck, "The Negro Drug Addict as an Offender Type," *Journal of Criminal Law, Criminology and Police Science* (in press); Julian Roebuck and Mervyn Cadwallader, "The Negro Armed Robber as a Criminal Type: The Construction and Application of a Typology," *Pacific Sociological Review,* Spring, 1961, pp. 21-26. See also: Julian Roebuck, "A Tentative Criminal Typology of 400 Negro Felons," an unpublished study conducted in 1958 under the auspices of the Institute for Criminological Research, Washington, D.C.

[6] Roebuck and Johnson, *op. cit.*
[7] Maurice J. Fitzgerald, *Handbook of Criminal Investigation* (New York: Greenberg, 1951), pp. 119-125.

The "Nonspecialized" Offender

While specialization is common, any prison population will contain a sizable group of offenders (perhaps the largest group) who do not fall into any particular offender type. Several hypotheses might be advanced to account for this "jack-of-all-trades" offender: Perhaps he is socially mobile and switches to more "advanced" types of criminal activity as he learns more complex criminal techniques during and after incarceration. Perhaps he specializes in a branch of crime that requires a kind of criminal apprenticeship so that he can "learn the ropes." Perhaps he has not been selected for such specialized training by his more "sophisticated" compeers because of low mental ability or lack of industry, finesse, self-discipline, or opportunity.

This paper compares criminals whose arrest records do *not* evidence a specialization in crime with those others whose offenses jell into a specific type. It attempts to discern the characteristics which presumably dispose the jack-of-all-trades offender to his varying pattern of crime.

An Arrest History Typology

The sample of subjects used in this study consisted of 400 offenders selected at random from 1,155 Negroes who entered the District of Columbia Reformatory, Lorton, Va., between January 5, 1954, and November 8, 1955.[8]

The criteria used to separate criminals into different criminal pattern categories are based on the arrest history, which was chosen as our source

of information because it is specific and less likely to be distorted than other records. As Sutherland and Cressey (among others) have noted, the further one gets away from a criminal's arrest history, the more obscure and distorted become the facts of his criminal activities.[9] Other academic criminologists have made a limited use of the arrest histories of certain offender types for purposes of illustration and interpretation,[10] while institutional caseworkers and parole and probation officers have also made use of the arrest history in discussing criminal careers and in developing the case histories of offenders. (Police use of the arrest history has already been mentioned.) Because the official arrest history is useful in assessing an offender's criminal career, a more systematic analysis of this record is called for.

Our typology was developed from a longitudinal study of the offenses charged to individual offenders as revealed by their official arrest histories. An analysis of the configuration of each offender's total known arrests by criminal charge permitted us to observe the existence of a fixed pattern of criminal behavior, if such pattern existed. One of the basic assumptions underlying this typology and the research stemming from it is this: if noncriminals manifest a pattern in their legal activities, then contemporary behavioral theory leads us to assume that the illegal activities of

---

[8] The Reformatory was actually a penitentiary housing a heterogeneous group of felons who were serving sentences of various lengths ranging to life imprisonment.

[9] Edwin H. Sutherland and Donald R. Cressey, *Principles of Criminology*, 6th ed. (New York: J. B. Lippincott, 1960), pp. 25-30.

[10] Reckless, *op. cit.*, pp. 87-95, 119-128, 154-177; Paul W. Tappan, *Crime, Justice and Correction* (New York: McGraw-Hill, 1960), pp. 122-130, 138, 140, 149-150, 153-154, 166-167, 204-205, 226-229.

the criminal must also manifest an identifiable pattern.

In order to fall into a criminal type, an offender's arrest history had to satisfy at least one of the following criteria: (1) it had to show three or more arrests, *all* of which were for the same charge; or (2) an arrest history, which contained at least four arrests for a given charge *and additional arrests for other charges*, was divided into three sections and qualified for a single pattern if at least one of the four or more arrests for a given charge appeared in the last section of the arrest history and if the charge constituted at least 33 per cent of those charges which occurred in the last two sections of the arrest history.

When the number of arrests could not be divided into three equal sections, the latter sections were given more weight. For example, an arrest history containing five arrests was divided into three sections—1, 2, and 2. The first arrest constituted the first section, the second and third arrests the second section, and the fourth and fifth arrests the third section. Hypothetically, if the charge for the first arrest was robbery, the second arrest housebreaking, and the third, fourth, and fifth arrests robbery, we would have a pattern of robbery.[11] Using these criteria it is clearly possible to have a double or even triple pattern of criminality.

Of the 400 offenders, 150 showed a single pattern, 104 showed double patterns (drunkenness and assault, larceny and burglary), 43 showed a triple pattern (drunkenness, assault, and larceny), and 103 showed no pat-

[11] For more detailed examples of the methods used in determining the criminal pattern, see Roebuck and Johnson, *op cit.,* pp. 25-26.

tern. Of these last, 32 fell into a residual category of offenders with fewer than three arrests. The remainder, 71 offenders, formed the "no-pattern group" and are the major focus of this paper.

Quantitative Comparison

The 71 offenders showing no arrest pattern were compared (see Table, p. 177) with the remaining 329 offenders with respect to thirty-four characteristics taken from the life history of the offender: family and community background, peer and reference group relations, indices of personal disorganization and juvenile delinquency, marital history, work history. (All differences discussed below are significant to at least the .05 level as determined by chi-square tests.)

The men in the no-pattern (or, more precisely, the mixed-pattern) group were a literate (Stanford Achievement Test grade median of 5.2), young (median age 29.8), urban group (57 of the 71 reared in urban areas) with a mean IQ of 85.8 (low but approximately the same as the IQ for the entire sample). Logically we would have assumed that no-pattern offenders would vary in their level of intelligence and would consist, let us say, of one group so dull that more accomplished criminals would not teach them specialized criminal techniques, and of another group whose ability was high enough to permit them to "advance" to other levels of crime, thus entering them into the "mixed-pattern" category. However, we found that the 71 members of the no-pattern group did not vary significantly more in their IQ than the members of other offender types.

COMPARISON OF NO-PATTERN OFFENDERS WITH ALL OTHER OFFENDERS

Selected Social and Personal Attributes	No Pattern (N-71) N.W.C.*	All Others (N-329) N.W.C.	Sign. of X²	Selected Social and Personal Attributes	No Pattern (N-71) N.W.C.	All Others (N-329) N.W.C.	Sign. of X²
Reared in more than one home	41	120	.01	Weak parental family structure	37	177	N.S.
Mother figure Southern migrant	37	137	N.S.**	Weak parental family ties	58	224	.05
Mother figure domestic servant	62	237	.01	Reared in rural area	14	52	.05
Dependent family	61	235	.05	Reared in slum area	68	183	.01
Family broken by desertion	39	101	N.S.	Living in slum when arrested	65	236	.01
Demoralized family	60	136	.01	History of school truancy	46	157	.05
Criminality in family	38	133	.05	Disciplinary problem at school	41	147	.01
Mother figure dominant	44	175	N.S.	Street trades as juvenile	48	155	.01
Inadequate supervision—father	66	130	.01	No marital ties	49	239	N.S.
Inadequate supervision—mother	64	218	.01	Juvenile delinquent companions	63	176	.01
Conflict in family	54	180	.01	Member delinquent gang	33	109	.05
Overt hostility toward father	62	99	.01	Adjudicated juvenile delinquent	36	137	N.S.
Overt hostility toward mother	8	61	N.S.	Committed as juvenile	31	115	N.S.
Disciplinary problem at home	33	86	.01	Police contact prior to 18	54	150	.01
History of running away	51	134	.01	Criminal companions as juvenile	30	133	N.S.
Inveterate nonprofessional gambler	45	125	.01	Drug addict	11	53	N.S.
Problem drinker	26	167	.05	Positive attitude toward work	17	136	N.S.

*Number With Characteristic.
**Not Significant.

No-pattern offenders, when compared with the remainder of the sample, were significantly more often reared in more than one home, had mothers who were domestic servants, and came from economically dependent, demoralized, and criminal families. They had greater conflict within their family, less adequate supervision by the father, to whom they expressed more hostility, and had weaker parental ties. They were disciplinary problems at home, from which they more frequently ran away, and disciplinary problems in school, from which they were more often truant. As juveniles, no-pattern offenders worked in street trades, had delinquent companions, were members of delinquent gangs, and had police contacts prior to age eighteen. As to geographical environment, they were more often reared in slums and were more frequently residents of slum areas when arrested. They gambled significantly more often but were problem drinkers less often than the sample as a whole.

These offenders compared unfavorably with the remainder of the sample in twenty-two of the thirty-four attributes (see Table), while they compared favorably in only one—problem drinking. Their environment appears to have been far more criminogenic than that of the rest of the sample.

Qualitative Comparison

Our major question, however, was not why these men were criminals, but why they showed no pattern (or a mixed pattern) of crime—an absolute answer to which was not reached through analysis of the quantitative data. The most significant qualitative difference between them and the other offenders was, from the beginning to the end of their criminal careers, their extreme naïveté in the ways of crime.

Take, for example, their typical burglaries. Usually, they did not specialize in any one type of building; they moved from private dwellings to apartment houses and from warehouses to stores. Nor did they specialize in the type of property they would steal. To use one offender's language: "We took everything that wasn't nailed down." "Everything" generally included money, jewels, furs, clothing, radios, television sets, checks, whiskey, cigarettes, etc. Vans for stolen goods or other means of transportation were rarely provided for. Seldom did they make a "connection" with a "fence" *prior* to the offense or carefully time the execution of the crime. Once planned, the crime would generally be carried out regardless of unexpected obstacles—the appearance of an extra policeman, a cruising squad car in the vicinity of operation, a change in a policeman's timetable of rounds, a change or addition of a lock on a door, failure of a lookout to show up, etc. These offenders would blunder through these difficulties with false courage and a capricious hope for lucky breaks. The following remark by one of those interviewed illustrates the point:

Once I got started, I had to go on with it . . . break on in and take the chance. You start thinking about the bread and you got to go. When I'm there set to go, the rollers [police] just got to get me, if they get me. The bust [arrest] just have to come.

Prior to the commission of the crime, these offenders did not make use of skillful "casing procedures." Tight organization was rare; they did not operate within a definite group of criminal acquaintances led by a fixed leader.

Most no-pattern offenders, in discussing their juvenile delinquent activities, indicated that they had done some form of stealing before they were twelve. Although most of their delinquent activities appeared to have taken place in groups, they also mentioned stealing as "loners":

I stole clothing from stores with two or three fellows. Most of the time I stole with the other boys when we took a car or something. Sometimes when I saw a good chance I made my own score. I stole money from home, too, by myself.

From their discussions of juvenile gang activity, they were obviously followers rather than leaders. They neither planned nor schemed, and their stories did not highlight the physical courage and the flair for violence generally attributed to gang leaders. Moreover, they voiced no strong identification with a gang:

There was five of us. We stole a lot of junk here and there in stores. Sometimes we stole a car. Tom divided the loot. He could beat up anybody in the block. Tom knew when a score was ripe. He could smell a cop a mile away. I didn't get busted stealing with Tom. But then he was bossy. Sometime I go along. Sometime I not go along. I just copped anything that wasn't nailed down.

As adults, their associations with other criminals were of a fluid variety —acquaintances but not strong brotherhoods in crime. Gang behavior was not evident:

I ran with a few dudes I had done a bit with sometimes. We stumbled into each other at a bash [a get-together] or something, you know. They're O.K., but I'm not with them all the time. Sometimes we score together, then I don't see them in a long time, you know.

In discussing their criminal associates they disclosed some knowledge of and some contact with underworld activity—the illegal sale of whiskey and drugs, prostitution, and gambling, though they didn't seem to belong to any organized underworld activity. Speaking in the criminal argot, offenders would make remarks like these:

Sure, sure I know studs who sell whiskey and some who sell drugs. I know some pimps and a whole lot of whores. You get to know these people, but I ain't never been tied up with that stuff. No sort for me. Like other hustlers, I knew what was happening, but I really wasn't in the know. I wasn't inside no big operation.

The qualitative material gleaned from the interviews suggested that these men never developed professional roles in the higher echelons of the underworld because of their clumsiness, lack of self-discipline, frequent arrests and incarcerations, inability to settle down into one type of crime, and their lack of opportunity for intimate association with more "sophisticated" criminals. An example:

Well, you know, some time I thought about the big time. You got to work hard at one kind of game for that. I had to have quick bread though, all my life. I had to get what I could get. You know, any way I could get it. I grew up in the bottom with the small hustlers. The Cadillac boys didn't have nothing to do with us. One time I knew a numbers man pretty good. I asked him for a job many times. He say, "Man, what you talking about? You just don't have the class for the numbers." I say, "Well, I can learn." He say, "Hell, man, you been arrested for every petty crime in the book. You been locked up too much. All the cops know you too good. You got jail fever." He say I should put the life down and get me a lunch pail. I guess he was right. Here I am in the joint again. I just couldn't settle down to no one type of hustle. Some small scores and many busts is the story of my life. I'm a jack-of-all-trades and no master of none.

For the most part, the no-pattern group consisted of a mildly antisocial, nonprofessional bunch of grown-up juvenile delinquents. They were reared in lower-class, demoralized families and they grew up in neighborhoods where older delinquent youths taught them to steal at an early age. They were products of the city slums and were loosely attached to the lower echelons of the underworld, resembling a group theoretically delineated by Walter C. Reckless as offenders with "ordinary criminal careers," in that ordinary criminal activities were a definite part of their life scheme.[12]

These institutionalized offenders (all of them had served time before, averaging 2.5 felonies per man) derived their meager economic support from their criminal activities (only nine had regular work histories). Unskilled, barely literate, and intellectually inferior, they had been indoctrinated with the "fast buck" philosophy of life, though they were a far cry from being clever enough to live by it. Therefore, they kept coming back to jail. A number of their lengthy arrest histories (mean average arrests—18.3) revealed extensive criminal activity that progressed from the less serious (petty larceny, car theft, shoplifting) to the more serious (grand larceny and burglary) types of offenses, without, however, a specialization in any one type of offense. The district attorney's reports on all crimes for which they had served felony sentences showed various low levels of *modus operandi*.

---

[12] Reckless, *op. cit.*, pp. 153-179.

Docile, easygoing followers, they were easily talked into taking appreciable risks for small "scores." They were not vicious, extremely courageous, or colorful. They evinced no marked bitterness toward the police or the courts, as a rule accepted their sentences philosophically, and made good prison adjustments. "Don't do the crime unless you can do the time" was a quite prevalent motto. They were that drab material which makes up most of a prison's population. Although not hardened criminals, many were vaguely aware that crime had not paid off *for them*, and most of them expressed hazy notions of "straightening up."

Conclusion

While the quantitative analysis does not indicate conclusively why these no-pattern offenders did not develop criminal skills and specialization, the qualitative data do point to two probabilities. The first is that since such a thing as criminal progression (from unskilled to skilled varieties of crime) does exist, albeit to only a small degree in the careers of these offenders, it therefore should follow that criminal progression takes place most frequently *within a certain specific criminal type.* (That is, given a first offense—numbers, burglary, etc. —the offender may "progress" by acquiring new skills from more seasoned criminals. Once committed to a particular skill, the offender is not very likely to progress along other lines.) The second is that these offenders were "marginal men" who had, as adults, only superficial acquaintances with other criminals—a commonly found characteristic which might account for their classification as "mixed pattern—no progression."

They conceived of themselves as introverted. All of them expressed a dislike for large groups, crowds, and noise, and desired to do their time in a cell. They were apprehensive about the D.C. Reformatory's open-dormitory housing facilities, and four of them asked for transfers. This fact suggests that these no-pattern, or mixed-pattern, offenders had limited contact with criminals because of their psychological make-up and hence were limited in what they could learn. This lack of learning made them "losers" with long records and little evidence of skill. In turn, being losers, they were avoided by fellow criminals who could teach them more skilled criminal techniques. This cycle of avoidance, naïveté, incarceration, and more avoidance may well be the cause of the lack of pattern or progression in the careers of the 71 offenders.

BRIXTON, LONDON:

A DRUG CULTURE WITHOUT A DRUG ECONOMY?

*It is a shared belief that in some London inner city areas the growth of drug markets provides high illegal earnings for street sellers and distributors. Among such areas Lambeth, but more particularly Brixton, are deemed to be prosperous drug markets where large illicit profits are produced. **Vincenzo Ruggiero** tries to identify the dimension and features of the drug economy in Brixton.*

The qualitative research on which this article was based, conducted between June and December 1992, funded by the Lambeth Drugs Prevention Unit (Home Office), was wider in scope than the present article, as it aimed to assess the perceptions of the drug phenomenon among groups of inhabitants in central Lambeth. It focused on a variety of themes such as: the dimension of drug abuse, the availability of drugs, the existence of a drug problem and the drug economy in the area, the causes of drug abuse and preventive drug policies. The following pages are confined to the information, suggestions and perceptions of informants with regard to dimension of the drug economy in the area under investigation.

Interviews were conducted with habitual and occasional users, street dealers, drug agency workers and social workers. A total number of approximately 100 persons was involved in the interview process. Despite the relatively small sample and the limitations inherent in qualitative and ethnographic research such as the present project, in this article an embryonic picture emerges of how those who inhabit the drug economy in Brixton perceive the characteristics of this economy.

DEMOGRAPHIC DATA

Lambeth has the second largest population in inner London, with some 234 000 people officially living in the borough. It is a multicultural community with over 30% of the population coming from black or other ethnic minorities. Almost one in five of Lambeth's households are single-parent families. Almost 80% of Lambeth's employment is in services and public administration. About 33 510 people were unemployed in March 1992 – that is, one in four of the borough's work force. The percentage increase in unemployment in the period 1989–91 was 49.3% (PSI, 1992).

The government considers Lambeth to be the fourth most deprived borough in the country (London Borough of Lambeth, 1991; Lambeth Services, 1992). Almost 29% of the estimated adult population are claimants receiving income support or supplementary benefit. The percentage is higher when only people aged 60 and over are considered: 35.1%, which compares with 19.3% in England as a whole. This seems to suggest that deprivation in Lambeth increases during the course of individuals' lives, and afflicts the more disadvantaged in their most vulnerable life period: from retirement to death. Mortality ratios, which are also associated with poverty and deprivation, increased well over the national average between 1977 and 1990 (PSI, 1992). Homelessness rose from 2.4 per 1000 households in 1980 to 6.4 in 1991 (PSI, 1992).

In spite of all the above, financial aid from central government, during the 1980s, declined in real terms. These figures suggest a deterioration in general social conditions in Lambeth over the last two decades. It is worth noting that, back in the 1960s, Lambeth was already regarded as a deprived area, suffering from major social and environmental problems, where 'the place and its people have been left behind by prosperity, and this gap has been widening' (Shankland et al., 1977, p. 1). The above figures also demonstrate that recommendations put forward in the mid-1970s as regards improvement in the area went largely unheeded.

DEPRIVATION AND DRUG ABUSE

The demographic data may lead one to think that an area such as Lambeth, officially described as a deprived area, is more likely than other areas to be affected by drug abuse. However, the association of drugs with deprivation is far from clear and straightforward. Drug use affects both deprived and affluent areas; social conditions seem to determine, at most, the motivation pattern, the effects and the degree of risk related to drug use. It is true that some unemployed youths may find in the drug scene a vicarious occupational arena providing them with income, sociability and a life structure (Allen and Jekel, 1991). Nevertheless, it seems also true that unemployment may be an outcome rather than a cause of drug use, and that in some classes it is the availability of money rather than the lack of it which may lure certain individuals into the drugs business (Reuter, McConn and Murphy, 1990; Ruggiero, 1992; Ruggiero and Vass, 1992).

If drug use involves diverse social groups and classes, its impact varies. The condition in which drugs are used, their quality, the expectations of users, along with their lifestyle, determine the degree of severity of what is termed a 'drug problem'. Disadvantaged individuals may find in drug use a supplementary source of disadvantage, thus adding to their social vulnerability. Others may find in drug use an additional vehicle of group sociability. Some others may discover in the commercial use of drugs a parallel source of economic advantage.

There are drug economies virtually devoid of a drug culture. Here, a well-structured drug business may be in operation which does not foster distinctive, visible attitudes among both suppliers and customers. In some areas, for instance, the supply of drugs occurs in a protected environment, and use takes place in safe conditions. Here, discretion keeps the official agencies at bay (Arlacchi and Lewis, 1991). By contrast, some areas present themselves with a drug culture which is virtually devoid of a drug economy in the sense that suppliers and customers do not participate in a lively, prosperous illegal economy. Here, both dealers may be very visible, unwittingly contributing to the shaping of stereotypes attached to them and the area where they reside. These areas, where well-structured remunerative illegal transactions rarely take place, may become a high-profile target for the intervention of official agencies.

These hypotheses formed the premise to discussions and interviews with individual or groups of informants. Their views are collected below.

A DRUGS ECONOMY IN LAMBETH?

A group of social workers suggested that drugs are tolerated in Lambeth because they provide an alternative economy where deprived people find a source of income. On the other hand, a very frequent comment of my informants was that the reputation of central Lambeth produces an imaginary magnification of the actual dimension of the drugs economy. It was felt, for example, that because the area is notoriously poor, there is a tendency to think that there must be a lot of drugs around. This may prompt the authorities to act accordingly, thus creating a vicious circle whereby more police activity in the area leads to more arrests being made and more drugs found.

The reputation of Lambeth as a prosperous drugs market may also cause strange incidents. Buyers may be attracted to the demand area and find drug supply insufficient. This leads to the appearance on the scene of improvised suppliers who are incapable of 'doing the job properly'. In the words of a user:

> Here, the chances of getting oregano instead of 'grass' are very high. For this reason it's always best to have personal contacts, or to cultivate particular dealers. If you know somebody, you buy from them. The word gets around that there is a serious dealer and you try and contact him.

It may happen that bogus drugs are sold in certain periods because somebody is holding on to the good-quality drugs for a while, with the intention of bringing them back afterwards at higher prices. This was said to have happened around last Christmas, when revellers who were getting ready for partying found unprecedentedly high prices. Another user explained:

> Many cocaine users would come to this area to score. They think they can find anything they want here. They are usually whites who believe both the hype and the rumour that prices are lower here. They do not know, and probably they are not in a position to check, what they are getting. This also applies to cannabis. Those who come from other areas to buy cannabis make us laugh. We call the stuff they get 'Brixton bush'. Young people know that customers come from all over London, and of course they don't always have the good-quality drugs to sell, so they just offer what comes handy.

In effect, some cannabis dealers stock two different qualities – one for their clients and friends, and the other for occasional customers allured by the reputation surrounding the area. Some of the users I contacted argued that the 'incompetence' and dishonesty of some dealers make the whole drug trade unreliable. Many resident users go elsewhere to buy, in order both to find better deals and to escape what they see as a heavily policed environment.

A social worker gave yet another example of the outcome of the area's reputation. In her experience, car thieves come to this area because they believe that this is a no-go area for the police. They are so instructed by those who commission theft from them. But, she explained:

> They are all caught, because on the contrary this area is under strict control. When these youths are arrested, everybody is puzzled. Social workers and the police find it hard to understand, because they think they know all the 'problem' youths who live in the area. Only eventually do they find out that these youths don't live here.

The crime/drug connection has spawned extensive research, but yielded very contradictory results (Inciardi, 1984; Cohen, 1989; Mott, 1991; Dorn et al., 1992). However, if we concede that a portion of drug users do resort to acquisitive offences, what kind of offences and what type of economy these generate deserve thorough examination. Less than half the users interviewed admitted to committing offences in order to finance their habit. A similar proportion emerged when drug agency workers were asked to estimate the percentage of users/offenders known to them.

In the view of most drug workers, the drug economy in central Lambeth is a domestic, petty, hand-to-mouth economy. In a sense, this informal economy mirrors the regular exchange of things and little amounts of money which occurs in some housing estates. Small quantities of drugs are sometimes exchanged, borrowed or sold, just as sums as low as £10 are sometimes lent to neighbours. A drug worker noted that when drug users turn to burglary, they reveal how hopelessly unskilled they are:

> The number of burglars arrested while holding stolen goods at home is perhaps an indication of their professional inadequacy and their little knowledge of networks where the goods can be circulated.

The success claimed by the police in fighting burglaries may be the result of the increasing professional inadequacy of burglars rather than of 'Police patrols, both uniformed and plain clothes, together with extensive use of our Scenes of Crime staff' (Metropolitan Police, 1991, p. 2). A number of informants confirmed that many drug users who turn to burglary are more likely than other burglars to confine themselves to this professionally inadequate milieu.

The limited scope of the drug economy is with regard to heroin in particular, whose consumption is felt to be as steady as the money circulation connected to it. The development of a genuinely commercial spirit within the heroin economy seems therefore unlikely. Furthermore, heroin still requires users to adopt a set, albeit vague, of 'counter-values'. Heroin users often feel they have something in common, and in the name of their tacit complicity, social, racial, and sometimes even gender differences among them may blur.

The cocaine market is generally seen as more conducive to a commercial spirit and thus to harsh competition. Because the drug suits diverse lifestyles and social groups, conflicts emerging in the cocaine milieu resonate with or mimic the conflicts in law-abiding milieu. Race differences are strongly felt, and hierarchies identified and respected. In sum, the cocaine scene is more problematic because it is more conformist. In the view of a drug worker:

> Cocaine may constitute a realistic career choice – more so than other drugs. It is true that there are probably still some old-style bohemian-type

cocaine dealers, who use the substance and share it with their peers. But in general commercial relationships prevail in the cocaine market and very ambitious individuals force their way into it. For these reasons perhaps the cocaine economy is more problematic.

The prevailing feeling among my informants was that little money is accumulated in the area through drug selling. The paucity of the drug economy was interpreted as a sign that profits go to other city areas where police control is not as strict. In other words, investors and large distributors are said to reside out of central Lambeth. If large distributors operated in central Lambeth, this would result in more money circulation being visible. This would also be apparent in more licit businesses being set up with the proceeds of drug selling.

A group of youth workers argued that, as distribution becomes more hidden and dangerous, more professional people are needed especially among the high- and middle-rank dealers. These preferably move out of central Lambeth, if they have ever lived in the area. In Lambeth, instead, they may find young people who are prepared to 'work' for them at street level. As a social worker stressed:

> Some youths do not get much out of it. They are exploited. All they get is prison.

The role of these vulnerable street workers seems exactly that: to be arrested. They are there to feed the criminal justice system. This was the opinion, among others, of some occasional cannabis users:

> Only the small fish are left here. They are very well known, and are exposed to high risk. Even we know them, although we only buy drugs occasionally. This tells you how well known they must be around here. They are probably left alone because the police try to see if they lead them to someone bigger, like their suppliers. They have a very stressful life, and hate their work, because theirs is not a career.

Some dealers are also engaged in other activities which supplement their income from drugs. Claiming state benefits, selling stolen goods and petty theft are among them. Although periodically apprehended, they are forced to inhabit this petty economy, especially if they are users as well as dealers. Some of them may start a career with the desire of escaping the boredom of a regular low-paid job. In this sense, most of the

users I talked to thought that a residual 'glamour' is attached to the drug world, as it appears to be a 'free' and exciting world. But, as they soon realise, 'In fact it also involves a lot of work'.

Speaking from personal experience, a crack dealer described the drugs economy in central Lambeth in the following terms:

> There are about 12 middle-range distributors who never go on the street in this area. They take between 50% and 70% of the street value of the substances sold. In turn, they buy in other areas. It is very rare that distributors here are in direct contact with importers, or are importers themselves. These middle-range distributors are in contact with street sellers, and it is here that problems start. Those who operate at street level are unreliable, and what is happening now is that many users go somewhere else to choose their own supplier. It is also happening that users prefer to buy from white dealers, who are seen as more serious. Among dealers you now find ordinary people who just get up promptly in the morning to do their job. They have a mortgage to pay, children to maintain.

From this testimony, it seems that the more disadvantaged people in central Lambeth are not only denied an official and acceptable legal occupation, they are even denied the possibility of a career in illegal activities. The majority of my informants felt that the community does not benefit from the drug economy operating in the area. The proceeds of drug distribution, it was argued, may at most feed individual flashy consumption. As a social worker lamented:

> What we see here is a few big cars and some portable phones. But this is not big money, as some are inclined to think. What annoys me is: all right, drugs are producing a lot of money, but none of that money is then invested in this community. All we've got left here is some gold and gaudy clothes for a few dealers.

That lament alluded to the notion that a criminal trade is a true economy only when it converts some of its proceeds into legal enterprises. This is, in effect, the case in countries where prosperous illegal economies exist, and where an indicator of the dimensions of structured criminal activities is the degree to which these activities establish links with legal activities. Most of my informants suggested that disadvantaged people in

Brixton are doomed, as they lack opportunities and infrastructures to change their condition. When trying to venture into some sort of business, frequently they are denied bank loans. This lack of infrastructure and finance reverberates in the illegal economy, which remains sloppy, amateurish.

For example, is it not surprising that a market of counterfeit goods is non-existent in the area? This is a typical feature of deprived areas in most European cities, where goods such as designer-label clothes are in high demand. In these cities, underground economies flourish, both at retail and production level, and they service a vast clientèle who cannot afford the original variety of those goods (Casillo, 1990; Ruggiero, 1993). Label clothes, and also other 'good-brand' commodities, are thus available at low prices. None of this happens in Brixton, where, as a cannabis dealer noted:

> We don't have a chance to set up a business like that, firstly because we are refused bank loans, and secondly because we would be immediately caught. That's why you either buy expensive goods or just get trash. As for clothes, this is a general feature in England: you can only be smart if you are rich... look how easy it is to tell class differences in this country.

My informants also disputed another assumption which is frequently put forward by both the local and the national press. This regards the increasing use of firearms as an indication that a real drugs economy has by now developed in Lambeth, and that a war is being waged for territory control. A recent barrage of media coverage on this issue conveyed the notion that a well-structured market has taken shape where groups compete with a view towards establishing monopolistic conditions (*Guardian*, 10 August 1991; Mitchell, 1991; *South London Press*, 1 May 1992; *Zilkha*, 1992; *South London Press*, 16 October 1992). The reality in central Lambeth seems to be different. Here, the use of firearms is either independent of the drug market or marks a phase which precedes the involvement of organised groups in it. Some armed robberies, my informants emphasised, are carried out because they allow a sort of preliminary accumulation of funds, which will eventually be invested into drugs. Sometimes the investors contact experts in armed robberies and commission the operations. Only afterwards do some of these 'entrepreneurs' try to buy quantities of drugs with a view to launching them on the market. This market is still far

from being rigidly structured, let alone presenting with monopolistic features or tendencies. The drug market seems as chaotic as drug use, and allows for ventures of diverse individuals, often improvised dealers, and unlikely firms.

Violent episodes occurring in the drug economy are not perceived as symptoms of the increasing stakes involved in it. It is felt that there is no rational relationship between risks and benefits for those involved in the drug economy. Nor does the degree of violence observed in this economy lend itself to accurate calculation on the part of those who deploy it (De La Rosa et al., 1990). This is also the case with predatory activities in Brixton. Even robberies do not necessarily bring large amounts of money. The local press describes, in thorough detail, armed robberies which yield average sums of £50. Details are not spared even when, as it frequently happens, robberies are only attempted. Mugging, given the modest amounts of money involved, is becoming a sort of violent begging.

A drug worker argued that the degree of violence in the drug business is just a reflection of the increasing level of violence in society as a whole. He also argued that this produces self-images among users and small dealers which are disproportionate with their actual calibre:

> Among my clients I don't see any Dillinger or Al Capone, but they all think they are gangsters. Somebody made them think they are – perhaps the media or the police. In fact they delude themselves: they think they are making a career, but they are just setting up the scene for themselves. They are vulnerable and obvious, they'll never make it to the top.

Among my informants, violence was more associated with alcohol rather than with drug use.

A dealer suggested that even so-called Yardies (alleged professional criminals and illegal immigrants from Jamaica) would find it hard to put some kind of order into what seems a very low-profile and confused economy (Headley, 1992). He hypothesised:

> The Yardies don't have a chance to develop their business because other gangs of white professional criminals would not allow them to. I also suspect that the white gangs themselves fuelled the panic about the Yardies, because they saw them as dangerous competitors. They must have informed the police, who in fact got information about the

Yardies that they would never have picked up by themselves.

This informant added that traditional white groups already involved in the underground economy contributed to the creation of the Yardie phenomenon and the scare attached to it. He concluded that 'this country is a bastion of racism', and the blacks are not even given the opportunity to improve in alternative or illegal businesses.

This point also emerged among both habitual and occasional users. As mentioned above, many black dealers are regarded as cheats, and therefore they find it hard to climb the criminal career echelon. Those who make it are highly stigmatised, not so much for being drug dealers as for being entrepreneurs. The moral disapproval of relatively prosperous black drug distributors hides a subtle resentment against the black population, rather than against drug barons. The blacks who succeed, even in crime, are somehow seen as overturning the 'natural' order of society. They are not expected to become suppliers but confine themselves to the role of users, as the whites are 'naturally' to occupy the leading positions in the drugs and other economies.

A dealer claimed that even in the crack business, allegedly controlled by black entrepreneurs, the position of the blacks is in fact confined to the lower strata of the distribution chain. They would buy cocaine from white large suppliers, and then 'wash it' before selling on the street. The good stuff, he said, is kept outside of Lambeth:

> Good cocaine is found in areas with a better reputation than this one. If a police raid in Lambeth seizes £800 worth of crack, this means that the same raid in Hampstead would seize £1 million worth of cocaine. Some time ago, for example, the local place where I used to buy was raided. But those who supplied my suppliers were not; they still operate undisturbed. They have both the good stuff and the money.

The disorganisation of the drug market in central Lambeth is confirmed by a number of episodes. People without any previous experience may be approached and asked if they want to be involved in drug selling even before they are asked to buy drugs. What commercial efficiency can neophytes offer? Lacking apprenticeship, they are inevitably caught, and often do not know why: they do not envisage this possibility. As an ex-user said:

The principle used to be: if you can't do the time, don't do the crime. Nowadays, they cannot do the crime and cannot do the time either. They don't plan what they do; they don't calculate the effects. My boyfriend, who was a small dealer, had a big shock when he was brought to prison; he never imagined his life ending up like that.

Users may be incapable of committing remunerative offences, and resort to stealing from people who are most close to them. Their victims include relatives, friends, and other users. However, most of the users I talked to claimed their 'honourability' in the choice of targets. Attacking a person on the street, for example, was said to be a taboo, whereas shoplifting was presented as a favourite activity. Moral principles mixed with a vague political awareness were implied in this claim: stealing from large companies (big stores and the like) is not regarded as so socially damaging as stealing from vulnerable people.

Many users do not like the drug scene; they just like drugs. Therefore, the choice as to which illegal activity, if any, they engage in is promoted by their unwillingness to be bogged down in the drug market. Their dislike includes images and stereotypes superimposed on them by outsiders, who tend to see them as callous and indiscriminate predators. Is this one of the reasons why they keep a low criminal profile? At Mainliners, a local drug agency, this point was endorsed as follows:

> Drug-related crimes are not as many as people think. In this area we didn't have a real hard drugs epidemic, one which would be visible through the dramatic increase of property crime. Property crime is relatively independent of drugs. In this sense, the ordinary residents in Lambeth may not perceive the existence of a drug problem in their area. However, it's also difficult to draw precise boundaries, because people are mobile. Some may go to other areas both to steal and to score. This perhaps happens because central Lambeth is heavily policed.

It may happen that youths are 'hired' by adult groups to commit offences. These groups, a social worker said: 'know juvenile law and youth courts, and calculate that the youths, when apprehended, will only be cautioned or get a community order'. But again, these offences were said to be very selective, as they do not target passer-by strangers and normally are not associated with drug use. Drug-related offences may be directed against the very enclave of users, or even by users against themselves. Prostitution, for example, in the words of a drug agency manager:

Re-establishes sex roles within a setting that one would think less conservative than the official society. The sex industry in this country is now bigger than it's ever been. Some female drug users continue their career as prostitutes even after coming off drugs. This is degrading and dangerous, and explains how people who most suffer the consequences of drug-related crime are users themselves and their limited milieu.

Self-inflicted crime and harm were also part of the argument put forward by an ex-drug user. After being arrested, he addressed the youths with a message depicting drug offenders as their own main victims. In a letter to a local paper he wrote:

I write this letter from a cage of my own making. At the beginning of 1991 I embarked upon my first venture into crack [...] I am not stupid, I knew of the dangers. I'd heard the stories and even knew people whose lives had been destroyed – and ended – by crack. No one put a gun to my head and said take a 'lick' or smoke. I did so freely, thinking I could control it. I was different. I was not going to fall into the trap of those weak-minded souls who get themselves shacked to the drug, I thought. In my arrogance I did not notice my life slipping away from me [...] Don't use crack. Do not fall into the trap. No one controls crack. It controls you (*The Voice*, 24 December, 1991).

It is worth adding that 'control', as described by the above ex-user, should be understood as a process which compounds users' dependence on drugs with their dependence on the drugs economy. Do drugs act as employers of last resort, the equivalent of MacDonalds (Davies, 1990)?

CONCLUDING REMARKS

All users and dealers interviewed agreed that the drug economy in Brixton and Lambeth is not as prosperous as it is widely assumed to be. Here, those who supply users, in turn, are supplied by larger distributors who reside outside the borough. This may be the result of former institutional intervention during the mid-1980s, which presumably displaced large drug distributors to less 'suspect' areas. This may also indicate, as some of my informants argued, that not only do impoverished areas fail to set up legal businesses, they also find it hard to establish illegal ones.

There is a drug culture in Brixton, there is also a visible drug scene in the area, although this is devoid of a real drug economy. This is true if we accept the notion that prosperous drug economies are able, and in a sense are forced, to invest illegal proceeds in legal enterprises. In Brixton, this occurs to a negligible degree.

The relative deprivation of Brixton, and the poverty of its drug economy, also reverberate in the pattern of its illegal activities. Social disadvantage is reflected even upon the very pattern of drug use in the area. It is not by chance that the most harmful drug used in Brixton is temazepan, a very cheap drug, which is legal to possess and use, though not to supply. According to the drug outreach worker for West Lambeth Health Authority, there are two particular problems associated with this drug. Firstly, arrest, as the users are unaware of the obvious disturbance of their speech and behaviour caused by this drug, while these effects of the drug do not escape police attention. Secondly:

Temazepan, despite assurances to the contrary from manufacturers, remains injectable and is frequently injected. Recent changes in the constitution of the gel within the capsules has made the drug more hazardous. Injection causes severe problems with circulation, severe abscesses and often results in the loss or permanent disabling of limbs and digits. This is caused by the gel re-solidifying within the body (HIV/Drugs Outreach Worker, 1992, p. 5).

In a marginalised situation, and within a petty drug economy, also the use of cocaine and its derivatives may be more problematic than in affluent contexts. For example, a paradox is apparent whereby crack users are increasingly vulnerable also because the price of cocaine is increasing. In other words, marginalised crack users are affected by the consumer demand of middle-class cocaine users (Williams, 1990). The former are constantly forced to step up their earning in order to catch up with prices. In brief, problematic use is also fostered by non-problematic use. Finally, marginalisation also affects the way in which drugs are administered and the effect they produce. In Brixton, for example, many cocaine users who cannot buy large quantities of the substance may resort to injecting it. Because these users tend to associate risk exclusively with heroin use, and because they are sexually active and likely to share syringes, it would come as no surprise if HIV soon spread faster among cocaine users than among opiate users.

Many literary classics have explored the magic properties of drugs. The exploration of the 'mediocre' human condition showed that the humans are not mediocre creatures after all. This seemed to apply to everyone: drugs were deemed 'democratic'. They were supposed to offer revelations without regard to the merits of the person using them (Paz, 1990). The reality today seems more mundane. The dreams induced by drugs in poets and in ordinary people are increasingly different.

Vincenzo Ruggiero
Reader in Criminology and Social Studies, School of Social Work, Middlesex University

REFERENCES

Allen, D.F. and Jekel, J.F. (1991) Crack. The Broken Promise. London: Macmillan.

Arlacchi, P. and Lewis, R. (1991) Droga. Il caso Verona. Bologna: Il Mulino.

Casillo, S. (1990) Il trionfo delle aziende fanstasma, Micromega, 4, 143-160.

Cohen, P. (1989) Cocaine Use in Amsterdam. Amsterdam: Instituut voor Sociale Geografie, Universiteit van Amsterdam.

Davies, M. (1990) City of Quartz. London: Vintage.

De La Rosa, M., Lambert, E. and Gropper, B. (Eds), (1990) Drugs and Violence: Causes, Correlates, and Consequences. Rockville, MD: National Institute on Drug Abuse.

Dorn, N., Murji, K. and South, N. (1992) Traffickers. Drug Markets and Law Enforcement. London: Routledge.

Guardian (1991) Yard squad to combat drug gangs. 10 August.

Headley, V. (1992) Yardie. London: The X Press.

HIV/Drugs Outreach Worker (1992) Final Report. London: West Lambeth Health Authority.

Inciardi, J. (1984) The War on Drugs. Heroin, Cocaine. and Public Policy. Palo Alto, CA: Mayfield.

Lambeth Services (1992) Living in Lambeth. Annual Report 1991–92. London: Lambeth Council.

London Borough of Lambeth (1991) Lambeth Statistics. London: Lambeth Reference and Information Service.

Metropolitan Police (1991) Policing Brixton. The Annual Report of the Brixton Division of the Metropolitan Police. London: MET.

Mitchell, M. (1991) Vicious circles. Time Out, 14–21 August.

Mott, J. (1991) Crime and heroin use. In Whynes, D.K. and Bean, P.T. (Eds), Policing and Prescribing. The British System of Drug Control. London: Macmillan.

Paz, O. (1990), Alternating Currents. New York: Arcade.

PSI (Policy Studies Institute) (1992) Urban Trends 1. A Report on Britain's Deprived Urban Areas. London: PSI.

Reuter, P., McConn, R. and Murphy, P. (1990) Money from Crime. A Study of the Economics of Drug Dealing in Washington, DC. Santa Monica, CA: Rand Corporation.

Ruggiero, V. (1992) La roba. Economie e culture dell'eroina. Parma: Pratiche.

Ruggiero, V. (1993) The Camorra: clean capital and organised crime. In Pearce, F. and Woodiwiss, M. (Eds), Global Crime Connections. Dynamics and Control. London: Macmillan.

Ruggiero, V. and Vass, A. (1992) Heroin use and the formal economy: illicit drugs and licit economies in Italy. British Journal of Criminology, 32, 273–291.

Shankland, G., Willmott, P. and Jordan, D. (1977), Inner London: Policies for Dispersal and Balance. Final Report to the Lambeth Inner Area Study. London: HMSO.

South London Press, 1 May 1992, Yardies evil.

South London Press, 16 October 1992, Drug barons 'rule of terror'.

Voice (1991) Letters: Don't crack up on crack. 24 December.

Williams, T. (1990) The Cocaine Kids. New York: Addison-Wesley.

Zilkha, E.F. (1992) New team for war on drugs. Streatham & Clapham Guardian, 10 September.

[22]

SOCIOLOGICAL ANALYSIS OF CONFIDENCE SWINDLING

EDWIN M. SCHUR

The author has been Research Assistant to the late Professor George Dession and to Professor Richard C. Donnelly of the Yale University Law School. He worked with them on a number of projects, including the drafting of a new Puerto Rican Criminal Code. Mr. Schur was recipient at Yale of the Felix Cohen prize in legal philosophy and the Scharps prize for work in criminology and criminal law. He has published in THE NATION, MEDICAL ECONOMICS and in SOCIAL PROBLEMS. In 1955 he participated in the Planned Parenthood Federation of America's Conference on Abortion.—EDITOR.

INTRODUCTION

Almost twenty years ago L. L. Bernard, noting the prevalence of various types of fraud in American society, stated: "We have reached the fraud stage of social control in the evolution of successsion of forms in social control."[1] There seems little doubt that today we are still in what Bernard terms the fraud stage of development. Swindling appears to be a strongly entrenched national phenomenon, many instances of which are reported daily in newspapers throughout the country.

Though fraud of course takes on a wide variety of forms, from a sociological view almost all fraud can be seen to contain the kernel of the "confidence game" procedure —the creation, by one means or another, of a relation of confidence, through which a swindle is effected. All types of con games fall into a general pattern which may be described briefly as follows. The swindler (or swindlers, for several racketeers often band together to form a "con mob") selects a person who appears likely to be a good "sucker" (or, in the argot of the con man, "mark"). After establishing some degree of rapport with the mark, and once he sees that the mark will trust him, the con man tells the mark of a dishonest scheme by which they can make some money. The mark gives the swindler his money, which he never again sees. Because he has placed his confidence in the con man, it never occurs to the mark (until it is too late) that he is the object rather than the co-perpetrator of the swindle.

Unfortunately there is no way to accurately gauge the extent of criminal fraud in the United States today. Victims of con games (who, themselves, sought to gain dishonestly) rarely report their losses; many victims of related types of fraud never fully realize they were "taken." And where the loss is small, the victim often prefers not to bother getting involved with the police. Thus especially in the realm of fraud, "crimes known to the police" fall far short of crimes actually committed.

Despite the uncertainty, experts agree on the magnitude of the fraud problem. According to Maurer, it may well be that "The three big-con games, the wire, the rag, and the pay-off, have in some forty years of their existence. . . . produced more illicit profit for the operators and for the law than all other forms of professional crime (excepting violations of prohibition law) over the same period of time."[2] And

---

[1] BERNARD, L. L., SOCIAL CONTROL, New York: Macmillan, 1939, p. 36.
[2] MAURER, DAVID, THE BIG CON, Indianapolis: Bobbs-Merrill, 1940, p. 17.

296

the most recent edition of the late Professor Sutherland's competent text reports: "It is probable. . . that fraud is the most prevalent crime in America."[3]

Current efforts to curb fraud are typically ineffectual. As noted above, the reporting of fraudulent crimes is minimal. Then too, the variety of statures relevant to various kinds of fraud is, in many jurisdictions, close to chaotic: "Enact, as Colorado has done, some two dozen statutes on the general topic of obtaining property illegally and confusion is bound to result."[4] In some states, there are separate statutes covering larceny, embezzlement, false pretenses, confidence game, and forgery. This may enable a defendant to play one provision off against another—against a larceny charge raising a defense that the evidence shows embezzlement, then reversing his stand in a subsequent embezzlement trial. Composite larceny statutes in New York and California undoubtedly simplify the law-enforcement-prosecution task. New York's law is particularly well-drafted in that it makes irrelevant the thorny questions of possession as against title which plague prosecutors in many states.[5]

Another difficulty for prosecutors arises because of the general rule of criminal law that a false pretense or representation, to be indictable, must be an untrue statement regarding a past or present fact. While a leading California decision recently held that false promises are false pretenses[6], the outdated common law doctrine is still the majority rule. Exacting evidenciary requirements under specific statutes, together with the possibilities of professional swindlers "fixing" cases, further inhibit successful prosecution of fraud.

Even where statutes have been simplified so that the required proof would not hinder prosecution law-enforcement authorities and courts seem reluctant to give fraud laws a broad application, particularly where a segment of the business community might be imperiled. For instance, under the Federal Mail Fraud Act, there need be no showing that anyone is in fact defrauded and promissory fraud as well as misrepresentation of past and present fact is indictable; yet the government has relied largely on the noncriminal "fraud order" technique, rather than using the criminal sanctions also provided by the Act. An important element seems to be the "reluctance to stigmatize the overzealous advertiser as a criminal."[7]

Where sanctions are imposed in swindling cases, they are rarely stringent; prison statistics show that, generally, sentences imposed in this country for fraud are relatively light. Fraud offenders, then, are rarely uncovered and even more rarely prosecuted; of those who are prosecuted, most are at least able to avoid serious punishment. The con game, perhaps the nucleus of much American fraud, is particularly untouchable because of the victim's equivocal position.

The extent to which particular criminal statutes are unenforceable should not be attributed to chance factors. If the law's efforts to curb fraud seem of no avail, the

[3] SUTHERLAND, EDWIN H., PRINCIPLES OF CRIMINOLOGY, New York: Lippincott, 5th ed. rev. Cressey, 1955, p. 42.

[4] HEGARTY, JAMES E., *False Pretenses, Confidence Game and Short Check in Colorado*, 25 ROCKY MTN. L. REV. 325 (1953).

[5] NEW YORK PENAL LAW, Sec. 1290 (Clevenger-Gilbert, 1951).

[6] *People v. Ashley*, 267 P2d 271 (1954), *cert. den.* 348 U. S. 900 (1954); Note, *False Promises as False Pretenses*, 43 CAL. L. REV. 719 (1955).

[7] Note, *The Regulation of Advertising*, 56 COL. L. REV. 1018,1041 (1956).

answer lies not merely in the cleverness of the swindler and the inadequacy of current police techniques for fraud-detection. To understand the real meaning of the fraud problem in America, one must turn to an analysis of the social dynamics of fraud and the con game within the modern American social system.

SWINDLING AS INTERACTION

An important element in an analysis of fraud (particularly in the confidence game situation) centers around the fact that the con game is, in a very real sense, a *game*. Though the term con game probably originated with the situations in which a swindler would induce his victim to compete in a "game of chance" (from which the swindler had carefully eliminated the chance element), it has been carried over to cover quite (superficially) different situations. Perhaps too little attention has been paid the interesting fact that confidence rackets are called "games", while most other criminal offenses receive (even from their practitioners) far less playful appellations.

Sociology has long recognized the great significance, for understanding human action, of play and games. Georg Simmel wrote:

> All the forms of interaction or sociation among men—the wish to outdo, exchange, formation of parties, the desire to wrest something from the other, the hazards of accidental meetings and separations, the change between enmity and cooperation, the overpowering by ruse and revenge—in the seriousness of reality, all of these are imbued with purposive contents. In the game, they lead their own lives; they are propelled exclusively by their own attraction. For even where the game involves a monetary stake. . . . to the person who really enjoys it, its attraction rather lies in the dynamics and hazards of the sociologically significant forms of activity themselves. The more profound, double sense of "social game" is that not only the game is played in a society (as its external medium) but that, with its help, people actually "play" "society.".[8]

As George H. Mead suggested, the development of the human "self" may be illustrated by the child's participation first in play and later in the organized game. In the earlier stage of pure play the child typically "takes on" the roles of particular persons he sees about him; he plays at being other people. In the organized game stage, there is more complex role-playing, the self emerges through the creation of a "generalized other", and the game has rules which must be followed.[9] Interestingly enough, the confidence game would seem to embody aspects of both these stages. Certainly the "taking on" of another's role, the playing at being someone else, so characteristic of Mead's pure-play stage, is a prime factor in confidence swindling. At the same time there is little doubt that, at least from the swindler's standpoint, the con game has rules which must be followed and is the sort of game where "taking the attitude of the other" (one of Mead's favorite phrases) may be vitally necessary. Maurer notes, "Big-time confidence games are in reality only carefully rehearsed plays in which every member of the cast except the mark knows his part perfectly."[10]

[8] WOLFF, KURT H. (ed. and tr.), THE SOCIOLOGY OF GEORG SIMMEL, Glencoe: The Free Press, 1950, pp. 49–50.

[9] MEAD, GEORGE H., MIND, SELF AND SOCIETY, Chicago: Univ. of Chicago Press, 1934, 1950, pp. 152–164.

[10] MAURER, *op. cit.*, p. 108.

Traditionally, criminology has studied crime and the criminal. Little attention has been paid the victim of criminal offenses; in many instances this is a grave shortcoming. Hans von Hentig pointed out an important but typically ignored fact when he wrote that, "In a sense the victim shapes and moulds the criminal."[11] This holds particularly true for most fraud situations. As Maurer explains:

> A confidence man prospers only because of the fundamental dishonesty of his victim. . . . As the lust for large and easy profits is fanned into a hot flame, the mark puts all his scruples behind him. . . . In the mad frenzy of cheating someone else, he is unaware of the fact that he is the real victim, carefully selected and fatted for the kill. Thus arises the trite, but none the less sage maxim: "You can't cheat an honest man."[12]

Similarly, Professor Sutherland quotes one professional con man as follows: " 'A confidence game will fail absolutely unless the sucker has got larceny in his soul.' "[13] And as Sutherland went on to note, there is no known case of a prospect declining to continue with a scheme once he learned it was dishonest.

One writer has argued that the victim's state of mind is completely irrelevant to the question of whether the crime of false pretenses is committed in a particular case:

> Whether the swindler obtains the confidence of his victim seems entirely unimportant if in fact the swindler intended to defraud and actually does defraud his victim. . . . the fraudulent trick or device is undoubtedly what causes the unwary citizen to lose his property. . . . To reason otherwise would seem almost to promote dishonesty, and cheating, and to reward artful treachery.[14]

While this approach might make it easier for prosecutors to proceed under false pretenses laws, it clearly fails to do justice to the actual dynamics of the fraud situation. Is it really the trick or device which "undoubtedly. . . causes" the citizen to lose his property? At best, that is only part of the true picture.

Confidence swindlers are generally recognized to be the elite of the underworld. Proceeds from such fraud can be exceptionally large, the con man tends to be his own boss (even where several swindlers form a mob), and unlike the "heavy rackets" swindling involves no violence. While factors such as these help to account for the swindler's high status in the underworld, there are satisfactions still more basic to the swindling process which accrue not only to the polished professional confidence man but all the way down the line to the small-time sharper.

One writer comments, for example, that "Above all, every deception, every imposture is an assumption of power. The person deceived is reduced in stature, symbolically nullified, while the imposter is temporarily powerful, even greater than if he were the real thing."[15] It may well be that from the psychodynamic standpoint, the assertion of power over the victim is as important to the swindler (though perhaps not on the conscious level) as is obtaining the sought-after money or property.

---

[11] VON HENTIG, HANS, THE CRIMINAL AND HIS VICTIM, New Haven: Yale Univ. Press, 1948, p. 384.

[12] MAURER, *op. cit.*, p. 16.

[13] SUTHERLAND, EDWIN H., THE PROFESSIONAL THIEF, Chicago: Pheonix Books, 1937, 1956, p. 69.

[14] ATTWELL, JOSEPH J., *The Confidence Game in Illinois*, 49 NORTHWESTERN UNIV. L. REV. 737, 751 (1955).

[15] KLEIN, ALEXANDER (ed.), GRAND DECEPTION: THE WORLD'S MOST SPECTACULAR AND SUCCESSFUL HOAXES, IMPOSTURES, RUSES AND FRAUDS, New York: Lippincott, 1955, p. 13.

Indeed the concepts of power and power relations seem quite appropriate to an analysis of defrauding. To some extent at least, we may even apply to the fraud situation a few of the ideas currently used in the analysis of small group interaction processes. For in a sense rivalry, coalition and strategy are of the very essence of the confidence game. (It is interesting to note in this regard that the term "payoff," which features significantly in the analytic scheme developed by von Neumann and Morgenstern,[16] is also the label given by professional criminals to several of the more ambitious of the traditional confidence games).

We have seen that the victim has an active role to play in bringing about his own downfall. Invariably, the swindler convinces the victim that together they can swindle a third party; this third party, too, must be reckoned with in studying the structure of power relations inherent in the confidence game situation. One way of picturing such a *triad* would be to say that the victim enters into a spurious coalition with the swindler against an imaginary third party. The would-be alliance between the con man and his victim is, of course, based wholly on a lie. But as Simmel aptly stated: "However often a lie may destroy a given relationship, as long as the relationship existed, the lie was an integral element of it. The ethically negative value of the lie must not blind us to its sociologically quite positive significance for the formation of certain concrete relations."[17] Though the victim's alliance with his swindler is indeed, as he will eventually discover, a spurious one, it is his belief in the lie and his confidence in the coalition which induces him to act as he does.

Basic to the widespread willingness to play the role of victim in such dramas would seem to be the desire to get "something for nothing." Again there may be the power element; the attempt to best a third party may underlie the victim's eagerness. But it is also interesting to note that potential victims do not seem to learn from their own or others' past experiences; indeed awareness of the widespread existence of swindling seems to help little in putting a swindle-prone public on its guard. This may suggest the presence of a desire (conscious or unconscious) to be victimized. Modern psychology has stressed the need for punishment which plays an important role in unconscious life, particularly among criminal offenders; this need is often illustrated by the frequency with which offenders betray themselves by leaving some telltale clue at the scene of the crime. A similar mechanism may operate to promote a willingness to be defrauded.

The potential victim is probably quite aware that the plan of action his confidant proposes is "wrong." Under such circumstances, he may harbor a strong ambivalence about winning; he may almost sense that he is to be swindled, but may unconsciously desire to be punished for his own wrongdoing. The question whether such self-defeating mechanisms should be attributed to a basic "death wish" or masochism must be left to the psychoanalysts.

A STRUCTURAL IMMORALITY

Most American studies of fraud and related offenses have been oriented to the individual offender, whose depredations are usually explained in terms of what may

---

[16] VON NEUMANN, JOHN AND OSKAR MORGENSTERN, THEORY OF GAMES AND ECONOMIC BEHAVIOR, Princeton: Princeton Univ. Press, 1947.
[17] WOLFF, *op. cit.*, p. 316.

be called a "situational approach." Thus the conclusion of Lottier, based on first-hand study of embezzlers in a court's psychopathic clinic: "In every case, without exception, a critical tension situation of one kind or another invariably preceded the embezzlement behavior."[18] Similarly Cressey, in his recent book, OTHER PEOPLE'S MONEY, developed a modified situational theory of trust violation:

> Trusted persons become trust violators when they conceive of themselves as having a financial problem which is non-shareable, are aware that this problem can be secretly resolved by violation of the position of financial trust, and are able to apply to their own conduct in that situation ver-balizations which enable them to adjust their conceptions of themselves as users of the entrusted funds or property.[19]

Such theories may have validity with reference to the "chance offender" (assuming for the moment that the "chance" offender is not merely a persistent offender who got caught early in the game); to explain the persistent swindler we need a theory which transcends the situational approach. In any case, since various types of fraud abound in modern American society, we must look to our present social system for clues to explain the great drawing-power the roles of swindler and victim currently display.

C. Wright Mills, who has perhaps sensed the crux of the problem, states:

> Many of the problems of "white-collar crime" and of relaxed public morality, of high-priced vice and of fading personal integrity, are problems of *structural* immorality. They are not merely the problem of the small character twisted by the bad milieu. And many people are at least vaguely aware that this is so. As news of higher immoralities breaks, they often say, "Well, another one got caught today," thereby implying that the cases disclosed are not odd events involving occasional characters but symptoms of a widespread condition. There is good probative evidence that they are right.[20]

In attempting to understand how such a "widespread condition" influences crime patterns, we should perhaps take for a lead the notion of the French sociologist Gabriel Tarde that "All the important acts of social life are carried out under the domination of example." Tarde asserted that: "Criminality always being. . . a phenomenon of imitative propagation. . . the aim is to discover. . . which among these various spreadings of example which are called instruction, religion, politics, com-merce, industry, are the ones that foster, and which the ones that impede, the expan-sion of crime."[21]

One system of values which may foster crime, and particularly fraud, in our society, is that relating to the phenomenon of salesmanship. As Sutherland notes, "The confidence games are based essentially on salesmanship. . . . "[22] To a great extent our society is built on salesmanship, and the term implies much more than the mere sale of material goods. In an era when an increased premium is being put on "idea men," the ability to "sell a bill of goods" (in the figurative sense as well as the literal) takes on added importance. It is just this ability which the successful con man must demon-

---

[18] LOTTIER, STUART, *A Tension Theory of Criminal Behavior*, 7 AMER. SOCIOL. REV. 840 (1942).

[19] CRESSEY, DONALD R., OTHER PEOPLE'S MONEY: A STUDY IN THE SOCIAL PSYCHOLOGY OF EMBEZZLEMENT, Glencoe: The Free Press, 1953, p. 30.

[20] MILLS, C. WRIGHT, THE POWER ELITE, New York: Oxford Univ. Press, 1956, pp. 343–344.

[21] TARDE GABRIEL, PENAL PHILOSOPHY, tr. Howell, Boston: Little Brown, 1912, p. 362.

[22] SUTHERLAND, PRINCIPLES OF CRIMINOLOGY, p. 233.

strate. Closely related to "selling a bill of goods" is the cultural stress on "putting across" one's "personality." We are all quite familiar with the importance in modern American society of being "well liked," of getting along and of being a "good mixer." These socially-sanctioned attributes are the very hallmark of the experienced swindler. Maurer notes that con men, ". . . have cultivated the social side more than any other criminal group. They are able to fit in unobtrusively on any social level . . . . Although their culture is not very deep, it is surprisingly wide and versatile."[23]

Though women frequently act as lures or accomplices in certain con games, full-fledged confidence swindling seems to be primarily a male offense in this country. Since nothing is required for the commission of fraudulent acts which would be beyond the physiological capacities or social opportunities of women, the fact that swindlers are predominantly male tends to underscore the influence of general social values in shaping patterns of fraud. The specific attributes of the swindler tend to be typically male attributes under our present social system. This is generally true of the ability to sell things and of having a successful "personality;" certainly, "coming up with an idea," "putting an idea across" and convincing others are held to be almost exclusively within the masculine domain. It may be interesting also to note that the role of confidant (which the swindler usually takes on, often with great success), be it in the form of priest, lawyer, doctor or psychoanalyst, is characteristically taken by a male in our society. Quite likely, we should expect an increase in female fraud in the future. Otto Pollak has noted that, ". . . an increase in female crimes against property is a concomitant of the social emancipation of women."[24] As the "idea woman" comes more and more into vogue, the "confidence woman" may cease to be a rarity. What affect this will have on the total extent of fraudulent crime remains to be seen.

Reinforcing the rationalizations which the social system provides the swindler, and further inciting his depredations, is the seemingly unlimited supply of victims. Businessmen seem particularly likely marks; as von Hentig has noted, "There is. . . general consensus that businessmen are excellent victims in all respects."[25] This must be at least partly attributed to certain values of the business community which seem to underlie the trend to what Mills terms a "structural immorality." As Donald Taft comments:

> . . . success is based somewhat increasingly upon financial gain similar to that of the banker or speculator rather than upon that of the old-fashioned industrialist whose fun was in the day's work. Whatever the economists may say, speculative gains look more like luck than hard work, and more nearly approximate the something for nothing philosophy of the pickpocket.[26]

Similarly, a probable influence on victim behavior is risk-taking, a generally approved activity which appears in numerous forms throughout our social life. The high value placed on risk-taking underlies the characteristic zeal for success which has played an integral part in shaping patterns of American social mobility. As Geoffrey Gorer has

---

[23] MAURER, *op. cit.*, p. 186.

[24] POLLAK, OTTO, THE CRIMINALITY OF WOMEN, Philadelphia: Univ. of Pennsylvania Press, 1950, p. 75.

[25] VON HENTIG, *op. cit.*, p. 435.

[26] TAFT, DONALD R., CRIMINOLOGY, New York: Macmillan, rev. ed. 1950, p. 231.

observed, "Gambling is. . . a respected and important component in many business ventures. . . . Like the gambler 'for fun' the American businessman is generally prepared to take proportionately far greater risks than his European equivalent."[27]

The victim, then, like the swindler, can easily take advantage of conflicting and overlapping patterns of expected behavior to justify his participation in fraudulent schemes. And in the swindler, who is the idea man, the convincer, (and who thus in part typifies the leader), the victim may see something of his own (real or hoped-for) image; it may be this image to which he responds.

IMPLICATIONS FOR THE SOCIOLOGY OF CRIME

According to Professor Sutherland's "differential association" theory, "A person becomes delinquent because of an excess of definitions favorable to violation of law over definitions unfavorable to violation of law."[28] While the impact of such "definitions" is evident in much of what I have suggested above, it may be more useful to view value orientation on the social-system level, rather than membership in particular social groups within that system, as the prime vehicle for assimilation of the definitions. Furthermore, at least insofar as it is offered as a general theory of all crime, the differential association theory is negligent in limiting the subject matter of criminology to the understanding of the individual offender. As Clarence Jeffery has remarked in his highly valuable article, "Crime must be studied as an aspect of institutional systems. Institutions, not individual offenders, should be the subject matter of criminology." Under such an approach, "The concept of cause is replaced by one of function."[29]

"Structural-functional" sociology indeed offers much that is fruitful for analysis of the sociology of crime. According to this view, "deviance is always relative to a given institutionalized value-pattern system. . . . "[30] Sutherland at least sensed this basic unity of legality and illegality, as evidenced by his thesis that essentially the same sort of processes which result in lawful behavior also result in unlawful behavior.

Structural-functional analysis makes clear that a given item may have "diverse consequences, functional and dysfunctional, for individuals, for sub-groups, and for the more inclusive social structure and culture."[31] Thus crime, usually thought of as negative and disorganizing, can serve positive as well as negative functions within the social system. While there has been some recognition of possible economic functions of crime[32], other social functions of crime are less frequently recognized.

The distinction between "manifest" and "latent" functions, "aids the sociological interpretation of many social practices which persist even though their manifest purpose is clearly not achieved."[33] This idea may be particularly useful in analysis

[27] GORER, GEOFFREY, THE AMERICAN PEOPLE, New York: Norton, 1948, p. 178.

[28] SUTHERLAND, PRINCIPLES OF CRIMINOLOGY, p. 78.

[29] JEFFREY, CLARENCE R., *Crime, Law and Social Structure. Part I: Methodology*, 47 J. CRIM. LAW, CRIMINOL. & POLICE SCI. 423 (1956).

[30] PARSONS, TALCOTT, THE SOCIAL SYSTEM, Glencoe: The Free Press, 1951, p. 283.

[31] MERTON, ROBERT, SOCIAL THEORY AND SOCIAL STRUCTURE, Glencoe: The Free Press, 1949, 1951, p. 32.

[32] HAWKINS, E. R. AND WILLARD WALLER, *Critical Notes on the Cost of Crime*, 26 J. CRIM. LAW AND CRIMINOL. 684 (1936).

[33] MERTON, *op. cit.*, p. 64.

of seemingly unenforceable criminal laws; I have elsewhere tried to apply such an analysis to our current laws against abortion.[34] Since our fraud laws are rarely applied, and when applied do not seem effective, why do we maintain them in their present form? The answer may lie in the important functions served by the practices nominally sought to be outlawed; we might well ask ourselves—could we really afford to effectively curtail fraud?

Structural-functional analysis has underscored the fact that in order to eliminate an existing social structure one must first provide the necessary "functional alternatives." This should make evident the futility of attempting to curb fraud by merely increasing penalties. Rusche and Kirchheimer have quite rightly stressed this "uselessness of shifting penal policies as a weapon against socially determined variations in the crime rate."[35] Just what sort of adjustment in the social system must be made is uncertain, but the idea that radical changes are needed is not new. Sutherland, for example, recognized that "adequate control of professional crime cannot be attained by proceeding against thieves one at a time either by punitive or by reformative policies. Control calls, in addition, for modifications in the general social order out of which professional theft grows."[36] Perhaps the only real hope for a major reduction of fraud lies in such changes as may gradually result from an informed questioning of some of our prevailing social value systems.

Criminology has been seriously hampered in the past by its refusal to abandon the "social welfare approach" in favor of a truly sociological orientation. The former, as Kingsley Davis suggests, labors under the like-causes-like fallacy, here the idea that evil causes evil. To adopt a genuinely sociological mode of analysis, criminology must first of all recognize that "the contramoral is always functionally related to the moral. . . . "[37] With such recognition as a starting point, the phrase "sociology of crime" begins to take on real meaning.

[34] SCHUR, E. M., *Abortion and the Social System*, 3 SOCIAL PROBLEMS 94 (1955).

[35] RUSCHE, GEORG AND OTTO KIRCHHEIMER, PUNISHMENT AND SOCIAL STRUCTURE, New York: Columbia Univ. Press, 1939, p. 201.

[36] SUTHERLAND, THE PROFESSIONAL THIEF, p. 229.

[37] DAVIS, KINGSLEY, *Illegitimacy and the Social Structure*, 45 AMER. J. SOCIOL. 215 (1939).

[23]

THE SOCIAL ORGANIZATION OF BURGLARY*

NEAL SHOVER
University of Tennessee

The social organization of systematic burglary is discussed and briefly compared to earlier work on systematic offenders. Salient aspects of both the internal and external social organization of burglary are presented, especially as these are related to the problems of burglary. It is suggested that burglary continues to be more like the social organization of professional theft, as this was presented by Sutherland, than check forgery and armed robbery, as these have been depicted in recent literature. Some possible reasons for this are presented. Finally, it is suggested that the social organization of burglary can be expected to continue to change as a result of macrolevel changes in the economy and in the nature of security forces.

One of the contributions of American sociologists to the analysis of crime was the early recognition that certain types of criminal pursuits could, like legitimate occupations, be studied as structured and collective activity (Sutherland, 1937; Hollingshead, 1939; Hall, 1952). It was recognized that these structures, or *behavior systems,* commonly consist of distinctive argot, an ideology of defense and legitimation, esoteric knowledge, behavioral norms, and more or less stable relationships between the occupational practitioners and a host of others on whom they are dependent for their successful work performance. Sutherland (1937) applied this sensitizing and organizing concept of the behavior system to theft, insightfully tracing the structure of *professional theft* and the crucial contingencies without which a career as a professional thief could not be realized. This analysis is intended as a continuation in the same tradition. It explicates some of the characteristics of the social relationships which enable one type of burglary offender, the "good burglar," to carry on his activities. The nature of the social relationships between working burglars, and also the relationships between

* I am grateful to Donald Cressey and Carl Bersani for comments on an earlier version of this paper.

burglars and quasi-legitimate members of the host society, are sketched.

LITERATURE

For Sutherland, the utility of the concept of professional theft as a behavior system stemmed, in part, from the implications this has for attempts to control professional crime and to understand the activities and careers of thieves (1937:229). However, following Sutherland, others have found that systematic check forgery (Lemert, 1958) and armed robbery (Einstadter, 1969; Camp, 1968) do not appear to conform very closely to this model of professional theft. Unlike the thieves which Sutherland studied, check forgers and armed robbers operate more independently of one another and are not necessarily dependent upon established offenders for tutelage and support. Moreover, they do not maintain on-going relationships with quasi-legitimate members of the wider society, such as fences and fixers. Thus far, however, burglary and the men who commit it have not been the objects of systematic study.

METHODS

Four different sources of materials were used for this study. First, I read 34 autobiographies of thieves—primarily, though not exclusively, burglars—in their entirety. In addition, 12 novels or journalistic accounts of crime and the activities of criminals were read (e.g., Davis, 1944).[1] Second, a total of 47 interviews were conducted with men incarcerated in the various branches of the Illinois State Penitentiary system. Third, on the basis of these interviews, a lengthy questionnaire was constructed and administered to an additional 88 inmates, in small groups of from three to 12 men at a time. And fourth, interviews were conducted with seven unincarcerated burglars or former burglars, one former fence, and one very peripheral associate of a gang of former bank burglars. All nine of these men were contacted and interviewed without the assistance or cooperation of law enforcement or correctional agencies. Table 1 contains limited demographic data on the three different samples. All materials were collected by the author personally.

The collection of data by prison interview and questionnaire proceeded in two steps. First, interviews were conducted with 25 inmates in various Illinois penal institutions; a topical guide was used to provide minimal structure for these interviews. (The same guide was used to abstract and

[1] A copy of the list of sources is available upon request from the author.

classify material from the autobiographies.) These interviews each lasted approximately one hour. Following the completion of these initial interviews, the questionnaire was constructed, pretested, and revised. Questionnaire respondents all were new admissions to the Illinois State Penitentiary system for burglary or some related offense (e.g., possession of burglary tools) during the period of the study. Only those men were asked to fill out the questionnaire who were shown by routine testing to be reading at or above a seventh grade level. The questionnaire was usually administered during the first month in the institution, usually in groups of from three to 12 men at a time. Thirteen men declined to complete the questionnaire, in most cases because of suspicion of the author's motives, and in the remaining cases because of feelings of extreme naivete about burglary.

Prison interview respondents were purposively selected, primarily from new admissions to the various institutions. At all times in the selection of interview respondents, I sought to maximize differences in criminal sophistication for comparative purposes. Those respondents who were more criminally sophisticated were all selected by snowballing, after I had made an initial contact with one good

TABLE 1

DEMOGRAPHIC CHARACTERISTICS OF THE SAMPLES

	Mean ($\overline{X}$) Age	Race		N
		White	Black	
Prison Interview Sample	23.4	38	9	47
Prison Questionnaire Sample	24.6	71	16	87[a]
Free World Interview Sample	31.6	9	0	9
Total	24.6	118	25	143

[a] Does not include one case for which no records were available.

burglar. Several of these men were at that time serving sentences for some offense other than burglary; however, each of them had at some time in his life been a skilled burglar. Interviews with 13 men were tape recorded and several of the men were interviewed two or more times. Participation by all respondents was completely voluntary. I repeatedly informed those who participated that "there is no way that you can either be helped or hurt by this."

The use of the questionnaire, autobiographies, and free-world interviews were intended to provide a crude triangulation of methods (Denzin, 1970), which was considered especially important in view of the understandable controversy surrounding the use of captive samples (cf. Polsky, 1967; Lemert, 1968). It was recognized, however, that each of the varied methods and research settings contains its own often unique threats to validity. Through the use of a combination of methods and settings, an attempt was made to deal with these validity problems. A more extended discussion of these issues and the methodology can be found in an earlier report (Shover, 1971).

FINDINGS

In the following discussion I present materials on both the *internal* and *external* social organization of burglary. I use the former to refer to the organization of burglary "crews" (i.e., their division of labor) and how they actually operate when "taking off" scores. By the external social organization of burglary, I refer to the relationships between burglars and those outside of their crews with whom they tend to maintain symbiotic social relationships. It is first necessary, however,

to discuss the meaning of the concept *good burglar,* since the materials presented here are intended to apply to this type of offender.

The designation "good thief" or "good burglar" is one which is applied selectively by thieves themselves to those who (1) are technically competent, (2) have a reputation for personal integrity, (3) tend to specialize in burglary, and (4) have been at least relatively successful at crime; success in turn is determined by (1) how much money one has made stealing, and (2) how much time, if any, he has done. The good burglar, then, is the man who generally confines his stealing activities to burglary, has been relatively successful, has a reputation as "good people," and is technically competent. At times such a person would be referred to by the more generic designation as a good thief. But in either case the qualitative distinction is most important (cf. Morton, 1950:18-19).[2]

Of the total number of respondents interviewed for this study, only ten men were considered to be good burglars. These determinations were made on the basis of peer evaluations and material elicited during the interview which indicated past success and sophistication in burglary. All of these men had, at some time, supported themselves solely by criminal activities, the shortest for one year and the longest for approximately 20 years—without incarceration. Of the total questionnaire sample (88), only 20 men were classified as good thieves.

[2] An extended discussion of how the social organization of contemporary systematic burglars compares to the behavior system of professional theft as sketched by Sutherland is beyond the scope and space limitations of this paper. I touch upon this issue in the conclusion of this paper.

This was done on the basis of an arbitrary scoring system applied to (1) the largest sum of money ever received from a single score, and (2) the kind of techniques used to enter places and/or open safes.[3]

Internal Social Organization

Skilled burglary by necessity is a social enterprise. Successful good burglars rarely work alone. The problems simply of managing the act requires at least two persons, frequently more. The work is often physically demanding, very time consuming, and must be performed under the apprehension of potential discovery, injury, or arrest. All of these problems must be dealt with, typically by task specialization among members of the burglary crew or "gang." The membership of these crews is in a nearly constant state of flux, as some thieves are arrested, drop out of crime, or are discarded by their crime partners for one reason or another. Although disparate crews may know one another, may hang out in the same joints, and may be linked together to some extent by occasionally overlapping memberships, it is the individual crew which forms the basic unit of social organization among working burglars. These crews are formed from the pool of available manpower which frequents the bars and lounges where thieves hang out, or they may be formed as a result of the assistance of tipsters and fences,

who often will introduce burglars to one another.[4]

The key to understanding the social world of the good burglar is found in the recognition that he and his associates form a *category* of individuals, not a society or organization. As Goffman (1963:23-24) defines it,

> The term category is perfectly abstract and can be applied to any aggregate, in this case, persons with a particular stigma. A good portion of those who fall within a given stigma category may well refer to the total membership by the term "group" or to an equivalent, such as "we" or "our people". Those outside the category may similarly designate those within it in group terms. However, often in such cases the full membership will not be part of a single group, in the strictest sense; they will neither have a capacity for collective action, nor a stable and embracing pattern of mutual interaction. What one does find is that the members of a particular stigma category will have a tendency to come together into small social groups whose members all derive from the category, these groups themselves being subject to overarching organization to varying degrees. And one also finds that when one member of a category happens to come into contact with another, both may be disposed to modify their treatment of each other by virtue of believing that they each belong to the same "group". Further, in being a member of the category, an individual may have an increased probability of coming into contact with any other member, and even forming a relationship with him as a result. A category, then, can function to dispose its members to group-formation and relations, but its total membership does not thereby constitute a group.

Two men, occasionally three, are usually the largest number of men

---

[3] In order to be considered a good burglar a respondent must have (1) received $4,000 or more on his largest score, and either (2) opened a safe at some time by drilling or burning, or (3) entered a place at some time by cutting a hole in the roof or wall. For a more extended discussion of the scoring system used to categorize the sample, see Shover (1971).

[4] Braly (1967:233-34) refers to the underworld as a "loosely cohesive and always shifting sub-world which include[s] a small manpower pool, fed by a trickle of youngsters outgrowing the teen gangs, and another trickle of men out on parole."

who will remain together in burglary activities over a relatively long period of time. They tend to confine their burglaries with this same "partner," crew or gang. Whenever the problems expected on some particular score necessitate additional manpower, a not uncommon occurrence, someone who is known to them will be "filled in" for the job. The person who is filled in will be selected on the basis of his trustworthiness, specialized competence, and availability at the time the score is being planned. If he performs well on one job, he may be asked in on other jobs where a person with his qualifications is needed.

As I have indicated, the locus of much of the contact between members of the category of thief or burglar is the hangout, usually a bar, lounge, or restaurant. Gould, *et al.* (1968) have similarly called attention to these hangouts as the places where thieves may recruit partners. In these hangouts thieves spend much of their free time in drinking and socializing. Here they exchange technical information, gossip about one another, talk about "old scores," and plan future ones. The significance of the hangout can be seen in the following remarks, which also tell a great deal about the process by which crews are formed and the loosely knit relationships between working crews.

Q: What are the determinants of whether or not a person gets taken in, or rather taken along, with a good group?

A: Generally you have to know somebody on the crew. Like when I came out of the joint in Iowa I came back to Chicago and I was going out with one guy, a guy I grew up in the neighborhood with. We were going into this joint where the thieves hang out and we made some nice jewelry scores . . . And when we went into

this joint I got in touch with a couple of fences through the guy that had [owned] this joint . . . One particular night this one crew was in there and I got introduced and he more or less told them that I was alright, good people, a good thief and making it. I had a good score that I had looked at so I ran it down to them. So we went over and looked at it and everybody liked it. We all went together and made the score. Owing me something, a couple of weeks later they went out and scored a wholesale house and they called me for a fill in.

For awhile then I didn't work with that crew. But I got filled in with another crew because they needed someone on the radio. One of the guys was in the hospital so I filled in with the crew on a couple of scores. Then I went back to work with the first crew on another score. And [then] this guy that owned the joint, he more or less started working with one guy from this crew and one guy from another crew. They filled-me-in and we had our own crew. And we started operating as a crew—but then we also worked intermittently too with other crews (Prison interview, May 1, 1970).

As a consequence of these networks of relationships, even though the actual span of social organization is extremely limited, working thieves in even large cities often will know one another, although they may never have worked together.

It's like everybody that is stealing—when you have several crews in a certain area —they generally know each other . . . even though it's no big organization thing—20 or 30 burglars and we all have some kind of conspiracy—it's just close knit groups and we all know each other. If you don't know them all you know two or three here and there, or one of your partners knows two or three, or a couple dudes you don't know. It's hard to explain. Over the years you get to know everybody (Prison interview, May 1, 1970).

Burglary crews, when working, usually function on a partnership basis (cf. Einstadter, 1969). Such differentiation of authority as does exist is usually grounded in marked internal differences in age, criminal experience, or skill. Rarely, however, is there a formally designated leader (cf. De-Baun, 1950). Tasks during scores are allocated on the basis of personal strengths and weaknesses, or personal preferences. An easy informally arrived at consensus seems to be the rule here. It is not uncommon for crews to contain at least one man whose mechanical prowess is quite high as evidenced, among other things, by his ability to open safes. Nor is it uncommon to find at least one man who seems to have a particularly good "eye for money" (i.e., who excels at locating potentially lucrative scores). Although each partner might keep his eyes open for "something that looked good," one of them would be more talented along these lines.

Potential scores are located through tips or direct personal selection. The burglar's various "connections" or *occupational contacts* (cf. Katz, 1958) are the most important source of tips. Burglars themselves often locate potential scores in a number of different ways. During their free time, for example, they will often go on automobile trips for hundreds of miles into nearby cities and towns looking over a variety of places. On "scouting trips" of this nature they will be especially alert for places similar to those they have made in the past (since chain stores, for example, will frequently purchase the same type of money safes for all of their stores). Having once located a potential score, one or more of the crew will visit the place to make some preliminary observations. This can range from driving past a few times in an automobile to possibly walking around the place or even climbing to inspect the roof during non-business hours. During these early observations the location of the safe is of upmost importance. If it is located near a front window where there is no cover for anyone who would be trying to open it, and if it is also anchored to the floor, it represents a formidable challenge, one which will under most circumstances simply be passed up. On the other hand, if the safe is located in an area of the place which affords cover, the burglars will investigate further. In addition to providing cover from outsiders, the location of the place itself is extremely important. It should, ideally, provide privacy and more than one "out" or avenue of escape. If the place is "bugged," the burglars must determine what type of "bug" it is and the points of vulnerability. If it is a "safe score," they must determine, as precisely as possible, what type of safe it is. If it is a "merchandise score," they will need to know precisely what is to be taken and its location.

To get to and from the score, plans must be made for some kind of transportation. A "work car" is used for this purpose. A stolen car or a used car, commonly purchased for cash under an assumed name, is kept hidden away until needed. A truck might be obtained and used in a similar manner. Occasionally, when the risks and stakes dictate, more than one car or truck will be used during a score; one vehicle might be a legitimate one—valid title and license plates—while one or more others are stolen.

The score itself, as I have emphasized, is planned so that each participant knows exactly what he is expected to do. Three or four men are the most typical size of a crew who take off a score; but here again there is variation, depending upon unique circumstances and conditions. One man is usually left "on point" as a lookout.[5] He can be stationed anywhere that provides good visual coverage of the immediate area, either inside or outside of the place. Depending upon the distance of his station from the building, he might use a walkie-talkie to provide instant warning. Another man will "sit on the calls," listening to police calls on a portable radio, again so that instant warnings of detection can be provided. Another confederate might drive a "pick-up car." Occasionally both the "radio man" and the "point man" will be one and the same person. Most commonly, one or two others will actually make the entry and do the necessary work. This can involve opening a safe and/or preparing merchandise to be hauled away.

Preparations are frequently made in advance for the means and route of escape. The destination is fixed, especially if the burglary involves merchandise. Generally, in such a case, the first stop will be a "drop" where the fence or one of his agents will inspect the proceeds and arrange for it to be cut up and moved on. If multiple vehicles are used in leaving the score, a legitimate car may be used as a "crash car." The driver of this car will follow the vehicle containing the merchandise and see to it that no one overtakes it from the rear. In the event of failure, and one or more of

the participants are arrested, those who escaped are ready and expected immediately to post bail for them.

Members of the crew usually share equally in the proceeds of a score (even "ends"). Any expenses incurred during the planning and carrying out of the score are also shared equally. (And it should be noted that the tools required are sometimes quite expensive.) If there is a "tipster" involved, he will receive an agreed upon percentage of the gross proceeds, frequently a flat ten percent.

External Social Organization

The most important of the social relationships which the good burglar maintains with persons outside his group are closely related to the problems he faces in this work. Collectively these social relationships are known as one's "connections;" the person who is "well connected" has been fortunate in establishing and maintaining a particularly profitable set of such relationships. Systematic burglars face several problems in their work; and their connections are particularly important in helping them to cope with these problems.

First, the good burglar must know before burglarizing a place that it would be worth his while to do so. He wants, above all, to avoid unnecessary exposure to the "bitch of chance" (Braly, 1967:233); so he tries, if possible, to assure himself in advance that a score will be rewarding. Second, if he steals a quantity of merchandise— or anything else that he cannot sell directly—he must have a safe outlet for it; he must be able to sell it without risk to himself of detection. And third, in the event of his arrest, he must be able to so thwart the criminal justice system, so that he either goes

---

[5] Cf. Einstadter (1969) for an excellent discussion of the social roles involved in heists. Einstadter, it should be noted, was only concerned with the *internal* social organization of armed robbery.

free or else receives an extremely light sentence for his crime(s). The first of these problems, the informational one, is handled by connections with "tipsters;" the second problem, the merchandising problem, is handled by relationships with the "fence;" the third is handled by attorneys, bondsmen, and occasionally, the "fix."[6]

The Tipster

A tipster (also known as a "spotter" or "fingerman") is a person who conveys information to a burglar about some premises or its occupants which is intended to aid in burglarizing those premises. Among even moderately successful burglars, tipsters represent an important connection and source of information.

> Your professional burglars depend on information. Any time you read about a darn good burglary, they didn't just happen to be walking along the street and say, Here's a good looking house, let's go in there. They depend upon information from strictly legitimate fellas (Martin, 1953:68).

Tipsters are of several types. Many of them (perhaps the majority) are fences who convey tips to thieves as a way of controlling their inventory. Another type is the ex-thief who holds legitimate employment but still maintains friendships with his old associates. A third type is the active thief who learns about some potentially lucrative score but cannot make it himself because the finger of suspicion would immediately be pointed at him.

---

[6] In many cities gambler and loan-sharks are also important sources of support for working thieves. Because of their contacts in diverse social circles they are often instrumental in the integration of criminal networks, and in the integration of criminals with quasi-legitimate business and professional men.

And finally, another type of tipster is what Hapgood (1903:262) referred to as the "sure thing grafter." This is a person, usually an older thief, who has become extremely selective in his scores. Whenever he hears about a score but does not want to make it himself, he may pass on the tip to some other thief of his acquaintance.

Tipsters of all four types are aware of the value of good information to the burglar; and should they ever receive such information, they are ready to pass it along to someone who can use it. Besides receiving tips from such individuals, the good burglar will, however, occasionally receive information from persons who are not so well informed on burglary and the role of the tipster. This may involve purchasing information from a person who is known to have it; while at other times it may involve the utilization of the knowledge of a personal friend—who may be employed on the premises or may have learned about it some other way.

> . . . in all walks of life you've got people who are morally dishonest. They won't go and steal something themselves. But they'll buy something stolen if they get the right price and they'll give you a little information too. As long as they don't get hurt. Those people are usually legitimate businessmen. They're in a position to give you a lot of information that you couldn't get otherwise. About the protection of different places. About the assets of different places. And the different security measures of different business houses (Martin, 1953:65).

Or the burglar may take a more active part in the search for information.

> . . . This particular place was here in town. I knew a girl that knew a girl that worked there. So I approached this girl and said "Hey I'd like some information about this place. Why don't you ask her and see what she says 'cause I'll pay her

for it?' . . . So this girl came back and said, 'Yeah, the 15th and 31st there's money there 'cause they cash company payroll checks' . . ." Then I sent back for some specific information, what kind of safe it was and how the alarm was tied in . . . We got the place and then I gave this other girl $500 and I never heard anymore about it (Free world interview, March 30, 1971).

Having briefly considered the activities of the tipster, we might now inquire as to just who he is; what kinds of legitimate occupational roles do tipsters occupy? It must be emphasized at the outset that tipsters are not confined to any particular social strata. They are found at all levels of the social structure. As one thief has remarked: "There are some amazing people who come to you with information—people you just wouldn't believe could do such things" (Crookston, 1967:127). The following specific examples of the legitimate occupations of tipsters are mentioned in the autobiographical literature: night watchman (Genet, 1964:58), window cleaner (Page, not dated:76-77), prostitute (Wilson, 1964:57), attorney (Black, 1926:141; Crookston, 1967:128; Jackson, 1969:121-122), coal deliveryman (Martin, 1953:65), catering service employee (Malcolm X, 1964:140), jeweler, gambler, detective, and used car dealer (Barnes, 1971:51-68). In addition, the questionnaire sample was asked if they had "ever received a tip on a place to burglarize." Of the total sample of 88 men, 61 percent replied in the affirmative. These men were then asked to indicate the legitimate occupation of one such person. Responses were given by 26 men, as shown in Table 2. The data presented in this table should not be interpreted as a representative picture of the larger population of tipsters. It is presented

TABLE 2
LEGITIMATE OCCUPATIONS REPORTED FOR 26 TIPSTERS

Occupation	N
Tavern Owner or Bartender	7
Owner or Employee of Victimized Place	5
Repairman or Deliveryman	3
Beautician	2
Businessman (unspecified)	2
Other (e.g., police officer, janitor, shipping clerk)	7
Total	26

here only as a means of emphasizing the diversity of backgrounds of tipsters.

There is reason to believe that the success of a burglar is directly related to the size of the geographical area over which he maintains connections such as relationships with tipsters (and fences). Some men scarcely know anyone outside of their own city, while others can count on receiving information and assistance from persons in widely separated parts of the United States—or even nearby countries such as Canada and Mexico. The following is a typical account of how these far flung connections are established:

Q: How did you get connected as well as you were?
A: Well, first I was thrown in jail with a man who was pretty well respected throughout the country. I made three or four trips across the country with him, meeting friends of his. And then it just more or less snowballed. It developed that a person in one city [would] say. "If you're going to Miami stop and see so-and-so, tell him I sent you. [There] may be something laying around you can pick up" . . . (Free world interview, May 27, 1971).

The value of connections such as these can be appreciated.

Q: You've seen a lot of men, then, who never really amounted to anything stealing. Why was it that they never progressed or became more proficient?

A: Well, one reason is lack of intelligence. [Others are] a lack of connections, a lack of integrity—nobody would trust them—and possibly just no ambition.

Q: You mentioned connections. Do you think they're important.

A: Highly important—well, it depends. Some people are born, raised, steal, and die in the same town. They never get out of the state. They might get out of the city to go to the county jail or penitentiary, then back home. Every policeman in the city knows who they are after they've fallen a couple of times on petty stuff . . . They don't travel far and fast enough.

Q: In what way were connections important to you?

A: They're what I just said in an indirect manner. Because if you're far enough away and fast enough away—through connections—then the local heat don't even bother you. If somebody robbed a safe for $50,000 on westhill today, who would get the blame for it? Where would they start sweeping? All the known safecrackers in this area. Certainly no farther away than Toledo. But suppose someone flew in here from Los Angeles and flew out. He's just about as safe as he can be. Because nobody knows he was here, he don't know anybody in the town except the man who sent for him [tipster]. So he does his little piece of work and goes. The cops are running around picking up everybody in town. But they're not bothering him. You couldn't do that without connections (Free World interview, June 9, 1971).

The Fence

A fence is a person who buys stolen merchandise, or some other type of commodities (e.g., a coin collection), generally for purposes of resale, which he knows or strongly suspects are stolen. As in the case of tipsters, fences are stratified such that some are better able than others to dispose of a more diversified line of products, a larger quantity of products, and to handle more frequent purchases of products. Additionally, fences can be ordered hierarchically on the basis of how deeply and heavily involved they are in the purchase of stolen goods (cf. Hall, 1952:155-64; 218-9). The lowest level of fence would be the "square john," who purchases an occasional item from a thief for his own use; the highest level fence would be the person who is able to dispose of nearly any type and quantity of merchandise on the shortest of notices. If it were not for the existence of fences, thieves would have great difficulty disposing of the merchandise they steal. Indeed, systematic theft would be a quite different sort of enterprise without them.

Fences, as already suggested, are one of the most common sources of tips for good burglars. The reason for this is related to the fence's need to exercise some control over the nature and quantity of his inventory. "Giving up scores" (tips) to burglars is one tested and proven technique for doing so. Evidence indicates that this is a very common practice on the part of fences (cf. Malcolm X, 1964:144). In fact, it is this practice which seems to be largely responsible for the fence's having a ready buyer for his products before the thief even "takes off" the score. Giving up scores works, then, to the advantage of both the burglar and the fence. The latter must be seen as occupying a dual role in the behavior system of theft; he purchases stolen goods and simultaneously gathers information about future scores to which the good burglar can be tipped off. By searching out the kinds of merchandise he wants, and then giving the score to burglars, he is able to control his inventory.

But leaving aside the fence's role as a buyer of stolen merchandise, we find that sometimes their relationships with burlgars is considerably more complex. Frequently, for example, the fence will be in a position to provide the burglar with several social services (cf. Martin, 1953:98-99). For example:

> I had . . . this one fence I was doing a lot of business with and he was giving me scores, too . . . . He wasn't a juice man [loan shark] but if you needed $500 and you did a lot of business with him, if you sold to him regularly, there was no problem . . . . If you had any problem and you needed money quick, say to go out of town to look at something, or if you got sort of short, he could come up with a G-note (Prison interview, March 13, 1970).

Moreover, because of their business contacts, fences occasionally learn about legitimate businessmen or business employees who have gotten themselves into some potentially embarrassing problem. For many of them, this is the kind of problem which could be solved by a contracted "burglary" (cf. Crookston, 1967:143-144). The fence can put the businessman in touch with a burglar; and the two of them can reach an agreement which works to the benefit of each. Still another service which the fence can provide for the burglar is the introduction of solitary burglars to established crews or gangs, thus helping to link together disparate elements in the thief category.

With few exceptions fences maintain some sort of role in the legitimate business world. Most of them do appear, in fact, to be businessmen of one kind or another. According to burglars, there are primarily three reasons

for this. First, it is usually only the businessman who has on hand at any given time the ready cash required in dealings with thieves. Second, businessmen can utilize the contacts and knowledge acquired in their legitimate business activities to evaluate and dispose of illicit merchandise (cf. Hall, 1952:156-57). And third, the fence can use his legitimate business transactions to mask his illicit dealings, thereby, making it more difficult for law enforcement officials to build a case against him (cf. Yoder, 1954).

Again, the members of the prison questionnaire sample were asked to indicate the legitimate occupations of "two persons you have personally known who bought stolen merchandise." A total of 61 replies were received and are listed in Table 3. There is strong support here for the assertion that most fences are persons who are engaged in some kind of legitimate business. As in the case of Table 2, which listed the occupations of tipsters, these data are not presented as

TABLE 3
LEGITIMATE OCCUPATIONS REPORTED FOR 61 FENCES

Occupation		Frequency
Tavern owner or Bartender		14
Store owner or Business owner (unspecified)		9
Other business owner		14
service station	4	
restaurant	3	
automobile dealer	3	
pawn shop	2	
barbershop	2	
Policeman		3
Insurance broker		2
Automobile mechanic		2
Television repairman		2
Other (e.g., alderman, jewelry salesman, auctioneer)		15
Total		61

representative of the total population
of fences, rather they are presented
only to give some idea of the types of
legitimate occupations found among
fences. Actually we would probably
be justified in assuming that the data
in Table 3 are representative of the
smaller scale, and less successful,
fences.

Bondsmen and Attorneys

Bondsmen and attorneys occupy
positions in legitimate society which
carry with them the socially sanctioned
approval to associate, at least to some
extent, with persons who are known
to be criminals. That some of them are
corrupted in the process is common
knowledge (cf. Goldfarb, 1965); of
much more fundamental consequence,
however, for the stability and perpetu-
ation of the activities of professional
criminals—and this includes the good
burglar—are the routinized working
relationships and understandings which
have emerged out of this socially sanctioned link between the underworld
and quasi-representatives of the criminal justice system.

For both the attorney and the
bondsman there are two extremely important consequences of prolonged
contact with members of the underworld. The first of these is a knowledge of the differences in personal integrity which exist among some of the
criminal offenders with whom they
have contact. The second is a recognition that there are constraints which
operate so as to reduce the risks which
are run by anyone, who in doing business with thieves, crosses the line of
unethical or illegal behavior. Both the
attorney and the bondsman learn
rather quickly that some members of
the underworld are more trustworthy
than others. One result of this is recog-

nition that they need not fear the consequences of unethical or illegal transactions so long as they are selective in
the types of clients with whom they
have potentially embarrassing dealings. Moreover, they learn that members of the underworld usually cannot
divulge their guilty knowledge anyway
because they themselves would stand
to lose much by doing so. They would
be sufficiently stigmatized by such disclosures as to make it difficult to acquire competent legal counsel and the
services of bondsman on any subsequent criminal charges. This sets the
stage for the emergence and flowering
of a number of quasi-ethical practices
and working relationships.

It must be noted that these practices
are further stimulated, and possibly
even generated, by certain characteristics of the problems faced by criminal
lawyers and bondsmen generally in
their work. The former, for example,
unlike his corporate counterpart, routinely deals with clients who have little
ready cash with which to compensate
him for his services.

> Now a criminal lawyer has to give credit,
> and the main reason for this is that
> burglars and armed robbers, if they had
> any money, they wouldn't be out stealing,
> they'd be partying. It's as simple as that.
> If they have money, they're partying, and
> when they're broke, they start to stealing
> again. If they get caught while they're
> stealing, they're broke (Jackson, 1969:
> 136).

One result of this is likely to be the
attempt by his clients to obtain his
services by offering other types of consideration (Carlin, 1966). Among
these other kinds of consideration are
such things as the sexual favors of
wives or girl-friends, and property,
both real and personal, some of which
is almost certainly stolen. The good
thief's ability to manipulate the crim-

inal justice system cannot be comprehended unless it is recognized that he differs greatly from the petty thief and first time offender in his knowledge of the workings of the system. Unlike them, he has had a great deal of contact with the various actors which comprise it.

When the good burglar is arrested —as he frequently is—he can count upon receiving the services of both a bondsman and an attorney, even if he has virtually no ready cash. In lieu of a cash down payment the thief will be able to gain his release from confinement, and also preliminary legal representation, on the basis of his reputation and a promise to deliver the needed cash at a later date. He will then search for one or more suitable burglaries (or some other type of crime) which holds out the promise of a quick and substantial reward— so that he can pay his attorney and bondsman. On occasion he will resort to high interest loan sharks ("juice loans") in order to quickly acquire the sums of cash which his attorney and bondsman demand for their services. This period of time when the thief is trying to acquire the cash which he so desperately needs is a particularly stressful one for him. Often he will resort to high risk scores which he would under normal circumstances have passed up. One consequence of this high risk stealing is likely to be another arrest, sometimes in a distant jurisdiction, thus only intensifying his problems.

The principal strategy which the good thief's attorneys use appears to be delay, in the hope that some kind of unforeseen contingency will arise which permits him to gain his client's release or, failing that, to strike a particularly favorable bargain. The fix, which once was relatively common in many American jurisdictions (cf. Byrnes, 1969), has become a much less predictable and available option for the good thief.[7] Admittedly, however, this is an area in which there has never been any thorough research. Nevertheless, if it is true that the fix has become less available for the good thief—as some have contended (cf. Gould *et al.*, 1968)—this could account in part for the alleged decline in the ethical standards of thieves in their dealings with one another (cf. Gould *et al.*, 1968); in a situation in which the probability of serving some time in prison has increased, it would be expected that the willingness of thieves to "cooperate" would similarly increase. And this could lead to a number of working relationships between thieves and the police (cf. Chambliss and Seidman, 1971:486-8). This also is an area in which more empirical research is needed.

In addition to what has already been noted about the relationships between good burglars and bondsmen and attorneys, other matters should be briefly mentioned. The latter have been known on occasion to provide tips to burglars on places to burglarize. In addition, some of them are alleged occasionally to purchase stolen property from burglars. Finally, in those unusual cases in which the fix can be arranged, attorneys, of course, act as the go-between in working out the details.

---

[7] Space precludes a discussion of the fix as it exists today; however, there is no doubt that the fix is still used in criminal cases. But there is real doubt about how often it is available to the *burglar*. My own views on the contemporary availability of the fix are quite similar to those expressed by Gould, *et al.* (1968) and Jackson (1969).

CONCLUSION

It should be clear on the basis of what has been said here that an understanding of the activities of the systematic burglar must take into account the social matrix in which he carries on his work, indeed on which he is dependent. To this extent the burglar remains more like the professional thieves which Sutherland sketched, and less like the systematic check forgers studied by Lemert (1958). In some respects, then, the social organization of burglarly has continued *relatively* unchanged—at least in comparison with the considerable changes which have occurred in the social organization of check forgery.

Yet even as this is written there is reason to question how much longer it will remain so. For there seems to be near universal consensus that things are changing. In addition to interviews with burglars, the field work for this project included interviews with representatives of two large urban police departments, employees of two safe manufacturers, and a burglary underwriter for a large insurance company. One of the points which was made by all of these respondents was their belief that sophisticated burglary is a declining occupation (cf. Gould, *et al.,* 1968). Again and again I was told, by thieves as well, that "there's no money in burglary anymore." Two reasons are cited for this change. First, security technology is becoming increasingly sophisticated and represents an ever more formidable challenge to the burglar, which means that many of those offenders who remain in burglary must increasingly confine themselves to easier—and less lucrative—scores. Gone are the days when even a reasonably talented burglar could blow a safe with soap and "oil." Secondly, historical changes in the economy have made cash a declining medium of exchange. There simply is not that much *cash* in safes anymore. Instead, checks and credit cards are used, and it is in the fraudulent manipulation of these that future criminal opportunity will increasingly be found. To the extent that these changes in the economy do in fact produce changes in the attractiveness and social organization of burglary, it will parallel the changes which made check forgery a different kind of offense from what it had been in the very early years of the 20th century (Lemert, 1958).

Another change which many of those interviewed mentioned spontaneously is the gradual erosion of "the Code" among thieves. All seem to agree that the "solid," ethical career criminal seems to be giving way to the "hustler," an alert opportunist who is primarily concerned only with personal—as opposed to collective—security (cf. Irwin, 1970:8-15; and Gould *et al.,* 1968). Rare is the contemporary autobiography which does not mention and bemoan this trend (cf. MacIsaacs, 1968:93-94; Crookston, 1967:140-141). It is always possible that the image of the past is more romance than reality and that this could account in part for the poor showing of our contemporaries (cf. Jackson, 1969:34-36). We are seriously handicapped here by the absence of any reliable comparative data from earlier periods. Despite this problem, however, it does seem to be true that, compared to the past, when infractions of the code occur today, there is surprisingly little imposed in the way of negative sanctions. This has not, however, altered the strong lip service accorded the code.

Any attempt to explain the apparent changes in burglary and burglary offenders must also take account of improvements in the performance of agents of social control, specifically the police. The existence, for example, of criminal records for police departments who draw upon the services of the FBI has surely done much to eliminate the informational vacuum in which the systematic offender can maneuver in anonymity—and safety. Similarly, the improvement of police technology, which has had the effect of tightening internal controls in police departments (Bordua and Reiss, 1966), has made it more difficult to bargain with isolated individual police officers for their freedom.

Because all of the changes mentioned here are likely to continue, it is reasonable to expect further decline in the ranks of men who approximate the ideal of the good thief.

REFERENCES

Barnes, Robert Earl
1971 Are You Safe from Burglars? Garden City, N.Y.: Doubleday.
Black, Jack
1926 You Can't Win. New York: A. L. Burt.
Bordua, David J. and A. J. Reiss, Jr.
1966 "Command, control and charisma." American Journal of Sociology 72(July): 68-76.
Braly, Malcolm
1967 On the Yard. Boston: Little, Brown.
Byrnes, Thomas
1969 Professional Criminals of America. New York: Chelsea House (original published in 1886).
Camp, George M.
1968 "Nothing to lose: A study of bank robbery in America." Unpublished Ph.D. Dissertation. Yale University.
Carlin, Jerome

1966 Lawyer's Ethics. New York: Russell Sage Foundation.
Chambliss, Wm. and Robert B. Seidman
1971 Law, Order, and Power. Reading, Mass.: Addison-Wesley.
Crookston, Peter
1967 Villain. London: Jonathan Cape.
Davis, Clyde B.
1944 The Rebellion of Leo McGuire. New York: Farrar and Rinehart.
DeBaun, Everett
1950 "The heist: The theory and practice of armed robbery." Harpers (February): 69-77.
Denzin, Norman K.
1970 The Research Act. Chicago: Aldine.
Einstadter, Werner J.
1969 "The social organization of armed robbery." Social Problems 17 (Summer): 64-82.
Genet, Jean
1964 The Thief's Journal (trans. by Bernard Frechtman). New York: Grove Press.
Goffman, Erving
1963 Stigma. Englewood Cliffs, N.J.: Prentice-Hall.
Goldfarb, Ronald
1965 Ransom. New York: Harper and Row.
Gould, Leroy, Egon Bittner, Sol Chaneles, Sheldon Messinger, Kriss Novak, and Fred Powledge
1968 Crime As a Profession. Washington, D.C.: U.S. Department of Justice, Office of Law Enforcement Assistance.
Hall, Jerome
1952 Theft, Law and Society (revised edition). Indianapolis: Bobbs-Merrill.
Hapgood, Hutchins
1903 Autobiography of a Thief. New York: Fox, Duffield.
Hollingshead, A. B.
1939 "Behavior systems as a field for research." American Sociological Review 4(October): 816-822.
Irwin, John
1970 The Felon. Englewood Cliffs, N.J.: Prentice-Hall, Inc.
Jackson, Bruce
1969 A Thief's Primer. New York: Macmillan.
Katz, Fred E.
1958 "Occupational contact networks."

Social Forces 37(October): 52-55.

Lemert, Edwin
1958 "The behavior of the systematic check forger." Social Problems 6 (Fall): 141-149.
1968 "Book review." American Journal of Sociology 73(March): 649-650.

MacIsaacs, John
1968 Half the Fun Was Getting There. Englewood Cliffs, N.J.: Prentice-Hall.

Malcolm X (with the assistance of Alex Haley)
1964 The Autobiography of Malcolm X. New York: Grove Press.

Martin, John Bartlow
1953 My Life in Crime. New York: Signet Books.

Morton, James (Big Jim) (with D. Wittels)
1950 "I was king of the thieves." Saturday Evening Post (August

5, 12, and 19): 17-19, 78-81; 28, 92, 94-96; 30, 126, 128, 130-132.

Page, Sir Leo
n.d. The Young Lag. London: Faber and Faber.

Polsky, Ned
1967 Hustlers, Beats and Others. Chicago: Aldine.

Shover, Neal
1971 "Burglary as an occupation." Unpublished Ph.D. Dissertation. University of Illinois (Urbana).

Sutherland, Edwin
1937 The Professional Thief. Chicago: University of Chicago Press.

Wilson, Brian
1964 Nor Iron Bars a Cage. London: Wm. Kimber and Co.

Yoder, Robert M.
1954 "The best friend a thief ever had." Saturday Evening Post 227 (December 25): 18-19; 72-73.

The Howard Journal Vol 31 No 4. Nov 92
ISSN 0265–5527

The Socially Bounded Decision Making of Persistent Property Offenders[1]

NEAL SHOVER and DAVID HONAKER

Neal Shover is Professor of Sociology and David Honaker doctoral student,
Department of Sociology, University of Tennesee, USA

Abstract: The rapid ascendance of deterrence theory and other rational-choice interpretations of criminal behaviour in the 1970s was matched until recently by a failure to examine empirically the criminal decision making of serious offenders. This paper reports the results of an ethnographic investigation of criminal decision making by a sample of persistent property offenders. Following brief introductory comments, we describe our research objectives and methodology. Then we describe salient features of the decision-making processes employed by members of the sample. We argue that improved understanding of criminal decision making by persistent property offenders is gained by exploring how their utilities are shaped and sustained by the lifestyle characteristic of many of them. We suggest that offenders' efforts to acquire the financial and social capital needed to enhance, sustain, or restore enjoyment of this lifestyle may generate a bounded rationality in which they discount or ignore the formal risks of crime.

The 1970s were marked by the eclipse of labelling theory as the dominant individual-level criminological theory and by the reappearance of interest in approaches originally advanced by classical theorists. Economists and cognitive psychologists along with many in the criminological mainstream advanced an interpretation of crime as *choice*, offering models of criminal decision making grounded in the assumption that the decision to commit a criminal act springs from the offender's assessment of its anticipated net utilities (for example, Becker 1968; Heineke 1978; Carroll 1978; Reynolds 1985). This movement in favour of rational-choice approaches to crime spurred empirical investigation of problems that heretofore were limited primarily to studies of the death penalty and its impact on the homicide rate.

Early investigations of a rational choice interpretation of crime reported a weak but persistent relationship between the certainty of punishment and rates of serious property crimes (Blumstein, Cohen and Nagin 1978). It was recognised, however, that an understanding of criminal decision making also requires knowledge about individual perceptions and beliefs about legal threats and other constraints on decision making (for example, Manski 1978). Investigators moved on two main fronts to meet this need. Some used survey methods to explore differential involvement in minor forms of deviance in samples of restricted age ranges, typically high school and college students (for example, Waldo and Chiricos 1972). Alternatively they examined the link between risk assessments and criminal participation in samples more representative of the general population (for example, Tittle 1980). Serious shortcomings of these studies are that most either ignore the potential rewards of crime entirely or they fail to examine its emotional and interpersonal utilities. Still other investigators turned attention to serious criminal offenders and began expanding the narrow existing knowledge base (for example, Claster 1967), chiefly through the use of cross-sectional research designs and survey methods.

For more than a decade now, investigators have studied offenders' attitudes toward legitimate and criminal pursuits, their perceptions of and beliefs about the risks of criminal behaviour, and their estimates of the payoffs from conventional and criminal pursuits (for example, Petersilia *et al.* 1978; Peterson and Braiker 1980). These studies raise serious questions about the fit between offenders' calculus and *a priori* assumptions about their utilities and criminal decision making. One investigation of 589 incarcerated property offenders concluded, for example, that the subjects apparently do not utilise 'a sensible cost-benefit analysis' when weighing the utilities of crime (Figgie International 1988, p. 25). They substantially underestimate the risk of arrest for most crimes, routinely overestimate the monetary benefit they expect, and seem to have 'grossly inaccurate perceptions of the costs and benefits associated with property crime' (Figgie International 1988, p. 81). Unfortunately, both design and conceptual problems undermine confidence in the findings of this and similar studies. Cross sectional survey methods, for example, are poorly suited for examining dynamic decision-making *processes*. Most such studies also fail to examine offenders' estimates of the likely payoffs from non-criminal alternatives or their non-monetary utilities, such as emotional satisfaction (Katz 1988).

As newer, empirically-based models of criminal decision making have been developed (for example, Clarke and Cornish 1985; Cornish and Clarke 1986), a growing number of investigators are using ethnographic methods to examine the offender's criminal calculus, often in real or simulated natural settings (for example, Carroll 1982; Carroll and Weaver 1986). The research reported here continues this line of ethnographic inquiry by using retrospective interviews to examine criminal decision making by serious and persistent property offenders. The focus of our attenton is the decision to commit a crime rather than the target-selection decision that has received substantial attention elsewhere (for example, Scarr 1973; Repetto 1974; Maguire 1982; Bennett and Wright 1984a; Rengert and Wasilchick 1985; Cromwell, Olson and Avary 1991). The first objective is to examine how closely the decision to commit crime conforms to a classical rational choice model in which decisions assumedly are based largely on an assessment of potential returns from alternative courses of action and the risk of legal sanctions. A second objective is to examine the influence of the lifestyle pursued by many persistent property offenders on the salience of their utilities and the risks they assess in criminal decision making.

Methods and Materials

The materials for analysis were collected during 1987 and 1988 as part of a larger study of crime desistance. From the population of all men incarcerated in Tennessee state prisons during 1987 we selected a sample of recidivists with a demonstrated preference for property crimes who were also nearing release from confinement. To select the sample, members of the research team first examined Tennessee Board of Parole's records to identify offenders incarcerated in Tennessee state prisons whose parole was imminent. We then used Department of Corrections' records to cull the list of all but those (i) with at least one prior felony confinement, and (ii) whose previous or current confinement was for serious property crime. Next the researchers visited prisons, primarily those located in the mid- and eastern areas of the state, and explained the study to and requested research participation from potential subjects. After meeting individually with approximately 75 inmates we reached our sample size objective of 60 subjects. Fifty-eight members of the sample had served at least one prior prison sentence and the remaining two had served one or more jail sentences. They had served time primarily for armed robbery, burglary, or theft. By limiting the sample as outlined we sought to approximate a population of career criminals, a type of offender that has received substantial attention from scholars and policy makers (Petersilia 1980; Blumstein *et al.* 1988). Subjects ranged from 23 to 70 years of age, with an average age of 34.1 years. In addition to the sample's adult criminal and incarceration profile, 47% (n = 28) of the men also had served one or more terms of juvenile confinement. Every member of the sample was interviewed approximately one month prior to release from prison. All data used in the present study, however, were collected in post-release interviews with the men.

Seven to ten months after their release from prison we successfully traced, contacted, and interviewed 46 of the original sample of 60 men (76.7%). (In addition, we established contact with one subject who declined our request for an interview, and with close relatives of another who failed to respond to repeated requests that he contact us.) Semi-structured ethnographic interviews were the principal data-collection technique. The interview included questions about the former prisoners' activities and living arrangements following release, self-report items measuring post-release criminal participation, and questions about the context of re-involvement in crime. They were paid $100 for completing the interview, all of which were audio tape recorded and transcribed for subsequent analysis. Fourteen subjects were in jail or prison again when interviewed, but most were interviewed in their former or newly established home communities.

Part of the interviews produced detailed descriptions of the most recent, easily recalled property crime that each subject had committed in the free world prior to the interview. They described either crimes they had committed prior to incarceration or, for those subjects who were locked up when interviewed, their return to jail or prison. Our objective was to gain through the repeat offender's eyes an understanding of the decision to commit specific criminal acts. We asked our subjects to focus their recollection on how the decision was made, and to provide a detailed account of the potential risks and rewards they assessed while doing so. The result was 40 usable descriptions of crimes and attempted crimes, which included 15 burglaries, twelve robberies, five grand larcenies, four unarmed robberies, two auto thefts, one series of cheque forgeries, and one case of receiving and concealing stolen property. Transcripts of the interviews were analysed using *The Ethnograph*, a software package for use on text based data (Seidal, Kjolseth and Seymour 1988). Use of this software enables us to code and to retrieve for analysis segments of interview text.

Findings

Analysis reveals the most striking aspect of the subjects' decision making for the crimes they described is that a majority gave little or no thought to the possibility of arrest and confinement. Of 34 subjects who were asked specifically whether they considered the risk of arrest or who spontaneously indicated whether they did so, 21 (62%) said they did not. The comments of two subjects are typical:

Q: Did you think about . . . getting caught?
A: No.
Q: [H]ow did you manage to put that out of your mind?
A: [It] never did come into it.
Q: Never did come into it?
A: Never did, you know. It didn't bother me.

Q: Were you thinking about bad things that might happen to you?
A: None whatsoever.
Q: No?
A: I wasn't worried about getting caught or anything, you know. I was a positive thinker through everything, you know. I didn't have no negative thoughts about it whatsoever.

The 13 remaining subjects (38%) acknowledged they gave some thought to the possibility of arrest but most said they managed to dismiss it easily and to carry through with their plans:

Q: Did you worry much about getting caught? On a scale of one to ten, how would you rank your degree of worry that day?
A: [T]he worry was probably a one. You know what I mean? The worry was probably one. I didn't think about the consequences, you know. I know it's stupidity, but it didn't – that [I] might go to jail, I mean – it crossed my mind but it didn't make much difference.

Q: As you thought about doing that [armed robbery], were there things that you were worried about?
A: Well, the only thing that I was worried about was – . . . getting arrested didn't even cross my mind – just worrying about getting killed is the only thing, you know, getting shot. That's the only thing.. . . But, you know, . . . you'd have to

be really crazy not to think about that . . . you could possibly get in trouble. It crossed my mind, but I didn't worry about it all that much.

Some members of our sample said they managed deliberately and consciously to put out of mind all thoughts of possible arrest:

When I went out to steal, I didn't think about the negative things. 'Cause if you think negative, negative things are going to happen. And that's the way I looked at it. . . .

I done it just like it was a job or something. Go out and do it, don't think about getting caught, 'cause that would make you jumpy, edgy, nervous. If you looked like you were doing something wrong, then something wrong is 'gonna happen to you . . . You just, you just put [the thought of arrest] out of your mind, you know.

Q: Did you think about [the possibility of getting caught] very much that night?
A: I didn't think about it that much, you know.. . . [I]t comes but, you know, you can wipe it away.
Q: How do you wipe it away?
A: You just blank it out. You blank it out.

Another subject said simply that 'I try to put that [thought of arrest] the farthest thing from my mind that I can'.

Many subjects attribute their ability to ignore or to dismiss all thought of possible arrest to a state of intoxication or drug altered consciousness:

Q: You didn't think about going to prison?
A: Never did. I guess it was all that alcohol and stuff, and drugs. . . . The day I pulled that robbery? – no. I was so high I didn't think about nothing.

Another subject told us that he had been drinking the entire day that he committed the crime and, by the time it occurred, he was in 'nightlight city'.

While it is clear that the formal risks of crime were not considered carefully by most members of the sample, equally striking is the finding that very few thought about or assessed legitimate alternatives before opting to commit a criminal act. Of 22 subjects who were asked specifically whether they had done so, 16 indicated they gave no thought whatsoever to legitimate alternatives. The six subjects who did either ignored or quickly dismissed them as inapplicable, given their immediate circumstances.

We recognise the methodological shortcomings of the descriptions of criminal decision making and behaviour used as data for this study. Since the subjects were questioned in detail only about specific offences they could remember well, the sample of descriptions may not be representative of the range of crimes they committed. By definition, they are memorable ones. Moreover, the recall period for these crimes ranged from one to 15 years, raising the possibility of errors caused by selective recall. Whether or not this could have produced systematic bias in the data is unknown. We cannot rule out the possibility that past crimes are remembered as being less rational than they actually were at the time of commission. Such a tendency could account in part for our interpretation of the data and our description of their style of decision making. The fact that we limited the sample to recidivists means also tht we cannot determine how much their behaviour may reflect either innate differences (Gottfredson and Hirschi 1990) or experiential effects, that is, the effects of past success in committing crime and avoiding arrest (Nagin and Paternoster 1991). It could be argued that the behaviour of our subjects, precisely because they had demonstrated a willingness to commit property crimes and had done so in the past, limits the external validity of their reports. Given sample selection criteria and these potential data problems, generalisations beyond the study population must be made with caution.

This said, we believe that the remarkable similarity between our findings and the picture of criminal decision making reported by others who have studied serious property offenders strengthens their credibility significantly. A study of 83 imprisoned burglars revealed that 49% did not think about the chances of getting caught for any particular offence during their last period of offending. While 37% of them did think about it, most thought there was little or no chance it would happen (Bennett and Wright 1984a, *Table A14*). Interviews with 113 men convicted of robbery or an offence related to robbery revealed that 'over 60 per cent . . . said they had not even thought about getting caught'. Another 17% said that they had thought about the possibility but 'did not believe it to be a problem' (Feeney 1986, pp. 59–60). Analysis of prison interviews with 77 robbers and 45 burglars likewise revealed their 'general obliviousness toward the consequences [of their crimes] and no thought of being caught' (Walsh 1986, p. 157). In sum, our findings along with the findings from other studies suggest strongly that many serious property offenders seem to be remarkably casual in weighing the formal risks of criminal participation. As one of our subjects put it: 'you think about going to prison about like you think about dying, you know'. The impact of alcohol and drug use in diminishing concern with possible penalties also has been reported by many others (for example, Bennett and Wright 1984b; Cromwell, Olson and Avary 1991).

If the potential legal consequences of crime do not figure prominently in crime commission decision making by persistent thieves, what *do* they think about when choosing to commit crime? Walsh (1980, 1986) shows that typically they focus their thoughts on the money that committing a crime may yield and the good times they expect to have with it when the crime is behind them. Carroll's (1982) data likewise indicate that the amount of gain offenders expect to receive is 'the most important dimension' in their decision making while the certainty of punishment is the least important of the four dimensions on which his subjects assessed crime opportunities. Our findings are consistent with these reports; our subjects said that they focussed on the expected gains from their crimes:

I didn't think about nothing but what I was going to do when I got that money, how I was going to spend it, what I was going to do with it, you know.

See, you're not thinking about those things [possibility of being arrested]. You're thinking about that big pay check at the end of thirty to forty-five minutes worth of work.

[A]t the time [that you commit crime], you throw all your instincts out the window. . . . Because you're just thinking about money, and money only. That's all that's on your mind, because you want that money. And you throw, you block everything off until you get the money.

Although confidence in our findings is bolstered by the number of points on which they are similar to reports by others who have explored crime commission decision making, they do paint a picture of decision making that is different from what is known about the way at least some of them make target selection decisions. Investigators (for example, Cromwell, Olson and Avary 1991) have shown that target decisions approximate simple common-sense conceptions of rational behaviour (Shover 1991). A resolution of the problem presented by these contradictory findings is suggested by others (Cromwell, Olson and Avery 1991) and also apparent in our data: criminal participation often results from a *sequence* of experientially and analytically discrete decisions, all of potentially varying degrees of intentional rationality. Thus, once a *motivational* crime commission decision has been made, offenders may move quickly to selecting, or to exploiting an apparently suitable target. At this stage of the criminal participation process, offenders are preoccupied with the *technical* challenge of avoiding failure at what now is seen as a *practical task*. As one subject put it: 'you don't think about getting caught, you think about how in hell you're going to do it *not* to get caught, you know'. His comments were echoed by another man: 'The only thing you're thinking about is looking and acting and trying *not* to get caught'. Last, consider the comments of a third subject: 'I wasn't afraid of getting caught, but I was cautious, you know. Like I said, I was thinking only in the way to prevent me from getting caught'. Just as bricklayers do not visualise graphically or deliberate over the bodily carnage that could follow from a collapsed scaffold *once there is a job to be done*, many thieves apparently do not dwell at length on the likelihood of arrest or on the pains of imprisonment when proceeding to search out or exploit suitable criminal opportunities.

The accumulated evidence on crime commission decision making by persistent offenders is substantial and persuasive: the rationality they employ is limited or bounded severely (for example, Carroll 1982; Cromwell, Olson and Avary 1991). While unsuccessful persistent offenders may calculate potential benefits and costs before committing criminal acts, they apparently do so differently or weigh utilities differently than as sketched in *a priori* decision making models. As Walsh (1980) suggests, offenders' 'definitions of costs and rewards seem to be at variance with society's estimates of them' (p. 141). This does not mean their decision making is *irrational* but it does point to the difficulties of understanding it and then refining theoretical models of the process. Our objective in the remainder of this paper is an improved understanding of criminal decision making based on analysis of the socially anchored purposes, utilities, and risks of the acts that offenders commit. Put differently, we explore the contextual origins of their bounded rationality.

Lifestyle, Utilities and Risk

It is instructive to examine the decision making of persistent property offenders in context of the lifestyle that is characteristic of many in their ranks: *life as party*. The hallmark of life as party is the enjoyment of 'good times' with minimal concern for obligations and commitments that are external to the person's immediate social setting. It is a lifestyle distinguished in many cases by two repetitively cyclical phases and correspondingly distinctive approaches to crime. When offenders' efforts to maintain the lifestyle (that is, their party pursuits) are largely successful, crimes are committed in order to sustain circumstances or a pattern of activities they experience as pleasurable. As Walsh (1986) puts it, crimes committed under these circumstances are 'part of a continuing satisfactory way of life' (p. 15). By contrast, when offenders are less successful at party pursuits, their crimes are committed in order to forestall or avoid circumstances experienced as threatening, unpleasant or precarious. Corresponding to each of these two phases of party pursuits is a distinctive set of utilities and stance toward legal risk.

Life as Party

Survey and ethnographic studies alike show that persistent property offenders spend much of their criminal gains on alcohol and other drugs (Petersilia *et al.* 1978; Maguire 1982; Gibbs and Shelley 1982; Figgie International 1988; Cromwell, Olson and Avary 1991). The proceeds of their crimes, as Walsh (1986) has noted: 'typically [are] used for personal, non-essential consumption (for example, 'nights out'), rather than, for example, to be given to family or used for basic needs' (p. 72). Thieves spend much of their leisure hours enjoying good times. Our subjects were no different in this regard. For example:

I smoked an ounce of pot in a day, a day and a half. Every other day I had to go buy a bag of pot, at the least. And sometimes I've went two or three days in a row.. . . And there was never a day went by that I didn't [drink] a case, case and a half of beer. And [I] did a 'script of pills every two days.

While much of their money is consumed by the high cost of drugs, a portion may be used for ostentatious enjoyment and display of luxury items and activities that probably would be unattainable on the returns from blue-collar employment:

[I]t was all just a big money thing to me at the time, you know. Really, what it was was impressing everybody, you know. 'Here Floyd is, and he's never had nothing in his life, and now look at him: he's driving new cars, and wearing jewelry', you know.

Life as party is enjoyed in the company of others. Typically it includes shared consumption of alcohol or other drugs in bars and lounges, on street corners, or while cruising in automobiles. In these venues, party pursuers celebrate and affirm values of spontaneity, autonomy, independence, and resourcefulness. Spontaneity means that rationality and long-range planning are eschewed in favour of enjoying the moment and permitting the day's activities and pleasures to develop in an unconstrained fashion. This may mean, for example, getting up late, usually after a night of partying, and then setting out to contact and enjoy the company of friends and associates who are known to be predisposed to partying:

I got up around about eight-thirty that morning. . .

Q: Eight-thirty? Was that the usual time that you got up?

A: Yeah, if I didn't have a hang over from the night before. . .

Q: What kind of drugs were you doing then?

A: I was doing . . .Percodans, Dilaudid, taking Valiums, drinking . . .[A]nyway, I got up that morning about eight-thirty, took me a bath, put on some clothes and . . . decided to walk [over to his mother's home]. [T]his particular day, . . . my nephew was over [there].. . . We was just sitting in the yard and talking and drinking beer, you know.. . . It was me, him and my sister. We was sitting out there in the yard talking. And this guy that we know,. . . he came up, he pulled up. So my nephew got in the car with him and they left. So, you know, I was sitting there talking to my sister.. . . And then, in the meantime, while we was talking, they come back, about thirty minutes later with a case of beer, some marijuana and everything,. . . and there was another one of my nephews in the car with them. So me, two of my sisters, and two of my nephews, we got in the car with this guy here and we just went riding. So we went to Hadley Park and . . . we stayed out there. There were so many people out there, they were parked on the grass and things, and the vice squad come and run everybody away. So when they done that, we left. . . . So we went back out [toward his mother's home] but instead of going over to my mother's house we went to this little joint [tavern]. Now we're steady drinking and smoking weed all during this day. So when we get there, we park and get out and see a few friends. We [were] talking and getting high, you known, blowing each other a shotgun [sharing marijuana].

Enjoyment of party pursuits in group context is enhanced through the collective emphasis on personal autonomy. Because it is understood by all that participants are free to leave if they no longer enjoy or do not support group activities, the continuing presence of each participant affirms for the remainder the pleasures of the lifestyle. Uncoerced participation thus reinforces the shared assumption that group activities are appropriate and enjoyable. The behavioural result of the emphasis on autonomy is acceptance of or acquiescence in group decisions and activities.

Party pursuits also appeal to offenders because they permit conspicuous display of independence (Persson 1981). This generally means avoidance of the world of routine work and freedom from being 'under someone's thumb'. It also may include being free to avoid or to escape from restrictive routines.

I just wanted to be doing something. Instead of being at home, or something like that. I wanted to be running, I wanted to be going to clubs, and picking up women, and shooting pool. And I like to go [to a nearby resort community] and just drive around over there. A lot of things like that.. . . I was drinking two pints or more a day.. . . I was doing Valiums and I was doing Demerol.. . . I didn't want to work.

The proper pursuit and enjoyment of life as party is expensive, due largely to the costs of drugs. As one of our subjects remarked: 'We was doing a lot of cocaine, so cash didn't last long, you know. If we made $3,000, two thousand of it almost instantly went for cocaine'. Some party pursuers must meet other expenses as well if the lifestyle is to be maintained.

Believe it or not, I was spending [$700] a day.
Q: On what?
A: Pot, alcohol, women, gas, motel rooms, food.
Q: You were living in hotels, motels?
A: Yeah, a lot of times, I was. I'd take a woman to a motel. I bought a lot of clothes. I used to dress pretty nicely, I'd buy suits.

Party pursuits require continuous infusions of money and no single method of generating funds allows enjoyment of it for more than a few days. Consequently, the emphasis on spontaneity, autonomy, and independence is matched by the importance attached to financial resourcefulness. This is evidenced by the ability to sustain the lifestyle over a period of time. Doing so earns for offenders a measure of respect from peers for their demonstrated ability to 'get over'. It translates into 'self-esteem ... as a folk hero beating the bureaucratic system of routinized dependence' (Walsh 1986, p. 16). The value of and respect for those who demonstrate resourcefulness means that criminal acts, as a means of sustaining life as party, generally are not condemned by the offender's peers.

The risks of employing criminal solutions to the need for funds are approached blithely but confidently in the same spontaneous and playful manner as are the rewards of life as party. In fact, avoidance of careful and detailed planning is a way of demonstrating possession of valued personal qualities and commitment to the lifestyle. Combined with the twin assumptions that peers have chosen freely and that one should not interfere with their autonomy, avoidance of rational planning finds expression in a reluctance to suggest that peers should weigh carefully the possible consequences of whatever they choose to do. Thus, the interaction that precedes criminal incidents is distinguished by circumspection and the use of linguistic devices that relegate risk and fear to the background of attention. The act of stealing, for example, is referred to obliquely but knowingly as 'doing something' or as 'making money'.

[After a day of partying,] I [got] to talking about making some money, because I didn't have no money. This guy that we were riding with, he had all the money.. . . So me and him and my nephew, we get together, talking about making some money. This guy tells me, he said, 'man, I know where there's a good place at'.
Q: Okay, so you suggested you all go somewhere and rob?
A: Yeah, 'make some' – well, we called it 'making money'.

Q: Okay. So, then you and this fellow met up in the bar . . . Tell me about the converation?
A: Well, there wasn't much of a conversation to it, really.. . . I asked him if he was ready to go, if he wanted to go do something, you know. And he knew what I meant. He wanted to go make some money somehow, any way it took.

To the external observer, inattention to risk at the moment when it would seem most appropriate may seem to border on irrationality. For the offender engaged in party pursuits, however, it is but one aspect of behaviours that are rational in other respects. It opens up opportunities to enjoy life as party and to demonstrate commitment to values shared by peers. Resourcefulness and disdain for conventional rationality affirm individual character and style, both of which are important in the world of party pursuits (Goffman 1967).

Party Pursuits and Eroding Resources

Paradoxically, the pursuit of life as party can be appreciated and enjoyed to the fullest extent only if participants moderate their involvement in it while maintaining identities and routines in the straight world. Doing so maintains its 'escape value' but it also requires an uncommon measure of discipline and forbearance. The fact is that extended and enthusiastic enjoyment of life as party threatens constantly to deplete irrevocably the resources needed to sustain enjoyment of its pleasures. Three aspects of the life-as-party lifestyle can contribute to this end.

First, some offenders become ensnared increasingly by the chemical substances and drug using routines that are common there. In doing so, the meaning of drug consumption changes:

See, I was doing drugs every day. It just wasn't every other day, it was to the point that, after the first few months doing drugs, I would have to do 'X amount' of drugs, say, just for instance, just to feel like I do now. Which is normal.

Once the party pursuer's physical or psychological tolerance increases significantly, drugs are consumed not for the high they once produced but instead to maintain a sense of normality by avoiding sickness or withdrawal.

Second, party pursuits erode legitimate fiscal and social capital. They can not be sustained by legitimate employment and they may in fact undermine both one's ability and inclination to hold a job. Even if offenders are willing to work at the kinds of employment available to them, and evidence suggests that many are not (Cromwell, Olson and Avary 1991), the time schedules of work and party pursuits conflict. The best times of the day for committing many property crimes are also the times the offender would be at work and it is nearly impossible to do both consistently and well. For those who pursue life as a party, legitimate employment often is foregone or sacrificed (Rengert and Wasilchick 1985). The absence of income from non-criminal sources thus reinforces the need to find other sources of money.

Determined pursuit of life as party also may affect participants' relationships with legitimate significant others. Many offenders manage to enjoy the lifestyle successfully only by exploiting the concern and largesse of family and friends. This may take the form of repeated requests for and receipt of personal loans that go unreturned, occasional thefts, or other forms of exploitation:

I lived well for awhile. I lived well . . . until I started shooting cocaine real bad, intravenously.. . . [A]nd then everything, you know, went up in smoke, you know.

Up my arm. The watches, the rings,. . . the car, you know. I used to have a girl, man, and her daddy had two horses. I put them in my arm. You know what I mean?. . . I made her sell them horses. My clothes and all that stuff, a lot of it, they went up in smoke when I started messing with that cocaine.

Eventually, friends and even family members may come to believe that they have been exploited or that continued assistance will only prolong a process that must be terminated. As one subject told us, 'Oh, I tried to borrow money, and borrow money and, you know, nobody would loàn it to me. Because they knew what I was doing'. After first refusing further assistance, acquaintances, friends, and even family members may avoid social contacts with the party pursuer or sever ties altogether. This dialogue occurred between the interviewer and one of our subjects:

Q: [B]esides doing something wrong, did you think of anything else that you could do to get money?. . . Borrow it?
A: No, I'd done run that in the ground. See, you burn that up. That's burned up, right there, borrowing, you know.. . . Once I borrow, you know, I might get $10 from you today, and, see, I'll be expecting to be getting $10 tomorrow, if I could. And then, when I see you [and] you see me coming, you say, 'no, I don't have none' . . . [A]s the guys in the penitentiary say, 'you absorb all of your remedies', you see. And that's what I did: I burned my remedies up, you know.

Last, when party pursuits are not going well, feelings of shame and self-disgust are not uncommon (Frazier and Meisenhelder 1985). Unsuccessful party pursuers as a result may take steps to reduce these feelings by distancing themselves voluntarily from conventional others:

Q: You were married to your wife at that time?
A: Yeah, I was married. . .
Q: Where was she living then?
A: I finally forced her to go home, you know . . . I made her go home, you know. And it caused an argument, for her to go home to her mother's. I felt like that was the best thing I did for her, you know. She hated me . . . for it at the time, didn't understand none of it. But, really, I intentionally made her go. I really spared her the misery that we were going to have. And it came. It came in bundles.

When party pursuers sustain severe losses of legitimate income and social resources, regardless of how it occurs, they grow increasingly isolated from conventional significant others. The obvious consequence is that this reduces interpersonal constraints on their behaviour.

As their pursuit of life as party increasingly assumes qualities of difficulty and struggle, offenders' utilities and risk perceptions also change. Increasingly, crimes are committed not to enhance or sustain the lifestyle so much as to forestall unpleasant circumstances. Those addicted to alcohol or other drugs, for example, must devote increasing time and energy to the quest for monies to purchase their chemicals of choice. Both their drug consumption and the frequency of their criminal acts increase (Ball *et al.* 1983; Johnson *et al.* 1985). For them, as for others, inability to draw on legitimate or low risk resources eventually may precipitate a crisis. One of our respondents retold how, facing a court appearance on a burglary charge, he needed funds to hire an attorney:

I needed some money bad or if I didn't, if I went to court the following day, I was going to be locked up. The judge was going to lock me up. Because I didn't have no lawyer. And I had went and talked to several lawyers and they told me . . . they wanted a thousand dollars, that if I couldn't come up with no thousand dollars, they couldn't come to court with me.. . . [S]o I went to my sister. I asked my sister, I said, 'look here, what about letting me have seven or eight hundred dollars' – which I knowed she had the money because she . . . had been in a wreck and she had gotten some money out of a suit. And she said, 'well, if I give you the money you won't do the right thing with it'. And I was telling her, 'no, no, I need a lawyer'. But I couldn't convince her to let me have the money. So I left. . . I said, shit I'm fixin' to go back to jail.. . . [S]o as I left her house and was walking – I was going to catch the bus – the [convenience store] and bus stop was right there by each other. So, I said I'm going to buy me some gum.. . . [A]nd in the process of me buying the chewing gum, I seen two ladies, they was counting money. So I figured sooner or later one of them was going to come out with the money.. . . I waited on them until . . . one came out with the money, and I got it.

Confronted by crisis and preoccupied increasingly with relieving immediate distress, the offender eventually may experience and define himself as propelled by forces beyond his control. Behavioural options become dichotomised into those that hold out some possibility of relief, however risky, and those that promise little but continued pain. Legitimate options are few and are seen as unlikely solutions. A criminal act may offer some hope of relief, however temporary. The offender may imbue the criminal option with almost magical prospects for ending or reversing the state of discomfort:

I said, 'well, look at it like this':if I don't do it, then tomorrow morning I've got the same [problems] that I've got right now. I could be hungry. I'm going to want food more. I'm going to want cigarettes more. I'm going to want everything more. [But] if I do it, and if I make it, then I've got all I want.

Acts that once were the result of blithe unconcern with risk can over time come to be based on a personal determination to master or reverse what is experienced as desperately unpleasant circumstances. As a result, inattention to risk in the offender's decision making may give way to the perception that he has *nothing to lose*:

It . . . gets to the point that you're into such a desperation. You're not working, you can't work. You're drunk as hell, been that way two or three weeks. You're no good to yourself, and you're no good to anybody else. Self-esteem is gone [and] spiritually, mentally, physically, financially bankrupt. You ain't got nothing to lose.

Desperate to maintain or re-establish a sense of normality, the offender pursues emotional relief with a decision to act decisively, albeit in the face of legal odds recognised as narrowing. By acting boldly and resolutely to make the best of a grim situation, one gains a measure of respect, if not from others, then at least from oneself.

288

I think, when you're doing . . . drugs like I was doing, I don't think you tend to rationalize much at all. I think it's just a decision you make. You don't weigh the consequences, the pros and the cons. You just do it.

You know, all kinds of things started running through my mind. If I get caught, then there, there I am with another charge. Then I said, well if I don't do something, I'm going to be in jail. And I just said, 'I'm going to do it'.

The fact that sustained party pursuits often causes offenders to increase the number of offences they commit and to exploit criminal opportunities that formerly were seen as risky should not be interpreted as meaning they believe they can continue committing crime with impunity. The opposite is true. Many offenders engaged in crimes intended to halt or reverse eroding fortunes are aware that eventually they will be arrested if they continue doing so:

Q: How did you manage not to think about, you know, that you could go to prison?
A: Well, you think about it afterwards. You think, 'wow, boy, I got away with it again'. But you known, sooner or later, the law of averages is 'gonna catch up with you. You just can't do it [commit crime] forever and ever and ever. And don't think you're not 'gonna get caught, 'cause you will.

Bennett and Wright (1984a) likewise show that a majority of persistent offenders endorse the statement that they will be caught 'eventually'. The cyclical transformations of party pursuits from pleasant and enjoyable to desperate and tenuous is one reason they are able to commit crimes despite awareness of inevitable and potentially severe legal penalties.

The threat posed by possible arrest and imprisonment, however, may not seem severe to some desperate offenders. As compared to their marginal and precarious existence, it may be seen as offering a form of relief:

[When he was straight], I'd think about [getting caught]: I could get this, and that [penalties] . . . [A]nd then I would think, well, I know this is going to end one day, you know. But, you know, you get so far out there, and get so far off into it that it really don't matter, you know. But you think about that. . . . I knew, eventually, I would get caught, you know. . . . I was off into drugs and I just didn't care if I got caught or not.

When I [got] caught – and they caught me right at the house – it's kind of like, you feel good, because you're glad it's over, you know. I mean, a weight being lifted off your head. And you say, well, I don't have to worry about this shit no more, because they've caught me. And it's over, you know.

In sum, due to offenders' eroding access to legitimately secured funds, their diminishing contact with and support from conventional significant others, and their efforts to maintain drug consumption habits, crimes that once were committed for recreational purposes increasingly become desperate attempts to forestall or reverse uncomfortable or frustrating situations. Pursuing the short-term goal of maximising enjoyment of life, legal threats can appear to the offender either as remote and improbable contingencies when party pursuits fulfil their recreational purposes or as an acceptable risk in the face of continued isolation, penury, and desperation.

We analysed the descriptions of crime provided by our subjects, and their activities on the day the crime occurred. We focussed specifically on: (i) the primary purpose of their crimes, that is, whether they planned to use the proceeds of crime for pleasure or to cope with unpleasant contingencies, and (ii) the extent and subjective meaning of their drug use at the time they decided to commit the crime in question. Based on the analysis, we classified the crimes of 15 subjects as behaviours committed in the enjoyment of life as a party and 13 as behaviours committed in order to enhance or restore enjoyment of this lifestyle. The twelve remaining crimes could not be classified because of insufficient information in the crime descriptions or they were isolated criminal acts that do not represent a specific lifestyle. Two subjects, for example, described crimes that were acts of vengeance directed at the property of individuals who had treated them or their relatives improperly. One of the men related how he decided to burglarise a home for reasons of revenge:

I was mad. . . . When I was in the penitentiary, my wife went to his house for a party and he give her a bunch of cocaine. . . . It happened, I think, about a week before I got out. . . . I just had it in my mind what I wanted to do: I wanted to hurt him like I was hurt. . . . I was pretty drunk, when I went by [his home], and I saw there wasn't no car there. So, I just pulled my car in.

The other subject told how an acquaintance had stolen drugs and other possessions from his automobile. In response the subject 'staked out the places where he would be for several days before I caught him, at gun point, [and] made him take me to his home, [which] I ransacked, and found some of the narcotics that he had stolen from me'. Although neither of these crimes was committed in pursuit of life as party, other crimes committed by both these subjects during their criminal careers did occur as part of that lifestyle. Other investigators have similarly reported that revenge is the dominant motive in a minority of property offences (for example, Cromwell, Olson and Avary 1991, p. 22).

Implications

We have suggested that daily routines characteristic of the partying lifestyle of persistent and unsuccessful offenders may modify both the salience of their various decision utilities and their perceptions of legal risk in the process of their crime commission decisions. This is not to say that these decisions are irrational, only that they do not conform to decision making as sketched by rational choice theories. Our objective was not to falsify the rational choice approach to criminal decision making, for we know of no way this could be accomplished. Whatever it is, moreover, rationality is not a dichotomous variable. Indeed, offenders' target selection decision making appears more rational in the conventional sense than do crime commission decisions.

The lesson here for theories of criminal decision making is that while

290

utilities and risk assessment may be properties of individuals, they also are shaped by the social and personal contexts in which decisions are made. Whether their pursuit of life as party is interpreted theoretically as the product of structural strain, choice, or even happenstance is of limited importance to an understanding of persistent offenders' discrete criminal forays. What is important is that their lifestyle places them in situations that may facilitate important transformations in the utilities of prospective actions. If nothing else, this means that some situations more than others make it possible to discount or ignore risk. We are not the first to call attention to this phenomenon:

> [The] situational nature of sanction properties has escaped the scales and indicators employed in official record and self-report survey research. In this body of research an arrest and a year in prison are generally assumed to have the same meaning for all persons and across all situations. The situational grounding of sanction properties suggests [,however,] that we look beyond official definitions of sanctions and the attitudinal structure of individuals to the properties of situations. (Ekland-Olson *et al.* 1984, p. 174)

Along the same line, a longitudinal survey of adult offenders concludes that decision making 'may be conditioned by elements within the immediate situation confronting the individual . . . [such that] perceptions of the opportunity, returns, and support for crime within a given situation may influence . . . perceptions of risks and the extent to which those risks are discounted' (Piliavin *et al.* 1986, p. 115). The same interpretation has been suggested by Shover and Thompson (1992) for their failure to find an expected positive relationship between risk estimates and crime desistance among former prison inmates.

In light of the sample and data limitations of this study we cannot and have not argued that the lifestyle we described *generates* or *produces* the characteristic decision making behaviours of persistent property offenders. The evidence does not permit such interpretive liberties. It does seem reasonable to suggest, however, that the focal concerns and shared perspectives of those who pursue life as party may function to *sustain* offenders' free-wheeling, but purposeful, decision making style. Without question there is a close *correspondence* between the two. Our ability to explain and predict decision making requires that we gain a better understanding of how utilities and risk perceptions are constrained by the properties of situations encountered typically by persons in their daily rounds. In other words, we must learn more about the daily worlds that comprise the immediate contexts of criminal decision making behaviour.

Note

This research was supported by grant No. 86-IJ-CX-0068 from the US Department of Justice, National Institute of Justice (Principal Investigator: Neal Shover). Points of view or opinions expressed here do not necessarily reflect the official position or policies of the Department of Justice. For their critical comments while the paper was in gestation we are grateful to Derek Cornish and to participants in a March 1991 colloquium at the Centre for

Socio-Legal Studies, Wolfson College, University of Oxford. Werner Einstadter, Michael Levi, Mike Maguire, and anonymous reviewers also provided helpful comments.

References

Ball, J. C., Shaffer, J. W. and Nurco, D. N. (1983) 'The day-to-day criminality of heroin addicts in Baltimore: a study in the continuity of offense rates', *Drug and Alcohol Dependence, 12,* 119–42.

Becker, G. (1968) 'Crime and punishment: an economic approach', *Journal of Political Economy, 76,* 169–217.

Bennett, T. and Wright, R. (1984a) *Burglars on Burglary,* Aldershot: Gower.

Bennett, T. and Wright, R. (1984b) 'The relationship between alcohol use and burglary', *British Journal of Addiction, 79,* 431–7.

Blumstein, A., Cohen, J. and Nagin, D. (Eds.) (1978) *Deterrence and Incapacitation: Estimating the Effects of Criminal Sanctions on Crime Rates,* Washington, DC: National Academy of Sciences.

Blumstein, A., Cohen, J. and Farrington, D. P. (1988) 'Criminal career research: its value for criminology', *Criminology, 26,* 1–36.

Carroll, J. S. (1978) 'A psychological approach to deterrence: the evaluation of crime opportunities', *Journal of Personality and Social Psychology, 36,* 1512–20.

Carroll, J. S. (1982) 'Committing a crime: the offender's decision', in: J. Konecni and E. B. Ebbesen (Eds.), *The Criminal Justice System: A Social-Psychological Analysis,* San Francisco: W. H. Freeman.

Carroll, J. S. and Weaver, F. (1986) 'Shoplifters' perceptions of crime opportunities: a process-tracing study', in: D. B. Cornish and R. V. Clarke (Eds.), *The Reasoning Criminal: Rational Choice Perspectives on Offending,* New York: Springer-Verlag.

Clarke, R. V. and Cornish, D. B. (1985) 'Modeling offenders' decisions: a framework for research and policy', in: M. Tonry and N. Morris (Eds.), *Crime and Justice: A Review of Research,* Vol. 4, Chicago: University of Chicago Press.

Claster, D. S. (1967) 'Comparison of risk perception between delinquents and nondelinquents', *Journal of Criminal Law, Criminology and Police Science, 58,* 80–6.

Cornish, D. B. and Clarke, R. V. (Eds.), *The Reasoning Criminal: Rational Choice Perspectives on Offending,* New York: Springer-Verlag.

Cromwell, P. F., Olson, J. N. and Avary, D. W. (1991) *Breaking and Entering: An Ethnographic Analysis of Burglary,* Newbury Park, Ca: Sage.

Ekland-Olson, S., Lieb, J. and Zurcher, 1. (1984) 'The paradoxical impact of criminal sanctions: Some microstructural findings', *Law and Society Review, 18,* 159–78.

Feeney, F. (1986) 'Robbers as decision-makers', in: D. B. Cornish and R. V. Clarke (Eds.), *The Reasoning Criminal: Rational Choice Perspectives on Offending,* New York: Springer-Verlag.

Figgie International (1988) *The Figgie Report Part VI – The Business of Crime: The Criminal Perspective,* Richmond, Va: Figgie International Inc.

Frazier, C. E. and Meisenhelder, T. (1985) 'Criminality and emotional ambivalence: exploratory notes on an overlooked dimension', *Qualitative Sociology, 8,* 266–84.

Gibbs, J. J. and Shelley, P. L. (1982) 'Life in the fast lane: a retrospective view by commercial thieves', *Journal of Research in Crime and Delinquency, 19,* 299–330.

Goffman, E. (1967) *Interaction Ritual,* Garden City, NY: Anchor.

Gottfredson, M. R. and Hirschi, T. (1990) *A General Theory of Crime,* Stanford, Ca: Stanford University Press.

Heineke, J. M. (Ed.) (1978) *Economic Models of Criminal Behavior*, Amsterdam: North-Holland.

Johnson, B. D., Goldstein, P. J., Prebel, E., Schmeidler, J., Lipton, D. D., Spunt, B. and Miller, T. (1985) *Taking Care of Business: The Economics of Crime by Heroin Addicts*, Lexington, Mass: D.C. Heath.

Katz, J. (1988) *Seductions of Crime*, New York: Basic Books.

Maguire, M. in collaboration with T. Bennett (1982) *Burglary in a Dwelling*, London: Heinemann.

Manski, C. F. (1978) 'Prospects for inference on deterrence through empirical analysis of individual criminal behavior', in: A. Blumstein, J. Cohen and D. Nagin (Eds.), *Deterrence and Incapacitation: Estimating the Effects of Criminal Sanctions on Crime Rates*, Washington, DC: National Academy of Sciences.

Nagin, D. S. and Paternoster, R. (1991) 'On the relationship of past to future participation in delinquency', *Criminology, 29*, 163–89.

Persson, M. (1981) 'Time-perspectives amongst criminals', *Acta Sociologica, 24*, 149–65.

Petersilia, J. (1980) 'Criminal career research: a review of recent evidence', in: N. Morris and M. Tonry (Eds.), *Crime and Justice: An Annual Review of Research*, Vol. 2, Chicago: University of Chicago Press.

Petersilia, J., Greenwood, P. W. and Lavin, M. (1978) *Criminal Careers of Habitual Felons*, Washington DC: US Department of Justice, National Institute of Law Enforcement and Criminal Justice.

Peterson, M. A. and Braiker, H. B. (1980) *Doing Crime: A Survey of California Prison Inmates*, Santa Monica, Ca: Rand Corporation.

Piliavin, I., Gartner, R. and Matsueda, R. (1986) 'Crime, deterrence, and rational choice', *American Sociological Review, 51*, 101–19.

Rengert, G. F. and Wasilchick, J. (1985) *Suburban Burglary*, Springfield, Ill: Charles C. Thomas.

Repetto, T. A. (1974) *Residential Crime*, Cambridge, Mass: Ballinger.

Reynolds, M. O. (1985) *Crime by Choice: An Economic Analysis*, Dallas: Fisher Institute.

Scarr, H. A. (1973) *Patterns of Burglary* (2nd ed.) Washington, DC: US Department of Justice, National Institute of Law Enforcement and Criminal Justice.

Seidel, J. V., Kjolseth, R. and Seymour, E. (1988) *The Ethnograph: A User's Guide* (Version 3.0), Littleton, Co: Qualis Research Associates.

Shover, N. (1991) 'Burglary', in: M. Tonry (Ed.), *Crime and Justice: An Annual Review of Research*, Vol. 14, Chicago: University of Chicago Press.

Shover, N. and Thompson, C. Y. (1992) 'Age, differential expectations, and crime desistance', *Criminology, 30*, 89–104.

Tittle, C. R. (1980) *Sanctions and Deviance: The Question of Deterrence*, New York: Praeger.

Waldo, G. P. and Chiricos, T. G. (1972) 'Perceived penal sanction and self-reported criminality: neglected approach to deterrence research', *Social Problems, 19*, 522–40.

Walsh, D. (1980) *Break-Ins: Burglary from Private Houses*, London: Constable.

Walsh, D. (1986) *Heavy Business*, London: Routledge and Kegan Paul.

Date submitted: November 91
Date accepted: April 92

[25]

EDITORIALS

THE PROFESSIONAL THIEF

The skilled pickpockets, confidence men, shoplifters, check writers, and certain other offenders may be regarded as professional thieves. This profession has a complex of skilled techniques, status, consensus, organization, and segregation in the underworld. They depend primarily on their wits, "front," and talking ability; they must be good actors. By these characteristics they are differentiated from non-professional thieves, and also from professional criminals in other rackets.

The earnings of some members of this profession are envied by people in legitimate occupations. Eddie Jackson (misnamed the Immune, for he spent a larger part of his life in prison than most professional thieves) said it was a poor week when he got less than $1500 for his personal income. Jackie French had a famous week in Florida in February, 1922, when he took $345,000 from three victims in confidence games. The states' attorney of Cook County, Illinois, stated in December, 1934, that Joseph (Yellow Kid) Weil and his troupe in six months took more than a million dollars from victims in confidence games. It is reported that the federal authorities are planning to accuse William Elmer Mead, professional confidence man, known as the Christian Kid, of income tax shortage of $60,000 during the years 1921-1928, due to failure to report his gains from swindles.

These professional thieves are able to pursue their occupation successfully for three principal reasons: First, they select the rackets in which conviction is very improbable. In some of the rackets the victim is induced to undertake an illegal act and is therefore not willing to bring accusations against the thief; this is true especially in confidence games and the "shake" (shake-down in connection with income tax frauds and homosexuality). Also, the stores are very reluctant to accuse a person who looks like a legitimate customer of theft, and the thieves look like legitimate customers. It is very difficult to secure sufficient legal evidence to convict a pickpocket. Second, the thieves have perfected their techniques by training and experience, both from the point of view of the criminal act and from the point of view of avoiding incriminating evidence. A shoplifter saw in a department store a bundle of men's suits which had just been unpacked; he went back around the corner, took off his coat and hat and put a pencil behind his ear so that he would look like an employee of the store, returned and picked up from the pile all the suits he could carry, took the service elevator to the ground floor, walked out the door, and stepped into a taxicab. In the confidence game the "build-up" is so convincing that many victims insist on going through with the swindle even after they have been warned by the police or by bankers that they are being swindled. Third, the thief works on the assumption that he can fix practically every case against him. He is arrested frequently but because of his ability to fix cases he is seldom sent to prison. The arrests are inconvenient, but bad weather is inconvenient also and persons do not give up their business because of bad weather. The thief takes the arrests as a matter of course and is not disturbed.

Cases against the professional thief are fixed sometimes by his own efforts, sometimes by efforts of political office-holders, and most frequently by a professional fixer for professional thieves. The fixing is accomplished principally by inducing the victim to drop the prosecution in return for restitution of property. Then, in order, assistance is rendered by policemen, prosecutors, clerks, bailiffs, and judges. The policemen, clerks, and bailiffs generally receive cash for their services after each act of assistance; the prosecutors and judges are likely to receive Christmas presents, loans which are not repaid, or contributions to campaign expenses.

This fixing of criminal cases is a specific instance of the modern social disorganization. First, the victim looks at the theft from the point of view of his own interest and has practically no consideration of the general social welfare; in this respect he has the same point of view as the professional thief. When he drops the prosecution he is not only acting from a narrowly individual point of view but also he is committing a technical crime. Second, the office-holder who accepts gifts for protecting the thief is a part of a political organization which, in general, is engaged in predatory control. The patronage system which is for the welfare of the party organization and in opposition to the general social welfare is an illustration of this predatory control. Other illustrations may be found in the methods of enacting and blocking legislation, the methods of voting, taxing, and granting contracts and franchises. The fix in professional crime is a part of this system of predatory control. The police and the courts are selected as agents to protect the general society against crime; under orders from the party organization or on payment of money they pervert their function and protect the thieves. Not every policeman or prosecutor does this, to be sure. In order to secure a conviction it is necessary to have the cooperation of victim, police, prosecutor, clerks, bailiff, judge, jury, and perhaps grand jury. The thief works on the assumption that he can always find a weak link in this chain and that it is only a matter of using ingenuity to find where the chain can be broken most easily.

EDWIN H. SUTHERLAND.

New Society 6 January 1983

Ducking and diving

Laurie Taylor looks back over his travels among the crime professionals

I never got used to the violence. I would be sitting with John McVicar in this or that club, chatting to Geoff or Phil or Tommy about some detail of their criminal dealings, flicking the tape recorder on and off, glancing at my list of questions, when—*bang bang bang*—in came another horrific story about how Mike had got smashed to pieces in a fight last night outside the Landsdowne, or how Ted and his brothers had knifed Big George at the dog track the night before. Even rather fastidious con men like Geoff would join in, pressing for more details, nodding enthusiastically at each twist and turn of the dramatically lurid description.

At least this stopped me from slipping into any sort of "loveable rascal" view of the underworld. There wasn't anything loveable about the stories, or their reception. At first some of the stories seemed so nasty that I assumed the teller was going over the top—that he was revealing some unfortunate pathological obsession. But I soon realised that nobody except me ever blanched. Neale's little story of how, at one time, he had sorted out some would-be gangsters who were threatening his club, was normal enough to rate no more than a few understanding nods:

"I thought: Well, I've had enough of you cunts. You gotta do what you gotta do, and I had this little penknife on me. And I could give someone some treatment. *Phhooo!* I was on 'em like a fucking dose of . . . they said something to me . . . and I was on them like a dose of salts. Sticking it right in their fucking head. About twenty times they was on the floor, bleeding profusely, with blood spurting up the walls, and then I done two more an' all—I do for *him*. I do for *him*. Right away. Right up. In the throat. And one in the fucking eye."

And as so often, there was more to come. Gangsters—whether would-be or successful—come in families. So, once Neal had started, he had to go on with his campaign. The next night he was round to see the rest of his enemies. Face to face:

"I said: 'I hear you're fucking looking for me. Well, you don't have to look for me. '*Cos here I am*! Then I hammered the geyser in front of them. A spade. I did have him. I did see to him an' all—and I fucking give him one. I stuck a blade right up this throat. And down he went, didn't he? With a blade protruding out of his fucking throat. He didn't feel too good then, did he? Over he went, didn't he? But I said, 'I hear you're looking for me.' 'Cos I can see them, and I know they're bullies. And they didn't fancy anything else."

Much of this violence was there to en-force existing rights. No other legal or quasi-legal sanctions could be invoked in a community of villains. So gangsters would be hired to protect gambling or drinking clubs, and get a share of the profits in return for their readiness to hand it out—or, more usually, as payment for a reputation which simply kept the troublemakers away.

But it is in the nature of violence that it resists strict regulation. It gets out of hand. Becomes an end in itself. The Krays were always the favourite example. They—and, in particular, Ronnie—went just that bit too far, even for most of the hardened villains at the Landsdowne. Phil summed up the general attitude:

"You see," he said, "Ronnie would really go over the brink. *Go over the brink.* And do more damage than he'd intended to do, *and* more than he should do—being a gangster . . . So people was absolutely in fucking fear of their lives with them. Nobody could say or speak anything. They went too fierce . . . And that was the trouble: 'Cos when you lose that with people, you've lost everything. I'll tell you why. 'Cos you'll never get the gist of nothing. When you've got just yes-men, you're in danger. You'll never get your cards marked."

I never heard anyone complain about the actual morality of the Krays' actions. The people they beat and shot were thought of as fair game: they had stepped out of line, and should have known better. It was just that too much violence, too much terror, might be tactically wrong. The limits were purely practical.

Self-righteousness

Not that anyone I met in my six months of trailing around with John McVicar could have been called amoral. Quite the contrary. I have never met a group of people who had such a pronounced sense of justice and right and equity, who spoke so much of principles and what was fair and reasonable. There was quite enough moral self-righteousness around to wallpaper a seminary.

Mike, for example, belonged to a rather smart health club in Mayfair. It was one of those executive gymnasiums where you are expected to exercise for half an hour before retiring to your own cubicle for a special massage and a large gin and tonic. Recently, the proprietors of this club had found out from somewhere (probably a police officer client) that Mike had done a spell in prison. He had been promptly excluded. "I mean! Is that fair? Because someone's been inside." This was directed at me, not John. Surely, as a criminologist, I should be properly outraged. "Because of

14　　　　　　　　　　　　　　　　New Society 6 January 1983

what someone's done in the past? Don't you think it's diabolical?"

Well—yes. On the face of it. But hardly enough to have anyone searching for the phone number of the National Council for Civil Liberties. All the crowd round us in the Landsdowne, who were looking equally shocked at the behaviour of the health club, knew full well that Mike was still an active villain, and had been out robbing that very morning. There were excellent contemporary reasons for excluding him from any straight club. But this didn't make a scrap of difference. The essential moral point was that the club had no way of *proving* this—and so Mike was innocent. Not just technically—but actually.

It was, I suppose, a judicial morality, born out of dozens of courtroom experiences; a view of the world in which doing it and getting away with it didn't count. Because no one could prove it. And the hypocrisy of the straight world, that characteristic which made it so eminently suitable for plunder, was its readiness to suspect duplicity when none was apparent; to fabricate evidence when none was immediately available.

"Plunder" is just about the best word for the professional's attitude to his activity and his prey. Villains distinguished themselves from the "cowboys" and the amateurs by the *systematic* and *wholesale* way in which they wrested profits from the straight world. Hoisters cleared complete racks of silk shirts; con men "worked" book after book of travellers' cheques; armed robbers cleaned out security vans; burglars emptied hundreds of country houses. Day after day. Week after week.

Lord Snooty's pals

And the evidence of the sorties into banks and homes and shops had to be just as flamboyant as the raids themselves. Always wodges of notes—ten, twenties, fifties. Denominations which I had to peer at to distinguish would be casually picked off from a fat roll and left lying as payment on bars and restaurant tables. And if you were in the money, then you had to live a luxury life of almost comic extravagance:

a Lord Snooty Rolls-Royce, a great *Dandy* roll of notes, a Desperate Dan magnum of champagne, and a *Beano*-size cigar. I remember asking Geoff what he really liked about the life.

"Well, I'm a natural. I mean, I *am* a natural. I love it. I love it. I love the high life . . . I love the . . . going out to wine and dine, the fucking champagne, and the birds, and living it up, and first class on the airplanes. Champagne fucking Charlie. You know. Ducking and diving; and, you know, wining and dining."

"Ducking and diving" is the other theme that kept coming through. Villains had to "stay sharp—right to the bottom of the glass." The belief was that, everywhere you went, there were gaps you could squeeze into: many of them created by those very hypocrites who were for ever pronouncing on the infamy of professional criminals. Neal explained it to me:

"Everybody, whatever walk of life, they're looking for perks. Millionaires look for perks. They're all at it. They're all at the fucking cheating game. No matter where

Biff Products

New Society 6 January 1983

they are, they're cheating. All you gotta do as a villain is to look for what they're cheating at. And once you know what they're creating at, where the readies are coming from, then you can move in."

Neal, like everyone else, called this (with no ironic inflection) "looking for clues": "When you ride about, you always find clues; always looking for clues, always riding about, and if I see something—Ah, that's a fucking clue."

A contagious frenzy

Everything in this world was sharpened up. You kept alert, moved quickly, stayed out late, drove at speed, made snap decisions. There was a contagious frenzy about it all. Everyone else was left standing at the lights. It was what Mark Benney in his 1930s novel, *Low Company*, nicely called "the fierce pulse of anti-social life."

This pulse was also what separated this crowd of villains, in their own minds, from the lumpen proletariat; from all those whose lives plodded between the fixed points of bingo—telly—Clacton—and the *News of the*

World. It would have taken someone braver than me to point out how much the villains' ideal version of fast luxury living—with all its cigars and champagne and Rollers—was rooted in the very social stratum they affected to despise.

"Don't be so superior," said one journalist who had listened to me for half an hour while I chatted on in this way about villains and their values: their rationalisations; their sentimental East-Endery; their crass attitudes to women, and any form of sensibility. "They're almost due to become a protected species. The police are on to them. All those computer records on how they work, all those supergrasses, and new ways of interrogation. And the profits aren't big. I doubt if altogether they take as much in a year as half a dozen big inside City frauds. There are probably more professional criminals pass across our television screen in a single year than actually roaming the streets of London. They're dodos compared to all the hooligans and bootboys and psychopaths."

Nobody down at the Landsdowne club

ever felt quite so sorry for themselves. Part of being a professional criminal was being able to shrug off even the worst "knockbacks." You didn't discuss the odds against you, the prospect of prison: and when it came to the final reckoning, you didn't pretend you were other than you were.

On the last night I was there, Neal was talking loudly about a villain he had once worked with on a very profitable and long-running job. As far as I could gather, it involved taking charge of parcels delivery at Kings Cross. Both of them had got prison sentences for their part in it, but Neal's mate had insisted on going round the actual prison, and still pleading innocence. The governor had come to see if he felt the same way:

"Ah, Greenwood," he says. "Do you also say you're innocent in this matter?" "*Innocent!*" I said. "*Innocent! 'Innocent' be fucked.* Course I'm not 'innocent.' I've had it good now for five years. Plenty of fucking money. Plenty of fucking women. Good time I've had. So fuck ya."

This concludes the series

[27]

Journal of Criminal Justice, Vol. 2, pp. 113-129 (1974). Pergamon Press. Printed in U.S.A.

OPERATIONAL PARAMETERS
IN THE STOLEN PROPERTY SYSTEM[1]

MARILYN WALSH

Research Scientist
Law and Justice Study Center
Battelle Memorial Institute
Seattle, Washington

and

DUNCAN CHAPPELL

Director
Law and Justice Study Center
Battelle Memorial Institute
Seattle, Washington

ABSTRACT

*The operational steps involved in the theft of property are
identified and discussed with central attention being given to
the criminal receiver of stolen goods—the "fence." Both the
likely and unlikely divisions of labor in the stolen property
marketplace are analyzed as are the functional progressions of
events in the theft industry. The analysis is based on a field
research project.*

A PROPERTY THEFT ORIENTATION

Perhaps no area of contemporary criminal activity holds more potential for improved
understanding and successful intervention through analytical reorientation than does that
of property theft. This area of crime is by no means new, a situation which may in fact
constitute the greatest barrier to fresh thinking on the subject. Centuries of experience with
thefts of property have given us a fairly strong conceptualization of this crime area, a
conceptualization which centers almost exclusively on the thief. There is of course nothing
illogical or erroneous about a concern for this individual; it is he after all who steals the
property. What is argued here, however, is that an exclusive concentration on the thief yields
a myopic view of the process of theft, a view which draws the boundaries of the crime too
tightly around that individual. It is a view which tends therefore to consider each incident of
theft as a unique event, determined and constrained by the motivations, needs, and skills of
the perpetrator. This "conventional view of theft" (if we can use this phrase) prescribes a

response to this crime area which largely consists of a fairly sophisticated sorting process, linking one individual (or one group of individuals) with each event as it occurs.

Such an "individualistic" approach to crime and criminals is not, of course, confined to the property theft area. Cressey (1972:19), for example, suggests that it is the most prevalent approach to crime in general.

> Consistently, both the popular and scientific tendency is to view the criminal's behavior as a problem of individual maladjustment, not as a consequence of his participation in social systems. Perhaps it is for this reason that in criminology we have had thousands of studies that have sought some damaging trait in the personalities of individual criminals, but very few studies of the organizational arrangements among criminals who commit crimes in concert.

The tendency toward an individualistic interpretation of criminal behavior cannot be laid to the idiosyncracies of either the public or the scientist, but rather is undoubtedly influenced by the nature of the legal systems, with their concepts of individual responsibility and intent, upon which most democratic societies are based. But while such an interpretation may conform well to the needs of a legal system, it may have the additional effect of causing us to ignore some important dimensions of contemporary criminal behavior. Cressey (1972:18) puts it this way:

> In such nations it is the duty of criminal justice agents to subject individual criminals to punishment, regardless of race, religion, social status or organizational memberships. Such agents, then, must be much more concerned with collecting evidence that will lead to trials of individuals than with evidence about the relationships among criminals or about the structure and operations of illicit organizations.

It is the perspective of this paper that property theft is one area of criminal behavior that has sorely suffered both conceptually and practically from a failure to probe "the relationships among criminals (and) . . . the structure and operations of illicit organizations." Perhaps the most glaring evidence of this failure concerns what the President's Crime Commission (1967:99) called the "little research . . . done on fencing," i.e., on the criminal receiver of stolen property. This crime figure, although tallying an impressive list of protestations to his importance over several centuries, (Colquhoun, 1806; Association of Grand Jurors of New York County, 1928; Hall, 1968) has remained little explored, while his relationship with the thief has been virtually ignored by the criminologist.[2] But if the popular and scientific tendency has been to overlook the fence, the police detective assigned the responsibility of dealing with property theft has not found it possible to do so. Instead, as the authors discovered in the course of an ongoing study of patterns of criminal receiving, police detectives possess a great deal of information about the fence. Other researchers have reported similar experiences (Mack, 1964 and 1970).[3]

Because the police know about the fence does not imply that his activities are either successfully or efficiently interdicted, for the police agency is as influenced by an individualistic approach to crime as is the social scientist. Thus the bulk of enforcement resources and activity against theft is directed to the thief, and the situation in which police effort is devoted directly and *exclusively* to the fence appears to be rare indeed. The criminal receiver remains a curiosity to the criminal justice system, being infrequently arrested and even less often convicted.

The police insist that the reason for the poor enforcement record vis a vis the fence lies in the unworkability of the laws in this area; but it is equally obvious that much information regarding the fence possessed by police agencies remains poorly systematized and underutilized, often resulting in less than satisfactory enforcement strategies and tactics. It is the purpose of this paper to demonstrate how a careful systematizing of existing intelligence materials on fences and thieves can yield valuable information not only about the relationships between these individuals but also about the "structure and operations of illicit organizations" facilitating property theft. Such information, it is thought, can be additionally useful in the restructuring and reorienting of our popular, scientific *and* official responses to this area of crime.

The model of property theft employed here—the Stolen Property System—is an operationally based one, derived from the authors' research into patterns of criminal receiving in a large urban area of the northeastern United States.[4] As part of this study, access to police intelligence reports on the activities of burglars and fences has been obtained, as well as records of these activities maintained in a special investigative unit in the office of the district attorney. References to specific police reports, etc., found below are drawn primarily from these sources.

THE SCOPE AND DIMENSIONS OF THE STOLEN PROPERTY SYSTEM[5]

The Stolen Property System (hereafter SPS) is that set of individuals *and their interactions* which locates, plans, facilitates, and executes the extraction of property from an owner (in most cases the rightful possessor) *and* its transfer to a new owner. Ideally this system will have six functioning modes:

1. *Research and planning mode*—The determination of a demand for an item(s), its location, and how best it can be acquired.
2. *Extraction mode*—The actual separation of property from its owner (the theft).
3. *Exchange mode*—The transfer of the item from the extractor to the marketer (the person who will offer it for sale).
4. *Marketing mode*—This includes transportation and storage, demand analysis (marketing information subsystem), packaging and advertising (any necessary modifications in property prior to resale).
5. *Redistribution mode*—The determination of where, when, and at what price the item will be resold.
6. *Evaluation mode*—The analysis of the feedback to the system as to its performance.

In its simplest form, the SPS can consist of but a single individual as in the case of the thief peddling his own merchandise. In this situation, mode 3 would be combined with mode 2 into a single operation. At the uppermost level of complexity, the SPS can contain many individuals (the maximum number being indeterminate) as in the case of a truck hijacking. In this situation, the planning mode (mode 1) alone will require either the accurate forecasting of the behaviors of shipper, dispatcher, and driver, *or* the enlistment of the aid of one or all of these individuals.[6] It is important to note that whether the SPS consists of one or a dozen individuals, *all* of its operations must be performed. If this is not done by those within the system, then it will be undertaken by its clients or by others in the environment.[7] An abridged version of the SPS, then, does not imply a functional curtailment, but rather a combining of functions into fewer operational steps.

There is some evidence that the SPS in its simplest form does in fact occur. Eric Pace (1971) noted that the low prices which fences were offering to addicts for stolen property were forcing addicts to sell the merchandise themselves. It is clear, however, that the nature of the SPS is such that its most frequent manifestation consists of a division of labor between *at least two* individuals—the thief and the fence. Robert Earl Barnes[a] explained it this way:

> A thief who steals merchandise is like bread without yeast, no good, just as yeast is an essential element in the making of good bread, the 'Fence' is the essential element in any accomplished act of thievery whenever merchandise is involved.

This basic division of labor between the thief and fence occurs roughly at mode 3, with modes 1 and 2 generally allocated to the thief and modes 4 through 6 to the fence. The relationship between the thief and the fence in mode 3, though little studied, is essential.[9] It is also precisely that interaction which the conventional view of theft fails to recognize and account for.

The theoretical character of the relationship between thief and fence is best described by the mixed-motive bargaining situation.[10] The thief is motivated to cooperate with the fence in order to divest himself of the stolen property, yet at the same time, he is motivated to compete with the fence in achieving the best price for the merchandise. The fence is in a similar situation. By the very nature of his role, he is in the market for stolen property (hence he will want to cooperate with the thief) and yet his profit margin depends upon how well he can compete with the thief for a favorable price on the goods. The pressures to cooperate are perhaps greater for the thief, since the consequences of failing to reach an agreement are likely to be more significant for him; i.e., the possibility of being caught with the goods in hand. The fence runs no risk, particularly in the short run, if a deal is not consummated. The consequences of protracted bargaining situations may, however, result in sharply decreasing his sources of supply as he gains the reputation of being an unfair bargainer. Dealings between thief and fence, as with all commercial dealings, are strengthened by *consistency* and *reliability*. Therefore, although fence and thief are motivated to compete with each other regarding the exchange value of stolen property, the clear bias for both is toward the establishment of cooperation. The thief-fence relationship is not unique in this respect for as Deutsch (1949) has explained, cooperative interests must be strong enough to overcome competitive interests if mixed-motive bargainers are to reach agreement.

The SPS is clearly able to foster the kind of cooperation necessary in the exchange mode (mode 3) to keep a continual supply of stolen goods flowing toward the fence. But were the exchange of goods the only dimension of the interaction between these two crime figures, the SPS model would be of little analytical value. In effect it would make it difficult to sustain the concept of the SPS as a total, integrated system, for the SPS could be regarded instead as the face-off of two stolen property mechanisms, one belonging to the thief and one to the fence. The relationship between thief and fence at mode 3, while essential, does not move us much beyond the individualistic tendencies of the conventional view of theft. If we are to appreciate instead the organizational quality of property theft crimes, it is necessary to explore further the interaction patterns of fences and thieves in other parts of the SPS.

FURTHER DIMENSIONS OF THE STOLEN PROPERTY SYSTEM

In confining our attention to the thief-fence interaction at mode 3 (exchange) in the SPS, we stipulated that the system's division of labor allocated modes 1 and 2 to the thief and modes 4 through 6 to the fence. This is, of course, the most elementary form of that relationship, and while useful in elucidating some dimensions of the thief-fence interaction, it tends to shroud some of the more complex and more insightful relationships existing between these two individuals.

In order to understand more complex thief-fence relationships and to achieve a greater appreciation for the role of the criminal receiver, two important axioms regarding the SPS must be introduced:

A. *The effectiveness of the SPS does not require a single and specific division of labor to obtain.* That is, no particular allocation of the activities in the system is essential to its successful functioning.

B. *The functional integrity of the SPS is not disturbed by a nonsequential performance of its modes.* What this means is that although we have set down the logical progression of activities in the SPS in modes 1 through 6, this does not imply that they must be performed in that order.

These axioms emphasize at least two origins of *variety* in the SPS, and it is this variety which makes the system both interesting and analytically complex.

A. *Divisions of Labor*

We will begin our deeper analysis into the SPS by looking more closely at the questions raised by the first axiom. It should be noted here that although this axiom states that varying division-of-labor arrangements are possible in the SPS, it does not suggest that they are all equally likely. We will discuss three different modal allocations most descriptive both of what is and what is not likely to occur within the SPS. First, we will look at the division of labor between thief and fence in mode 1 (research and planning). Next we will look at the labor-sharing activities of these individuals at mode 2 (extraction). Finally, we will discuss the contributions of thief and fence in mode 4 (marketing).

1. *The division of labor between thief and fence in the planning of a theft.*

To begin, it should be noted that the fence, as the buyer of the thief's produce, always has some *implicit* influence over the planning of a theft through his power to reward. Thus those items for which the fence is willing to pay more will be more often sought by the thief and this will, of course, affect his choice of target. The fence's patterns of reward mediation therefore becomes the "Invisible Hand" guiding the thief toward the selection of what property he will steal. This "guidance" is felt not only by the junkie but also by the professional thief.

ITEM 1: (interview with Greg, professional burglar)[11]

I stole a beautiful pair of Imperial jade earrings one time and couldn't get rid of them. This just isn't a colored gem city (diamonds are biggest here) so a lot of fences won't touch things like rubies and saffires[sic], etc. Only Mr. A handled that sort of stuff. *Until I got connected with him,* there was no percentage in taking colored gems.

ITEM 2: (from police activity reports)

Received info from informer that of all the cabbies fencing hot stuff in the _____ St. area, Mr. X is doing the most business. It is reported that he pays $20 for stereo players taken from cars while others are only paying $15, further stated that he keeps stuff in trunk of the cab.

ITEM 3: (from statement of Joe, a semi-skilled burglar, to district attorney)

We could only get scrap prices from fences for stuff like silverware and tea sets, etc., so D (other burglar) said we were better off to steal the metals themselves. That's when we started working the warehouses and railroad yards.

A thief's selection of targets and items for theft is similarly influenced by the number of fences he knows and the degree of specialization in which they engage. Thus in item 1 Greg's acquaintance with Mr. A accrued to him rewards for property that had previously been unsalable. A burglar who only knows fences who handle TVs and clothing is likely to limit his thefts to those items.

The fence's "Invisible Hand" in mode 1, however, is not nearly always so invisible. Witness the following police activity report entries:

ITEM 4: (from police activity report)

Info that M (who fences from his auction house) is now selling insurance. What he does is visit older people who have money and antiques around and then fingers them for burglaries. Stuff all comes to him.

ITEM 5: (police activity report)

Mrs. _____ recent victim of a house burglary, says she has made purchases in antique store owned by T. T has been suspected of setting up wealthy clients for years.

ITEM 6: (police activity report)

Info that Greg's gang (prof. burglars) is fencing stuff through X who works for a detective agency and gives the burglars floor plans and info on security devices.

In these items, we see the fence who, by virtue of his business or occupation, is in a position to know individuals who possess valuable property, the nature of that property, or something about their movements. By sharing this information with thieves, he becomes the engineer, the prime mover, of the theft. Implied in most of these arrangements, of course, is the agreement that he will receive the property once it has been stolen. The increased role of the fence as "set-up man" in mode 1 also increases his power vis a vis the thief since is control over valuable theft information has an impact upon the thief's livelihood and future. The thief who needs this information must be willing to accept completely the fence's terms. If he does not come to terms, the fence with complete knowledge of who committed the theft, is in an excellent position to "set-up" the thief as well. This is why some professional thieves prefer to rely on their own research and planning rather than risking an indenture (however brief) to the receiver.

2. *The division of labor between fence and thief in the extraction mode.*

Labor sharing between fence and thief in the actual theft can take two forms. The fence can actually participate in the theft or he can offer technical advice on its commission. The former arrangement is an extremely unlikely situation in the SPS.

ITEM 7: (Robert Earl Barnes)

Seldom does the 'fence' ever participate in the actual thievery of the merchandise. . . (He) is the individual who takes no chance of apprehension by the police while the actual offense is being committed. . . .

ITEM 8: (interview with Greg, a professional thief)

I know the fence's job is a lot more lucrative and a lot safer (than that of the thief) because he never actually steals anything himself. But it just isn't as exciting.

Even though, then, the fence's participation in the theft's commission is highly unlikely, there is some evidence that he can assist in the offense in ways other than setting it up. He can, for example, instruct the thief as to techniques to use in avoiding suspicion and apprehension.

ITEM 9: (police activity report)

. . .went to the jail and talked with _____ He said recent daytime burglaries are being set up by Mr. L. He tells the junkies to go from door to door and if someone answers to attempt to sell him a *Reader's Digest*.

ITEM 10: (police activity report)

. . .word is that X tells burglars to sit on stuff til they call in and only to come to the store during regular hours.

Little evidence could be found of a more active role taken by the fence in the extraction mode. Instead his involvement here appears limited to the giving of advice or admonition to the thief. It is probably fair to say, therefore, that a division of labor in the SPS which allocates mode 2 to the fence is a highly unlikely arrangement and for all intents and purposes can be eliminated from consideration.

3. *The division of labor between fence and thief in the marketing mode.*

It is probably necessary to restate the activities which occur in the marketing mode of the SPS since it covers three general areas: an analysis of demand in the stolen property economy (a marketing information subsystem); activities related to the transportation and storage of property; and, finally, activities related to packaging and promotion (the modifications necessary in the preparation of stolen property for resale). As can be imagined, mode 4 is an extremely complex and comprehensive component of the SPS. This is in general the fence's milieu; and it is because of his skills in organizing and coordinating the various activities in this mode that he can command a lion's share of the rewards which the SPS has to offer. (Robert E. Barnes suggests that he pays a " 'bucket of coal' for a bucket of diamonds.")

The quality of the demand analysis conducted by the fence will depend upon his individual business acumen. If he distributes stolen property through his own retail outlet, he must anticipate the future demands of his customers and determine what he needs to buy from his "suppliers." Similarly, he must decide what mix of stolen versus legitimate property e wants to maintain; this again will affect his buying habits. He will also need to analyze the market he serves to discover the different segments it contains and the varying tastes that he should satisfy in his product line. If the fence does not sell directly to the public but instead to other middlemen or to retail establishments, his demand analysis will follow the same general pattern as above but will depend as well upon the quality of the contacts he makes in the legitimate market place and the guidance they can provide.[12] The fence, then, faces many of the same dilemmas as any legitimate marketer. There is no one formula for success, only the expertise which past success and failure teaches. (An accommodation to the difficulties in demand forecasting and analysis used in both legitimate and illegitimate market places will be discussed below when the nonsequential function of the SPS is considered).[13] There is little question, however, that the demand analysis function is an all-fence activity.

The other two activity areas in mode 4, though directed by the fence, can be shared with the thief. This is particularly true of the transportation and storage function where the evidence suggests that often an equal responsibility obtains. Consider the case in which the fence employs a "drop" where property is to be abandoned by the thief. The former pays for the storage facility while the latter must be responsible for transportation.

ITEM 11: (police activity report)

. . .what happens is that burglars are told to take stolen property to a drop at _____ St. and stash it in the garage until X (fence) can be called. He comes to the drop and if property is worth buying he opens his store for burglars to deliver it that night. Most of the stolen property is kept in a back room of the store and guarded by a police dog (kept mostly for protection against the police).

A similar arrangement has the fence financing both transportation and storage functions.

ITEM 12: (police activity report)

. . .went to cell block of county jail re: arrest of A and B (burglars) last night inside the _____ TV store. Both gave sworn statements and also stated that they were to drop the TVs at a gas station on _____ and _____ streets. They were to meet a blue van truck at the gas station between midnight and 1 a.m. . . . B admitted to a previous burglary the night before in which they took 6 TVs and 4 stereos and sold them to Mr. Y (fence) after making a deal with him at the _____ bar and grill. They took this loot to the same gas station and put it in a blue truck and were paid $225 by unknown W/M. They were to do the same thing last night.

The "drop" is only one technique which the fence uses to facilitate the safe transport and storage of stolen property while at the same time insuring against his being found in "possession" of it. The rental of warehouse facilities serves a similar purpose.

ITEM 13: (police activity report)

Info that Mr. A (fence) not only owns the appliance store on _____ St., he also has the store across the street and rents a storage area further down the block.

ITEM 14: (police activity report)

Detectives _____ and _____ rec'd info that Mr. X is into stolen property again. Heard he has a warehouse on _____ St. where he stores these items.

It is clear that the storage function is the sole responsibility of the fence since the thief has at this point relinquished control over the property to him. Similarly, any further transportation that may be required is also the fence's concern. Some fences pursue occupations in the trucking and storage industries which are tremendous assets to their illegal business endeavors. Two individuals in the data base, for example, jointly own three moving and storage firms, with a dozen vans and numerous warehouses. Two of their legitimate businesses did a gross in 1969 of $96,000 and police won't attempt to estimate their profits from criminal receiving. These individuals also appear to provide transportation facilities for other fences in the city. Witness the following note from police files:

ITEM 15: (police activity report)

. . .suspicious activity at _____ Avenue re: building being used as warehouse for storage of stolen TVs and hi fis (foreign mfg.)—Detectives observed male get out of car and use key to gain entrance—car registered to Mr. C. who is suspected of being a fence. To add to suspicions, when TV's were moved across state to the present location at above-mentioned warehouse, the mover was X owner of _____ Moving and Storage (fencing outlet).

We have seen that activities related to transportation and storage in the SPS can be shared by fence and thief. The sharing of responsibility for these functions is not, however, haphazard nor random in nature. Instead it is determined by the degree of control which each is considered to exercise over the stolen property at a given point in time. Thus, any storage or transportation activities that are required, pursuant to an agreement reached in the exchange process (mode 3), are likely to be performed by the thief. Once this exchange agreement has been satisfied, any further need for transport or storage becomes the fence's responsibility. To require the thief to perform such functions beyond those pursuant to the exchange process would be to defeat his prime motivation for making an agreement with the fence, which is to divest himself of the stolen property. Similarly, to require the fence to perform these functions prior to an exchange agreement would force him to exercise control over property which he has not as yet decided to purchase. Both thief and fence recognize that their possession of (i.e., effective control over) stolen property requires the performance of certain activities; neither, however, will be willing or likely to assume responsibility for such activities once possession has been relinquished or before it has been undertaken.

The final activity area in mode 4 of the SPS is the preparation of property for resale. This is almost exclusively the province of the criminal receiver who, following the exchange with the thief, becomes the new *seller* of the merchandise. It is the fence who takes responsibility for decisions relating to modification of the goods prior to sale, in what quantities he will sell the goods, and in what manner he will present the items to potential customers. With some items, such as automobiles, the fence will find it important to remove or disguise identifying numbers while keeping the make and model apparent. In other cases, with fair-traded appliances for example, it may be more important to disguise make and model than identifying numbers. The type of customer which the fence serves, whether retail or wholesale, corporate or individual, knowledgeable or naive, will determine the quantities in which the merchandise is sold and the manner in which it is promoted. The planning and coordination of activities in the packaging and promotion area emphasize again the organizational know-how and financial base which a fence needs to operate efficiently. It also serves to explain why he may not be able to "afford" to reward the thief too generously for his efforts.

There are certain limited cases in which the thief shares responsibility for preparing stolen property for resale. One such case is that of the professional jewel thief.

ITEM 16: (interview with Greg, professional burglar)

> As soon as we finished a job we always went back to my apartment. There I'd remove all the stones from their settings, weigh them, appraise them and put them in jeweler's paper to protect them.

Greg explained that this was done for two reasons: first, as a form of protection. Often the only identity possessed by a gem is its setting. By removing a gem from its setting, then, its identification becomes much more difficult so that even upon apprehension by the police he and his associates had a good chance of not being charged with anything. Second, Greg found that he could make better deals with fences with loose stones since he had saved them the trouble of removing the settings. In addition, the origins of the items could remain somewhat obscure protecting both of them.

The professional thief is probably one of the few classes of thieves who has sufficient skill or motivation to perform such preparatory activities. It is obvious that he does not perform them as a favor to the fence but out of his own self-interest. This activity area in mode 4, then, is similar to the area of transportation and storage where activities are performed by the individual in control of the property. Because of the nature of the packaging and promotion activities and the point in time in which they occur, it is the fence who in nearly all situations is in possession of the merchandise. Responsibility for these activities, therefore, falls primarily on him. From our review of mode 4 activity areas it also becomes quite clear that the fence is the prime mover in the marketing process of the SPS.

B. *Nonsequential activity performance*

The second axiom of the SPS relates to the nonsequential nature of the functioning modes. In order to demonstrate the sort of variety which this axiom suggests, we will discuss three modal configurations in the SPS: (1) the system beginning at mode 2 (extraction) and proceeding spontaneously; (2) the system beginning at mode 1 (planning), moving to mode 3 (exchange agreement) then to mode 2 (extraction) and finally proceeding to modes 4 and 5; (3) the system beginning at mode 5 (redistribution) then moving to modes 1, 3, 2 and 4 in that order. Each of these configurations represents not only different degrees of *determinateness* in the SPS, but also different degrees of *integrative control* exhibited by the fence.

1. *The SPS beginning at the extraction mode 2, having eliminated a research and planning phase.*

This configuration can be termed the "cheapest opportunity" model. It is likely to be initiated by the least skilled thief or the addict thief. Because of the lack of planning involved, it will also be the least determinate, least integrated and least efficient model in the SPS for one of two reasons. First, it is unlikely to yield property of great resale value since its targets must be those which can be attacked spontaneously and with a minimum effort. For example:

ITEM 17: (police radio message item)

B & E at pawnbroker's shop on _____ St. Window broken and two trays
of jewelry removed. Assailant believed to be on foot.

In some cases this model of the SPS will yield nothing at all and instead will serve only to
create a disturbance within the environment surrounding the system.

ITEM 18: (police activity report)

Alarm sounded at warehouse on _____ Avenue. Two w/m seen
running from building. Would-be thieves didn't have time to get anything.
Pct 2 will put a patrol car in the area in case they try again.

The second reason why the "cheapest opportunity" model is inefficient is that it fails to
predetermine a demand for merchandise. For example, consider the luckless thieves below
who managed to steal merchandise of some value but whose lack of planning rendered it not
only valueless to them but also incriminating.

ITEM 19: (police activity report)

X and Y (thieves) were arrested this AM in the act of trying to peddle meat
from the _____ warehouse. They did not have a refrigerated truck so
most of it had already started to spoil when recovered.

This model, if it is to be effective at all, requires the existence of the generalist fence who
is willing to handle a wide range of items of varying quality and indeterminate quantity.
The SPS does of course provide for this sort of individual in the form of owners of
secondhand and general merchandise outlets and used furniture and appliance stores.[14]
Fences who engage in this sort of trade do so because they can acquire property very cheaply
from hard-pressed thieves whose lack of planning has put them in precarious possession of
stolen property. If, then, the thefts initiated under this model are of the "cheapest
opportunity" variety, they are also of the least rewarding variety to the thief. For the fence
they also represent the "cheapest opportunity" since they comprise the best bargains he can
get from any set of thieves.

If this model is to have any determinateness, it is the fence who must introduce it by
manipulating the rewards offered in the exchange mode. By giving such direction to the
thief's activities, the fence is not generating a planning process but only narrowing the
range of products which he is likely to encounter. This can help make the thief a bit more
predictable and the system a bit more determinate and efficient. This model of the SPS
remains, however, the least integrated configuration.

2. *The SPS in the modal sequence of planning (mode 1), exchange (mode 3), extraction
(mode 2), marketing (mode 4), and redistribution (mode 5).*

This is the "exchange-oriented" model of the system in which thefts are planned but not
carried out until the terms of the exchange agreement and the responsibilities for activities
pursuant to that agreement are determined. This model is significantly more determinate
and efficient than is the "cheapest opportunity" model, although this is only true through
the exchange-extraction processes. The marketing and redistribution modes retain an
indeterminate quality in this model. The degree of integration in the "exchange-oriented"

model depends upon who generates and plans the theft and who initiates the terms of the exchange agreement. Two basic situations are possible: the thief-generated pact, and the fence-generated pact.

The thief-generated pact is the situation in which the thief assures a market for the theft he envisions by making preliminary arrangements with a fence to buy the product of his activities. In some sense, then, it is the thief's insurance policy which he hopes will prevent him from being caught holding stolen property unnecessarily.

ITEM 20: (Robert E. Barnes)

one. . . must always remain conscious of the fact, it is impracticable for the thief to steal what he cannot sell. What should be of vital importance to law enforcement officials is the fact that semi and professional thieves *seldom steal before they sell*, thus proving the fact that all major crimes whereas [sic] merchandise is involved would never occur if there were no outlets for this merchandise.

In many cases the professional thief wants more than the assurance of a market, he may also want to make sure that his efforts will be sufficiently rewarded before attempting a "big score."

ITEM 21: (interview with Greg, professional burglar)

. . . we had been casing this place in _____ (a nearby city) where this lady was supposed to have $100,000 worth of jewelry in the house. I called Mr. A (jewel fence) at home and asked him if he could come up with $30,000 cash if it were necessary. "Yes," he said *"if* the stuff was worth it."

Perhaps the most important element of the above statement is the fence's "if." It is clear that the professional thief can succeed in getting some assurances from the fence but it is unlikely that he can force any binding agreement upon the fence before he has seen the merchandise. Robert E. Barnes, for example, maintains that fences are notorious for promising to pay a certain price prior to thefts of goods and then reneging on the agreement later. The thief-generated pact under the exchange-centered model of the SPS, then, does not display very much integration. All it really does is assure the thief of a buyer and notify the fence as to the type of property he is likely to receive and when.

The fence-generated pact is somewhat different. Here a high degree of integration can be introduced into the system as the fence has the opportunity to *specifically* direct the activities of the thief and to positively determine the products he will acquire. The fence who plans the theft and who provides information important to its commission is also in a position to extract from the thief a *specific* exchange agreement. This makes for a highly rationalized extraction process which has been preplanned with an exchange phase that is predetermined. The integrative control of the fence over the exchange-extraction processes produces a more efficient and determinate model of SPS behavior.

3. *The SPS beginning at the redistribution phase (mode 5) and proceeding through mode 1 (planning), mode 3 (exchange), mode 2 (extraction), and mode 4 (marketing).*

This final modal configuration of the SPS is by far its most complex and sophisticated sequence. The most apt term for this configuration is the "production to order" model.

What happens in this case is that no activities relating to a theft are initiated until an order for the merchandise has been received. Once this order is received, the theft is planned; an exchange agreement decided upon; the extraction carried out; and the marketing activities completed. And all of the above processes are coordinated and directed by the fence.

The "production to order" model is an accommodation made in the legitimate marketplace to avoid the stacking up of inventory surpluses and gluts in the marketing process. The fence uses the model for similar reasons but has the advantage over the legitimate marketer that his suppliers (thieves) are likely to produce goods quicker than is the legitimate manufacturer who supplies the legitimate businessman. The model, then, is likely to be much more effective within the SPS than it has been found to be in the legitimate marketplace.[15]

The most frequently cited example of the "production to order" model in the SPS is the auto theft ring. Instances have been reported of automobiles being stolen to meet the exact specifications of buyers, with color and bogus engine numbers added before resale. Robert Earl Barnes suggests that the "production to order" model is not limited to the stolen auto area, being particularly prevalent in the hijacking and cargo theft arena (U.S. Senate, 1973: 162):

> Prior to any hijacking, the merchandise has already been sold to underworld sources, and once the crime has been set-up, and carried out by the thieves, the merchandise is extremely difficult to recover, as it may go out for resale on the legitimate market to as many as 50 to 100 middle men.

Both the "cheapest opportunity" and "exchange-centered" models of the SPS require the fence to have increasing amounts of control over the forces of *supply* in the system. The "production to order" model requires of him the ability to generate the forces of *demand* as well. Demand control by the fence is somewhat more amorphous than is supply control. It will depend on such things as his individual abilities to forecast the desires of disparate customers; the kinds of contacts he has been able to cultivate at the wholesale and retail levels of the legitimate marketplace; and often upon his particular occupation.[16] For example, the two individuals described below pursue legitimate occupations of which generating orders for merchandise is an integral part. Their additional abilities to initiate an illegitimate supply process, allows them to operate a tight and effective stolen property distribution system.

ITEM 22: (police activity report)

Mr. T who is a salesman for the _____ Company, a manufacturer and distributor of clothing, is also a fence. Was seen last night with a load of clothes in car. Day crew check any recent clothing store burglaries in area.

ITEM 23: (police activity report)

Mr. S who owns a jewelry manufacturing company is alleged to be fencing for some of our better burglars. He supposedly has nationwide customers and contacts. Should be kept in mind whenever jewelry is taken in residence jobs.

The control which the fence has over the sequencing of events in the SPS under the "production to order" model makes it possible for him to bring the forces of demand and supply into a fairly stable equilibrium. This makes the model highly efficient and determinate. It also serves to protect all of the persons involved since by insuring that all aspects of the system are coordinated beforehand, stolen property can move swiftly to its final destination, minimizing the risk of either thief or fence being found in possession of it.

The limits upon the "production to order" model are of two orders. The model is limited, first, by the individual ability of the fence to generate demand (i.e., contacts and outlets to do business with him.) Second, the model hinges upon the amount of organizational and financial resources at the fence's disposal which can facilitate the completion of all activities based in mode 4, the marketing mode. This is perhaps the more important limitation since it defines the size and scope of his operation. No matter how organizationally skilled the fence, if he cannot command the use of storage and transport facilities—or cannot finance the performance of such activities by others—his business volume will remain small. The "production to order" model need not, then, be characterized by large scale operations. Instead this model describes a highly integrated, tightly controlled and finely precisioned model of the SPS in which the fence is both the orchestrator and the central character.

IDENTIFYING THE ROLE OF THE FENCE

What is immediately apparent from the discussions of division of labor and sequence configuration in the SPS, is the wide-ranging role played by the fence in the theft of stolen property. This actor, completely ignored by the conventional view of theft, can be seen to be much more than an innocuous mechanism by which the thief converts property to cash. On the contrary, the criminal receiver is often the planner, the initiator, and the contractor for theft. These additional roles assumed by the fence help to explain, first, the origins of the *incentives* for theft which, despite the volume of space in criminological literature devoted to thieves, has remained an area little developed; and second, the process by which *opportunities* for theft are generated. Thus, the fence by virtue of his occupation or station is often in a position to develop information vital to the successful commission of a theft which in most cases could not be generated by the thief himself. Without such a service provided by the fence, many thieves might be considerably less productive—if not less successful. Robert E. Barnes tells of his relationship with a jeweler-fence (U.S. Senate, 1973:162):

> In _____ (large city) one jeweler supplied me with over one hundred fifty names, addresses, amount of jewelry within the premises, time the family worked, telephone numbers of the home, and then purchased the stolen jewelry for about ten percent of its actual value after I burglarized the residents. The fact remains if I had not been given these addresses by this so-called legitimate businessman those families would still possess their jewelry today.

Once we have seen the fence as author of both the incentive and the opportunity for theft, we can appreciate more fully the compelling nature of his exchange relationship with the thief. We can also begin to see the thief as little more than an instrument of the fence—a highly visible but relatively minor cog in a giant distribution circuit. This should tell us why our efforts to combat theft by concentrating on the minor character who is the thief have been less than successful. In doing so we have concentrated upon eliminating the most easily replaceable functionary in the SPS without in any way dampening that system's incentives, altering its opportunity structure, or hampering its ability to dispose of stolen property rapidly and efficiently.

EVALUATING THE STOLEN PROPERTY SYSTEM

One final mode in the SPS is left for our consideration, mode 6 (evaluation). Any system desiring to grow and maintain itself must seek feedback. In addition it must be capable of evaluating the feedback it receives for validity and usefulness and be willing to incorporate the modifications which such feedback suggests. Often a system's feedback will be internally generated, that is the individual components of a system will monitor each other's activities. Alternatively a system can employ outside evaluators to review its operations and procedures and suggest revisions. Finally, a system can interpret its operational effectiveness through the feedback given by the several environments in which it finds itself. This latter evaluative source, nature, though often fickle, is presumed to favor no one and hence can comprise a system's least biased feedback mechanism.

The SPS must be characterized as a highly successful distribution mechanism in the American economy. Over the decade of the 1960's, the theft rate grew 180 percent (Hoover, 1970); and the SPS showed itself to be both flexible enough and efficient enough to absorb this expansion comfortably. It is now estimated that in the area of cargo theft alone, the SPS annually handles a volume of goods valued at $1.5 billion (U.S. Senate 1973:2). Such a system must continually seek and carefully analyze feedback. The fence who occupies the central position in the SPS has the best opportunity to make such an analysis. He will be influenced of course by the demands, the suggestions, and the dilemmas of both his suppliers and his customers, but he is also likely to be influenced by the feedback received from the environment.

What is the nature of this feedback? Clearly, the environment offers little challenge to the techniques and procedures of the SPS. The SPS faces an economy of mass-produced and mass-owned goods whose anonymity is insured because of poor identification and bookkeeping systems; it operates in a world of commerce dominated more often by "terms of sale" than by origin of goods; it sees a society in which "the paraphernalia of lawful enterprise"[17] carries a seal of legitimacy; it finds a criminal justice system that is avidly pursuing thieves, and a social science establishment that continues to view crime as a curiosity rather than as a major, organized American industry.

This resounding support given the SPS by its several environments can only be characterized as encouraging for it. It also makes it difficult to evaluate the SPS's true effectiveness, for in many ways that remains to be tested. If it is to be tested, a major reorientation must occur in the area of property crime. To accomplish this reorientation three important steps must be taken. First, the outmoded conventional view of theft must be discarded in favor of a more operationally descriptive definition of the theft process. Second, the enforcement emphasis placed upon the thief must be shifted and additional resources allocated to the investigation of the criminal receiver. Finally, the police detective and the scientist must be willing to form a partnership in which the systematizing of information and the sharing of experience and skills can contribute to a new technology to respond to a 20th century theft industry. Unless these minimum steps are taken the SPS will continue to operate unchallenged. Quite clearly, and literally, that is something we cannot afford.

MARILYN WALSH AND DUNCAN CHAPPELL

FOOTNOTES

¹This paper is an abridgment of a paper presented at the 44th national meeting of the Operations Research Society of America, 12-14 November 1973 in San Diego, California.

²An interesting recent exception is MacIntosh (1971).

³Carl Klockars, who recently completed doctoral work at the University of Pennsylvania (Philadelphia, Pennsylvania), relating to criminal receiving, has reported similar experiences of police knowledgeability to the authors.

⁴Portions of this research were supported by funds made available from the National Science Foundation, Grant No. 20-477. Because of the conditions under which the research was conducted and the nature of many of the materials used, the location of the data site cannot be revealed.

⁵The Stolen Property System Model and the discussion of its dimensions and scope are taken from Walsh (1974).

⁶A fascinating account of the complex planning and execution of truck hijacking can be found in U.S. Senate (1973).

⁷For example, it is conceivable that the SPS makes use of the extensive advertising efforts of the legitimate marketplace. Such well-developed preselling of merchandise removes from some fences the necessity of carrying on their own promotional campaigns.

⁸Robert Earl Barnes, a convicted professional thief who is now serving time at the Federal Correctional Institution in Sandstone, Minnesota, wrote a rather lengthy letter about fences to the U.S. Senate Select Committee on Small Business (U.S. Senate, 1973:158-63).

⁹A point elaborated on by Chappell and Walsh (1974).

¹⁰This discussion is taken from Walsh (1974). It is a much abridged version of a chapter which relies heavily upon the contributions of sociologists and social psychologists to the theory of games, a further development of which is not considered relevant to the discussion here.

¹¹The individual identified as Greg is a young, professional thief who became the chief informant witness for the district attorney in a series of theft prosecutions. The authors were much enriched by the access given to this individual and his willingness to be interviewed.

¹²The discussion here is based upon descriptive data of actual fences and fencing operations found at the data site. Since the aim of this paper is a theoretical rather than a descriptive portrayal of the SPS, details of such persons are not included although some of the dimensions of the fence's demand analysis relate to the situations of receivers in the sample.

¹³Specifically under the "production to order" model.

¹⁴Generalist fences were found to represent only six percent of the sample of fences studied.

¹⁵Again it should be emphasized that this model is limited in the legitimate market to large unit value items designed primarily for industrial users and to craft and specialty items in the consumer market. Although "production to order" is analogous to a catalogue buying system, the latter situation requires that someone hold an inventory of already finished goods, usually at a central warehouse or distribution center. A description by a burglar of a "production to order" fencing operation will be found in U.S. Senate (1973:30-36).

¹⁶Again this discussion focuses on those variables thought to influence the situations of fences observed at the research cite.

¹⁷Hall's characterization of how criminal receivers operate in order to escape public notice (Hall, 1952).

REFERENCES

Association of Grand Jurors of New York County (1928). *Criminal Receivers in the United States*. G.P. Putnam's Sons, 200 Madison Avenue, New York, New York 10016.

Chappell, D., and Walsh, M. (1974). "Receiving Stolen Property: The Need for Systematic Inquiry into the Fencing Process." *Criminology* 11:484.

Colquhoun, P. (1806). *A Treatise on the Police of the Metropolis*. Reprint of the seventh London edition. Smith, Patterson Publishing Corporation, 23 Prospect Terrace, Montclair, New Jersey 07042.

Operational Parameters in the Stolen Property System   129

Cressey, D.R. (1972). *Criminal Organization: Its Elementary Forms.* Harper and Row, Publishers, 10 East 53rd Street, New York, New York 10022.

Deutsch, M. (1949). "A Theory of Cooperation and Competition," *Human Relations,* 2:129-52.

Hall, J. (1952). *Theft, Law and Society,* second edition. Bobbs-Merrill Company, 4300 West 62nd Street, Indianapolis, Indiana 46268, p. 195.

Hall, J. (1968). "Theft, Law and Society—1968." *American Bar Association Journal,* 54:960-7.

Hoover, J.E. (1970). *Uniform Crime Reports.* Federal Bureau of Investigation. U.S. Government Printing Office, Washington, D.C. 20402.

MacIntosh, M. (1971). "Changes in Organization of Thieving." In *Images of Deviance,* Cohen, ed. Penguin Books, Ltd., Harmondsworth, Middlesex, England.

Mack, J. (1964). "Full Time Miscreants, Delinquent Neighborhoods and Criminal Networks." *British Journal of Sociology,* 15:38-53.

Mack, J. (1970). "The Able Criminal." Report to the Current Research Seminar of the Sixth World Criminological Congress, Madrid, Spain.

Pace, E. (1971). "Shift in Crime Patterns Adds to 'Fences' Here." *New York Times,* 12 October, pp. 1 & 31.

President's Commission on Law Enforcement and Administration of Justice (1967). *Task Force Report: Crime and Its Impact—An Assessment.* U.S. Government Printing Office, Washington, D.C. 20402, p. 99.

U.S. Senate (1973). *Criminal Redistribution Systems and Their Economic Impact on Small Business.* Report of the Select Committee on Small Business, 93rd Congress, 1st Session. U.S. Government Printing Office, Washington, D.C. 20402.

Walsh, M. (1974). "Criminal Receiving: A Study of the Fence and How he Operates." Doctoral dissertation, School of Criminal Justice, State University of New York at Albany, Part III, Chapter B.

[28]

FILM CHRONICLE

THE GANGSTER AS TRAGIC HERO

America, as a social and political organization, is committed to a cheerful view of life. It could not be otherwise. The sense of tragedy is a luxury of aristocratic societies, where the fate of the individual is not conceived of as having a direct and legitimate political importance, being determined by a fixed and supra-political—that is, non-controversial—moral order or fate. Modern equalitarian societies, however, whether democratic or authoritarian in their political forms, always base themselves on the claim that they are making life happier; the avowed function of the modern state, at least in its ultimate terms, is not only to regulate social relations, but also to determine the quality and the possibilities of human life in general. Happiness thus becomes the chief political issue—in a sense, the only political issue—and for that reason it can never be treated as an issue at all. If an American or a Russian is unhappy, it implies a certain reprobation of his society, and therefore, by a logic of which we can all recognize the necessity, it becomes an obligation of citizenship to be cheerful; if the authorities find it necessary, the citizen may even be compelled to make a public display of his cheerfulness on important occasions, just as he may be conscripted into the army in time of war.

Naturally, this civic responsibility rests most strongly upon the organs of mass culture. The individual citizen may still be permitted his private unhappiness so long as it does not take on political significance, the extent of this tolerance being determined by how large an area of private life the society can accommodate. But every production of mass culture is a public act and must conform with accepted notions of the public good. Nobody seriously questions the principle that it is the function of mass culture to maintain public morale, and certainly nobody in the mass audience objects to having his morale maintained.[1]

[1] In her testimony before the House Committee on Un-American Activities, Mrs. Leila Rogers said that the movie *None But the Lonely Heart* was un-

240

At a time when the normal condition of the citizen is a state of anxiety, euphoria spreads over our culture like the broad smile of an idiot. In terms of attitudes towards life, there is very little difference between a "happy" movie like *Good News,* which ignores death and suffering, and a "sad" movie like *A Tree Grows in Brooklyn,* which uses death and suffering as incidents in the service of a higher optimism.

But, whatever its effectiveness as a source of consolation and a means of pressure for maintaining "positive" social attitudes, this optimism is fundamentally satisfying to no one, not even to those who would be most disoriented without its support. Even within the area of mass culture, there always exists a current of opposition, seeking to express by whatever means are available to it that sense of desperation and inevitable failure which optimism itself helps to create. Most often, this opposition is confined to rudimentary or semi-literate forms: in mob politics and journalism, for example, or in certain kinds of religious enthusiasm. When it does enter the field of art, it is likely to be disguised or attenuated: in an unspecific form of expression like jazz, in the basically harmless nihilism of the Marx Brothers, in the continually reasserted strain of hopelessness that often seems to be the real meaning of the soap opera. The gangster film is remarkable in that it fills the need for disguise (though not sufficiently to avoid arousing uneasiness) without requiring any serious distortion. From its beginnings, it has been a consistent and astonishingly complete presentation of the modern sense of tragedy.[2]

In its initial character, the gangster film is simply one example of the movies' constant tendency to create fixed dramatic patterns that can be repeated indefinitely with a reasonable expectation of profit. One gangster film follows another as one musical or one Western follows another. But this rigidity is not necessarily opposed to the requirements of art. There have been very successful types of art in the past which developed such specific and detailed conventions as almost to make individual examples of the type interchangeable. This is true, for example, of Elizabethan revenge tragedy and Restoration comedy.

American because it was gloomy. Like so much else that was said during the unhappy investigation of Hollywood, this statement was at once stupid and illuminating. One knew immediately what Mrs. Rogers was talking about; she had simply been insensitive enough to carry her philistinism to its conclusion.

[2] Efforts have been made from time to time to bring the gangster film into line with the prevailing optimism and social constructiveness of our culture; *Kiss of Death* is a recent example. These efforts are usually unsuccessful; the reasons for their lack of success are interesting in themselves, but I shall not be able to discuss them here.

For such a type to be successful means that its conventions have imposed themselves upon the general consciousness and become the accepted vehicles of a particular set of attitudes and a particular aesthetic effect. One goes to any individual example of the type with very definite expectations, and originality is to be welcomed only in the degree that it intensifies the expected experience without fundamentally altering it. Moreover, the relationship between the conventions which go to make up such a type and the real experience of its audience or the real facts of whatever situation it pretends to describe is of only secondary importance and does not determine its aesthetic force. It is only in an ultimate sense that the type appeals to its audience's experience of reality; much more immediately, it appeals to previous experience of the type itself: it creates its own field of reference.

Thus the importance of the gangster film, and the nature and intensity of its emotional and aesthetic impact, cannot be measured in terms of the place of the gangster himself or the importance of the problem of crime in American life. Those European movie-goers who think there is a gangster on every corner in New York are certainly deceived, but defenders of the "positive" side of American culture are equally deceived if they think it relevant to point out that most Americans have never seen a gangster. What matters is that the experience of the gangster *as an experience of art* is universal to Americans. There is almost nothing we understand better or react to more readily or with quicker intelligence. The Western film, though it seems never to diminish in popularity, is for most of us no more than the folklore of the past, familiar and understandable only because it has been repeated so often. The gangster film comes much closer. In ways that we do not easily or willingly define, the gangster speaks for us, expressing that part of the American psyche which rejects the qualities and the demands of modern life, which rejects "Americanism" itself.

The gangster is the man of the city, with the city's language and knowledge, with its queer and dishonest skills and its terrible daring, carrying his life in his hands like a placard, like a club. For everyone else, there is at least the theoretical possibility of another world—in that happier American culture which the gangster denies, the city does not really exist; it is only a more crowded and more brightly lit country —but for the gangster there is only the city; he must inhabit it in order to personify it: not the real city, but that dangerous and sad city of the imagination which is so much more important, which is the modern world. And the gangster—though there are real gangsters—is also, and primarily, a creature of the imagination. The real city, one might say, produces only criminals; the imaginary city produces the gangster: he is what we want to be and what we are afraid we may become.

Thrown into the crowd without background or advantages, with only those ambiguous skills which the rest of us—the real people of the real city—can only pretend to have, the gangster is required to make his way, to make his life and impose it on others. Usually, when we come upon him, he has already made his choice or the choice has already been made for him, it doesn't matter which: we are not permitted to ask whether at some point he could have chosen to be something else than what he is.

The gangster's activity is actually a form of rational enterprise, involving fairly definite goals and various techniques for achieving them. But this rationality is usually no more than a vague background; we know, perhaps, that the gangster sells liquor or that he operates a numbers racket; often we are not given even that much information. So his activity becomes a kind of pure criminality: he hurts people. Certainly our response to the gangster film is most consistently and most universally a response to sadism; we gain the double satisfaction of participating vicariously in the gangster's sadism and then seeing it turned against the gangster himself.

But on another level the quality of irrational brutality and the quality of rational enterprise become one. Since we do not see the rational and routine aspects of the gangster's behavior, the practice of brutality—the quality of unmixed criminality—becomes the totality of his career. At the same time, we are always conscious that the whole meaning of this career is a drive for success: the typical gangster film presents a steady upward progress followed by a very precipitate fall. Thus brutality itself becomes at once the means to success and the content of success—a success that is defined in its most general terms, not as accomplishment or specific gain, but simply as the unlimited possibility of aggression. (In the same way, film presentations of businessmen tend to make it appear that they achieve their success by talking on the telephone and holding conferences and that success *is* talking on the telephone and holding conferences.)

From this point of view, the initial contact between the film and its audience is an agreed conception of human life: that man is a being with the possibilities of success or failure. This principle, too, belongs to the city; one must emerge from the crowd or else one is nothing. On that basis the necessity of the action is established, and it progresses by inalterable paths to the point where the gangster lies dead and the principle has ben modified: there is really only one possibility—failure. The final meaning of the city is anonymity and death.

In the opening scene of *Scarface,* we are shown a successful man; we know he is successful because he has just given a party of opulent proportions and because he is called Big Louie. Through some monstrous lack of caution, he permits himself to be alone for a few moments. We understand from this immediately that he is about to be killed. No convention of the gangster film is more strongly established than this: it is dangerous to be alone. And yet the very conditions of success make it impossible not to be alone, for success is always the establishment of an *individual* pre-eminence that must be imposed on others, in whom it automatically arouses hatred; the successful man is an outlaw. The gangster's whole life is an effort to assert himself as an individual, to draw himself out of the crowd, and he always dies *because* he is an individual; the final bullet thrusts him back, makes him, after all, a failure. "Mother of God," says the dying Little Caesar, "is this the end of Rico?"—speaking of himself thus in the third person because what has been brought low is not the undifferentiated *man,* but the individual with a name, the gangster, the success; even to himself he is a creature of the imagination. (T. S. Eliot has pointed out that a number of Shakespeare's tragic heroes have this trick of looking at themselves dramatically; their true identity, the thing that is destroyed when they die, is something outside themselves—not a man, but a style of life, a kind of meaning.)

At bottom, the gangster is doomed because he is under the obligation to succeed, not because the means he employs are unlawful. In the deeper layers of the modern consciousness, *all* means are unlawful, every attempt to succeed is an act of aggression, leaving one alone and guilty and defenseless among enemies: one is *punished* for success. This is our intolerable dilemma: that failure is a kind of death and success is evil and dangerous, is—ultimately—impossible. The effect of the gangster film is to embody this dilemma in the person of the gangster and resolve it by his death. The dilemma is resolved because it is *his* death, not ours. We are safe; for the moment, we can acquiesce in our failure, we can choose to fail.

Robert Warshow

Name Index